AMERICAN
COMIC BOOK
CHRONICLES

THE 1990s
1990–1999

By JASON SACKS
and KEITH DALLAS

Dedication
To all comic shop retailers. Without them, there is no comic book industry.

Writer: Jason Sacks
Editor: Keith Dallas
Logo Design: Bill Walko
Layout: David Paul Greenawalt
Cover Design: Jon B. Cooke
Proofreader: Scott Peters
Publisher: John Morrow

TwoMorrows Publishing
10407 Bedfordtown Drive
Raleigh, North Carolina 27614
www.twomorrows.com • 919-449-0344
email: twomorrow@aol.com
Second Printing • December 2020 • Printed in China
ISBN 978-1-60549-084-7

Table of Contents

Introductory Note about the Chronological Structure
of American Comic Book Chronicles

The monthly date that appears on a comic book cover doesn't usually indicate the exact month the comic book arrived at the newsstand or at the comic book store. Since their inception, American periodical publishers—including but not limited to comic book publishers—postdated their issues in order to let vendors know when they should remove unsold copies from their stores. In the 1930s, the discrepancy between a comic book's cover date and the actual month it reached the newsstand was typically one month. For instance, *Detective Comics* #1 is cover-dated March 1937, but actually went on sale one month earlier in February. Starting in 1940, comic book publishers hoped to increase each issue's shelf life by widening the discrepancy between cover date and release date to two months. In 1973, the discrepancy was widened again to three months. The expansion of the Direct Market in the 1980s, though, turned the cover date system on its head as many Direct Market-exclusive publishers chose not to put cover dates on their comic books while some put cover dates that matched the issue's release date.

This all creates a perplexing challenge for comic book historians as they consider whether to chronologize comic book history via cover date or release date. The predominant comic book history tradition has been to chronologize via cover date, and *American Comic Book Chronicles* is following that tradition. This means though that some comic books that were released in the final months of one year won't be dealt with until the chapter covering the following year. Each chapter, however, will include a yearly timeline that uses a comic book's release date to position it appropriately among other significant historical, cultural and political events of that year.

- Keith Dallas, with the
assistance of Ray Bottorff, Jr.

Note on Comic Book Sales and Circulation Data

Determining the *exact* number of copies a comic book title sold is problematic, regardless if the sales outlet under consideration is the newsstand or the Direct Market. The best one can hope to learn is a close approximation of a comic book's total sales. This is because the methods used to report sales figures were (and still are) fundamentally flawed.

For decades, most comic books sold on the newsstand printed an annual "Statement of Ownership, Management and Circulation" in one of their issues as was required by the United States Post Office for all periodicals with Second Class Mail subscribers. These statements divulged—among other information—a comic book title's average print run, average paid circulation, and average returns from the newsstand. The data in these statements were as accurate as the publishers could provide. The publishers certainly knew how many copies they printed, but they relied on the distributors to inform them of how many copies were sold on the newsstand and how many unsold copies were being "returned" for a refund. Most distributors actually didn't return unsold copies—or even stripped covers of the unsold copies—back to the publishers; instead they sent to the publishers affidavits of the number of unsold copies they destroyed. In essence, an "honor system" was in place that relied on the newsstand distributors to be truthful about the number of copies bought by consumers and the number of unsold copies being destroyed. And perhaps unsurprisingly, once the publishers couldn't dispute what the distributors were reporting in their affidavits, the whole system became corrupted with distributors skewing sales data in their favor.

This reality makes it all the more understandable why comic book publishers in the early 1980s looked to the Direct Market as a replacement sales venue. Under the Direct Market system, comic book stores had to keep

whatever copies they couldn't sell. However, this fact doesn't necessarily make determining exactly how copies a comic book title sold less problematical. That's because Direct Market distributors didn't require their retailers to keep track of how many comic books were purchased by their consumers and how many comic books became unsold inventory.

The discrepancy between number of copies ordered by retailers and the number of copies purchased by consumers can be significant, especially in the speculator-driven market of the 1990s. For example, in 1993 comic book retailers ordered over 1,750,000 copies of Valiant Comics' *Turok, Dinosaur Hunter* #1. Months after the issue's release, though, the fan press reported that retailers were stuck with cases of unsold copies. Supply had so greatly outstripped demand that Capital City Distribution President John Davis wondered aloud if even 200,000 copies of the issue had been purchased by consumers. The same speculation can be applied to other high profile comic books of the 1990s, like 1991's *X-Men* #1 and 1992's *Superman* #75.

American Comic Book Chronicles then recognizes the flawed nature of newsstand and Direct Market circulation data but is resigned to the fact that they are also the only data available and will consider them close approximations of a comic book's total sales numbers.

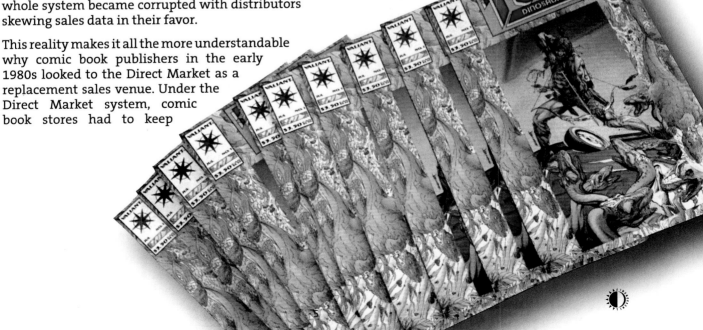

INTRODUCTION & ACKNOWLEDGMENTS

The Most "Interesting" Decade in Comic Book History

The ancient Chinese proverb "may you live in interesting times" most likely didn't originate in China. For one thing, the adage can't be directly translated into Chinese. For another, the earliest known use of the expression has been traced not to some Oriental wise man, but to a mid-twentieth century British statesman who mistakenly believed it to be Chinese.

Regardless of the proverb's origin, astute readers know that it is a curse rather than a blessing because the adjective "interesting" is not meant to be synonymous with "gratifying" or "entertaining" but with "chaotic" or "volatile." For that reason, I can think of no better expression to sum up the comic book industry during the 1990s. Arguably, no other decade in comic book history was as volatile as the final decade of the twentieth century. The 1990s began in euphoria with publishers capitalizing on the rapid increase of specialty comic book stores. Not only did the expansion of the Direct Market allow for high profile comic books from the early 1990s to be sold in the millions of copies, it also enabled the success of new publishers like Image and Valiant. Unfortunately, the proliferation of comic book stores was fueled by speculators. Simply put, too many comic book consumers were only interested in the secondary market value of their purchases. Comic books were seen as commodities expected to quickly skyrocket in value. As history has proven time and again though, all sales booms that are driven by speculation are bound to crash, and when the 1990s speculator boom crashed, it decimated the Direct Market to the point where recovery became a daunting, seemingly impossible task. At decade's close, a "successful" comic book sold over 50,000 copies per issue. In the span of ten years the range of the industry's fortunes had truly run the gamut.

Partly because of the market's volatility, the 1990s commonly gets assessed as "the worst decade in comic book history." The other part of that evaluation entails the quality (or lack thereof) of the material produced during the decade. The widespread belief is that style was valued over substance, so the stereotypical 1990s comic book has a lenticular die-cut cover and a mediocre story that relies too much on splash pages and battle scenes. Oh, and, of course, the issue comes polybagged. Frankly, this is an unfair characterization, especially if the person making it also implies that "bad comic books" didn't exist *until* the 1990s. Pick a random comic book from *any* decade in comic book history, and chances are it will be trite, derivative and eminently forgettable. Therefore, a true assessment of a decade's contribution to comic book history should involve the consideration of its best—rather than its worst—works. As far as the 1990s are concerned, then, we should be looking at the stark magnificence of Frank Miller's *Sin City* or the charm of Jeff Smith's *Bone*. The poignant perspective of Kurt Busiek and Alex Ross's *Marvels* or the originality of Mike Mignola's *Hellboy*. The rebellious provocation of Warren Ellis and Darick Robertson's *Transmetropolitan* or the obscene blasphemy of Garth Ennis and Steve Dillon's *Preacher*. Or we can just limit our judgment to *anything* written by Neil Gaiman or Alan Moore during the 1990s as it was all impressively sophisticated and erudite. These are just a few of the many works produced in the 1990s that deserve a place among the greatest comic books ever published, and one of this volume's goals is to show how interesting comic books were as the twentieth century came to a close, and not just in the proverbial sense.

During the production of this volume, the authors contacted various professionals who were part of the comic book industry during the 1990s to gain their insight and learn their experiences, so heartfelt thanks goes to the following people for responding to our queries: Shon Bury, J.M. DeMatteis, Danny Fingeroth, Hart Fisher, Paul Levitz, Ron Marz, Dave Olbrich, Wendy & Richard Pini, Whilce Portacio and Roy Thomas. Kurt Busiek deserves special recognition for his numerous detailed responses which proved invaluable in our attempt to get the facts straight.

Dean Compton of the Unspoken Decade and John Wells both provided vital feedback, and their eagerness to assist us throughout the composition of this volume was tremendously appreciated. This volume would have been considerably poorer without their input, so we are in their eternal debt.

Finally, we thank Daniel Elkin for his keen assistance, Julie Dietel for performing some emergency copy-editing at the eleventh hour and, of course, David Greenawalt for yet another beautifully designed volume of *American Comic Book Chronicles*! Excellent work, as always, David! ◖

1990

I WONDER HOW THOR MANAGES.

Swing Time

For many comic book publishers, creators and retailers, the dawn of the 1990s was the best of times. Fully recovered from the black-and-white boom and bust of the late 1980s, the comic book industry was experiencing a renaissance: of sales, of critical attention and of diverse, quality material. Fueling it all was the ever-expanding Direct Market of comic book shops which definitively proved itself a profitable alternative to the antiquated—and corrupt—newsstand system. Meanwhile, the runaway success of Tim Burton's 1989 *Batman* film, starring Jack Nicholson and Michael Keaton, promised a new link between Hollywood and the comics industry, just as a new generation of comic book celebrities became affixed to some of the most popular series of the time.

As the decade began, most newsstand-distributed comic books—from publishers like Archie, DC, Harvey and Marvel—cost $1, but overall, the price points ran the gamut. DC's Superman titles (*Action Comics, Adventures of Superman* and *Superman*) were cover-priced at 75¢. Deluxe-format comics cost twice as much or more. The Batman-featured *Legends of the Dark Knight* and Marvel's *Marc Spector: Moon Knight* cost $1.50 while *Legion of Super-Heroes* cost $1.75. Above that, DC and Marvel charged $3.95 (and sometimes $4.95) for their squarebound books. Direct Market-exclusive publishers strove to keep their price points competitive: Eclipse sold *Miracleman* for $1.50 while *Mike Grell's Sable* (published by First) cost $1.75. Innovation Publishing's *Justice Machine* had a $1.95 price point.

For kid-friendly publishers who were out of favor in the Direct Market, the newsstand was still a vital source of revenue. While **Archie Comics** refreshed its line with titles like *Explorers of the Unknown* and *Riverdale High* as well as a Teenage Mutant Ninja Turtles/Archie crossover, **Harvey Comics** struck a deal with the pop music group New Kids On the Block and published 44 issues starring the teen idols between 1990 and 1991. Unseen in comic books since the Whitman line ended in 1984, the Warner Bros. line of cartoon characters made a tentative return in 1990, as well. In the same time frame as the year's merger of Warner Communications and Time, Inc., DC published Bugs Bunny for the first time in a three-issue mini-series and the short-lived *Looney Tunes Magazine* and *Tiny Toons Adventures Magazine*.

A growing number of comic book publishers aggressively courted the bookstore market with new graphic novels and reprint collections. Matching the *Marvel Masterworks* line of hardcovers, which premiered in 1987, DC began producing *DC Archives* in 1989 with inaugural volumes that reprinted the very earliest Batman and Superman stories from the late 1930s and early 1940s. More recent material, like Frank Miller's *Daredevil* and Alan Moore and David Lloyd's *V For Vendetta* received the trade paperback treatment. Eclipse released an adaptation of J.R.R. Tolkien's *The Hobbit* by David Wenzel, and First Comics revived *Classics Illustrated*, last seen in 1969, with new adaptations of such literary works as Herman Melville's *Moby Dick* (by Bill Sienkiewicz), Mark Twain's *The Adventures of Tom Sawyer* (by Michael Ploog), and Charles Dickens' *A Christmas Carol* (by Joe Staton), among others, for $3.75 each. Each of these projects was an attempt to gain a foothold in the bookstore marketplace to varying degrees of success.

Despite the industry's overall bullish disposition, some creators lamented the limited opportunities offered to them. The black-and-white bust of two years left lingering scars but did little to diminish the number of comic book publishers operating in 1990: *Amazing Heroes* #179 (May 1990) listed comics from 73 different com-

panies. The reality, however, was that very few publishers could offer creators gainful employment. As one commentator noted at the time, Comico was facing bankruptcy and First and Eclipse were "abandoning monthly titles for the sake of albums, anthologies, reprints, and sundries. The resulting vacuum leaves the Big Two [i.e. DC and Marvel] looking more and more like the lone reliable places for a big paycheck" (Kreiner 3).

Among the literary adaptations published in 1990 were The Hobbit *and* Moby Dick.

But at least the decade began with more than a dozen distributors servicing the comics business, including not only the far-reaching Diamond, Heroes World and Capital City but also smaller operators like Comics Hawaii, New Jersey's Superhero Enterprises and Portland, Oregon's Second Genesis. Retailers in most parts of the country tended to order the latest comic books from the distributor nearest them since most distributors relatively carried the same material as their competitors.

As sales surged at the beginning of the decade and money was made, new publishers joined the field and new creators became stars. Much of the industry was euphoric, a mood that would last several years... until hubris and inattention brought an end to the party.

The Big Business of Marvel Comics

In 1990, **Marvel Comics** had one of the biggest years in its history. Shipping over 115 million copies of comics and magazines, Marvel also moved strongly into publishing squarebound comics and softcover and hardcover graphic novels (Humphrey 15).

Marvel boasted one of the most diverse lines in comics, publishing not just super-hero comics but also war titles (*The 'Nam*), humor (*Groo*) and science fiction (Marvel's Epic line was filled with science fiction adventure titles such as *Alien Legion*, *Interface*, *Open Space* and *Stalkers*). What's more, Marvel offered several comics directed at kids. As much as 10% of Marvel's output in a given month were "entry-level comics" including *Camp Candy*, *ALF* (adapting the popular TV sitcom character), *Brute Force*, *Heathcliff*, and *Police Academy*, among others. In 1991 Marvel would expand that line, including a comic version of the rappers Kid 'n Play and *Bill and Ted's Excellent Comic Book*, following on the heels of an adaptation of *Bill and Ted's Bogus Journey*, written and illustrated by indie comics darling Evan Dorkin.

Marvel's owner was Revlon chairman **Ronald O. Perelman**, who purchased the company in early 1989 for $82.5 million, outbidding a group that included former Marvel editor-in-chief Jim Shooter. In an autumn 1990

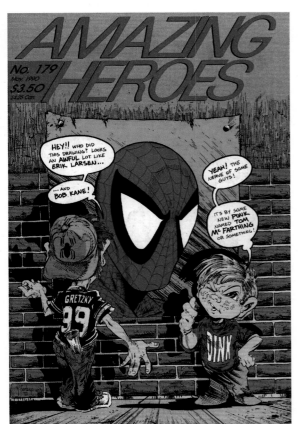

Self-mocking cover by Todd McFarlane from the fanzine **Amazing Heroes**. Spider-Man TM and © Marvel Characters, Inc.

TIMELINE: 1990

A compilation of the year's notable comic book history events alongside some of the year's most significant popular culture and historical events. (On sale dates are approximations.)

January 9: Written by Louise Simonson and drawn by Rob Liefeld, *New Mutants* #87 introduces Cable, a gun-toting mutant soon to become one of Marvel's most popular characters of the decade.

March 18: Disguised as policemen, two men steal art from a museum in Boston, including masterpieces by Rembrandt, Vermeer, and Degas and an ancient Chinese bronze beaker valued at $300 million.

February 11: After 27 years of captivity as a political prisoner opposing Apartheid, Nelson Mandela is released from a South African prison.

April 8: *Twin Peaks*—a murder mystery co-created by David Lynch—premieres on the ABC television network. Soon the entire country will be asking, "Who Killed Laura Palmer?"

April 24: A symbol of the 1980s era of Wall Street greed, "junk bond" financier Michael Milken pleads guilty to six felonies in connection with the largest securities fraud case in history.

May 19: Madonna's dance-pop single "Vogue" becomes the #1 song on *Billboard's* Hot 100 chart.

June 15: A feature film version of *Dick Tracy*—based on Chester Gould's comic strip detective—arrives in movie theaters. Despite tremendous publicity and fanfare, along with the star power of such actors as Warren Beatty, Al Pacino and Madonna, the film proves to be a disappointment at the box office.

JANUARY	**FEBRUARY**	**MARCH**	**APRIL**	**MAY**	**JUNE**

January 18: The mayor of Washington D.C., Marion Barry, is arrested for possession of crack cocaine during an FBI sting operation. He is subsequently sentenced to six months in prison.

LEAN, GREEN, AND ON THE SCREEN EVERYWHERE.

March 30: A big-screen version of Kevin Eastman and Peter Laird's *Teenage Mutant Ninja Turtles* arrives in movie theaters. The film would gross more than $201 million worldwide.

April 24: The space shuttle Discovery blasts off from Cape Canaveral, Florida, carrying the $1.5 billion Hubble Space Telescope. Once in orbit, Hubble broadcasts images of deep space that revolutionize man's understanding of the universe.

April 8: Ryan White—who gained national attention when he was expelled from school after contracting the AIDS virus—dies at the age of 18 from complications of the disease. After his death, Congress passes the "Ryan White CARE Act" which funds health care for uninsured AIDS patients.

June 19: Over two million copies of the debut issue of *Spider-Man*—written and drawn by Todd McFarlane—are distributed to comic book stores and newsstands. In a sign of things to come, Marvel offers multiple variations of the issue including polybagged copies and gold-tinted and silver-tinted covers.

June 26: President George Bush—who ran for office in 1988 on a pledge of "no new taxes"—publicly concedes that increased taxes need to be combined with spending cuts in order to reduce the national deficit.

---

article, *Forbes* magazine ranked 47-year-old Perelman as the third-richest American through his investments in cosmetics, camping gear, an artificial sweetener company and a drug company. Marvel staffers, though, privately referred to their new Revlon Cosmetics boss by a different name: "the lipstick guy" (Howe 313).

Many doubted Perelman had any genuine interest in—or affection for—comic books. The new owner, though, clearly grasped the profitable potential of his new possession. He referred to Marvel Comics as "a mini-Disney" whose fictional characters could be lucratively branded and marketed (Raviv 12). To that end, Perelman pushed for the production of more crossover "event comics," beginning with 1989's "Inferno," a multi-part story that ran through *Uncanny X-Men*, *New Mutants* and *X-Factor*, with circulation-boosting tie-ins with other comics including *Daredevil* and *Fantastic*

Four. Perelman also encouraged the promotion of Marvel's most popular creators. The immediate result was that Marvel's sales surged dramatically and net income doubled.

Marvel's editor-in-chief **Tom DeFalco** supervised a large crew of editors that included Craig Anderson, Bobbie Chase, Dan Chichester, Don Daley, Bob Harras, Terry Kavanagh, Ralph Macchio, Howard Mackie, Carl Potts and Jim Salicrup. Together, that team was responsible for releasing approximately 70 comics a month. DeFalco drew less attention to himself than his outspoken editor-in-chief predecessor. Unlike Jim Shooter, who always seemed to have his tall frame in front of the comics media, DeFalco was more of a behind-the-scenes presence, making sure his editors received his full support. The last thing DeFalco wanted was a continuation of the poor office morale that plagued the end of Shooter's tenure. At the same time, DeFalco held his editors

responsible for maintaining the integrity of Marvel's characters, and now his subordinates were monetarily incentivized: like writers and artists, editors received bonus payments for best-selling books (Howe 314).

Marvel's core super-hero line had seldom been stronger than it was in 1990. The company dominated the Direct Market with a juggernaut group of titles that was steadily accumulating new series, and Marvel's most talked-about comic book of the year starred its most iconic super-hero and its most popular artist.

The Adjectiveless Spider-Man

By 1990, *Amazing Spider-Man* had turned into one of Marvel's best-selling comics, with an average monthly circulation of 334,893 — the highest the title had achieved since 1969. Much of the success could be attributed to artist **Todd McFarlane**, a 28-year-old Canadian who entered the comics field through a back-up

July 25: Sam Grainger—an inker best known for his Marvel Comics work during the 1960s and 1970s on titles like *Avengers*, *Incredible Hulk* and *X-Men*—dies at the age of 60 due to diabetes-related complications.

August 2: Iraqi President Saddam Hussein invades the neighboring nation of Kuwait on the pretense that Kuwait is stealing oil that rightfully belongs to Iraq. Within two days, Kuwait is completely conquered. The invasion—and subsequent annexation—of Kuwait is condemned internationally, setting up a historic military operation the following year.

September 5: Jerry Iger—a cartoonist who partnered with Will Eisner to become one of the earliest comic book "packagers" in the 1930s—dies at the age of 87.

September 13: *Law & Order*—a police procedural and courtroom drama created by Dick Wolf—premieres on the NBC television network. The show would last 20 seasons, winning numerous awards along the way.

October 4: *Beverly Hills, 90210*—a drama starring Jason Priestley and Shannon Doherty as two teenagers from Minneapolis who move with their family to Beverly Hills, California—debuts on the FOX television network. The show eventually becomes the most watched program on television, spawning various spin-offs and imitations.

October 9: David Souter is sworn in as a U.S. Supreme Court judge, filling the seat vacated by William Brennan.

November 27: British Conservative John Major succeeds Margaret Thatcher as Great Britain's Prime Minister.

December 26: According to the 1990 census, over 249 million people are living in the United States, an increase of 23 million people since 1980.

JULY	AUGUST	SEPTEMBER	OCTOBER	NOVEMBER	DECEMBER

July 27: The first episode of *Swamp Thing*—starring Dick Durock as DC Comics' heroic muck monster—debuts on the USA cable television network. The show would last three seasons and a total of 72 episodes.

September 20: The first episode of *The Flash*—starring John Wesley Shipp as DC Comics' Fastest Man Alive—debuts on the CBS television network. Airing in the same Thursday night time slot as NBC's *The Cosby Show* and FOX's *The Simpsons*, *The Flash* is canceled after one season.

November 15: The producer of the pop music band Milli Vanilli publicly confirms rumors that the lead duo had not performed the actual singing on any part of their debut album, *Girl You Know It's True*. Milli Vanilli are subsequently stripped of the Grammy Award they received in 1989 for "Best New Artist."

December 22: Trade-union activist Lech Walesa becomes Poland's first popularly elected president.

---

feature in Epic Comics' *Coyote* #11 (March 1985) before moving on to draw 24 issues of DC's *Infinity Inc.* and three parts of the "Batman: Year Two" story arc in *Detective Comics*. He then began a memorable long run on *Incredible Hulk* with writer Peter David that garnered both men some major accolades, including a "Best Artist" Eisner Award nomination for McFarlane in 1988.

When McFarlane took over *Amazing Spider-Man* with issue #298 (March 1988), his depictions of the web-slinger and his cast deviated radically from everything that had come before. Spider-Man's costume had enormous white eyes, and the hero contorted in anatomically impossible poses. Some readers—and Marvel staffers—were aghast, but many more were captivated by the dynamic vividness of McFarlane's depictions.

McFarlane became a bona fide star... but one with a stick in his craw. The problem was that while McFarlane's vivid work was driving *Amazing Spider-Man*'s success, the artist didn't have total creative control. David Michelinie remained the title's writer. As McFarlane explained later in the year, "I guess I was getting a little restless on the *Amazing Spider-Man* book. I figured the only way I could have control over what I wanted to draw was to write the book. It was not so much that I wanted to be a writer, but I wanted to have more freedom on the writing side of it" (Sanderson 18).

So with issue #328 (Jan. 1990)—featuring a knock-down, drag-out battle between Spider-Man and the Hulk (and a cover in which a punch from Spider-Man causes the Hulk to smash through the comic logo)—McFarlane quit *Amazing Spider-Man* and told his editor, Jim Salicrup, to attach him to a title he could both write and draw. (Erik Larsen, fresh off a five-issue stint on *The Punisher* and soon to be an important figure in McFarlane's life, became the new

artist on *Amazing Spider-Man*.) Considering his inexperience as a writer, McFarlane expected Salicrup to assign him to an under-performing series where he could prove himself (Howe 319). Little did McFarlane know that the Marvel editors had been talking for some time about starting a fourth new Spider-Man series (to join *Amazing Spider-Man*, *Spectacular Spider-Man* and *Web of Spider-Man*) and that became the book McFarlane was offered to write and draw. McFarlane admitted at the time, "It wouldn't have been my choice to bring in a fourth Spider-Man book, but I wasn't fool enough to say no to it" (Wong 25).

With this new Spider-Man series, McFarlane wanted to pay homage to the history of the character while at the same time update him for a modern audience. He figured the best way to do that was renovate one of the villains originally created by Stan Lee and Steve Ditko. Unfortunately,

Promoted as an "Issue #1 Collector's Item," **Spider-Man** #1 was published in multiple versions, which helped spur sales of some 2.35 million copies. TM and © Marvel Characters. Inc.

McFarlane soon discovered that all of the villains he wanted to use were already allocated for the other Spider-Man books—one of the pitfalls of having so many series devoted to one character. So McFarlane instead settled for a villain he last drew in *Amazing Spider-Man* #313 (March 1989): the Lizard.

The first issue of **Spider-Man** (or as some clever fans called it, "The Adjectiveless Spider-Man") launched a five issue story arc titled "Torment" that prominently features the Lizard. As the story progresses, however, readers soon learn that a mysterious femme fatale, someone who hadn't been seen in a Spider-Man comic book in over eight years, has been secretly manipulating the Lizard for her own nefarious ends.

Carol Kalish, Marvel's Vice President of New Product Development, gave comic shop retailers their own version of *Spider-Man* #1 that they could sell exclusively to their customers. It was the same comic book except with a silver-tinted cover. Meanwhile, Marvel's Director of Sales presented the newsstand dealers with a version of the comic book that came wrapped in a polybag (stamped with a banner that reads "Marvel Collector's Item—Issue #1"). Upon learning this, the Direct Market retailers demanded that they receive polybagged copies too (Howe 321-2). Wal-Mart, coincidentally, received copies that had a gold-tinted cover.

The multiple versions of *Spider-Man* #1 created a challenge for the consumers who wanted every one of them in order to make their collections "complete."

Others who wanted to read the issue feared the opening of the poly-bag would ruin the comic's value. They ended up buying two copies and keeping one sealed. Retailers anticipated the demand and ordered appropriately. By the time *Spider-Man* #1 arrived in comic book stores on June 19 (cover date Aug. 1990), it had the largest print run of any comic in recent history with some 2.35 million copies distributed to stores and another 500,000 copies held as overruns. (As a token of gratitude, Marvel later provided Direct Market retailers with a copy of the issue with a platinum-tinted cover. Ironically, the thicker paper stock used for the platinum-tinted version of the cover didn't work well with the printing process as the color broke all along the spine of the comic.)

The massive sales guaranteed the setting of an industry trend. Soon, not only Marvel but many other comic book publishers would employ the variant cover strategy as a means to boost sales. Indeed, variant covers became one of the most iconic aspects of the 1990s comic book industry.

As some might have expected, sales of *Spider-Man* #1 were so huge that they caused a small recession in the sales of other comic books. Since most comic shops had limited financial resources, and since so many shops invested so heavily in *Spider-Man* #1, retailers didn't have enough cash flow to order some of the middle-tier Marvel and DC titles, though they did squeeze out enough for their most popular independent comics. As Mel Thompson of the *Comics Speculator* newsletter noted, "The heavy sales of *Spider-Man* #1 affected titles like *West Coast Avengers*, not [Fantagraphics'] *Usagi Yojimbo*" (Humphrey 17). To make matters worse, many retailers over-ordered the comic and the supply of *Spider-Man* #1 exceeded its demand in many shops, resulting in stores getting stuck with dozens—or even hundreds—of extra copies that had to be either kept in inventory or sold at a discount at conventions. The glut even caused some stores to go out of business (Humphrey 17).

All in all, though, the new *Spider-Man* title was a tremendous success, one that confirmed the notion that a new generation of popular creators was now ruling the comic book galaxy. "When I came back to do *Spider-Man*," McFarlane boasted, "I was hotter than ever" (Dean 12). It was a fact that wasn't lost on many of his peers, including a 22-year-old artist from Anaheim, California: **Rob Liefeld**. A life-long comic book fan who had been dreaming of being an artist since childhood, Liefeld broke into the industry

in 1988, drawing a short story in DC's *Secret Origins* #28 and then the five-issue *Hawk and Dove* mini-series. A year later, Liefeld went over to Marvel where, after some fill-in jobs, he was eventually assigned the regular art duties on ***New Mutants***, starting with issue #86 (Feb. 1990). (Coincidentally enough, Liefeld's cover to that issue was inked by Todd McFarlane.) While not as detailed or polished as McFarlane's work, Liefeld's artistry nonetheless possessed a forceful energy.

Written by **Louise Simonson**, *New Mutants* had been steadily shedding readers over the previous several years to the point where it became Marvel's lowest-selling X-Men-related book. In 1989, its monthly sales average was just over 210,000 copies – almost half of the best-selling *Uncanny X-Men*'s 410,000 copies per issue. As 1990 dawned, editor **Bob Harras** recognized that *New Mutants* needed a creative spark, so he sought to introduce a new leader for the super-hero group, a more action-oriented figure who could serve as a foil for the X-Men's longtime mentor, Professor Xavier. As Simonson seized upon the idea of a military leader, Liefeld—approached separately by Harras—started sketching. One of his designs was a muscular soldier with a bionic eye. Harras approved the design and the character was added to *New Mutants*. The hitch was that the character didn't yet have a name. On his sketches, Liefeld labelled the man "Cyber." Harras thought "Quinn" or "Quentin" would be better. In her scripts, Simonson referred to the character as "Commander-X," though she saw that as just a placeholder name. Finally, Liefeld suggested "**Cable**." That name stuck (Cronin #201).

New Mutants #87 (March 1990), the second issue of Liefeld's tenure on the title, introduces Cable as a white-haired, gun-toting, tough-as-nails time traveler from the future. Cable stands opposed to another Liefeld-designed character, Stryfe, the silver-armored leader of the Mutant Liberation Front who also makes his debut in the same issue.

New Mutants *#86 marked the beginning of Rob Liefeld's run on the title. In his second issue, Liefeld introduced the gun-toting, tough-as-nails time traveler Cable.*
TM and © Marvel Characters. Inc.

The story hints at a mysterious relationship between Cable and Stryfe. In fact, the relationship was so mysterious that neither Harras, Simonson nor Liefeld had worked it out before the characters appeared in print. By the time readers learned who Stryfe really was in 1991, the *New Mutants'* creative direction—and creative team—had changed in a very dramatic way.

New Mutants aside, the X-Men titles were never more popular than they were at the beginning of the decade. **Marc Silvestri** had been intermittently drawing *Uncanny X-Men* since 1987. In 1990, he would become the new regular penciller on *Wolverine*, starting with issue #31 (cover-dated September). That move cleared the way for artist **Jim Lee** to transition from *Punisher War Journal* to *Uncanny X-Men*, just in time for Marvel's major crossover event for 1990: **"The X-Tinction Agenda."**

Told in nine parts—spread out evenly among *Uncanny X-Men*, *X-Factor* and *New Mutants*—"The X-Tinction Agenda"

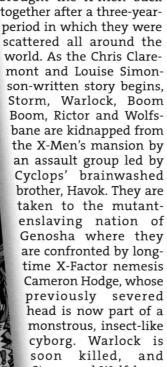

brought the X-Men back together after a three-year-period in which they were scattered all around the world. As the Chris Claremont and Louise Simonson-written story begins, Storm, Warlock, Boom Boom, Rictor and Wolfsbane are kidnapped from the X-Men's mansion by an assault group led by Cyclops' brainwashed brother, Havok. They are taken to the mutant-enslaving nation of Genosha where they are confronted by long-time X-Factor nemesis Cameron Hodge, whose previously severed head is now part of a monstrous, insect-like cyborg. Warlock is soon killed, and Storm and Wolfsbane

1990's "The X-Tinction Agenda" reunited the X-Men in a storyline that helped spur a major 1991 event. TM and © Marvel Characters, Inc.

Gambit debuted in full in Uncanny X-Men *#266.*
TM and © Marvel Characters, Inc.

undergo the same brainwashing performed on Havok. The remaining X-Men—whose membership now includes a charismatic rogue named **Gambit** who first appeared in a cameo in *Uncanny X-Men Annual* #14 (July 1990) before being cover featured in *Uncanny X-Men* #266 (Aug. 1990)—join up with X-Factor, Cable and the New Mutants to fly to Genosha to save their teammates.

After much fighting, the combined mutant teams defeat the Genoshan forces and Cameron Hodge's head is buried alive under the Genoshan capitol building by an earthquake caused by the New Mutant Rictor. Storm and Wolfsbane are freed of their brainwashing but Wolfsbane finds herself permanently trapped in her lupine form. She and Havok—also returned back to normal—opt to stay in Genosha to help rebuild the country and improve relations between the human and mutant populations.

With all the mutants reunited, the stage was set for a radical change to the X-Men franchise that would occur the following year.

Marvel's Vigilantes of Vengeance

In the early 1990s, crime in America was at thirty-year highs, a fact which caused a great deal of public concern. That national anxiety helped fuel a trend that carried over from the 1980s: America's fascination with fictional loners who took the law into their own hands. No comic book character epitomized this trend more than **The Punisher**. Marvel's resident vigilante was approaching the zenith of his popularity in 1990 as the eponymous star of not only two solo series (*Punisher* and *Punisher War Journal*) but also a black-and-white reprint magazine, various graphic novels (like Gregory Wright and Tod Smith's *Punisher: No Escape* and Chuck Dixon and Jorge Zaffino's *Punisher: Kingdom Come*) and even a descriptive weapons manual titled *Punisher Armory* (first issue cover-dated July 1990).

Capitalizing further on the violent loner trend, Tom DeFalco asked his staff to pitch ideas for a revival of **Ghost Rider**, the demonic motorcyclist first introduced in 1972 but seldom used since his series was cancelled in 1983. **Howard Mackie** proposed completely abandoning the previous Ghost Rider—including his alter ego, Johnny Blaze—in favor of a brand new version to fit the times. DeFalco agreed, and Marvel's new "Spirit of Vengeance" was soon born.

Written by Mackie with art by Javier Saltares, *Ghost Rider* #1 (May 1990) introduces Danny Ketch, who—along with his sister, Barbara—visits Harry Houdini's grave on Halloween night. There they stumble upon a fight between the forces of infamous gangster the Kingpin and those of a new villain named Deathwatch. After Barbara is shot through the chest with a crossbow bolt, Danny attempts to flee the scene on a motorcycle he finds in a nearby junkyard. This motorcycle, though, has a glowing mystic sigil and when Danny touches it, both he and the vehicle are transformed. With a fire-emblazoned skull, Danny now rides an ultra-modern motorcycle with wheels of flame. Danny becomes the Ghost Rider. He confronts his attackers with his "Penance Stare," which forces them to psychically feel all the pain they have ever inflicted on others in their lives. By issue's end, Barbara has been brought to a hospital where she lies in a coma. Danny, on the other hand, is left to ponder what happens next.

What happened next for Marvel was that *Ghost Rider* became its latest smash hit. For many years afterwards, *Ghost Rider* consistently ranked as one of the best-selling comic books of the month, and that kind of achievement ensured that its lead character would appear in numerous other mini-series and one-shots as well as a guest star in other Marvel comics. (Appropriately, Ghost Rider and Punisher frequently appeared in each other's titles.) Series editor Terry Kavanagh attributed the success of the new Ghost Rider to Mackie's vision: "We have a different incarnation than that of the first series, and I think the current character is perfectly fitted to the '90s" (Sellers 30).

Ghost Rider showed the mystical spirit reborn in a new human host. The series quickly became a bestseller. TM and © Marvel Characters, Inc.

Updating a different 1970s Marvel anti-hero for the 1990s were writers Dwayne McDuffie and Gregory Wright, who—along with artists Jackson Guice and Denys Cowan—produced a four-issue squarebound series for the cyborg assassin **Deathlok**. No longer Luther Manning—the American soldier reanimated in a post-apocalyptic future—the new Deathlok was Michael Collins, a pacifist scientist who discovers his cybernetics research is being used for a Roxxon Oil project that will create a murderous humanoid cyborg. When Collins protests, he is sedated by his boss, Harlan Ryker, who transplants Collins' brain into the cyborg and then sends him to a South American country to slaughter rebel guerillas who oppose Roxxon's interests. Collins' persona awakens during the mission, and once he is able to assert his control over the cyborg's programming, he vows revenge against his former boss. The mini-series performed well enough for Marvel to launch an ongoing *Deathlok* series in 1991.

Even **Doctor Strange** embraced the darker side in 1990, though he still trod in mystical realms rather than the "real world." *Doctor Strange, Sorcerer Supreme* was a mid-selling title in 1990 under the writing of Roy and Dann Thomas and the art of Jackson Guice but it played a key part in Marvel's continuity. In the five-part "Vampiric Verses" storyline, which ran from issue #14 (Feb. 1990) to #18 (June 1990), vampirism was returned to the Marvel Universe after it was banished several years before. This deep dark mystical tale involved Brother Voodoo and the evil Varnae and firmly established that vampires could be found in Marvel Comics again. In an odd turn of events, the cover of *Doctor Strange, Sorcerer Supreme* #15 was the subject of a lawsuit. Drawn by Jackson Guice, the comic's cover featured a woman's face in sharp close-up. But the woman's face wasn't that of an ordinary artist's model. It was the face of Amy Grant, a singer best known for her Christian devotional music, taken from the cover of her album "Amy Grant – the Collection." She didn't like having her face on the cover of a comic that included vampires, so in April, Grant sued Marvel in U.S. District Court – not for image copyright but for associating her image with the occult. She feared that association could hurt her standing in the Christian music community. A sealed out-of-court settlement was reached in early 1991.

Marvel's other new vigilante series included the four-issue *Nomad*, which starred Captain America's former sidekick Bucky, and the ten-issue *Foolkiller*. Written by Steve Gerber and drawn by Joe Brozowski (under the pseudonym J.J. Birch), *Foolkiller* features Kurt Gerhardt, a broken man with a bad marriage, a murdered father and some major mental problems. He becomes inspired by a TV appearance of the previous Foolkiller (also created by Gerber in the 1970s) to rid the world of all the fools who inhabit it. "It's a character study of someone who may or may not be a psychopath," Gerber commented. "It's a very dark series. It's one of the strangest books I've ever written" (Barnum 14). Considering the legendary "strange" books that Gerber had written up to that point (such as *Omega the Unknown, Howard the Duck, Guardians of the Galaxy*, among others), that was certainly saying something.

The Guardians of the Future

Coincidentally, Tom DeFalco—prompted by weekly office discussions of the latest episode of *Star Trek: The Next Generation*—opted to revive the sci-fi oriented **Guardians of the Galaxy** in 1990. Created by Arnold Drake and Gene Colan in 1968 and then resurrected by Steve Gerber in 1974, the Guardians hailed from the 31st century and consisted of spiritual archer Yondu, the time-lost Vance Astro, muscleman Charlie-27, crystalline Martinex, fiery Nikki and the mysterious Starhawk and Aleta.

Cover to the first issue of Jim Valentino's
Guardians of the Galaxy. TM and © Marvel Characters, Inc.

DeFalco worked up his own ideas for the new series but instead approved a proposal pitched by someone else: former independent comic book creator—and frequent *What If?* contributor—**Jim Valentino**.

Valentino confessed that his *Guardians of the Galaxy* (first issue cover-dated June 1990) was "not a science fiction series. This is a straight-ahead, balls-out, 100-miles-an-hour super-hero series" (Sacks 57). Indeed, the series was firmly rooted within the Marvel universe, just one set more than 1000 years in the future. The plot running through the first six issues involves the team's search for Captain America's shield on a planet inhabited by a civilization based on Iron Man's armor and technology. Later issues feature futuristic versions of Phoenix and Ghost Rider.

While not one of Marvel's bestsellers, *Guardians of the Galaxy* proved popular enough for Valentino to earn wider recognition from fandom... which he would put to good use in 1992.

A comic book creator who had already earned considerable recognition from fandom was **John Byrne**. With extended, memorable runs on such series as *Uncanny X-Men*, *Fantastic Four* and *Superman*, Byrne earned himself a devoted audience, one that would follow the creator to whatever new title he attached himself. Byrne began the new decade having finished up his seven-issue collaboration with writer Archie Goodwin as the penciller on *Wolverine*. He had also quit *Avengers West Coast*, which he had written and drawn for a year. As Byrne explained years later, the bone of his contention with *Avengers West Coast* was Tom DeFalco:

We writers and editors were summoned to [DeFalco's] office for the purpose of concocting the latest . . . shudder...Summer Crossover. As I had a storyline coming up in *Avengers West Coast* that would be pretty cosmic and wide reaching, I offered it as the basis for the Crossover. [DeFalco] said no, he didn't want to do that for the Crossover. So Howard Mackie (*Avengers West Coast*'s editor) and I returned to our jobs on the book, and went ahead with the story as planned. One month before we got to the Big Reveal, as it were, [DeFalco] suddenly noticed we were doing the storyline he had "rejected." He ordered us to change it, immediately. Howard protested— [DeFalco] had not said we could not do the storyline, only that he did not want to use it for the Crossover. Finally [DeFalco] pulled rank—we MUST change our story, as we did not have "permission" to do it. (Permission was needed only if stories caused major changes to characters or continuity. This did neither.) Since there was nothing I could do with all my months' setup, other than the story as planned, I quit in protest, with Howard's support (Byrne).

For his first project of the 1990s, then, Byrne turned to one of his favorite—

and one of Marvel Comics' oldest— characters: **Namor, the Sub-Mariner**.

At various points in his history, the Prince of Atlantis had been portrayed as either a villain or a hero. John Byrne, though, gave Namor a completely different role. He turned him into a businessman. With a cover blurb that reads "Out of the depths... and into the 90's!," *Namor, The Sub-Mariner* #1 (April 1990) begins with its protagonist discovering a box of buried treasure. With these new found riches, Namor buys a small company and becomes its CEO, out to save the world's oceans from such threats as oil spills and environmental terrorists. Namor soon learns, however, that the problems in the royal suite are very different from those in the boardroom.

One of the most unique Marvel comic books of the decade, *Namor, the Sub-Mariner* explored not just environmental and corporate issues, but also such real-world matters like the reunification of Germany in the aftermath of the fall of the Berlin Wall. This is not to say *Namor* lacked the kind of super-heroics one would expect from a Marvel comic book. Indeed, Byrne seemed to enjoy immersing the series into Marvel Comics continuity. Later issues show Namor, Captain America and the original Human Torch reunited as The Invaders. Another story arc

In 1990 John Byrne launched a new series starring one of his favorite characters, Namor the Sub-Mariner.
TM and © Marvel Characters, Inc.

presents the resurrection of Iron Fist, who had died at the end of the series he shared with Power Man in 1986. What made *Namor* one of Byrne's most distinctive projects, though, was his use—starting with issue #4—of Duo-Shade art boards which allowed for the creation of some of the most nuanced shading of Byrne's career.

Byrne also took over the writing chores on **Iron Man**, beginning with issue #258 (July 1990) which launched the "Armor Wars II" storyline. There was one catch: Byrne had no idea what "Armor Wars II" was about. The story was conceived by Bob Layton, *Iron Man*'s previous writer and co-author of the popular "Armor Wars" from 1987 and 1988. "Armor Wars II" was advance solicited to the Direct Market, but Layton quit *Iron Man* so suddenly that the title's editor, Howard Mackie, didn't get the chance to learn what Layton planned for the story arc. Mackie approached Byrne for help. Because of the advance solicitation, "Armor Wars II" had to be published or else retailers could return unsold copies for a full refund, potentially costing Marvel a significant amount of money. Byrne had no affinity for Iron Man and the prospect of developing someone else's story idea wasn't particularly appealing to him. What *was* appealing to him, though, was the opportunity to collaborate with *Iron Man*'s artist **John Romita Jr.**, so Byrne agreed to take on the assignment (Byrne).

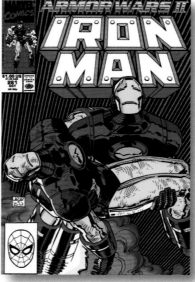

John Byrne agreed to write "Armor Wars II" without knowing what was planned for the event. TM and © Marvel Characters, Inc.

Given the nature of the creation of "Armor Wars II," it is little surprise that it has no true thematic parallels to the original "Armor Wars," which presented an obsessed Tony Stark on a mission to disable every armored hero and villain he suspects has stolen his technology. "Armor Wars II," on the other hand, has villainous industrialists taking control of Tony Stark's central nervous system and a subplot involving the Mandarin retrieving one of his power rings with the aid of the monster Fin Fang Foom. The story arc lasted nine issues, after which Romita Jr. left the series in order to work on a Howard Mackie-written graphic novel titled *Hearts of Darkness* which starred Ghost Rider, Wolverine and the Punisher. Replacing Romita Jr. on *Iron Man* was Paul Ryan, and Byrne remained on the title until issue #277 (Feb. 1992).

Meanwhile, writer/artist **Walter Simonson** assumed the reins of one of the titles Byrne previously made a mark on: *Fantastic Four*. With issue #333 (Nov. 1989), Steve Englehart's two and a half year tenure on *Fantastic Four* came to an acrimonious end with Englehart seething over—what he described as—arbitrary editorial decisions that mangled his carefully laid out plotlines. Simonson could relate to that frustration. When he was writing *Avengers* in 1988, Simonson got permission to add Mr. Fantastic and Invisible Woman to the team, so he worked out storylines that involved the characters. Soon after he did so, Simonson was informed that Mr. Fantastic and Invisible Woman would be rejoining the Fantastic Four and that Simonson could only use them in *Avengers* for one issue. After he did so in issue #300 (Feb. 1989), Simonson quit *Avengers*, annoyed for the same reasons that Englehart was. A year later, Simonson agreed to take over *Fantastic Four*, and he couldn't help but admire the irony of his situation: "I had all these stories lined up for *Avengers*. They were stories that, among other things, involved Reed and Sue. I just pulled the stories over to the *Fantastic Four*" (Nolen-Weathington 65).

Just as he revived a previously moribund *Thor* in 1983 by adding wild vitality to the stories

Walt Simonson's cheeky new Fantastic Four mocked its own ambitions as "The World's Most Commercialist Comic Magazine!" TM and © Marvel Characters, Inc.

of the God of Thunder, Simonson injected an element of energetic insouciance to the story of Marvel's First Family. One need only look at the cover to Simonson's first issue on the series—*Fantastic Four* #334 (Dec. 1989)—for proof: against a background of underwhelming B-list super-villains participating in Marvel's "Acts of Vengeance" crossover event, the Thing mockingly asks, "Yer kiddin', *right*?" Simonson repeated the cover gag for the next two issues. After that, he began playing with the title's long-standing banner "The World's Greatest Comic Magazine!" *Fantastic Four* #337 (Feb. 1990) declares itself "The World's Latest Comic Magazine!" Ten issues later, the series was billed as "The World's Goofiest Comic Magazine!"

In 1990 Frank Miller resurrected Elektra for a hardcover graphic novel.
TM and © Marvel Characters, Inc.

The most amusing banner belonged to *Fantastic Four* #348 (Jan. 1991) which reads, "The World's Most Commercialist Comic Magazine!," and for good reason: standing in for the Fantastic Four were Spider-Man, Wolverine, Ghost Rider and the Hulk. The idea started with Simonson who wanted to use Spider-Man as a guest star in the series. Kurt Busiek, then working in Marvel's sales department, joked that Simonson should use *all* the Marvel characters who were popular at the time, not just Spider-Man, but Ghost Rider, Wolverine and the Punisher as well. Guest artist Art Adams told Simonson that he'd rather draw the Hulk than the Punisher, so Simonson obliged (even though he couldn't resist having the Punisher make a cameo in issue #349) (Nolen-Weathington 69). Appropriately, the second printing for *Fantastic Four* #348 has a gold-tinted cover.

Another key 1980s Marvel creator returned to the company in 1990 to produce some of the most unique work of his career.

Frank Miller's Final Elektra Story

Since finishing the "Batman: Year One" story arc in 1987, writer/artist **Frank Miller** hadn't done any work for either Marvel or DC Comics. The man who became an industry superstar with 1986's *Batman: Dark Knight* spent the last couple of years in Hollywood, writing the screenplay to *Robocop 2*. His comic book work was limited to drawing covers for First Comics' *Lone Wolf and Cub*. He was lured back to Marvel to produce a graphic novel that was first teased in fanzines in the mid-1980s, starring two characters that were not only very familiar to Miller, but also ones that first earned him the admiration of comic book critics and

fans ten years earlier: the blind super-hero Daredevil and his former lover, the assassin Elektra.

In the 80-page deluxe hardcover *Elektra Lives Again*, Matt Murdock (a.k.a. Daredevil) is haunted by the memory of Elektra, dreaming that she's being chased by the people she's killed. He then becomes obsessed with the idea that she has returned from the dead. As he tracks down his former paramour, she fends off reanimated ninjas that have been conjured by the Hand. Little do Daredevil and Elektra know that the Hand has also resurrected Bullseye, the villain who previously murdered her. During a confrontation at a church—where Elektra is dressed in a white nun's habit—Bullseye delivers Elektra a second mortal wound, although she manages to decapitate him before she herself expires in Daredevil's arms. The hero has once again experienced the loss of his lover, and in the end, he—and the reader—are left wondering if Daredevil's despairing state of mind has caused him to imagine all these tragic events.

Already recognized as an artist with a penchant for crafting scenes of graphic violence, Miller was given even more creative leeway as *Elektra Lives Again* was published under Marvel's adult-oriented Epic Comics imprint with a "Suggested for Mature Readers" label. With the expert aid of his wife, colorist Lynn Varley, Miller took full advantage, providing many blood-soaked images that stood in stark contrast to the book's overall somber palette.

The New Warriors were a new teen group for the 1990s.
TM and © Marvel Characters, Inc.

Elektra Lives Again won Miller an Eisner Award for Best Graphic Album, but if fans had any hopes that Miller would soon be producing more stories for the "House of Ideas," they would have to wait a while. He was already busy tackling other projects that would be released by another publisher. But *Elektra Lives Again* at least gave Miller the opportunity to write one final story for the character he created back in 1980, and in many ways, the graphic novel serves as a creative segue, a line of demarcation between the kind of work that Miller produced in the 1980s and what he would produce for the rest of the 1990s.

New Warriors for a New Decade

While Walter Simonson used "Acts of Vengeance" to create some fun in *Fantastic Four*, Tom DeFalco used the 1989 crossover event to introduce Marvel's first super-hero group for the 1990s. DeFalco had wanted to launch a team of teenaged super-heroes and he learned from a newsstand distributor

that skateboarding magazines sold best among young adults (DeFalco 243). As the writer of *Thor* #411 (Dec. 1989), then, DeFalco collected several of Marvel's existing teen characters: the mutants Firestar and Marvel Boy, Namor's cousin Namorita, the space adventurer Nova and the Steve Ditko-created Speedball. Leading them was a brand new character who rode a motorized skateboard. His name was Night Thrasher, and the team was **The New Warriors**.

Seven months later, the group appeared in its own title. Written by **Fabian Nicieza** and pencilled by former *Marvel Comics Try-Out* winner **Mark Bagley**, *New Warriors* #1 (July 1990) begins with a flashback to a time when Night Thrasher first assembles the team of young heroes to help him in a mysterious cause. Initially, the other heroes don't much like Night Thrasher, but they decide to stick around, principally to make sure Night Thrasher doesn't do anything too crazy.

Nicieza, whose last ongoing writing assignment was Marvel's *Psi-Force*, the New Universe title that was cancelled with its June 1989 issue, jumped at the chance to write the new series: "I took the assignment for two reasons. First, I saw a lot of potential in these characters that had already been deemed useless. And secondly, I really wanted to write a monthly book." Nicieza presented the New Warriors as characters who struggled not only with their superpowers but also the inherent difficulties of their emerging adulthood. As Nicieza joked, "I guess you could say that *New Warriors* is, well, a book about deep, meaningful themes with fight scenes as well" (McElhatton 42).

Jokes aside, Nicieza and Bagley turned a market-research-driven gimmick into one of Marvel's most underrated series with solid storytelling, smart characterization and plots that

played out over the long term. From the start, the New Warriors was an inclusive group, more a club for super-powered teens than a formal organization. Nicieza soon introduced new characters like Silhouette, Rage, Turbo and Sprocket to the group while other young heroes from the Marvel Universe, like Cloak and Dagger, appeared as guest stars. With such a large cast, Nicieza enjoyed focusing on duos in the team such as Speedball and Rage, who had a strong buddy-movie connection, or the emotional relationship between Nova and Namorita.

Nicieza and Bagley's work on *New Warriors* would eventually earn them assignments on higher profile Marvel books. After *New Warriors* #25 (July 1992), Bagley left the series to begin a four year run on *Amazing Spider-Man*. Nicieza continued writing *New Warriors* until issue #53 (Nov. 1994) during which time he was writing several mutant books and being dubbed "the busiest man in comics" by *Wizard Magazine*. Despite this, Nicieza considers the first 25 issues of *New Warriors* that he produced with Bagley the best of his career (Wheeler).

Spider-Man in Scotland

Not everything Marvel published in 1990 seemed dictated by market research or the drive to maximize profits. For instance, a very different take on teen life was delivered by Elaine Lee and Steve Leialoha with their six-issue *Steeltown Rockers*. A "straight" drama, without costumes or superpowers, *Steeltown Rockers* features a bunch of kids who live in a depressed town where the steel industry had dried up. Concluding that the only thing to do when your town is dying is to have fun, the kids form a rock band. Lee wrote the rock opera *Starstruck* while Leialoha played in the fan band "Seduction of the Innocent," so the creative pair were duly qualified to produce a soap opera centered on wild drummers, family conflicts and teen jealousies.

Maybe the strangest Marvel Comic of its era was the inexplicable *Street Poet Ray*, a kind of rap haiku comic by Michael Redmond and Junko Hoshizawa that was first published in 1989 by Blackthorne Publishing (where it sold 25,000 copies) before being picked up by Marvel as a squarebound comic. Though the original comics had a decent circulation, appearing in 13 college newspapers, traditional Marvel Comics readers found the book baffling and quickly turned it into a running joke.

Meanwhile, **Charles Vess**, the legendary fantasy artist, brought his talents to the Marvel Universe with the painted hardcover graphic novel *Spider-Man: Spirits of the Earth* (July 1990), placing the web-slinger in—of all places—Scotland. "I have a fixation on Scotland," Vess confessed in an interview published in 1990. "I'm sort of a 'Scotti-o-phile' – I've got 'Highland Fever'" (Henkel 10). One day when Vess was sharing his love for Scotland, Marvel editor Jo Duffy suggested he create a graphic novel set in that country with a Marvel hero as its star. Vess played with a few ideas and landed on the concept of inverting the old trope of the "country mouse in the big city."

TM and © Marvel Characters, Inc.

It took Vess two years to finish the lush, fairytale-like story, which has Mary Jane Watson inheriting a castle on the Scottish Highlands. She and Peter Parker fly over for a second honeymoon where they discover a local castle haunted by a spectral knight who is hell-bent on ridding the town of its villagers. Things get worse as the local version of the Hellfire Club shows up. Vess described his work as "like an Uncle Scrooge adventure story drawn more realistically" (Henkel 11).

Good Times at DC Comics

With its crossover events and superstar artists, Marvel dominated the 1990 comic book marketplace, accounting for more than half of its sales. A third of the market's sales went to Marvel's closest competitor, **DC Comics**.

As the 1990s began, DC was on a high from the success of the 1989 *Batman* film. A genuine cultural phenomenon, the movie boosted the sales of Batman-related comics, particularly 1989's *Arkham Asylum* hardcover graphic novel that retailed for $24.95. In light of that, DC solidified its super-hero line with several contemporary-feeling new titles as well as a handful of more experimental books with higher price points that were aimed at older readers. Late-shipping comics as well as the subsiding boom from the *Batman* movie caused DC's sales to suffer some slippage as 1990 went on (Humphrey 15). That fact didn't diminish the company's overall outlook as **Paul Levitz**—then DC Comics' Publisher and Executive Vice President—told *American Comic Book Chronicles*, "We were certainly feeling good about the rapid growth the comic shop side of the business had shown in 1989, and were optimistic about ways to continue it. The graphic novel program, both collected and

original, was starting to gain steam. Overall, it was a good time."

Jenette Kahn relinquished her role as DC's Publisher in March 1989 but remained the company's President and Editor-in-Chief. With **Dick Giordano**, DC's Vice President of Editorial, the duo formed an editorial team that had all been with the company for almost ten years. Not surprisingly, then, DC's line of comics exhibited a stability of writers, artists and editors working together for a long time on their titles. The Superman books, for instance, were managed under tenured editor **Mike Carlin** and had used the same roster of creators, with few variations, for most of the previous year. The same was true of DC's other major characters, including the Batman titles, *Wonder Woman,* and breakout hits like *Sandman.*

Though selling fewer comics than Marvel, DC promoted major events in its titles, and no event was more celebrated than a monumental change in its most iconic character: in the double-sized *Superman* #50 (Dec. 1990), Clark Kent asks Lois Lane to marry him. The proposal, written by Jerry Ordway and with art by most of DC's Superman crew including Dan Jurgens, Brett Breeding, Kerry Gammill, Curt Swan, Ordway, and Dennis Janke, happened at the end of the "Krisis of the Krimson Kryptonite" storyline in which a dying Lex Luthor, in alliance with the mischievous other-dimensional magic creature Mr. Mxyzptlk, steals Superman's powers using red kryptonite. While the depowered Superman fights for justice (and desperately dreams for his powers to return), he wrestles with a more existential dilemma: whether to propose to Lois after several years of romance as they both worked on the floor of the Daily Planet. Superman's time without his super-powers makes him appreciate what it truly means to be human, and that seals his decision. Somewhat surprisingly, though, Clark doesn't tell Lois that he's Superman until several weeks later in *Action Comics* #662 (Feb. 1991), with a cover that shows a shocked Lois removing Clark's glasses and a caption that reads, "At long last... the secret revealed!" After she considers the revelation, Lois decides to accept Clark's proposal.

Clark Kent and Lois Lane's decades-long romance finally reaches its consummation when she accepts his marriage proposal. TM and © DC Comics.

Carlin and the Superman creative team met each year for a creative summit that mapped out the storylines for the Man of Steel and his supporting cast for the following twelve months. At the summit to plan 1990's stories, the topic of marriage came up and the consensus was that it was a logical progression to have the characters get engaged. In fact, the team's first thought was that Clark would ask Lois to marry him and that Lois would say no. But as Carlin remembered, "Literally while Jerry Ordway and I were plotting that issue at his house, it didn't feel right that she would say no. She had liked Clark enough to date him, and she had gotten Superman out of her system by that time, so she would logically say yes" ("DC in the 90's").

The characters had dictated the plotline, and DC's executives trusted Carlin and his team to make the right decision, so the engagement was approved. For the next few months the Superman team ran a subplot that showed Clark and Lois planning their wedding. In 1992, however, events would transpire that would cause the wedding to be postponed indefinitely.

Digitalized Dark Knight

Over in the **Batman** books, much of the attention was paid to a brand new **Robin**. Introduced in 1989, and with that year's "A Lonely Place of Dying" arc depicting his origin, Tim Drake was a harder-edged "Boy Wonder" created in response to some readers' frustrations with the previous Robin, Jason Todd, who was killed in a notorious storyline in 1988. Unlike his predecessors, the thirteen-year-old Drake was a natural detective with amazing computer skills but he wasn't the greatest fighter or acrobat when he started his career. He had to learn as he went along. This allowed readers to empathize with the young man and watch his progress as he grew into being a worthy partner to the Caped Crusader. In 1990, Drake and the Batman fought some of the series' most iconic villains, including the Penguin, the Joker and the Riddler. Tragically, slow-acting poison from the Obeah Man causes Drake's mother to die and his father to fall into a coma.

Finally, at the end of the year, Tim officially became Robin and donned a new costume that was the result of a call put out by DC and its parent company, Warner Bros. At that time Warner Bros. was considering featuring Robin in a sequel to the *Batman* movie and needed a more modern costume than the old suit with bare legs and booties.

Twelve artists were approached, and each was promised a stipend of $1000 just for submitting a new costume design. Classic Batman artist **Neal Adams**, however, made a counterproposal; he asked to be paid $12,000 but *only* if his design was accepted over all the others. If his design was rejected, Adams agreed not to be paid at all. Adams tackled the new costume as a problem-solving exercise: the yellow cape needed a black exterior so Robin could disappear inside it. He gave Robin ninja boots for gripping items in his toes, pockets on his legs instead of a utility belt, and red leggings to keep him warm. Adams's design was selected over his competitors.

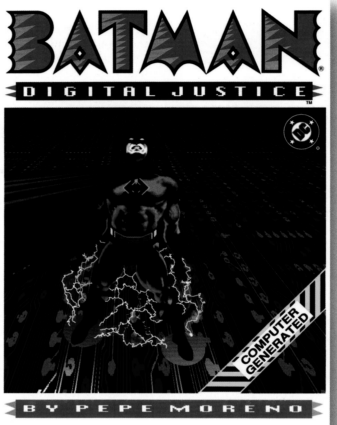

Pepe Moreno's Batman: Digital Justice *was an innovative computer-generated graphic novel that received widespread coverage.* TM and © DC Comics.

One of the most unique books of 1990 was the 98 page hardcover *Batman: Digital Justice* by Pepe Moreno with dialogue by Doug Murray. An internationally popular cartoonist, Moreno's work appeared in the U.S. in *Heavy Metal, The 'Nam, Creepy* and *Epic Illustrated* (for which he produced the standard-format *Generation Zero*, reprinted as a graphic novel by DC Comics in 1991). Though most of his comics work before *Digital Justice* was produced in the standard pencils-and-inks way that most comics were created, Moreno's love for technology led him to create *Digital Justice*, DC's first fully computer-generated graphic novel. He spent a year putting the book together using a combination of 3-D modeling, vector illustration and CAD programs in conjunction with image editing software—much of which was still in Beta at the time—on a Macintosh II computer with an 8bit/32bit color board, a system palette of 16,000,000 possible colors, 8MB of RAM, a removable 45 MB hard disk drive and a 19" Trinitron monitor. The lettering was designed to duplicate the look and charm of traditional comic book hand-lettering.

Released in February 1990, *Digital Justice* delivers a cyberpunk take on Batman, a tale of a far future Gotham City in which Batman is long dead, the police force is corrupt and the grandson of James Gordon is the only good policeman. An investigation reveals that an evil virus has taken over the city: the Joker virus. Gordon then dons the familiar black suit, modified to be computer-generated, and attempts to stop the virus. This action-packed drama, all presented in a virtual world that reflects the unreality of the future, adds familiar yet strange versions of many of Batman's regular cast: a cyber-skateboarding Robin, a future pop star version of Catwoman with questionable motives, and ultimately a virtual version of Batman himself who confronts and defeats the evil Joker.

Upon its release, *Digital Justice* became a topic of discussion in hundreds of magazines and led to Moreno attending and speaking at conferences and seminars worldwide. The concept of "digital art" was new at the time, so Moreno—backed by his decade of experience creating standard art—often had to defend himself against those who did not see his new work as "real art."

The Fastest Man on Television

The sequel to Burton's *Batman* movie wouldn't arrive in theaters until 1992. Until then, DC Comics fans would have to turn on their television sets to get their super-hero fix. On July 27, the USA cable network launched a low-budget version of *Swamp Thing*, starring the same actor who portrayed the heroic muck monster in two film versions, Dick Durock. The more auspicious DC Comics super-hero show, though, premiered on September 20, 1990 on the CBS television network: *The Flash* starred former Emmy Award-winning soap opera star **John Wesley Shipp** as DC Comics' Fastest Man Alive.

The series' genesis began two years earlier when Warner Bros. wanted to develop television movies featuring some of DC's characters. Producers **Danny Bilson** and **Paul De Meo** proposed a dystopian allegory titled *Unlimited Powers* that would have included several DC characters, including The Flash. Ultimately, their proposal wasn't approved, but when Jeff Sagansky became president of CBS Entertainment in January 1990, he gave the pair the green light to develop an hour-long Flash television show. (It didn't hurt that Sagansky grew up reading DC Comics.)

Evoking the aesthetics of Burton's *Batman* movie, *The Flash* television show was expensive to produce. At $1.6 million, each episode's budget matched *Star Trek: The Next Generation* as the most costly of all television shows at the time. The pilot episode alone cost $6 million, and the Flash's suit—designed by *Rocketeer* artist Dave Stevens—cost $100,000 to make.

The show presents an origin familiar to all Flash fans: after being doused in chemicals due to a lightning strike, Central City police scientist Barry Allen discovers he can move at near limitless speeds, a super-power which he uses to fight crime as The Flash. Initial episodes played out like standard police procedural shows with The Flash confronting gangsters, drug dealers and thieves. Midway through the season, however, the show shifted to include some of the Flash's

John Wesley Shipp starred as Barry Allen in CBS-TV's The Flash.
TM and © DC Comics.

famous Rogues' Gallery villains, including Captain Cold, Mirror Master and the Trickster (played by Mark Hamill, who achieved fame in the 1970s as Luke Skywalker in *Star Wars*).

CBS decided to air *The Flash* on Thursdays at 8 p.m., a timeslot that had been dominated by NBC's *The Cosby Show* for many years. It was a shrewd counterprogramming move on CBS' part: as the popularity of *The Cosby Show* showed signs of waning, CBS was seizing the opportunity to lure young viewers over to its new action-oriented super-hero show. Unbeknownst to CBS executives, the fledgling FOX network had the same idea. FOX moved its top-rated *The Simpsons* cartoon series from Sunday nights to the same Thursday timeslot that *The Cosby Show* and *The Flash* were going to occupy. Entering its second season, *The Simpsons* had already established itself as one of television's most hip, cutting-edge shows. In a 1990 *Los Angeles Times* article, Danny Bilson confessed, "The last thing we want to do is to be up against *The Simpsons*" (King). As FOX had hoped, the media spent a lot of its time predicting how well the irreverent animated series would fare against one of the most popular sitcoms in television history. With nearly everyone focused on the "Bill vs. Bart" showdown, *The Flash* found itself at a loss for attention.

As a countermeasure, CBS gave *The Flash* a major promotional push during the summer of 1990, including teaser ads during July's baseball All-Star Game, displays at malls and K-Marts, four-minute promos at Six Flags Amusement Parks, and much more. Despite this—and despite all of the show's state-of-the-art special effects—*The Flash* couldn't attract the kind of audience it needed to remain on the air. A move away from *Cosby* and *The Simpsons* to an 8:30 p.m. timeslot—an unusual starting time for an hour long program—didn't make an impact, and at times, the show seemed cursed. In January 1991, a new episode of *The Flash* was pre-empted by CBS' news coverage of the Iraq War. CBS eventually moved the show to Saturday nights... where it was pre-empted once again in early May 1991 for an announcement that President George Bush had been rushed to the hospital with heart problems. Bush recovered, which is more than could be said for *The Flash*; it was cancelled after only one season and 22 episodes. Its final installment—with Mark Hamill reprising his role as the maniacal Trickster—aired on May 18, 1991.

Meanwhile, *The Flash* comic book continued to present the exploits of Barry Allen's protégé Wally West, as written by William Messner-Loebs and drawn by Greg LaRocque. The Flash's longtime comrade **Green Lantern** returned to his own series after his previous run had ended with the ill-fated *Action Comics Weekly*, with an

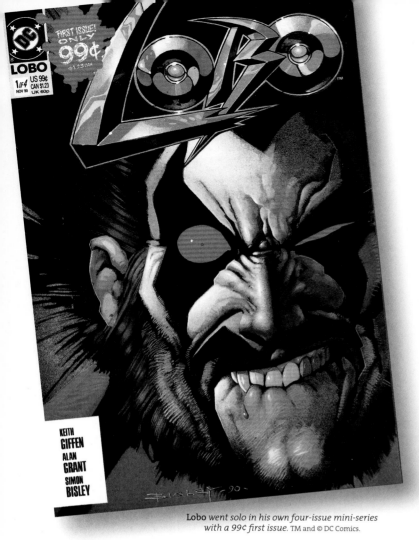

off. In all previous stories, the Rann citizenry hailed Strange as a hero, but in this story he's held in contempt. Rann's problem is that all life is growing increasingly sterile to the prospect of eventual extinction. Rann's only light of hope comes from Adam and his Rannian wife Alana's unborn child. The Zeta beam is upgraded to a meta-Zeta beam, which will allow Adam to live forever on Rann, but Strange discovers problems on Rann that he had never suspected existed. What's more, when another Earthman comes to Rann, Strange's status is worsened by a political revolution that breaks out on the planet.

The three-issue story gives Adam psychological depth by defining the reasons why he is compelled to fight to save an alien planet and why he feels alienated from Earth. It provides views of Adam's childhood, especially his troubled relationship with his father. The series also shows how technology on Rann triggered emotional and political consequences as the machines have taken control of all human actions, leaving people with little to strive for. The series even explores the complexities of alien sex.

Bruning and the Kuberts presented a radically different view of Adam Strange, one that generated its share of controversy. Some commentators complained that the series betrayed the action hero's core values while others felt that a deep examination of Strange's personality and motivations was long overdue. Regardless of the approach, DC never revisited this line of continuity in future Adam Strange stories.

DC Comics' Main Man

A much more traditional take of an established character was presented by writer **Alan Grant** and artist Val Semeiks. *The Demon* #1 (July 1990) features Etrigan, the hellish monster created by Jack Kirby in 1972 and then reinvented by Alan Moore in 1984 as a rhyming fiend. As his new series opens, Etrigan has engineered a coup that has placed him in command of Hell. Unfortunately, Etrigan soon finds himself deposed and he returns back to Earth, where he has an encounter with Batman in *Demon* #3 and a plot that has him opposed to fellow Kirby creation Klarion the Witch Boy.

Etrigan wasn't the only anti-hero Alan Grant would be handling in 1990. He also co-wrote the first mini-series to star someone who would become one of DC Comics' most iconic characters of the decade: **Lobo**. Co-created by **Keith Giffen** and first introduced in *Omega Men* #3 (June 1983), Lobo was an indestructible, brash, alien mercenary with a penchant for vulgarity, murder and torture. As he made guest appearances throughout the 1980s in other Giffen-written titles like *Justice League International* and *L.E.G.I.O.N. '89*, Lobo became more and more popular with DC's readers to the point where his own mini-series was warranted.

Plotted by Giffen and scripted by Grant, the four-issue *Lobo* retconned its protagonist's origin: Lobo was now "The Last Czarnian," the sole survivor of his race. The only reason why no other Czarnians existed was because Lobo himself slaughtered everyone on his home planet. This

issue cover-dated June 1990. Set up by the six-issue *Green Lantern: Emerald Dawn* mini-series, Hal Jordan's new adventures (which also featured fellow Lanterns John Stewart and Guy Gardner) were written by Gerard Jones and illustrated by Pat Broderick. Guy Gardner, by the way, continued to be one of the stars of J.M. DeMatteis and Keith Giffen's best-selling *Justice League America* series.

The Zeta Beam Strikes — But What Does it Hit?

Buoyed by the success of edgier, more contemporary-minded revivals of older characters like Animal Man, the Doom Patrol and Green Arrow, as well as the war-weary "Five Years Later" Legion of Super-Heroes, DC continued its process of updating many of its established characters for the 1990s.

Among those characters was **Adam Strange** who received his own three-issue mini-series in 1990. Written by Richard Bruning and illustrated and colored by Joe Kubert's sons, Andy and Adam Kubert, *Adam Strange* followed on ideas set into motion by Alan Moore three years earlier in *Swamp Thing* #58-59 during the swamp creature's space adventures. The mini-series posits an "everything you know is wrong" take on the optimistic space-faring hero who was drawn with futuristic flair in the 1960s by Carmine Infantino. Adam Strange is an ordinary Earthman transported by a Zeta beam to the distant planet Rann who returns to his home planet when the beam's energy wears was but a small taste of the kind of dark humor that *Lobo* provided. The series clearly reveled in its own perverse excesses. It parodied the bloodletting violence of such fan-favorite super-heroes as Wolverine in the most outrageous ways possible. Making it even further outlandish was the surreal work of **Simon Bisley**, the British artist who previously contributed to DC's *Doom Patrol* and stories featuring Judge Dredd and other heroes in his country's popular *2000AD*.

The *Lobo* mini-series was so successful that DC published several other *Lobo* mini-series and one-shots—such as 1991's *Lobo Christmas Paramilitary Special* in which the Easter Bunny hires Lobo to kill Santa Claus—before launching an ongoing series in 1993. Before the end of the decade, Lobo was starring in intercompany crossovers, like 1995's *Judge Dredd/Lobo*. All of this confused Keith Giffen, who reflected years later, "I have no idea why Lobo took off. I came up with him as an indictment of the Punisher, Wolverine, bad-ass hero prototype and somehow he caught on as the high violence poster boy. Go figure" (Offenberger).

On The Road to Vertigo

While *Lobo* deliberately catered to the crudest of sensibilities, DC Comics also published a group of more sophisticated titles that targeted a more erudite reader: *Animal Man*, *Doom Patrol*, *Hellblazer*, *The Sandman* and *Swamp Thing*. Under the auspices of editor **Karen Berger**, most of these books carried a "Suggested for Mature Readers" label.

As the year began, **Grant Morrison** was writing three of these titles—*Animal Man*, *Doom Patrol* and *Hellblazer*—but he soon relinquished control of two of them. Jamie Delano became the new regular writer on *Hellblazer* with issue #28 (April 1990). Four months later, DC published Morrison's final issue of *Animal Man*, #26 (Aug. 1990) in which the titular super-hero literally met his maker. In a clever postmodern twist on the *deus ex machina* literary device, Animal Man talks to "Grant," who explains that everything that Buddy Blank has experienced—all the death and pain that he suffered—has been heaped upon him by a malevolent, selfish writer. Grant then sends Animal Man back to his everyday world as it was when the series began, a fine meditation on the transitory power of comic book stories.

The writing reins on *Animal Man* were passed on to fellow Brit **Peter Milligan** who also added to DC's slate of "mature" titles by reviving Steve Ditko's cult classic super-hero series *Shade the Changing Man*. Illustrated by rising star **Chris Bachalo**, Milligan's new series reinvented Shade (last seen in the pages of *Suicide Squad*) as an alien poet sent to Earth to stop a growing tide of madness from consuming the planet. Shade's M-Vest—previously established as a device that allowed Shade to distort his own appearance—became the "Madness Vest," capable of warping reality. The head-trippy double-sized first issue (July 1990) reincarnates Shade in the body of a serial killer on death row. He quickly befriends Kathy George, daughter of two of the serial killer's victims and the couple fall in love (though both are concerned that

they are inadequate for each other) as they journey deep into America's creative unconsciousness to find the evil known as the American Scream.

Through this concept, Milligan and Bachalo investigate the nooks and crannies of American history, albeit in a surreal way. One issue presents an eloquent take on the JFK assassination. In another segment, the pair visit Hollywood and see actual casting couches attack starlets. As the comic wrapped up its first arc with *Shade* #18 (Dec. 1991), the American Scream is revealed to be a malignant alien dream of the United States – a bizarre idea that perfectly complemented a comic that veered between reality and unreality, sometimes on the same page.

Meanwhile, *Swamp Thing*—written by Doug Wheeler and drawn by Pat Broderick—dealt with the aftermath of the birth of Swamp Thing's daughter, Tefé Holland. **Neil Gaiman's** *The Sandman* spent the first part of 1990 wrapping up the "The Doll's House" story arc—with one memorable issue featuring a clandestine convention of serial killers—before moving on to a series of self-contained stories billed as "Dream Country."

The Sandman was quickly becoming recognized as one of the most literary titles in comic book history,

Shade the Changing Man *pursued The American Scream, a malignant alien dream of the United States.* TM and © DC Comics.

particularly as it fleshed out its pantheon of mythological characters: Destiny, Death, Destruction, Desire, Despair, Delirium and of course, Dream himself, a.k.a. Morpheus. It was at this time that *Sandman* became a regular Eisner Award nominee. For work published in 1990, Gaiman won the Eisner Award for Best Writer, *Sandman: The Doll's House* won the award for Best Graphic Album: Reprint, and *Sandman* itself won Best Continuing Series. What's more, *Sandman* #19 (Sept. 1990) won 1991's World Fantasy Award for Best Short Fiction. Drawn by Charles Vess, the issue takes place in 1593 as William Shakespeare's theatrical company performs *A Midsummer Night's Dream* in front of an audience of faeries, including ones who are represented in the play, in order to fulfill a previous bargain between Morpheus and Shakespeare: in exchange for the ability to write, Shakespeare will provide Morpheus with two of his plays.

Sandman wasn't the only book Gaiman was working on for DC Comics in 1990. He also produced *Swamp Thing Annual* #5, a fill-in issue of *Hellblazer* (#27, March 1990) and most significantly, the four-issue ***Books of Magic*** mini-series which chronicled the adventures of Tim Hunter, an English teenager who finds out he is fated to be the greatest wizard in the DC Universe. Seven years before the publication of J.K. Rowling's first *Harry Potter* novel, DC's bespectacled magician goes on a quest to achieve his destiny. At each stage he is accompanied by one of DC's mystical heroes. Each of the four issues was painted by a different artist and explores unique corners of DC's cosmology. In "Book One: The Invisible Labyrinth," with art by John Bolton, the Phantom Stranger shows Tim the history of the DC Universe. In "Book Two: The Shadow World," with art by Bo Hampton, John Constantine and Hunter explore the current world. In "Book Three: The Land of Summer's Twilight," with art by Charles

Neil Gaiman explored The Books of Magic *with artists John Bolton, Bo Hampton, Charles Vess and Paul Johnson.* TM and © DC Comics.

Vess, Doctor Occult takes Hunter to the worlds of Faerie, Gemworld, Skartaris, King Arthur's Camelot and other mystic realms. Finally, in "Book Four: The Road to Nowhere," with art by Paul Johnson, Mister E and Hunter travel to the universe's possible future.

While perfectly suited for the series, Gaiman wasn't the first writer attached to *Books of Magic*. As the letters page in *The Spectre* #12 (March 1988) makes clear, the project was initially assigned to J.M. DeMatteis, along with artists Jon J. Muth and Kent Williams. Before work on the series began, however, the artists stepped away, quickly followed

by DeMatteis. If DeMatteis had remained, *Books of Magic* would have read like a kind of storybook, with writing on one page and art on the other (Cronin #271). With DeMatteis gone, Karen Berger approached Gaiman to take over the project, describing it as a "Who's Who" guide for DC's magical characters. Gaiman initially demurred, but after a day's consideration, he figured out how to approach the story. The mini-series was successful enough for DC to launch an ongoing *Books of Magic* series in 1994, written by John Ney Rieber and illustrated by Gary Amaro and Peter Gross.

At the same time that Gaiman handled DC's complement of notable magicians, writer **Howard Chaykin** and artist **José Luis García-López** presented a unique, edgy take on DC's classic science fiction characters with the three-issue Prestige format ***Twilight***. Chaykin took some of DC's most clean-cut space-farers—Tommy Tomorrow, the Star Rovers, Manhunter 2070, Space Cabbie and Star Hawkins—and revised them as complex, often deeply disturbed individuals, occupying a faraway utopia that is tainted by human weakness and fallibility. The main plot has Star Rover Karel Sorenson becoming a living god with his former ally, the renegade hero Tommy Tomorrow, attempting to stop him. According to *Twilight*, the previous incarnations of these characters were mere simulacra of reality. The brutal reality was that space in the far future will be a very rough place with few heroes.

Outside the DC Universe

A very different DC science fiction series was the six-issue *World Without End*, written by Jamie Delano with painted art by John Higgins. An allegorical adventure with fantastical imagery and outrageous language, *World Without End* related a war between the sexes in the far future, on a world that literally grew over our current one.

One of the oddest DC mini-series of the year was the squarebound four-issue *Breathtaker*, created—and owned—by writer Marc Hempel and painter Mark Wheatley. Addicted to finding true love, Chase Darrow is an incredibly beautiful and exciting woman, with all sorts of men falling for her. Unfortunately, loving Chase means death. Her lovers literally age and die, though they die in bliss. Chase is traumatized by her power but finds it hard to fight her addiction. She comes to the attention of the world's only super-hero, called

OH GOD.

PLEASE.

NOT AGAIN.

Marc Hempel and Mark Wheatley produced a super-hero horror story with Breathtaker.
Breathtaker TM and © Mark Wheatley and Marc Hempel.

The Man, who finds himself falling for the charms of the beautiful woman.

This super-hero horror story was the work of the team who created First Comics' unique science fiction comic *Mars* in the 1980s, and Hempel and Wheatley used their connection to former First editor Mike Gold, who had subsequently moved on to DC, to help them place *Breathtaker* there after Comico rejected it. Gold accepted the project within an hour of it reaching his desk, then it took three months to iron out contracts before the comic was fully greenlit. The series received very positive reactions from critics, though it didn't sell very well.

Tom Veitch and Bryan Talbot had an equally askew look at super-heroes in their squarebound four-parter *The Nazz*. The story of a sexy guru who turns out to be a power-hungry monster, *The Nazz* has a different narrator with each issue. In combination with Bryan Talbot's idiosyncratic artwork, Veitch delivers a more Eastern view of super-heroes than traditional American comics do.

DC also continued its **Piranha Press** imprint, which was launched in 1989 by editor **Mark Nevelow** as a diverse line of eclectic creator-owned comics and graphic novels intended, in part, to compete with independent comics. In 1990 Piranha released its biggest hit: **Kyle Baker's *Why I Hate Saturn***. With text (almost all dialogue) beneath black-and-white images, the 208-page *Why I Hate Saturn* tells the story of a female writer for a *Details*-like magazine in New York City who finds her life taken over by her visiting sister who thinks she's Queen of the Leather Astro-Girls of Saturn. The sisters clash, and wacky hijinks ensue – but not the kind a reader might expect, as Baker explores relationships, family, sex, New York City life, and much more. Baker's affection for his characters gives the book its charm, and the story careens around in unexpected but delightful directions. The book won a Harvey Award, earned a rave from *Rolling Stone* magazine and finished on *The Comics Journal*'s list of 100 Greatest Comics of the Twentieth Century.

Aces High

Nominated for the same Harvey Award that *Why I Hate Saturn* won was another DC Comics graphic novel. It was written and painted by artist **George Pratt**, who grew up a big fan of the war comics that DC published in the 1960s and 1970s. In 1989, Pratt was doing gallery work in New York City to support himself when he decided to pitch a project to DC. Reflecting on the work he had done for the Vietnam War-focused *Eagle* magazine as a college student, Pratt felt he had a lot to say about Vietnam that could be expressed through a story featuring a character created by Robert Kanigher and Joe Kubert in 1965: the World War I German fighter pilot Hans Von Hammer, a.k.a. Enemy Ace. DC accepted Pratt's proposal, and he produced a 128-page fully painted graphic novel titled *Enemy Ace: War Idyll*.

An intense, impressionistic story in which Von Hammer reminisces about his military exploits to a Vietnam War reporter, *War Idyll* conveys the incredible thrills and horrors of the Great War, emphasizing the deep scars that the conflict left on both Von Hammer and his country. Flashbacks reveal how the former Enemy Ace came to hate war: his slow change from an aristocratic Prussian to an honor-bound flying ace to a man ashamed of all his wartime actions. Pratt created a realistic story that emphasizes the profound pain caused by war, and he went out of his way to provide authentic details: he built an exact scale model of a German Fokker DR-1 fighter plane in his studio and flew in an old open cockpit Stearman biplane owned by fellow artist Herb Trimpe.

DC promoted *War Idyll* by publishing *Enemy Ace Special #1* (Oct. 1990) three months prior to the graphic novel's release. The issue reprinted Von Hammer's first two appearances (from 1965's *Our Army at War* #151 and #153) and included an introduction by Pratt. Unfortunately, *War Idyll* didn't sell particularly well, perhaps undermined by its subject matter and $24.95 price point. If nothing else, though, the graphic novel earned Pratt a job offer at the

George Pratt delivered a unique take on a DC icon in Enemy Ace: War Idyll.
TM and © DC Comics.

Joe Kubert School of Cartoon and Graphic Art due to his modern take on Kubert's classic comic character.

Ken Steacy delivered a very different kind of flying epic for DC with his creator-owned four-part deluxe mini-series *Tempus Fugitive*. The light, breezy time travel chase story allowed Steacy to indulge in one of his favorite passions: drawing airplanes from many different eras. As Steacy admitted at the time, the series was "an excuse to draw my favorite planes. It covers the entire history of powered flight, starting with World War I and ending up at the turn of the next century," including the planes at Area 51 (Harrington 119).

A Dark Horse for Publisher of the Year

Though Marvel and DC dominated market share in 1990, they were hardly the only publishers making a mark on the industry. One company that was steadily becoming more prominent was **Dark Horse Comics**. Capital City Distribution even named Dark Horse its "Publisher of the Year" for 1990 because it "achieved share numbers impressive for an independent." Dark Horse's most popular title, *Aliens*—based on James Cameron's 1986 sci-fi film—sold a phenomenal 400,000 copies per issue in 1990, putting it on par with the sales performance of *Uncanny X-Men* (Groth 6). That was a tremendous achievement for the Portland, Oregon-based publisher then entering its fifth year of business.

Having successfully weathered the devastating aftershocks of the black-and-white bust of the late 1980s, Dark Horse began the new decade in much better shape than most of its competitors, particularly Comico, Eclipse and First Comics. Publisher **Mike Richardson** shepherded a varied slate of titles. On one hand were the licensed properties like Robert E. Howard's *Cormac Mac Art* (written by Roy and Dann Thomas with art by E.R. Cruz) and mini-series devoted to the *Aliens* and *Predator* film series. During a mutual brainstorming session, the writers and artists of the *Aliens* and *Predator* comic books came up with a winner of an idea: a comic book that set the two sci-fi franchises against each other. To that end, Dark Horse published the four issue *Aliens vs. Predator*. Written by Dark Horse's vice president Randy Stradley, the story actually begins in *Dark Horse Presents* #34-36 (Nov. 1989-Feb. 1990) and involves the inhabitants of a colonized planet who just want to live their lives as simple ranchers. Unbeknownst to them, the Predators have traditionally used their planet as a hunting ground, and now they're back to hunt new prey: Aliens. The colonists find themselves caught in the middle of the conflict. *Aliens vs. Predator* #1 (June 1990) sold a remarkable 325,000 copies.

By the summer of 1990, Dark Horse added another James Cameron sci-fi film property that NOW Comics had been licensing for the past two years: *The Terminator*. Written by John Arcudi and drawn by Chris Warner, the Dark Horse version of *The Terminator* evokes the original Arnold Schwarzenegger action flick as a small band of soldiers travels back in time from the future to present-day Los Angeles. Following them are three Terminator cyborgs who are programmed to ensure that their machine-ruled future isn't undermined.

Frank Miller and Dave Gibbons united for the sci-fi adventure Give Me Liberty. TM and © Frank Miller, Inc. and Dave Gibbons

Besides the licensed fare, Dark Horse's catalog was also filled with titles created by some of the most respected independent talents in the business: Bob Burden's quirky *Flaming Carrot Comics*, Paul Chadwick's meditative *Concrete*, Bryan Talbot's visionary time travel sci-fi series *The Adventures of Luther Arkwright*, and Elaine Lee and Michael Kaluta's whimsical science fiction adventure *Starstruck*. As well, writer Jerry Prosser and artists Arnold and Jacob Pander—who achieved fame in the late 1980s for their work on Matt Wagner's *Grendel* series—produced *Exquisite Corpse*, a three issue non-linear story about the life and death of a serial killer. The three unnumbered issues could be read in any order, ultimately affecting the reader's interpretation.

As avant-garde as *Exquisite Corpse* was, the truly revolutionary work that Dark Horse published in 1990 was the squarebound four-issue mini-series ***Give Me Liberty***, produced by two of the most popular creators in the industry: *Batman: The Dark Knight* creator **Frank Miller** and *Watchmen* artist **Dave Gibbons**.

With a title derived from Patrick Henry's famous Revolutionary War declaration ("give me liberty or give me death!"), *Give Me Liberty* was initially planned as a serious political tale. The creators, though, eventually opted for a different approach. As Miller explained, "We both spontaneously decided we *didn't* want to take it in that direction. Our feelings were that there had been a glut of stories dealing with soul-searching in the American heartland, books expounding on the state of man, the universe and the U.S. political system. We decided to make it more action-packed, more fun, a story that basically encapsulated the joy of comics" (Nutman 15).

The story follows the life of African-American Martha Washington as she moves through the dystopia of her near-future society — from her birth in extreme poverty to her stay in a mental institution to her exemplary service in the military. While the series provides its fair share of political statements—especially in its depiction of ghettoized minorities and an America that has been literally fractured by all-powerful corporations—*Give Me Liberty* is more farce than overtly ideological treatise. Despite its seemingly grim trappings, the story has a hopeful, even absurdly humorous, edge as Martha maintains her principles against great opposition. In their decision to infuse humor in *Give Me Liberty*, the creators of two of the graphic novels that helped usher in a new level of seriousness in comic books turned the tables a bit and showed that there was light at the end of a dark night. *Give Me Liberty* #1 sold 120,000 copies (Humphrey 20), and the mini-series won the Eisner Award for "Best Finite Series."

Frank Miller wasn't done winning Eisner Awards for his 1990 work, however. Besides being recognized for *Elektra Lives Again* and *Give Me Liberty*, Miller also won the Eisner Award for "Best Writer/Artist Team" with **Geof Darrow** for their three-issue magazine-sized **Hard Boiled** for Dark Horse Comics about a Los Angeles family man who discovers he is actually a homicidal robot. Unit Four—codenamed "Nixon"—must lead the revolution to liberate the other enslaved robots. Unfortunately, his human programmers have other plans.

If *Give Me Liberty* was a tale ultimately about hope and perseverance, then *Hard Boiled* was about future doom and corrupted humanity. The story's bleak world view was made all the more vivid by the eye-popping detail of Geof Darrow's art. A disciple of master cartoonist Jean Giraud (a.k.a. "Moebius"), Darrow had been published primarily in France until Giraud introduced him to Miller. After *Hard Boiled*, Miller and Darrow would go on to collaborate on other projects, and Darrow's work would capture the attention and respect of not only his peers but people outside the comic book industry as well.

Jim Shooter's Valiant Return to Comics

In 1986 Western Publishing, a large company that printed such items as Little Golden Books and children's coloring books (and which had a successful comic publishing business that was shuttered in 1984), attempted to purchase Marvel Comics. The deal ultimately fell through when Western chairman Richard Bernstein became fed up with the negotiation tactics of Marvel's owners, Cadence Industries (Shooter, "The Web of the Snyder—Part 1"). Around the same time, Marvel's editor-in-chief **Jim Shooter** met entertainment mogul **Steve Massarsky**, who was planning a live-action stage show featuring some of Marvel's characters. Several months after Western's attempted takeover, and on the same day in 1987 that Massarsky was granted his license to produce his stage show, Shooter was fired as editor-in-chief. Despite the dismissal, Marvel's executives recommended to Massarsky that Shooter write the stage play. As the two men worked together, they discussed the idea of co-founding a new comic book company.

First, though, Shooter wanted Massarsky to help him buy Marvel Comics from the company who ended up purchasing Marvel from Cadence: New World Entertainment. The two men made their bid in 1989, but that ultimately proved fruitless. As Massarsky explained, "We didn't have [the right] financing together. We had the Chase Manhattan Bank interested in being our ventured group, but they weren't putting up any equity. In order to make a deal like this, you need both equity and debt financing. We kind of went into the deal with no equity, just somebody saying, 'I'll lend you some money', and in the end, we weren't among the bidders finally put together" (*The Beginning of the Valiant Era* 13). Massarsky and Shooter then joined one of Marvel's two final bidders, Shenkman Capital, on the pretense that Shooter and his team would be good managers for Marvel. It was all for naught as the highest bidder, Ronald O. Perelman, head of Revlon Cosmetics, purchased Marvel Comics for $82.5 million.

Massarsky and Shooter moved on. They explored the idea of buying Harvey Comics' Richie Rich and Casper the Friendly Ghost. Separately, Shooter also approached Bernstein about licensing some of Western Publishing's old comic book characters like

Detail from Miller and Geof Darrow's Hard Boiled.
TM and © Frank Miller and Geof Darrow.

Jim Shooter's Valiant Comics debuted in 1990 with adaptations of Nintendo video games.
Super Mario Bros and Zelda TM and © Nintendo of America Inc.

Doctor Solar: Man of the Atom, Magnus: Robot Fighter, and Turok: Son of Stone. Bernstein agreed to hold the characters until Shooter could raise the necessary funds (Shooter, "The Web of the Snyder—Part 1"). That funding eventually came from the Triumph Capital firm. In November 1989, then, Shooter and Massarsky officially started their own comic book company with Shooter providing the managerial expertise and Massarsky—whose clients included Cyndi Lauper, Aerosmith and the World Wrestling Federation—providing the connections to the entertainment industry. They named their new company Voyager Communications but their releases were branded as **Valiant Comics**.

Not wanting to stop with the Western Comics characters, Jim Shooter set his sights on other properties to license. Among the ones that he considered were pulp heroes the Shadow and the Green Hornet (the latter of which was being published by NOW Comics) as well as the classic comic strip *Terry and the Pirates*. One licensor suggested Valiant publish comics that featured characters associated with one of Massarsky's clients: the ultra-popular Nintendo Entertainment System. In 1990, Valiant debuted its "Nintendo Comics System" with four titles: *Captain N: the Game Master*, *Game Boy*, *Link: the Legend of Zelda* and *Super Mario Bros*. The releases were intended less for comic shops and more for mass retail stores, like K-Mart and Toys "R" Us. In other words, less for comic book collectors and more for the kids who bought Nintendo games.

Two key figures in Valiant's eventual success worked on the Nintendo comics. Longtime Marvel artist **Bob Layton** drew interiors and covers for several of the titles. He soon became Shooter's editor-in-chief. Likewise, **Janet "Jay Jay" Jackson** served as both one of Valiant's colorists and Shooter's right-hand assistant. In addition, future Valiant mainstays such as Steve Ditko and Joe Quesada produced work for the Nintendo comics. Quesada's first ever comic work appeared in *Captain N: the Game Master* #3 (July 1990).

Unfortunately, many video game fans despised the Nintendo comics, mostly because they included plots that were very different from those in the games and featured off-model versions of the characters, or starred characters with no video game presence at all. Reader complaints, though, were the least of Valiant's worries. The more troubling problem was that Valiant couldn't turn a profit on the books. Nintendo promised Shooter and Massarsky access to the mailing list of the two million subscribers to the in-house *Nintendo Power* magazine as well as store displays for Valiant's comics to be sold right next to the video games. Shooter and Massarsky were provided with neither (Shooter, "Ditko at Valiant and Defiant—Part 1").

The Nintendo comics were a financial fiasco and a major miscalculation for the market that Shooter, Massarsky and their team were trying to reach. Right from the start, Jim Shooter's return to comics had gotten off on the wrong foot. His company was quickly losing money and facing imminent closure. Making matters worse was the cancellation of a seven-part series of bi-monthly reprints of Western's *Magnus, Robot Fighter* comics. Though the first 96-page issue with a $7.95 cover price was announced to come out August 16, 1990, it never appeared because pre-orders came in well below the 100,000 copy threshold that Valiant needed to break even. Valiant also initially planned on publishing an all-new Magnus title beginning in July but that fell through as well (Powers 14).

Despite the unpromising start, Shooter wasn't about to give up, and Magnus would end up a big part of Valiant's publishing plans for the following year. In fact, the classic character would be the linchpin for a whole new line of comics that would reverse Valiant's fortunes.

Small Press Survival

As Jim Shooter strove to get Valiant Comics up off the mat, other comic book publishers found themselves on the verge of throwing in the towel, including some that had thrived during the 1980s. **NOW Comics**—which published not only the aforementioned *Green Hornet* and *The Terminator* but also adaptations of *Married with*

Children, *The Real Ghostbusters* and *Speed Racer*, among other titles—filed bankruptcy documents in the U.S. District Court in Chicago claiming $1.4 million in liabilities against $300,000 in assets. The company disappeared from comic shops in August but returned briefly in November with a smaller line-up. NOW owner Tony Caputo had claimed to be looking for investors, including the man who had purchased bankrupt Comico, Andrew Rev, and educational publisher General Learning Corp. (Humphrey).

Eclipse Comics released more and more squarebound comics such as Jon J. Muth's four-issue adaptation of the classic German silent crime film *M*; *Orbit*, which adapted science fiction stories by Isaac Asimov; *Fly in My Eye*, adapting works by horror author Clive Barker; and Grant Morrison and Ian Gibson's three issue *Steed and Mrs. Peel*, based on the British *Avengers* television show. One of Eclipse's few remaining ongoing series was the Eisner Award-nominated **Miracleman**, now written by Neil Gaiman, who replaced Alan Moore (and also

received Moore's 30% ownership stake in the character). *Miracleman* #17 (June 1990) begins "Book Four: The Golden Age," a six-issue set of stand-alone stories that explored the utopia that Miracleman had created for humanity at the end of Alan Moore's tenure on the title. Elsewhere, **First Comics** announced late in the year that it would no longer publish monthly comics such as *Badger*, *Dreadstar* and *Grimjack* in favor of its line of *Classics Illustrated* comics.

In the same year that *Spider-Man* #1 sold over two million copies, some of the quirkier comics struggled to find an audience. Among the books that sold less than 3000 copies per issue were Julie Doucet's *Dirty Plotte*, Jim Woodring's *Jim*, Joe Sacco's *Yahoo* and Terry LaBan's *Unsupervised Existence* (Groth 6). **Martin Wagner**—who self-published the anthropomorphic *Hepcats*—also saw his sales in the 3000 copy range but rather than just market his drama about four college friends to the comic shops, Wagner offered incentives like sketches for fans who sent him cash in the mail.

Scott Rosenberg folded his Sunrise distributorship in 1988 but he plugged along with his conglomerate of black-and-white comic book companies—Aircel, Adventure and Eternity—that served as imprints of the other company he owned, **Malibu Comics**. One of Aircel's 1990 releases was **Men in Black**. Created and written by Lowell Cunningham and illustrated by Sandy Carruthers, the three-issue series features Jay and Kay as two agents of a clandestine organization that investigates paranormal activity like extra-terrestrials, lycanthropes and supernatural beings. *Men in Black* and its 1991 sequel, *Men in Black II*, were essentially ignored by comic book patrons. In 1997, however, the series became the inspiration for a blockbuster film starring Will Smith and Tommy Lee Jones. Fittingly, Cunningham wrote the comic adaptation of the film based on his original comic.

One of 1990's most fateful launches was Fantagraphics' *Hate*, the creation of writer/artist **Peter Bagge**. At the age of 32, Bagge was no comic book rookie. He began his career ten years earlier self-publishing three issues of *Comical Funnies*, which introduced the fictional Buddy Bradley and his dysfunctional suburban New Jersey family (loosely based on Bagge's own life). From 1983 to 1986, Bagge served as the managing editor for *Weirdo* magazine—founded by one of Bagge's idols, legendary cartoonist Robert Crumb—before continuing Buddy Bradley's story in Fantagraphics' *Neat Stuff*. When that series ended in 1989, Buddy had run away from home after a series of calamitous events. In *Hate*, Buddy moves to Seattle, living life as a grunge slacker. In doing so, both the character and the series embodied an early '90s zeitgeist, of a youth culture that rejected ambition and careerism and embraced disaffection and cynicism. *Hate*, though, was more than just an expression of changing social attitudes. It was also an evocation of the underground comix movement of the 1960s and 1970s as Bagge's highly stylized artwork presented characters with elastic arms, bulbous noses and giant mouths who evinced grand emotions, overreacting to every perceived slight.

Through its various printings, *Hate* #1 sold about 40,000 copies and later issues consistently sold between

Peter Bagge's **Hate** *embodied an early '90s zeitgeist.*
TM and © Peter Bagge.

Gilbert Hernandez's Birdland *was one of the first releases from Eros Comix.* TM and © Gilbert Hernandez.

20,000 and 25,000 copies — big numbers for an alternative comic book (Sally). The series and its creator also received a considerable amount of critical praise and honors. Nominated for two 1991 Eisner Awards and six 1991 Harvey Awards, Bagge won the Harvey for Best Cartoonist and *Hate* won the Harvey for Best New Series. It would hardly be the last time either the creator or the series found itself on the awards ballot.

Hate was just one of many highly regarded books that **Fantagraphics** released. The Seattle-based company—having recently moved from Los Angeles—also continued to publish two of the most influential comics news magazines: *The Comics Journal* and *Amazing Heroes*. In the face of some nasty budget shortfalls, however, Fantagraphics sought to supplement its revenue with a pornographic imprint: **Eros Comix**. Along with some predictably suggestive titles (e.g. *Time Wankers*), Eros also featured work by well-known comic book creators. For instance, *Megaton Man* creator Don Simpson (using the pseudonym Anton Drek) wrote and drew *Wendy Whitebread, Undercover Slut* about a policewoman posing as a prostitute who wore her badge tied to her g-string. The comic went through five printings. Future Eros series included *Birdland* by *Love and Rockets'*

Gilbert Hernandez and *Ironwood* by *Elementals'* creator Bill Willingham.

Comic book porn proved profitable enough for other publishers to join the parade, like Kitchen Sink and Rip Off Press. Apple Comics, known for comics like *Blood of Dracula*, *Thunderbunny* and Don Lomax's *Vietnam Journal*, opened its "Forbidden Fruit" line with titles such as *The Adventures of Misty*, *Sexy Superspy* and *Sindy*. Slave Labor Comics published *One-Fisted Tales*, and popular cartoonist Phil Foglio preceded the trend with his own *xXxenophile*.

From Turtles to Tundra

Six years after their debut as a small press black-and-white comic book, the **Teenage Mutant Ninja Turtles** had become a pop cultural phenomenon. They were everywhere. Besides the ongoing Mirage Studios comic book—which in 1990 had guest contributions from artists like Richard Corben, Rick Veitch, Michael Zulli and Mark Bodé, the son of legendary underground comic creator Vaughn Bodé—Archie Comics had its own series titled *Teenage Mutant Ninja Turtles Adventures*, based on the animated television show which, starting in September 1990, aired in both weekday afternoon syndication and on the CBS network's Saturday morning slate. The Turtles had their own Nintendo video game, their own cereal, their own frozen pizza, their own Hostess Pudding Pie, and most impressively, their own live-action feature film which arrived in movie theaters on March 30, 1990. Playmates Toys produced the ultrapopular Teenage Mutant Ninja Turtles action figures while other companies fought to have the Turtles' likenesses on their products: school supplies, Pez dispensers, skateboards, bed sheets and comforters and lots, lots more.

With merchandising alone grossing $400 million, the Turtles' co-creators **Kevin Eastman** and **Peter Laird** had hit a gold mine beyond their wildest dreams ("From Hither and Yon…"). That success, though, caused the pair tremendous headaches as well: endless meetings with lawyers, harassment from people obsessed with the Turtles, and, maybe most importantly, no time for the creation of comic books. Eastman felt like he was moving away from the art form that he loved.

So full of cash and idealistic fervor, Eastman decided to create **Tundra Publishing**, a place where creators could put together the works that they had always dreamed of producing, far from commercial considerations. The creators would have final say over every aspect of the work, be given a generous royalty, and have traffic managers rather than editors. Profits would be split 80/20 after costs were recovered, with 80% going to the creator. Eastman saw it as being the Apple Records of comics, an emulation of the record label that the Beatles created at the peak of their success that empowered musical artists.

Unfortunately, just as Apple Records was a financial black hole, so too became Tundra. As Eastman reflected several years later, "I thought I would spend a year forming this company that would break all the rules. I'd bring all these talented people and then expect them to climb inside my head, read my mind and try to make these impossible things happen" (Groth 62). Eastman intended to start the company small and build from there, but as Steve Bissette reported, "By the time [Eastman] went to his first convention as 'Tundra,' he returned with something like 70 projects. [laughs] It was mind-bogglingly out of control in its first few months, a Taj Mahal built upon no foundation to speak of — other than *money* and good will, in copious amounts" (Thompson 49). Among the comic projects that Eastman committed to during the 1990 San Diego Comic Con were *Cages* by *Arkham Asylum* artist Dave McKean, a reprint of the British graphic novel *Violent Cases* by McKean and Neil Gaiman and *No Man's Land* by *Enemy Ace: War Idyll* painter George Pratt. At that same San Diego Con, Eastman approached Mike Richardson with a proposal to merge Dark Horse Comics and Tundra, but Richardson turned him down cold. Kitchen Sink Press publisher Denis Kitchen, on the other hand, *was* interested in aligning his company with Eastman's. It would turn out to be a fateful decision in the future of both men and both companies.

Big Ideas/Big Numbers

Just as Kevin Eastman got Tundra off the ground, two other creators sought to advance comic book storytelling to its next level. One of them was a new-

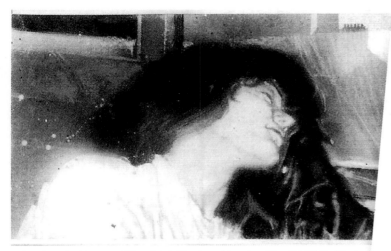

Alan Moore had huge ambitions for **Big Numbers**, *his series with artist Bill Sienkiewicz.*
TM and © respective copyright holder.

comer to the industry. The other was the most highly respected comic book writer of his time.

The newcomer was 23-year-old **Chris Oliveros** of Montreal, Canada. Inspired by Art Spiegelman's *Raw* comic magazine, Oliveros launched a comic book company called **Drawn & Quarterly**. As Oliveros related in 2003, "I was about 15, and I remember seeing the first issue of *Raw* when it came out... and it was like a revelation to me. Before then I had only known what most people consider to be standard comics, and then all of a sudden I saw this magazine that showed you could really do anything with comics both graphically and story-wise. It really sort of turned the whole definition of comics on its head. From then on I really had a very keen interest in somehow being involved in the medium myself" (Duncan). Drawn & Quarterly's first publication was a black-and-white comic magazine of the same name. The first issue (Spring 1990) featured work by many prominent alternative cartoonists: Peter Bagge, Joe Matt, J.D. King and Dennis Worden, among others. The next issue (Oct. 1990) included work by creators like Richard Sala, Frank Stack, and Julie Doucet. Later issues added Mary Fleener, Chester Brown, Joe Sacco, David Mazzucchelli and Daniel Clowes to the roster of talent featured in its pages. As the decade went on, D&Q would become an important publisher of emerging talents and among the first to give solo comic series to Adrian Tomine, Julie Doucet, Jason Lutes, Joe Matt, Chester Brown and Debbie Drechsler, all major lights in alternative comics during the 1990s. Fleener began a solo run with her own series, *Slutburger Stories*, though Rip Off Press in 1990. Her art style, described by critic Kevin W. Hall as "like a comic by Picasso" (Hall 79), was picked up by Drawn & Quarterly in 1991.

Besides Oliveros, the other person on a mission to elevate comic book storytelling was **Alan Moore**. The body of work Moore produced for DC Comics throughout the 1980s (specifically *Swamp Thing, Watchmen, Batman: The Killing Joke* and *V For Vendetta*) earned him the standing as one of the leading innovators of the comic book medium. By 1990, however, he had divorced himself from his former employer, upset with how DC both tried to foist a rating systems onto its creators and withhold from him and Dave Gibbons royalties earned from the sale of *Watchmen* merchandise.

Going forward, Moore's ambition was to create the kind of books that he felt DC Comics—or any other mainstream company—wouldn't publish. As Moore himself put it, "If you had got your own comics company, you weren't restricted by people at DC or Marvel, what could you do? How far could you go?" (Millidge 164).

His first work for the new decade, then, was a square, 10"x10", 12-issue series called ***Big Numbers***. Illustrated by **Bill Sienkiewicz**, *Big Numbers* explored the way that the creation of a California-style shopping mall affected the lives of forty diverse people in a thinly veiled version of Moore's British hometown of Northampton. The mall was both a literal reality—pushing aside nursing homes and child care centers—and also a figurative sign of the complex future that the town was facing. This visionary comic integrated varied topics like speed metal, British economic policies, LSD, poetry, computers and fractal numbers. (The comic was initially announced as *The Mandelbrot Set*, in honor of mathematician Benoit Mandelbrot's exploration of fractal numbers and chaos theory. Mandelbrot, though, asked Moore to change the title of the series.)

Big Numbers promised to be the strangest, most experimental work of Moore's career, with a plot so complex that the noted writer had to chart it out on extremely long sheets of paper just so he could follow the flow of his own story. Using royalties from *Watchmen*, Moore self-released *Big Numbers* through his **Mad Love Publishing**, and the first two issues both came out in 1990, three months apart. Everything seemed like it was going as planned.

But it wasn't. As later years would prove, Moore's groundbreaking work would never come to a conclusion, even with outside forces attempting to help out.

X-Year

Impressed by the sales revenue generated in 1990, the executives at **Marvel Comics** delivered a mandate to their editor-in-chief for 1991: don't just match the previous year's performance; do better. With Marvel about to become a publicly traded company on the New York Stock Exchange, potential investors needed assurances of sales growth. Nonetheless, **Tom DeFalco** felt he was in a bind as he cried to his editors, "How the hell are we gonna do better than that?" (Howe 325).

The problem wasn't going to be whether Marvel would continue to dominate comic book market share. Indeed, Marvel's share grew dramatically in 1991, peaking at 68.38% of all comics sold in July 1991. The same month, DC's sales comprised 19.8% of the market, which meant that all other publishers combined accounted for less than 12% of the market (Humphrey 11). The company with the third largest share for the month was Dark Horse Comics with a mere 2.3% of the market. For the entire year Marvel published 91 of the top 100 best-selling comics. The only non-Marvel books to crack the top 50 bestsellers were all four issues of DC's *Robin II* mini-series.

For Marvel, dominating market share was *fait accompli...* but also something that was no longer good enough for Marvel's executives. They wanted more, and they looked at 1990's *Spider-Man* #1 as the standard: every year going forward, Marvel needed comic books that sold millions of copies. Nothing less than annual record-breaking sales events would suffice. With that expectation hanging over him, DeFalco turned to the one Marvel property he knew could deliver the results his superiors wanted: the **X-Men**.

X Marks the Top

DeFalco ordered the creation of a new X-Men comic book. While editor **Bob Harras** initially had concerns that the marketplace wouldn't support yet another Marvel mutant title (to go along with *Uncanny X-Men, Wolverine, X-Factor, Excalibur* and *New Mutants*), he eventually realized a new X-Men book gave him the opportunity to make some big changes that he felt were long overdue.

Harras started with *New Mutants*, which had been suffering a creative schism for nearly a year. Writer **Louise Simonson** and artist **Rob Liefeld** had incompatible approaches to the series. Liefeld's layouts emphasized action-packed violence, foiling Simonson's attempts to keep *New Mutants* focused on young characters struggling with both their powers and immaturity. Increasingly frustrated with the fact that her dialogue and plots would be frequently changed without her approval (or even her consultation), Simonson finally faced facts: Harras had cast his lot with Liefeld, and it was time for her to move on. After ten years working at Marvel, first as an editor and then as a writer, Louise Simonson abandoned *New Mutants* (and her other longtime assignment, *X-Factor*) and figuratively walked across the street to DC Comics where she helmed a new

New Mutants #98 introduced a trio of new characters, including Deadpool. TM and © Marvel Characters, Inc.

Superman title, *Superman: the Man of Steel*, starting in May.

Liefeld's handpicked replacement for Simonson, **Fabian Nicieza**, took over *New Mutants* with #98 (Feb. 1991), an issue which introduced three more action-oriented characters: Domino, Gideon and the motor-mouthed, psychotic mercenary Deadpool. With Simonson gone, *New Mutants* finally became the book that Liefeld always wanted it to be. The young artist, though, had ambitions beyond creative control; Liefeld wanted to

turn *New Mutants* into one of Marvel's tentpole titles. Backed by Nicieza and Marvel's Director of Marketing Sven Larsen, Liefeld approached DeFalco about cancelling *New Mutants* and relaunching it as a new series. Liefeld even promised his editor-in-chief that the rebrand would be a huge hit. That confidence was music to DeFalco's ears, and he and Harras approved the plan (Howe 326).

With issue #100 (April 1991) the *New Mutants* series ended with a jawdropping cliffhanger: on the final page, Stryfe removes his helmet to reveal he looks exactly like his arch-nemesis Cable. (Readers would have to wait a few years to learn that Stryfe is Cable's clone.) The story continued four months later in the debut issue of a new series titled *X-Force*, the new name for the Cable-led team whose membership consisted of Boom Boom, Domino, Feral, Shatterstar, Warpath and the final holdout from 1982's original *New Mutants* cast, Cannonball. X-Force moves into a new base of operations to continue its battle against Stryfe's Mutant Liberation Front. With that, Marvel had a mutant group for the 1990s, one completely divorced from

the X-Men's decades-old purpose of mutants seeking peaceful co-existence with the humans who fear and hate them. Liefeld and Nicieza turned that premise on its head; Cable's pro-active militancy had *X-Force* fighting a war where they attacked—and sometimes killed—the enemies who sought to destroy them.

Liefeld's forceful artistry perfectly suited *X-Force*'s displays of violence, and the new series cemented his status as one of Marvel's most popular artists. At the same time, however, Liefeld acquired more detractors than seemingly any other creator in the comic book industry. In nearly every comic book fanzine, a debate about Liefeld raged on. Many commentators complained that his work was too undisciplined and too reliant on splash pages. One writer encapsulated the debate well by saying "[Liefeld's] style remains controversial in its flaunting of traditional pacing, proportion and perspective" (McCallum 57). The worst accusation directed at Liefeld was that he often copied other artists' work. For instance, a two-page spread in *New Mutants* #100 shows Shatterstar thrusting his sword behind him

Spinning out of **The New Mutants**, *the first issue of Rob Liefeld and Fabian Nicieza's* **X-Force** *sold over four million copies.* TM and © Marvel Characters, Inc.

TIMELINE: 1991

A compilation of the year's notable comic book history events alongside some of the year's most significant popular culture and historical events. (On sale dates are approximations.)

January 16: With Iraq refusing to withdraw its forces from Kuwait, Operation Desert Storm commences. Coalition forces—led by the United States and Great Britain—begin bombing Iraqi targets.

February 14: *Silence of the Lambs*—starring Jodie Foster as a rookie FBI agent and Anthony Hopkins as serial killer Hannibal Lecter—arrives in movie theaters. The film will win five Academy Awards, including Best Picture.

March 3: After a high-speed car chase, four Los Angeles police officers pummel Rodney King with batons when he resists arrest, even after he has been subdued. A local resident records the assault on video, which is soon broadcast around the country. The police officers are subsequently charged with use of excessive force.

April 4: Graham Ingels—the comic book artist most famous for drawing EC's horror titles of the 1950s (*Tales from the Crypt, The Haunt of Fear* and *The Vault of Horror*)—dies of cancer at the age of 75.

June 25: A civil war erupts in Eastern Europe when Croatia and Slovenia proclaim independence from Yugoslavia.

JANUARY	FEBRUARY	MARCH	APRIL	MAY	JUNE

January 17: Iraq launches Scud missiles into Israel. U.S. Patriot surface-to-air missiles soon protect Israel (and Saudia Arabia) from further Scud attacks.

February 24: Coalition forces, led by U.S. General Norman Schwarzkopf, launch a ground assault against Iraqi troops. Four days later, President Bush declares that "Kuwait is liberated, Iraq's army is defeated."

March 11: The second Teenage Mutant Ninja Turtles movie, *The Secret of the Ooze*, arrives in movie theaters. It earns over $78 million at the box office.

April 26: The U.S. government reports the nation has sunk deeper into recession as the gross national product shrinks to 2.8 percent.

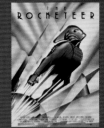

June 21: *The Rocketeer*—based on Dave Steven's 1980s comic book—premieres as Walt Disney's latest feature film. Starring Billy Campbell, Jennifer Connelly and Timothy Dalton, and written by the *Flash* television show's executive producers Danny Bilson and Paul De Meo, the movie earns over $46 million at the box office.

to impale his attacker. The same spread—identical in perspective, character stance and panel placement—can be found in Frank Miller's 1983 mini-series *Ronin*.

Regardless, *X-Force* #1 was essentially "critic proof," especially since it came polybagged with one of five different X-Force trading cards inside. In order to obtain a complete set of cards, collectors had to purchase five copies of the issue (and many purchased a sixth copy so as to be able read the issue while keeping the other five copies sealed in the polybag). Comic shop retailers ordered the issue by the case load, and as a result, over four million copies of *X-Force* #1 were distributed to stores, outperforming 1990's *Spider-Man* #1 by more than a million copies. Tom DeFalco had his first blockbuster hit of the year. He didn't have to wait long for his second.

The "X-Tinction Agenda" crossover event of 1990 began the reset of the X-Men franchise by reuniting the founding members with the current team. The issues that followed presented the return of Professor Xavier from outer space, culminating with *Uncanny X-Men* #280 (Sept. 1991) in which Xavier defeats a psychic monster known as the Shadow King at the cost of the use of his own legs. Once again confined to a wheelchair, Xavier resumes his role as mutantkind's mentor, just in time for the debut of the X-Men's new monthly book, which was simply titled ***X-Men***.

Marvel promoted the new *X-Men* title many months before the release of its first issue, and it became the most eagerly anticipated new comic book of the year. Even *Marvel Age* #104, Marvel's in-house hype fanzine that spotlighted the new series, sold out at several retailers (Chun 75). When the first issue finally arrived at stores in August (cover date October), Marvel adopted a similar publishing strategy that it did with *Spider-Man* #1 and *X-Force* #1: entice collectors to buy multiple copies. To that end, *X-Men* #1 had four versions of the same issue, each with a different cover. Put together, the four interlocking covers form an homage to Jack Kirby's 1963 cover to the original *X-Men* #1 which shows the team attacking its longtime archenemy Magneto *en masse*. Those four covers were released individually over four consecutive weeks, from August 13 to September 3. Marvel then issued a deluxe version of *X-Men* #1 on September 10, with a foldout that included all four covers in one expanded image. Printed on glossy paper, the deluxe edition retailed for $3.95 and outsold all the other versions (which cost $1.50 each) by a wide margin.

Ultimately, an unprecedented 8.1 million copies of *X-Men* #1 were distributed to newsstands and comic shops, a figure exceeding the rest of Marvel's Direct Sales circulation for that month combined, and one-third of Diamond Distribution's entire comics business for August 1991 ("From Hither and Yon..."). However, retailers dramatically

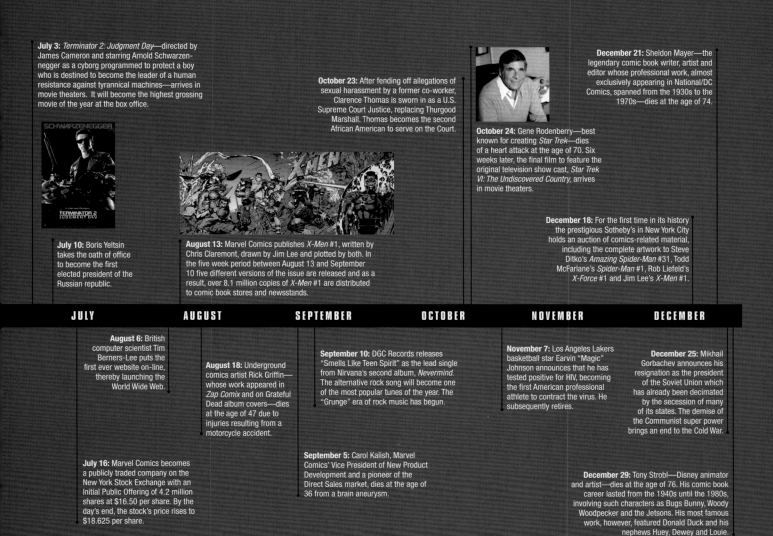

July 3: *Terminator 2: Judgment Day*—directed by James Cameron and starring Arnold Schwarzenegger as a cyborg programmed to protect a boy who is destined to become the leader of a human resistance against tyrannical machines—arrives in movie theaters. It will become the highest grossing movie of the year at the box office.

July 10: Boris Yeltsin takes the oath of office to become the first elected president of the Russian republic.

October 23: After fending off allegations of sexual harassment by a former co-worker, Clarence Thomas is sworn in as a U.S. Supreme Court Justice, replacing Thurgood Marshall. Thomas becomes the second African American to serve on the Court.

August 13: Marvel Comics publishes *X-Men* #1, written by Chris Claremont, drawn by Jim Lee and plotted by both. In the five week period between August 13 and September 10 five different versions of the issue are released and as a result, over 8.1 million copies of *X-Men* #1 are distributed to comic book stores and newsstands.

October 24: Gene Rodenberry—best known for creating *Star Trek*—dies of a heart attack at the age of 70. Six weeks later, the final film to feature the original television show cast, *Star Trek VI: The Undiscovered Country*, arrives in movie theaters.

December 21: Sheldon Mayer—the legendary comic book writer, artist and editor whose professional work, almost exclusively appearing in National/DC Comics, spanned from the 1930s to the 1970s—dies at the age of 74.

December 18: For the first time in its history the prestigious Sotheby's in New York City holds an auction of comics-related material, including the complete artwork to Steve Ditko's *Amazing Spider-Man* #31, Todd McFarlane's *Spider-Man* #1, Rob Liefeld's *X-Force* #1 and Jim Lee's *X-Men* #1.

| JULY | AUGUST | SEPTEMBER | OCTOBER | NOVEMBER | DECEMBER |

August 6: British computer scientist Tim Berners-Lee puts the first ever website on-line, thereby launching the World Wide Web.

August 18: Underground comics artist Rick Griffin—whose work appeared in *Zap Comix* and on Grateful Dead album covers—dies at the age of 47 due to injuries resulting from a motorcycle accident.

September 10: DGC Records releases "Smells Like Teen Spirit" as the lead single from Nirvana's second album, *Nevermind*. The alternative rock song will become one of the most popular tunes of the year. The "Grunge" era of rock music has begun.

November 7: Los Angeles Lakers basketball star Earvin "Magic" Johnson announces that he has tested positive for HIV, becoming the first American professional athlete to contract the virus. He subsequently retires.

December 25: Mikhail Gorbachev announces his resignation as the president of the Soviet Union which has already been decimated by the secession of many of its states. The demise of the Communist super power brings an end to the Cold War.

July 16: Marvel Comics becomes a publicly traded company on the New York Stock Exchange with an Initial Public Offering of 4.2 million shares at $16.50 per share. By the day's end, the stock's price rises to $18.625 per share.

September 5: Carol Kalish, Marvel Comics' Vice President of New Product Development and a pioneer of the Direct Sales market, dies at the age of 36 from a brain aneurysm.

December 29: Tony Strobl—Disney animator and artist—dies at the age of 76. His comic book career lasted from the 1940s until the 1980s, involving such characters as Bugs Bunny, Woody Woodpecker and the Jetsons. His most famous work, however, featured Donald Duck and his nephews Huey, Dewey and Louie.

over-ordered the issue. Thousands, and perhaps millions, of copies didn't sell through at comic shops because owners stockpiled them as investments. After speaking to twenty comic shops across the country several months after *X-Men* #1 had been released, *The Comics Journal* reported that over half the stores had copies of *X-Men* in stock. Herb McCaulla, president of Southern Fantasy Distributors, stated that some of his accounts had cut back on future purchases or even gone out of business because they purchased too many copies of *X-Men* #1. Most of his clients sold out of the deluxe version of the comic with the gatefold cover, but others had troubles. On the other hand, John Davis of Capital City Distribution believed that few of his client stores lost money with *X-Men* #1, "Most stores sold so many copies that it was still profitable, and those remaining copies are going to be sold over time" (Humphrey 13-14).

Two X-Men titles allowed for the mutant super-hero group to be separated into two teams. *X-Men* featured the "Blue" team: Cyclops, Wolverine, Beast, Psylocke, Rogue and Gambit. In the opening issues of the new title, they engage their former ally, Magneto, as the master of magnetism declares his Earth-orbiting asteroid base a safe haven for any mutant. To protect mutantkind, Magneto has seized several nuclear missiles from a sunken Soviet submarine, an act that puts Earth's world powers on alert. Meanwhile, starting with issue #281 (Oct. 1991), *Uncanny X-Men* presented the

"Gold" team: Marvel Girl, Storm, Archangel, Iceman and Colossus. They confront the next generation of Sentinel robots as well as a time-displaced mutant warrior from a dystopian future. His name was **Bishop**, and he would become the X-Men's next new member. (Furthermore, the title that used to star the original X-Men—*X-Factor*—was also revamped. Starting with issue #71 (Oct. 1991), writer Peter David and artist Larry Stroman provided banter-filled mayhem with an eclectic cast of throwaway mutants: Havok, Polaris, Wolfsbane, Quicksilver, Madrox the Multiple Man and a hulking bruiser who names himself "Strong Guy." To get a sense of the kind of comical tone that David and Stroman injected into the series, one need only look at *X-Factor* #71's title: "Cutting the Mustard.")

The X-Men franchise was truly entering a new age, a perception reinforced by the fact that the person steering it was no longer the one who had been at its helm since the mid-1970s, writer **Chris Claremont**. Instead, the series' new creative architects were its rising superstar artists: **Jim Lee** on *X-Men* and **Whilce Portacio** on *Uncanny X-Men*. Like Louise Simonson before him, Claremont had fallen out of favor with Bob Harras. Indeed, Harras had spent much of the previous year undoing many of the changes Claremont made to the X-Men (e.g. removing the team from exile, returning Professor Xavier from outer space, restoring Magneto as a villain, et al). By the time *X-Men* #1 was

In part due to its multiple interlocking covers, **X-Men** *#1 by Chris Claremont and Jim Lee sold an unprecedented 8.1 million copies to comic shops.* TM and © Marvel Characters, Inc.

published, Claremont had been removed completely from *Uncanny X-Men* and his role on *X-Men* had been reduced to writing dialogue over Jim Lee's plots. Even that limited task became arduous because Lee couldn't meet his deadlines. With artwork being delivered to him late, Claremont often had only one day to write dialogue before sending pages to the printer (Howe 328).

Before long, Claremont had enough of the situation and he quit. His final issue was *X-Men* #3 (Dec. 1991), not that Marvel promoted that fact with any kind of fanfare. The printed acknowledgement of Claremont's departure was almost unnoticeable. A small caption at the top of the first page of *X-Men* #3 declares, "Stan Lee proudly presents Chris

Claremont's final issue of the X-Men." An even smaller caption in the issue's final panel reads, "CSC – 1976-1991 – Fin." And that was it. There was no editorial that waxed poetic about Claremont's contributions to Marvel's most popular property and no farewell column from Claremont himself. The longest-running tenure of any creator on any title in Marvel Comics history ended quietly, and business went on as usual. Within a few months, the *X-Men's* letter column was being filled not with missives that lamented Claremont's exit but with breathless praise of Jim Lee's work. Some letters that the editors selected to run even suggested that the series was better off without Claremont. Consider the column in *X-Men* #9 which contains a letter that reads, "...I was extremely worried that the X-Men would just not be the same [with Claremont gone]. But after issues #4 and #5, I can see that my fears were groundless. For the first time in what seemed like ages, we actually had an issue that seemed more devoted to the X-Men's personal lives than just another mindless slugfest..."

With Claremont gone, the person responsible for writing the dialogue for both X-Men titles was someone Claremont had been at odds with many times over the past decade: his former X-Men collaborator, **John Byrne**. Some fans erroneously assumed Byrne accepted the assignments in order to settle a score with Claremont or prove he was the better writer. Byrne's real reasons were far more opportunistic: he knew working on the X-Men would earn him far more money than he was making from his underperforming *Namor* series. He told one interviewer at the time, "The X-Men are going to pay my mortgage" (O'Neill 4). While that may have been true, Byrne soon found his task to be both extraordinarily challenging and unappealing. First, the X-Men characters themselves had changed so much since he was last involved with them over a decade ago that he had no connection to them (Byrne, "Questions About Aborted Storylines"). Second, Lee and Portacio continued to miss their art deadlines and like Claremont before him, Byrne found himself rushed to write dialogue as fast as he could.

The situation came to a head when Harras asked Byrne to dialogue an entire issue overnight. Byrne threw up his

Jim Lee, Whilce Portacio and John Byrne delivered the second mutant team in **Uncanny X-Men**. TM and © Marvel Characters, Inc.

hands in exasperation and refused to do it. Scrambling, Harras turned to Fabian Nicieza to pull the all-nighter. Nicieza turned him down too. Harras's last resort was someone who had recently begun writing *Excalibur* after producing various stories in *Marvel Comics Presents* for the previous two years: **Scott Lobdell** (Howe 329-330).

Lobdell proved he could handle the deadline pressures, so much so that Harras quickly made him the full-time scripter of both X-Men titles. With that, John Byrne's work was done. The fan favorite creator contributed to just five issues of *Uncanny X-Men* and two issues of *X-Men* before he was replaced by a 30-year-old with very little track record in comics. Lobdell, though, would take full advantage of the opportunity Harras provided him. The inexperienced tyro became one of the chief creative forces of the X-Men franchise for most of the 1990s, contributing to its most significant story arcs, crossover events and spinoffs.

To Infinity and Beyond

The generational process that pushed older creators aside and helped elevate Byrne and Claremont in the 1980s was now lifting Lee, Liefeld, Portacio, Nicieza and Lobdell to be the most famous comic creators of their era. Some of the older creators, though, still had some marks to make on the industry. One of them was **Jim Starlin** who had an eventful decade during the 1980s. From creating Marvel's first graphic novel (*The Death of Captain Marvel*) to launching Epic Comics' first creator-owned series (*Dreadstar*) to writing a Prestige format four issue Batman mini-series (*Batman: The Cult*), Starlin's work was varied, provocative and more often than not, very popular with the fans. But it was the 1988 story that killed Jason Todd—the second Robin—that got Starlin in trouble. "A Death in the Family," written by Starlin, allowed fans to dial a 1-900 number at 50¢ per call to determine whether Jason Todd would live or die at the hands of the Joker. In a close count, the fans voted to kill Robin. Several months after the publication of Robin's demise, *Comics Buyer's Guide* #805 (April 21, 1989) ran an interview in which Starlin asserted that had fans voted to keep

Robin alive he would have put the Boy Wonder into a coma to remove him from the series (Salerno 3). Unsurprisingly, DC Comics didn't take kindly to the suggestion that the 1-900 vote essentially had no bearing on Jason Todd's ultimate fate and a spokesperson officially refuted Starlin's claims. Before 1989 ended, Starlin found himself without any DC assignments, and he could only conclude that the *CBG* article resulted in him being blacklisted.

So Starlin returned to Marvel Comics. He converted his and Bernie Wrightson's sequel to *Batman: The Cult* into a four-issue Prestige format Punisher mini-series titled *P.O.V.* As Starlin later admitted, "some of the characters from *The Cult* got converted over almost wholesale" (Best). Starlin also assumed the writing chores on *Silver Surfer* with issue #34 (Feb. 1990). That assignment allowed him to return to one of his favorite creations: **Thanos**, the cosmic madman originally influenced by Jack Kirby's New Gods villain Darkseid. As *Silver Surfer* #34 and #35 reveal, the personification of Death has brought Thanos back from the realm of the dead in order to correct a universal imbalance: there are more people alive than have ever died. After *Silver Surfer* #38, the story continues in a two-issue Prestige format series titled *Thanos Quest* (cover-dated August and November 1990) where the "Mad Titan" collects the six Infinity Gems together as a weapon of unlimited power. With the Infinity Gauntlet in his possession, Thanos has become a god. The stage was set for Marvel's best-selling crossover event of 1991: the six-issue ***Infinity Gauntlet*** mini-series.

Throughout *Infinity Gauntlet* #1 (July 1991), Thanos strives to impress his

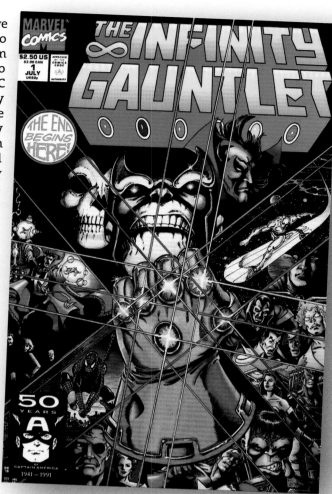

The cosmic The Infinity Gauntlet *by Jim Starlin and George Pérez was the best-selling crossover of 1991.* TM and © Marvel Characters, Inc.

beloved Death. Among other things, he builds a shrine to her and he turns the space pirate Nebula (who claims to be Thanos's grand-daughter) into a grotesque zombie. Finally, with the power of the Infinity Gauntlet, Thanos causes half the people in the universe to simply blink out of existence. Captain America watches his fellow Avengers Hawkeye and Sersi vanish in front of his eyes. Other casualties include the Fantastic Four, Alpha Flight and Daredevil. In *Infinity Gauntlet* #3 (Sept. 1991), Adam Warlock—a cosmic super-hero whom Starlin famously handled in the 1970s—assembles some of Earth's mightiest beings to oppose Thanos: Captain America, Thor, Spider-Man, the Hulk, Iron Man, Namor, Wolverine, Cyclops, She-Hulk, Nova and Doctor Doom, among others. One by one, though, Thanos slays each of those super-powered characters with ease. The Mad Titan's omnipotence is then challenged by the supreme beings of the Marvel Universe, among them Galactus, the Celestials, Chronos, Eon and the Stranger. But they all soon become his captives. Thanos even overcomes Eternity, the embodiment of the entire Marvel Universe. With that, he has become the ruler of all reality... until the decrepit Nebula staggers towards the arch-villain's abandoned body and removes the Infinity Gauntlet from his hand. With newfound power, Nebula regains her vitality and restores the universe to how it was before Thanos wielded the Gauntlet (most of the super-heroes lose their memories of everything that had happened). The mini-series ends with Adam Warlock gaining control of the Gauntlet and vowing to safeguard it. Thanos, on the other hand, goes into exile on a remote world to live out his life as a simple farmer.

Infinity Gauntlet was one of the most popular comics of 1991, with all six issues finishing among the top 100 best-selling comics of the year. In addition, the titles that crossed-over into the event—*Doctor Strange, Incredible Hulk, Quasar, Silver Surfer* and *Sleepwalker*—enjoyed a sales boost. A follow-up series was launched two months after lhe release of *Infinity Gauntlet #6*; *Warlock and the Infinity Watch* teamed Adam Warlock with other cosmic characters like Pip, Moondragon, Gamora and Drax as they protected the Infinity Gauntlet from falling into the wrong hands. Additional related series included 1992's *Infinity War* and 1993's *Infinity Crusade*. All three follow-up series were written by Jim Starlin.

George's War Wounds

The artist who drew the first several issues of *Infinity Gauntlet* was **George Pérez**, a very fitting choice considering Pérez's fan appeal and aptitude for drawing crowded panels. Unfortunately, Pérez couldn't maintain his interest in the project. He explained, "I was becoming overly critical of the books I was working on. With *Infinity Gauntlet*, I felt that the story did not warrant six double-sized books.... It seemed that Thanos was just talking to the heroes, knocking them back, talking, they come back, he knocks them back,

Ron Lim replaced George Pérez as artist on Infinity Gauntlet *starting with issue #4.*

TM and © Marvel Characters, Inc.

he talks some more—it seemed really, really padded to me" (Nolen-Weathington 60-61). Pérez's disinterest caused his production to slow down further and further as the series went on. By the time work on issue #4 was under way, Tom DeFalco stepped in and replaced Pérez with **Ron Lim**, the regular artist on *Silver Surfer*. Pérez had no problem being dismissed. Indeed, as far as Pérez was concerned, Lim should have been the first person tapped to draw *Infinity Gauntlet* since he had also drawn the *Silver Surfer* issues that led into the mini-series event (Nolen-Weathington 60). To show the readers he had no ill will at being replaced, Pérez inked Lim's covers for *Infinity Gauntlet* #5 and #6.

Pérez probably shouldn't have agreed to take on *Infinity Gauntlet* in the first place, considering he was already busy working on a major crossover event for **DC Comics**. Originally called "The Holy Wars" (a title DC deemed too religious), **War of the Gods** was intended to both celebrate the 50th anniversary of Wonder Woman's first appearance in 1941 and conclude Pérez's five-year run as the writer on *Wonder Woman*.

The year began with the Amazons beginning a goodwill tour of the outside world in the double-sized *Wonder Woman* #50 (Jan. 1991). In succeeding issues the goddess Circe commits a series of brutal murders in which precious artifacts are stolen. She then frames the Amazons for the crimes. Tensions rise to a fever pitch, and Steve Trevor is ordered to attack Themyscira. The next part of Circe's scheme unfolds in *War of the Gods* #1 (Sept. 1991) when she manipulates the Greek and Roman gods to rage war against each other. The Greek gods call upon Wonder Woman to battle Captain Marvel, the possessed champion of the Roman pantheon. As Circe's magic begins to ravage the world over, Earth's super-heroes intervene and the *War of the Gods* story spins out into over a dozen DC titles including *Animal Man*, *Batman*, and *Superman: Man of Steel*, to create a grand story arc encompassing the entire DC Universe.

That was the plan, at least. The execution of that plan proved less than successful for a variety of reasons. Pérez spent a year plotting the *War of the Gods* event, but when it came time to coordinate the mini-series with other DC titles, Pérez's editor, Karen Berger, went on maternity leave. Her absence caused a breakdown in interoffice communications that, according to Pérez, undermined the entire event: "By the time the

series was coming out it was quite obvious that, in some cases, I had done overviews that the creators of the tie-in books never saw—the editors never got them to them. So there was a crossover that no one seemed to know anything about" (Nolen-Weathington 59). In the confusion, several tie-in issues shipped out of order or didn't properly indicate their "War of the Gods" chapter number. Extra issues of *Captain Atom* and *Hawk & Dove*—already slated to be cancelled—had to be added to DC's production schedule, and the cover to *Justice League Europe* #31 didn't even carry the "War of the Gods" banner. Some tie-in issues shipped late, which allowed retailers to return unsold copies to their distributors for credit, an allowance many shop owners took full advantage of. Frank Magiaracina of Friendly Frank's Distribution reported that "we probably got 40% to 60% of them back. Usually we get just a few back" (Humphrey 11).

As far as crossover events went, it was hardly DC Comics' finest effort. Mercifully, *War of the Gods* only lasted four issues. The concluding chapter ended the conflict with Circe's death and the dispersal of the warring gods. A month later DC published *Wonder Woman* #62, the final issue of Pérez's tenure on the series. Appropriately, the

George Pérez spearheaded one of DC Comics' major 1991 events, **War of the Gods,** *which centered on Wonder Woman.* TM and © DC Comics.

cover banner reads, "An Era Ends For Wonder Woman." As they rebuild their war-destroyed homes, the Amazons have come to peace with mankind to the point where men are allowed on Paradise Island for the first time.

Pérez crafted a fitting conclusion to his run on the title... with one exception: he wasn't allowed to marry off Steve Trevor and Etta Candy, a plot thread he had been developing since the series began. That task was passed on to the next writer on *Wonder Woman*, William Messner-Loebs (O'Neill, "War of the Gods"). For Pérez, that proved to be the final slight at the end of a difficult year. *Wonder Woman* #62 was the last DC comic book that Pérez would work on for several years to come.

Armageddon Now

At the same time *War of the Gods* launched, a different DC Comics crossover event was wrapping up: "**Armageddon 2001**." Written by Archie Goodwin, drawn by Dan Jurgens and Dick Giordano and edited by Denny O'Neil, *Armageddon 2001 Special* #1 (May 2001) begins in the year 2030 where a dystopian Earth is ruled by an armored overlord named Monarch. One scientist, Matthew Ryder, discovers that in the year 2001, one of Earth's super-heroes turned evil, killed all of the other super-heroes and then conquered the world. Ryder, though, can't figure out exactly which super-hero betrayed his comrades, so he hatches a plan to travel

back in time to the year 1991, determine Monarch's true identity and stop the villain ten years before his rise to despotism. As Ryder traverses the time stream, the temporal energies transform his body. He becomes Waverider with the ability to see a person's possible future life. Arriving in 1991, Waverider endeavors to use this power to learn which super-hero will become Monarch.

The story continued through twelve DC Annuals released between early April and late August. In each Annual Waverider comes in contact with various super-heroes and learns what the future could hold in store for each of them. For instance, in *Superman Annual* #3 (written by Jurgens and pencilled by Dusty Abell), Waverider sees the Man of Steel attempting to destroy the world's nuclear weapons but getting killed by Batman in the process. A different future presented in *Action Comics Annual* #3 (written by Roger Stern and pencilled by Tom Grummett) has Superman becoming President of the United States. In *Hawk and Dove Annual* #2 (written by Barbara Kesel and pencilled by Curt Swan, among others) the daughter of Hawk and Dove battles Monarch. Elsewhere, *New Titans Annual* #7 (written by Marv Wolfman and pencilled by Tom Grindberg) introduces the Team Titans, future offshoots of the Titans who would receive their own title in 1992.

Besides providing visions of the future lives of various DC super-heroes, "Armageddon 2001" functions as a kind of murder mystery, enticing readers to look for clues planted within the Annuals in order to deduce which hero was fated to become Monarch before the answer was fully revealed in the story's final installment, *Armageddon 2001 Special* #2 (Oct. 1991). For many fans, the real clues were found in the comic news media's advance reports, where the absence of a *Captain Atom Annual* in the crossover and the upcoming cancellation of his title made Captain Atom the number one suspect. As Dan Jurgens recalled, that assertion soon became disseminated via a premium-rate telephone service: "There was a 900 service that somebody set up that supposedly gave you inside secrets of the comic book industry. And somewhere along the line, that 900 service started saying that Monarch was going to be Captain Atom" (Bruck 49). One need only read the end of *Justice League Europe Annual* #2 to get the hint that Captain Atom was indeed the man Waverider was looking for. Nonetheless, many DC staffers felt they had a problem on their hands: the Captain Atom report— whether leak or theory— became so widespread

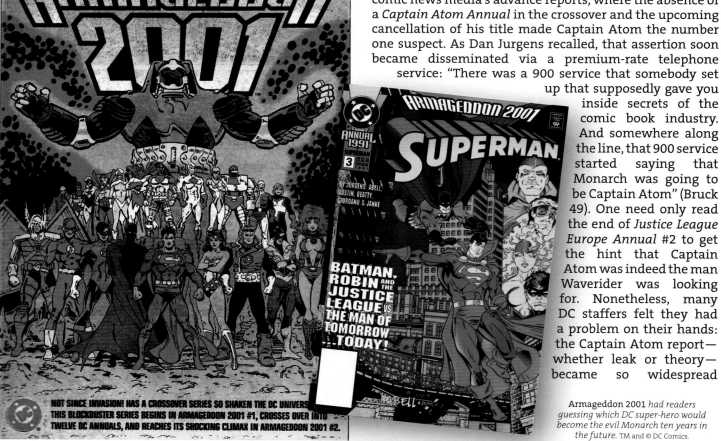

Armageddon 2001 had readers guessing which DC super-hero would become the evil Monarch ten years in the future. TM and © DC Comics.

among fandom that it was feared that too many readers would feel let down if the rumor proved true. So rather than keep the story the way it was originally plotted, a last-minute change was made.

When *Armageddon 2001 Special* #2 arrived in stores, readers discovered that the super-hero who becomes Monarch is Hank Hall, a.k.a. Hawk of *Hawk & Dove*. Ironically, in the rush to swap out Captain Atom with a super-hero readers wouldn't suspect, the one character who *couldn't possibly* become Monarch based on what had already been presented in the Annuals was selected. *Hawk & Dove Annual* #2 showed not only Hawk fighting and dying at Monarch's hands but also Waverider witnessing many possible futures and definitively ruling out Hawk and Dove as candidates to become Monarch: "No matter the future, [Hawk and Dove] fought [Monarch] but never became him." Compounding matters, Hawk has to act out of character in order to become Monarch; inexplicably, he murders Dove, the love of his life.

In a case of "can't win for losing," DC faced the wrath of many fans who cried foul at *Armageddon 2001*'s altered resolution. Nothing could be done after the fact, though, and DC was just going to have to live with the consequences. A direct sequel to the storyline appeared as *Armageddon: the Alien Agenda,* a four issue mini-series that premiered one month after "Armageddon 2001" ended. That story—written by Jonathan Peterson and illustrated by a different artist for each issue—has Captain Atom chasing Monarch in a time-spanning tale that journeyed from the primordial past to ancient Rome to the American Old West to the atomic bomb explosions during World War II.

As a result of a last-minute change, Hawk became revealed as Monarch instead of Captain Atom.
TM and © DC Comics.

Robin received his own bestselling mini-series in 1991.
TM and © DC Comics.

Boy Wonder Blockbuster

"Armageddon 2001" and "War of the Gods" were DC's two biggest crossover events of 1991. None of the books associated with those events, however, turned out to be bestsellers. The title that *did* become DC's hit of the year featured the most recognizable supporting character in all comic books.

After Tim Drake first donned the **Robin** costume at the end of 1990, DC took steps to make him more prominent throughout 1991. For the first time in comics history, the Boy Wonder starred in his own title. Written by Chuck Dixon, drawn by Tom Lyle and Bob Smith with covers by Brian Bolland, the five issue *Robin* mini-series (first issue cover-dated Jan. 1991) has Batman sending Tim Drake around the world in order to be sufficiently trained to be his sidekick. Under the tutelage of expert martial artist Lady Shiva, Robin overcomes the threats of King Snake and Lynx and returns to Gotham City as a self-assured crimefighter, ready to serve at Batman's side.

When the first two issues of the mini-series sold well enough to earn additional print runs (*Robin* #1 even received a third printing after the second one sold out), a second Robin mini-series was assured. Seven months after the final issue of the first mini-series was published, the first issue of *Robin II* arrived in stores. As the cover's "Joker's Wild" subtitle indicates, the second mini-series (four issues instead of five) has Robin singlehandedly dealing with the Joker, who has escaped Arkham Asylum while Batman

As this panel from Batman/Judge Dredd: Judgment on Gotham *shows, the graphic novel's two title characters don't get along well.*
Batman TM and © DC Comics. Judge Dredd TM and © Rebellion.

is out of town. The creative team remained Chuck Dixon, Tom Lyle and Bob Smith.

For *Robin II*, DC decided to take a page out of Marvel's playbook: the first issue was released with five different covers. (A polybagged "Collector's Set" offered all five covers for a $7.50 retail price.) Going one step further, Bruce Bristow, DC Comics' Vice President of Sales and Marketing, came up with the novel idea of imbedding a hologram card on the covers. Each issue carried a different hologram: Robin for issue #1, Batman for issue #2, the Joker for issue #3 and the Bat-signal for issue #4. The combination of variant covers and hologram trading cards resulted in massive sales for the *Robin II* mini-series. Capital City Distribution alone ordered 322,250 copies of issue #1.

The success of this mini-series set the stage first for *Robin III: Cry of the Huntress*, a six-issue mini with lenticular covers, which premiered with a December 1992 cover date and then an ongoing *Robin* series in 1993. Tim Drake was here to stay as a worthy and unique new Robin.

The Dark Knight Meets The Dredd Judge

In 1991 Batman took part in a crossover that was both intercompany and intercontinental. ***Batman/Judge Dredd: Judgment on Gotham*** teamed DC's Dark Knight with the authoritarian law enforcement officer made famous by the British comic magazine *2000 AD*. Four years in the making, the deliriously surreal 64-page one-shot came courtesy of a creative team that knew both protagonists very well: writer Alan Grant had already produced long runs on *Batman* and *Detective Comics*, and he and fellow writer John Wagner, along with artist Simon Bisley, delivered many of Judge Dredd's wildest stories.

Judgment on Gotham begins when Dredd makes a dimensional jump to Gotham City, where he kills several people, and then jumps back to his dystopian home of Mega City One. Batman follows him, only to be confronted first by Mean Machine Angel and then by Dredd himself. Angel transports back to Gotham while Dredd arrests Batman for possession of illegal weapons. In jail, Batman convinces the telepathic Judge Anderson that he is a hero, and the two go back to Gotham, followed by Dredd. Once

there, the trio discover that Batman's enemy the Scarecrow has partnered with Dredd's enemy Judge Death. The two villains have made their way to a heavy metal concert in which the band Living Death is playing. After Judge Death slaughters the metal band, Batman, Anderson and Dredd defeat the arch-villains. Afterwards, Dredd insists that Batman return to Mega City One to serve out his sentence, but Anderson persuades Dredd to drop the charges against him. As they leave, Dredd shows his respect for Batman by calling him "a bit of a tough guy."

Grant and Wagner enjoyed playing with the contrasts between Batman and Dredd: "The differences between them are greater than their similarities. The similarity is that they're both *really* tough. The difference is that Batman has a heart, whereas Dredd *doesn't*. Dredd obeys the law, whether the law is right or wrong; Batman tried to serve the interests of justice. He tries to be fair" (Nicholls 76). The excitement and tension on the page was matched by stress behind the scenes because Bisley was very slow delivering his artwork. In fact, the final few pages of *Judgment in Gotham* arrived at DC's offices in New York at the last possible minute to avoid a long delay in the book's release. So as to not interfere with the promotion of the *Batman Returns* film, DC's editorial team determined that no Batman crossovers would be published in 1992. That meant all art for *Batman/Judge Dredd* had to be completed and in DC's offices no later than Thanksgiving weekend 1991. However, the usually diligent Bisley struggled mightily to meet the tight deadline. In the end, an editor from *2000 AD* had to grab Bisley's art pages and scramble to an airport to catch an intercontinental flight, just so the completed book could reach New York in time to be released before the embargo (Bishop 151). The creative team's efforts earned *Judgment on Gotham* an Eisner Award nomination for best new graphic album as well of sales of over 200,000 copies in North America. Grant and Wagner would go on to produce more Batman/Judge Dredd crossovers: *Vendetta in Gotham* in 1994 and *The Ultimate Riddle* in 1995.

Meanwhile, DC continued to revive characters that hadn't been used in a long time. For instance, writer **Jeph Loeb** and artist **Tim Sale** helmed ***Challengers of the Unknown*** (first issue cover-dated March 1991), an eight-issue mini-series that presents the Challengers as a team of washed-up men and women who own a theme park devoted to the team and its villains. By the end of the series, the Challengers have been radically revamped for the 1990s with a new reason to be teamed up, new concepts for the characters and a new approach to their stories. Though the creative team had plotted a regular series for the reinvented Challengers, DC chose not to pick it up. Regardless, the mini-series was an impressive comic book debut for the 32-year-old Loeb. A Hollywood transplant who had co-written such mid-1980s films as *Commando* (starring Arnold Schwarzenegger) and *Teen Wolf* (starring Michael J. Fox), Loeb would go on to produce several high-profile comic book projects with Sale and other artists (including Rob Liefeld) throughout the 1990s and beyond.

OMAC: One Man Artistic Creator

Phil Foglio was the main force behind the revival of a concept originally created in 1968 by Carmine Infantino, Joe Orlando, E. Nelson Bridwell and Bob Oksner: ***Angel and the Ape***. In Foglio's madcap four-issue mini-series, beautiful private investigator Angel O'Day teams up with talking ape Sam Simeon, an artist for "DZ Comics" who has psychic powers descended from Flash villain Gorilla Grodd.

John Byrne, on the other hand, wanted to revive Kamandi, the post-apocalyptic character Jack Kirby had created for DC in 1972. Editor Jonathan Peterson, though, told Byrne that another creative team had beaten him to the punch, so he suggested Byrne tackle a different 1970s Kirby character: **OMAC: One Man Army Corps**. Kirby's original conception for OMAC was a rejected proposal for a new Captain America that posited a wimp named Buddy Blank in a strange, dystopian future. Blank transforms himself into the powerful OMAC with the help of the amazing satellite Brother Eye. In Byrne's reboot (which was dedicated to Kirby), everything in the future is destroyed, but things aren't as they seem to be. What OMAC perceives as reality is actually an alternate timeline, and he must go back in time to 1929 in order to set the past straight.

Byrne insisted that the four-issue Prestige format mini-series be printed in black-and-white. Because of concerns that a black-and-white book wouldn't sell well, DC stipulated that the subsequent trade paperback collection be colored. That edict forced Byrne to modify his artistic approach. Like he had been doing in Marvel's *Namor* series, Byrne used Duo-Shade art boards for *OMAC* to give his art the kind of layered texture found in Wally Wood's classic work in *MAD* magazine. To accommodate DC's plans, though, Byrne had to send in his pages to be photostated for the trade paperback before he added gray tones for the black-and-white series. As luck would have it, the photostated pages got lost, forcing DC to abandon the

John Byrne adapted Jack Kirby's vision of the future in his black-and-white **OMAC** mini-series. TM and © DC Comics.

OMAC trade paperback collection altogether (Byrne, "JBF Reading Club: *OMAC* #1").

Elsewhere, writer Grant Morrison and artist Duncan Fegredo rebooted yet another obscure DC character with the three-issue squarebound ***Kid Eternity***. This dark and surreal vision features a young man who dies before his time and is fated to wander the Earth as a ghostly spirit accompanied by his partner and guardian Mister Keeper. However, as this series reveals, Kid Eternity has been a pawn in the war between the Lords of Order and the Lords of Chaos, and he and Mister Keeper have been exiled to Hell. Only stand-up comedian Jerry Sullivan, comatose victim of a car accident, can save the heroes. Morrison's disorienting and scattered script imbues the series with a supernatural strangeness.

Another squarebound comic from DC in 1991 was a different unique take on the super-hero genre. The six-issue *The Griffin* by writer Dan Vado, penciller Norman Felchle and inker Mark McKenna told the lighthearted story of an American teenager who is kidnapped and becomes an alien super-hero. He escapes the aliens after spending twenty years with them and returns to Earth as a man out of time. The series was first published in 1988 by small California company Slave Labor Graphics, at which Vado was the publisher. For DC the series was rewritten and redrawn, with an added conclusion.

Written by Roger Stern with art by Kerry Gammill and Dennis Janke, the 48 page *Superman For Earth* one-shot aimed to expand awareness of environmental issues in the spirit of Earth Day. It ties the wedding plans of Superman and Lois Lane together with their concerns for the health of the planet. On assignment at an ecological symposium in Metropolis, Lois learns about the terrible effects of acid rain, toxic waste and greenhouse gases. Alarmed by Lois's findings, Superman undertakes a campaign of his own by declaring, "A thousand Supermen could not do all that is necessary to save this world. We are, all of us, part of the problem... we must all be part of the solution." By the end of the one-shot, Earth is not saved — but contact information for 25 environmental organizations is included in the back of the comic so that ordinary readers can do their part.

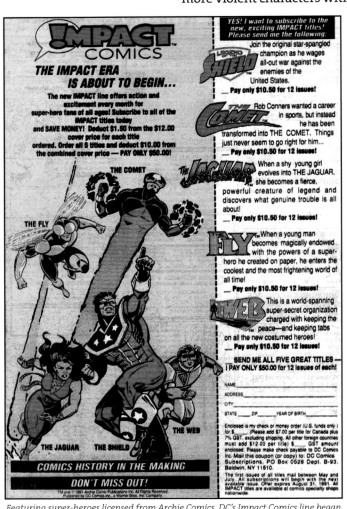

Featuring super-heroes licensed from Archie Comics, DC's Impact Comics line began with five ongoing series. All characters TM and © Archie Comic Publications, Inc.

Super-Heroes with !mpact

Just in time for the summer, a new line of comic books appeared in stores and on newsstands: **Impact Comics** (or perhaps "!mpact Comics," depending on how one reads the logo). What some readers may not have known, unless they gazed upon the comic's indicia, was that Impact was actually a DC Comics imprint. What most readers couldn't have known was the long buildup to Impact's launch.

The line was initially conceived four years earlier in conversations between DC's Director of Editorial Development Mike Gold and its distribution chief Matt Ragone. The two men were frustrated by the lack of "entry-level" comics on the stands, particularly comics aimed at kids under the age of 13. Because DC's main line of comics was so complex and interlocked, both men felt there was no way for younger readers to jump on board, and Gold

decided to correct that problem. Hoping to avoid having to create characters from scratch, Gold began looking around for a pre-existing set of characters that DC could license. He considered the Gold Key super-heroes (i.e. Doctor Solar, Magnus: Robot Fighter, Turok, et al.), then looked at Wally Wood's T.H.U.N.D.E.R. Agents before finally settling on a group of costumed heroes owned by Archie Comics. **The Mighty Crusaders** (i.e. The Comet, The Fly, The Shield, et al.) were actually scheduled to be rebranded in 1989 as darker, more violent characters within a new Archie imprint called Spectrum Comics. Michael Silberkleit and Richard Goldwater, Archie's respective Chairman and President, got cold feet on the plan when faced with the prospect of negative mainstream media attention. With the Mighty Crusaders back on the market, Mike Gold swooped in, and after a quick negotiation, DC signed a renewable three-year license for the characters. With that, Gold's Impact Comics was a go.

Gold mostly assigned up-and-coming creators to each series: Mark Waid and Tom Lyle on *The Comet*; Len Strazewski and Mike Parobeck on *The Fly*; William Messner-Loebs, David Antoine Williams and Jose Marzan Jr. on *The Jaguar*; Mark Wheatley and Rick Burchett on *The Black Hood*; Strazewski, Tom Artis and Bill Wray on *The Web*; Waid, Grant Miehm and Jeff Albrecht on *The Legend of the Shield*. To a limited degree, Archie gave DC the freedom to have its creators change these established characters to suit their purposes. Therefore, the Black Hood became a silent vigilante; the Jaguar became a Brazilian-American who fought crime with her feral powers; the Web became an organization that kept both heroes and villains under its surveillance; the Shield became a soldier with an indestructible suit of armor; the Fly became a high school student who discovered a mystical amulet; and the Comet became a college kid who wanted to become a hero.

The initial Impact titles were rolled out individually over a span of two months. *The Shield* #1 arrived in stores on May 28, 1991 and was soon followed by *The Comet* (released on June 4) and *The Jaguar* (June 18). *The Fly*, *The Web* and the informational *Who's Who in the Impact Universe* then premiered in July. Characters soon began crossing over into each other's titles. A core universe became complete when *The Black Hood* joined the line in mid-October (cover date December).

Despite quality content, Impact Comics didn't sell well.

Impact Comics achieved decent sales early on. A good presence on the nation's newsstands at places like supermarkets and convenience stores allowed for impulse purchases from the parents of younger readers. But by the early 1990s the comic book industry had almost completely bypassed newsstands in favor of Direct Market stores, and more and more comic store consumers were purchasing titles based on their "collectability." Impact Comics was anything *but* collectible. They had no secondary market value to speak of and they didn't rely on sales enhancements like variant covers. In other words, Impact Comics, despite its charm, was anachronistic, out of step with the way the comic book industry was evolving. As a result, as the months wore on, Impact's sales dropped, steadily and consistently.

As Impact's first year ended, plans for a team title started to come into place. *Crusaders* #1 (May 1992) assembled The Web, The Shield, The Jaguar, The Fly, The Black Hood and The Comet. In a late attempt to attract collectors, the issue even came with three bound-in trading cards. By this point, however, the Impact line had begun falling apart amid changing editors and creative teams. Though Mark Waid and Brian Augustyn plotted *Crusaders* past issue #12, DC ordered that the line be canceled with issue #8 (Dec. 1992), which wrapped up the initial burst of the Impact line with a cover blurb that reads, "They're gone! The last crusade!" Two months later, the publication of *Crucible: the Final Impact* #1 (Feb. 1993) was intended to set up Phase Two of the Impact Universe, focusing on heroes still on Earth as the Crusaders fought battles in space in their own series. Sales needed to be sensational for the line to continue. They were merely adequate. The line was killed with *Crucible* #6, though first issues of new series *Wrath of the Comet* (by Waid and Dave Cockrum),

The American Shield (by Augustyn, Waid, Steve Carr and Daryl Skelton) and *Mark of the Black Hood* (by Augustyn and Chuck Wojtkiewicz) were already partially completed.

The Impact line was hardly the only 1991 effort to use licensed characters to appeal to the shrinking entry-level audience. Marvel had success with a pair of *Barbie* and *Barbie Fashion* titles (each cover-dated January 1991) that eventually tallied fifty-plus issues apiece. **Harvey Comics**, along with relaunching its flagship *Casper*, *Richie Rich*, *Wendy* and *Hot Stuff* titles with new first issues, unleashed a flood of titles based on the New Kids On the Block pop group as well acquiring the rights to new comic books featuring Felix the Cat, Tom & Jerry, and Woody Woodpecker.

Disney, which had begun directly producing comic books in 1990 after ending its license with Gladstone, primarily owned its own characters but it published a notable one-shot in 1991 based on Dave Stevens' popular 1980s creation, the **Rocketeer**. After several years of development, the high-flying hero finally took flight in a Walt Disney feature film in 1991 that was adapted by Peter David and Russ Heath for comics. Featuring Billy Campbell in the title role as pilot Cliff Secord, *The Rocketeer* was more a critical success than a financial one. Whether it was the 1930s setting or the film's old-fashioned qualities, viewers didn't turn out in the numbers that Disney hoped and plans for two sequels were soon dropped.

Back in the comic book industry, another publisher was placing its bets not on a man from the past but a man from the future.

Based on the Dave Stevens creation, **Rocketeer** *was a major Disney release.*

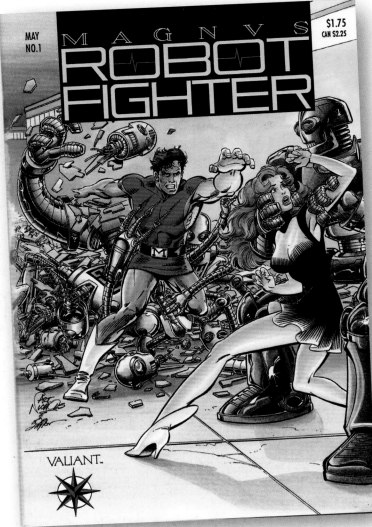

Valiant Comics launched its action heroes line with Magnus Robot Fighter.
TM and © Random House. Inc.

Robot Fighter, Valiant Savior

In 1990, the Nintendo video game titles released by **Valiant Comics** proved to be a major money-losing flop. Publisher **Steve Massarsky**, though, wasn't about to give up, so he turned to one of the other clients he represented as an entertainment agent: the World Wrestling Federation. *WWF Battlemania* (first issue cover-dated Aug. 1991) was a magazine-sized comic that portrayed wrestlers like modern day super-heroes. The magazine sold 300,000 copies per month, one-third of them in England (Sellers 38). Unfortunately, Valiant's editor-in-chief **Jim Shooter** found working with the WWF a "nightmare." As he recalled, "They'd been uncooperative on every front. They honored none of their promises about helping us market our books. They were insane with regard to approvals. No drawing we made of their wrestlers was ever adequate" (Shooter). Consequently, *Battlemania* only lasted five issues.

It was another swing and a miss for Massarsky, and the grim reality was that the projects he was lining up only moved Valiant closer and closer to bankruptcy. Luckily for everyone involved, Shooter recognized the situation and took steps to change it before it was too late. In a move that would end up saving Valiant, Shooter redirected the company's focus to the Gold Key characters he licensed from Western Publishing at an affordable cost.

Published in March 1991 (cover date May), *Magnus Robot Fighter* #1 featured writing by Shooter, pencils by Art Nichols and inks by Bob Layton. The title protagonist lives in the future city of North Am in which robots satisfy all human needs. When a group of robots called the Freewills rebel against their human masters, Magnus must become the savior of mankind. That first issue sold 90,000 copies, not one of the year's bestsellers but a decent enough performance to give Shooter and his staff confidence that they were on the right track. Sales dropped to 60,000 copies with *Magnus* #2 then stayed at that amount for several issues afterwards (McClellan). One incentive readers had for sticking with the series was the promise of a free, mail-away comic book: the first eight issues of *Magnus* included a coupon. Collected together, the eight coupons could be redeemed for *Magnus* #0, an issue that was both a limited edition collectible and a prequel chapter to the overall series.

The mail-away zero issue was only the first of several different gimmicks that Valiant utilized to brand itself as a different kind of comic book company. Another example is *Magnus* #5 (Oct. 1991), which was published as a flip-book: a new Magnus adventure on one side and the introduction of a futuristic Japanese warrior named Rai on the other side. The flip-book arrangement continued through *Magnus* #8 (Jan. 1992), and the world of Rai proved popular enough with the fans to receive its own title two months later.

Well before then, however, Valiant spotlighted another Gold Key character with *Solar, Man of the Atom*. The first issue—written by Shooter, pencilled by Don Perlin and inked by Layton—premiered in June 1991 (cover date Sept.). In an homage to the original version of the character, Valiant's Solar was Dr. Phil Seleski, a physicist who gets exposed to lethal doses of radiation during the emergency shutdown of a nuclear reactor. Rather than killing him, the radiation gives Seleski the ability to manipulate all forms of energy, which reminds him of the Doctor Solar superhero he grew up reading about in Gold Key comics.

For many readers, *Solar* was Valiant's most attractive title because it boasted the work of legendary artist **Barry Windsor-Smith**, both on the covers and in eight-page

Valiant editor-in-chief Jim Shooter and publisher Steve Massarsky.
Photo courtesy of Jim Shooter.

backup stories. Having just wrapped up a thirteen-chapter Wolverine origin serial for *Marvel Comics Presents*, Windsor-Smith was hired to be Valiant's creative director. It was the kind of hire Valiant needed to further legitimize itself because by 1991, Windsor-Smith was synonymous with creative excellence. Whether it be for his singular artwork in the 1970s on *Conan the Barbarian* or later as a fine art painter, Windsor-Smith was one of the most admired and respected professionals in the comics industry. His involvement helped Valiant gain much-needed attention and blossom into something bigger and better than it was at the time.

FROM **THIS**...COMES THE HERO!

Boasting covers by Barry Windsor-Smith, Solar, Man of the Atom *became Valiant's second action title.* TM and © Random House. Inc.

As 1991 ended, Valiant was the tenth largest publisher in the Direct Sales comics market, controlling only 0.64% of all sales. One short year later, Valiant would command a much larger market share — of a much larger comic market.

The Dark (Horse) Empire

As Valiant grew, so too did **Dark Horse Comics**. Besides the *Aliens*, *Predator* and *Terminator* mini-series, Dark Horse's line of film adaptations added two new franchises in 1991. The first was Indiana Jones. The four issue *Indiana Jones and the Fate of Atlantis* (first issue cover-dated March 1991) by William Messner-Loebs and Dan Barry told a thrilling tale of the high-adventure hero. It met with good success, but Dark Horse's second new license of 1991 was such a hit that it became one of the most reprinted books in Dark Horse's history. Written by **Tom Veitch** and illustrated by **Cam Kennedy**, *Star Wars: Dark Empire* (first issue cover-dated Dec. 1991) actually originated with a completely different series on which the duo collaborated: Epic Comics' *The Light and Darkness War*. When that series concluded in 1989, Kennedy and Veitch wrote a letter to George Lucas to ask if they could revive the *Star Wars* comic book, which was no longer being

Star Wars: Dark Empire was a major hit for Dark Horse Comics. TM and © Lucasfilm Ltd.

published by either Marvel (which had cancelled not only the main title in 1986 but also the *Droids* and *Ewoks* spin-offs in 1987) or the small independent Blackthorne (which had released a trio of 3-D specials in 1987 and 1988). Three days later, Lucas replied, requesting copies of *Light and Darkness*. Within a week of that book being sent to Lucas, Veitch and Kennedy had the comic book rights to the *Star Wars* franchise.

At first, Veitch offered the series to Archie Goodwin, former writer of the *Star Wars* newspaper strip and then editor of Marvel's Epic Comics line. Goodwin enthusiastically accepted the assignment, but when he defected to DC Comics, the *Star Wars* project got bogged down at Marvel. Eventually, Veitch persuaded Lucasfilm to negotiate with Dark Horse Comics, pointing to the *Aliens* comic book as an example of the publisher's outstanding work with licenses. Dark Horse and Lucas soon signed a contract, and for the next twenty-three years, Dark Horse was *Star Wars'* comic book home.

Dark Empire is notable for its extension of the *Star Wars* mythos beyond the parameters of the original film trilogy. The six-issue bi-monthly mini-series takes place six years after the end of *Return of the Jedi*, by which point the

Rebel Alliance has established a New Republic that controls three-quarters of the galaxy. The former Empire, though, still hasn't completely expired, and the story's main threats are a clone of the villainous Emperor Palpatine (killed at the end of *Return of the Jedi*) as well as the returned bounty hunter Boba Fett (seemingly killed at the beginning of *Return of the Jedi*).

Dark Empire's popularity was in no small part due to Kennedy's hand-colored art and Dave Dorman's regal covers, both of which captured the power and atmosphere of the original films. Dark Horse published two follow-up mini-series, *Dark Empire II* in 1994 and *Empire's End* in 1995, featuring, among other things, Princess Leia and Han Solo's children: the twins Jacen and Jaina and youngest son, Anakin.

Now Entering Sin City

Having already produced the *Give Me Liberty* and *Hard Boiled* mini-series for Dark Horse Comics, **Frank Miller**'s next project for the company would arguably be his most seminal work of the decade. **"Sin City"** first appeared in the one-shot *Dark Horse Presents Fifth Anniversary Special* (April 1991) before continuing as a serial in *Dark Horse Presents* #51-62 (May 1991-June 1992). Miller both wrote and drew the story as a bleak, crime noir saga in which a hulking professional hitman named Marv is framed for the murder of a prostitute. After a series of increasingly brutal events, Marv discovers that the real murderer is a cardinal of a church who turns out to be both a serial killer and a cannibal. In a vicious scene, Marv confronts and kills the priest. However, the police catch up with Marv, and the story ends with the professional executioner being executed in the electric chair for his crimes.

A fan of hard boiled fiction since he was a young child, Miller even included crime stories he had drawn in the portfolio he brought to New York in 1976 when he began searching for comic book work. Even though no company was publishing crime comics at that time, Miller ended up infusing noir elements in his comic book assignments, most notably *Daredevil*. Miller described his time in Hollywood in the late 1980s as purgatory, so when he returned to comic books, he vowed to create the kind of crime stories he wanted to write and draw at the beginning of his career. What Miller most loved about the genre was the opportunity to do something different with the comic book medium: "It was a chance to do stories with people, with motivations that were outside the norm of comic books. That is, people who would do things because of sex, for instance, or perversion, rather than it just being some mad scientist who wants to conquer the world, and doing the lonely, disenfranchised hard boiled hero" (Brayshaw 64). Miller adopted a hard-edged black-and white art style for the series that

deepened his characters' experiences with a noir intensity. He imagined his stories taking place in a fairly realistic world but his artistry implied the characters' inner lives.

By 1992 the original "Sin City" storyline was collected as a graphic novel which won the Eisner Award for Best Graphic Album for reprinted modern material. ("Sin City" garnered Miller two other Eisner Awards that year for Best Penciller/ Inker for a black-and-white comic book and Best Writer/ Artist.) Miller would continue to produce *Sin City* comics and graphic novels for Dark Horse throughout the 1990s.

Bad Girl Bloodlust

For most of the 1960s and 1970s **Stanley Harris** co-owned Myron Fass Enterprises, publisher of such Warren-derivative titles as *Witches' Tales*, *Tales from the Tomb* and *Weird Vampire Tales*, among many other schlock books. After a falling out with Fass (which, according to legend, involved a fistfight and/or a pistol whipping), Harris founded **Harris Publications** and acquired the rights to Warren's magazines from James Warren. (In 1985 Harris published *Creepy* #146, the magazine's final issue.) Amassing a lineup of 70 special interest magazines that included *Guitar World*, *Bowhunting* and *Dog News*, Harris decided to launch his own comics line in 1991.

The first Harris Comics release was *Creepy: the Classic Years*, a 143-page trade paperback that reprinted twenty stories from James Warren's defunct magazine. Behind a new Michael Kaluta cover, *Classic Years* reproduced the work of such creators as Neal Adams, Gene Colan, Steve Ditko,

Frank Miller's **Sin City** *presented a noir storyline.* TM and © Frank Miller Inc.

Frank Frazetta, Archie Goodwin, John Severin, Alex Toth, Al Williamson and many others. A distribution arrangement with Dark Horse Comics enabled Harris to then publish a trade paperback collection of **Vampirella** stories from the 1970s that had the scantily-clad space vampire battling a vicious cult. That set up the September 1991 launch of the first new Vampirella series in nearly a decade. With a title that referenced the famous slogan Ronald Reagan used during the 1984 Presidential election, the four issue *Vampirella: Morning in America* was written by **Kurt Busiek** and illustrated by Louis La Chance and John Nyberg with covers by Michael Kaluta.

By 1991, Busiek already had a long list of professional credits to his name, including work on Marvel's *Power Man and Iron Fist*, DC's *Red Tornado* and *Legend of Wonder Woman* mini-series and Eclipse's *Liberty Project*. The person recruiting Busiek to write *Vampirella* was his longtime friend—and new Harris editor—Richard Howell. Leaving his staff job at Marvel (where, among other tasks, he worked on *Marvel Age*), Busiek tackled his new assignment with a devotional relish. He spent a month in Harris Publications' back room reading old Vampirella stories and taking extensive notes. The end result was a deep, complex cosmology that Busiek developed for the vampire super-heroine, a background that he put to good use, not only for *Morning in America* but also the follow-up series *Vampirella Summer Nights* (Aug. 1992) and *Vampirella* (first issue cover-dated Nov. 1992).

Busiek's work on *Vampirella* came at the beginning of a new comic book trend: the rise in popularity of a group of female characters labeled as "**Bad Girls.**" In contrast to the voluptuous-yet-pure-hearted "Good Girls," the Bad Girls were characterized by their indiscriminate bloodlust, their supernatural/occult origins and, perhaps most tellingly, their enormous breasts. *Evil Ernie* #1 (Dec. 1991), created and written by **Brian Pulido**, illustrated by Stephen Hughes and published through Eternity Comics, introduced one of the most iconic of all Bad Girls: **Lady Death**, a vicious demoness cast out of Hell by Satan himself. She served as the muse for Evil Ernie, an undead psychotic killer. Just as Death goaded Thanos into attempting to annihilate the Marvel Universe, Lady Death pushes Evil Ernie to destroy the world in nuclear genocide. Unlike the end of *Infinity Gauntlet*, the world actually ends at the conclusion of the first *Evil Ernie* mini-series, with Ernie's face shown in the atomic mushroom cloud.

With her skimpy leather bikini, long flowing white hair, enormous jeweled sword and porn star physique, Lady Death was *the* prototypical Bad Girl. *Evil Ernie*, though, was hardly an immediate hit upon its first release. Retailer orders of each issue of the mini-series were low. (Capital City Distribution only ordered 2500 copies of the first issue.) That meant Brian Pulido would have to wait for the Bad Girl trend to gain more steam if Lady Death was going to catch on with readers. The good news for Pulido is that he didn't have to wait long for that to happen. By 1994, Pulido—now co-founder and President of **Chaos! Comics**—began publishing multiple *Lady Death* mini-series, all of which sold very well for him. As far as the comic that started Pulido's career, *Evil Ernie* #1, its relative scarcity

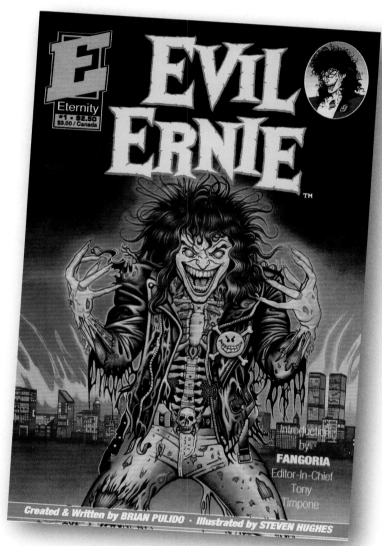

Brian Pulido's Evil Ernie *introduced the decade's most popular "bad girl," Lady Death.* TM and © Dynamite Characters, LLC

assured its secondary market value would skyrocket, and it became one of the most highly sought-after back issue comic books for the remainder of the decade.

Bone Sticks Out

Perhaps because it lacked the dark, violent tone that was so in vogue that year, or perhaps because it was a small-press comic released by a generically-named publishing house featuring work by an obscure creator, one of the most auspicious debuts of 1991 slipped past the notice of most comic book fans. Within a few years, though, **Jeff Smith's** *Bone* would become both a best-selling comic book and an award-winning one. *Bone* told the story of three anthropomorphic cousins named Fone Bone, Phoney Bone and Smiley Bone who live in a *Lord of the Rings*-inspired fantasy world populated by kind dragons, stupid rat creatures and a beautiful and sympathetic girl named Thorn who just might be fated to be the most important person in her world. The deep, delightful plot unfolds slowly and steadily over the course of the series, with plenty of dramatic twists and turns that alternate between the hilarious and the tragic.

Smith's approach to *Bone* was fresh and unique for its time, with an art style that was reminiscent of classic comic strips and Disney cartoons. In fact, for a time, *Bone* ran in the *Disney Adventures* anthology digest intended for elementary school children. Deeply influenced by Walt Kelly's seminal *Pogo* comic strip, Smith delivered characters as memorable and vivid as those of the great cartoonist while bringing a 1990s sensibility to his work, especially in the naturalistic way that the characters interacted and the tough lead female character Thorn, who could be as prickly as her namesake.

Bone began as doodles Smith made as a child. He had been drawing the Bone cousins for almost as long as he could hold a pencil. While attending Ohio University, Smith used the characters for a daily newspaper strip titled *Thorn*. Smith was then recruited by the newspaper syndicates but he declined the opportunity to work for them, thinking that they offered bad deals for creators since few new cartoonists were able to own their own strip. Smith instead moved on to co-found an animation studio, Character Builders, before selling it to devote himself full-time to *Bone* and its parent company, Cartoon Books. The decision to sell his business paid off because *Bone* became one of the true runaway hits of the decade, garnering nearly universal critical acclaim as well as love from its fans. The sincerity of the strip and quality of the work Smith presented seemed a counterpoint to the relentless sales gimmicks and hype that much of the rest of the comics industry offered in the 1990s. *Bone* truly did take readers to a different place.

TM and © Jeff Smith.

The Fans Follow the Wizard

One of the most important publications in the comic industry in the 1990s wasn't a comic book itself but rather a magazine that covered the medium. **Wizard: the Guide to Comics** debuted in July 1991. As published by 22-year-old **Gareb Shamus**, *Wizard*'s first several issues had rudimentary graphics, a large typeface and articles that sometimes seemed tangential to comics. By issue #7 (Feb. 1992), however, *Wizard* was printed in full color on slick paper with strong production values. Those attributes set *Wizard* apart from its nearest competitor, Fantagraphics' *Amazing Heroes*, which was printed on black-and-white newsprint. *Amazing Heroes* had premiered in 1981 as a light, fun alternative to *The Comics Journal*, offering interviews and news on upcoming titles as well as a robust reviews section, intelligent columnists and a strong editorial voice. It avoided discussion of the secondary market and what comic books were worth. *Wizard*, on the other hand, embraced the speculators' mentality. Collectability became the magazine's *raison d'etre* as it often breathlessly promoted the industry's newest releases with effusive articles and interviews. Moreover, unlike its more history-minded contemporaries and predecessors, the upstart viewed most anything published prior to 1980 as beyond its scope or interest.

Wizard was originally produced as a giveaway newsletter at The Wizard of Comics and Cards, a comic book and trading card store in Nanuet, New York that Shamus's parents opened in 1988. Gareb and co-worker Pat McCallum released three monthly eight-page newsletters for the store's club members before deciding to turn their work into something that could appeal to a wider, national audience. The team produced an "ashcan" mock-up of the magazine that was essentially an up-to-date back issue price guide with scant editorial content. Walter Wang, former co-owner of comics distributor Comics Unlimited, persuaded Shamus and McCallum to fill out the magazine with additional columns, articles and interviews. To do so, Shamus and McCallum recruited Patrick Daniel O'Neill, the senior contributing writer for *Comics Scene,* to become *Wizard*'s editor. O'Neill brought with him additional writers, filling out *Wizard*'s staff (McCallum 74-75).

Shamus handed out copies of *Wizard* #1—with a Spider-Man cover drawn by Shamus family friend, Todd McFarlane—at the 1991 San Diego Comic Con but found little interest. "It was amazing how many people didn't want it," Shamus told an interviewer in 2005. "It was very humbling" (Gustines). Shamus and his staff didn't give up, though. They kept publishing the magazine even as it bled money. By the time *Wizard* #7 was released, sales figures had bottomed out... but that was also the issue that included a long feature on Valiant Comics, including a cover by Barry Windsor-Smith. Soon after, Valiant's titles experienced a surge in sales. That was the first indication that *Wizard* was a viable promotional vehicle. The other comic book companies quickly sought *Wizard*'s attention, creating a symbiotic relationship between the magazine and the publishers it covered. Before long, *Wizard* offered mail-away "half" issues (e.g. *Lady Death* #½, *Vengeance of Vampirella* #½, *X-Men* #½, among many others) that the publishers exclusively provided to the magazine—a strategy that had never been tried before. These were often ashcan previews of upcoming new releases that contained a handful of story pages along with design sketches and other content. The interdependence between *Wizard* and the publishers assured the magazine grew in visibility and popularity until its sales eventually exceeded 100,000 copies an issue.

Wizard's favorite word was "hot" (like "hot new comics"), and one of its favorite features was its monthly "Top 10" list of the most popular writers and artists working in the industry. In providing these arbitrarily determined "hot" lists, however, *Wizard* was essentially attempting to control fans' perception on what comic books—and which comic book creators—deserved recognition and fame. This attempt to control perception extended to the magazine's lengthy price guide section which often contradicted values listed in the *Overstreet Comic Book Price Guide*. Prior to *Wizard*'s launch, *Overstreet* was generally accepted within the industry as having the most authoritative guide, but *Wizard*'s burgeoning popularity soon changed the minds of retailers and consumers alike. Before long, many people believed *Wizard* provided the most definitive secondary market values.

As a result, Overstreet, and all the other existing comic book-focused periodicals, had to take countermeasures. As John Jackson Miller, then an editor for Krause Publications, publisher of the weekly *Comics Buyer's Guide* newspaper, attests, "*Wizard* really was our Moby Dick... the presence of *Wizard* did provide a great example of what was possible for a comics magazine, and it definitely caused us to work harder" (Miller). Starting in 1993, Overstreet began producing two monthly magazines: *Overstreet's Comic Book Marketplace* (which offered its own comprehensive price guide) and *Overstreet's Comic Book Monthly* (relaunched as *Overstreet's Fan* in 1995). Meanwhile, **Hero Illustrated** (first issue cover-dated July 1993) attempted to stake a slightly higher ground. Still including a price guide for the first two years of its existence before dropping it to great fanfare, *Hero* paid more attention to indie comics than *Wizard*, still maintaining a focus on more mainstream fare. Early issues of *Hero* included mini comics of *Bone* and *Madman*.

One casualty of *Wizard*'s success was the magazine it supplanted: *Amazing Heroes*. With *Wizard* and its imitators flooding the market, *Amazing Heroes* saw its sales drop so dramatically that cancellation couldn't be avoided. The final issue was #202/203 (July 1992), a double-sized flip book. *Amazing Heroes* and *Comics Journal* publisher Gary Groth felt *Wizard* represented all that was bad about the comics industry in 1991, calling it "the most promi-

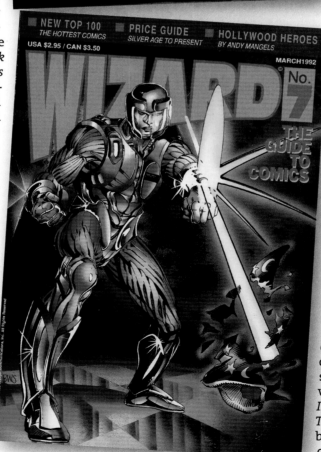

Wizard *magazine presented a slick, collector's approach to comic book news which often set fandom's agenda in the 1990s.*
Spider-Man TM and © Marvel Characters, Inc. X-O Manowar TM
and © Valiant Entertainment LLC.

nent propagandizer on behalf of contentless, collectible comics" (Groth, "Illiteracy," 4).

And Then My Troubles Began

In 1989 Penguin Books assumed the publishing responsibility for the acclaimed literary comics anthology *RAW*, previously self-published by **Art Spiegelman** and his wife Francoise Mouly. *RAW*'s 228-page final volume, released in 1991, included a cover by underground comix great Robert Crumb which showed a kneeling turbaned man who prays, "Please God—I'm afraid! Make them stop destroying the planet (and also maybe put an end to the Teenage Mutant Ninja Turtles)." Interior stories were produced by some of the comic book world's leading lights, including José Muñoz and Carlos Sampayo, Aline Kominsky-Crumb, Kaz, Chris Ware, Drew Friedman, Richard Sala, Gary Panter, Alan Moore, Mark Beyer and many others.

Arguably, the most notable part of *RAW*'s final volume was the tenth (and penultimate) chapter of Spiegelman's magnum opus, **Maus**, the anthropomorphic story of Spiegelman's father's life before, during and after his captivity during World War II at Auschwitz's concentration camp with Jews depicted as mice and Germans as cats. In late October 1991 Pantheon collected Spiegelman's final five chapters and published it as a sequel to the *Maus* book it released in 1986. *Maus II: A Survivor's Tale: And Here My Troubles Began* received a front-page review in *The New York Times Book Review*—the first graphic novel that had ever received that honor—with Holocaust scholar Lawrence L. Langer showering Spiegelman's work with praise. By December *Maus II* had entered both *The New York Times* and *Publisher's Weekly* bestseller lists... albeit in different categories. The *Times* wryly noted that "*The Times* has it under fiction, reasoning that the events,

Art Spiegelman's second volume of Maus, *released in 1991, won a special Pulitzer Prize.* Maus TM and © Art Spiegelman.

though real, did not happen to animals. *Publisher's Weekly* has it under nonfiction." Besides being nominated for the 1991 National Book Critics Circle Award in the Biography/ Autobiography category, *Maus II* won both an Eisner and Harvey Award in 1992. That same year, the entire *Maus* story was bestowed with a special Pulitzer Prize. Clearly, Art Spiegelman was doing his part to dispel the commonly held assumption that the comic book format was unsophisticated and strictly for juveniles.

Escaping Comics Cages

Dave McKean was trying to do his part as well. Primarily known as a painter, especially on 1989's best-selling *Arkham Asylum* graphic novel, McKean used a different art style for *Cages*, a ten-issue limited series launched through **Kevin Eastman's Tundra Publishing**. As described by McKean, *Cages* "follows the interweaving lives of a bunch of people who live in the same building. There are fantasy elements that weave through it, but what I'm trying to set up in the beginning is a down-to-earth, simple story about these people" (Johnson 26). But things aren't quite as quotidian as they seem, as running alongside the core story are mythical folk tales, full of surreal and fantasy images. The series celebrated the complex elements of everyday life in light and funny ways.

In contrast to his previous work, McKean simplified his storytelling technique for *Cages*. Gone were the abstract paintings and shocking collages for which he was well known, and in their place was more conventional black-

and-white linework. With *Cages*, McKean hoped to show that comics could—and should—escape their genre trappings and appeal to a thoughtful reader, like one who could enjoy independent films. The comic was critically lauded… but it didn't sell well. In fact, because of *Cage's* production costs, Tundra lost money on every copy of the book that was sold. According to a report of a May 21, 1991 Tundra meeting, "*Cages* is presently selling at $3.50. It has been determined that Tundra loses five cents on every copy of *Cages* that it sells." That sad reality applied to nearly the entirety of Tundra's output. Of Tundra's eight releases, only three of them had the prospect of turning a profit, and that was only if the book's entire print run sold out (Groth 83). The underground-feeling *Beer Nutz* by Wayno, the dark *Rain* by Rolf F. Stark and the nostalgic *Fun Boys Summer Special* by Jeff Bonivert demonstrated the wide range of Tundra's catalog, but nearly all the 1991 releases failed to attract significant reader interest.

While Tundra proved extremely unprofitable for Kevin Eastman, a different publishing venture had the potential to reverse his fortunes. Since the late 1970s *Heavy Metal* magazine printed the work of some of the finest avantgarde cartoonists from both Europe and America. Eastman was an avid fan. One day French graphic novel publisher Fershid Bharucha introduced Eastman to *Heavy Metal's* owner, James Jimirro. Eastman learned then that Jimirro wanted to sell the publishing rights to *Heavy Metal*—which at that time was generating annual revenues of $300,000—in order to subsidize the other magazine he

Dave McKean's Cages *attempted to transcend comics' genre trappings.* Cages TM and © Dave McKean.

owned, *National Lampoon*. After a payment of $500,000 Eastman was the new *Heavy Metal* publisher.

In the wake of such 1980s successes as *Dark Knight*, *Watchmen* and *Maus*, more and more mainstream book publishers looked to release their own graphic novels and comic anthologies. In late August 1991, Collier Books (an imprint of the giant Macmillan Publishing Company) published **The New Comics Anthology** as a 287-page large size trade paperback with a fashionable design and high cover price of $19.95. Edited by Bob Callahan with advice from Art Spiegelman, *New Comics* collected the work of some of the best-known cartoonists in America alongside relative newcomers. Classic underground creators like Kim Deitch, Spain Rodriguez, Justin Green and Bill Griffith were placed next to emerging cartoonists like Daniel Clowes, Robert Sikoryak, Peter Kuper, Mary Fleener, Joe Sacco and Charles Burns. Unfortunately, the book had many flaws (possibly due to the fact that it was rushed out to be available at college bookstores at the beginning of the school year): art was reproduced from comics rather than original art pages; story pages were printed out of order; one story was missing several pages; and one cartoonist's name was misspelled. *The New Comics Anthology* didn't sell well and quickly ended up in bookstore remainder bins.

Collier Books had unfulfilled ambitions for **The New Comics.**

Mazzucchelli Goes Independent

After collaborating with Frank Miller on two of the most acclaimed stories of the 1980s—the *Daredevil* "Born Again" and "Batman: Year One" arcs—artist **David Mazzucchelli** decided to turn away from super-hero comic books, going so far as to decline an offer to illustrate *X-Men* in 1990 (Roth 50). He wanted to produce more personal works. To that end, Mazzucchelli took some time away from comics to both enroll in printmaking classes and study underground comics. When he re-emerged in 1991, Mazzucchelli self-published a gorgeous comic that was a work of art on its own: **Rubber Blanket**, named after a tool publishers used to transfer ink from the printing plates to the printing surface in offset printing. The oversized black-and-white magazine – 9x12 in size – featured material mainly by Mazzucchelli but also by artists Richmond Lewis, David Hornung, Ted Stearn and the team of Massimo Semerano and Francesca Ghermani.

To emphasize his break from mainstream comics, Mazzucchelli adopted a radically different art style from the one he used at Marvel and DC, a style that used thick, expressionistic lines. The subject matter of his stories was also varied and unconventional. For instance, "Discovering America" in *Rubber Blanket* #2 presents a man whose mapmaking skills parallel his adventures in love, and "Big Man" in issue #3 is a parable about a giant who washes ashore to a small rural village. Mazzucchelli released three issues of *Rubber Blanket* over three years, eventually earning an Eisner Award nomination for Best Anthology in 1993. He was one of the few artists who eschewed the lure of the lucrative pay that could be obtained by drawing Marvel Comics in favor of producing something more creatively self-rewarding.

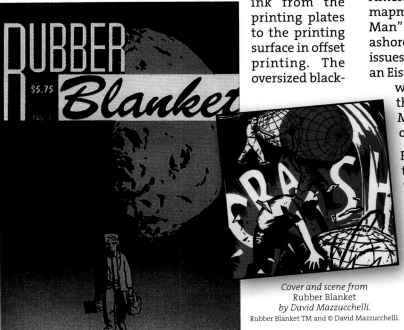

Cover and scene from
Rubber Blanket
by David Mazzucchelli.
Rubber Blanket TM and © David Mazzucchelli.

By the end of 1991, however, Marvel's star artists began to wonder why they couldn't have the best of both worlds. Why couldn't they create—and keep—their own properties that would earn them both personal satisfaction *and* substantial amounts of money? A creator revolution was at hand, one that would not only change the landscape of the comic book industry in permanent ways but also upend its hegemony.

In 1991, Marvel and DC Comics controlled a vast share of the comic book marketplace. That would not be the case in 1992.

1992

CHAPTER THREE

Nirvana

The tremendous fan appeal of artists like Jim Lee, Rob Liefeld and Todd McFarlane led comic books into an unprecedented era, a time when creators were treated like rock stars and their comics sold as many copies each month as popular rock albums sold in a year. Just as grunge rockers Nirvana's album *Nevermind* and its feature single "Smells Like Teen Spirit" dominated radio play and record sales with a fresh sound for the 1990s, the new comic book artists presented a furiously energetic spirit that many fans considered revolutionary.

According to John Davis, co-owner of Capital City Distribution, total industry sales for 1992 were up at least 25% from 1991, a continuation of several years of rapid growth. In fact, the comics industry cumulatively generated more than $500 million in total sales, the first time that milestone was achieved. Marvel continued to lead the market with a share of around 45%, but that percentage was down significantly from its high of 68.38% for comics sold in July 1991. DC's overall sales in 1992 dropped 6.5% from the previous year, but DC had perhaps the greatest impact on the market. This led to a feeling of diversity in the medium — at least among publishers who produced mainstream material. The fastest growing publishers were the "middle three" companies Malibu, Valiant and Dark Horse (which Capital jointly named Publisher of the Year). A new imprint boosted the sales of the formerly small Malibu Comics to over 19% of the market in September 1992. Speculator and fan interest raised Valiant's market share from 0.64% to 4.11% while Dark Horse's sales, fueled by its growing line of licensed comics, increased a proportionally smaller amount, from 3.71% in 1991 to 5.55% in 1992.

A few naysayers, though, warned that the industry's growth resembled an inflated balloon that was about to pop. These detractors foretold the comic book industry would suffer the same fate as the oversaturated collectible sports card business which, as 1992 dawned, was beginning to crash. For several years, both Marvel and DC Comics tapped into the lucrative card business by releasing their own popular collectible card sets (like a 1991 X-Men set that included cards autographed by Jim Lee). Now the shoe was on the other foot: sports card shop owners began selling comic books to turn their foundering finances around. The foreboding reality, however, was that both the comic book and sports card businesses utilized similar sales strategies. Like sports card companies, comic book publishers grew their readership by promoting the "collectability" of their releases (i.e. polybagged issues, exclusive covers). For their part, an increasing number of consumers bought into the speculation frenzy, allowing an emphasis on the resale value of a comic book to outweigh considerations of its quality. Collectors routinely bought stacks of copies of the latest mega-hyped comic with dreams of flipping it a few months later for big money without ever even opening the book. "One to read, one to bag" was the mantra of the day.

Perhaps unsurprisingly, the independent publishers that didn't cater to the collectors' mentality had a rough year. In the second half of 1992, publishers outside the top five split about 12% of the total comics market, which meant miserably low sales for many (Groth, "The Two Daves", 6). Fantagraphics Books canceled eight ongoing series to concentrate mainly on graphic novels and the thriving Eros Comix line. Four Fantagraphics employees were laid off in October 1992. Tundra Press's revenue actually increased 50% between 1991 and 1992, as its comics sold anywhere between 10,000 and 40,000 copies an issue. However, Tundra was still unable to turn a profit due to fixed high production costs. Other publishers tried unique ways to expand their reach. For example, Ron Turner of distributor/ publisher Last Gasp traveled on the 1992 alternative music Lollapalooza tour promoting his comics. Kitchen Sink Publishing sold items like candy bars, neckties and collectible cards to help diversify its product line. Several other publishers had trouble paying their creators on schedule. While NOW Comics emerged from bankruptcy with back debts to sort out, Comico went into bankruptcy in February 1992, leaving some creators waiting many months for payment. It took over two years for artist Ho Che Anderson to be paid for a story he drew. And prominent 1980s publisher Eclipse Comics had major cash flow problems that caused the late release of many comics, including the popular Neil Gaiman-scripted *Miracleman*, thereby crippling Eclipse's cash flow even more.

Though all comic publishers had their fair share of significant releases in 1992, a new publisher dominated the attention of the comic book industry.

Image Is Everything

Rob Liefeld, **Todd McFarlane** and a few of their artistic colleagues practically owned the comics world. Their Marvel series were perennial bestsellers, and under Marvel's incentive plan, they were earning an income that might have been the envy of some movie stars. Despite their success, the young turk creators felt increasingly frustrated with what they saw as a deep disrespect from Marvel's editors and executives. The stars were furious that merchandise that featured their artwork, such as T-shirts and posters, was released without credit or compensation, and that they earned no royalties from international reprints. For McFarlane, matters came to a head over an editorial decision. As McFarlane's *Spider-Man* series was born, the writer/artist was given freedom proportional to the sales he received. However, as the series went on, the company began pulling back some of McFarlane's creative control, to the point that editorial interference became a

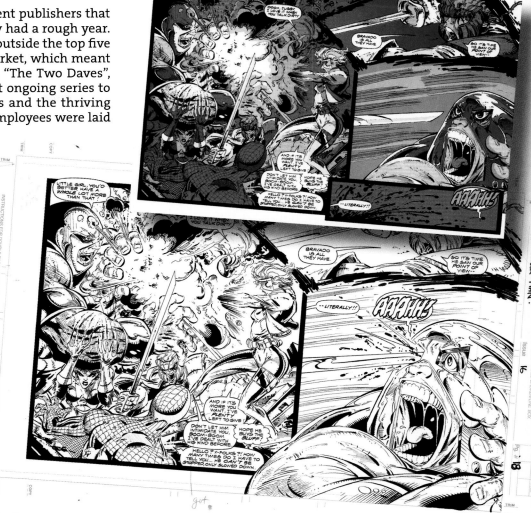

Angered by his editor's refusal to allow a sword pierce Juggernaut's eye, Todd McFarlane quit his assignment on **Spider-Man**. TM and © Marvel Characters, Inc.

regular occurrence. Finally, an editorial mandate to alter a scene in *Spider-Man* #16 (Nov. 1991) caused McFarlane to quit. In the midst of a pitched battle between Spider-Man, X-Force and Juggernaut, a sword is thrust through Juggernaut's eye. McFarlane's editor, Danny Fingeroth, along with Marvel's editor-in-chief Tom DeFalco, demanded that the panel not show the sword piercing the villain's eye as the depiction wouldn't be approved by the Comics Code Authority. After all, kids read Spider-Man comics. McFarlane complied but that was the last straw for him. The change was no more or less important to him than any other change that was requested of him, but he felt that with his first child soon to be born, and money in the bank, it was a good time for him to take a break from comics.

Meanwhile, several other Marvel artists had a fateful meeting at the 1991 San Diego Comic Con, held over the July 4th weekend. One night Rob Liefeld, writer/artist on *X-Force*, **Jim Valentino**, writer/artist on *Guardians of the Galaxy*, and **Erik Larsen**, artist on *Amazing Spider-Man*, dined with longtime friend **Dave Olbrich**, publisher of **Malibu Comics**. A survivor of the black-and-white boom and bust of the 1980s, Malibu was releasing comics under several imprints including series based on popular older films such as *Planet of the Apes*, *Re-Animator*, *Robotech* and

TIMELINE: 1992

A compilation of the year's notable comic book history events alongside some of the year's most significant popular culture and historical events.
(On sale dates are approximations.)

January 14: In *Alpha Flight* #106, written by Scott Lobdell and drawn by Mark Pacella and Dan Panosian, Northstar becomes the first Marvel Comics super-hero to be identified as a homosexual. As a result, the issue receives national media attention.

February 8: The 16th Olympic Winter Games opens in Albertville, France. Americans Kristi Yamaguchi and Nancy Kerrigan win the gold and bronze medals in women's figure skating respectively.

March 6: Widespread concerns about the "Michelangelo" computer virus (set to trigger on the birthday of the famous Renaissance painter) prove mostly unfounded as only several thousand computer systems around the world become infected.

April 29: After a jury acquits four police officers in the beating of Rodney King, rioting erupts in Los Angeles. Three days of violence result in the deaths of 55 people and nearly $1 billion worth of property damage. In an attempt to restore calm, King publicly appeals, "Can we all get along?"

April 6: A civil war breaks out in northern Bosnia between the Bosnian government and local Serbs who lay siege to the capital of Sarajevo. The conflict lasts almost four years, resulting in the deaths of thousands of soldiers and civilians.

May 19: Vice President Dan Quayle denounces the inner cities' "poverty of values," taking specific aim at the television show *Murphy Brown* for having its title character decide to bear a child out of wedlock.

May 22: Johnny Carson ends his nearly 30-year tenure as the host of NBC's *Tonight Show*, telling his audience, "I bid you a very heartfelt good night." He is succeeded by comedian Jay Leno.

June 3: EC Comics and *Mad* magazine publisher William Gaines dies in his sleep at the age of 70.

June 18: Revolutionary Comics publisher Todd Loren is stabbed to death in his San Diego apartment. No one is arrested for his murder, and the case is never solved.

JANUARY | FEBRUARY | MARCH | APRIL | MAY | JUNE

February 17: Two days after a jury rejects his insanity plea, Jeffrey Dahmer is sentenced to life in prison for the mutilation and murder of 15 men and boys in the Milwaukee, Wisconsin area.

February 1: Marvel Comics artists Erik Larsen, Jim Lee, Rob Liefeld, Todd McFarlane, Whilce Portacio and Jim Valentino meet at Marc Silvestri's Malibu, California home to officially found Image Comics.

April 16: The first Image comic book—Rob Liefeld's *Youngblood* #1—arrives in Direct Market stores.

April 8: Retired professional tennis player Arthur Ashe reveals he has AIDS, contracted from a blood transfusion he received years earlier.

June 6: Former Marvel Comics publisher Martin Goodman dies at the age of 84 of natural causes.

June 19: *Batman Returns*—directed by Tim Burton and starring Michelle Pfeiffer as Catwoman, Danny Devito as the Penguin, and Michael Keaton as the Caped Crusader—opens in movie theaters. While not as successful as 1989's *Batman*, *Batman Returns* ultimately becomes the third highest grossing movie of the year.

May 19: In Long Island, New York, 17-year-old high school student Amy Fisher shoots Mary Jo Buttafuoco in the face, seriously wounding her. It is soon revealed that Fisher is having an affair with Buttafuoco's 36-year-old husband, Joey. Fisher is subsequently sentenced to prison, Joey Buttafuoco pleads guilty to statutory rape, and the whole sordid affair becomes one of the most infamous crimes of the decade, the subject of numerous books and television specials.

Northstar TM and © Marvel Characters, Inc. Batman TM and © DC Comics. Youngblood TM and © Rob Liefeld Inc.

Flesh Gordon along with a small line of original comics. In 1987, Olbrich had offered Liefeld the chance to create his own comic for Malibu. Four years later, Olbrich's offer was still open, and Liefeld was now giving it some serious consideration. Liefeld wanted his Marvel colleagues to give it their consideration as well, so to put the idea in their heads, Liefeld asked Olbrich during the dinner if Malibu would also be willing to publish comics created by Valentino and Larsen. Olbrich quickly said he would (Khoury 133).

After the convention, Liefeld contacted Olbrich to propose a new series that could be published through a new Malibu imprint that would be called **Image Comics**. Liefeld teased his potential new comic book, *The Executioners*, in a full-page ad that ran in the September 9, 1991 issue of popular fan publication *Comics Buyer's Guide*. The new comic's logo emphasized the "X" in the team name and even looked similar to the original logo for Marvel's *X-Factor* title. Above the logo, bold text declared, "From the creator of the smash summer hit X-FORCE!" The depicted characters—described as "rebel mutants"—resembled heroes appearing in *X-Force*. After he saw the ad, Bob Harras, the editor of Marvel's mutant line, called Liefeld and angrily told him that Marvel was considering legal action to remove Liefeld from *X-Force* if he pursued this new series (Khoury 63). Liefeld and Olbrich backed off from their plans.

Simultaneous to his *Executioners* announcement, Liefeld also considered returning to DC Comics to create a Teen Titans spin-off mini-series. As Liefeld explained, "My favorite characters as a kid were the X-Men and the Teen Titans... *The New Mutants* was my way of doing my own version of the X-Men, and *X-Force* is kind of that now. I always loved [*Teen Titans*], and it was like, 'Wow, if I could do the Titans and the X-Men at the same time, I could die a happy man'" (Walko). The mini-series—to be titled either *Team Titans* or *Titans Force*—would have been co-written by regular *Titans* writer Marv Wolfman and starred Green Arrow's former sidekick Speedy as the leader of a West Coast contingent of the Teen Titans. Other members would have included Two-Face's daughter Harlequin and Legion of Super-Heroes member Blok. The deal ultimately fell through, however, when Liefeld and DC's Vice President of Editorial Dick Giordano couldn't come to an agreement on financial terms. Liefeld asked for $100,000 per issue, similar to the royalties he was receiving at Marvel, but DC proved unwilling to match (Liefeld).

Summer turned to Fall, and as Liefeld continued to draw *X-Force*, he spoke frequently to the comic book professionals he felt closest to: Larsen, McFarlane and Valentino. Liefeld kept pressing each of them to join him in his Image Comics endeavor, a new line of comic books where they could all continue producing their lucrative work for Marvel

July 17: Veteran Marvel Comics writer Bill Mantlo—best known for his long runs on *Incredible Hulk*, *Micronauts* and *ROM* as well as co-creating the Rocket Raccoon and Cloak & Dagger characters—is struck by a car while rollerblading. As a result of the accident, Mantlo's brain suffers irreversible damage.

August 11: The biggest shopping mall in the nation, the Mall of America, opens in Bloomington, Minnesota.

August 24: Hurricane Andrew smashes into Florida causing the death of 55 people and record damage. At the time it is the most expensive natural disaster in U.S. history.

July 25: Marvel Entertainment Group acquires Fleer, one of the nation's largest trading card companies, for $265 million.

October 31: *X-Men* debuts on the FOX television network as a Saturday morning cartoon. The show will last five seasons, 76 episodes in total.

November 17: Written and pencilled by Dan Jurgens, *Superman* #75 presents the death of the fabled Man of Steel after a pitched battle against the monstrous Doomsday. Available in both regular and polybagged editions, six million copies of the issue are distributed to comic book stores and newsstands.

November 28: Whitney Houston's song "I Will Always Love You" peaks at #1 on the pop singles chart, staying there for 14 weeks.

| JULY | AUGUST | SEPTEMBER | OCTOBER | NOVEMBER | DECEMBER |

July 30: Comic book artist and Superman co-creator Joe Shuster dies at the age of 78 of congestive heart failure.

September 7: *Batman: The Animated Series* debuts on the FOX television network. Produced by Bruce Timm, Eric Radomski, Paul Dini and Alan Burnett, the Emmy Award winning show will last four seasons, 85 episodes in total.

November 3: Democratic governor of Arkansas Bill Clinton is elected the 42nd President of the United States, defeating incumbent Republican George Bush. Third party candidate Ross Perot wins 19% of the popular vote.

July 25: The 25th Summer Olympics open in Barcelona, Spain. A "Dream Team" of professional basketball players—including Michael Jordan, Larry Bird, and Magic Johnson—win the goal medal for the United States.

October 3: Irish rock singer Sinead O'Connor becomes the talk of the nation when she appears on NBC's *Saturday Night Live* and rips up a picture of Pope John Paul II declaring, "Fight the real enemy!"

December 8: As part of Operation Restore Hope, U.S. Marines land on the beaches of Somalia, an African country where millions are starving, to protect food and medicine supplies from local warlords and gangs.

---

while engaging in a side-venture that they would own. McFarlane was the easiest of recruits since he had an axe to grind with Marvel and already started his sabbatical from comics. With little to lose by moving to a new company, McFarlane began advocating for more creators to join the Image Comics club. The independent-minded Valentino felt a resonance in his peers' mission, but with a large family to feed, it was important to Valentino that he remain attached to his Marvel assignments while also working on his own creation.

The process of starting the Image line of comics gained significant momentum when Liefeld and McFarlane set their sights on Marvel's "golden boy," **Jim Lee**. From Liefeld and McFarlane's point of view, Lee was the one creator who would cause Marvel the most pain if he chose to defect to another company. The problem was that Lee had little—or no—motivation to take a chance on a creator-owned undertaking considering how profitable his *X-Men* work was. Regardless, Liefeld and McFarlane kept at him, and Lee soon found his attitudes turned around. In December 1991, the prestigious Sotheby's held an auction of comics-related material. Marvel invited several of its creators to attend the event, among them Lee, Liefeld and McFarlane (whose respective original artwork for *X-Men* #1, *X-Force* #1 and *Spider-Man* #1 was included in the auction). Marvel even paid their airfare to New York City… but

Marvel didn't pay for the airfare for any of the creators' spouses. That lack of generosity rubbed Lee the wrong way as McFarlane explained, "Jim does his homework. He knows he's probably brought in 22 million dollars in the last three months… [Marvel] can't even spring for a $200 plane ticket? When they started saying that kind of stuff, that's when they pushed the wrong buttons" (Howe 337).

The day before the auction Lee, Liefeld and McFarlane ran into another Marvel creator who traveled to New York City: famed *Wolverine* artist **Marc Silvestri**. Led by a fired-up McFarlane, the three creators pitched Silvestri on joining them in their new venture. For Silvestri, it was an easy sell, "when I talked to Todd, literally within 30 seconds it was 'yes.' I was again ready for something new, and again I wasn't quite sure if I wanted to stay in comics, but this was something exciting. Yeah, I'll take that gamble. What's the worst that could happen?" (Khoury 118). After their impromptu meeting, Silvestri went off to tour the city while the other three artists—along with McFarlane's wife Wanda and their four-month-old baby Cyan—trooped up to the offices of Marvel President **Terry Stewart** where a tense confrontation commenced sometime before 7PM.

As the meeting began, the group let Stewart know that they were dissatisfied with their situation at Marvel. As

After CBG *ran this ad for Rob Liefeld's* Executioners *comic book, Marvel Comics threatened to sue.*
TM and © Rob Liefeld Inc.

it turned out, that general sentiment was the only thing that all the creators could agree upon. By nearly all accounts, the meeting went terribly for everybody. McFarlane charged into the conversation ready for a fight with a belligerent attitude that was different from Liefeld and Lee's more conciliatory approach. Before long, the creators began to make demands of Stewart. One creator asked for 75% of the profit of every book he worked on. Another asked for 90%. Each of the young men had a slightly different vision of what he wanted from Marvel. At one point a creator asked for Marvel to pay to fly and host himself and his wife at conventions, something Marvel already did. That thread devolved into a conversation about paying friends to fly and putting the creators up in the nicest hotels in the city. Tom DeFalco—who inadvertently wandered into the meeting halfway through—wasn't necessarily opposed to any of the demands... until the creators stipulated that they would get to choose the creative teams that would succeed them whenever they left a title. DeFalco balked at that.

As the meeting dragged on, Stewart casually proposed the artists take over Marvel's Epic Comics imprint with their new creations. The catch was that Stewart essentially offered Lee, Liefeld and McFarlane the same deal that any other creator working

on an Epic comic book would receive: a 50/50 split of character ownership with Marvel. As Jim Lee reflected, Stewart's offer demonstrated the difference in perspective between Marvel and its star artists, "there was a wide, wide rift between how we perceived ourselves and what they valued us as creators, and I think they felt that they would survive without us" (Khoury 52). To say the least, the Epic Comics proposition was neither accepted nor even appreciated by the three creators.

It was getting late in the evening, and everybody was exhausted by the volatile displays of emotion. By 9:30 the meeting concluded with Stewart imploring the artists to make a list of their demands and present those demands to Marvel management for negotiation the next day. But the creators never came back to Marvel. Later that night they agreed upon a publishing and distribution deal with Malibu Comics.

The next day Lee, Liefeld and McFarlane went up to DC's offices, where they gathered all the DC editors to make an announcement. Pulses raced as people grew excited about the prospect that Jim Lee, the industry's best-selling artist, might be coming to work for DC. As McFarlane remembered it, the creators dropped a proverbial bomb when they declared,

"He's not going to work for you either, we just quit Marvel. We just told Marvel we're not going to work for them, and we just thought we'd give the same courtesy to you, that we're not working for you either" (Sacks, "Image Comics 20th Anniversary").

Later that day, the new Image creators issued a press release announcing that some of the most popular artists in comics were leaving Marvel in order to start their own company. It was an early Christmas gift that shook the mainstream comics industry. Though Lee and Silvestri weren't included in the very first announcements of the new line, they soon signed on as Image founders as did one more Marvel defector: Jim Lee's studio-mate and *Uncanny X-Men* writer/artist **Whilce Portacio**.

For a month, the seven creators—Todd McFarlane, Rob Liefeld, Jim Lee, Erik Larsen, Marc Silverstri, Jim Valentino and Whilce Portacio—discussed their plans amongst themselves and worked on their new characters and comics. Then on February 1, 1992, the group gathered at Silvestri's Malibu, California beach home for a series of meetings to officially form Image Comics. The enthusiasm at Silvestri's house was infectious as each creator described the books he would be releasing to the oohs and aahs of his friends. The Image founders also

(Standing) Erik Larsen, Rob Liefeld, Todd McFarlane, Marc Silvestri, Jim Valentino. (Sitting) Hank Kanalz, Jim Lee.

finalized their deal with Malibu, talked marketing with Gareb Shamus, publisher of then-new *Wizard* Magazine, and discussed newsstand distribution with Harold Anderson of Anderson News. The seven men agreed to their company bylaws and determined that all the Image founders would be equal shareholders in the new company. They further agreed that Image itself would own nothing other than the Image "I" logo and that all work created by the Image founders would remain exclusively their own. Finally, the founders agreed that anyone could leave the group at any time and that they could invite new creators to join. In fact, feelers quickly went out to popular Marvel artists Larry Stroman (then drawing *X-Factor*), Dale Keown (then on *The Incredible Hulk*) and Sam Kieth (artist of stories for *Marvel Comics Presents*).

The next day, the team convened at the new offices of Malibu Comics to begin a week-long series of discussions about the affiliation between Image and Malibu. Before invited press—including writers from *Amazing Heroes* and *Wizard*—the Image founders described their plans for their own series and a shared Image Universe that would resemble the Marvel Universe. Each artist brought along story pages and sketches of their new characters, and photocopies were passed out to everyone in attendance. After fielding questions from the press, the Image creators and Malibu representatives secluded themselves so they could work out the nuts and bolts of their partnership (Mason, "The First Image Press Conference"). Among other things, Malibu agreed to have no editorial involvement with any of the Image titles, though the publishing house would manage all the logistics of "Image Comics Press" (as they were then called), including administrative, production, advertising and marketing services. Profits on all the Image titles would be split, with 90% going to the applicable Image creator and 10% going to Malibu (which also collected a small fee per comic to cover overhead). While the Image creators received the lion's share of profits, Malibu's executives were nonetheless delighted: given how popular the Image creators were, ten percent of profits still amounted to a potential financial windfall.

Something unique that Malibu offered to Image was its state-of-the-art coloring service. By 1992, computer-produced coloring was relatively new to comics, and Malibu was one of the first publishers to fully invest in it. According to an *American Comic Book Chronicles* interview with Tom Mason, one of Malibu Comics' founders, the quality of Malibu's coloring—particularly on a special *Puppet Master* comic book that had been commissioned by Full Moon Studios—impressed the Image creators so greatly that combined with everything else being provided, it was the final assurance the group of Image creators needed to cast their lot with Malibu rather than go with another publisher like Dark Horse Comics (which was briefly considered as a partner company). With their relationship cemented, Malibu charged right ahead with promoting Image Comics at an annual retailers' meeting in Hawaii later in February. Besides handing out promotional material and Image hats, Malibu representatives showed off galleys of the first wave of Image titles.

When the Image Founders appeared at the 1992 Chicago Comicon, thousands of fans waited hours in line for their autographs.

As everyone waited for the first Image titles to reach stores, the founders kept talking to the press, and their rhetoric consistently embodied a revolutionary zeal. By casting off their former corporate masters, they all refused to suffer the same fate as Jack Kirby who co-created many of Marvel's most iconic characters only to become increasingly frustrated by the fact that he had no ownership of them. Image sought to invert the prevailing hegemony by having comic book writers and artists retain full ownership of the characters that they created. The creators, and not the publishers, would be the ones who prospered from their characters' ancillary rights. As Jim Valentino declared in a fiery spring 1992 interview, "It is the right to own your creations outright, to benefit from them in whatever way possible and more importantly, not to be told by a corporation that your contributions are insignificant and your relative worth to a project you've created is minimal" (Stephenson 22).

The tables had been turned. Marvel promoted Lee, Liefeld and McFarlane as the next generation of comic book superstars, and now those very superstars were leading an insurrection. In addition, because of their Marvel

Flipbook covers to Rob Liefeld's **Youngblood** *#1, the first Image Comics release.*
TM and © Rob Liefeld Inc.

Comics accomplishments, the Image founders had the highest kind of name recognition among fandom. They told anyone and everyone that they didn't need Marvel to continue to succeed in the comic book business, and for the most part that was absolutely true.

The formation of Image Comics received mainstream news media coverage, including articles in *The Los Angeles Times*, *USA Today*, *Newsweek* and *The New York Times*, among others (Mason 1). Within the comic book industry, Image was garnering all the attention. Fan interest turned into a frenzy that came to a head on the July 4th weekend in 1992 when all seven Image founders appeared together in person for the first time in public at the Chicago Comicon. Though the convention was held in the very large Ramada O'Hare Hotel, which had plenty of space for over 200 attending professionals, it still wasn't big enough to accommodate the throng of fans who came to meet the Image founders. The crowd became so overwhelming that the organizers had to move the Image creators off the convention floor and outside into a pavilion. Over 2500 people waited for hours on lines outside of the convention center, just for the opportunity to get an autograph. As Jim Valentino remembered, "All we saw was an endless stream of belt buckles and

that was it. You sign your name, look up, 'Hi, how're you doing?' Sign your name, look up, 'Hi, how're you doing?'" (Sacks, "Jim Valentino"). Liefeld went above and beyond the call of duty by holding a 24-hour autograph session from Friday afternoon to Saturday afternoon (Todorovich).

Undeniably, the Image founders were the rock stars of the comic book world, but their role within that world was somewhat contradictory. Image was the Biblical figure of David, the underdog who bravely set out to take on a seemingly unbeatable opponent. But given how popular creators

like Jim Lee, Rob Liefeld and Todd McFarlane were at the time, Image was also simultaneously Goliath, the giant who had the power to crush everything in its path. For proof, one need only consider comic book sales for August 1992 when, for the first time since the dawn of the Direct Market, DC Comics was pushed to third place in the Capital City Distribution sales chart. That month, Marvel sold 38.79% of all comics distributed to Direct Market stores while Malibu/Image earned a 17.86% share, good enough to edge out DC at 17.35%. Making that achievement all the more remarkable was the fact that Image released only six comic books that month (in comparison, Marvel and DC released 93 and 61 books respectively). Marvel's sales also declined by 9.13% from the month before, a sure sign that Image was going to give Marvel a run for its money.

On April 16, 1992, Image launched its inaugural series, Rob Liefeld's **Youngblood**, featuring a team of super-heroes who work for the government to stop threats against the United States. The first issue is divided into two stories. The front half presents the Youngblood "home team": Bedrock, Combat, Chapel, Vogue, Diehard and its leader Shaft. The flip side of the issue presents the Youngblood "away team": Brahma, Riptide, Photon, Psi-Fire, Cougar and its leader Sentinel. While Liefeld had created most of these super-heroes during his teen years, some of them resembled existing DC Comics characters that

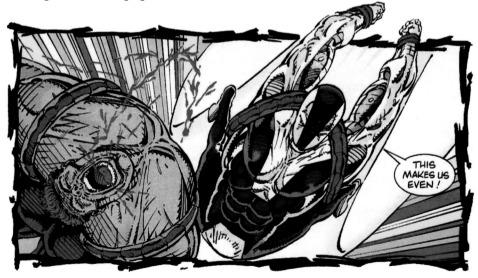

Youngblood *displayed the kind of non-stop action that made Liefeld popular.*
TM and © Rob Liefeld Inc.

Liefeld had intended on using in his aborted *Team Titans* mini-series. Shaft, Vogue and Bedrock were derivatives of Speedy, Harlequin and Blok respectively. In addition, Liefeld originally conceived Combat as a Kh'undian warrior and Die Hard as a S.T.A.R. Labs android (Walko).

Youngblood #1 displayed the kind of non-stop action that made Liefeld such a popular comic book artist in the first place, but years later the creator expressed disappointment with the quality of his work:

"The first issue of *Youngblood*. I wasn't aware. I was completely just not aware of the importance that book would hold in the scheme of things. It should have been a lot better than it was. And it could have been. And I think I was just thoroughly distracted, and caught up in the hype, and caught up in... I was kind of confused. I had never started my own business, and hiring people. I just... I let the deadline creep up on me and then it got the best of me, and I didn't perform well and as a result, it's an awful piece." (Fisher 28)

Regardless, *Youngblood* #1 sold extremely well. At 930,000 copies, it was the best-selling comic book that wasn't published by Marvel or DC in many years (Lissau 184). The initial

Early promotional ad for Spawn.
TM and © Todd McFarlane Productions, Inc.

Todd McFarlane's Spawn *was an immediate blockbuster hit.*
TM and © Todd McFarlane Productions, Inc.

print run sold out so quickly that a second printing was ordered almost immediately (the second printing had a gold border in order to differentiate it from the first printing and also to ensure readers that it was valuable and special). Golden Apple Comics in Los Angeles held a signing with Liefeld on *Youngblood*'s debut night. The media attention was remarkable. "We had three TV news crews, two radio stations, newspapers, and sold 3000 comics during a seven-hour period," said Golden Apple owner Bill Leibowitz. Golden Apple only sold one copy of *Youngblood* #1 per customer but distributed other free comics for everybody in line, which Leibowitz described as "a very Guns 'n Roses crowd," many of whom later returned to shop in his store (Sodaro 71-72).

Each of the Image founders had his own characters ready to go when the line debuted, but none was more prepared than Todd McFarlane. Debuting in May 1992, *Spawn* is the story of Al Simmons, a former U.S. Marine turned CIA operative who is murdered and sent to Hell. Once there, he makes a deal with a devil named Malebolgia to be resurrected so he can see his wife, Wanda, one last time. Upon returning to the land of the living, however, Simmons finds himself horribly disfigured and worse, five years have passed since his death. In that time,

Wanda has re-married—to Simmons' former best friend—and given birth to a baby girl. Simmons is then confronted by the Violator, a demon who disguises himself as an obese clown. The Violator was sent to Earth to prepare Simmons for service in Hell's army, but Simmons rebels against his Hellbound masters. Residing in the alleys of "Rat City" with the homeless, Simmons uses the awesome powers given to him by Malebolgia to battle street gangs and organized crime. As Spawn, Simmons employs brutal crime-fighting methods, even going so far as to mutilate a pedophile.

Spawn #1 had a print run of 1.7 million copies, and because he owned the entire intellectual property, McFarlane earned more money from that comic than he did from his work on *Spider-Man* #1, which sold nearly twice as many copies. McFarlane re-emerged from his parental leave—and a flirtation with the idea of creating sports trading cards under his "Front Row" imprint—with one of the earliest and most popular Image series, and with a character that he had conceived years previously. McFarlane created Spawn in the late 1970s, during his fandom days. Though some readers didn't like the violence or Satanic elements of the series, *Spawn* was consistently one of the top ten best-selling comic books during the entire decade of the 1990s.

The next Image release was the three-issue mini-series **Savage Dragon** by Erik Larsen. The first issue (cover-dated July 1992) shows a powerfully built green man with a fin on his head lying naked in the middle of a burning field in Illinois. Upon waking in a hospital, this man confesses to having no memories of who he is or where he came from. Chicago Police Department Lieutenant Frank Darling nicknames him "Dragon" and gets him employed at his cousin's shipyard warehouse. What Darling really needs, though, is the Dragon on the police force, especially since Chicago is being overrun by super-powered mobsters and maniacs. Initially reluctant, the Dragon becomes an officer after the murder of his employer.

While McFarlane created Spawn when he was 16, Larsen created the Dragon when he was only 10 years old. Ten years later, in 1982, the Dragon made his first appearance in a fanzine titled *Graphic Fantasy* that Larsen and two friends self-published. Shortly thereafter, Larsen began his professional comic book career, contributing to several of Bill Black's AC titles. The Dragon wasn't completely abandoned, however, as Larsen managed to insert him into two 1985 issues of Gary Carlson's *Megaton* comic book. From there Larsen took on bigger and better projects, drawing *DNAgents* for Eclipse in 1986-7 and *Doom Patrol* for DC Comics in 1988. After a five issue run on *The Punisher*, Larsen took over *Amazing Spider-Man* when McFarlane left the series in 1989 and surprisingly found that sales went up with him performing the artistic chores.

In his earliest incarnation, the Dragon wore a dragon-faced mask and a Captain Marvel-like cape. Later, Larsen humorously had the cape rip whenever the Dragon walked through a door. By 1992, Larsen had spent significant time away from the Dragon, which gave him the opportunity to revamp the character for his own Image series (Mason, "Interview with Erik Larsen"). *Savage Dragon* was an unapologetic "old school" super-hero romp, and Larsen delighted in presenting a seemingly endless parade of oddball heroes and villains, many of whom were revived from his childhood days.

Jim Lee's final work on *X-Men* appeared in issue #11, released in June. Two months later, his new Image comic book debuted. *WildC.A.T.s* offered a very different super-hero team than the one Lee just finished working on for Marvel. As Lee

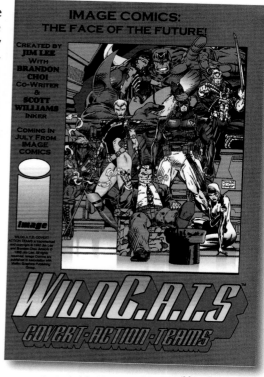

Jim Lee's debut Image series was WildC.A.T.s.
TM and © WildStorm Publications, an imprint of DC Comics.

commented, "I immediately started thinking about a concept of how I could get a team together who don't want to be celebrities. So I knew right away that it would be a covert team, a team with a hidden agenda. I always liked the concept of a team that had something to prove, or who did something that not everybody knew about" (McCallum 29). The Covert Action Team (C.A.T.) is a secretive group of super humans fighting to save the world against a cabal of Daemonites. Led by the dwarfish Jacob Marlowe, a.k.a the Lord Emp, the WildC.A.T.s consist of Void, an enigmatic woman who can bend space and time; Spartan, an artificial man with enhanced strength, speed and agility; Zealot, a Zen weapons master; Voodoo, a tempstress who can project an aura of "animal attraction"; Maul, a strong man who can enlarge himself at the expense of his intelligence; Grifter, a loner gunman; and Warblade, who can alter the many metal parts of his body. *WildC.A.T.s* #1 was the best-selling comic of its release month with over one million copies distributed to stores. (*X-Men*, on the other hand, was the fourth best-selling book on Diamond Comics Distributors' sales charts that month).

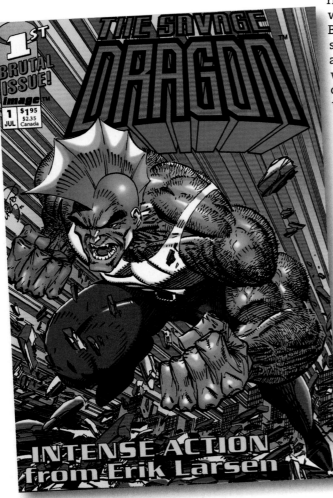

Erik Larsen's **Savage Dragon** *stars a green-skinned powerhouse who joins the Chicago police department.* TM and © Erik Larsen.

Youngblood #2 contained a preview of Jim Valentino's controversial Image series ***Shadowhawk***. As described by Valentino, "Shadowhawk is the mystery-man concept taken to its ultimate extreme. He doesn't come out of the shadows and doesn't let anyone see him unless he's after the person" (Chrissinger 43). From his first story onward, Shadowhawk broke the spines of evil-doers in a reflection of a series that Valentino referred to as "very dark, very gritty, very realistic and very character driven" (Stephenson 25). The lead character is so mysterious that practically nothing about him is revealed: not his secret identity, not his origin, not even his personal characteristics. With this hidden background and with everyone against him—police, super-heroes and criminals alike—it's fair to wonder whether Shadowhawk is a hero or a villain... or someone who doesn't easily fit into a specific category. *Shadowhawk* #1 (Aug. 1992) had a special die-cut cover in which the character's mask was outlined in silver against a black background.

This dark avenger was first conceived by Valentino in 1989 when Archie

Jim Valentino's Shadowhawk *debuted at Image with embossed covers and back-breaking violence.* TM and © Jim Valentino.

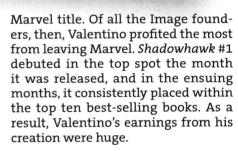

Comics was planning a relaunch of its super-hero line as the more violent Spectrum Comics (starring the same characters that eventually became the centerpieces of DC's cheerful and young-reader-oriented Impact Comics line). Valentino proposed a new take on Archie hero The Fox that set the black-clad hero as a Batman counterpart: a furtive, barely-seen figure who avenges evil in his own dark ways. When Archie cancelled the Spectrum imprint before a single issue was published, Valentino moved on to his breakthrough Marvel series, *Guardians of the Galaxy*. In one *Guardians* storyline, Valentino considered changing the name of team member Starhawk to Shadowhawk. Marvel's management wouldn't allow it, however, and suggested Valentino use the name for a new series. Ultimately, that proposal sat unsold on a Marvel editor's desk before Image started up. As with Jim Lee on *X-Men*, Valentino stayed on *Guardians of the Galaxy* for several months after Image was announced. His plots continued up to *Guardians* #29 (cover date Oct. 1992). (Valentino had actually plotted the series all the way to issue #51.) Sales on *Guardians* were solid but not nearly as high as Marvel's mutant or Spider-Man titles. It ranked as the thirtieth best-selling comic book released in June 1992, mid-range for a

Marvel title. Of all the Image founders, then, Valentino profited the most from leaving Marvel. *Shadowhawk* #1 debuted in the top spot the month it was released, and in the ensuing months, it consistently placed within the top ten best-selling books. As a result, Valentino's earnings from his creation were huge.

Marc Silvestri launched ***Cyberforce*** in October. An X-Men-influenced super-hero action series with science fiction elements, *Cyberforce* featured a group of cybernetically-enhanced mutants who opposed CyberData, a nefarious corporation with designs of ruling the world. Cyberforce consisted of four-armed leader Stryker, the energy sword-emitting Cyblade, the force-blasting Heatwave, the big bruiser Impact, the speedster Velocity, and finally, the series' early breakout star Ripclaw, a Native American with extended bear-like claws. Silvestri had initially conceived *Cyberforce* as a new Marvel Comics series, but when he cast his lot with Todd McFarlane and company, Silvestri decided to make *Cyberforce* his first work for Image Comics (Khoury 120). He was handsomely rewarded for his decision as over 850,000 copies of *Cyberforce* #1 were sold to Direct Market stores.

The inaugural Image titles established that they were operating within the

Marc Silvestri's Cyberforce *fused super-hero and science-fiction elements.* TM and © Top Cow Publications, Inc.

same fictional universe as each creator's characters guest-starred in other creators' books. For example, Spawn appeared in *Shadowhawk* #2 while *WildC.A.T.s'* Jacob Marlowe had a cameo in *Cyberforce* #1. Youngblood was featured in both *WildC.A.T.s* #2 and *Savage Dragon* #3. Before long, however, the founders avoided having guest stars from other Image titles as they built up their own plot threads for their own individual sets of characters.

Starting in August, readers had the opportunity to order an exclusive comic book, *Image* #0, by mailing coupons included in seven other Image books: *Cyberforce* #1, *Shadowhawk* #1, *WildC.A.T.s* #2, *Savage Dragon* #3, *Spawn* #4, *Youngblood* #0 and the second issue of Rob Liefeld's second Image series *Brigade*. Readers were informed, however, that they couldn't mail photocopies of the coupons. The coupons had to be cut out of each comic book. Therefore, those readers who wanted to keep their Image collection in pristine condition had no choice but to buy additional copies. Eventually released in October 1993, *Image* #0 included four-page stories by each of the Image founders, except Whilce Portacio who only contributed to the issue's cover.

In fact, Portacio was also the only founder who didn't launch his own Image series in 1992. He initially agreed to illustrate

Though Whilce Portacio's **Wetworks** *was announced as an Image launch title, it didn't debut for several years.* TM & © WildStorm Publications, an imprint of DC Comics.

The Huntsman, a title created by **Chris Claremont**, the former X-Men scribe. Claremont had even been promoted as a founder in some of the first advertisements for Image Comics, and as he reflected, "If things had come together the way Jim (Lee) and I discussed them, I would have been part of the core group" (O'Neill 35). Unfortunately for Claremont, Portacio eventually opted out of the project in order to create his own comic book.

The first ad for Image Comics listed Chris Claremont, among other creators.

Portacio admitted to the press, "The appeal of doing my own concept was just too great to pass up!" (Kanalz 6). With Portacio out, Claremont had trouble finding a quality artist who was free to work on *The Huntsman*. Ironically, they were all either working on Image comics or another title published elsewhere. Spelling out the situation, Claremont said, "I would love to engage Todd, Jim, Marc Silvestri, Larry Stroman and Dale Keown to draw issues of *Huntsman*. I don't think it will happen anytime soon, because why should they?" (O'Neill 35). Thus, Claremont was unable to move ahead with *The Huntsman*, and his opportunity to join Image during its inception passed. The Huntsman did, though, appear as a featured character in two Image series: *WildC.A.T.s* (issues #10-13, April-Sept. 1994) and *Cyberforce* (issue #9-11, Dec. 1994-March 1995) with Claremont writing all seven issues. After that, the Huntsman never appeared in comics again.

Instead of collaborating with Claremont, Whilce Portacio created **Wetworks**, an action-oriented comic book about a team of black ops soldiers who battle supernatural forces. The first issue was solicited for an October 1992 release, and pre-orders were so high that *Wetworks* #1 was set to become the best-selling comic book for that month…, but it didn't work out that way. When October came and went, *Wetworks* #1 was nowhere to be found. The only Portacio work that fans could read was a four page *Wetworks* preview in the back of *WildC.A.T.s* #2. Furthermore, it wouldn't be until 1994 before *Wetworks* #1 was actually published. The sad reality was that Portacio's professional life had been disrupted by a personal tragedy: his sister—who worked as a receptionist for his and Jim Lee's studio—passed away. The loss devastated Portacio so much that he had to stop working on comics for an extended period of time.

The first Image comic book produced by a creator who was not a founder was **Dale Keown**, a Canadian artist then popular for his work on the Peter David-scripted *Incredible Hulk*. Keown was someone the Image founders had tagged for recruitment before they launched their line because he was another young turk whose energetic work excited the comic book fanbase. The prospect of plucking another popular artist away from Marvel was particularly appealing to Todd McFarlane. At first, Keown proved reluctant to leave Marvel as the Hulk was his favorite character to draw, and he enjoyed collaborating with Peter David. Ultimately, though, the lure of artistic comradery—and financial riches—was too much to pass up: "I really liked the idea of these young guys all getting together and creating their own studio. I liked that idea" (Khoury 198). Given his success on—and fondness for—*Hulk*, it was little surprise that Keown chose to create his own heroic monster for Image. *Pitt* starred a savage alien giant and his half-brother, a young boy named Timmy, as they attempt to elude the Creed, the alien race responsible for Pitt's creation. After debuting in a back-up story in *Youngblood* #4, the Pitt starred in his own title, the first issue of

Image soon broadened its offerings by publishing work not produced by one of its founders, like Dale Keown's Pitt. TM and © Dale Keown

which sold over a million copies. *Pitt* #1 was solicited for a November 1992 release but the actual publication of the issue was delayed for many months, something that would become a troubling trend for both Keown and Image Comics in general.

The sales success of Image's titles combined with the firebrand mentality of its creators was bound to have a polarizing effect on comic book readers, critics and professionals alike. While younger readers relished Image's hyperkinetic storytelling, many older readers seemed put off by it. Their frustrations were given voice by critics like *The Comic Journal*'s R. Fiore who declared, "The art of Todd McFarlane and Rob Liefeld is all surface and no feeling" (Fiore 22).

Inevitably, Image became the target of various parodies, including Fantagraphics' *WildB.R.A.T.s* (an acronym for "Bad Redundant Art Teams") as well as *Doom Force Special* #1 (July 1992) by Grant Morrison and a team of artists which pitilessly mocked Rob Liefeld's comics and artwork. (To its credit, Image proved willing to lampoon itself with *Stupid* #1 (May 1993), a parody of Spawn by Doug Rice and Hilary Barta as well as the two issue *Splitting Image* (March and April 1993), in which Don Simpson told a slightly satirical story about the founding of Image.)

The professional reaction to Image seemed split between those who felt the whole endeavor was receiving more attention—and more money—than it really deserved and those who were simpatico with the Image founders' anticorporate mission statement. Scott McCloud, writer/artist of *Zot!* and one of the comic book industry's most prominent champions of creators' rights told *The Comics Journal*, "Image is a very radical thing. There are a lot of people who think that Image comics are like neo-conservative status quo comics. But actually it's a pretty radical take on the

superhero comic—quite a shift from what the status quo was only a few years ago. It's very interesting. It's very incomprehensible for some of us, writers and artists of a certain generation or older. But it struck a responsive chord, and I've been urging people not to dismiss them too quickly" (Harvey 68). By the end of 1992, if any disapproving fan, professional or critic hoped that Image would suffer a quick demise, he was in for a big disappointment. For better and for worse, Image's standing would only increase over the coming years, and in 1993, Image's very reputation would be the subject of a public debate between two of the industry's most prominent creators.

The Unity of Valiant

With radical layouts and multiple splash pages, the Image Comics creators frequently approached comic book storytelling in unorthodox ways. **Valiant Comics**, on the other hand, utilized traditional storytelling techniques (like symmetrical panel grids) and became the comic book industry's other major success story of 1992. Emphasizing character over creator and story over flash, Valiant grew its line slowly and systematically. While Image founded itself as a loose confederation of seven different entrepreneurs who went in seven different directions, Valiant practiced unity. Valiant's tightly integrated line of comics had a unified approach, a unified art style, a unified grounding in the real world, and a unified staff. Most of Valiant's team – writers, artists, editors, production workers, and even sales staff – worked in one large space, nicknamed "knob row," where ideas and jokes flowed easily.

In 1992, Valiant went from being a niche publisher that released wrestling comics and a handful of Gold Key hero revivals to a larger line of realistic-feeling super-hero titles. Valiant's most important figure was its President, **Jim Shooter**, who stressed that Valiant's stories take place in "the world outside your window," mirroring the approach Shooter had in 1986 when his New Universe imprint was rolled out at Marvel.

The cornerstone series of the unified Valiant universe—and perhaps the comic most dear to Shooter's heart—was *Harbinger*. Written by Shooter and illustrated by his young, talented protégé **David Lapham**, *Harbinger* had parallels to the X-Men in its story of misunderstood, super-powered teenagers on the run. The lead character is Peter Stanchek, a powerful psionic who flees from the malicious Harbinger Foundation and its CEO, the megalomaniacal Toyo Harada. Peter, along with his girlfriend Kris Hathaway, gathers together a group of young allies to help him bring down Harada: Faith Herbert, a cheerful, overweight girl with flying powers who dubs herself Zephyr but whose friends

Valiant Comics expanded in 1992 with a slate of new characters in an interlocking universe.
TM and © Valiant Entertainment LLC.

call her Zeppelin; the illiterate and brutish John Torkelson, nicknamed Torque, who has superhuman strength; and the flirtatious Charlene Dupre, or Flamingo, whose pyrokinetic powers, beauty and high heels betray a crippling lack of self-esteem. *Harbinger* focused tightly on the relationships between these characters, with a naturalistic style that fit Shooter's vision of the comic reflecting the real world. Just like it did with *Magnus* the year before, Valiant inserted coupons in the opening issues of *Harbinger*. Readers who collected the coupons found in the first six issues could redeem them for a free copy of *Harbinger* #0.

Shooter created the Harbinger characters in 1987 as a movie treatment for Paramount Pictures. Though the head of production at Paramount said he "loved" the treatment, he asked Shooter to rewrite it as a comedy so it could feature box office superstar Eddie Murphy. Shooter declined and pulled back the property, which he then revived for Valiant with a few changes (Shooter).

The next new original Valiant series, *X-O Manowar* (first issue cover-dated Feb. 1992), starred Aric, a resourceful yet furious Visigoth warrior who is kidnapped by spider aliens and held captive on their

X-O Manowar *was one part* Conan the Barbarian *and one part* Invincible Iron Man.
TM and © Valiant Entertainment LLC.

spacecraft for over 1500 years. When the aliens' ship is attacked, Aric dons a powerful suit of armor which he uses to escape the spacecraft and return to Earth where he's an incredibly powerful man out of time. Pitched by longtime *Iron Man* artist **Bob Layton** in the summer of 1991 as "a barbarian from outer space with high tech alien armor," the series shows Aric finding his way in the modern world while intermittently getting involved in Toyo Harada's latest scheme. That cross-title continuity, casting Harada as a nemesis in several series, demonstrated the way the Valiant universe stitched itself together. The aliens featured in *X-O* are the same ones that appeared in other Valiant comics, and readers eventually learn that Aric was freed when the aliens' ship was destroyed by another Valiant super-hero, Solar, Man of the Atom. Written first by Shooter and comics veteran **Steve Englehart** before Layton assumed the reins with issue #5, *X-O Manowar* progressed in real-time with each issue narrating events 30 days beyond those of the previous issue. Aric grows and changes as the series progresses, eventually becoming a corporate CEO who settles happily into late 20th century life. The title of the series came from Valiant Director of Sales Jon Hartz, who suggested that the character be called X-O because he wears an exo-skeleton.

Rai, which had been running as a backup series in *Magnus Robot Fighter*, received his own comic with *Rai* #1 (March 1992) written by David Michelinie, with art by Joe St. Pierre and Charles Barnet. A uniquely dark and emotionally complex series, *Rai* touched on elements of honor, inheritance, politics and betrayal, depicting an isolated man, the inheritor of his family's heroic mantle, in an even more isolated environment desperately trying to determine the right thing to do – and often failing. The series was set in a bizarre future Japan that orbits the Earth in a durable plastisteel animal frame launched after the defeat of the spider aliens in the *Magnus* backup. Though *Rai* had a more high-concept storyline compared with other Valiant series, its art and approach fit the Valiant house style. At the end of its initial eight-issue run, Rai lies dead, the city has crashed back to Earth, and despair pervades the Japanese citizens. In an era filled with exuberance, the dark tone of *Rai* stood out as a bracing antidote.

The Valiant line next expanded with the Englehart-scripted **Shadowman** (first issue cover-dated May 1992) which portrayed a mystically-powered musician from New Orleans. Dark and disturbing, Shadowman is a true being of the night who lives in his own mysterious world. Shooter, Englehart and artist David Lapham took pains to make the comic as authentic as possible. Lapham traveled to New Orleans and took extensive photos of the city, while Englehart studied the city's jazz scene so that he could portray it accurately.

By early 1992, most Valiant titles sold between 25,000 and 30,000 copies per issue. While that was unspectacular, *Wizard* magazine at least took note of an upward trend when the price guide in its fifth issue posed the rhetorical question, "Has anyone noticed that all of the Valiant titles are slowly climbing up the price charts?" Two months later, *Wizard* #7 featured a cover of X-O Manowar by Barry Windsor-Smith and interviews with Windsor-Smith and Shooter. That same month, *Solar* #10 (cover date June 1992) combined an all-black embossed cover with the introduction of a new character named **Eternal Warrior**, whose life spanned centuries. The issue's initial print run of 40,000 copies quickly sold out, forcing the order of a second print run to satisfy demand. To borrow *Wizard*'s catch phrase, Valiant was suddenly "hot." Comics that Valiant released not even a year prior were now fetching high prices on the back issue market, and new Valiant releases began selling over 100,000 copies per issue (McLelland). This dramatic escalation in reader interest coincided with the publication of Valiant's first summer crossover event, **Unity**.

Encompassing Valiant's entire catalog of titles—*Harbinger, Magnus Robot Fighter, Rai, Shadowman, Solar, Man of the Atom, X-O Manowar* and two new series, *Archer & Armstrong* and *Eternal Warrior*—*Unity* centers on Erica Pierce, one of Solar's physicist colleagues who goes mad when she gains god-like powers. Seeking to repair a timeline that has been damaged by Solar's adventures, Pierce vows to reset the entirety of history: "I will bring order and unity to all existence... and this time creation shall have a just God!" In the event's first chapter, the 16 page *Unity* #0 (Aug. 1992)—written by Shooter, drawn by Windsor-Smith and offered free of charge so as to hook readers—all the Valiant heroes are transported to an alternate future world to fight a war against Pierce, renamed Mothergod. By event's end—with *Unity* #1 (Oct. 1992)—Erica is defeated but the Valiant universe has been drastically—and permanently—changed. Both Rai and Harbinger member Torque have died, Shadowman

The **Unity** *crossover helped propel Valiant's sales into the stratosphere.*
TM and © Valiant Entertainment LLC.

has found love, and a new member of the Valiant universe has been spotlighted, the Native American dinosaur hunter—and former Gold Key Comics hero—**Turok**. *Unity* #1 was Valiant's best-selling comic book up to that time, and in its wake, Valiant's entire line got a sales boost with some titles selling up to 150,000 copies per issue. The Valiant universe had a tight, interconnected continuity which many fans found attractive, so much so that they passionately hunted down Valiant back issues, driving secondary market values even higher. By December 1992, seven of the top 10 most sought-after back issues listed in *Wizard* #17 were Valiant comic books.

Unity reset Valiant's status quo. Before the crossover, Valiant's sales were barely strong enough to keep the company in business. Post-*Unity*, sales improved so much that Diamond Comics Distribution declared Valiant its "Publisher of the Year" for 1992. Former Valiant editor Jeff Gomez attributes the line's success to the men behind it: "The initial artistic chemistry at Valiant, when Jim Shooter and Barry Windsor-Smith were spearheading the direction of the superhero universe,

was a rare flashpoint in the history of comics. Those were unique, personal and passionately-told stories" (McLelland).

One of the secrets of Valiant's success came from its personal touch with readers and retailers. The Valiant office often rewarded people who helped in the company's success by providing them with comics that had special covers. Similar in concept to gold records given to stores that helped a musician achieve huge sales, Valiant sent gold logo variants to retailers and consumers who the Valiant team felt went above and beyond the call of duty to support the company. Those comics could be retained for the pleasure of owning a rare collectible or immediately resold for big bucks. For instance, a special *Unity* #0 variant had a red cover banner rather than the blue one found on all the other copies. The red banner variants were specially shipped to select shop owners and resold for as much as $125.

November 1992's *Rai* #0, written by David Michelinie and illustrated by David Lapham and Tom Ryder, pulled together all the elements that helped Valiant achieve its success. Beneath a striking cover that silhouetted Rai against a rising sun, the issue provided a glimpse into the future of the Valiant Universe. Among other things, *Rai* #0 features a crucial new character named **Bloodshot**, a nanite-enhanced soldier who escapes the grasp of those who made him powerful with the help of a Geomancer (introduced during the *Unity* crossover). The issue also reveals the fates of many of Valiant's other key characters, including the death of Shadowman fighting his nemesis Master Darque, the transformation of Archer from *Archer and Armstrong* into a guru of sorts, the disappearance of Peter Stanchek, and the continued rise in power of Toyo Harada to the point where he controls two-thirds of the Earth. *Rai* #0 was a near-instant sellout, quickly gaining value on the secondary market and a seemingly permanent place in *Wizard* magazine's Top 10 list of most sought-after back issues.

Valiant's final new series for 1992 spun out of *Harbinger*. **H.A.R.D. Corps** presents a group of super-powered Vietnam War veterans banded together to oppose Toyo Harada. The first issue (cover-dated Dec. 1992) offered something no other Valiant comic book could: a gatefold cover drawn by none other than Image Comics founder Jim Lee. Initially declining to

Rai #1 (top) told the future history of the Valiant Universe. **Hard Corps** *#1 (bottom) featured a cover by Image Comics co-founder Jim Lee.*
TM and © Valiant Entertainment LLC.

draw the cover for Valiant because he was too busy with *WildC.A.T.s*, Lee changed his mind when Steve Massarsky offered him something the artist really wanted: tickets to a U2 concert. Lee wanted to attend the rock band's show when they reached his home city of San Diego, but to Lee's chagrin, the concert was sold out. When Lee mentioned that fact to Massarsky, the Valiant publisher used his connections in the entertainment industry to secure a pair of tickets, which Lee accepted in exchange for his work on the cover.

The appearance of Jim Lee's artwork on a Valiant comic book was a pleasant surprise. The later news that Jim Shooter was leaving the company was nothing short of an unexpected shock. Five years after he was fired as Marvel's editor-in-chief, Shooter was now out at Valiant Comics. Some claim that Shooter was let go because he had become too difficult to work with, requiring his personal approval of every new release, which bogged down Valiant's production process. For a publisher that prided itself on always shipping its comics on time, the delays became untenable. Shooter, however, offered a different explanation for his departure. In a June 21, 1993 *Forbes* magazine article Shooter claimed he was pushed out of Valiant in a power play by two members of the board: Massarsky and his paramour (and later wife) Melanie Okun. A rift had developed between Shooter and Massarsky that dated back to Massarsky's decision to publish the money-losing Nintendo and WWF wrestling comics. A year later, with Valiant finally turning handsome profits, Massarsky wanted to sell the company to a group of investors that would secure movie deals and better newsstand distribution while keeping all of Valiant's executives on staff. Upon seeing the particulars of the proposed sale, however, Shooter realized he was being handed the short end of the stick. For instance, he was being asked to sign a ten-year contract that stipulated his employment could be terminated if he failed to "engender good morale." As Shooter explained, "let's say I piss off Bob Layton one day, they could fire me and claw back all my stock with no compensation, leaving me with nothing... How long do you think, in that ten year period, it would take for me to piss somebody off? A letterer or a colorist for instance? The janitor? An intern?" (Irving). Sensing a trap, Shooter refused to sign the contract. That defiance only delayed the inevitable as the company's board of directors soon fired him. In an arbitrated settlement, Shooter received several hundred thousand dollars from Valiant. As it turned out, that was a fraction of what Shooter would have yielded had he not been let go.

Meanwhile, Bob Layton became Valiant's new editor-in-chief, and he would steer the company into its most successful days... right before its spectacular downfall.

Doomsday for Superman

While Valiant and Image distinguished themselves as the comic book success stories of 1992, the year's most important comic book event actually belonged to **DC Comics**. It involved nothing less than the death of the most iconic character in comic book history, **Superman**.

The epic storyline that led to Superman's death started in September 1992 as three of DC's Superman titles (in order of release: *Superman: The Man of Steel* #17, *Adventures of Superman* #496 and *Superman* #73) provided a four-panel teaser of a gloved fist punching a steel wall and a bottom caption that declares, "Doomsday is Coming!" In the fourth Superman title that month, *Action Comics* #683, the fist has finally punched through the steel wall and the caption ominously announces, "Doomsday is here!" Then in October's *Superman: The Man of Steel* #18—written by Louise Simonson with art by Jon Bogdanove and Dennis Janke—the creature breaks free from his prison and begins a mindless rampage through the countryside on his way to

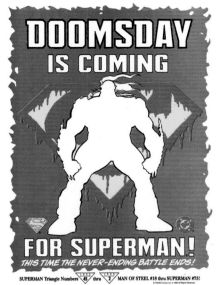

Doomsday proved to be a fateful opponent for Superman. TM and © DC Comics.

his ultimate destination: Metropolis. The Justice League intercepts... only to be savagely beaten back. Superman enters the fray just in time to hear Booster Gold describe the monster as "Doomsday."

The next four Superman issues, released over consecutive weeks, show the trail of destruction produced by the Man of Steel's battle with Doomsday. As the story progresses, each issue's panel count decreases. *Adventures of Superman* #497 is presented entirely with four-panel pages, *Action Comics* #684 with three-panel pages and *Superman: The Man of Steel* #19 with two-panel pages. The story's final chapter, *Superman* #75, consists entirely of full splash pages. In that fateful issue, written and drawn by **Dan Jurgens**, Superman and Doomsday have reached Metropolis and furiously fight each other with their last ounces of energy. The force of their blows shatter skyscraper windows. As the story climaxes in front of the *Daily Planet* building, the two adversaries manage to land one final vicious punch on each other. It is enough to stop Doomsday once and for all, but victory comes at a terrible cost. A shattered Man of Steel lies in the arms of a disconsolate Lois Lane. He is gone. Superman is dead.

"The Death of Superman" received national media attention well in advance of *Superman* #75's arrival in stores. CNN Headline News covered the event in its September 5, 1992 rotation with the suggestion that DC Comics decided to kill off the Man of Steel because he was "dated"; his "boy scout" adventures were no longer appealing to the comic book readers of the early 1990s who preferred more

violent characters like Wolverine and the Punisher. Similar coverage ran in dozens, if not hundreds, of other outlets. The Death of Superman became a pop cultural phenomenon, which took DC completely by surprise, as Superman editor **Mike Carlin** explained:

"Last March [1992], we told all the distributors that we were killing Superman and heard not a peep out of anybody. Not until it got into the newspapers did it start blowing wide open, and we couldn't control it. Many people complained about the hype that we got, and it wasn't us. We couldn't stop it if we wanted to." (McTigue 5)

On November 17, 1992, the day *Superman* #75 was published, lines stretched outside comic shops as fans and non-fans alike clamored for copies. People who had never before set foot in a comic book store waited hours to buy the story of the death of one of America's greatest icons, undoubtedly assuming the issue was a worthwhile investment that was guaranteed to increase in value in the years ahead. Many local news stations televised interviews with consumers who described their plans to keep their copies of *Superman* #75 stored away until it was time to cash them in for enough money to pay for their children's college education costs.

DC released several editions of *Superman* #75. Besides the standard edition that retailed for $1.25, there was also a "deluxe" edition with a tombstone cover that had the engraved words "Here Lies the World's Greatest Hero." A polybagged "Memorial" set that retailed for $2.50 consisted of a copy of the issue, a memorial poster, commemorative stamps, a Daily Planet obituary, a black mourning armband, and an exclusive Skybox trading card. Finally, a 10,000 copy "Platinum" edition of *Superman* #75 was made available first to any comic book retailer with a business card and resale certificate before being sent to readers who wrote the best fan letters about "The Death of Superman" and the subsequent "Funeral for a Friend" story arcs. Those platinum editions quickly increased in value to over $100 per copy.

Superman #75 went through four printings, totaling six million copies. On the day of the issue's release, $30 million of comic book revenue was generated nationwide (Miller). The blockbuster sales of the "Death of Superman" stand out even more when compared to sales from earlier in the year. During most of 1992, the Superman family of titles had been hovering at the bottom of the Top 100 best-selling comic books

The cover to the deluxe edition of **Superman** #75 resembled a tombstone. TM and © DC Comics.

list. For example, Diamond Comic Distributors ranked *Superman* #71 as the 91st most popular comic in the month of July, with *Action* #681 and *Adventures of Superman* #494 occupying the 98th and 99th spots respectively. In September, Capital City Distribution ordered 19,250 copies of *Superman* #73. That quantity increased tenfold two months later when Capital ordered 281,400 copies of *Superman* #75.

The "Death of Superman" storyline actually happened because another storyline fell through. In planning out each year's worth of adventures, all the Superman writers and artists took part in a creative retreat. Going into 1992, the Superman comics had already progressed the plot thread in which Clark Kent proposes marriage to Lois Lane in *Superman* #50 (Dec. 1990) by showing the couple plan their wedding in issues throughout 1991. Editor Mike Carlin and his team planned to have Lois and Clark finally tie the knot... but then the *Lois and Clark: the New Adventures of Superman* television show was announced as being in the works for 1993. Since that series planned to feature a flirtatious relationship between its two lead characters, the Superman comics team decided it would be premature to have Clark and Lois marry in the comics. Carlin picks up the story:

[The change] was our doing, not Warner Brothers or the TV show's doing. We felt that if there was going to be a *Lois and Clark* TV show on the air, and they were going to play it along the lines we do, where Lois and Clark would actually build a romance, we wanted to maybe get to the altar at the same time. So basically we put it off for a while. ("DC in the 90's")

If Superman wasn't going to get married, then the comic book creators had to figure out something else to do with him. Ideas were bounced around during the retreat, until writer/artist Jerry Ordway jokingly suggested that Super-

Superman's funeral was attended by ordinary people and heroes alike. TM and © DC Comics.

man should die. It wasn't the first time Ordway had sarcastically made that suggestion, and just like before, his colleagues chuckled at the thought of DC's flagship character being killed off.

But then the creators began to give the idea serious consideration, until they all decided it was indeed the best option. A significant problem to be solved, however, was determining how the Man of Steel would die. Who could kill him? The creators considered Superman's entire rogues gallery and found them all to be wanting. None of them could appropriately serve as Superman's killer. While diabolically brilliant, neither Lex Luthor nor Brainiac could equal Superman's physical power. As Dan Jurgens explains, the creators all concluded that in order for Superman to die, a new nemesis had to be created for him, "We had done so many business-suit villains, so many lame old boring guys. We had to have something that could pound the crap out of Superman — that raised the stakes" (Christensen and Seifert 85). The villain, unnamed at the time of his conception, was a force of nature, primal rage incarnate and capable of destroying enormous sections of Metropolis all by himself. After finally coming up with the name of Doomsday, the creators decided to keep the villain's background a mystery, in part to leave readers guessing about his origin and in part to keep the story focused on Superman himself rather than on the villain who causes his demise.

The unprecedented media attention paid to the Death of Superman influenced rival comic book publishers to satirize the event. Like DC's "Memorial" edition of *Superman* #75, Parody Press' *The Deaths of Stupidman* #1A and #1B came polybagged with a poster, an obituary, mock Stupidman postage stamps, and a coupon that readers could send in for free used Stupidman Kleenex. One of the most surprising comments on the death of Superman came from legendary Superman artist **Curt Swan**, who said, "I think the 'death' story came out of the blue. There was no build-up, no suspense developed. Superman had no foreboding of some force out there that would conquer him. It all happened too quickly" (Swan 9).

The Dark Knight Returns

Even though 1992 was the year Superman died, DC Comics' other flagship character received his fair share of fanfare as well, especially since the sequel to his 1989 blockbuster film was scheduled to arrive in theaters. Once again directed by **Tim Burton** and starring Michael Keaton, *Batman Returns* has the Caped Crusader opposing the sociopathic Penguin (played by Danny DeVito) who seeks to become the next mayor of Gotham City. Aiding Penguin is Max Shreck (Christopher Walken), an evil businessman who will go to any lengths to protect his self-interests, even murdering his secretary Selina Kyle (Michelle Pfeiffer) when he suspects she knows too much about his wrong-doings. However, thanks to the mysterious intervention of a clutter of stray cats, Kyle is resurrected and as **Catwoman**, she vows revenge on her former boss.

Batman Returns presents many of the same elements that made Burton's first movie so distinctive: a surreally noir depiction of Gotham City, a multifaceted performance by Michael Keaton as both Batman and Bruce Wayne, and cackling, over-the-top villains. Burton, though, originally didn't want to make a second Batman movie, especially when Warner Bros. rehired the first movie's screenwriter **Sam Hamm** over Burton's objections. After Hamm submitted a draft of *Batman Returns* that had the Penguin and Catwoman pursuing hidden treasure, Burton replaced Hamm with **Daniel**

Waters, who previously scripted a couple of notorious action comedies: 1990's *The Adventures of Ford Fairlane* (starring standup comedian Andrew Dice Clay) and 1991's *Hudson Hawk* (starring Bruce Willis). In revising Hamm's script, Waters brought Harvey Dent (a.k.a. Two-Face) and Robin into the story. African-American actor Marlon Wayans agreed to play Robin in both *Batman Returns* and a sequel, and he even attended a wardrobe sitting. But then Burton and his staff decided to save the Boy Wonder for the next Batman movie. Uncredited screenwriter Wesley Strick subsequently removed Dent and Robin from *Batman Returns* when he polished the final script.

Batman Returns portrayed the tumultuous romance between Michael Keaton's Batman and Michelle Pfeiffer's Catwoman. TM and © DC Comics.

Several actresses were considered to play Catwoman before the role was finally given to Michelle Pfeiffer. Annette Bening was the first actress to be cast but had to drop out after she became pregnant. Jennifer Jason Leigh, Madonna and Bridget Fonda were also in the running. One person who felt very strongly that she was the perfect choice to play Catwoman was former *Blade Runner* actress Sean Young, who previously lost roles as Vicki Vale (*Batman*, 1989) and Tess Trueheart (*Dick Tracy*, 1990). When she learned that Burton refused to even consider her for the role, much less let her read for the part, Young put on a cat suit and showed up at the office of *Batman* producer Mark Canton to plead her case. When that didn't get her anywhere, Young went public with her passion by appearing on *The Joan Rivers Show* as Catwoman (Gerosa).

Batman Returns premiered June 19, 1992, and grossed over $162 million in the United States. Though Warner Bros. was disappointed that the sequel earned far less than Burton's first *Batman* film (which had grossed over $251 million domestically in 1989), *Batman Returns* was undeniably a smash hit, finishing as the third highest-grossing film of the year in the United States, behind Disney's *Aladdin* and *Home Alone 2*. *Batman Returns* was also nominated for two Academy Awards, for Best Visual Effects and Best Makeup.

Batman Goes Back to the Future

Three months after the premiere of the *Batman Returns* movie, another Batman adaptation made its debut. On Monday, September 7, 1992, the FOX television network aired the first episode of the groundbreaking **Batman: The Animated Series**. For many years, television cartoons—particularly ones that involved super-heroes—featured uninspiring design work and insipid scripts. From its initial episode, however, *BTAS* embodied a more sophisticated aesthetic; art deco cityscapes grounded Batman in a dynamic, intriguing Gotham City.

With 60 episodes in its first season, *BTAS* presented a wide range of adventures, some new and some based on classic tales from Batman comic books. In one of the most moving episodes, "Perchance to Dream," Batman wakes up and discovers that there is no Batcave and that his parents are still alive. "The Man Who Killed Batman" features a low-level gangster who believes he's killed the Dark Knight only to find out that he's very much mistaken. "Moon of the Wolf," adapted from a Batman story by Neal Adams and Denny O'Neil, pits Batman against a werewolf. To be expected, the series heavily relies upon Batman's familiar rogues gallery. The Joker, Two-Face, The Penguin, The Riddler, Catwoman, The Scarecrow, Mr. Freeze, Poison Ivy, Clayface and Ra's al Ghul each appear in several episodes. One of the most memorable Joker episodes was "The Laughing Fish," a cartoon version of Steve Englehart and Marshall Rogers's classic story from 1977. Comic writers such as

O'Neil, Gerry Conway and Elliot Maggin wrote for *BTAS*, which helped the show remain true to its comic roots.

Batman: The Animated Series emerged in the wake of the success of Burton's first *Batman* movie. The studio wanted ancillary material to support the film series, so Warner Bros. executive Jean MacCurdy approached animation industry veterans **Paul Dini**, **Bruce Timm** and **Eric Radomski** and tasked them with creating a new Batman cartoon. The team came up with a distinctive and powerful art design for the new show. Strongly influenced by the classic 1930s art deco Superman cartoons produced by the Fleischer Studios, *Batman: The Animated Series* had an idiosyncratic, throwback visual style that helped it stand out from other animated shows. As Dini remembered, "We wanted to make something completely different looking than anything that had been on television before" (Hansen 12). The quality of that approach helped bring aboard award-winning producer Alan Burnett (known for his work on *Duck Tales: The Movie*, *Pirates of Dark Water* and *The Smurfs*): "[MacCurdy] showed me a promo clip by co-producers Bruce Timm and Eric Radomski, and I couldn't believe my eyes. It was the *best* action/adventure animation I had ever seen for television" (Jankiewicz 34).

Maybe most importantly for the show's eventual success, the producers chose an actor with a voice that was pitch perfect for Batman. **Kevin Conroy** was a former soap opera star and Shakespearean actor whose voice had a range and gravitas that simultaneously made Batman heroic and Bruce Wayne sympathetic. Equally as important, the Joker also had a strong audio impression as *Star Wars* actor **Mark Hamill** performed the role of Batman's arch-nemesis with an energy, humor and

Batman: the Animated Series.
TM and © DC Comics.

verve that truly turned him into the character that viewers loved to hate. The real breakout star of the show, however, was the Joker's assistant, **Harley Quinn**, clad in a traditional court jester outfit. She was the Joker's "gal Friday," his muse and assistant who was always ready with a quick quip and a deadly attack. As voiced by **Arleen Sorkin**, the squeaky Harley loved her "Mister J" and would do anything to help him.

Perhaps the biggest struggle experienced by the show's producers was their continuous battle with the network's Standards and Practices team. While restrictions about displays of violence in children's programming had loosened up somewhat since the 1970s and the days of the *Super Friends* cartoon, there was still *a lot* that couldn't be shown in 1992, like gunfire or death. This left Timm, Radomski, Dini and Burnett in a bit of a bind. Batman's origin episode, for instance, couldn't show Bruce Wayne's parents being gunned down, despite the fact that their murder was the impetus for Bruce donning a cape and cowl. Any character who was pushed out of a window always had to land in water with a reassuring splash. The producers' battles with the censors extended beyond displays of violence and included whether or not the Penguin could smoke a cigarette or Batman could kiss Catwoman.

Batman: The Animated Series was an unqualified hit with both fans and critics, earning strong ratings and multiple daytime Emmy Award nominations as well as influencing the future of animation. The show inspired a new generation of animation auteurs by proving that imaginative programming could be produced relatively cheaply. It also helped a whole new generation of kids to discover iconic super-heroes. DC Comics capitalized by launching a comic book set in the TV show continuity. Written by Kelley Puckett with art by Ty Templeton and Rick Burchett, *The Batman Adventures* (first issue cover-dated Oct. 1992) presented self-contained adventures intended for kids (and kids at heart).

Since Batman was at the center of many fans' attention in 1992, DC launched another new ongoing

Debuting in 1992, Azrael would become an important Batman supporting character. TM and © DC Comics.

Batman series. ***Batman: Shadow of the Bat*** (first issue cover-dated June 1992) became DC's fourth monthly Batman title, joining *Batman*, *Detective Comics* and *Legends of the Dark Knight*. The Caped Crusader now had as many ongoing series as Superman. To distinguish *Shadow of the Bat*, Brian Stelfreeze painted the first 50 covers of the series, and each cover had a distinctive border to frame Stelfreeze's work. The new series was created by two men who had collaborated together on many Batman stories: writer **Alan Grant** and artist **Norm Breyfogle**. Their initial *Shadow of the Bat* story, "The Last Arkham," had Batman pretend to go insane in order to go undercover in Arkham Asylum. While there, he met the institution's new administrator Jeremiah Arkham and discovered that the hospital's

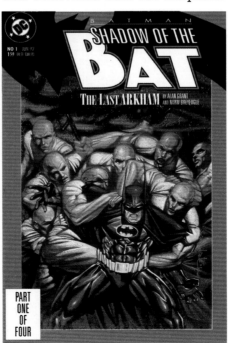

Shadow of the Bat *debuted a new Batman series.*
TM and © DC Comics.

builder had provided serial killer/prisoner Victor Zsasz with the means of coming and going at will. New character Zsasz—who would become one of Batman's most popular villains in the '90s—had no qualms about who he murdered. He kept track of his killings by cutting hash marks on his body.

Meanwhile, **Chuck Dixon** and **Tom Lyle**—who had helmed both *Robin* mini-series of the previous two years—were installed as the regular creative team on *Detective Comics*, starting with issue #644 (May 1992). Having already made third-generation Robin Tim Drake his own, Dixon was poised to become one of the key voices in the 1990s Batman series. Issues #647-649 introduced the Spoiler, the heroic teenage daughter of Silver Age villain Cluemaster and a character destined to become a beloved supporting cast member. Following Lyle's departure with *Detective* #649, **Graham Nolan** moved in to succeed him as Dixon's most popular artistic collaborator of the decade. Among their first joint efforts was the return of the Huntress to the Batman series in *Detective* #652-653 (Oct.-Nov. 1992).

Little noticed at the time, one 1992 mini-series would emerge as crucial to Batman continuity in 1993. The four-part *Batman: Sword of Azrael* (Oct. 1992 to Jan. 1993) introduced Jean-Paul Valley, an assassin of the mysterious Order of St. Dumas. Written by Denny O'Neil and illustrated by Joe Quesada and Kevin Nowlan, the mini-series ends with Valley training with Bruce Wayne—important foreshadowing for Valley's future in Batman continuity.

Bwaa-Ha-Ha No More

As Batman received a new, darker comic book, DC Comics' most prominent team titles also took a turn for the more serious. Since commandeering the **Justice League** in 1987, writers **Keith Giffen** and **J.M. DeMatteis** had crafted action/adventure stories where hilarity ensued. Plots were outrageously over-the-top, and the Justice Leaguers themselves—almost exclusively supporting characters of the DC universe—often displayed downright goofy behavior: Martian Manhunter became addicted to Oreo cookies, Blue Beetle and Booster Gold concocted get-rich-quick schemes, and Green Lantern Guy Gardner managed to rub everyone in the worst way possible. In short order, *Justice League* had morphed into *Justice League International* (and eventually into *Justice League America*) and then spun out into new titles like *Justice League Europe* and the 80-page *Justice League Quarterly*. Giffen and DeMatteis were responsible for all of it, and as a result, by the early 1990s the two creators were burned out. As Giffen later explained, "It reached a point wherein I knew that there were so many more Justice League stories to be told, but there were no more I wanted to tell" (Johnson 14). Giffen and DeMatteis jointly decided to step away. A sixteen-issue story arc titled "Breakdowns" that crossed over between *Justice League America* (#53-60, Aug. 1991 - March 1992) and *Justice League Europe* (#29-36, Aug. 1991 - March 1992) allowed the two writers to clear the deck for the creative team that would follow them. Over the course of "Breakdowns," an assassination attempt puts Justice League benefactor Max Lord into a coma, prompting the United Nations to disband both Leagues. After an all-out fight in Manhattan between the extraterrestrial bounty hunter Lobo and the destructive behemoth known as Despero, the former League members travel to the Pacific island of Kooey Kooey Kooey to rescue Lord whose body has been psychically possessed by a villain named Dreamslayer. Fully recovered after Dreamslayer's defeat, Max Lord endeavors to restore the Justice League... only to have the superheroes walk away from him, one after the other. With that, an era had ended.

The Giffen/DeMatteis Justice League was no more.

Max Lord wasn't finished, however. He reappeared just one month later in *Justice League Spectacular* #1, written by Dan Jurgens and Gerard Jones and drawn by Jurgens, Ron Randall, Rick Burchett and Randy Elliott. In the 38-page one-shot (published with two different covers), Lord has secretly funded the Royal Flush Gang to take a Florida amusement park hostage. As Lord had hoped, over a dozen super-

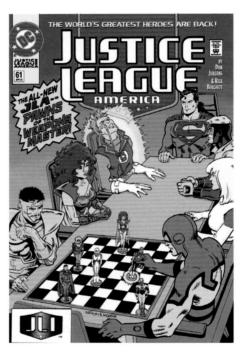

After the "Breakdowns" story arc, the Justice League titles received new creative teams. TM and © DC Comics.

heroes—including iconic DC Comics characters who hadn't been Justice League members for several years like Batman, Superman, Green Lantern Hal Jordan and Aquaman—converge to defeat the Gang. Afterwards, they agree to reinstate the Justice League as two distinct groups.

Written and drawn by Dan Jurgens, *Justice League America* casts Superman as the leader of a team that confronts a series of villains who first appeared in JLA stories from the 1960s and 1970s, specifically the Weapons Master and Starbreaker. (The cover to *JLA* #61 (April 1992) is an homage to 1960's original *JLA* #1.) Along with Blue Beetle, Booster Gold, Guy Gardner, and Fire and Ice, the team also includes new members Maxima and Bloodwynd (who has a mysterious backstory that is teased over several issues). *Justice League Europe*, on the other hand, as written by Gerard Jones and drawn by Ron Randall, features Batman, Aquaman, Flash, Power Girl, Elongated Man, Doctor Light and Crimson Fox. Both series take a decidedly more conventional approach than the irreverent one incorporated by Giffen and DeMatteis and by the end of 1992, sales on *Justice League America* climbed to their highest levels in years, due in part to a special Superman funeral issue (*JLA* #70, Jan. 1993). After that, though, sales dropped back to their previous levels.

Meanwhile, former *Justice League* artist **Kevin Maguire** latched onto a new series in 1992, though one with an unusual gimmick. Written by Marv Wolfman, **Team Titans** bore no relation to Rob Liefeld's abortive 1991 proposal of the same name (other than the fact that both were Titans spinoffs). Instead, *Team Titans* starred five futuristic characters who were featured in 1991's *New Titans Annual* #7, part of DC's "Armageddon 2001" crossover event: Killowat, Mirage, Nightrider, Redwing and Terra, a doppelgänger of the original Terra who infamously betrayed the Teen Titans in 1984.

Team Titans #1 arrived in stores in late July (Sept. 1992 cover date). Rather than release one version—or even one version with multiple covers—DC published *five* unique editions of the first issue. Each edition contained a different 18-page lead story that

> YOU ARE *WRONG*, LOUIS SNIPE. THERE *IS* A HEREAFTER. THERE *IS* JUSTICE.

> AND *YOU* ARE FACING *BOTH*.

John Ostrander and Tom Mandrake collaborated on a new volume of The Spectre. *TM and © DC Comics.*

presented the origin of one of the title's lead characters (one edition presented Mirage's origin, another starred Nightrider, another focused on Terra, and so on). Following each origin story was the same 22-page story that featured the entire team. That meant that fans who wanted to read all the origin stories of the new team had to buy all five editions of the first issue – each with a cover price of $1.75.

DC's editorial team wanted *Team Titans* to mirror Rob Liefeld's approach to comics: high-energy stories that emphasized dynamic action over characterization and story complexity. Marv Wolfman and Kevin Maguire, however, wanted the series to be more character-driven. Thus the creators and editors were continually arguing over the direction of the series.

As Phil Jimenez (who drew one of the first issue origin stories before assuming art chores on the series with issue #7) recalled, "From literally the first issue, it was a struggle editorially to the point that the book just fell apart on us completely" (Cadigan 214). As a result, the comic survived only two years before being cancelled.

The Reborn Spirit of Vengeance

One of DC's lesser known characters made a memorable return with a first issue cover-dated December 1992. Writer—and former theology student—**John Ostrander** joined artist **Tom Mandrake** to deliver a new take on **The Spectre** whose last series was cancelled in 1989. Under Ostrander and Mandrake, the all-powerful supernatural protagonist was both a hard-as-nails 1930s policeman and the embodiment of the avenging wrath of the murdered dead. Mandrake's forceful art emphasized the horror of the Spectre's abilities while Ostrander explored intriguing moral quandaries. In the opening twelve-issue storyline Corrigan befriends a lonely hospital social worker who has AIDS and is being stalked by a serial killer. In another memorable tale that reflected the then-current wars in the former Yugoslavia, the Spectre kills everybody in the fictional country of Vlatava because of its dark history of ethnic cleansing, civil war and retribution. In yet another story, the Spectre threatens to kill everyone in the State of New York to prevent the execution of an innocent man.

Ostrander and Mandrake's re-imagined version of the Spectre has a deep Biblical motif. He is the resurrected Spirit of Vengeance—literally the Wrath of God. Furthermore, Ostrander and Mandrake revealed that the Spectre, humanized as police officer Jim Corrigan, is a fallen angel named Aztar who had participated in Lucifer's rebellion but then repented. Aztar serves his penance as the embodiment of God's anger. He is returned to Earth, not just to punish evil, but also to figure out why evil happens. The critically-acclaimed and brutally intense series lasted 62 issues—all of them written by Ostrander—before its run ended with its February 1998 issue.

I See the Darkness

Following the format of 1991's "Armageddon 2001," DC's major crossover event of 1992 involved two 56-page "specials" that served as bookends for 18 Annuals. Written by Robert Loren Fleming and Keith Giffen and illustrated by Bart Sears, *Eclipso: The Darkness Within* aimed to position Eclipso as one of the DC Universe's most formidable villains. In a reinvention of the character originally created by writer Bob Haney in the 1960s for *House of Secrets*, Eclipso is a banished angel who caused the Great Flood of Noah's Ark, among other legendary disasters. His power level—and arrogance—rivals Darkseid's as then-DC Comics editor Michael Eury attested, "[Eclipso] could probably kick Darkseid's butt. We'll probably never mention this but in our back story we establish that he is on par with Darkseid, and on occasion Darkseid will drop in on Eclipso's castle on the moon, and they play chess together" (Bartilucci 32).

Similar to the Spectre, Eclipso is God's Spirit of Wrath but with the power to take possession of peoples' minds and turn them evil through the "Heart of Darkness," a black diamond first mined on Darkseid's homeworld of Apokolips. Over the course of 18 Annuals, Eclipso amasses an unstoppable army by "eclipsing"

The first issue of DC's Eclipso: the Darkness Within *crossover included an embedded plastic gem. TM and © DC Comics.*

many of the DC Universe's most powerful characters, including Lobo, Green Lantern Hal Jordan, Power Girl, Wonder Woman, the Flash and the Creeper, among others. (The "eclipsed" super-heroes are identified by their two-toned faces.) As shown in *Eclipso: The Darkness Within* #2 (Oct. 1992), Eclipso is stopped thanks to the timely intervention of L.E.G.I.O.N.'s Vril Dox and the noble sacrifice of Will Payton, Starman. The eclipsed super-heroes are then returned to normal. An *Eclipso* ongoing series—by the same creative team of Fleming, Giffen and Sears—launched one month after the conclusion of the crossover event.

Arguably, what made *Eclipso: The Darkness Within* most memorable wasn't its sprawling story or its featured villain or even the death of

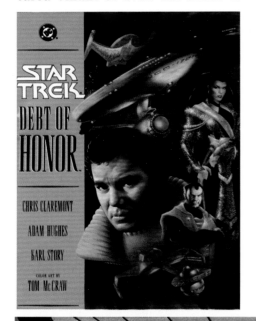

Starman (an unremarkable super-hero whose career began a mere four years earlier in 1988). Instead, for many fans the most memorable—and notorious—aspect of the event was the gimmick DC used for *The Darkness Within* #1. Bart Sears's cover depicts a close-up of Eclipso holding a jewel over his right eye. For novelty sake, copies of the issue that were distributed to Direct Market stores had a plastic purple gem attached to their cover. This became problematic for both collectors and retailers for a couple of reasons. First, the gem became easily detached, and second, if it didn't detach, any comic book placed adjacent to *The Darkness Within* #1 became damaged because the gem would poke through plastic sleeves and backing boards. In either case, fans were forced to purchase a copy at a newsstand dealer—where copies didn't have a gem on their cover—if they wanted to keep their collection in mint condition.

Paying Debts

While focusing its efforts on its core super-heroes, DC didn't lose sight of its popular licensed properties. In 1992 DC continued publishing two ongoing **Star Trek** comic books, one based on the original series (written by Howard Weinstein and principally drawn by Gordon Purcell) and the other based on *The Next Generation* (written by Michael Jan Friedman with art by Peter Krause, Carlos Garzon and Ken Penders). DC's other notable Star Trek publication for 1992 was **Debt of**

Honor, a 96-page hardcover graphic novel written by Chris Claremont and drawn by budding superstar **Adam Hughes**.

Retailing for $24.95 (a softcover version released later in the year cost $14.95), *Debt of Honor* was the first true *Star Trek* graphic novel. It depicts a major threat that has been building in the galaxy throughout James T. Kirk's entire career, from his start as an ensign, to his days as an admiral, and finally to his time commanding the Enterprise after the events of *Star Trek VI*. Captain Kirk and the crew of the Enterprise battle a fleet of evil invaders bent on destroying wide swaths of the space quadrant. Claremont emphasizes characterization in his story, adding a creative relationship with a smart female Romulan captain to the mix and making an effort to include familiar faces as supporting characters. Artists Adam Hughes and inker Karl Story went to great lengths to make sure that they accurately captured likenesses and costumes appropriate for the story, and their space scenes were highly acclaimed by reviewers.

Witness to the X-cution

Claremont's former employers, **Marvel Comics**, adjusted to life without its most popular artists. That included mainstream media reports that advanced the notion that Marvel had taken a painful body blow from the defections. A February 17, 1992 article in *Barron's* financial magazine was emblematic. Guest columnist Douglas Kass, a Wall Street analyst, testified that "almost every [comic book] dealer I've talk to has observed that Marvel is becoming 'old hat' and lacks innovation and creativity." The article reported that Marvel "pushed through another price hike in January and increasingly resorts to gimmickry to break down consumer resistance." Kass had serious qualms about the viability of those gimmicks: "I saw boxes upon boxes filled with unsold copies of the highly promoted premiere issues of *X-Men* and *X-Force*—titles that were introduced nearly six months ago" (Kass 64). The day after the *Barron's* article was published, Marvel's stock price dropped $11.37 per share to close at $54.62 (still more than 300% higher than its IPO just eight months

Chris Claremont and Adam Hughes produced **Star Trek: Debt of Honor** *for DC Comics.* TM and © DC Comics.

million purchase of sports card manufacturer Fleer whose sales contributed strongly to Marvel's bottom line. The nearly $240 million of debt absorbed by Marvel in the purchase would have long-lasting ramifications on the company's ability to remain profitable.

Sales growth assurances aside, Marvel's editors were in a panic to find replacement artists on the books that had been abandoned by the Image defectors. Taking over the art chores on *X-Force* with issue #10 (May 1992), Mark Pacella and Dan Panosian mimicked Rob Liefeld's style, making the transition easier for readers and allowing Marvel to keep a similar look for the series. *X-Force*'s writer, Fabian Nicieza, would soon become one of the most ubiquitous writers on Marvel's mutant comics, as he also took over *X-Men* (with art by Art Thibert and Panosian). The other popular mutant scribe, Scott Lobdell, remained on *Uncanny X-Men* (drawn by Tom Raney

and later Brandon Peterson). For *Wolverine*, which had been pencilled by Marc Silvestri since 1990, Larry Hama continued as writer with artist Mark Texeira now at his side. When Larry Stroman left his gig on *X-Factor*, art responsibilities got passed on to Jae Lee. Replacing Jim Valentino on *Guardians of the Galaxy* were writer Michael Gallagher and artists Kevin West and Steve Montano.

And then there was the adjectiveless *Spider-Man* series which no longer had a set creative team after Erik Larsen's departure with issue #24 (July 1992). For nearly the next two years, *Spider-Man* was variously handled by writers Howard Mackie, Terry Kavanagh, Tom DeFalco, Don McGregor, Ann Nocenti, Steven Grant, David Michelinie and J.M. DeMatteis and artists Larry Alexander, Chris Marrinan, Mark Bagley, Marshall Rogers, Bob McLeod, Tom Lyle, Klaus Janson and Jae Lee. The ever-shifting creative team approach was Marvel's reaction to the desertion of the Image creators. Artist Greg Capullo, who replaced Mark Pacella as the artist on *X-Force* with issue #15 (Oct. 1992), recalled how the formation of Image Comics compelled Marvel to stop shining a spotlight on its creators:

> I think the thing that was bugging me—[Marvel] stopped

previously). Other news outlets took notice. CNN TV's *Moneyline* stated that Marvel's "brain drain" was luring readers away from the characters with whom they had invested their money and attention.

Marvel's response, as reported by CNN, was that "creative people are secondary to the comic book characters." Internally, Marvel's executives were confident the company wouldn't miss a beat without the likes of Lee, Liefeld, McFarlane and the others. Indeed, sales on the best-known Marvel books actually went up in 1992. For instance, the average monthly paid circulation for *Amazing Spider-Man* rose from 340,977 in 1991 to 544,900 in 1992. It climbed even further to 592,442 in 1993, a full year after the old creative team had left the title. Overall, Marvel's 1992 revenue nearly doubled 1991's $115 million, and new series that debuted with sales of 500,000 copies were considered disappointments (Howe 341). However, Marvel's total 1992 earnings were inflated by the company's $265

"X-cutioner's Song" was a massive crossover that attempted to keep fan attention on the mutant titles after Jim Lee's departure. Each issue was polybag sealed with a collectible trading card. TM and © Marvel Characters, Inc.

promoting the talent that was on the book. And, you know, understandably. They had just been stung. They promoted all these guys and pushed them to the forefront and made them superstars, and then the superstars left. Me being a loyal player... it bugged me that they weren't doing anything on the artists' behalf that way. (Voger 80)

Continuing its reliance on crossover events to drive sales, Marvel released two major ones in 1992. **"X-Cutioner's Song"** ran throughout all four **X-Men** team books (*Uncanny X-Men, X-Men, X-Factor* and *X-Force*) as a 12-issue story arc. For added collectible value, each issue came sealed in a polybag with a different X-Men trading card.

"X-Cutioner's Song" begins in *Uncanny X-Men* #294 (Nov.

1992) where Professor Xavier speaks at the One World Harmony concert in New York's Central Park, an event intended to promote social diversity. As he delivers an eloquent speech about how humans and mutants can peacefully co-exist, Xavier is shot with a bullet that infects him with the lethal techno-organic virus. Shockingly, the shooter appears to be X-Force's leader, Cable. Simultaneous to that event, X-Men nemesis Apocalypse kidnaps Jean Grey and Cyclops in order to steal their DNA. It is soon revealed that Apocalypse is really a disguised Mr. Sinister who in turn informs the X-Men that the person responsible for shooting Xavier isn't Cable but his doppelgänger, the villainous Stryfe. The X-Men then team up with the real Apocalypse who purges the Professor's body of the techno-organic virus in time to save him. Elsewhere, Stryfe tortures Cyclops and Jean Grey for ruining his life, an accusation which baffles the heroes since they had never before met the man. Cyclops and Jean finally escape as the storyline's grand finale takes place on the Moon, where Stryfe has built a giant time portal. The climactic battle has Cyclops activating the portal (on Cable's orders), causing a vortex that engulfs Cable and Stryfe both. In the end, Cyclops and Jean suspect that either Stryfe or Cable is their time-displaced son, Nathan Christopher Summers.

The same month that "X-Cutioner's Song" concluded with *X-Force* #18 (Jan. 1993), Marvel released a one-shot titled *Stryfe's Strike File*, which presented all the event's trading cards as if they were Stryfe's secret files on various mutants in the Marvel universe, including ones that hadn't yet been introduced in the comic books. By the end of the one-shot, Xavier has destroyed the files rather than allow them be discovered by his X-Men. Another "X-Cutioner's Song" tie-in, of sorts, was the two issue *Cable: Blood and Metal* (Oct.-Nov. 1992). Written by Fabian Nicieza and drawn by John Romita Jr. and Dan Green, the mini-series fills holes in Cable's history, particularly his opposition to Stryfe in the past, present and future.

"X-Cutioner's Song" had been in the works well before Jim Lee, Rob Liefeld and Whilce Portacio left Marvel Comics. Even after those three creators officially co-founded Image Comics, they all declared their intention to pull double-duty: continue working on their X-Men assignments while also developing their new creator-owned titles. But as the weeks rolled on, no new pages were produced by the trio, and eventually everyone concluded the obvious: the Image creators were fully divorced from Marvel Comics. Fabian Nicieza, for one, accused his former collaborators of deliberately keeping Marvel hanging:

In my opinion, they were waiting as long as they possibly could in order to sabotage the production of ["X-Cutioner's Song"]. The longer they waited under the assumption that they'd still be drawing those issues, the harder it was

"X-cutioner's Song" kicks off with the apparent assassination of Professor X.
TM and © Marvel Characters, Inc.

Despite its flaws, the **X-Men** *animated series became iconic.* TM and © Marvel Characters, Inc.

going to be to get quality artists to draw it, the harder it was going to be to write it. They were hurting, for no reason, the people they'd work with for the last several years, who's helped them get to that level. To this day, I think that was a little bit of hypocrisy and mean-spiritness. (Howe 340)

At a creative retreat, the X-Men creators—writers Fabian Nicieza, Scott Lobdell and Peter David along with editor Bob Harras—decided to proceed with the crossover as planned in order to make sure readers didn't lose sight of the X-Men family of titles as more and more fan attention was being diverted to Image Comics. "X-Cutioner's Song" had two main objectives. First, it would feature the X-Men's greatest enemies: Apocalypse, Mr. Sinister and Stryfe. (The idea of resurrecting Magneto—assumed to be dead at the time—was even entertained with David sarcastically suggesting that Magneto use his powers to pull Wolverine's adamantium skeleton out of his body. Ultimately, the creators opted to save Magneto's resurrection—and David's idea—for a 1993 event (Cronin).) The second objective of "X-Cutioner's Song" was to reveal the true origins of Cable and Stryfe, with one being the son of Scott and Jean Summers and the other being a clone. As "X-Cutioner's Song" drew to a close, however, the creators decided to keep Cable and Styfe's true identities a mystery so that a forthcoming *Cable* ongoing series could finally reveal all the secrets.

Animated X

In 1989 Marvel Productions created a half-hour animated pilot titled "Pryde of the X-Men" as part of a planned syndicated X-Men cartoon series. Unfortunately, Marvel's funding problems halted the production of any more episodes. A couple of years later, in 1991, the new FOX network wanted to make a splash with its "FOX Kids" Saturday morning programming, so FOX executive Margaret Loesch—who previously served as Marvel Productions' President and CEO—greenlit a 13-episode run of **X-Men**, starring Professor Xavier, Cyclops, Jean Grey, Wolverine, Storm, Rogue, Gambit, Beast and Jubilee. The first episode aired on October 31, 1992, and the series garnered such high viewer ratings throughout its first season that a second season was put on the schedule. *X-Men* would end up lasting five seasons, 76 episodes in total, the longest-running animated TV show based on a Marvel Comics property.

The series became a touchstone for many super-hero fans as it often adapted stories directly from the X-Men comic books. For instance, a two-part first season episode adapts Chris Claremont and John Byrne's classic "Days of Future Past" story, while other episodes showcase such fan-favorite characters as Alpha Flight, Cable, Bishop and Longshot. The mutant super-heroes battle Magneto, Apocalypse and the Sentinels, among other iconic X-Men villains.

Behind the scenes, the show was plagued by delays at launch. The series' producers, Saban Entertainment and Marvel, contracted with a company called AKOM (Animation Korea Movie) to create the animation. AKOM, however, did a subpar job. The first episode had hundreds of animation errors, such as a shirtless Magneto, characters not appearing on view screens, and characters who didn't cast shadows. The second episode was equally as bad. Delivered by hand to a FOX executive five days before the show was slated to air, some fifty scenes were missing from the required set. This necessitated an all-night editing session to assemble the second episode. After the third episode aired on November 27, FOX put the show on hiatus in order to get the animation problems fixed once and for all. *X-Men* returned to TV screens in January 1993 with a re-airing of the first episode that had all its errors corrected. AKOM lost the *X-Men* contract, as they had the *Batman: The Animated Series* contract previously (Mangels 34).

The Avengers Storm the Galaxy

Marvel's second major comic book crossover event of 1992, "**Operation Galactic Storm**," spanned issues of *Avengers, Avengers West Coast, Captain America, Iron Man, Quasar, Thor* and *Wonder Man*. This nineteen-chapter epic had the **Avengers** intervening in a galactic war between the alien Kree and Shi'ar Empires and showed the physical and emotional consequences of that intervention. It was a quasi-sequel to the famous Kree/Skrull War story arc of the early 1970s, which saw the Avengers caught in the middle of a conflict between two alien races.

The grand adventure blossomed out of a storyline in the Mark Gruenwald-written *Quasar* series that presented the cosmic hero facing a challenge that is too big for him to handle: the use of a Stargate by warring alien races that threatens to destabilize the Earth's sun. As an active member of the Avengers, Quasar seeks his teammates' help, and that request births this sprawling tale. Over twenty Avengers gather to handle the threat presented by the alien invaders, and the Avengers split into three teams

that most of the events of the war, including the explosion of the bomb, have been manipulated by the Kree Supreme Intelligence, an organic construct composed of the greatest minds in Kree history. In a staggering revelation, the Supreme Intelligence claims he used the bomb against his own race, hoping that its radioactive effects would trigger their evolution, which had been stalled for thousands of years. The Avengers then argue amongst themselves about what they should do next. One faction believes that the Supreme Intelligence should be executed immediately for its genocidal act. A different group, led by Captain America, vehemently oppose that idea and calls for a vote. The majority decide that the Supreme Intelligence should live. Upset by the voting results, Iron Man recruits the other dissenting Avengers—Black Knight, Hercules, Sersi, Thor, Vision and Wonder Man—and the lot of them attack the Intelligence, seemingly killing it. Disillusioned and demoralized by the events in which they participated, the Avengers return to Earth emotionally broken and battered. Unbeknownst to any of them, the Intelligence has survived the attack.

The events of "Operation Galactic Storm" had long-reaching effects on the Avengers, creating a rift that would never be fully healed. In fact, the schisms would eventually lead to the end of the Avengers West Coast, as that team of heroes took a more proactive role to their mission in 1993. It also led to a series of follow-up storylines in *Avengers* and other comics.

Taking its name from "Operation Desert Storm," the U.S. military's term for the 1991 Persian Gulf War, "Operation Galactic Storm" was tightly planned by the title's creative teams. "We got together with everyone on this one, and threw out ideas," *Avengers* group editor Ralph Macchio declared. "Everybody contributed, from writers and pencillers all the way down to letterers and colorists" (Meredith 24). Mark Gruenwald, Bob Harras and Fabian Nicieza outlined the story, then held a creative summit to hash out the details.

The Super-Hero Who Came Out of The Closet

The formation of Image Comics and the death of Superman were the two biggest comic book industry stories of 1992. The Marvel comic book that received the most mainstream media attention the same year wasn't *X-Men* or *Avengers*. Surprisingly, it was one of Marvel's lowest-selling titles, **Alpha Flight**. Written by Scott Lobdell and illustrated by Mark Pacella and Dan Panosian, *Alpha Flight* #106 (March 1992) confirmed a longtime rumor among comics fans: Canadian super-hero Northstar was gay. The revelation comes in the middle of a slugfest where another Canadian super-hero called Major Mapleleaf tries to shame Northstar for not caring about gay people like his son who died of AIDS. In response, Northstar declares, "For while I am not inclined to discuss my sexuality with people for whom it is none of their business – *I am gay!*" After the battle ends, Northstar holds a press conference in which he publicly announces his sexual orientation.

In *Alpha Flight*'s earliest issues, published in the mid-1980s, writer/artist John Byrne had subtly hinted about Northstar's homosexuality as he had always imagined

to fight their perilous battles: one team each for the Kree and the Shi'ar and the final team to deal with the conflict as it affects Earth. As the Avengers engage with the alien races, the team discovers that the Shi'ar have developed an incredible weapon called the Nega-Bomb that is able to devastate an area as large as the entire Kree Empire. One Avengers team is able to convince Shi'ar Queen Lilandra to not use her ultimate weapon, but Skrull agents, who hate the Kree, steal the massive bomb even though the Vision and Wonder Man are inside it. The two Avengers try to defuse the explosive device but the Skrulls are successful at detonating it in the midst of the Kree Empire. Billions of Kree are killed across many light years of space.

Though that was perhaps the most destructive moment ever published by Marvel up to that time, the most fateful moment of the storyline happens next. The Avengers gather on the Kree homeworld of Hala and soon discover the character to be gay. Byrne, though, hadn't been allowed to portray Northstar's sexual orientation, in part because the Comics Code Authority didn't allow it. Code restrictions had eased by the early 1990s, so with his editor's blessing Lobdell "outed" Northstar once and for all, "Everyone working in comics and many fans knew he was gay. But no one in the comic book universe seemed to know it. His homosexuality seemed to be something of a secret to his fellow heroes and the Canadian population as a whole" (Furey).

By 1992, homosexual comic book characters were nothing new. Fantagraphics' *Love and Rockets* had been featuring gay and lesbian characters for a decade, as had DC's mature reader-oriented *Sandman* and *Doom Patrol*. Gay characters could even be found in some of DC's non-mature reader series. Extraño, a super-hero who was a member of the New Guardians, was written in the late 1980s as a gay man, and the former

In Alpha Flight *#106 Northstar announces he's gay, the first Marvel super-hero to do so.* TM and © Marvel Characters, Inc.

villain Pied Piper revealed he was gay in a 1991 issue of *The Flash*. Northstar, however, was different because he became the first *established* Marvel character to out himself as a homosexual. That distinction was significant enough to garner media attention from dozens of outlets,

attention that proved to be mostly positive and praise-worthy. *The New York Times*, for instance, declared, "Mainstream culture will one day make its peace with gay Americans. When that time comes, Northstar's revelation will be seen for what it is: a welcome indicator of social change" ("The Comics Break New Ground").

Marvel's publicity department, though, seemed ill-prepared and "skittish" about the interest *Alpha Flight* #106 received (David 100). Staffers initially offered a terse "no comment" to media interview requests, and there were reports that Marvel's controversy-adverse head Ron Perelman was furious over the comic. Marvel Comics president Terry Stewart called *Alpha Flight*'s editor, Rob Tokar, into his office for an explanation, even though Tokar wasn't the one who signed off on the story. (That honor belonged to Bobbie Chase, who Tokar replaced when editorial assignments got shuffled.) Tokar vociferously defended the issue as the kind of social progressivism that Marvel used to pride itself on. It was a message that apparently hit home, as Stewart allowed Tokar to be interviewed by *U.S. News & World Report* about Northstar's homosexuality (Howe 352-3).

Within a week of its release, *Alpha Flight* #106 sold out its initial print run of 60,000 copies and a second print run of another 60,000 copies also sold out. After all that, Northstar's sexual orientation was never mentioned again in the comics during the 1990s, not even in his 1994 solo mini-series.

Blazing Vengeance

As it had been since its launch in 1990, *Ghost Rider* remained one of Marvel's best-selling titles. The series' writer, **Howard Mackie**, noted that whenever Johnny Blaze, the previous Ghost Rider, guest-starred, sales went up even further, so the decision was made to create a spin-off series that featured both the new version of Ghost Rider, Danny Ketch, and the previous version. In *Ghost Rider/Blaze: Spirits of Vengeance* (first issue cover-dated Aug. 1992), Blaze travels the country with his carnival, fighting evil beings with a mystical motorcycle and a sawed-off shotgun that shoots hellfire. As the series proceeds, readers learn that Blaze is a focal point for magic, attracting

The popular Ghost Rider *spun out a companion series,* Spirits of Vengeance, *in 1992.* TM and © Marvel Characters, Inc.

it from all over the spiritual world. *Spirits of Vengeance* #1 was part of a six-issue crossover event titled "Rise of the Midnight Sons" that involved two *Ghost Rider* issues as well as the debut issue of three new supernaturally dark series: *Morbius: The Living Vampire*, *Nightstalkers* and *Darkhold: Pages from the Book of Sins*. Every "Midnight Sons" issue came polybagged with a fold-out poster.

Besides the three new supernatural titles, Marvel also launched three new series that carried the promotional tag "Big Guns." As the name suggests, the lead characters of these series wielded guns: *Nomad* (written by Fabian Nicieza and drawn by Samuel Clarke Hawbaker and Mark McKenna), *Silver Sable and the Wild Pack* (written by Gregory Wright and drawn by Steven Butler and James Sanders III) and *Punisher: War Zone* (written by Chuck Dixon and drawn by John Romita Jr., and Klaus Janson). As Marvel's third ongoing *Punisher* series, *War Zone* premiered with an embossed, die-cut wraparoun d cover.

The Spider-Man comics were also doing well for Marvel, and to celebrate the web-head's 30th anniversary, Marvel provided special hologram covers for *Spectacular Spider-Man* #189, *Web of Spider-Man* #90, *Amazing Spider-Man* #365 and *Spider-Man* #26. These special comics—which carried a cover price of $2.95 (or $3.50 in the case of *Spider-Man* #26) as opposed to the $1.25 cover price on most other Marvel issues—were created through a laborious design process by John Romita, Sr. David Dann then sculpted a three-dimensional figure which was finally laser-photographed at Holografx.

Epic's Dinosaurs: A Celebration *presented a realistic account of how dinosaurs lived.*
TM and © Steve White.

Crazy Good

Through its **Epic Comics** imprint, Marvel continued to publish unique, diverse material. *Sinking* by writer James Hudnall and artist Rob Ortaleza explores the childhood, adolescence and adult life of Ted Smith, a man suffering from paranoid schizophrenia. The fully painted 80-page story earned an Eisner Award nomination for Best New Graphic Album. Epic also released a sequel to Ted McKeever's critically acclaimed *Metropol*, the allegorical story of a city plagued by demons and angels. Taking place one year after 1991's twelve-issue Epic series, the three-part *Metropol A.D.* has five remaining angels planning to rid the world of demons... until one discovers that she's pregnant. Quite different from McKeever's supernatural allegory, Epic also published four issues of *Dinosaurs: A Celebration*, a realistic account of how dinosaurs lived. The short comic stories, with expository text serving as chapter dividers, detail the facts of dinosaur existence. Intended as a kind of dinosaur encyclopedia, the series also reveals the state of paleontological knowledge in the early 1990s.

One of the surprise hits for Marvel in 1992 was a comics adaptation of the popular Nickelodeon cartoon **The Ren & Stimpy Show**, about a crazed Chihuahua and a dim-witted cat who engage in silly, gross hijinks. Premiering in August 1991, the *Ren & Stimpy Show* quickly became a pop cultural phenomenon, with producer John Kricfalusi's creations merchandised on T-shirts, posters and toys. Marvel acquired the license to the cartoon and provided perhaps the strangest comic enhancement of all time: the first issue came polybagged with a noxious "Air Fouler." If fans ignored Ren's admonition and unsealed the polybag ("You eediot! You opened the bag! Now the comic ees worthless!!"), they found a comic as madcap and bizarre as any being published. Written by Dan Slott and illustrated by Mike Kazaleh (the team had paired a year earlier on *Mighty Mouse* #10, in which the flying rodent meets TV talk show host David Letterman), *Ren & Stimpy* was a consistent seller in Marvel's line of comics for several years, and the first issue was highly sought-after in the secondary market.

Marvel 2099: the Future Is Now

Marvel expanded its super-hero universe into the future with the launch of four new titles that all take place in the year 2099. As an imprint, **"Marvel 2099"** depicts a dystopian world in which America is a police state ruled by mega-corporations. One new 2099 series debuted every month between September and December of 1992, and Marvel was so excited about the project that specially-produced "2099" neon signs and LED clocks were made available to comic shops.

The imprint got kicked off with **Spider-Man 2099**, previewed in the celebratory *Amazing Spider-Man #365* (Aug. 1992) before the first issue was launched a few months later. Written by Peter David and drawn by Rick Leonardi and Al Williamson, *Spider-Man 2099* stars Miguel O'Hara, a brilliant genetic scientist who resigns from Alchemax, a major genetics company, after a human test subject dies during an experiment. Rather than accept his resignation, Tyler Stone, Alchemax's Vice President, poisons Miguel with a powerful drug called Rapture. Miguel tries to cure

The Marvel 2099 line debuted with **Spider-Man 2099** and a new webslinger, Miguel O'Hara.
TM and © Marvel Characters, Inc.

himself via a genetic re-sequencing process that he had been developing. Little does Miguel know that his procedure has been sabotaged, resulting in an explosion. Managing to survive, Miguel discovers his DNA has been radically altered. He now possesses the proportional agility, speed and strength of a spider, along with fangs and spiked fingers. To disguise himself, Miguel dons a red and blue costume he once wore for a Mexican festival, but people begin to recognize him as a legend from generations past, Spider-Man. Unlike Peter Parker, Miguel shoots webs directly from his forearms, and the venom from his fangs causes temporary paralysis.

One month after the debut of *Spider-Man 2099*, **Ravage 2099** #1 offered a rare treat: it was one of the last comic books scripted by **Stan Lee**. Accompanied by artists Paul Ryan and Keith Williams, Stan Lee wrote the first eight issues of *Ravage 2099*, delivering a politically aware story about Paul-Phillip Ravage, a company CEO who is framed for murder after he begins questioning Alchemax's methods. In response, Ravage becomes a fugitive vigilante, out to combat political corruption and corporate pollution. **Doom 2099** #1 followed in November (cover date Jan. 1993), with a script by John Francis Moore and art by Pat Broderick. Doctor Doom finds himself transported to a future Latveria where he has been deposed and a mercenary robber baron named Tyger Wylde is in control of his country. Doom thus becomes a freedom fighter, even as he considers whether he's the real Doctor Doom because his face isn't scarred and he's much younger than he should be. The final inaugural "2099" title, **Punisher 2099** (first issue cover-dated Feb. 1993), was written by Pat Mills and Tony Skinner with art by Tom Morgan. The comic tells the story of Jake Gallows, a member of the Public Eye Police Force whose family is gunned down

on orders by a psychotic businessman. After he discovers the original Punisher's war journal—which closes with the directive, "You who find this, I charge you to carry on my work"—Gallows takes on the legacy of the Punisher, meting out vicious justice on the criminals of the future.

Each "2099" book sold extremely well on launch, especially *Spider-Man 2099*, the first issue of which was the best-selling comic book in Direct Market stores for September 1992. *Ravage 2099* and *Punisher 2099* had impressive unveilings as well. Their first issues were the third best-selling books for their respective months. Subsequent months didn't produce significant dropoff in sales for the "2099" titles, either. *Spider-Man 2099*, for instance, remained among the top ten best-selling comic books for several months.

The "2099" line was first conceived in 1990 by Stan Lee, who wanted to build his own corner of the Marvel Universe. Lee called it "The Marvel World of Tomorrow," and he recruited **John Byrne** to be his co-architect. As Byrne related several years later, "[Stan] wanted me to be the 'Jack Kirby' who would help him create that universe" (Braden 34). Upon being assured he would have complete creative freedom, a flattered Byrne readily came on board. Already in the process of formulating his own new comic book series set in the future, Byrne simply amended it for Lee's project. He plotted and drew a 64 page "Marvel World of Tomorrow" one-shot that would set the stage for Lee's new fictional universe (Byrne). But after Byrne submitted his pages for Lee to script, he received back a twelve-page memo from Marvel's editorial department, detailing a multitude of changes that needed to be made, including the insertion of specific references to Marvel continuity. The memo made Byrne realize that, despite Lee's assurances, he didn't have creative autonomy, after all. Ultimately, Marvel's editors would have final say over how the books would turn out. With that, Byrne quit the project, and his pages have never been published.

With Byrne gone, "The Marvel World of Tomorrow" was changed to "Marvel 2093" (when it was presumed that the line would be launched in 1993) before finally becoming "Marvel 2099."

John Byrne's X-Men Next Men

Byrne now had 64 pages of artwork that he didn't know what to do with. Luckily for Byrne, his good friend, writer Roger Stern, had a keen suggestion: submit the work to **Dark Horse Comics**. When Byrne did, the Portland, Oregon publisher eagerly accepted the material and even proved willing to publish any other work that Byrne wanted to pitch. So Byrne also proposed a team book he had been developing for several years. In fact, this team first appeared in prototypical form in 1986's *History of the DC*

Original character designs for John Byrne's Next Men as they first appeared in the History of the DC Universe Portfolio. TM and © John Byrne.

One month after *Dark Horse Presents* #57 was released, the first issue of *Next Men* (a.k.a. *John Byrne's Next Men*) arrived in comic shops in January 1992. Fans and critics alike showered the new series with praise. (Along with his work on Marvel's *Namor* and *She-Hulk*, *Next Men* helped Byrne earn a 1992 Eisner Award nomination for Best Writer/Artist.) What's more, Dark Horse ordered a second print run of *Next Men* #1 when the first printing quickly sold out. While that was an impressive feat, *Next Men* didn't come close to selling as many copies as the popular Image titles did, a fact that Byrne seemed stoic about:

> I had my turn. I was exactly where Todd [McFarlane] and Jim [Lee] and the rest of the Image guys were 10 years ago, when there were no royalties and no creator ownership. When I was No. 1 dog, I didn't make a billion dollars. Todd happened to happen when he did make a billion dollars. (Duin and Richardson 66)

While Byrne was no longer one of the "hottest" creators in the comic book business, undoubtedly, he still had legions of fans devoted to his work. That following would soon aid Byrne as he teamed up with other

Universe Portfolio. Included with portraits of Batman, Superman, Sgt. Rock, Wonder Woman and other DC characters that other artists produced was a John Byrne-drawn plate titled "Freaks" that displayed five completely new characters that were intended to be introduced into DC's super-hero universe. That introduction never happened, however, and over the ensuing years, Byrne completely revamped the characters into an entirely different concept, a group he dubbed **Next Men**. Byrne later confessed that he deliberately chose a name that "sort of sounded like 'X-Men'" in order to lure in readers who enjoyed super-hero comic books. Any similarity between Next Men and X-Men ended with the name, though, as the former was more a science fiction concept than a super-hero one (Cooke 58).

With some dialogue changes, Byrne reconfigured the 64-page story he had produced for Stan Lee into a Next Men prequel. Dark Horse published it in November 1991 as a graphic novel titled *John Byrne's 2112.* By that time, the Next Men had already made their debut two months earlier in *Dark Horse Presents* #54 (Sept. 1991), part of a four issue serial that ended in *DHP* #57 (Dec. 1991).

The Next Men were five teenagers who had been raised since

infancy within a virtual reality world as part of a secret bio-engineering experiment to create the perfect soldier: "Project Next Men." When the teens escape their confinement, they discover they all have super powers: Jack has uncontrollable strength, Danny can run at superhuman speed, Bethany is invulnerable, Jasmine can perform amazing acrobatic feats, and Nathan has mutated eyes that allow him to see through anything. Together, the Next Men have to make their way in a strange, new world that is none too kind to them.

John Byrne's Next Men presented Byrne's take on super-hero teams. TM and © John Byrne.

Roy Thomas and Mike Mignola adapted *Bram Stoker's Dracula* for *Topps Comics*.
TM and © Columbia Pictures Industr

The Revolutionary Situation

One of the saddest events of 1992 involved energetic comic book publisher **Todd Loren**, who was found dead in his San Diego apartment on June 18, 1992, after being stabbed fifteen times in his bed. Loren was 32 years old at the time and was experiencing good success with his two comics lines: **Revolutionary Comics**, which released unauthorized profiles of sports stars and rock and roll musicians, and the pornographic **Carnal Comics**. Loren also sold pornographic videos through ads in gay newspapers. Loren's murder was never solved, although years later, some wondered if the killer might have been Andrew Cunanan, a disturbed young man who went on a killing spree in 1997, taking the lives of at least five men (including clothing designer Gianni Versace) before committing suicide. Like Loren, Cunanan had frequented San Diego's gay social scene in the early 1990s.

After Loren's murder, his parents, Herb and Marilynn Shapiro, assumed the day-to-day operations of their son's company and quickly encountered deep financial problems. There was unexpected competition as new publishers, including Malibu and Personality Comics, entered the music biography field. In addition, a foray into newsstand release in 1992 started with promise but resulted in dramatically decreased profits due to an ill-advised decision to produce more expensive color comics. The problems weren't all outside of Revolutionary's control, however. There were production problems during that time as well. For instance, a page from a Kareem Abdul-Jabbar biography inadvertently was included in a Wilt Chamberlain biography. Perhaps those problems weren't surprising as Loren's parents struggled mightily with the loss of their son. Herb Shapiro reflected, "The first six or seven months after Todd's death were a lot of chaos. It took me a good six months to get refocused so that I could fully concentrate on what was going on here" (Powers 11).

The Shapiros attempted to merge Revolutionary with sports card publisher Sportstime in 1992, but when the merger ultimately didn't happen, Revolutionary began to fall behind in its payments to creators. After several years, the Shapiros finally got the company's finances straightened out, and Revolutionary Comics continued to be published throughout the 1990s.

Rise to the Topps

With so many comic book companies entering into the trading card business, it seemed inevitable that a trading card company would enter into the comic book business, especially considering where the flooded trading card market was headed. Industry wide trading card sales tumbled 20% between 1991 and 1992. The company that best recognized that this downward trend was a serious problem was Topps whose CEO declared, "There has been a sea change out there. This is not just a blip" (Lesly). In a preemptive move to protect its assets, Topps decided to expand outside the sports trading card arena. In March 1992, Topps announced the formation of its own comic book division, **Topps Comics**, to be run by former Marvel Comics editor, **Jim Salicrup**.

From the start, Topps Comics sought to license various movie and television show properties. To that end, Topps' first comic book release was a four-issue adaptation of the Francis Ford

Coppola film *Bram Stoker's Dracula* by writer Roy Thomas, penciller Mike Mignola and inker John Nyberg. With a $2.95 price tag, *Bram Stroker's Dracula* #1 (Oct. 1992) was released one month prior to the movie's opening in theaters and included four Topps collectible cards with each copy of the comic. In a sign of the times, a variant edition of the first issue was made available to retailers who pre-ordered at least 50 copies of *Dracula* #3. The variant had a unique cover printed on heavy stock with a crimson foil-embossed logo.

The Topps Comics line would expand considerably in 1993, with even more Dracula books, like Roy Thomas and Esteban Maroto's three-part *Dracula: Vlad the Impaler*—which purported to present the "true story" of the bloodsucker—and Don McGregor and Thomas Yeates's two issue *Dracula vs. Zorro*—which pitted the ageless vampire against the famous Southern California cavalier. Among other movie and TV show adaptations, Topps would also offer a line of comics

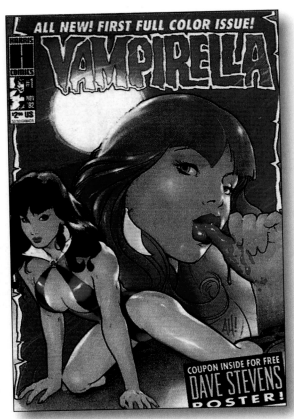

Rising superstar artist Adam Hughes provided vivid covers for Harris Comics' Vampirella. TM and © Dynamite Characters, LLC.

featuring characters created by one of the most revered creators in comic book history.

Vampirella Draws Blood

Harris Publications had its own popular creature of the night, **Vampirella**, and after the success of 1991's four-issue *Vampirella: Morning in America* mini-series, Harris expanded its line of comics in 1992. *Creepy: the Limited Series* was a four-issue anthology that included four 12-page stories per issue. Among the well-known creators who contributed were Peter David, Gene Colan, Carmine Infantino, Jo Duffy, Jim Mooney, Tom Sutton, Jackson Guice and Colleen Doran. *Vampirella Summer Nights* included a tale by writer Steve Englehart and artists J.J. Birch and John Nyberg in which Vampirella meets horror comics hosts Uncle Creepy and Cousin Eerie. That one-shot then led into the five issue *Vampirella* series (first issue cover-dated Nov. 1992), written by Kurt Busiek and illustrated by Louis Small Jr. and Jim Balent, with eye-catching covers by one of the new masters of pretty girl art, Adam Hughes. Balent would become well known himself for his renditions of

beautiful women, and each issue of *Vampirella* included a coupon that could be redeemed for a poster drawn by yet another artist known for his portrayal of female beauty, Dave Stevens. Busiek bowed out halfway through *Vampirella* #2 (Feb. 1993) to be replaced with writer Tom Sniegoski.

Harris also released ***Twister*** #1, a serial killer story by James Hudnall and Bill Koeb. The book was slated to run four issues, complete with trading cards of the serial killers of the comic's universe, but the series was cancelled after one issue due to poor sales. Harris would release five more individual comic issues in 1993, another eleven in 1994 (including James Hudnall's *Harsh Realm*, which would eventually be adapted for the small screen as a FOX television show), and would average one comic per month over the rest of the decade. The company would sporadically announce and promote new ongoing series that ultimately would only have one issue appear, such as the star-spanning science fiction series *Q-Unit*, announced with great fanfare in 1993. That comic appeared in shops with December 1993's first, trading card-enhanced issue, only to never appear again.

Ice Ice Baby

In 1992 **Tundra Publishing**'s independent-minded line was producing a wide range of titles that included super-hero, horror, humor and underground-type comics. Tundra's "creator's edge" focus intended to give writers and artists the same kind of creative freedom that founder **Kevin Eastman** and his partner Kevin Laird enjoyed when they created the Teenage Mutant Ninja Turtles. Tundra editors were more traffic managers than overseers, and creators were put on a lax schedule that would ensure the highest level of quality. That, at least, was Eastman's hope.

Tundra released 29 new comic book titles in 1992, representing

unique approaches to the medium, like Al Columbia's nightmarish one-shot *Doghead* or Bo Hampton's lavish squarebound adaptation of *The Legend of Sleepy Hollow*. Impressively, many Tundra creators—and titles—were nominated for various Eisner Awards. For instance, Mark Martin's *20 Nude Dancers 20*—which reprinted one-page strips originally published in the *Comics Buyer's Guide*—received a nomination for Best Humor Publication. Simon Bisley received a nomination for Best Painter for his contribution to Michael T. Gilbert's *Mr. Monster Attacks*, which revived the popular 1980s pulp hero. Rick Veitch's *Bratpack*—a dark satire of the "kid sidekick" trope—was nominated for Best Finite Series.

Also nominated for Best Finite Series was Tundra's action/adventure comic book ***Madman***, about a disfigured, amnesiac crimefighter named Frank Einstein who arms himself with a yo-yo, a slingshot and a very odd attitude toward life. *Madman*'s creator, **Michael D. Allred**, imbued the series with an extraordinarily unique Pop Art style, and for his efforts, he was nominated for both Best Writer/Artist and Best Penciller/Inker awards.

Mike Allred's quirky **Madman** was one of Tundra Publishing's standout titles. TM and © Michael Allred.

No Tundra publication received more Eisner nominations than *Taboo*, **Steve Bissette**'s trade paperback-sized horror anthology that was co-produced with his own Spiderbaby Graphics. Every issue of *Taboo* presented short, shocking stories, expertly vetted by Bissette to avoid horror clichés. Bissette wanted to disturb his readers and force them to see horror in a different light. Aiding that endeavor was material from some of the finest comic creators of the era; *Taboo* was the home for the serialization of Alan Moore and Eddie Campbell's highly acclaimed Jack The Ripper novel, *From Hell*, as well as Moore and wife Melinda Gebbie's exploration of Victorian era sex and pornography, *Lost Girls*. Also included in each issue was cartoonist Jeff Nicholson's "Through the Habitrails," a surreal and deeply upsetting look at corporate life that imagines workers as depersonalized and dehumanized rodents scurrying through mazes.

Taboo #6 notably started ***Sweeney Todd: the Demon Barber of Fleet Street*** by writer **Neil Gaiman** and illustrator **Michael Zulli**. The pair first worked together on DC Comics' *Sandman* #13 (Feb. 1990), a story that spans centuries as Morpheus grants immortality to a man living in the late 14th century and then pays him a visit every 100 years. Gaiman and Zulli both enjoyed their research for that issue and agreed it would be fun to work together on another historical tale. Since the two men were fascinated by the story of Sweeney Todd, the Victorian-era Penny Dreadful character who murders his barber shop customers and has his neighbour bake them into meat pies, they chose that as the subject of their next collaboration. Inserted into *Taboo* #6 was a sixteen-page *Sweeney Todd* promotional pamphlet, featuring historical information written by Gaiman and preliminary sketches drawn by Zulli. *Taboo* #7, also published in 1992, then provides a 26-page *Sweeney Todd* "prologue," which explains that Gaiman and Zulli were using Sweeney Todd to reflect on legendary towns, urban legends, the nature of stories themselves, and the small things that would be necessary for a demon barber to be successful at using humans for meat.

Gaiman and Zulli's work was assured to be intelligent, sophisticated and beautifully rendered... but unfortunately, the prologue was the last *Sweeney Todd* material to see print. Gaiman and Zulli were prepared to produce additional chapters, but Bissette informed Gaiman that they would have to wait until Bissette was able to clear out the considerable backlog of content that was scheduled to appear in *Taboo*. That never happened as *Taboo* #9 (1995) proved to be the final issue of the anthology. As a result, Gaiman and Zulli never completed their *Sweeney Todd* story.

Tundra's output for 1992 was considerable, but in actuality, it should have been even greater. There were still other comics that should have been released but weren't because the creators hadn't finished them, despite the fact that they got paid good advance money for those projects. Indeed, in some cases, a creative team received a $10,000 advance to have a book ready for print in seven months, only for

Neil Gaiman and Michael Zulli debuted their ill-fated version of Sweeney Todd *for Steve Bissette's* Taboo *anthology.* TM and © Neil Gaiman and Michael Zulli.

Eastman and his team to find out seven months later that the creative team hadn't even started on the book. With the advance money already spent, the creators had to seek other work in order to pay their bills. Compounding matters was the fact that the Tundra books that were published weren't selling enough copies to cover costs, never mind turn a profit. *Madman* #1, for instance, only sold 13,000 copies, which didn't justify the $12,000 advance that Michael Allred was paid (Groth, "Eastman", 84).

Kevin Eastman was earning considerable money through Teenage Mutant Ninja Turtles licenses, which he used to invest in expensive sub-companies for Tundra: a British division ("Tundra U.K."), a pre-press house, a public relations and design company, a recording studio and a movie production company. The plan was to give Tundra enough support that it would eventually become financially self-sustaining. But one by one the sub-companies themselves began hemorrhaging money, and Eastman would learn in 1993 that even his TMNT riches would have its limits.

1993

CHAPTER FOUR

Feeling Vertigo

Thanks in large part to the death of Superman, new consumers—many of whom had no prior interest in comic books—were frequenting comic shops, where they found a dazzling array of product from new publishers like Image and Valiant Comics. Offering new fictional universes and characters different from those that had come before, these new publishers held the promise of becoming the next Marvel or DC. Excitement about that potential caused many collectors to buy extra copies of their titles as investments, which subsequently drove sales on those comics to unprecedented levels for new publishers.

Many in the comic book industry were earning exceptional amounts of money as the sales euphoria of 1992 continued into 1993. Retailers ordered approximately 190 million total comics in February 1993. Only two months later, orders more than doubled to over 400 million units. The most popular comic books sold a million copies per issue, and many mid-range titles sold over 100,000 copies. As Chicago-area retailer Gary Colabuono reported, "In the spring weeks of '93 we were doing $1,300 more [per week] than our summer weekly average" (Reynolds 28). Overall, industry sales jumped from an amazing $500 million in 1992 to an astonishing $800 million in 1993, with much of that growth coming from Valiant and Image. The success of those industry upstarts spurred the formation of even more new comic book companies as well as new imprints from established publishers.

Even Marvel and DC got into the new imprint act, just as their dominance of the marketplace became seriously threatened. According to Diamond Comics Distributors, the country's largest wholesaler of comics, history was made in February 1993 as for the first time since the formation of the Direct Market, none of the top five comics that retailers ordered for the month was published by either Marvel or DC. Four of the five comics came from Image while the other was released by Valiant. Marvel had the sixth, seventh and eighth highest-ordered books, while DC's bestseller finished in the 24th position. Evidently, a revolution was at hand.

At the same time the comics market grew, the trading card market had collapsed. Much to their chagrin, card collectors discovered that their once valuable premium sports cards were now relatively worthless. As a result, both card store owners and card collectors shifted their attention to comics. Comics industry consultant Mel Thompson conservatively estimated that 6,000 of the 12,000 card dealers operating in 1992 had added comics to their product inventory by

1993, and that many of those stores experienced sales gains from doing so (Reynolds 27). The card store owners often saw comics as a mirror image of the other product they sold: something to be marketed as a collectible rather than as a form of entertainment. As more and more comic lines emerged in 1993 and growth seemed endless, plans were born by three companies to create nationwide chains of comic shops. Big Entertainment, Starlog Franchising Corporation and Classics International Entertainment all announced initial stock offerings in September 1993 to fund the purchase of comic shops. As Thompson stated, "The existing direct market is on the close order of a billion dollars a year at retail. My belief is that there's at least a billion dollars of business out there that can and will develop over the next ten years" (Powers and Groth 9).

Thompson's outlook, however, proved to be wildly over-optimistic. By the end of 1993 comic book sales in America followed those of trading cards and were tumbling downward at a startling rate. The bubble had burst as the bottom dropped out of the comics sales boom. For the month of November 1993, Capital City reported that the market had shrunk to 200 million units sold — half its size from just seven months before. It was a startling turn of events. The jubilation of the spring season turned into outright panic by the end of autumn as many retailers discovered they had over-ordered comics they could not sell. Making the industry downturn all the more painful was the realization that much of it was self-inflicted. And the publisher at the center of it all was Image Comics.

Image Runs Free

Image Comics was the comic book industry's biggest success story of 1992 but Image's upstart creators didn't receive all the profits from the sale of their books. Instead, Malibu Comics printed and arranged distribution of Image's line in exchange for 10% of the net profits. It didn't take long for the Image founders to decide they should manage their affairs entirely on their own. As Erik Larsen put it, "It just seemed to many of us that, well, even at a 90/10 split, what the hell [is Malibu] doing?... It eventually came down to just, 'Enh, let's just do this on our own. We don't need them. It's not that complicated'" (Khoury 29). The Image founders incorporated their line as an independent company, Image Comics Inc. Each partner was asked to put some money into a fund to cover start-up costs. All of the original Image rebels invested their share with the exception of Whilce Portacio who was too preoccupied with the recent death of his sister to continue as an Image partner.

As 1993 began, then, Image was truly independent with a greatly expanded lineup that included titles spearheaded by creators who weren't Image founders. Besides Dale Keown's *Pitt*, Image also published Hilary Barta's *Spawn* parody *Stupid*, Al Gordon and Jerry Ordway's sci-fi adventure *Wildstar: Sky Zero*, Keith Giffen's outrageously violent *Trencher*, Mike Grell's Native American-themed *Shaman's*

In 1993, Image Comics published Sam Kieth's **The Maxx**, *a bizarre series that would later become an MTV animated series.* TM and © Sam Kieth.

Tears, and Todd Johnson and Larry Stroman's *Tribe*, about a group of African-American super-heroes. With sales of around a million copies, *Tribe* #1 (April 1993) was the best-selling comic ever produced solely by African-American creators. Likewise, *Shaman's Tears* #1 (May 1993) proved to be one of Mike Grell's most successful publications, with orders exceeding 500,000 copies (Pinkham 27).

Former *Sandman* artist **Sam Kieth** revamped a character he created for a 1983 issue of Comico's *Primer* anthology in order to produce the most off-beat of Image's "second year" titles: *The Maxx*. As first seen in *Darker Image* #1 (March 1993), and spun out into his own series the same month, Maxx is a purple costumed behemoth caught between two worlds. In the modern world he is a confused homeless man who often seeks the refuge of his social worker, Julie Winters. In the primitive Outback, however, Maxx is the ferocious protector of the Jungle Queen (who bears a striking resemblance to Julie). Kieth's over-the-top artwork combined with William Messner-Loeb's graceful writing creates a bizarre narrative that has Maxx questioning the reality of his experience. *The Maxx* became one of Image's most enduring series, running until the end of the decade.

TIMELINE: 1993

A compilation of the year's notable comic book history events alongside some of the year's most significant popular culture and historical events. (On sale dates are approximations.)

January 3: The first episode of *Star Trek: Deep Space Nine*, starring Avery Brooks as Commander Sisko, airs on syndicated television. The show will last seven seasons with its final episode airing on June 2, 1999. Malibu Comics will publish a *Deep Space Nine* comic book series from 1993 to 1995. A Marvel Comics series then runs from 1996 to 1998.

February 23: The first Milestone Comics title hits the stands with *Hardware* #1, written by Dwayne McDuffie and drawn by Denys Cowan and Jimmy Palmiotti.

February 26: A bomb explodes in the parking garage of New York City's World Trade Center, killing six and injuring over 1000 people. The crime was committed by four Islamic extremists who are eventually captured, convicted in court and sentenced to life in prison.

April 19: The 51-day siege of the Branch Davidian compound near Waco, Texas, ends in an inferno after federal agents try to force their entry. Dozens of people, including the Branch's leader David Koresh, die.

May 20: After 11 seasons, NBC's top-rated *Cheers* television show airs its final episode. An estimated 93 million viewers tune in.

June 11: The cloned dinosaur thriller *Jurassic Park*, directed by Steven Spielberg, opens in movie theaters. It will become the box office's highest-grossing movie of the year, over $357 million.

JANUARY	FEBRUARY	MARCH	APRIL	MAY	JUNE

January 12: DC Comics' Vertigo imprint officially debuts with *Death: The High Cost of Living* #1, written by Neil Gaiman and drawn by Chris Bachalo and Mark Buckingham. Other Vertigo titles include *Animal Man, Doom Patrol, Hellblazer, Sandman, Shade, the Changing Man* and *Swamp Thing*.

February 21: Legendary cartoonist and *Mad* magazine creator Harvey Kurtzman dies at the age of 68.

March 8: Created by Mike Judge, the *Beavis and Butthead* cartoon airs its first episode on MTV. The show will last until 1997 and its protagonists—two heavy metal music-loving teenage slackers—will become part of the cultural zeitgeist of the decade.

March 19: *Teenage Mutant Ninja Turtles III* arrives in movie theaters, eventually earning over $42 million at the box office.

May 25: In *Batman* #497, written by Doug Moench and drawn by Jim Aparo and Dick Giordano, the villainous Bane cripples the Batman by breaking his back over his knee. In Bruce Wayne's stead, Jean-Paul Valley, formerly the assassin known as Azrael, assumes the role of the Batman.

June 30: Dick Giordano retires as DC Comics' Vice President-Editorial Director in order to resume his former career as a freelance artist.

Batman, Superman and Death TM and © DC Comics. The Next Men TM and © John Byrne.

Darker Image #1 also introduced **Rob Liefeld**'s Bloodwulf, an obvious copy of DC Comics' Lobo character, and **Jim Lee**'s Deathblow, a special ops military thriller that led into its own title (first issue cover-dated May 1993). During the year, Lee's **Homage Studios** also released new super-hero titles like *Stormwatch* and *Union*, the latter of which featured the work of long-time Marvel artist Mark Texeira. Still more new super-hero comics came from Liefeld's **Extreme Studios** which launched new series like *Bloodstrike, Brigade, Prophet, Supreme, Team Youngblood* and *Youngblood Strikefile*. The plethora of twentysomethings that Extreme hired to work on these books earned salaries that rivalled those of film studio employees. Consider, for instance, artist **Stephen Platt** who burst onto the comic book scene in 1993 when Marvel assigned him to draw *Marc Spector: Moon Knight*. With a detailed art style that echoed the work of both Todd McFarlane and Jim Lee, Platt immediately gained the appreciation of fans and professionals alike while garnering considerable praise from *Wizard* magazine. Liefeld recruited Platt to Extreme Studios and agreed to pay him $40,000 for every issue's worth of work (pencils, inks and cover) – big money for someone who had recently graduated art school (Johnston).

Liefeld took the spending in stride because his career seemed to be on an unstoppable upswing. By 1993, the 25-year-old was such a player in the entertainment industry that *Entertainment Weekly* named him one of its "29 Most Important People Under 30." That kind of honor inevitably attracts the interest of Hollywood luminaries, like famous film director Steven Spielberg whose Amblin Entertainment optioned Liefeld's *Doom's IV* characters before the first issue even appeared in print. Liefeld was reportedly storyboarding and co-producing the film. Jim Lee and Todd McFarlane were also negotiating with Hollywood producers to place their comics (Barlow).

The Hollywood deals along with the other trappings of stardom proved to be a distraction to many of the Image founders, so much so that they began to neglect their comic book endeavors. In short order, Image became infamous for its failure to stick to a reliable production schedule. In fact, *every single* Image comic with an announced release date between January and March 1993 shipped late, sometimes months late. Case in point: Dale Keown's *Pitt*. That comic's first issue was solicited for a November 1992 release but didn't arrive in stores until January 1993. Readers then had to wait until July before they could buy *Pitt* #2. For the entire year, Capital City reported that Image only shipped 32.8% of all its comics on time, by far the lowest percentage of any of the major publishers (Malibu had second-worst on-time rate at 52.14%) (Markley 16).

With most publishers, such tardiness would have had little effect on retailers. Image, however, published some

August 24: Superman returns from the dead in *Superman* #82 as the "Reign of the Supermen" story arc concludes.

September 13: At the White House, Israeli Prime Minister Yitzhak Rabin and PLO Chairman Yasser Arafat sign a historic accord that grants limited autonomy to Palestine.

October 3: In Mogadishu, Somalia, a U.S. military operation intended to capture warlord Mohammed Farrah Aidid fails, resulting in the deaths of 18 U.S. soldiers and at least 500 Somalis. The shocking footage of two dead American soldiers being dragged naked through the streets of Mogadishu is broadcast on live television.

October 8: At Philadelphia's Comicfest convention, George Pérez moderates a debate between Peter David and Todd McFarlane on whether Image Comics—and its creators—have been treated fairly by the comic book news media.

November 9: The first issue of *Marvels*, written by Kurt Busiek with painted artwork by Alex Ross, arrives in stores. Besides cementing Busiek and Ross as industry superstars, *Marvels* would earn three Eisner Award nominations, winning the Best Limited Series and Best Publication Design categories. (Ross won the Eisner Award for Best Painter.)

November 11: John Stanley—the cartoonist best known for writing *Little Lulu* from 1945 to 1959—dies at the age of 79.

August 30: *The Late Show with David Letterman* premieres on the CBS television network.

November 23: Written by Ron Marz and drawn by Bill Willingham, *Green Lantern* #48 begins the "Emerald Twilight" story arc. Within three issues, Hal Jordan will turn into the villainous Parallax, responsible for the murder of the Green Lantern Corps, and Kyle Rayner will become Earth's new Green Lantern.

JULY	AUGUST	SEPTEMBER	OCTOBER	NOVEMBER	DECEMBER

September 10: *The X-Files*, starring David Duchovny and Gillian Anderson as FBI agents investigating paranormal and extraterrestrial activities, premieres on the FOX television network. Topps Comics will publish an *X-Files* comic book series from 1995 to 1998.

September 12: *Lois and Clark: The New Adventures of Superman*, starring Dean Cain and Teri Hatcher, premieres on the ABC television network. The show will last four seasons.

November 9: Ross Andru—the prolific comic book artist and editor who most famously contributed to *Amazing Spider-Man* and *Wonder Woman* in a career that began in the late 1940s—dies at the age of 66 of a brain aneurysm.

December 14: Hellboy—a hellspawn demon turned paranormal investigator created by Mike Mignola—makes his official debut in Dark Horse Comics' *John Byrne's Next Men* #21.

October 20: Gaylord Du Bois—the writer most famous for his 25-year tenure on *Tarzan* comic books from 1946 to 1971—dies at the age of 94.

---

of the best-selling comics of 1993. That fact made the impact of Image's publication delays far-reaching and devastating. Simply put, retailers found themselves in a vicious cycle: readers asked for the latest Image Comics, and retailers ordered enough copies to meet the high demand, but when the comics didn't ship on time, retailers were in a lurch because they had to wait (sometimes a very long time) for the opportunity to recoup their investment. New York retailer Alan Hanley claimed that at one point he had $500,000 of retail funds tied up in late-shipping Image comics. Consequently short on cash, retailers then couldn't order future products – or, in the worst case scenario, even pay their bills. Hanley explained how dire the situation became for many stores, "Every month, you convince yourself 'well, it's bad this month, but it's got to get better next month.' And next month it kept getting worse. You do that for a few months, realize

you're in a hole, and you cut expenses, which we did, but that doesn't mean you make up for the money you lost during those months" (Reynolds 29).

Retailer woes became even more magnified when readers began to lose interest in the late-shipping books. The copies that had originally been ordered to satisfy demand now sat unsold on store shelves. As Gary Colabuono testified at the time, "The sell-through [rate] since April has been the worst in my 15 years of retailing; the buying patterns have changed fundamentally" (Reynolds 29). Chuck Rozanski, owner of comic stores in Colorado and California, added, "[retailers] had no return privileges for books that were late shipping… I was at a couple of distributor meetings… where there was a near-riot among the retailers because they were so angry because they were stuck with all these late-shipping books that they didn't want

anymore. It killed them. It put them out of business" (Khoury 172).

In response, Diamond, Capital and other Direct Market distributors began to stipulate return privileges to Image on its late-shipping books. In an attempt to get its house in order, Image changed its charter so that no new title could be solicited for sale until at least an issue and a half had been fully completed (Butler 34). Image also cancelled four of its "second year" titles: *Shaman's Tears*, *Stupid*, *Trencher* and *Tribe*. Some commentators referred to the cancellations as "The Image Implosion," and in an interview published in the *Comics Buyer's Guide*, Image founder **Todd McFarlane** justified the cancellations as a business decision to oust creators who didn't deliver what they promised because they were late with their work: "we had people on board, and some of them were good people – [but] something just didn't work out right – and other guys were just taking

As Image Comics expanded, it included such titles as Jim Lee's **Deathblow**, *Keith Giffen's* **Trencher** *and Al Gordon and Jerry Ordway's* **WildStar: Sky Zero**.
Deathblow TM and © WildStorm Publications, an imprint of DC Comics. Trencher TM and © Keith Giffen. Stryke Force TM and © Top Cow Publications, Inc. Wildstar TM and © Al Gordon and Jerry Ordway.
Bloodstrike and Youngblood TM and © Rob Liefeld Inc.

advantage of us. So we said, 'Screw it. We're not going to sit here and make people rich by taking advantage of us'" (Butler 28). In the same interview McFarlane acknowledged the Image founders were being hypocritical for holding other creators to a standard that they couldn't hold themselves to. New rules were being implemented so that Image founders could be fired for chronic lateness or other transgressions. (McFarlane even stated that Whilce Portacio had been removed from Image's board of directors for lack of production.)

McFarlane's acknowledgement, however, didn't stop some commentators from roundly criticizing the Image founders for their actions. Image's most recognized detractor was Marvel Comics writer **Peter David**. In his weekly *CBG* column "But I Digress" David frequently took some of the Image founders to task, appraising their various published statements as arrogant, disrespectful or flat-out nonsensical. For instance, when learning about the cancellation of some of Image's "second year" titles, David accused the founders of treating other creators as poorly as they claimed Marvel treated them. By late September, McFarlane felt he had taken enough bashing. Labeling David's opinions as "uninformed information" and "out-and-out lies," McFarlane publicly challenged him to a one-on-one debate at the upcoming Comicfest convention in Philadelphia. David accepted the challenge.

On Friday, October 8, David and McFarlane entered a packed comic book convention panel room to debate the topic "Image Comics—Have they received fair treatment from the media?" Before the debate could get under way,

though, one of the participants demonstrated he was mainly interested in entertaining the audience. When introduced by moderator George Pérez, Todd McFarlane took off the bathrobe he was wearing to reveal yellow boxing trunks. Surrounded by Dallas Cowboys cheerleaders that he hired for the event, the bare-chested McFarlane then turned on a portable disc player which blasted the theme music to *Rocky*. Peter David wasn't amused. He had been called a liar, and now the person who called him that seemed determined to treat the day's affair as a farce. David, however, was dead set on defending his honor, and he came to the event dialectically loaded for bear. As the two creators addressed such topics as Image's treatment of its freelancers, the responsibilities of an op-ed columnist, and even the definition of "lie," David tore into McFarlane's statements without abandon. Perhaps the most memorable moment of the debate came when David accused McFarlane of paralogia, a state of illogical thinking. David provided the example of a schizophrenic patient who was convinced he was Switzerland when he connected two unrelated premises to arrive at an insane conclusion: "Switzerland loves freedom. I love freedom. I am Switzerland." David then pointed to McFarlane and shouted, "Ladies and gentlemen, Switzerland!" The crowd roared hysterically.

Representatives from *CBG*, *Hero Illustrated* and *Wizard* magazines served as judges for the debate, and in the end, both *CBG* and *Wizard* ruled that Image had been treated fairly by the media. The *Hero Illustrated* judge declared the debate a tie because the matter of media fairness wasn't truly addressed. All in all, then, McFarlane didn't fare too well in the debate, although David later posited that

McFarlane successfully used the debate to recast himself—and Image—in the role of "industry underdog" (David).

McFarlane was hardly an underdog when it came to comic book sales. His *Spawn* sold more copies than any other comic series published in 1993: 1,700,000 copies per issue (Millidge 198). Aiding sales was McFarlane's recruitment of four of the most highly regarded and independent-minded comic creators of the time to serve as guest writers for four consecutive issues. *Spawn* #8 (Feb. 1993), written by Alan Moore, features one of Spawn's victims, the serial killer Billy Kincaid, as he takes a torturous journey through Hell. Popular *Sandman* writer Neil Gaiman then wrote *Spawn* #9 (March 1993), which introduces the angelic hit woman Angela. Originally intended as a one-shot character, Angela would become a bone of contention between Gaiman and McFarlane in the years to come. Dave Sim wrote *Spawn* #10 (May 1993) for a $100,000 fee that he donated to the Comic Book Legal Defense Fund. The issue made a metafictional plea for creators' rights. Beyond that, it also introduced Sim's anthropomorphic aardvark Cerebus to any *Spawn* reader who wasn't familiar with the character. Partly because of the *Spawn* exposure, *Cerebus*, then in the midst of the complex "Mothers & Daughters" storyline, achieved its highest-ever readership. Frank Miller wrote the final guest-scripted *Spawn* issue (#11, June 1993), providing a story that led directly to a *Spawn/Batman* crossover, which was one of 1994's best-selling comics.

Alan Moore came to work for McFarlane in part because another Image founder had

reached out to him. In the spring of 1992, **Jim Valentino** asked artist **Steve Bissette** to approach Moore (with whom Bissette had a longtime working relationship) with the offer to guest write an issue of Valentino's *Shadowhawk*. Though initially turned off by the type of material that Image was releasing, Moore nonetheless applauded the new company's mission: "I thought, I didn't really like these things, but if they're pissing off the major companies, then it must be a good thing. If they're striking a blow for the independence of creators, then it's something I should get behind" (Millidge 195). Moore subsequently declined the invitation to write *Shadowhawk* and instead made a counterproposal. With artists Bissette and **Rick Veitch** designing the characters, Moore created a rip-roaring, lighthearted mini-series that evoked Marvel Comics of the early 1960s. Billed as "a bedazzling brace of barnstorming bargains from the bower of brilliance," *1963* featured transparent analogues to the Marvel Comics super-heroes

*Neil Gaiman created the heavenly hitwoman Angela for a one-issue guest assignment on **Spawn**. TM and © Todd McFarlane Productions, Inc.*

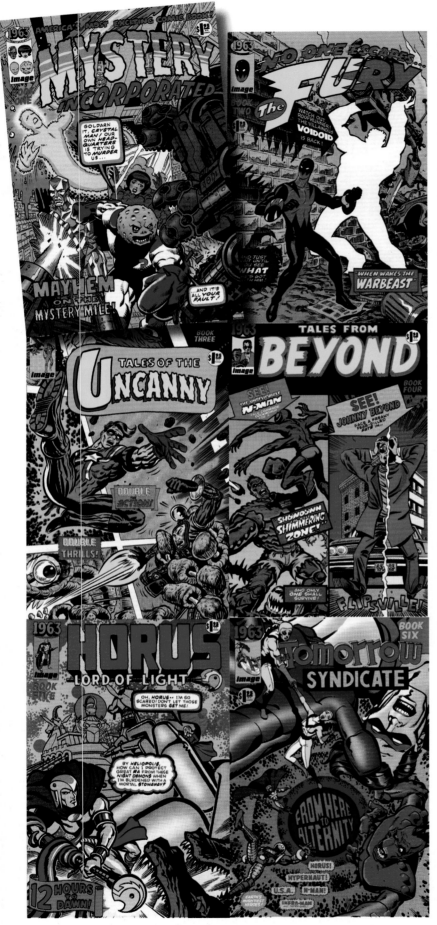

Affable Al" Moore and friends created the 1963 universe, a reaction to the Image style.
1963 delivered modern heroes with early Marvel Comics nostalgia.
TM and © Alan Moore, Steve Bissette and Rick Veitch.

that made their debut thirty years prior. Instead of the Fantastic Four, Spider-Man, Captain America, the Hulk, Thor and the Avengers, *1963* presented Mystery Incorporated, the Fury, U.S.A. (Ultimate Special Agent), N-Man, Horus and the Tomorrow Syndicate in tales that took place in 1963. Complemented by artwork by Veitch, Bissette, John Totleben, Don Simpson, and even *Watchmen* co-creator Dave Gibbons, Alan Moore's writing reads like a Stan Lee pastiche, with alliterative narration, corny in-jokes and charming asides, matched with fake ads, hyperbolic editorials and fan-gushing letters pages. Moore even eschewed his usual highly detailed scripts in favor of the traditional "Marvel method" of comic book production, where a writer first submits a plot breakdown and then provides dialogue only after pages have been drawn.

Through *1963*, Moore, Bissette and Veitch sought to demonstrate how much super-hero stories had changed over the course of thirty years, and not necessarily for the better. While the comic books of yesteryear may have been overly verbose and silly, they at least embodied a fun creativity, unlike the dour, dark, nihilistic narratives that were in vogue in the early 1990s, a comic book trend that Moore himself inadvertently inaugurated through his work of the late 1980s (most notably, *Watchmen*).

Each issue of *1963* sold between 300,000 and 500,000 copies, yielding substantial revenue for all the *1963* creators. For Bissette, it was "more money than I'd earned before or since" (Millidge 197). In fact, the royalties from *1963* helped fund independent, self-published comics such as Don Simpson's *Bizarre Heroes,* Steve Bissette's *Tyrant* and Rick Veitch's *Rare Bit Fiends.* The final issue of *1963* (Book Six, Oct. 1993) was intended to lead into an eighty page "Double Image Giant Annual," in which the throwback *1963* characters confront the modern day Image heroes (i.e. Spawn, WildC.A.T.S., Shadowhawk, Youngblood and Savage Dragon). However, due to contractual disputes that developed between Jim Lee and Rob Liefeld, work on that Annual never moved beyond the plotting stage. Those disputes would foreshadow future problems inside the once-brotherly Image cocoon.

The Deathmate Disappointment

1963 started with promise but ended with frustration. Another high-profile comic of 1993 also seemed to have great potential but resulted in disaster. Throughout the 1992 comic book convention season Image co-founder Jim Lee spoke with **Valiant Comics** Publisher **Steve Massarsky** and Vice President of Marketing **Jon Hartz** about the possibility of the two companies collaborating on a comic book event. Considering how popular both Image and Valiant had become, the idea seemed a surefire hit. Lee eventually brought Rob Liefeld into the discussion, and by the end of 1992, the two Image creators met with Massarsky and Hartz in Kansas City to work out the project details. What

Deathmate *crossed over the red-hot Valiant and Image universes, promising high sales and fan interest.* TM and © respective copyright owners.

followed was the first major comic universe crossover since 1982's *The Uncanny X-Men and The New Teen Titans*: a six-issue mini-series titled **Deathmate** that teamed up Image and Valiant's casts of characters. (In reality, the only Image characters featured in *Deathmate* were the ones owned by Jim Lee, Rob Liefeld and Marc Silvestri since they were the only Image founders who participated in the crossover.)

Each company agreed to supply creative personnel who would jointly create prologue and epilogue issues for the series. The remaining four issues were then evenly divided with Image and Valiant responsible for producing them on their own. These issues were each self-contained and identified by a color (Yellow, Blue, Red, Black) rather than a number. Theoretically, this arrangement would compensate for any production delays as it would allow the issues to be published in whatever order the creative teams finished them.

Fan anticipation ran high as house ads bombastically declared *Deathmate* "the Biggest Crossover Event in the History of Comics!!" Accordingly, the retailers placed big orders, not only of the comic books but also of Upper Deck *Deathmate* trading cards. Jim Lee reassured everyone that Image intended on living up to its end of the bargain, "I don't foresee any delays. Everyone knows these books are high-profile. There are a lot of people waiting on that project. We'll look especially bad if Valiant comes through

on their end and we don't, so there's a lot riding on this" (O'Neill 34). Like the fans, Valiant's executives were also very excited about the project, but when they negotiated the agreement with Image, they failed to consult one of their most important people: Valiant editor-in-chief **Bob Layton**. As Layton recalls, "[*Deathmate*] was jammed down our throats and we did our best to comply, although most Valiant creators thought it was a bad idea" (McLelland). And the Valiant creators turned out to be right. Despite Jim Lee's assurances, the project was immediately plagued with delays from the Image creators, causing Layton a tremendous amount of stress and frustration. In one memorable incident, Layton flew from New York to Southern California, then literally sat on Rob Liefeld's doorstep until Liefeld finished drawing his pages for *Deathmate Prologue*. Layton then inked the pages in an Anaheim hotel room before returning to the east coast. "What a pain in the ass that was!," Layton later complained. "There I was, with my own company to manage, and I was in California, managing someone else's people" (McLelland).

Thanks in no small part to Layton's efforts, *Deathmate Prologue* shipped on time at the end of June (cover date Sept. 1993). The lead story, written by Layton with art by Barry Windsor-Smith and Jim Lee, has Solar, Man of the Atom meeting *WildC.A.T.S.*'s Void in "unreality," a kind of time-space limbo. Instantly smitten with each other, the two cosmically powerful beings embrace. As they become fused together, the

However, slow production of the issues produced by Image handcuffed sales and helped drive comic shops into dire financial straits. TM and © respective copyright owners.

fabric of reality alters, and the Image and Valiant universes merge as one. Valiant then published *Deathmate Yellow* and *Deathmate Blue* in late July and early August, respectively. Produced by such Valiant Comics mainstays as Mike Baron, Bob Hall, Mike Leeke, David Michelinie, John Ostrander and Don Perlin, among others, the two issues present battles and team-ups involving Valiant heroes like Archer & Armstrong, Magnus Robot Fighter, Ninjak, Solar and Shadowman, and Image groups like Brigade, Cyber Force and WildC.A.T.S.

The two issues Image was responsible for—*Deathmate Black* and *Deathmate Red*—were originally solicited for late summer release. *Deathmate Black*—which introduced Gen[13], a teenage super-hero group co-created by Jim Lee, writer Brandon Choi and newcomer artist J. Scott Campbell—wasn't published until October. *Deathmate Red*—written and drawn by Rob Liefeld and predominantly featuring his Youngblood characters—came out in December, four months after its scheduled release date. Perhaps more embarrassing, Image ended up publishing *Deathmate Red after* the release of *Deathmate Epilogue*, the issue that concluded the crossover event. *Deathmate Red* was so late that Image resolicited it to give retailers the opportunity to cut their orders. The earliest *Deathmate* issues had print runs close to 500,000 copies. Upon re-solicitation, *Deathmate Red*'s print run dropped to 180,000

copies, and even that outstripped demand because by the end of the year, few cared anymore about the Image/Valiant crossover. As retailer Cliff Biggers explained, "*Deathmate* was a concept that we all thought was a great idea, until we had five, six, eight months to think about it. The lateness killed any reader interest in the book" (Dean 9). Once again, retailers got stuck with dozens if not hundreds of copies of a book they had no chance of selling.

When all was said and done, *Deathmate* became another bad Image Comics investment that retailers couldn't recoup. Appropriately then, *Deathmate* received Capital City's "Flop of the Year Award." The distributor noted, "If the entire crossover had come out on time, *Deathmate* would have been the success of the year" (Reynolds 33). Many consider *Deathmate* the comic book that singlehandedly put an end to the industry's prosperous times and the biggest reason why so many comic book stores closed its doors for good. In truth, there was plenty of blame to go around.

Bloodshot and the Valiant Comics Bubble

One of the companies at fault was *Deathmate*'s co-publisher, Valiant Comics. In 1992, Valiant's interconnected fictional universe became so popular that average monthly sales for each Valiant title increased from 30,000 copies to nearly 150,000 copies. The upward sales trend didn't stop there. Speculators fueled it even higher as they bought multiple copies of Valiant issues in the expectation of reaping considerable—and immediate—profit. After all, according to *Wizard* magazine's back-issue price guide, the earliest Valiant releases had skyrocketed in value in a relatively short period of time. But as Valiant continued to increase its print runs, Bob Layton grew concerned. He had been in the industry long enough to know that speculator bubbles inevitably pop. The longer Valiant catered to speculators, the more likely Valiant was threatening its own future viability. After Layton explained the situation to Steve Massarsky and Jon Hartz, the three of them agreed that Valiant would never print more than 500,000 copies of any single issue (McLelland).

That agreement was almost immediately broken with the release of *Bloodshot* #1 (Jan. 1993), written by Kevin Van Hook with art by Don Perlin and Bob Wiacek and a chromium cover by Barry Windsor-Smith. The issue reached comic shops the same day as the epochal *Superman* #75. Van Hook remembers, "At Forbidden Planet in [New York City], there were two lines around the block. One for each mega-hit selling book" (McLelland). *Bloodshot* offered an action-packed story starring Valiant's nanite-powered assassin, and the first issue sold 742,000 copies, a number spurred in part by the speculators' belief that the issue was a collector's item that would quickly increase in value. Several months after *Bloodshot* #1 hit the stands, however, *Wizard* reported that many retailers still had hundreds of copies of the $3.50 cover price comic on hand. That meant collectors were going to have to wait before they could sell their copies for a profit.

Meanwhile, Rai of the future returned in *Rai and the Future Force* #9 (May 1993) — assuming the numbering from the previous run of the series. Even though it lacked a

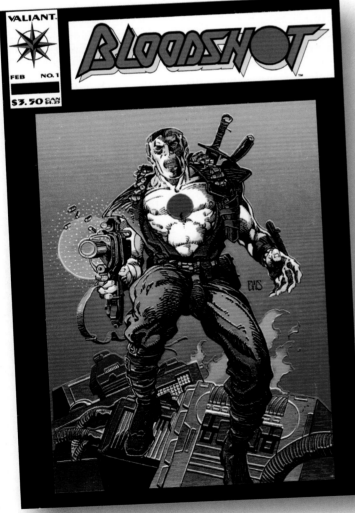

Bloodshot #1 sold 742,000 copies to dealers. Many fewer fans purchased copies.
TM and © Valiant Entertainment LLC.

special enhanced cover, the issue sold 900,000 copies. In a sign of the overheated comics market, 900,000 copies was only good enough to place *Rai* as the fourth best-selling comic of the month. Other prominent Valiant Comics bestsellers of 1993 included *Magnus Robot Fighter* #25 (June 1993) with a metallic silver cover that heralded a new direction for the series; *X-O Manowar* #0 (Aug. 1993), which included a chromium foil cover by Joe Quesada and Jimmy Palmiotti; *Secret Weapons* #1 (Sept. 1993), a book that teamed Bloodshot, Eternal Warrior, Livewire, Shadowman, Solar, Stronghold and X-O Manowar; and *The Second Life of Doctor Mirage* #1 (Nov. 1993), written by Bob Layton with art by Bernard Chang and Ken Branch. All of these issues finished at or near the top of the sales charts for their respective months.

Without a doubt, Valiant's most auspicious comic of 1993—and the book that most represents the speculation frenzy of the times—was **Turok, Dinosaur Hunter**. With a $3.50 cover price and chromium cover, *Turok* #1 (cover date July 1993) seemed specifically made for collectors. Retailers ordered 1,750,000 copies—only good enough for a fourth-place finish in the sales charts that month but still far more copies than reader demand warranted. Many retailers hoped to turn around their cache of copies for a quick profit. Instead, after being burned speculating on books like *Bloodshot* #1, many collectors skipped *Turok* altogether, or only purchased one copy. Consequently, retailers ended up stuck with cases of *Turok* #1, desperate to sell copies at pennies on the dollar. As Capital City President John Davis reported, "I'd be surprised if 200,000 [copies of *Turok* #1] actually sold to customers" (Deppey). Just like that, the speculators abandoned Valiant, causing retailers to decrease their orders of Valiant comics dramatically. As 1993 drew to a close, Valiant's monthly sales average had dropped from 300,000 to 75,000 copies per issue, a downward slide from which the company would never recover (McLelland). Even though Valiant maintained a high level of professional quality, its comics became symbols of a speculator-driven era.

Comic Book Universe Explosion

Image and Valiant's massive success was bound to prod other publishers to create their own new comic book universe. One of the most popular came from Image's old partner, **Malibu Comics**. Flush with cash after Image ended their business relationship, Malibu launched a new comic book imprint that was primarily writer-centric (whereas Image was artist-centric). The new line, which had the working title of "Megaverse," was founded after a 1992 summit meeting in Scottsdale, Arizona. That event, held at a posh resort, was attended by a dozen veteran comics and science fiction authors including Mike W. Barr, Steve Englehart, Steve Gerber, James Hudnall, Gerard Jones and Len Strazewski, as well as Nebula and Hugo Award-winning science fiction writer Larry Niven. At the end of those meetings, the writers had created a shared fictional universe that stressed characterization and storytelling and aimed to provide a fresh, innovative take on super-heroes. As Englehart commented at the time, "We looked at the superhero genre with new eyes, identifying the conventions that had become stale with age" (Grant 83).

Turok, Dinosaur Hunter #1 sold an astonishing 1.75 million copies to retailers — but only an estimated 200,000 copies reached customers. TM and © Random House. Inc.

Some of the finest artists in the comics industry were then tasked with providing interesting, contemporary designs for all the characters.

After learning that Palladium Books had already trademarked "Megaverse," Malibu rebranded its imprint as **Ultraverse**. What made working on an Ultraverse title particularly enticing for its creators was Malibu's Character Interest Agreement. Similar to the contracts that DC Comics offered at the time, Malibu's agreement didn't let a writer or artist own (or even co-own) the characters they created for the Ultraverse. Instead, the contract stipulated the payment of a small percentage of whatever money Malibu earned whenever an Ultraverse character was adapted for other media. Considering Malibu's commitment to use its Hollywood connections to bring its concepts to television and movie screens as well as home video, the Ultraverse creators were very hopeful that they could earn significant supplemental income.

With a distinctive line-wide trade dress and a handful of popular gimmicks such as incentive holofoil covers for retailers, Ultraverse made an impact in the crowded comics market. Between June and November 1993, Malibu unveiled twelve Ultraverse series: *Hardcase* by writer James Hudnall, with character designs by Dave Gibbons and art by James Callahan, stars an actor turned super-hero who returns to crime fighting after the death of his

Malibu Comics launched the Ultraverse in 1993 as a shared universe of twelve titles.
TM and © respective copyright owners.

former teammates; *Prime*, designed by Bret Blevins and drawn by Norm Breyfogle with writing by Len Strazewski, features a 13-year-old boy who is transformed into the most powerful super-hero alive; *The Strangers*, written by Steve Englehart and drawn by Rick Hoberg, with designs by Darick Robertson, tells the story of seven strangers on a San Francisco cable car that is struck by a bolt of mysterious energy which gives them incredible super-powers; *Freex*, designed by Walter Simonson and written by Gerard Jones and drawn by Ben Herrera, sends five teenage victims of an experiment gone wrong on the run; *Mantra*, designed by Adam Hughes with art by Terry Dodson and writing by Mike W. Barr, follows the adventures of a centuries-old warrior reincarnated in the body of a busty heroine; *Prototype*, by writer Len Strazewski and artist David Ammerman, opposes a man with the greatest armor on Earth against his two rivals with strong armor of their own; *The Solution* by James Hudnall, with art by Chris Wozniak and designs by Hong Nguyen, presents a group of super-powered martial artist mercenaries; *Firearm*, written by James Robinson with art by Cully Hamner and designs by Jerry Bingham, has a secret agent on a personal mission to stop all the super-powered "Ultras"; *Nightman* by Englehart and Robertson stars a man who wakes up from a coma and is able to hear evil intentions; *Sludge* by Steve Gerber with art by Aaron Lopresti and designs by Kevin Nowlan shows a gunned down corrupt police

officer given the opportunity to redeem himself after he is soaked in a puddle of experimental chemicals; *Solitaire*, written by Gerard Jones with art by Jeff Johnson, features an extremely rich man whose body is destroyed in a car accident. His evil, corrupt father rebuilds him through nanotechnology. From there the hero plots his revenge.

The final inaugural Ultraverse series, *Exiles*, stars eight Ultras who gained their super-powers after being exposed to a deadly virus. While Malibu led readers to believe the Steve Gerber-written series was an ongoing title like all the other Ultraverse titles, *Exiles* ended after only four issues with the unexpected death of nearly all the book's characters. To keep readers in the dark, Malibu even advance-solicited *Exiles* #5, an issue that Malibu never intended on publishing. Though Malibu took some flak for the deception, the stunt still captured many readers' imaginations and signaled to them that the Ultraverse was a line in which almost anything could happen.

With a million-dollar advertising budget, Malibu bought ads on MTV, on popular radio shows, and on the sides of buses. It also furnished short promo films for key characters, developed video games, and produced trading cards. Like many other publishers, Malibu offered exclusive mail-away comic books. Readers who sent in coupons from four of Malibu's comics and magazines received a free limited edition *Ultraverse* #0. Perhaps Malibu's most innovative idea was the "CD Romix" software that brought *Hardcase*, *Prime* and *Freex* comic books to life on computer screens. The programs included high-resolution graphics, voice acting, music and special effects, impressive features considering Microsoft's groundbreaking Windows 95 operating system wouldn't be available for another two years.

Malibu also published comic books outside its Ultraverse line. Sergio Aragonés created his new character Magnor for Malibu, with a unique 3-D foldout cover for the first issue. The comic was hyped on the shopping television channel QVC. Malibu also picked up the license to the new Star Trek television series *Deep Space Nine*, launching an adaptation with writing by Mike W. Barr and art by Gordon Purcell. *DS9* #1 (Aug. 1993) shipped with four variant covers: a drawn cover, a photo cover, a gold foil cover and a black foil cover.

Besides the "Ultraverse," Malibu launched another new imprint: **Rock-It Comix**. Billed as the only fully authorized line of comics about rock stars, Rock-It was a comic-magazine hybrid: each 48-page issue presented 24 pages of comic art and story with the remaining pages devoted to interviews, photos, fan letters and more. Debuting in November with a three-part profile of Metallica by James Donall and Dave Kendall, Rock-It continued into 1994 with comics featuring Ozzy Osbourne, Lita Ford, Black Sabbath, Pantera and Santana. The Rock-It imprint competed with Marvel Music, Revolutionary Comics and other companies that published biographies of popular rock stars in comic form.

While Malibu premiered the Ultraverse, **Harvey Comics** unveiled its brand new (and completely unrelated) "Ultracomics" line with a three-part mini-series by writer Dwayne McDuffie and artist Ernie Colón featuring the famous Japanese monster-fighting robot **Ultraman**. With painted covers by Ken Steacy, *Ultraman* (first issue cover-dated July 1993) was shipped polybagged with a mutant monster trading card and the comic's logo printed on the bag rather than the comic. This "virgin cover" was a first for Harvey. The Ultracomics imprint was Harvey's attempt to lure in more mature readers while still maintaining its children's comics line, which in 1993 included such recognizable licensed characters as the Muppet Babies, the Flintstones, Underdog and the Pink Panther. Ultraman would return the following year under a different Harvey imprint, "Nemesis," which also included adaptations of Mary Shelley's *Frankenstein* (titled *Frank*) and the television series *Seaquest*. Unfortunately, all of these series were quickly cancelled.

Along with Harvey, **Disney Comics** had been a prominent early 1990s source for children's titles but that came to an end in 1993. Confidently pulling the license from Gladstone in 1990, the publisher had aspired to greater profits by creating comic books in-house. Within a year, sales figures disproved that notion and, following a so-called "Disney Implosion," a scaled-down line stood in its wake. With no budget for hot new creators like Don Rosa and William Van Horn, editors were unable to attract a great enough fan base to satisfy executives. Consequently, Disney returned the duck and mouse license to Gladstone and six ongoing titles premiered in the summer of 1993: *Donald and Mickey*, *Donald Duck*, *Donald Duck Adventures*, *Uncle Scrooge*, *Uncle Scrooge Adventures* and *Walt Disney's Comics and Stories*. The license for more recent film properties landed elsewhere in 1994.

Although Disney comic books transitioned with no disruption in schedule, **Continuity Comics** couldn't say the same about its reliability in 1993. Begun in the 1980s by comics legend **Neal Adams** as an extension of his comics studio, Continuity developed a reputation for presenting slick art, unique characters and an irregular publishing schedule. The line also suffered low sales, with a nadir of 7000 copies sold to comic shops in 1992 (Samsel 56). After hitting that low point, Adams and his team put the line on hiatus while searching for a new backer. One stepped forward with a $500,000 investment, which allowed Continuity to launch its most ambitious project yet. "Deathwatch 2000" was a twenty-part storyline that encompassed its revived series *Armor*, *Megalith*, *CyberRad*

Continuity Comics trumpeted a 1993 team up between Valeria the She-Bat and Spawn, but it was never published.
Spawn TM and © Todd McFarlane Productions, Inc. Valeria the She-Bat TM and © Neal Adams.

and *Ms. Mystic* as well as new titles *Hybrid* and *Earth-4*. Typical for Continuity, all of these comics were released with enhanced covers. Also typical for Continuity, not all of the comics in the event were actually published. The final chapter, *CyberRad* #3, never saw print. To help promote "Deathwatch 2000," Continuity issued a trading card set which included art from the comics along with three original illustrations by Adams of basketball player Shaquille O'Neal, baseball player Ken Griffey Jr., and the first professional female hockey player, goalie Manon Rhéaume, as inserts. When "Deathwatch 2000" sold poorly as the 1993 boom turned to bust, Continuity tied its hopes for a revival to an unlikely source: Todd McFarlane. Adams and McFarlane agreed to publish a crossover between Spawn and Continuity's Valeria the She-Bat. Pages were drawn and included in the preview book *Comics Debut* #1 (June 1993). The project fell through, however, and McFarlane later crossed Spawn over with a much more famous bat as Spawn met Batman in 1994. Continuity published its final comics with a January 1994 cover date.

Dark Horse Comics jumped into the shared universe frenzy with Comics' Greatest World. TM and © Dark Horse Comics, Inc.

Dark Horse Greatness

At the same time that Malibu released its "Ultraverse," **Dark Horse Comics** embarked on the most aggressive expansion in its history by debuting its own super-hero imprint, the immodestly dubbed "**Comics' Greatest World**." Co-created by comic industry veterans Mike Richardson, Randy Stradley, Barbara Kesel, Jerry Prosser and Chris Warner, Comics' Greatest World introduced a variety of new costumed heroes dispersed among four different fictional cities: Arcadia, Golden City, Steel Harbor and The Vortex. CGW's architects considered the cities to have as much storytelling importance as the characters themselves and even went so far as to design the cities first before creating the super-heroes.

Published weekly from mid-June to late September, Comics' Greatest World was a sixteen-issue event. Each issue presented fifteen pages of story for the cover price of one dollar. With Ultraverse and Image titles costing $1.95 per issue, CGW provided readers with a real bargain. In fact, some of the hype for Comics' Greatest World revolved around the fact it offered an affordable interconnected storyline without any of the costly accoutrements (like enhanced covers).

Each month Comics' Greatest World spotlighted one of its fictional cities along with the heroes who inhabited them. The line launched in June 1993 with four Jerry Prosser-written adventures that take place in Arcadia, a corrupt city where organized crime lords are in cahoots with crooked politicians and corporate robber barons: *X* (drawn by Chris Warner and Timothy Bradstreet with a cover by Frank Miller), *Pit Bulls* (by Joe Phillips and John Dell III), *Ghost* (by Adam Hughes and Mark Farmer) and *Monster* (by Derek Thompson and Ande Parks). In July Dark Horse released four Barbara Kesel-written issues set in Golden City, a utopian land of opportunity: *Rebel* (by Tim Hamilton and Gary Martin with a cover by Jerry Ordway), *Mecha* (by Chuck Wojtkiewicz and John Lowe), *Titan* (by R. Brian Apthorp and Jimmy Palmiotti with a cover by Walter Simonson) and *Catalyst: Agents of Change* (by Damon Willis and Rick Magyar with a cover by George Pérez). In August Comics' Greatest World moved on to the run-down rambling hell-hole of Steel Harbor with four issues written by Chris Warner: *Barb Wire* (by Paul Gulacy and Dan Davis),

Comics' Greatest World debuted as weekly 16-page comics for $1 each. TM and © Dark Horse Comics, Inc.

The Machine (by Ted Naifeh with a cover by Mike Mignola), *Wolf Gang* (by Lee Weeks) and *Motorhead* — no relation to the heavy metal band — (by Vince Giarrano). Comics' Greatest World's final month brought readers to the futuristic Cinnabar Flats with writing provided by Randy Stradley: *Division 13* (by Doug Mahnke and Randy Elliott), *Hero Zero* (by Eric Shanower with a cover by Art Adams), *King Tiger* (by Paul Chadwick and Jimmy Palmiotti with a cover by Geof Darrow) and finally *Out of the Vortex* (by Bob McLeod with another cover by Frank Miller). Every issue included a one page "prologue sequence" scripted by Mike Richardson and drawn by Lee Weeks.

Dark Horse Creative Director Randy Stradley was realistic about the line's success at the time of launch, stating "at least it has the weight of sixteen issues tying it together" (Sodaro 43). Once the initial event concluded, Dark Horse gave several CGW concepts their own monthly ongoing series: *Barb Wire*, *Catalyst: Agents of Change*, *Out of the Vortex* and *X*.

Along with the Comics' Greatest World titles, Dark Horse continued publishing its diverse line in 1993, including *Star Wars*, *Aliens* and *Robocop* comics, an adaptation of the sci-fi horror film *Army of Darkness* with painted art by John Bolton, a small manga line, creator-driven comics such as *John Byrne's Next Men* and Frank Miller's *Sin City* and even oddball comics such as *Godzilla vs. Barkley*, which had professional basketball superstar Charles Barkley battling the King of Monsters in a story inspired by a popular series of Nike sneaker television commercials.

JIM SHOOTER PROUDLY ANNOUNCES
THE NEW MAJOR FORCE IN COMICS

DEFIANT™

Jim Shooter has gathered together the greatest universe builders in the business to create a super-heroic universe far beyond the imaginary limits.

DEFIANT

JIM SHOOTER IS MAKING COMICS HISTORY. AGAIN.

Plasm™, the first monthly series from DEFIANT debuts August 8.

The PLASM ZERO ISSUE™ trading card set—the prologue of the DEFIANT Universe—Debuts in June*

*Produced by The River Group under exclusive license from DEFIANT.

Jim Shooter's latest line of comics had a deliberately provocative name.

The Defiant Jim Shooter

Immediately after he was pushed out of Valiant in 1992, **Jim Shooter** worked on a plan that would return him to comics. At first, he attempted to purchase the West Virginia-based Innovation Publishing, best known for its adaptations of Anne Rice novels. When negotiations collapsed, however, Shooter decided to start afresh. Early in 1993, Shooter secured the backing of a collectibles company called The River Group and created a new comic book company with the appropriate name of **Defiant**. At Defiant, Shooter reunited with the core of his team at Valiant, bringing in former collaborators such as David Lapham and Steve Ditko, along with in-house team members such as Janet "JayJay" Jackson and a roster of talent that dated back to his days at Marvel. Shooter's plans were ambitious: he aimed to create a company that would rival Valiant's massive success.

The first release from Shooter's new company never reached the hands of most regular readers. *The Birth of the Defiant Universe* was a very special comic given away to retailers who attended 1993's 6th Annual Capital City Sales Conference. Touted as the most expensively produced comic book of its time, the issue had a translucent paper overlay atop a thick card stock cover while the interior pages were printed on high gloss heavy paper. All 1000 copies were signed and numbered by Shooter. As if to authenticate the issue's high worth, the comic came with an envelope that contained a pair of white gloves and a note that reads, "Defiant! The Gloves Are Off! (But put these on to preserve this incredible collectors' item!)." Inside the comic, characters break the fourth wall to tell readers about Defiant's forthcoming integrated fictional universe — including two series (*Truth and Beauty* and *Mongrel*) that Defiant never published.

Defiant's first official release was equally unconventional. The zero issue of its flagship title wasn't issued as a comic book at all. Instead, *Plasm* #0 came out as a set of collectible trading cards. When placed within a special binder, the cards formed one long comic book story. This unusual idea originated with the moguls of The River Group, who felt readers shouldn't have to wait until Defiant's scheduled August launch date to read its comics. The card set and binder was conceived as a way to build hype and give readers a unique collectible. Unfortunately, it was released when comic book readers were suffering from "universe fatigue." Too many other publishers had already launched their own fictional universes, and getting fans interested in yet another one was a daunting task. Reader apathy, combined with the unusually high price tag for the binder, translated to retailers having trouble selling *Plasm* #0. Definitely not the start Shooter hoped for his latest endeavor.

Only 5,555 of these tins will be produced!

*The first issue of **Warriors of Plasm**, Defiant's kickoff series, was released as a trading card set.*
TM and © EEP, L.P.

The Birth of the Defiant Universe *was a premium giveaway to retailers that included a set of cotton gloves.* TM and © EEP, L.P.

veteran comic book writer Len Wein, *Dark Dominion* explored the role of magic in the Defiant universe. Despite all the problems associated with *Plasm #0*, The River Group pushed Shooter to release a zero issue of *Dark Dominion* as a trading card set with art by Steve Ditko. Unsurprisingly, the new set did no better than its predecessor, and by April 1994, many store owners loudly complained about unsold *Dark Dominion* binders (if they bothered to carry them in the first place). In an effort to calm the waters, Defiant allowed retailers to trade in binders of cards for a special *Dark Dominion* trade paperback. The offer didn't help get Defiant back in the retailers' good graces.

Defiant's next comic, *The Good Guys*, debuted in November. All the characters in the comic were based on real children who entered a *Wizard* magazine contest to have their likenesses included as the main characters. The winners of the contest received a free trip to Disneyland for themselves and their family, as well as a stay at the plush Hyatt Regency Hotel. The prize also included a signing party at the nearby Mile High Comics Mega-Store in Anaheim. All the winners showed up at the event on time, all, that is, except for one. Laura Neale—whose likeness was used for a character named Flex—was in a terrible car accident two weeks before the signing. The car she was riding in was struck by a drunk driver, and her back was broken in the accident. Neale had to undergo ten hours of surgery to reconstruct her destroyed vertebrae. The

Equally as frustrating was that before Defiant's line launched, the company found itself fighting off a lawsuit from Marvel Comics. Marvel UK had a comic book in the planning stages titled *Plasmer*. Because *Plasmer* was similar enough in name to Defiant's *Plasm* (at least as far as Marvel saw it), Marvel claimed Defiant was violating its trademark. Though Shooter changed his comic's title to *Warriors of Plasm*, Marvel still sued Defiant — perhaps as a symbolic slap to its former editor-in-chief as well as an attempt to keep a spirited competitor out of the comics business. Defiant defended its copyright at a cost of more than $300,000 in legal bills, crippling the young company's cash flow. Adding to Defiant's woes, the suit scuttled a potential lucrative toy deal with Mattel.

Defiant's first true comics release was the renamed *Warriors of Plasm* #1 (Aug. 1993), written by Shooter and illustrated by **David Lapham**, whom Shooter referred to as "the best young guy I've seen since Frank Miller" (Sodaro 74). Shooter compared the world of Plasm with Valiant's Unity event (or the New Universe's White Event from the 1980s): a unifying force that grants powers to the real world. *Plasm* takes place in a dimension where all technology is based in biology, and all machines are actually living things. Lorca, a rebel from that universe, escapes to Earth and brings some of that dimension's power with him.

Defiant released its second title, *Dark Dominion*, in October. With a creative team of artist Joe James and

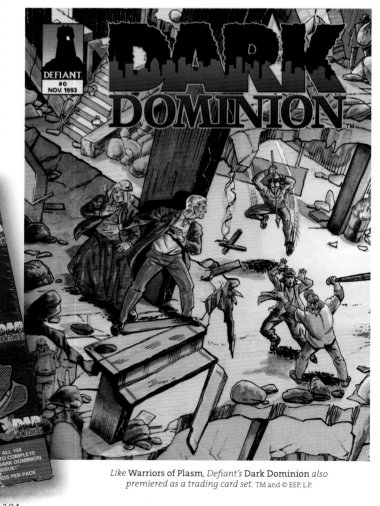

Like Warriors of Plasm, *Defiant's* Dark Dominion *also premiered as a trading card set.* TM and © EEP, L.P.

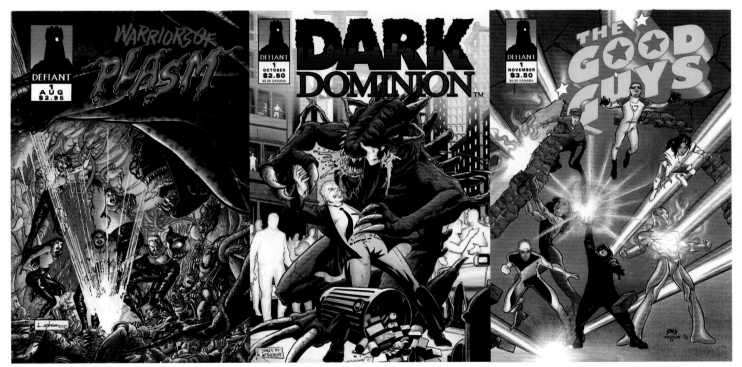

The Defiant Comics universe consisted of few super-heroes battling strange mystic threats. TM and © EEP, L.P.

team at Mile High made arrangements to video conference Neale from her home, but at the last minute, she showed up in person, and signed autographs from her wheelchair (Zuranski 20).

As 1994 would reveal, Shooter's new company wasn't destined to survive very long, but it at least outlasted the other comic company that Shooter tried to purchase. Unable to pull out of the deep financial hole it dug itself into, **Innovation Publishing** closed its doors on December 31, 1993. Former freelance writer **David Campiti** founded Innovation in 1988 with backing from a venture capital firm. That firm then helped Campiti receive funding from a private investor and the Ohio Valley Industrial and Business Development Corporation. All told, Campiti started Innovation with $350,000, but with those funds, he made some bad investments in 1988 and 1989 by publishing comics that didn't sell well, like *The Maze Agency*, *Hero Alliance* and *Power Factor*. After licensing Anne Rice's *The Vampire Lestat* in 1990, Innovation's fortunes seemed to be turning around. By 1991, adaptations of Anne Rice novels and the 1960s sci-fi television show *Lost in Space* sold 50,000 copies per issue. Other licensed titles—like adaptations of the sci-fi television show *Quantum Leap* and such horror movies as *Nightmare on Elm Street*, *Psycho* and *Child's Play*—helped Innovation rank between fourth and sixth in monthly market share throughout most of the year. Despite the fact that many of Innovation's titles sold well, the company remained unprofitable and payments to creators became more and more erratic. The poor choices for titles at launch consumed the company's cash reserves, and the high costs of licensing comics ate into the profit of the newer titles, sometimes cutting margins to the bone and in some cases — as with adaptations of Gene Wolfe's horror novel *Shadow of the Torturer* and Terry Pratchett's *The Light Fantastic* — causing Innovation to lose money on the projects. As editor-in-chief George Broderick noted,

"there were far too many vanity books, books that we were doing just because certain people on the staff liked them." With no indications of an improving cash flow and sales not growing even during 1992's market boom, Innovation went out of business at the end of 1993 (Powers 34-37).

A Dizzying New Perspective

For a variety of reasons, nearly all of the new comic book universes introduced in the early 1990s proved to be short-lived. The one new line that lasted the longest debuted in 1993, courtesy of **DC Comics** and its Eisner-Award winning editor, **Karen Berger**. In fact, DC's new line became so highly regarded and influential that it stands as one of the most important comic book developments of the decade.

Since the late 1980s, Berger had been cultivating a unique sensibility in the DC titles that she edited. With series like *Doom Patrol*, *Sandman* and *Hellblazer*, Berger fostered a more cutting-edge, *avant garde* approach than what was found in DC's mainstream comics. The series she guided weren't the best-selling comics in DC's line, but they received critical acclaim for their relative sophistication and innovation and also cultivated an older, more mature audience, a group that viewed comics more as literary works than as valuable collectibles.

In 1991, as Berger prepared to go on maternity leave, DC Comics' Publisher Paul Levitz and Managing Editor Dick Giordano asked her to develop a publishing plan that would help differentiate her collection of comics from the rest of the titles DC offered. During breaks from caring for her newborn son, Berger drafted a proposal that would create a new DC Comics imprint, one that would offer radical spins on new and existing DC characters to attract readers who were graduating from super-hero comics. As Berger put it, this new imprint would offer "contemporary fiction/pop culture comics that don't look or feel like mainstream

DC's Vertigo imprint officially launched with Death: The High Cost of Living. *TM and © DC Comics.*

popular *Sandman* supporting character Death. A three-issue mini-series, *Death: The High Cost of Living* (written by *Sandman* writer Neil Gaiman and illustrated by *Shade* artist Chris Bachalo) follows the adventures of Death on the one day that she assumes human form. Vertigo's "core" titles consisted of six existing DC series: *Animal Man* (rebranded as a Vertigo title with issue #57), *Doom Patrol* (rebranded with issue #64), *Hellblazer* (rebranded with issue #63), *Sandman* (rebranded with issue #47), *Shade, the Changing Man* (rebranded with issue #33) and *Swamp Thing* (rebranded with issue #129). One of DC's marketing strategies for Vertigo was to instill brand loyalty: to transform the regular readers of one of these core titles into devoted followers of the entire Vertigo line.

In February, Vertigo added the crime comic *Sandman Mystery Theatre*, by Matt Wagner and Guy Davis. That series was a semi-spinoff from *Sandman*, portraying the World War II-era adventures of the Golden Age Sandman, the man who temporarily picked up Morpheus' mantle during the 1930s and 1940s while Dream was trapped in a bottle. *Kid Eternity*—written by Ann Nocenti and drawn by Sean Philips—joined the line as a new Vertigo ongoing in March (May 1993 cover date). Eternity was another Golden Age hero given a post-modern spin, this one a follow-up of sorts to the 1991 Grant Morrison/Duncan Fegredo squarebound mini-series. *Kid Eternity* #1 sold 140,000 copies (a number that barely landed it in the top 100 comics for that month) (Robson). By the end of 1993 the Vertigo line included the ongoing company-owned series *Black Orchid* by Dick Foreman, Jill Thompson and Stan Woch, as well as the creator-owned

limited series *The Extremist* by Ted McKeever and Peter Milligan, *The Last One* by J.M. DeMatteis and Dan Sweetman and *Scarab* by John Smith, Scot Eaton and Mike Barriero. Each of these new titles, as well as one-shot comics like June's *Vertigo Visions: the Geek,* written by *Doom Patrol* writer Rachel Pollack and illustrated by budding indie comics superstar Mike Allred, originated from inside Vertigo itself. Other early Vertigo comics had their roots in an abortive comics venture.

One of Berger's key moves in creating Vertigo was rehiring her former assistant **Art Young** and assigning him to a British office, where he worked with Vertigo's many British creators. Young had left DC in 1991 to develop a competing line of mature comics at Disney. Touchmark Comics, named after Disney's adult-oriented Touchstone Pictures division, would produce titles completely different from Disney's *Mickey Mouse* and *Donald Duck* comics. At the 1991 San Diego Comic Con, Disney released a brochure that included a list of creators who would be working for Touchmark and information about some of the

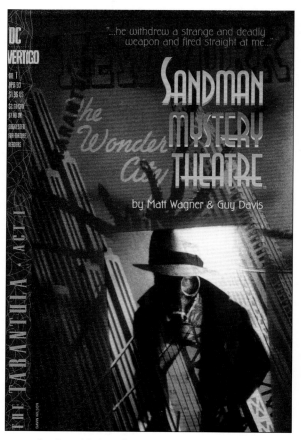

Sandman Mystery Theatre presented noir adventures of the Golden Age Sandman. TM and © DC Comics.

super-hero comics" (Groth 51). Berger's editorial goals were lofty; she wanted to shake up the status quo of the comic book industry. Fitting, then, that the new imprint she proposed for DC was called **Vertigo**.

With every issue carrying a "Suggested For Mature Readers" label, Vertigo stood out as much because of its unique storytelling approaches as by the characters it presented. As Berger described, "What makes a Vertigo book a Vertigo book is a certain sensibility that you will find in the approach to the material... the way the writer and artist make you see the world. It's ...a case of looking at reality in strange ways, or perhaps, seeing the strangeness in reality itself and projecting that strangeness for the reader to see" (Curtin 44).

Vertigo launched the first week of January 1993, with comics cover-dated March 1993. The first comic book to display the Vertigo logo featured the first titles that it was planning to publish. As the brochure described, "Touchmark's goal is to create books that are unique and innovative, and to do it with the top writers and artists in the field." Among the creators listed in the booklet were John Wagner, Jon J. Muth, Garry Leach, J.M. DeMatteis, Steve Yeowell, Dave McKean, George Pratt, Alan Grant, Duncan Fegredo, Sam Kieth, John Bolton, Kent Williams, Jamie Delano, Kelley Jones, Peter Milligan, Simon Bisley, Grant Morrison and Brian Bolland. The brochure also advertised three comics: *Sebastian O* by Grant Morrison and Steve Yeowell, *Mercy* by J.M. DeMatteis and Paul Johnson and *Enigma* by Peter Milligan and Duncan Fegredo. All three of those mini-series and one-shots, which had already been completed, moved to Vertigo after Touchmark failed to launch.

In its inaugural year, the Vertigo line sometimes followed the patterns of its parent company. One of those patterns was a crossover event presented through several Vertigo titles' Annuals. With December 1993 and January 1994 cover-dated titles, the *Children's Crusade* event delivered two bookend issues as well as *Black Orchid Annual #1*, *Animal Man Annual #1*, *Swamp Thing Annual #7*, *Doom Patrol Annual #2* and *Arcana: the Books of Magic Annual #1*. "The Children's Crusade" brought back the two dead schoolboys from *Sandman #25* with writing by Neil Gaiman and novelist Alisa Kwitney and art by Chris Bachalo. The crossover wasn't well received by either readers or the creators, and because of the negative reaction, Berger vowed to avoid any future Vertigo crossovers.

By the end of 1993, Vertigo had firmly established a distinctive audience, one that was more college educated and affluent than the typical comic book reader. Vertigo also managed to attract a significant amount of female readers. As Berger stated, at signings she saw "young guys in suits who just got out of work, and healthy adolescent high school and college people. It was still primarily male, but more women than I saw maybe five or six years previous" (Groth 55). She noted that the Vertigo tag had helped stimulate sales on certain titles by up to thirty percent above what they were before at certain shops, especially in college towns, noting that *Sandman* and *Shade* sold especially well to women. The line survived the comic book industry's 1993 downturn because it emphasized reading over collecting, and also because DC was aggressive about getting Vertigo Comics racked at receptive outlets such as Tower Records.

Kid Eternity was one of the Vertigo series that participated in The Children's Crusade *crossover.* TM and © DC Comics.

After being branded as a Vertigo title, Shade *received a boost in sales.* TM and © DC Comics.

Reaching a Milestone

As impressive and important as Vertigo's debut was, it still didn't match the fanfare attached to a different endeavor that involved DC in 1993: **Milestone Comics**, the first minority-owned comic book company. Milestone was co-founded by four African-Americans: **Derek T. Dingle**, Managing Editor of *Black Enterprise* magazine; **Dwayne McDuffie**, long-time comic book writer who co-created Marvel's much-loved *Damage Control*; **Michael Davis**, seasoned editor and comic book packager; and **Denys Cowan**, veteran artist who had been drawing for Marvel and DC for more than a decade, most notably on *The Question*. (Cowan achieved additional fame by appearing in an advertisement for Dewar's Scotch Whiskey in 1992). All four men felt the all-white casts found in the great majority of super-hero comic books didn't accurately reflect the expanding cultural diversity of the United States. Milestone, therefore, aimed to counteract this bias by producing action-oriented comics that showcased characters of varied cultural backgrounds. As Cowan explained, "We got together to fill what we saw as a lack of minority representation in comics" (Brown 27).

As early as 1991, Cowan and McDuffie contacted Paul Levitz to gauge DC's interest in financing Milestone. Levitz proved sympathetic to and intrigued by the company's goals, and the two sides eventually negotiated an unprecedented deal. Under their contract, Milestone controlled all copyrights, creative output and merchandising for its comics and characters while DC agreed to print, distribute and license Milestone's titles for a share of the profits and an annual fee that would vary between $500,000 and $650,000 (Brown 29). In essence, Milestone's relationship to DC was akin to a small independent film company attached to a larger studio.

Milestone's initial launch of four titles—each with an African-American lead character—began in late February 1993 with *Hardware* #1 (cover-dated April 1993). Written by McDuffie and drawn by Cowan and Jimmy Palmiotti, *Hardware* introduces Curtis Metcalf, a brilliant inventor for a giant corporation that turns out to be a front for organized crime. Furious at this revelation, Metcalf invents a state-of-the-art cybernetic suit, complete with laser cannons, plasma guns and jet packs that he wears in his personal battle with his former mentor and the evil company he created. As the series proceeded, the creative team made a point of portraying Metcalf as a complex man who wrestled with his anger in realistic ways, atones for the mistakes he makes early in his career, and even becomes allies with his original nemesis.

Milestone's second debuting series, *Blood Syndicate*, was perhaps its most controversial comic. Written by Ivan Velez Jr. and drawn by Chris Cross, it is the story of a super-powered, racially-mixed street gang more concerned about protecting their turf than doing

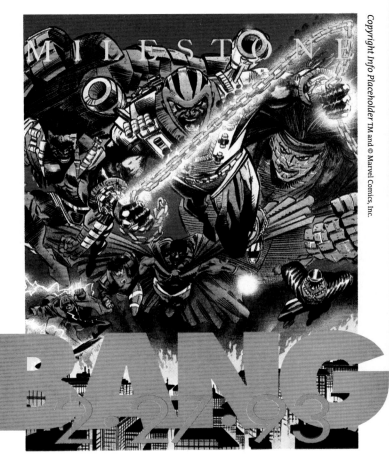

IF YOU'RE NOT THERE, YOU JUST WON'T GET IT.

HARDWARE #1
BLOOD SYNDICATE #1
BEGINNING IN FEBRUARY

good for others. Given the premise, *Blood Syndicate* was a violent comic book, a creative direction purposefully meant to unsettle readers according to Cowan: "A lot of the violence in *Blood Syndicate*, the down-and-dirty violence as well as the mental violence is much scarier because you can relate to it" (Nazzaro 49).

McDuffie and artist M.D. Bright delivered *Icon*, arguably Milestone's most traditional super-hero series. The flagship title of the line featured a character who is in many ways an African-American counterpart to Superman. The superhumanly powerful Augustus Freeman lives a long life as a wealthy and politically conservative man until one night a group of teenagers breaks into his mansion. Thanks to his great powers, Freeman easily chases the teenagers away, but among the perpetrators is Raquel Ervin, who soon joins the older man as his sidekick and takes on the nickname Rocket. Though the series has a traditional feel, *Icon* was also innovative in the dichotomous ideologies of its two lead characters: Freeman is a Booker T. Washington type who believes in success through perseverance while Rocket is more like W.E.B. DuBois, stressing the injustices of the society in which they live. The series doesn't shy away from the political ideas that the characters embody. In one storyline, Rocket gets pregnant and decides to keep her baby, becoming comics' first teen mom.

The Milestone heroes presented a grittier—and more culturally diverse—approach to the super-hero genre. TM and © Milestone Media Inc.

The final initial Milestone series was the lighthearted *Static*. Written by McDuffie and Robert Washington III, with art by John Paul Leon and Steve Mitchell, this comic features geeky fifteen-year-old Virgil Hawkins, who one day gets exposed to radioactive gas. He soon discovers he has electromagnetic powers that allow him to generate force fields, create lightning bolts and even fly. Similar to early

Spider-Man stories, Virgil's adventures are cheerful despite their real-world setting; the hero is always ready with a clever quip at the right moment.

The 300,000 copy print run of *Hardware* #1 nearly sold out during its first week of release, exceeding the expectations of both DC and Milestone's teams. After that, Milestone's comics were well received, but they seldom appeared on Capital City's monthly list of the top fifty best-selling comics. Uniquely, *Icon* #1 and *Blood Syndicate* #2 were rejected by the Comics Code and released without the Code seal due to their inclusion of racial epithets that were appropriate for their setting — bad guys say the word "nigger" in one comic and "spic" in another. As Milestone Associate Editor Matt Wayne noted, the usage was meant to be "a modern and honest reflection of this society and attitudes," adding that the terms were not used in a gratuitous or exploitative way (Ogg 12).

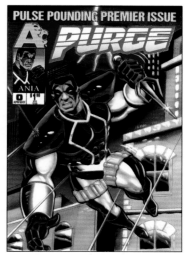

Purge publisher U.P. Comics was part of ANIA, a coalition of black comic book publishers. TM and © U.P. Comics.

Just as Milestone reached the nation's comic shops through its unique deal with DC, another set of African-American comics publishers banded together to present their own racially-mixed comics. ACB Comics, Hype Comics, U. P. Comics, Dark Zulu Lies, Africa Rising and Omega 7 joined forces to create **ANIA - the Association of Black Publishers** to promote their politically charged titles. Among them were *The Original Man*, about an omnipotent black hero; *Purge*, the tale of a man who tries to stamp out racism in his community; *Ebony Warrior*, a Fortune 500 manager by day and avenger at night; *Zwanna Son of Zulu*, an African student who returns from studies in the United States to find his old nation imperiled; and *Inner City Products*, about a group of rappers who clean up New York City through their product placement lyrics.

Though none of these series lasted beyond a handful of issues, ANIA engaged in an ongoing behind-the-scenes argument with the Milestone founders about the correct approach for presenting African-American heroes in comics.

Static and Icon were two of Milestone's most popular series. TM and © Milestone Media Inc.

Superman Returns — But Who Is He?

A month after **Superman** died battling Doomsday, DC's pantheon of super-heroes mourned his loss with the six issue "Funeral for a Friend" storyline that ran through all four Superman series (*Action Comics*, *Adventures of Superman*, *Superman* and *Superman: Man of Steel*) as well as one issue of *Justice League America*. The Man of Steel's funeral occurred in *Superman* #76 (Feb. 1993), after which characters had to accept a world—and readers had to accept a fictional universe—that didn't have a Superman.

The only Superman comics published with March 1993 cover dates were two one-shots: *The Superman Gallery*, a collection of pinups of the Man of Steel by a diverse group of artists including Todd McFarlane, Jack Kirby, Gil Kane, Kurt Schaffenberger and Moebius, and *The Legacy of Superman*, a 68-page anthology spotlighting the new heroes of Metropolis, including the Guardian, Rose and the Thorn, Gangbuster, Sinbad and Waverider. While that comic sold well enough to go through two printings, the more notable distinction is that for the first time in Superman's 55-year publication history, he did not appear as a character in any of DC's comics.

The Cyborg Superman, Superboy and Eradicator were three of the "replacement Supermen" from 1993's "Reign of the Supermen" story arc. TM and © DC Comics.

John Henry Irons, Steel, made his debut in "Reign of the Supermen". TM and © DC Comics.

Superman editor **Mike Carlin** originally had no intention of prolonging the Man of Steel's absence. He wanted to resurrect DC's most iconic character as early as April 1993 with the publication of *Adventures of Superman* #500 (cover date June 1993). However, once Carlin saw the massive reaction to the "Death of Superman" storyline, he changed his mind. His new plan was to tease readers about Superman's return for several months. When the double-sized *Adventures of Superman* #500 finally appeared in stores, it came with an enhanced cover that showed a ghost-like vision of Superman drifting among the clouds. A banner across the top of the cover rhetorically asked, "Back From The Dead?!" The issue's first story—the last Superman story to be written by Jerry Ordway for several years—opens with Pa Kent having an out-of-body experience after suffering a near-fatal heart attack. In that state, he encounters Clark Kent, and father and son have a heartfelt conversation. By the story's end, Lois Lane visits Superman's tomb only to discover an empty coffin. Then come the sightings as four beings claiming to be Superman have appeared. Each looks like a radically-altered Man of Steel, but which one is the real Superman?

The remaining June cover-dated Superman titles, all released on the same day in the last week of April 1993, moved the story of the Death of Superman to its next phase: a crossover story arc titled "**Reign of the Supermen.**" Beneath special cut-out covers, each of the Superman titles featured the adventures of a new contender to the role of Man of Steel.

Adventures of Superman #501 presented an all-new take on Superboy, this one wearing a leather jacket, fashionable sunglasses and a modern haircut. *Action Comics* #687 brought an enigmatic, emotionless survivor of the destruction of Krypton. In *Superman* #78 readers were greeted with a cybernetic version of Superman, while *Superman: the Man of Steel* #22 appropriately starred Steel, a normal human wearing a suit of armor that gave him strength and powers comparable to Superman, along with a matching hammer that he could use as a weapon.

TM and © DC Comics

Ensuing "Reign of the Supermen" chapters reveal that the new Superboy is a clone of Superman who was removed from his molding matrix too soon and thus isn't fully matured. Steel is John Henry Irons, a great scientist who created his powerful suit in part because of his love for Superman. The emotionless Kryptonian was a being designed not only to serve as a Superman stand-in but also to place a near-death Kal-El in the healing baths of a matrix chamber. In effect, this version of Superman resurrects the Last Son of Krypton. The Cyborg Superman proved not so helpful, though. Exposed as a vicious henchman of the evil villain Mongul, the Cyborg Superman destroys Green Lantern's home town of Coast City in *Green Lantern* #46 (Oct. 1993), murdering millions of people in the process.

"Reign of the Supermen" lasted four months, culminating in *Superman* #82 (Oct. 1993) as a now long-haired Superman is reborn wearing an all-black costume. Superman, Green Lantern, Steel, Supergirl and the new Superboy then engage the Cyborg Superman, and after a series of intense twists and turns, they finally defeat him. The immediate threat is ended and Superman is returned to life, but Coast City is devastated in the battle. That fact would serve as the catalyst for DC Comics' most status quo altering storyline of 1994.

As far as 1993 was concerned, however, "Reign of the Supermen" helped DC temporarily reign over the comic book marketplace. For the first time since 1987, DC Comics topped Capital City Distribution's sales charts with a 30.68% market share in April 1993, double its performance from the previous month. (Marvel's share dropped by 17 points in the same time period.) Three-quarters of DC's explosive sales came from its Superman titles. The only problem—and it was a significant one—was that while retailers ordered "Reign of the Supermen" issues in great numbers, the copies mostly remained unbought on the stores' shelves. Readers didn't seem as interested in "Reign of the Supermen" as much as they did in "Death of Superman" or even "Funeral for a Friend." Part of the indifference can be attributed to the hubbub around Image and Valiant Comics as some readers considered Superman to be "last year's news." Others, though, felt duped by the entire event. After all, Superman's death barely lasted nine months. Even fans who knew DC would inevitably bring back its greatest hero felt that was too short a time span. The other reason why retailers got stuck with so many unsold copies has less to do with Superman and more to do with the state of the entire industry: the comic book sales boom was over.

Superman returns in the conclusion to "Reign of the Supermen," but a vicious battle destroys Coast City.
TM and © DC Comics.

111

Lois Loves Clark

Meanwhile, the TV show that indirectly caused Superman's death premiered on the ABC network on September 12, 1993. ***Lois and Clark: the New Adventures of Superman*** starred two relative newcomers: former college football player Dean Cain as Clark Kent and the beautiful Teri Hatcher as Lois Lane. The show reflected the influence of John Byrne's 1980s reboot of Superman by positioning Clark Kent as Superman's dominant personality and showing him as an outstanding, award-winning journalist. What's more, rather than feature the kind of explosive action and adventure that one might expect from a super-hero show, showrunner Joy DeVine focused *Lois and Clark* as a romantic comedy, emphasizing the incongruous relationship between country kid Clark and city slicker Lois. DeVine hoped this approach would prove more appealing to a wider audience. The show also included Lex Luthor, portrayed by actor John Shea as a secretly evil millionaire philanthropist, and during the show's first season, Lex, Clark and Lois form an odd sort of love triangle. Luthor's attempts to woo Lois eventually succeed as she agrees to marry him, but she leaves Lex at the altar when she realizes she truly loves Clark. The *Los Angeles Times* called the premiere episode of *Lois and Clark* "relentlessly witty,"

praising "hunky" Dean Cain, and stating that *"Lois & Clark* is a series that flies" (Rosenberg).

Ratings for *Lois and Clark* were initially somewhat weak, especially since it ran opposite NBC's expensive—and heavily promoted—science fiction show *Seaquest DSV*, which starred veteran film star Roy Scheider as the captain of a futuristic submarine. *Lois and Clark*'s "rom-com" angle brought in some viewers but ABC executives soon decided the show needed more super-heroics. In the second half of the first season, then, more villains appeared, necessitating Cain to wear the Superman costume more often. But ratings didn't budge much. Once the first season ended, ABC fired LeVine and replaced her with Robert Singer, who turned the series into a screwball romantic comedy, with a stronger, better-written romance filled with silly misunderstandings, cute banter and an undercurrent of sweetness. As *Entertainment Weekly* critic Ken Tucker noted in a review of the show's second season, "It's the first Superman spin-off (including the feature films) that carries emotional weight" (Tucker).

Lois & Clark ran for four seasons, frequently teasing viewers with hints of a marriage between the two long-time icons. A 1996 storyline brought the pair to the altar, which was paralleled in the comics that year as well.

Breaking Bat

While 1992 was the year in which Superman was killed, 1993 was the year in which **Batman** was broken – literally. One of the most significant events in Batman history was conceived in late 1991, when editor **Denny O'Neil** led an offsite brainstorming meeting of the Batman creative teams where he proposed a radical idea: Bruce Wayne's retirement as the Caped Crusader. According to *Batman* writer Doug Moench, "Denny's original idea was to show Batman losing his stuff and getting burned out, with the whole process culminating with Bruce Wayne taking a big loss and then retiring" (Meth 29). Feeding off that idea, *Detective Comics* writer Peter Milligan then suggested a different character could become DC's new Dark Knight. O'Neil relished the opportunity to explore what it meant to be Batman, so he and his creators coordinated an epic storyline that would reach an astonishing climax in 1993.

As the drama of Superman's death played out, the Batman comics provided several indications that similarly big changes would soon happen to DC's other iconic hero. First, O'Neil, Joe Quesada and Kevin Nowlan collaborated on the four issue *Batman: Sword of Azrael* mini-series (first issue cover-dated Oct. 1992), which introduced the intense Jean-Paul Valley, a.k.a. Azrael, an armored assassin serving a mysterious cult called the Order of St. Dumas. That globe-spanning mini-series involved Valley and Wayne in an action-adventure yarn that put the two men in an uneasy alliance because of their differing approaches to violence. Azrael's cavalierly violent methods placed him in opposition with the classic DC hero who refused to ever take a life.

O'Neil next asked for a new villain who would prove to be Batman's equal, both physically and intellectually. That was a tall order as far as *Robin* writer **Chuck Dixon** was

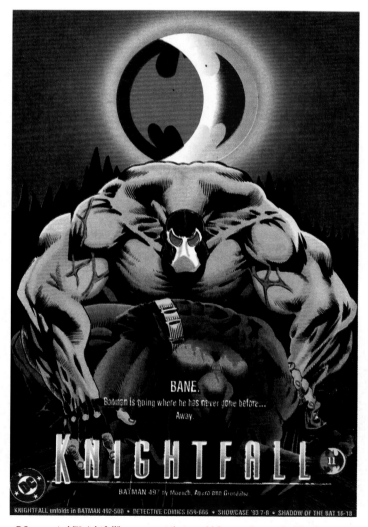

DC promoted "Knightfall" as an event that would forever change the life of Batman.
TM and © DC Comics.

Bane breaks Bruce Wayne's back in **Batman** #497. Art by the legendary Jim Aparo.
TM and © DC Comics.

Batman is really Bruce Wayne. Meanwhile, Robin recruits Azrael to aid them.

Eventually, Batman has to fight his way into Bane's inner circle, established inside Bruce's own home in Wayne Manor. Exhausted, the hero can barely lift his arms against his drug-enhanced nemesis. Finally in *Batman* #497 (July 1993), with Batman at his lowest ebb, the triumphant Bane lifts him over his knee and with a loud KRAKT! breaks Bruce Wayne's back. One of comics' greatest heroes is crippled, and DC implied the injury was permanent. After more than fifty years in the suit, Bruce Wayne might no longer be able to walk, much less fight crime. The comics world was shocked by the events, and protégé Jean-Paul Valley promised vengeance.

Three issues later, after some experimentation with the old costume, Valley assumes the mantle of Batman but with a very different cape and cowl. Jean-Paul Valley's Batman armor, as designed by Joe Quesada, reflected his relentless approach to fighting crime, a suit with incredible firepower built into it. Deadly weapons were literally at Valley's fingertips. It was a radical change that fit a new generation of comics readers. (Unfortunately for DC, the new costume first saw print on the cover of *Wizard* #24 (Aug. 1993), one month before DC meant to premiere it in the pages

concerned. He doubted that they could create anyone who could capture fans' attention and interest. O'Neil appreciated that kind of skepticism and consequently tasked Dixon with creating the most memorable villain possible. The product of Dixon's efforts was a vicious criminal named **Bane**. As detailed in the 55-page one-shot *Batman: Vengeance of Bane* (cover date Jan. 1993), written by Dixon and drawn by Graham Nolan and Eduardo Barreto, Bane was born and raised in a prison in the fictitious Caribbean island of Santa Prisca, eventually becoming one of its most hardened and fearsome inmates. A group of scientists later injected Bane with an experimental steroid called Venom which endowed him with super-human strength and stamina. After escaping the prison, Bane travels to Gotham City in order to confront Batman who he views as the manifestation of his deepest fears. As Dixon described him, Bane is "an evil version of Doc Savage" and a "screwed-up, crack-the-mirror version of Batman" (Meth 30, 32).

Three months after Bane's introduction, the nineteen-issue **"Knightfall"** story arc began in *Batman* #493 (March 1993), continuing not only in that title but also in *Detective Comics* and *Showcase '93*. In order to distract Batman so he can increase his power in Gotham City, Bane blows up Arkham Asylum, freeing dozens of villains from the insane asylum. The Caped Crusader is forced to confront several of his nastiest foes like the Mad Hatter, Scarecrow, the Joker and Poison Ivy. Observing the battles, Bane comes to realize that

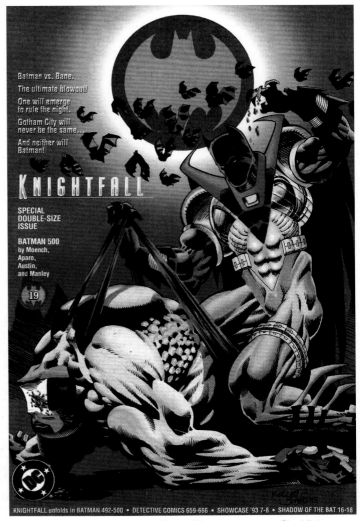

With Bruce Wayne crippled, Azrael stepped in as a new, more militant Batman, complete with cybernetic armor and deadly weapons. TM and © DC Comics.

of Diamond Distributors' *Previews*.) As a trained assassin, Valley was ready and willing to kill criminals in order to win his battles, a true Dark Knight who would do anything to triumph. That set the student apart from his mentor but also set Valley firmly in the 1990s ethos of increasingly violent lead characters.

In the fifty-six page celebratory *Batman* #500 (Oct. 1993), "Knightfall" comes to an end as Valley (soon to be nicknamed "AzBat" by the fans) avenges his predecessor's injury by defeating Bane. The next issue then kicked off "Knightquest" as readers followed the new Batman, not knowing when — or if — Bruce Wayne would ever again don his leather and spandex. They would have to wait until 1994 to learn the answer.

"Knightfall" was a hit as many of its chapters received second (and even third) printings. *Batman* #500 had the honor of being Diamond Distributors' top-selling comic released in August 1993. That issue, along with all the other "Knightfall" *Batman* issues, was drawn by the legendary **Jim Aparo**. According to Chuck Dixon, some of DC's executives wanted to inaugurate a new era in Batman history by having a new artist draw *Batman* #500. Denny O'Neil, however, insisted that the 61-year-old Aparo remain on the title until the start of "Knightquest." O'Neil felt Aparo deserved the royalties that the sales of *Batman* #500 would reap as a reward for remaining loyal to DC Comics even after Stan Lee personally tried to get Aparo to defect to Marvel many times over the previous

two decades. As Dixon put it, "It would have been a crime to hand ALL those #500 royalties to a first-time Batman artist who wouldn't even stay on the title for a year" (Dixon).

DC spun out two new series from "Knightfall." *Robin* #1 (Nov. 1993), written by Dixon and drawn by Tom Grummett and Scott Hanna, finally brought Batman's ward to his own ongoing comic after three separate mini-series earlier in the decade. As it did with *Batman* #500, DC released a standard newsstand version of *Robin* #1 as well as an embossed foil version. *Catwoman* #1, released the same month, did not have an enhanced version but did contain a story written by Jo Duffy and illustrated by Jim Balent and Dick Giordano.

Another notable Batman project of 1993 was the long-awaited *Batman/Grendel* intercompany crossover. Delayed due to legal issues surrounding Comico's change of ownership in the early part of the decade, the two-part square bound mini-series presented Matt Wagner's art deco version of Gotham City where Bruce Wayne faced off against the diabolical Hunter Rose (a.k.a. Grendel). Also published in 1993 was the first Batman Halloween special by Jeph Loeb and Tim Sale. *Batman: Legends of the Dark Knight Special* #1 (Dec. 1993) mixed

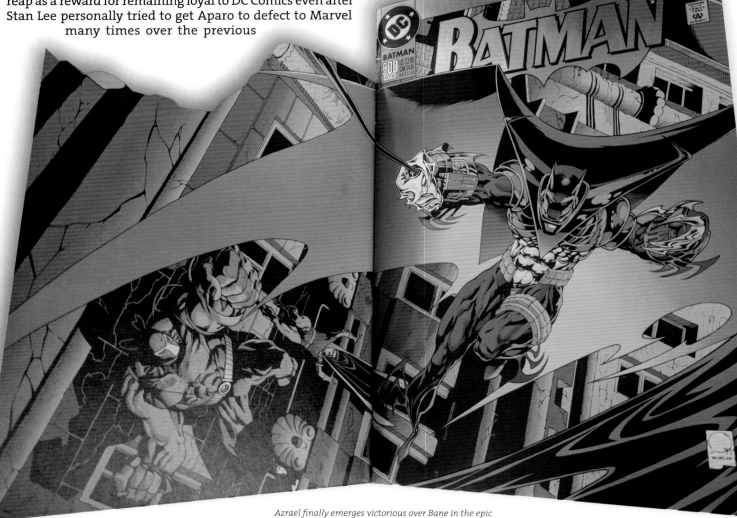

Azrael finally emerges victorious over Bane in the epic conclusion of "Knightfall" in **Batman** *#500.* TM and © DC Comics.

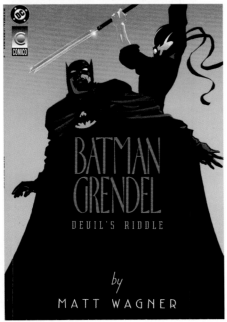

Robin went solo in 1993, as Batman met Grendel.
Robin, Batman TM and © DC Comics. Grendel TM
and © Matt Wagner.

a harrowing tale of the Scarecrow with a tragic romance in Bruce Wayne's life. The special proved so popular that a Loeb/Sale Batman Halloween book became an annual tradition, spawning a much-beloved mini-series in 1996.

Significant events occurred in DC's super-hero comics outside of its Superman and Batman lines. One of them included a six-issue story arc in **The Flash** written by **Mark Waid** and drawn by Greg LaRocque and Roy Richardson: "The Return of Barry Allen." Wally West had been running around as the Flash since the events of *Crisis on Infinite Earths* killed his

predecessor and uncle Barry Allen in 1985. In the ensuing years, Wally West distinguished himself as a worthy successor to Barry Allen's legacy, not only in his own series, but in such team titles as *New Teen Titans* and *Justice League Europe*. Despite this, many fans—and comic book creators—weren't happy that Wally West remained DC's "Fastest Man Alive." Mark Waid explained in a 2008 interview:

"Even though Wally West had been The Flash then for about six years, we continued to get pelted, month after month, with letters from fans demanding to know, 'When's Barry really going to come back and get rid of this upstart?' Even John Byrne. I'd asked him at some point about perhaps doing a one-shot or something, and in his characteristically caustic way, he stood there in the halls of DC and proclaimed that he would be glad to draw The Flash as soon as the *real* one comes back." (Wells 156-7)

In response to the clamor, Waid seemingly gave disgruntled fans exactly what they wanted; in *The Flash* #74 (April 1993) Barry Allen returns from the dead. This triggers ambivalent feelings in Wally. While thrilled that his mentor and boyhood idol has been miraculously resurrected, Wally nonetheless begins to suffer self-doubt and an inferiority complex, especially when Barry angrily asserts himself as the "real" Flash. In the end, though, Wally— and the readers— have been duped. It turns out "Barry Allen" is none other than Flash's nemesis from the 25th century, Eobard Thawne, a.k.a. Professor Zoom, in disguise. The story concludes in the fifty-four page *Flash* #79 (Aug. 1993) as Wally defeats Thawne and returns him back to the future. By that issue's

Catwoman leaped in her own series in 1993. TM and © DC Comics.

end, readers had no doubt as to who the Flash was, which was Mark Waid's intention all along: "My feeling was we needed a story that would establish several things. One was to show that we're never going to bring Barry Allen back. Wally is the first sidekick in comics history to actually fulfill the promise, to take up the mantle of his mentor. My job was to show people that Wally deserved the mantle and mystique" (Grant 81).

Two other DC series received spin-offs. *Legionnaires*—debuting with an April 1993 cover date with writing by Tom and Mary Bierbaum and art by

"The Return of Barry Allen" story arc left no doubt who was the true Flash of the 1990s.
TM and © DC Comics.

Chris Sprouse and Karl Story—presented a bright alternative to the bleak events found in the main *Legion of Super-Heroes* title (like the destruction of the Earth in *Legion* #38 (Dec. 1992)). *Justice League Task Force*—premiering with a June 1993 cover date with writing by David Michelinie and art by Sal Velluto and Jeff Albrecht— introduced a Justice League offshoot led by the Martian Manhunter who handpicked the members of his team based on the needs of their mission. The uber-popular anti-hero Lobo also received his own ongoing series with a Dec. 1993 cover date after many one-shots and mini-series. Alan Grant, one of the key writers of the "Main Man," wrote the comic while Val Semeiks and John Dell illustrated.

DC also revived the 1980s series *Outsiders*. Joining former members Geo-Force, Katana, Looker and Halo were new members Misfit, Faust and Sanction. The oddest touch of this Mike W. Barr-written series was that DC published two different first issues, both arriving in stores on September 28, 1993. *Outsiders* #1 featured the men of the team, while *Outsiders* #1 Ω featured the women. Both issues were drawn by Paul Pelletier and Robert Campanella who continued with the artistic chores on the series.

DC's big Annuals event for 1993 was "**Bloodlines**," a crossover that spanned 23 Annuals and then concluded with two *Bloodbath* specials, both written by Dan Raspler with art by Chuck Wojtkiewicz, Bill Willingham, Sal Velluto and Val Semeiks. The event showed an invasion of Earth by a group of xenomorphs who kill humans in order to extract their spinal fluid. A handful of humans survive the attack, develop super-powers and become known as the "New Blood." Each "Bloodlines" Annual introduces a new hero, with the plan to spin a few of these characters out into their own series. Eventually, a few "Bloodlines" heroes received their own title (*Hitman, Anima, Gunfire*) and four others earned their own mini-series (*Blood Pack, The Psyba-Rats, Loose Cannon, Argus*). Only *Hitman* had a substantial run, with a sixty-issue series that began in 1996. *Anima*, launched in 1994 as a kind of "punk rock super-heroine," received coverage in a number of national magazines, but only lasted sixteen issues. Her series was written by science fiction and fantasy authors Paul Witcover and Elizabeth Hand and illustrated by Malcolm Davis. *Anima* had a different viewpoint from most other comics, exploring a war between metaphysical beings who embodied Jungian archetypes via its

The "Bloodlines" crossover debuted a set of new characters, most prominently Hitman. TM and © DC Comics.

vast supporting cast. While *Anima* proved a bit out of step with its times, most of the rest of the "Bloodlines" heroes reflected the comic book zeitgeist with names like Ballistic, Shadowstryke and Terrorsmith. As a result, many critics ridiculed the "Bloodlines" event as epitomizing the comic book industry's bloodlust of the 1990s.

Tarnished Gold

Just as it fully embraced event comics and spun its edgier comics out to a new line, DC Comics also produced ambitious squarebound books. Among them were *Blackmask* by Brian Augustyn and Jim Baikie; an adaptation of *The Hitchhiker's Guide to the Galaxy* by John Carnell, Steve Leialoha and Denis Rodier; *Streets* by James Hudnall and John McCrea; and **The Golden Age** by **James Robinson** and Paul Smith.

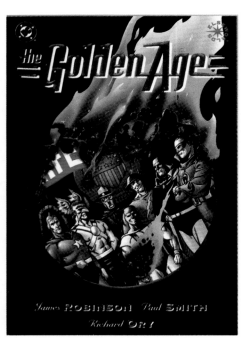

The Golden Age *set heroes from the 1940s, like the Justice Society, face to face with anti-communist hysteria and a turncoat villain.* TM and © DC Comics.

Of that group of titles, the breakout hit was *The Golden Age*, a four-issue Elseworlds series that earned comparisons to *Watchmen* for its grim but smartly written approach to DC's classic super-heroes and the way it depicted their reactions to the Cold War and the rise of Communism. Robinson was a British writer whose early work, including the 1989 black-and-white World War II story *London's Dark*, *Terminator* comics for Dark Horse, and a contribution to Eclipse's *Miracleman: Apocrypha*, caught the eyes of several editors in the United States. One of them was DC Comics' **Archie Goodwin** who employed the writer in 1992 for a three-issue arc on *Legends of the Dark Knight* (#32-34). Goodwin then encouraged Robinson to pitch him other stories. After mulling around an idea that they both eventually agreed wasn't quite thought through, Robinson and Goodwin crafted a comic story based on Robinson's love for the characters from the 1940s, not just the Justice Society of America but also heroes like Manhunter, Mr. America, Robotman and the Tarantula. *The Golden Age* weaves together several plot threads, each one exploring the characters' deep psychological conflicts before culminating in the jaw-dropping revelation that Hitler's brain was implanted into one of the former heroes. Robinson balanced his love for the characters with his innovative take on the genre: "I wanted to bring a sense of respect for those characters. So that hopefully while new readers would enjoy the story for the modernist way I depicted everything, older fans would still be able to see my love for the characters and the books because of it" (Spurgeon 78). Aided by Paul Smith's polished, cinematic art, Robinson's work on *The Golden Age* made him a rising industry superstar, and he was tasked with writing a sequel to the mini-series with the appropriate title of *The Silver Age*. Featuring art by Howard Chaykin, *The Silver Age* would have begun with Jim Harper, formerly the Golden Age Guardian, investigating a series of murders. Harper soon discovers there is more happening than he expected, with ramifications that go to the top of the American Cold War government. Detective J'onn J'onzz, a.k.a. the Martian Manhunter, gets assigned the case, and his investigation brings in a plethora of DC characters from the 1950s including the Flash, the Doom Patrol, Green Lantern, the Challengers of the Unknown and many more. Though *The Silver Age* was slated to appear in the summer of 1997, it was never published. Robinson instead co-created a very different legacy comic book for publication in 1994. It would cement him as one of the most important writers of the 1990s.

Marvel Falls from Grace

In 1993, **Marvel Comics** was in transition. No longer commanding monthly market shares over 50% as it did just a couple of years previously, the House of Ideas still typically controlled about one-third of the sales charts each month, including about a third of the best-selling comics in the top 10, top 50 and top 100 lists. That wasn't always the case, however. For instance, for the first time in the history of the Direct Market, Marvel placed only one comic among the best-selling twenty

comics in April 1993. With stockholders demanding revenue growth, Marvel couldn't—and wouldn't—sit idly as competitors ate away its market share. So, as a countermeasure against the sudden popularity of Image and Valiant, Marvel put even more attention-grabbing events on its docket and flooded an already crowded market with more titles under the presumption that when push came to shove, fans would spend their funds on Marvel than on the other publishers. That conceited line of thinking proved wrong.

In 1993 episodes of FOX's X-Men cartoon were made available on VHS.
TM and © Marvel Characters, Inc.

Marvel released an astonishing 128 comics with a November 1993 cover date, a 25% increase from twelve months prior, when it released 96 comics. By contrast, DC released 84 comics with November 1993 cover dates (including Vertigo and Milestone titles), and Image released 20. Capital City Distribution reported that despite its deluge of product, Marvel only accounted for 31.12% of the comics market dollar share for the month. DC accounted for 17.85%; Image 11.9%; Valiant, with a line of 14 titles, had 8.35%; Dark Horse, with 27 titles, had 4.77%; and all other publishers combined for 26.01%. By comparison, for cover date November 1992, Marvel had accounted for nearly 50% of the dollar share. So despite adding dozens of titles to its catalog, Marvel suffered a 19 percentage point drop in a year's time.

Marvel's executives, though, remained busy by further diversifying the line of companies that were under the Marvel corporate banner. In March 1993 toy manufacturer **Toy Biz** was granted exclusive, royalty-free rights to produce action figures based on Marvel characters in exchange for 46% equity in Toy Biz. The sale helped insulate Marvel somewhat from the ups and downs of the comic and card industries, but the person benefitting the most from the deal was someone who had just become one of Toy Biz's co-owners, **Avi Arad**. As a result of the purchase, the veteran toy designer now had a seat as a Marvel executive. Arad immediately became the executive producer of the immensely popular *X-Men* cartoon series, and along with Stan Lee, he fought to get Marvel's characters on movie and TV screens. It didn't take long for Arad to strike pay dirt as in October, he convinced Twentieth-Century Fox to distribute a soon-to-be-produced live-action X-Men movie. Arad also managed to kill a low-budget Fantastic Four film that was being co-produced by Roger Corman. Fearful that a schlock movie could inadvertently sabotage

IT'S MILLER TIME!

FRANK MILLER RETURNS TO COMPLETE THE ORIGIN OF THE CHARACTER HE MADE GREAT!

A 5-ISSUE LIMITED SERIES BY FRANK MILLER, JOHN ROMITA JR. & AL WILLIAMSON.

ALSO DON'T MISS DD'S NEW COSTUME IN DAREDEVIL #321!

Frank Miller revamped a Daredevil television movie treatment as **The Man Without Fear** *mini-series with art by John Romita Jr.* TM and © Marvel Characters, Inc.

future Hollywood negotiations, Arad offered to buy the Fantastic Four film prints for two million dollars. Corman and his partners accepted. Arad then made sure the movie was never released in theaters or on home video (Howe 356).

As far as the **Fantastic Four** comic book went, it experienced a major shakeup to its roster. Written by Tom DeFalco and drawn by Paul Ryan and Danny Bulandi, *Fantastic Four* #381 (Oct. 1993) ends with an astonishing cliffhanger: the disintegration of Mr. Fantastic and Doctor Doom. In the next issue Invisible Woman theorizes that Doctor Doom has merely teleported her husband rather than killed him, but Marvel put on the pretense that Mr. Fantastic had truly died. To wit, the title logo on issues #382-384 reads, "Fantastic Three." After that, other heroes, first the Sub-Mariner and then Ant-Man, join the team in Reed Richard's stead. The story developments seemingly confirmed the year's persistent rumor, made most notably by *Comics Buyer's Guide* columnist Tony Isabella, that *Fantastic Four* was slated to be canceled and replaced with a comic called *Fantastic Force*, though sales on *Fantastic Four* were reported to be solid and slightly on the rise (Grant 21). The truth of this matter would be revealed in 1994.

Meanwhile, **Frank Miller** returned to Marvel to script **Daredevil** once again, in the five-issue deluxe format mini-series *Daredevil: The Man Without Fear*. Paired with artist John Romita Jr., Miller retold Daredevil's origin with a special focus on Matt Murdock's college years in which he met the beautiful, exotic and deadly Elektra. Printed on slick paper with thick covers that contained gold embossing, *Man Without Fear* was one of the few Marvel releases of the year that was both a critical and financial hit, providing a satisfying story that helped to illuminate one of the most iconic characters in Marvel's lineup. Miller actually had written much of the first two issues of *Man Without Fear* as a plot synopsis for an unproduced *Daredevil* TV movie, then expanded on it when he and Romita Jr. decided to turn the script into a mini-series in 1987. It took Romita two years to illustrate the 148-page story and another four years for the book to reach the stands.

The main *Daredevil* title also received much attention in 1993, as the **"Fall from Grace"** storyline upended Matt Murdock's life and re-inserted Elektra into the current Marvel continuity. Under writer **D.G. Chichester** and artist **Scott McDaniel**, Daredevil is revealed in the press to be Matt Murdock, so the hero fakes his own death in order to protect his loved ones. During the seven-issue arc, Daredevil dons a new armored costume to replace his iconic red suit

Daredevil donned his "motocross outfit" and teamed with Elektra to fight Venom, Nightmare and other villains in the "Fall from Grace" storyline. TM and © Marvel Characters, Inc.

— in part to be able to deny that he's the same man. Often derided as Daredevil's "motocross outfit," this red, grey and white get-up made of biomimetic materials, along with shoulder pads and other protective appendages, offended many longtime fans and came to represent some of the poor decision-making Marvel made with its iconic characters during the 1990s. What's more, while "Fall from Grace" sold well, the storylines that followed it were perhaps overly complicated, thereby pushing readers away from the title in which they had just become interested.

Doctor Strange, Sorcerer Supreme #60 (Dec. 1993) signaled an offbeat new direction for Marvel's master of the mystic arts. Writer **David Quinn**, late of the indie hit *Faust*, took over the reins of the good Doctor's comic and moved it in a darker direction. *Strange* joined Marvel's "Midnight Sons" sub-line (which included such characters as Ghost Rider and Morbius, the Living Vampire) and soon was having unpredictable, mysterious adventures that both looked back at Strange's original Lee/Ditko stories and lived firmly in the 1990s. As Quinn reported, "Doctor Strange became 'Earth's Healer' as a way to work our destructive, selfish, suicidal culture into saving the planet" (Braden 30). In other words, Quinn turned the hero away from his mystic roots by having him defend the Earth's biosphere. Strange's actions in fighting doppelgangers that represented different areas of his personality intrigued readers who enjoyed the dark side of the Marvel Universe. As critic Ben Herman noted, "[Quinn's] writing is filled with energy and insane ideas and off-the-wall mystical concepts and the sort of dark lunacy typically associated with Neil Gaiman and Grant Morrison's work for DC/Vertigo" (Herman). Quinn's distinctive writing helped keep sales on *Doctor Strange* strong for several years.

Unfortunately, the same couldn't be said for several other Marvel series whose flagging sales designated them

Magneto removes the adamantium from Wolverine's skeleton at the end of the "Fatal Attractions" story arc. TM and © Marvel Characters, Inc.

for cancellation by the end of the year. Among them were *Alpha Flight, Avengers West Coast, Cage, Conan the Barbarian, Darkhold, Deathlok, Marvel Universe Master Edition, Marc Spector: Moon Knight, Nightstalkers, Original Ghost Rider, Quasar, Sensational She-Hulk,* and *Sleepwalker. Warlock Chronicles* was cancelled before a single issue was ever published.

Marvel's mutant titles celebrated the thirtieth anniversary of the first appearance of the **X-Men** with a storyline titled **"Fatal Attractions."** Playing out over six issues (*X-Factor* #92, *X-Force* #25, *Uncanny X-Men* #304, *X-Men* #25, *Wolverine* #75 and *Excalibur* #71), "Fatal Attractions" presents the event that Peter David suggested for 1992's "X-Cutioner's Song": in *X-Men* #25 (Oct. 1993), Wolverine attempts to gut Magneto with his claws and in response, the master of magnetism violently extracts all the adamantium metal from the feral mutant's skeleton. That moment triggers an equally shocking decision by Professor X who mindwipes Magneto and leaves his longtime friend and enemy in a coma. These two major events would have lasting effects. Without a metal-laced skeleton, Wolverine brandishes claws made only of bone. Even more importantly, in wiping Magneto's brain, Professor X unleashes an evil psychic entity called Onslaught who would play a major role in 1996 (and not just in the X-Men books). Though "Fatal Attractions" sold well (in part because of the hologram-enhanced covers), it didn't sell as well as previous mutant epics. *Wizard* speculated the sales drop might be a reflection of many fans' exhaustion of crossover story arcs.

Unfortunately for those fans, immediately following "Fatal Attractions," the X-Men starred in another crossover event. The five-part **"Bloodties"**—which involved *Avengers, X-Men, Avengers West Coast* and *Uncanny X-Men*— shows Fabian Cortez, a member of Magneto's Acolytes, engineering a civil war on Genosha and then kidnapping the baby daughter of Quicksilver and Crystal. The crossover prominently features the next major X-Men nemesis: Exodus, an incredibly powerful, centuries-old mutant with a complete disregard for the lives of regular humans. Writer

The Avengers and X-Men united for the "Bloodties" crossover.
TM and © Marvel Characters, Inc.

The Merc with a Mouth starred in his own limited series by Fabian Nicieza and Joe Madureira. TM and © Marvel Characters, Inc.

Another of Marvel's most popular anti-heroes received his own limited series in 1993 with the six-issue *Venom: Lethal Protector*. Written by David Michelinie (co-creator of the character) and drawn by Mark Bagley and Ron Lim, the series takes Venom's alter ego Eddie Brock to San Francisco after he and Spider-Man agreed to a truce. Once on the West Coast, Venom discovers a group of homeless people living underground. He soon must protect them (in his usual vicious way) from a super-armored gang calling itself The Jury. The first issue was printed with both a red foil cover and a rarer gold foil one. *Lethal Protector* initiated a series of rolling mini-series starring Spider-Man's arch-nemesis. As one mini ended, the next began. That way Marvel could continually stimulate sales while remaining flexible on creative teams.

Fabian Nicieza described the "Bloodties" conflict in grand terms: "The story we have now is completely about family but it's also completely about excessive use of power in a very volatile international situation" (Martin 9). The story also had resonance in the X-Men titles, especially in the way that Jean Grey and Cyclops could see their experiences with their own child repeated in the life of Crystal's baby.

The "Merc with a Mouth," **Deadpool**, received his first limited series, a four-issue story by Fabian Nicieza and rising artistic star **Joe Madureira**. The series focuses on the relationship between Deadpool, Kane and Slayback as all three mutants search for a mysterious "prize" mentioned in a will. Of course, this being a *Deadpool* comic, there's lots of wisecracking and one-liners throughout the four issues. Though Deadpool was presented as a villain in the mutant books, Nicieza didn't see him that way: "A villain's someone who's really evil and kicks kittens and the like — Deadpool's just a guy who'll do whatever it takes to get a paycheck," noting that he and Rob Liefeld "created someone that we found ourselves getting request after request to see again" (McElhatton 43-44). *Deadpool* #1 (Aug. 1993) had a unique embossed/debossed cover that both raised and lowered the letters of the logo to create a greater depth of field.

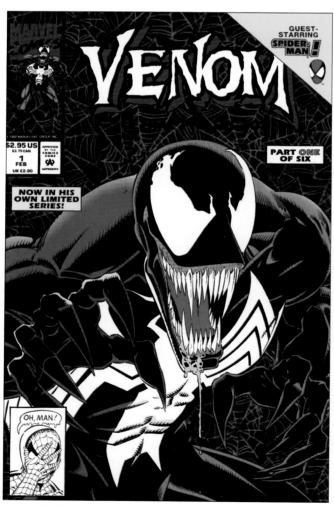

The first Venom limited series featured a foil-enhanced cover. TM and © Marvel Characters, Inc.

Spider-Man, by the way, had his hands full in 1993 dealing with a different symbiote: an insane serial killer named **Carnage** (previously introduced in late 1990 during Erik Larsen's run on *Amazing Spider-Man*). Combining the work of four writers (Tom DeFalco, J.M. DeMatteis, Terry Kavanagh and David Michelinie) and five pencillers (Mark Bagley, Sal Buscema, Ron Lim, Tom Lyle and Alex Saviuk), the fourteen-part **"Maximum Carnage"** set everyone's favorite web-slinger against a cadre of bloodthirsty psychopaths (Carnage, Shriek, Carrion, Demogoblin and Doppleganger) as they rampage through New York City. To stop the mayhem—which at one point has the villains turning the entire population of Manhattan into maniacal murderers—Spider-Man must enlist the help of such heroes as Black Cat, Captain America, Cloak and Dagger, Deathlok, Firestar, Iron Fist, Morbius and even Venom. (In an apparent jab at Todd McFarlane, one of the other heroes coming to Spider-Man's aid is the newly created Nightwatch, a masked man bearing an obvious resemblance to McFarlane's Spawn character.)

Upon hearing the storyline's premise, **J.M. DeMatteis** initially wanted no part of it. He told Spider-Man editor Danny Fingeroth that he had his fill of "the psychos and mass murderers running through the pages of half the comic books on the stands. (And those—Heaven help us—were the heroes!)" (DeMatteis). From DeMatteis's point of view, Peter Parker was the antithesis of the kind of violent super-heroes that had become fashionable in the early 1990s. Fingeroth, however, reassured the writer that emphasizing the title character's inherent decency and nobility was indeed the true goal of the story arc. That purpose brought DeMatteis on board, allowing him to be part of the setup of the story's climax: Spider-Man stopping Venom from killing Carnage in cold blood.

"Maximum Carnage" crossed over into every title that starred the web-slinger (*Spider-Man*, *Amazing Spider-Man*, *Spectacular Spider-Man* and *Web of Spider-Man*) but began in the debut issue of *Spider-Man Unlimited*, part of a group of new on-going, double-sized quarterly series that Marvel rolled out throughout 1993. The others were *2099 Unlimited*, *Fantastic Four Unlimited*, *Midnight Sons Unlimited* and *X-Men Unlimited*. Understandably, many readers and critics balked at the launch of another new Spider-Man (and X-Men) title, but again, Marvel's strategy to regain lost market share was to produce as many comic books as possible. As retailer Todd McDevitt of Evans City, PA, attested at the time, the strategy backfired: "They are finally losing it. There's too much product and too little money for Marvel Zombies to buy it all. I've seen a dip in every title they publish" (McDevitt 36, 38).

Journey to the Barkerverse

One of the ways Marvel added more product to the comics market was by following the example of other publishers and branding several new titles as a separate line of comics. Marvel's most heavily promoted new imprint was "**Razorline**," featuring new super-heroes created by famed British horror novelist **Clive Barker**. Dubbed the "Barkerverse," this collection of comic series aimed to make Marvel Comics more diverse by having a non-Comics Code-approved line partitioned away from the standard Marvel Universe. Razorline was different from the set of Barker-related titles published through Marvel's Epic Comics line. Those comics adapted properties from Barker novels and movies. Razorline, on the other hand, was composed of completely new ideas, which Barker pitched to a group of Marvel editors one day in 1993 over lunch in New York City. Barker declared that he had "a whole new bunch of worlds to conquer here, new characters, new concepts, new cosmoses" to deliver in their own series (Berry 80). Editor Carl Potts proposed that these comics be carved out as their own universe, and Barker ran with the idea, combining Marvel's traditional approach to super-heroes with his own dark vision of alternative worlds.

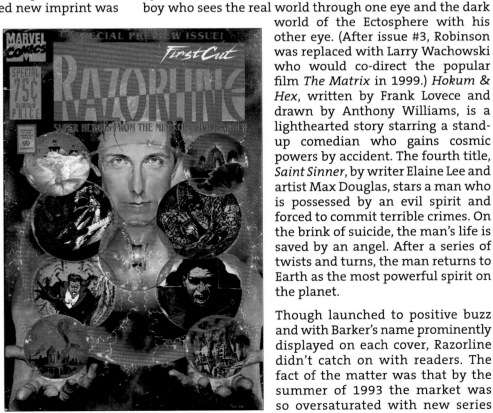

An army of carnage creatures battled Spider-Man and his allies in the "Maximum Carnage" crossover. TM and © Marvel Characters, Inc.

Clive Barker created super-heroes for Marvel's new Razorline imprint in 1993. TM and © Clive Barker

Each creative team on the four new titles worked from a bible created by Barker. The first Razorline comics arrived in stores in July 1993, starting with *Hyperkind*, about a group of super-heroes who pick up the reins from a previous team of heroes who had failed to stop an alien invasion. That series was written by Fred Burke and drawn by Paris Cullins. *Ectokid*, written by James Robinson and drawn by Steve Skroce, features a boy who sees the real world through one eye and the dark world of the Ectosphere with his other eye. (After issue #3, Robinson was replaced with Larry Wachowski who would co-direct the popular film *The Matrix* in 1999.) *Hokum & Hex*, written by Frank Lovece and drawn by Anthony Williams, is a lighthearted story starring a stand-up comedian who gains cosmic powers by accident. The fourth title, *Saint Sinner*, by writer Elaine Lee and artist Max Douglas, stars a man who is possessed by an evil spirit and forced to commit terrible crimes. On the brink of suicide, the man's life is saved by an angel. After a series of twists and turns, the man returns to Earth as the most powerful spirit on the planet.

Though launched to positive buzz and with Barker's name prominently displayed on each cover, Razorline didn't catch on with readers. The fact of the matter was that by the summer of 1993 the market was so oversaturated with new series and new universes, there was no room for imprints as unique as the

Barkerverse to stand out. By March 1994, Barkerverse titles were some of Marvel's lowest-selling comics. *Hyperkind* #9 placed 261ⁿᵈ in Capital City's sales charts for that month; *Ectokid* #9 was 269ᵗʰ and *Hokum & Hex* #9 finished as the 272ⁿᵈ best-selling comic – just three slots above *Barbie*, which had anemic sales in the Direct Market. No Razorline title lasted beyond its ninth issue. An announced second wave of titles included *Schizm* (written by Fred Burke), *Mode Exteme* (written by Sarah Byam), *Fusion Force*, and *Wraitheart* (by Frank Lovece and Hector Gomez), which would have integrated S.H.I.E.L.D. agents in its fifth issue. The industry downturn, however, caused several issues of all Razorline titles to be shelved after they were already written and drawn. Those stories have never been published.

Razorline wasn't the only Marvel imprint of 1993. That same year, Marvel also added several new series to Epic Comics' "Heavy Hitters" line, all of which were creator-owned titles united only by a common cover banner. Among the titles were Peter David and George Pérez's four issue mini-series *Sachs & Violens*; *Dragon Lines* by Peter Quinones and Ron Lim; *Law Dog* by Chuck Dixon and Flint Henry; the one-shot *Alien Legion: Binary Deep* by Dixon and Alcatena; the four-part *Untamed* by Neil Hansen; the two-part *War Man* by Dixon and Juan Zanotto; *Brats Bizarre* by Pat Mills, Tony Skinner and Duke Mighten; *Terrarists* by Pat Mills, Tony Skinner and John Erasmus; and a *Heavy Hitters Annual*. In addition, Marvel premiered two more lines of comics that year. Marvel UK launched the "Frontier Comics" line. Distributed in both the U.S. and U.K., this small imprint was intended to present mature readers titles free from the core Marvel line. Though books like *Bloodseed* (by Paul Neary) and *Children of the Voyager* (by Nick Abadzis and Paul Johnson) boasted quality creative teams, the comics were also lost in 1993's comics market, and sales were abysmal. And then there were the new titles from the Marvel U.K. "Pumping Iron" line that was distributed in the U.S., which included the four-issue *Die Cut*, the two-part *Die Cut vs. G-Force*; and the four-part *Plasmer* (the subject of Marvel's lawsuit against Jim Shooter's Defiant Comics).

Tundra Melts

While Marvel saw some of its imprints die on the stands, other publishers had even bigger problems. **Kevin Eastman** founded **Tundra Press** with the best of intentions, but by 1993 his company was collapsing under its own ambitions and lax scheduling. Tundra was hemorrhaging so much money that despite earning his portion of the $50 million his co-creation, the Teenage Mutant Ninja Turtles, netted in both 1991 and 1992, Eastman couldn't afford the huge financial losses that

Marvel expanded with the Frontier line of comics in the U.K. and more Epic Comics titles in the U.S.
TM and © respective copyright owner.

Tundra was suffering. The company invested in dozens of comics and graphic novels that either never came out, came out late, or came out at the wrong time for the marketplace. For instance, Eastman was a big fan of Alan Moore and Bill Sienkiewicz's ambitious *Big Numbers*, which stalled after Moore's Mad Love Publishing released two issues in 1990. Eastman made a deal with Moore to re-release the first two issues and arrange for foreign market licensing. Intervening to patch up a bumpy relationship between the series' two creators, Eastman successfully convinced Sienkiewicz to draw *Big Numbers* #3. The artist, however, had no desire to continue beyond that issue so Eastman contracted Sienkiewicz's assistant, Al Columbia, to complete the rest of the proposed ten-issue series. Eastman even paid Columbia an advance of $9,200 for his work on *Big Numbers* #4. As Columbia worked on the issue, however, he became more and more irritated that he would be producing art in Sienkiewicz's style rather than his own. That irritation made Columbia less and less diligent until he finally quit the project, destroying all the pages he had drawn in order to cover up the fact that he didn't finish the issue (Cronin). Eastman tried recruiting other artists such as Jon J. Muth, George Pratt and Kent Williams to produce the comic but they all declined. After an enormous investment of time, money and energy, Eastman cancelled the project. Once and for all, *Big Numbers* was dead (Groth 74-75).

Big Numbers was just one of several comic books Eastman paid for but never saw printed. Nonetheless, Tundra had several solid hits throughout 1992 and 1993. Along with a soon-to-be classic from Scott McCloud, Tundra released a serialized version of Alan Moore and Eddie Campbell's epochal *From Hell*, a deep probe into the Jack the Ripper murders. Each squarebound volume collected two stories originally published in the pages of *Taboo*, the anthology magazine edited by Stephen Bissette and also published through Tundra. In 1993 Tundra also premiered Michael Allred's wild and ginchy *Madman Adventures*, which sold out the 50,000 copy print run of its debut issue. Tundra's other notable 1993 releases included Rick Veitch's "heroic" characters in *Brat Pack* and *Maximortal*, *Sandman* cover artist Dave McKean's acclaimed slice-of-life comic *Cages*, Bo Hampton's horror graphic novel *The Upturned Stone* and other titles that cut across the entire spectrum of comics offered during that time.

Tundra also picked up the rights to **The Crow**, the acclaimed graphic novel saga of tragedy and retribution by writer/artist **James O'Barr**. Collecting the issues originally published by Caliber Comics in the late 1980s, Tundra's volumes quickly ran through four print runs, undoubtedly aided by the anticipation of the release of *The Crow* movie and the tragic news that its lead actor, Brandon Lee, was accidentally shot and killed during filming on March 31, 1993.

But no matter its successes in the comic book market, Tundra was in deep financial trouble. Few outside observers had much of an idea how bad Tundra's problems were. Indeed, in late March 1993, Eastman and Kitchen Sink Press publisher **Denis Kitchen** stunned the comic world with the announcement that Eastman had sold all of his Tundra assets to Kitchen. Eastman's dream was no more. He had sold out to a competitor – though things

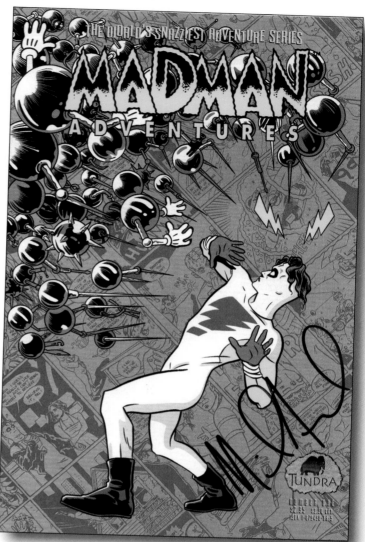

Madman Adventures was one of the series that moved away from Tundra Comics in 1993. TM and © Michael Allred

weren't quite as they seemed. It was originally announced that Kitchen paid Eastman one dollar to buy Tundra Press. In reality, Eastman paid Kitchen over $2 million to take over his foundering company. As part of the deal, Kitchen was only required to keep the projects alive that he wanted to publish. The transaction left Eastman with 49% equity in the merged company (which retained the name Kitchen Sink Press), and Eastman was removed from all day-to-day operations. As Eastman stated, "[Kitchen] took over the management, completion, re-negotiation, and ongoing interest in projects that he selected for Kitchen Sink from the Tundra library." The money paid for Kitchen's move from rural Wisconsin to Northampton, Massachusetts and all other company-related expenses. Eastman further agreed to pay the costs for any books that Tundra had commissioned but which Kitchen thought wouldn't be profitable. Among those books were compilations of Rolf F. Stark's *Rain*, Mark Martin's *Hyena* and John Bergin's *Bone Saw*. Kitchen could continue to publish profitable former Tundra series like *From Hell*, Bernie Wrightson's *Captain Sternn* and Mike Allred's *Madman*. Kitchen would also continue to capitalize on the success of *The Crow*, and he could do so without having to put any of his own money at risk. In the end, Eastman lost $14 million in three years publishing independent comic books (and owning ancillary companies) during a market boom (Groth 84-90).

With **Understanding Comics** *Scott McCloud delivered arguably the most important book about the comics format.* TM and © Scott McCloud

Comic Fans Understand *Understanding Comics*

Before Tundra became a historical relic, one of its final releases became one of the most important works ever published about comic books. **Understanding Comics** by **Scott McCloud** was a revolutionary examination of the theory and practice of comic book creation. McCloud, best-known at the time for his 36-issue series *Zot!* (published by Eclipse Comics from 1984 to 1991), developed a complex theoretical framework for understanding the comics medium, delivered in an elegant and charming artistic style that was tremendously effective at conveying the important ideas of the book.

Understanding Comics details the history of sequential art, from Egyptian tombs in 1300 B.C., all the way up to the modern day, while also providing a distinct definition of the term "comics": "Juxtaposed pictorial and other images in deliberate sequence, intended to convey information and/or produce an aesthetic response in the reader." Furthermore, through the book McCloud advances a unified

theory of comic art, delivering thoughtful takes on technique and perception, page design, rendering and style. *Understanding Comics* was like nothing that had been created about comics before. Previous attempts to explore the aesthetics of the comics medium, including work by comics legend Will Eisner, generally focused on comic art process and techniques. McCloud instead offered a drawn graphic novel that both discusses *and shows* the great power of the medium. In other words, by presenting *Understanding Comics* in comic form, McCloud reinforced the nearly limitless boundaries of the medium. *Understanding Comics* was therefore as much a polemic or demonstration of comics' potential as it was an exploration of McCloud's complex ideas.

Understanding Comics debuted to massive critical acclaim from readers, scholars and fellow cartoonists, and sold 30,000 copies in Direct Market stores by early 1994. *The Comics Journal* devoted a whole issue to the book, though influential editor Gary Groth referred to McCloud's ideas as overly mechanistic and was frustrated by McCloud's need to define everything. Garry Trudeau, popular cartoonist of the newspaper strip *Doonesbury*, gave the book a rave review in the February 13, 1994 *New York Times Book Review*, which earned *Understanding Comics* additional readers from outside the comics industry. The book was deeply significant to a generation of cartoonists and became one of the most frequently used texts in cartooning schools and graphic novel classes.

Eclipse in the Shadows

Scott McCloud's first significant comics work was published by **Eclipse Comics**. By 1993 that company had hit hard times, mainly due to poor cash flow and poor decision making. In the early 1990s, monthly comics were booming, with many comics from various companies selling in the hundreds of thousands of copies per issue. Eclipse co-owner **Dean Mullaney**, however, led his company in a different direction. Rather than launch a new line of comics

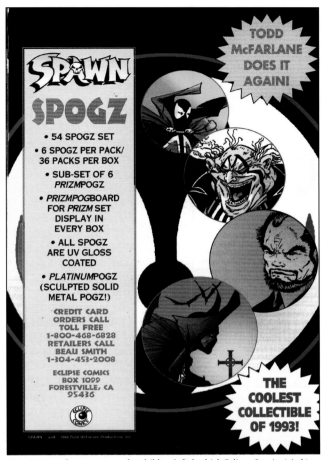

In 1993 pogs became a popular children's fad, which Eclipse Comics tried to cash in on with Todd McFarlane's Spawn. TM and © Todd McFarlane Productions, Inc.

that featured a new fiction universe, Mullaney instead focused Eclipse's efforts on an array of other products. With apparent financial backing from a contract with HarperCollins, signed in January 1993, Eclipse marketed traditional book stores with graphic novels that adapted literary properties such as *The Hobbit*, Clive Barker stories and the fantasy novel *Dragonflight*. Eclipse also produced trading cards with a slew of unusual sets like *Congressional Medal of Honor Trading Cards*, *Famous Comic Book Creators Trading Cards* and *Savings and Loan Scandal Trading Cards* along with more traditional sets like one that featured James Bond. Catching two trends in one product Eclipse also produced "Spogz," pogs (small circular playing disks that kids could trade and compete with) of Todd McFarlane's Spawn. Supplementing Spogs were three-ring binders and prism pogs that became hot commodities in elementary schools around the country.

Mullaney believed these new offerings would resolve the company's longstanding cash-flow problems which vexed many Eclipse freelancers and agents. Neil Gaiman, for instance, reported that he and artist Mark Buckingham received no money for their work on Eclipse's *Miracleman* between 1991 and 1993, nor did they receive any royalties from the publication of *Miracleman: The Golden Age* (released by Eclipse in 1992 as both a hardcover and trade paperback). In fact, Gaiman explained to the fan press that Eclipse had been negligent in its payments all the way back to the 1986 debut of *Miracleman*, with creator Alan Moore only receiving royalties on the first issue.

Miracleman #24, the second chapter of "The Silver Age" story arc, appeared in stores at the end of August, a full year after Eclipse published issue #23. Despite the massive popularity of the *Sandman* writer, *Miracleman* #24 sold less than 40,000 copies. Gaiman and Buckingham completed issue #25 but it would never see print as Eclipse cancelled the series. Soon to be tied up in litigation for many years, *Miracleman* #25 became one of comics' most notorious "lost stories."

Toren Smith, who Eclipse hired to translate and edit various Japanese manga like *Cyber 7*, *Appleseed* and *What's Michael*, also complained about money that was owed to him, "Eclipse has been paying late for the last three years. Their accountings have been peculiar, and I am now taking legal steps on behalf of myself and the Japanese to get what we're owed" (Powers 12). In December, Smith filed a lawsuit in California State Superior Court to recover past due advances and royalties.

By that time, Mullaney had already promised things would improve. He claimed his brother Jan "hadn't had the time" to manage accounts payable, adding "That's the main reason why I'm taking over that job to make sure people get their royalty statements on time." Unfortunately, things went from bad to worse as Eclipse also stopped paying Glass House Graphics, who represented several Brazilian artists, like Hector Gomez and Mike Deodato. Gomez completed 60 pages of painted art for Eclipse's Clive Barker adaptation *The Great and Secret Show* but didn't receive any of the $16,000 owed him for his work. At the October 1993 Philadelphia Comicfest, Mullaney told Glass House a check had been put in the mail, but as it turned out, Glass House never received it (Powers 38). As Glass House Graphics co-owner Dave Campiti explained:

We were doing a ton of work for Eclipse. The Barker stuff, a monthly *Miracleman* spin-off by Mike Deodato, Dean was having me arrange a license for [the film] *Die Hard*. Then everything fell apart — money stopped coming, royalties were no nowhere to be seen.... [Mullaney] was conveniently avoiding phone calls and faxes. Once in a blue moon I would get a fax dealing with maybe ten percent of the things I was asking about. (Reynolds 15-6)

As if matters weren't bad enough, Eclipse was rocked by another, more

Miracleman was knocked around by Eclipse Comics' financial strain. TM and © Marvel Characters, Inc.

THIS IS FIT TO PRINT NUMBER 482:
he promised her a layout table, but
office days and nights
side by side they
erased pages and cleaned up ligatures
When others had forgotten
how it should have been done
or typeset and pasted like demons
Rushing to Fed-Ex at closing time
eating Mexican at Joe's or Fonseca's
and then at Austin Street or
delaware Street or Lover's Lane
Collapsing with fatigue and pride
on the rug she imagined the future
damn you he said, so she
erased her mind and cleaned up spilled
Coffee and broken chairs
alone inside her head where it was
not unsafe and almost not unhappy
Going to the flea market
englishwoman or Midgley's or
the Vets, how slow you are he said, yet
The gifts of coffee and books and
homer laughlin were waiting at the
end of the road and
Records, too, and more, more, more,
except not because they must oh let's
avoid the sigh the not the
languor was not possible, of course,
Nor mutual assured devotion, yet
evenings on the couch, he with
warren G. Harding and Aimee
semple McPherson, and she with
Dean Hole on Roses, rendering
eidetic images of mission furniture,
architectural details, and a
neon sign they'd seen somewhere for
Him to copy, were a species of fulfillment
although that other stuff, you know,
simply out of the question, impossible,
Languor is unknown but anger is
everywhere within his grasp
fed Ex brings it daily
to anyone who has an address, including
Me
except on Sundays and Holidays
For time is of the essence and
orders not filled are insubordination
recalling his bitter coffee, she
Anxiously feared he'd switched brands
When have I ever lied, you stupid bitch

oh don't call me that
my own mother would not call me that
and your mother too,
never mind, we have each other
Now, don't we? Get the gluestick
and the grid ruler, quick, Fed Ex is here!
manic-depression alert!
emergency! Permanent lung
damage!
Jane Austen never knew a thing
about a deadline and i wish i
never had to go to bed
empty of all thought lest i dream of being
Kissed by the black dog of death
i'd rather be a common labourer
not a socialist malcontent, just a mason
grunting in the sun as Comrade Jack
sweeps by, all Martin Eden now, fully
bloated with undue ease,
unmindful of shared purposes that once
rewarded loyalty but never with languor
yah, boss, and here's yer yeller kid
With four words and aftra words
hung on the winding sheet like stains
onomatopoeia! ono!
He doesn't touch that stuff not now not
anymore he told her and she believed him
sigh avoid the sigh the not the
Bed of roses she expected, was it?
only yesterday she would have found it
not impossible to speak of
evenings on the couch with (he)
Coxey's Army or the Bonus March (she)
how to Make the Garden Pay
in languid green with gold stamping
perhaps, or fustian brown, embossed
silent for an hour at a time while
In the air between them Ricky
nelson Flaco Jimenez
Hank Williams Memphis Minnie the
east Texas Serenaders and Marty
robbins defined eternality
Believe it happened, because you have to
remember something and
anything is better than the black dog's kiss
it's Fed Ex time; you once were fed but
now you're ex

Cats twine around her thin ankles
and cry aloud for food and comfort
they'll get it, too, but later than they think

Heading this time by CHAMPION.
To see YOUR name in boldface type and your art or lettering here,
make FtP logos 8 1/2 inches wide by 3 inches deep and send photocopies to
catherine yronwode, p.o. box 1099, forestville, california 95436.

---

personal, development that involved its staff. At the end of summer 1993 Eclipse co-owner **Cat Yronwode** alleged that Mullaney, her husband, abandoned her and his company in order to run away with a new lover. Yronwode informed Eclipse's readers of her husband's secret affair in a unique way: via a coded message within a free verse poem that saw print in *The Comic Buyer's Guide* #1034 (Sept. 10, 1993) where Eclipse's weekly advertisement usually appeared.

All of Eclipse's financial stresses came to a head by the end of 1993 when Mullaney claimed he had never received any royalty payments from HarperCollins, effectively destroying any attempts to resurrect the company's finances. Months later, in September 1994, Toren Smith received a court judgment for $122,328 for the translation and packaging of two books for which he hadn't been paid. By that point, however, Eclipse had already liquidated its assets and sold its remaining graphic novel inventory to retailer Bud Plant, in advance of formally filing for bankruptcy. It was a sad end to the company that published one of the first American graphic novels and was a major industry player in the 1980s. The end of Eclipse Comics could be seen as the passing of the indie comics baton from one generation to the next. In a 1990s market that banked on youthful energy, new universes and flashy presentation, the publishers that thrived during the 1980s seemed outdated and irrelevant to many readers.

The King's Lost Heroes

Unlike Eclipse, **Topps Comics** expanded its roster of titles to include a couple more Dracula books, an ongoing *Zorro* monthly (written by Don McGregor and drawn by Mike Mayhew and John Nyberg), and adaptations of the latest *Friday the 13th* horror movie (written by Andy Mangels and drawn by Cynthia Martin) and Steven Spielberg's blockbuster thriller *Jurassic Park* (written by Walter Simonson and drawn by Gil Kane and George Pérez).

Topps also launched a new line of super-hero comics involving one of the most revered creators in comic book history: **Jack Kirby**. At the age of 75, Kirby had long since retired from regular comic book work, but Topps' new line, dubbed "The Kirbyverse," didn't need his services as a writer or artist. Instead, Topps just needed the characters he had created in years past that had never seen print. (Given Kirby's unparalleled creativity, Topps had a seemingly endless supply of characters to choose from.) Kirby also provided a brief story outline that would tie all the Kirbyverse titles together. "The Secret City" was an ancient civilization based on organic technology that was destroyed by an apocalypse — an event that was fated to repeat itself unless revived heroes from that civilization could stop it. While Kirby retained ownership of all the characters, Topps Comics' editor Jim Salicrup tapped veteran comic book writer **Roy Thomas** to flesh out Kirby's ideas.

The Kirbyverse line launched in April 1993 with three Roy Thomas-written one-shots, each with a cover produced from Kirby's character designs. Salicrup hired "Silver Age Marvel People" to work on the series. To that end, *Night Glider* was co-written by Gerry Conway and drawn by Don Heck, *Captain Glory* was drawn by Steve Ditko, and *Bombast* was co-written by Gary Friedrich and drawn by Dick Ayers and John Severin. (In an attempt to lure Image Comics' considerable fanbase, *Bombast* also guest starred Erik Larsen's Savage Dragon who beats up the title character without hardly breaking a sweat.) The following month began the four-issue *Secret City Saga* which teamed up the three super-heroes introduced in the one-shots. The artist initially paired with Thomas on *Secret City Saga* was the legendary Gil Kane, but he eventually withdrew from the assignment and was replaced with Ditko (Amash 36). Topps produced a free "zero" issue of *Secret City Saga* that included a cover by Walter Simonson who also drew the interior pages. Via a mail-in offer, readers could obtain either a gold foil or silver foil embossed version of the issue.

Later comics in the "Kirbyverse" included *Satan's Six*, a four-issue series by Tony Isabella, John Cleary and Armando Gil - with eight pages of art by Kirby (most likely produced during the 1970s) mixed in to the story. Kurt Busiek and Neil Vokes added the four-

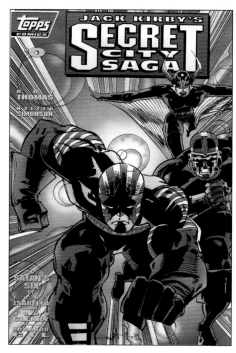

Topps debuted a line created by the King of comic book creators, Jack Kirby. TM and © Jack Kirby Estate.

issue *TeenAgents*, which premiered with an August 1993 cover date. Despite the inclusion of a deluxe trading card—produced by more contemporaneous creators like Bill Sienkiewicz, John Byrne and Arthur Adams—with each issue, none of the Kirbyverse titles sold well. Thomas believes the Kirbyverse was doomed from its start precisely because of Topps' decision to bag each issue with a trading card: "because the comics arrived at the comics stores in sealed if transparent bags, people couldn't open them and page through the comics to decide if they really wanted to buy them" (Amash 39).

Once the first issue of *Silver Star* appeared in October 1993, the decision had already been made to cancel the Kirbyverse. *Silver Star* was designated a four-issue mini-series, but only one issue ever appeared in stores. The same was true of *Victory*, by Kurt Busiek, Keith Giffen and Jimmy Palmiotti. Collecting all the heroes of the Kirbyverse, *Victory* was designated a five-issue mini-series, but Topps only published one issue (even though a second issue had been fully written and drawn). The cover to *Victory* #1 (June 1994) rhetorically asks, "Is this the end of the Kirbyverse!?" Most readers already knew the answer. Topps' line of Kirby-derived comics died with only a small fraction of its true potential tapped.

Hovering Below the Fray

While the big comic companies fought for market share, small press and self-publishers continued to release their idiosyncratic comics in 1993. *Cerebus* was a kind of central promotional house for many self-publishers, as **Dave Sim** took an active position in encouraging creators to go it alone. Besides advancing the sprawling "Mothers & Daughters" story arc, each 1993 issue of *Cerebus* also provided previews of upcoming books from other creators and Sim's own practical advice on self-publishing. For instance, *Cerebus* #170 (May 1993) included a seven-page article on how to market comic books. The comics featured in *Cerebus* in 1993 included *Exit* by Nabriel Kanan, *Wandering Star* by Teri Wood, *Nina's Adventures* by Nina Paley and work by Colin Upton. Sim's status with his peers would change dramatically in 1994 due to

an extremely controversial issue of *Cerebus*.

Many other creators worked as self-publishers in 1993. Jeff Smith continued to self-publish his highly acclaimed *Bone*. Along with writing *Catwoman* for DC, former Marvel writer and editor Jo Duffy self-published *Nestrobber*, a science fiction adventure illustrated by Maya Sakamoto and Colleen Doran. Steve Bissette launched his ambitious dinosaur epic *Tyrant* in 1993, funded in part by money he made from Image's *1963*, while James Owen

Jeff Smith continued self-publishing Bone.
TM and © Jeff Smith.

continued his *Starchild* saga. The Xeric Foundation, a non-profit organized by Peter Laird of *Teenage Mutant Ninja Turtles* fame to provide grants to small press comic artists, awarded money to four cartoonists for their work in 1993: Tom Hart for his *Hutch Owen's Working Hard*, Garret Izumi for his *Strip Down*, Scott Getchell for *Ritchie Kill'd My Toads* and Stephen Townsend for *The Hood: A Change from Within*. Between 1992 and 1994, the Foundation awarded over $170,000 to worthy cartoonists.

New publisher **Majestic Entertainment** released five titles in 1993 (three issues of *Legacy*, and one each of *Majestic* and *S.T.A.T.*), none of which made an impression in an overcrowded comic book marketplace. Like every other publisher, Majestic also released its

own trading card set. Majestic's set, though, didn't feature a licensed property or even its own characters. Instead, the *Comics FutureStars* trading card set showcased 100 artists who were seen as industry up-and-comers. Among the represented creators were Brian Michael Bendis (with his character Zora, whom he would include in his 2000 series *Powers*), David Mack (whose Kabuki would premiere in her own Caliber Comics series in 1994), Philip Hester, Stan Woch, Kyle Hotz, Batton Lash, Terry Dodson, Dan Brereton, Lea Hernandez, Andrew Pepoy and Mike Mayhew, among many others. Years later, Hester recalled how he became involved with the card set:

"The reason you see Stan Woch, Fred Schiller, Dan Lawlis, and me in this set is because we were all freelancers for Majestic at the time. Majestic, like Defiant, was banking on the success of comics that were compiled from trading cards. I did a forgettable comic called *STAT* (the super hero strike team Tonk & Big Guns belonged to) that I had to draw on a Watchmen grid since each page was composed of NINE separate cards. You had to buy pack after pack of *STAT* cards to get all the panels you then assembled in a binder, like *Warriors of Plasm*. It was horrifying. Plus, I had to draw in this grid, which would have been okay, EXCEPT I don't think the book ever came out as cards, just a regular comic (they saw the light at the last minute, I guess) which had super cramped, boring ass layouts." (Sims)

Although backed by a trading card company, Majestic's comics line never expanded past the handful of early series.

Majestic's trading card set was emblematic of 1993 in many ways: an upstart publisher attempted to find and encourage a team of new writers and artists to provide work, but its absurd ambitions and unrealistic business plan led it to failure. Majestic, like several other publishers in 1993, soon went out of business. As 1993 rolled into 1994, and as industry sales continued to tumble at 10% per month, Majestic would have a lot of company in the defunct publishers' club.

1994

CHAPTER FIVE

Counting Down
to Zero

The comic book crash of 1993 became an out-and-out catastrophe the following year. As swiftly as sales boomed in early 1993, they plummeted even faster in early 1994. The same speculators who believed "The Death of Superman," pre-*Unity* Valiant and early Image comics would make them rich learned by 1994 that nearly all their investments had not paid off. As investors moved to the next fad (in this case, non-sports cards and pogs), thousands of former fans followed them. Because of that attrition, thousands of comic shops nationwide closed their doors forever. As Fantagraphics Publisher Gary Groth reported, "I was told by Capital City Distribution that 2,000 of their retailers went out of business in a nine-month period. (Extrapolating from Capital's market share, we may estimate conservatively that 4,000 or more retailers have disappeared in the same period)" (Groth 13). In 1993 there were over 9,000 comic book retailers nationwide. One year later 40% of them were gone.

Milton Griepp of Capital City Distribution cited five reasons why sales were down: (1) speculators left the market, (2) popular franchises such as the X-Men were over-exploited, (3) there were too many new titles, (4) gimmicks and crossovers made it too complicated to follow a favorite character, and (5) late books made all these problems worse. Valiant Comics' Director of Marketing Marty Stever provided two more reasons for the sales crisis. He asserted that publishers released countless mediocre books because there weren't enough qualified creators. Stever also noted that books hyped as sure-fire investments became sales disasters (Grant 78). A retailer from Rochester, New York concurred with that assertion: "there's too much mediocre product on the market that is overpriced by publishers and that imitates each other's thrust" (Funk 22-4). Part of the problem was the sheer number of publications being released each month. *Wizard* counted the deluge as over 1,100 new issues per month, and as a result, "retailers are gunshy, under-ordering new releases to ensure they don't get stuck with unsold books" ("Wizard Market Watch" 141). The decimation of retailers then hurt publishers as well. At Marvel, line-wide sales fell 36% in the first six months of 1994 versus the last six months of 1993 (Howe 361).

Matters did not improve during the usually profitable summer months. According to Diamond Comic Distributors, industrywide sales during August "[have] not brought any release from the summer doldrums... We'd love to see a sign that the negative trends of the last few months have been reversed, but such is not the case" (Davis 55). Later in the year *Hero Illustrated* added, "the slowdown this Autumn was the most severe in several years" (Funk 22).

Publishers employed the usual strategies to try to boost sales: spinning new series out of major events, changing their most famous characters in radical ways, and presenting enhanced covers. Valiant even allowed retailers to exchange unsold books for collectible chromium books that could be quickly resold for a premium price ("An Interview with Valiant's Steve Massarsky" 9). Yet few of these tactics made any real difference. Over a dozen publishers went out of business in 1994 including longtime stalwarts Eclipse Comics and Fantagor Press, as well as newcomers Defiant, Triumphant and Ominous Press.

Malibu Moves to New York

A completely different fate befell **Malibu Comics**. By all appearances, Malibu seemed healthy and profitable as 1994 began. Its state-of-the-art digital coloring system was the envy of the industry, and Malibu's Ultraverse line distinguished itself for its imaginative super-hero stories as produced by quality creative teams. A new series, *UltraForce* (first issue cover-dated Aug. 1994), united several of the Ultraverse super-heroes. Written by Gerard Jones and with art by industry legend George Pérez, *UltraForce* became one of Malibu's bestselling titles. A cartoon featuring the team was set to premiere on the USA cable network in fall 1995, with a toy line following shortly thereafter. Malibu also attracted attention through its licensed series, delivering comics based on the popular video game *Street Fighter* and the latest *Star Trek* television show *Deep Space Nine*.

New imprint **Bravura** added to Malibu's prestige. Its small line presented stories and art by fan favorite creators like Howard Chaykin, Walter Simonson and Jim Starlin. Best of all for Malibu, Bravura didn't require a significant monetary investment. Much like the plan arranged with the Image founders, Malibu performed production work on the Bravura titles and then solicited and distributed those series without having to edit or manage them. The creators retained ownership of their properties. The new line emerged as the result of a friendship between Malibu's publisher Dave Olbrich and lawyer Harris Miller, an agent who represented many celebrated artists including Chaykin, Simonson and Starlin.

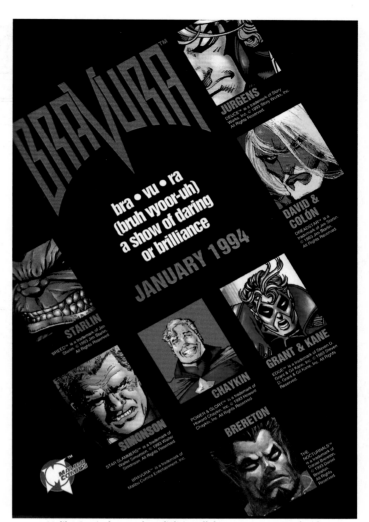

Malibu Comics house ad spotlighting all the creators associated with its Bravura imprint. TM and © respective copyright owner.

Bravura launched with Jim Starlin's 'Breed. TM and © Jim Starlin.

In an important symbolic move, Bravura debuted in January with Starlin's *'Breed*, a horror story about a man who discovers he's half demon. *'Breed* came to Malibu when the writer-artist took out an ad in *Comics Buyer's Guide* in which he described his project and requested interested publishers to contact him. While several publishers replied to the ad, Starlin chose Malibu because he believed the company offered him the best deal (McLaughlin 6).

A decade earlier, Starlin launched Marvel's creator-owned Epic imprint with his *Dreadstar*, so his move with *'Breed* could be seen as both history repeating itself and a good omen for Bravura. In February, Bravura launched its second title with Chaykin's *Power & Glory*, a satirical story about how style has replaced substance in everyday life (including the everyday life of a super-hero). In March, Steven Grant and Gil Kane's *Edge* hit the stands as a four-part mini-series. The plot presented an ordinary human nicknamed Edge who learns that an ostensibly heroic team called the Ultimates have a terrible secret. In a sign of the times, only the first three issues of *Edge* were ever published despite the fact Grant and Kane completed the fourth issue. In April, Starlin's *Dreadstar* returned to comic shops after a three-year hiatus. Written by Peter David with art by Ernie Colón, the new *Dreadstar* was set twenty years after the events of its earlier run and starred the original hero's daughter. Simonson's space opera *Star Slammers* began in May, extending a story that started a decade earlier as a Marvel Comics graphic novel. Bravura continued expanding throughout the year, with new titles such as *Nocturnals* by Dan Brereton, *Strikeback!* by Jonathan Peterson and Kevin Maguire, *The Man Called A-X* by Marv Wolfman and Sean McManus, and *Metaphysique* by Norm Breyfogle.

In combination with the licensed titles and the Ultraverse line, Bravura enabled Malibu to present itself as a publisher

TIMELINE: 1994

A compilation of the year's notable comic book history events alongside some of the year's most significant popular culture and historical events. (On sale dates are approximations.)

January 6: U.S. figure skater Nancy Kerrigan is assaulted at an ice skating rink, suffering a severe leg injury. The culprit is an associate of Jeff Gillooly, who concocted a scheme to remove Kerrigan from the upcoming Winter Olympics to improve the chances of his ex-wife, rival figure skater Tonya Harding, of winning a medal. Four men are later sentenced to prison, and while Harding denies involvement in the assault, she still receives a probationary sentence after pleading guilty to conspiracy to hinder prosecution.

February 12: The Winter Olympic Games open in Lillehammer, Norway. U.S. speedskater Bonnie Blair wins her fourth gold medal while Dan Jansen breaks an Olympic drought by winning his first gold medal. In ladies' figure skating Ukraine's Oksana Baiul wins the gold medal, Nancy Kerrigan overcomes her leg injury to win the silver medal, and Tonya Harding finishes in eighth place.

April 7: Video game developer Acclaim Entertainment agrees to purchase Voyager Communications, the parent company of Valiant Comics, for $65 million in cash and stock.

April 7: Civil War erupts in the African nation of Rwanda, a day after a mysterious plane crash claims the lives of the presidents of Rwanda and Burundi. In the months that follow, Hutu militia round up and slaughter hundreds of thousands of minority Tutsis.

April 8: Kurt Cobain, lead singer for grunge rock band Nirvana, dies at the age of 27 of an apparent self-inflicted gunshot wound.

May 13: *The Crow*, a supernatural action film based on James O'Barr's 1989 comic book series, opens in theaters, eventually grossing over $50 million domestically. Lead actor Brandon Lee, son of famous martial artist Bruce Lee, was accidentally killed during the film's production.

JANUARY	FEBRUARY	MARCH	APRIL	MAY	JUNE

January 17: An earthquake registering 6.7 magnitude strikes Southern California, killing at least 61 people and causing $20 billion worth of damage.

February 6: Comic book writer and artist Jack Kirby dies of heart failure at the age of 76. Universally recognized as one of the industry's most prolific, influential and innovative creators, The King's career began in the 1930s and continued until his death.

February 4: *Schindler's List*, a historical drama directed by Steven Spielberg and starring Liam Neeson as Oskar Schindler, a German businessman during World War II who saves over 1000 Jews from being sent to the concentration camps, opens in movie theaters. It will win seven Academy Awards, including Best Picture, Best Director and Best Screenplay.

April 22: Former U.S. President Richard Nixon, who resigned from office in 1975 in the wake of the Watergate scandal, dies at the age of 81, four days after suffering a stroke.

May 23: Don Thompson, a pioneer of comic book fandom and longtime co-editor of the influential *Comics Buyer's Guide* weekly newspaper, dies at the age of 58.

May 6: Murray Boltinoff, a comic book editor who worked for DC Comics from the 1940s to the 1980s, dies at the age of 83.

June 12: Nicole Simpson and Ronald Goldman are knifed to death outside her Los Angeles condominium. Five days later, her ex-husband, former professional football player O.J. Simpson is arrested for their murder, but not before he leads police on a slow-speed car chase on the Southern California freeways that is broadcast live all over the country. The "Trial of the Century" that pits the Los Angeles District Attorney's office against Simpson's high-priced "Dream Team" of lawyers begins in November.

---

of critically acclaimed, diverse material that was sure to appeal to every kind of comic book reader. Unfortunately, most of Malibu's offerings didn't sell well. In fact, by the middle of 1994, retailers reported that Malibu's sales had significantly declined from the previous year.

Malibu was in deep financial trouble, but only partly because of the grim sales trends. Bigger problems came from Malibu's attempt to develop video games based on the Ultraverse characters. Needing help from a company that had more experience with the video game market, Malibu allied itself with Worldwide Sports and Entertainment. The two companies essentially merged with equity stakes going both ways. Thanks to Worldwide's involvement, Sony reached a tentative deal to license a video game featuring Ultraverse hero *Prime* and also discussed games featuring *UltraForce* and *Firearm*. Soon thereafter, however, Worldwide and Malibu discovered that the development of these video games was costlier than they originally anticipated. Indeed, Malibu's games division began to hemorrhage money, over $200,000 a month, leading to a negative cash flow for the entire company. The situation became so dire that Worldwide stakeholders anxiously searched for potential partners to rescue them from a sinking investment. For several months, DC Comics appeared to be their savior. Behind the scenes, all conversations at that year's San Diego Comic Con pointed to a rapid consummation of a deal. DC

and Malibu even announced that their heroes would cross over into each other's comic book lines. That news received coverage in publications such as *Comic Shop News*. No crossover ever appeared, though, because shortly before executives put ink on paper to complete their merger, an unexpected new suitor arrived. Marvel Comics jumped in and quickly bid more money for Malibu than DC was willing to spend. It was an offer Worldwide and Malibu couldn't decline. Within a matter of weeks, then, DC's courtship was for naught. Marvel purchased Malibu and its video game division effective November 3, 1994.

Marvel president Terry Stewart characterized the acquisition as "a step in Marvel's plan to continue aggressive expansion in the industry" (Straub). Put another way, Marvel was protecting its own marketplace hegemony as Tom Mason, one of Malibu Comics' founders, explains in an interview for *American Comic Book Chronicles*:

The underlying theory was if DC buys Malibu Comics and Malibu Comics does another thing like an Image deal or DC is able to grow Malibu's market share in some way, DC would then become the number one comic book company, supplanting Marvel. And in Ron Perelman's business world, he had been leveraging Marvel's number one position against his other companies to get cash. He wouldn't be able to do that if Marvel suddenly fell to number two on his watch.

July 1: *The Shadow*, starring Alec Baldwin as the famous pulp hero who knows what evil lurks in the hearts of men, opens in theaters. The movie proves to be a disappointment at the box office, grossing only $32 million domestically.

July 12: Written and pencilled by Dan Jurgens with inks by Jerry Ordway, the first issue of *Zero Hour: Crisis in Time* arrives in stores. Promoted as the most important comic book event since 1985's *Crisis on Infinite Earths*, *Zero Hour* realigns DC Comics' continuity.

August 12: Professional baseball players go on strike rather than accept team owners' proposal to put restrictions on player salaries. When negotiations fail to bring the two sides together, the remainder of the season is cancelled, including the World Series.

August 12: To commemorate the 25th anniversary of the original Woodstock music festival, *Woodstock '94* opens in Saugerties, New York. Over 350,000 people attend the three day concert which includes performances by Nine Inch Nails, Red Hot Chili Peppers and Peter Gabriel, among many others.

September 22: Cartoonist Bud Sagendorf, who wrote and drew *Popeye* comic books and comic strips for many decades, dies from brain cancer at the age of 79.

September 22: *Friends*, a sitcom about six twentysomethings living in Manhattan and starring Jennifer Aniston, Courtney Cox, Lisa Kudrow, Matt LeBlanc, Matthew Perry and David Schwimmer, premieres on the NBC television network. The show will become one of the most popular programs of the decade, winning numerous Emmy and Golden Globe awards.

November 3: Marvel Comics announces it has purchased Malibu Comics. DC Comics had been negotiating to acquire the California-based publisher but ultimately lost to Marvel's late bid.

December 28: Marvel Comics announces it has purchased Heroes World, a New Jersey based comic book distributor.

December 5: A month after Republicans won enough mid-term elections to gain majorities in both houses of Congress, Newt Gingrich is elected the first Republican speaker of the House of Representatives in four decades.

| JULY | AUGUST | SEPTEMBER | OCTOBER | NOVEMBER | DECEMBER |

July 29: *The Mask*, an action comedy starring Jim Carrey and based on the Dark Horse comic book series created by publisher Mike Richardson, opens in movie theaters. It will gross nearly $120 million domestically.

July 6: *Forrest Gump*, a comedic drama directed by Robert Zemeckis and starring Tom Hanks as a good-natured simpleton who wins the love of his childhood sweetheart, opens in movie theaters. It will become the highest grossing movie of the year at the box office as well as the winner of six Academy Awards including Best Picture, Best Actor and Best Director.

September 5: Later declared by Charles Schulz as "one of the best comic strips of all time," Patrick McDonnell's charming newspaper strip *Mutts* makes its debut.

September 19: Operation "Uphold Democracy" is launched with some 3,000 U.S. troops peacefully entering Haiti to enforce the return of exiled President Jean-Bertrand Aristide.

September 5: John Morrow publishes his fanzine *The Jack Kirby Collector* #1, and forms TwoMorrows Publishing, devoted to documenting comics history and celebrating its creators.

October 14: *Pulp Fiction*, a violent crime drama directed by Quentin Tarantino and starring Samuel L. Jackson, John Travolta and Bruce Willis, opens in movie theaters. It will garner seven Academy Award nominations, winning the Best Screenplay category.

October 14: The Nobel Peace Prize is awarded to PLO leader Yasser Arafat, Israeli Prime Minister Yitzhak Rabin and Israeli Foreign Minister Shimon Peres for their efforts to establish peace between Palestine and Israel.

November 28: Writer and artist Frank Robbins, who created the *Johnny Hazard* comic strip in 1944 and also worked for DC and Marvel Comics in the 1960s and 1970s on such titles as *Batman* and *The Invaders*, dies of a heart attack at the age of 77.

November 18: Captain Kirk meets Captain Picard in *Star Trek: Generations*, the first movie to feature the characters from *Star Trek: The Next Generation*.

On the day of Marvel's purchase, Malibu president Scott Rosenberg released an internal memo that declared "this is a great day for all of us!" He went on to boast that Marvel will enable Malibu to enjoy "stronger distribution, sales, licensing and marketing" (O'Connor). Rosenberg would soon learn, however, what Marvel really had in store for Malibu. Indeed, after the sale, Malibu found itself with a budget slashed to the bone. By the end of 1995, the Bravura imprint had been shelved, and many of Malibu's titles had been cancelled, including *Deep Space Nine*. The Ultraverse line was reduced and rebooted with a completely new continuity. Marvel published several crossovers (including *Avengers/Ultraforce*, *Prime vs. the Incredible Hulk*, *Nightman vs. Wolverine* and *Ultraforce/Spider-Man*, among others), but after 1997 the Ultraverse characters were nowhere to be found. With that, Malibu Comics ceased to exist.

The Marvel/Disney/Harvey Comics

The acquisition of Malibu Comics was hardly the only deal **Marvel Comics** made in 1994. Another one strengthened Marvel's foothold in the kids humor genre as established licensed titles like *Barbie* and *Ren & Stimpy* were joined by hit contemporary **Walt Disney** properties. Comic books featuring decades-old characters like Uncle Scrooge and Mickey Mouse were being published (once again) by Gladstone, but Disney wanted a new partner to generate content featuring its animated film stars of the 1990s. Enter Marvel, which saw huge opportunities in an alliance with the Disney juggernaut. "Our readership is basically male," Marvel Specialty Sales Vice-President Jim Sokolowski noted. "While *Barbie* is the ideal comic book for young girls, it gets buried on the rack with all the other superhero products" (Raab 10). Adding Disney comics to the mix would result in enough different titles to justify a

comics shop rack exclusively featuring series marketed to children. Editor Hildy Mesnik added that one of the partnership's goals was to move beyond the shops: "We're looking into the newsstands, school catalogs, the Disney Stores and theme parks, and book stores" (Raab 11).

The collaboration kicked off in May with *Disney's The Lion King* #1, the first half of a two-part adaptation of the movie slated for a June 15 premiere. Ongoing series featuring *Beauty and the Beast*, *The Little Mermaid* and *Aladdin* followed during the summer. *The Disney Afternoon* joined the line-up in September with a mix of shorts starring TV animation features such as *Bonkers*, *Darkwing Duck*, *Goof Troop* and *TaleSpin*.

The new Disney comics had barely launched when Marvel scored another coup. In June, it acquired the worldwide publishing and distribution rights for **Harvey Comics**. The deal came on the heels of news that Harvey Comics Entertainment had suffered a loss in profits during its 1993 fourth-quarter. The downturn was blamed primarily on a decrease in revenues from HCE's film branch, and executives continued to pin their hopes on forthcoming movie adaptations of both *Richie Rich* and *Casper* (Neal 6). The underperforming comic books were apparently deemed expendable and the last issues went on sale in August 1994.

Marvel—which first tried to acquire the Harvey properties in 1982—was eager to snatch them up and enthusiastically proclaimed its intention to launch five titles in the fall of 1994 before expanding further in 1995. Instead, the best that Marvel could muster were adaptations of the *Richie Rich* and *Casper* live-action movies, respectively on sale in December 1994 and May 1995. It wasn't until 1997 that Marvel finally put together an ongoing *Casper* comic book.

Marvel Masters the Media

By 1994, Marvel was far more than just a comic book publisher. In fact, as the year started, comics only accounted for 37.3% of Marvel's total sales. (Just six years prior, in 1988, comics accounted for 90% of Marvel's total sales.) Card company Fleer produced more than 50% of Marvel's revenue in 1993 ("You Say You Want" 16), and throughout

1994, Marvel added to its non-comic book portfolio. In June, Marvel spent over $150 million to purchase the Panini Group, one of the largest producers in the world of children's collectible stickers and sticker albums. Later in the year, Marvel acquired Welch Publishing and its group of slick magazines for young readers, like *Barbie*, *Barney*, *Major League Baseball for Kids* and *Superman & Batman Magazine*. That meant a Marvel-owned subsidiary was publishing a magazine that featured DC Comics super-heroes.

Marvel had evolved into a vast media conglomerate that owned intellectual properties which could be marketed in a variety of ways: as video games, animated television shows, toys, action figures, children's books, stickers, trading cards and apparel. Unfortunately for Marvel, its aggressive expansion didn't help its stock market position. Marvel's stock price tumbled from a high of $35.75 in late 1993 to a low of $13.87 in spring 1994. That drop perhaps reflected concern from investors that Marvel's credit was over-extended. Financial analysts reported that Marvel had close to $400 million in debt by the end of the year. Those debts would cause problems for Marvel later in the decade.

In the meantime, Marvel moved boldly to promote its super-heroes as pop culture icons. The company licensed its characters to rides and attractions in Universal Studios' Islands of Adventure, a theme park in Orlando, Florida, that would open in 1999. Marvel executives explored the possibility of a chain of theme restaurants similar to Planet Hollywood or the Hard Rock Café. As part of that investigation, a team of managers discussed their plans with Planet Hollywood investors who were looking to expand their business. Those restaurants never opened. Marvel also stepped up production of video games starring its iconic heroes, setting up an in-house games studio to put its wares in the hands of as many gamers as possible. Marvel even debuted its own show on the Home Shopping Network. Writers, artists and editors appeared on HSN to sell collectible comics and other merchandise direct to consumers. Building on that success, Marvel noted in its 1994 stockholders report that it looked to open its own branded stores similar to Disney Stores. Located in shopping malls throughout the country, Disney Stores peddled products that featured iconic characters like Mickey Mouse and Donald Duck. The proposed Marvel Stores would sell clothing, artwork, video tapes and accessories, among other related products. One key question left unanswered by the report was whether Marvel Stores would also sell comic books.

Understandably, nervous retailers speculated that Marvel was looking to invade their territory. By the end of 1994, Marvel Stores remained just an idea, but Marvel had already started selling direct to consumers via a mail order system coined "Marvel Mart." The first Marvel Mart catalog appeared as an insert in *X-Men Adventures* #4 (May 1994), a comic book released to both newsstands and Direct Market stores. The cover blurb of the insert promised "8 pages stuffed to the staples with hard-to-find mighty Marvel merchandise," and the interior

Comic store owners believed Marvel Mart was Marvel's attempt to drive them out of business. TM and © Marvel Characters, Inc.

pages advertised a diverse selection of material, not only fresh hardcover books and trade paperbacks like *Marvel Masterworks* and *The Greatest Battles of the Avengers* but also branded products such as pins, caps, posters and phone cards. Many of the items listed in the catalog were already available in mainstream retail stores as well as in comic shops. What took most comic book retailers by surprise was that Marvel Mart also offered recent back issues including those of such hot series as *Daredevil: The Man Without Fear*. Back issues were traditionally available only through specialty retailers, who used them as a way of generating revenue from excess stock. Marvel Mart, therefore, encroached on the traditional role such stores had in the market. Making matters worse, the retail prices listed in Marvel's catalog were lower than what most shops charged.

Retailers across the country were furious about Marvel Mart, and they didn't hold back their anger. Many expressed concern that the catalog was merely Marvel's first step towards pushing retailers out of business in favor of stores owned and run by the company. Tensions ran high. Walter Wang, co-owner of a comic book distributor named Comics Unlimited Ltd., included a diatribe with his April 1994 *Dear Valued Retailer* monthly newsletter. Beginning with the capitalized declaration "WE'RE MAD AS HELL AND WE'RE NOT GOING TO TAKE IT ANYMORE," Wang's letter advised his retailers to "reduce [Marvel's] importance by issuing a 'wake-up call'" to the House of Ideas. He went on to instruct his clients to "promote other, direct-market-friendly publishers" and "reduce your Marvel back-issue budget." On May 18, just weeks after the dissemination of Wang's letter, Marvel retaliated by discontinuing sales to Comics Unlimited. Soon afterwards Wang sold his company to Diamond Distributors, increasing Diamond's market share. Other entrepreneurs would soon follow Wang's lead as Diamond began gobbling up its smaller competitors.

The next shoe dropped at the end of the year. On December 28, 1994, Marvel purchased New Jersey-based **Heroes World Distribution**. Created and co-owned by Marvel's former head of marketing, Ivan Snyder, Heroes World controlled 8% of the market share among distributors nationwide and specialized in distribution to shops on the Atlantic seaboard. Retailers knew that Marvel had bigger ambitions for Heroes World than just the urban east coast, and rumors abounded throughout the industry that Marvel would soon be distributing its comics exclusively through Heroes World. Those rumors proved well-founded as fallout from the Heroes World purchase would drive the biggest comics news of 1995.

Marvelution

Marvel's comic book line didn't escape the turmoil that affected the rest of the company. Indeed, in 1994 Marvel overhauled its editorial structure under a wide-ranging plan called "Marvelution." As Terry Stewart explained during a staff dinner, **Tom DeFalco**, having served as Marvel's editor-in-chief since 1987, would be promoted to Senior Vice President of Marvel Publishing. The editor-in-chief position would then be apportioned among five editors (Bob Budiansky, Bobbie Chase, Bob Harras, Mark Gruenwald

Among the items sold in Marvel Mart were paperbacks, posters, VHS cassettes and phone cards. TM and © Marvel Characters, Inc.

and Carl Potts) who would each be responsible for a specific group of titles. (For instance, Bob Harras remained in charge of all the X-Men affiliated books while Bobbie Chase shepherded a new imprint called "Marvel Edge" that included titles like *Doctor Strange*, *Ghost Rider* and *Incredible Hulk*.) All five editors-in-chief would report not to DeFalco but to Stewart and also be supervised by Marvel's Specialty Sales Vice-President, Jim Sokolowski (Howe 363).

Savvy Marvel staffers recognized that Stewart had effectively negated DeFalco's power within the company. In other words, DeFalco wasn't really being promoted; he was being pushed aside so Marvel's sales and marketing departments could assert their influence on the editors without DeFalco getting in the way. Going forward, each editor-in-chief had a revenue target to hit with his or her group of titles. The pressure to fulfill their sales quota separated the editors from each other, and in some instances, even created animosity as the editors tried to poach fan-favorite writers and artists from their colleagues' stables. In addition, editors now had little incentive to allow the characters under their control to guest star in another editor's comic book. As a result, characters became isolated within their own corner

The Spider-Man Clone saga began with the revelation that Peter Parker has a clone.
TM and © Marvel Characters, Inc.

to share Peter Parker's powers. Fans speculated for months about the identity of the mystery man until finally the enigma became resolved while Peter sits at Aunt May's bedside at the hospital. Glancing out the window of May's room, Peter is taken aback when he sees none other than Spider-Man swinging by! As revealed in *Spectacular Spider-Man* #216 (Sept. 1994), that other Spider-Man is the long-forgotten clone of Peter Parker who originally appeared in a storyline published two decades prior. In 1974 and 1975 Spider-Man was stalked by a renegade scientist called the Jackal who made clones of both Peter Parker and his recently deceased girlfriend Gwen Stacy. In *Amazing Spider-Man* #149 (Oct. 1975), during final battle with the Jackal, Peter confronts his own clone before triumphing over the Jackal. The clone seems to die when construction scaffolding crashes over him. Two issues later, Peter tosses his clone down a smokestack, where he believes the clone will be incinerated. Now nearly twenty years later, Peter discovers his clone had survived.

In August (cover date Oct. 1994) Marvel released two versions of all four Spider-Man titles. Retailing for $1.50, the newsstand versions present "Power and Responsibility," a story arc that has the two Spider-Men square off against each other before introducing a new villain named Judas Traveller who has taken over the Ravencroft Academy for the Criminally Insane. Traveller vows to kill all the Academy's inmates unless Spider-Man agrees to a confrontation. The deluxe versions of each issue, on the other hand, retailed

Calling himself Ben Reilly, the clone eventually reveals himself to Peter.
TM and © Marvel Characters, Inc.

of the Marvel fictional universe. As one Marvel staffer described the situation, "It would have been easier to have Spider-Man team up with Superman than to have Spider-Man team up with the X-Men" (Howe 365).

These matters were no longer Tom DeFalco's concern, though, because he was having no part of "Marvelution." He refused the promotion offered to him and instead became a freelance writer, continuing his work on *Fantastic Four* and *Thunderstrike* and picking up a new assignment on *Spectacular Spider-Man*.

The Return of the Spider-Clone

Speaking of **Spider-Man**, 1994 was arguably the worst year of Peter Parker's complicated life as he experienced a series of traumatic events that would have broken the spirit of most other men. First, Peter's parents appear to have been resurrected from the seeming dead but are later revealed as robots created by his longtime enemy The Chameleon. Then Aunt May, the woman who raised Peter, suffers a stroke. As if those miseries aren't enough, Peter's wife Mary Jane also leaves him because he can't control his anger. (As Spider-Man, Peter becomes so enraged that he almost beats the Scorpion to death.) All these problems are compounded by the return of an unexpected stranger to Peter's life.

Early in 1994, a mysterious character begins making cameo appearances in the pages of the four main Spider-Man titles. First shown only in the shadows, the man appears

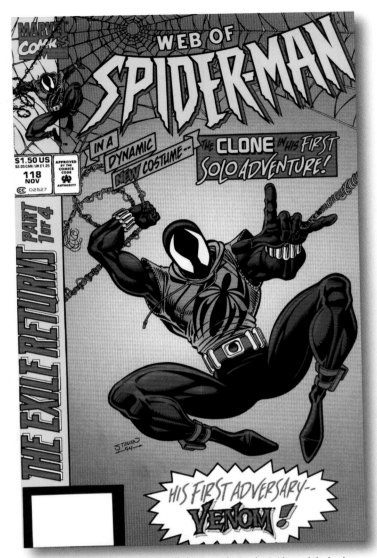

With a makeshift costume, Ben Reilly becomes the Scarlet Spider and the lead character of two Spider-Man titles. TM and © Marvel Characters, Inc.

Spider-Man. The twists and turns of Peter and Ben's lives would spin an even more tangled web in 1995.

Web of Spider-Man's writer **Terry Kavanagh** proposed the idea of reviving the spider-clone during a creative conference. After some resistance, editor-in-chief Tom DeFalco and editor Danny Fingeroth agreed to try out the concept. As *Spider-Man* artist Tom Lyle reported, "Danny Fingeroth at first… didn't want to do it. At first Tom DeFalco said no, too. My initial reaction was boy, we better do this right or this is going to stink" (Cadenhead, "Clones" 31). In a down market, sales on the Spider-Man books defied the trends, so much so that they became the only group of Marvel titles to meet its sales goal (Goletz). The sales boost was a trap though. The short-term storyline became a morass for the character and the company, and the spider-clone saga soon became emblematic of Marvel's problems in the 1990s.

Hoping for a Fighting Chance

One of Marvel's most iconic heroes also faced profound changes in 1994. In *Captain America* #425 (March 1994), the star-spangled Avenger learns he is dying from the same serum that first transformed him into a super-soldier. Cap discovers the more he exerts himself, the more he ravages his body. This terrible predicament was the main plot element behind the year-long "Fighting Chance" storyline, written by Mark Gruenwald and illustrated by Dave Hoover. A lesser man would have chosen to step away from battling villains in the face of this dreadful diagnosis, but Cap is a true hero. It is his nature to keep the world safe. Thus the star-spangled super-hero launches into battles with one super-villain after the next, including adversaries he had thought dead. As he struggles against his ever-decreasing strength, Cap finds himself in moral opposition to counterparts who combat evil more ferociously than he does. Among those are the hyper-violent Super Patriot (a Punisher analogue) and the vicious Americop (a Judge Dredd analogue). Captain America takes on a new protégé

for $2.95 due to its foil enhanced covers and the additional "flipbook" story included within: "The Double," documenting the life of the clone Spider-Man since his apparent demise in 1975. While Peter battles Traveller, his clone sits by May's bedside. As he chats with May, the clone reveals he's adopted the name **Ben Reilly**, the combination of Uncle Ben's first name and Aunt May's maiden name. May persuades Ben to help Peter, and as Ben swings away to save his clone-brother, it's clear the love between the clone and Aunt May is as strong as the man the clone resembles.

As Ben and Peter fight Traveller, their dichotomous personalities emerge. Ben is humorous and honorable while Peter is savage and insane. (Ben even has to stop Peter from using deadly force against the inmates.) After the heroes win, Ben decides to distance himself from Peter. In doing so, the clone stitches together his own version of the Spider-Man costume: a sleeveless blue sweatshirt with a spider emblazoned on the chest, worn over a red spandex body suit. A reporter for the *Daily Bugle* dubs the new hero the **Scarlet Spider**, a nickname Ben hates. Effective with the November 1994 cover-dated issues, the Scarlet Spider became the lead character in *Spider-Man* and *Web of Spider-Man*, while Peter continued to star in *Amazing Spider-Man* and *Spectacular*

in the beautiful and brutal Free Spirit, and together they encounter adversaries like Jack Flag, who resembles WildC.A.T.S. member Grifter and has his own ambitions to become the next Captain America. The storyline concludes in *Captain America* #436 (Feb. 1995) where Cap lies beaten and near death. Few readers would be prepared for what happened to the august Avenger in 1995.

Captain America's former ally U.S.Agent was a member of Avengers West Coast. As 1994 began, that longstanding

Captain America armored up in "Fighting Chance."
TM and © Marvel Characters, Inc.

Force Works spun out of Avengers West Coast. The first issue featured the death of Wonder Man.
TM and © Marvel Characters, Inc.

with his non-super-powered friends. The Hulk's best buddy, Rick Jones, marries his beloved and vivacious Marlo in *Incredible Hulk* #418 (June 1994), an issue that simultaneously embraces and rejects the storytelling clichés of super-hero weddings. Rick's bachelor party is suitably ridiculous, but when villains show up at the wedding, they're respectful and polite. Two issues after the wedding, a tragedy occurs. The Hulk's old friend Jim Wilson dies of AIDS in one of the most poignant issues of Peter David's decade-long run on the series. Most tellingly, *Incredible Hulk* #420 never reveals how Wilson contracted AIDS, which, as David explained, was the most appropriate creative decision to be made:

team was no more. *Avengers West Coast* was cancelled with issue #102 (Jan. 1994) and replaced with the grittier *Force Works* (first issue cover-dated July 1994). The Avengers editorial team created the new series (which had the working title of "Powerworks") to offer a contrast to the more conservative Avengers team. Force Works didn't seek to react to crimes in progress. Instead Iron Man, Scarlet Witch, U.S.Agent, Spider-Woman and Wonder Man coordinated pre-emptive strikes. That bellicose attitude had catastrophic consequences in the team's first adventure. Longtime Avenger Wonder Man is slain in the comic's premiere issue, replaced by the mysterious alien Century. *Force Works* #1, written by the team of Dan Abnett and Andy Lanning, included a unique cover that could fold out to become a 3D die-cut image that showed the death of Wonder Man. The initial few issues were drawn by Tom Tenney and Rey Garcia before a rotating team of artists took over.

1994 was a tough year to be a super-hero in the Marvel universe. In *The Incredible Hulk*, the Green Goliath had a year full of ups and downs. The green-skinned hero was intelligent, emotionally complex and always ready with a clever quip. In fact, he was mature enough to assume leadership of a team of immortals called the Pantheon while also spending time

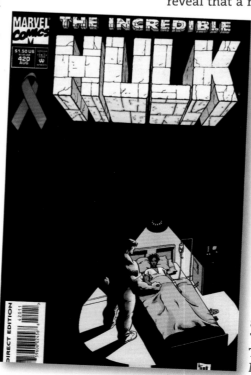

The Hulk's friend Jim Wilson dies of AIDS in one of the saddest issues of Peter David's long run on the series.
TM and © Marvel Characters, Inc.

"As that story developed, I realized I was in a no-win situation when it came to explaining just how Jim had contracted the disease. If I said he was gay, I'd be accused of feeding the gay-equals-AIDS mindset. If I said he got it through straight sex or a blood transfusion, I'd be accused of being too weasly to reveal that a mainstream Marvel character was gay. Ultimately, as I waffled, I realized that I had inadvertently backed into the point of the story. It didn't matter how he had contracted the disease. What mattered was that he had it and needed help and support." (David 58)

The Next Generation of Mutant

The Hulk celebrated a wedding in 1994. So too did Marvel's most popular mutants. After a romance that dated back to the 1960s and even survived Jean's apparent death, Scott Summers and Jean Grey finally marry in *X-Men* #30 (March 1994). Writer **Scott Lobdell** delivered a tale long on ordinary human drama but short on super-hero strife. Scott and Jean enjoy a romantic weekend to celebrate their love, complete with bachelor party and wedding shower. Life-long friend The Angel walks Jean down the aisle. The event's guest list includes all of Marvel's merry mutants... aside from a grouchy Wolverine, who skips the ceremony. The Summers's wedding reception is full of dancing, drinking and smiling friends. *X-Men* #30 provided a respite from the never-ending battles the mutants faced and reminded many readers why they loved the series.

Some of Marvel's other mutant titles, though, weren't as festive. Writer J.M. DeMatteis and artist Jan Duursema presented the death of team member Jamie Madrox in *X-Factor* #100 (March 1994). The Multiple Man contracts the horrible Legacy Virus and dies in agonizing pain. (Madrox's demise would last all of two years as *X-Factor* #128 (Nov. 1996), written by Howard Mackie and drawn by Jeff Matsuda, reveals that the virus only infected one of Madrox's duplicates. The real Madrox is alive and suffering from amnesia.)

The mutant crossover event of the year, **"The Phalanx Covenant,"** involved seven titles (*Uncanny X-Men*, *X-Men*, *X-Factor*, *X-Force*, *Excalibur*, *Wolverine* and *Cable*), carried out over nine issues, featuring a force of techno-organic aliens looking to assimilate the X-Men into its hive-minded collective. As expected, the crossover presents its fair share of

After decades of romance, Scott Summers and Jean Grey finally marry in **X-Men** *#30.*

X-Men heroics, but more notably, it collects a host of characters who will comprise Marvel's next new mutant team. Debuting in September (cover date Nov. 1994) with writing by Scott Lobdell and art by former *Shade the Changing Man* contributor Chris Bachalo, **Generation X** stars mutant teens who embody the cynical 1990s demographic group it's named after. Rather than the "Barbie and Ken" mutants (as Lobdell labelled them) who made up earlier X-Men teams, *Generation X* consists of Jubilee, a Chinese-American moving from the core mutant title to continue her education; Husk, the workaholic younger sister of X-Force member Cannonball, who can remove a layer of her skin in order to change into a variety of different substances, like metal or stone; Skin, a former L.A. gang member who can elongate the extra skin on his body; Synch, an African-American who can duplicate the powers of any mutant near him; Chamber, an antisocial Brit whose bio-blast power exploded his chest and jaw the first time he used it; Penance, a reticent girl with a diamond-hard, razor-sharp atrophied body;

and M, a spoiled rich Muslim with the powers of flight, strength, speed and psionic abilities. With powers and personalities like these, it's no wonder Bachalo noted, "a couple of [the characters] are very monstrous. Scott's taken more of a grisly look at them" (Sodaro 34). Despite this, the heroes of *Generation X* don't agonize much about their powers. Instead they love to have fun. That approach gave the new series a more youthful and contemporary mood than Marvel's other mutant series. *Generation X* also stood out because of its strong emphasis on characterization. Lodbell paid special attention to the struggles of the emotionally battered Chamber, who was changed forever on the terrible day his body exploded. The mutants are taken in by former X-Man Sean Cassidy (a.k.a. Banshee) and the reformed villain Emma Frost at her Massachusetts Academy, where Frost teaches the next generation of mutants on how to use their powers effectively. This latest mutant title was a huge hit, immediately placing among the industry's top ten best-selling titles. As 1995 dawned, *Generation X* and all the mutant titles would receive a dramatic reboot.

Scott Lobdell was responsible for another key moment in mutant history in 1994. He disclosed in *X-Men Unlimited* #4 (March 1994) that the years of rumors were true: Mystique, the former leader of the Brotherhood of Evil Mutants, was indeed Nightcrawler's mother. In a story illustrated by Richard Bennett and Steve Moncuse, the German X-Man meets his long-lost brother Graydon Creed who reveals their mother was the widow of a German count who threw young Kurt Wagner over a waterfall when she was fleeing from her ex-husband's henchmen. The husband was furious when he saw the blue-skinned beast to whom she gave birth. Fans speculated Nightcrawler's father might be Sabretooth (whose last name is also Creed), but that rumor was never confirmed in any Marvel comic book.

Marvels: Back to the Future

In 1994, the legendary **Stan Lee** was inducted into the Eisner Awards' Hall of Fame. Lee's professional career wasn't over yet, though, as he also received approval to develop a new Marvel Comics imprint from his base in Southern California. The suitably titled **Excelsior Comics** was initially intended to include four interconnected titles. After considering the idea of situating all the series ten years in the future, Lee and his writers instead kept their heroes in a contemporary setting. Many of the creators Lee worked with were film industry veterans new to the comic industry. Two contributors, however, had an extensive history with Lee. Writer **Roy Thomas** and artist **Sal Buscema** were assigned to an Excelsior series titled *Zarlok*, about an alien with super powers who came to Earth. Thomas completed plots for the first four issues, and Buscema was pencilling issue #3 when Marvel cancelled Excelsior Comics. No work created for the line was ever published (Amash 31-33).

Fans would have to wait before getting the chance to read any new Stan Lee material. Work he produced with Jack Kirby in the past, on the other hand, was the focus of a new deluxe format Marvel Comics mini-series, arguably the highest regarded Marvel publication of the 1990s. Debuting with a January 1994 cover date, *Marvels* represents pivotal events from the House of Ideas' continuity, including the Sub-Mariner's attack on New York City, the return of Captain America after years of hibernation and the threat of Galactus to the planet Earth. Bearing witness to all these events is the mini-series' narrator, *Daily Bugle* photojournalist Phil Sheldon, his commentary illuminating how everyday civilians perceive the "Marvels" (the term Sheldon uses for super-humans) as both awesome and terrifying. The mini-series' thematic arc is one of resignation as Sheldon retires from his job after witnessing Gwen Stacy's death, realizing the world can never truly appreciate the super-heroes who protect it.

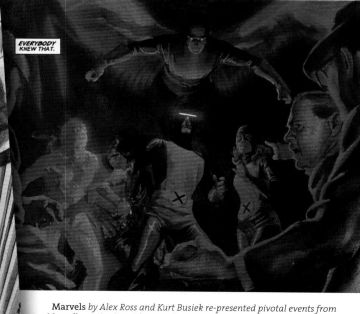

Marvels by Alex Ross and Kurt Busiek re-presented pivotal events from Marvel's continuity with a startling new verve. TM and © Marvel Characters, Inc.

Journeyman comic book scribe **Kurt Busiek** provided *Marvels'* nuanced narrative. The mini-series' photorealistic painted artwork that was one part George Pérez and two parts Norman Rockwell came courtesy of a 23-year-old graduate from the American Academy of Art in Chicago, **Alex Ross**. A lifelong super-hero fan, Ross previously paired with Busiek on a pitch to take over *Iron Man* when John Byrne left the title in 1992 (Cronin, #578). While that assignment ultimately went to Len Kaminski and Kevin Hopgood, Busiek and Ross discussed collaborating on a painted anthology series that would deliver new takes on crucial moments in Marvel Comics' history.

With that concept germinating, the artist found fill-in work. After Ross contributed to the *Miracleman: Apocrypha* mini-series, an Eclipse Comics editor sent his samples to horror novelist Clive Barker who subsequently forwarded them on to Marc McLaurin, the Marvel editor handling Barker's *Hellraiser* and *Nightbreed* comic books. McLaurin became an immediate fan of Ross's work and soon learned about the project that Ross and Busiek wanted to produce. McLaurin agreed to help get *Marvels* approved for publication. (Simultaneously, McLaurin convinced Ross to draw a story in *Hellraiser* #17, an assignment the artist hated because of his preference for super-hero stories.)

Despite some Marvel executives' fears that *Marvels* was both too expensive and lacked "hot" creators and characters, the mini-series became a smash hit. By 1995, retailers had sold over 600,000 copies of the individual issues, hardcover and trade paperback collections. Furthermore, *Marvels* was nominated for three Eisners, winning the Best Limited Series and Best Publication Design awards. Ross was personally nominated for two Eisners, Best Cover Artist and Best Painter, winning the latter award.

Marvels catapulted Busiek and Ross into superstar status, allowing both to work on more personal projects in the years to come. The mini-series also ushered in a wave of painted super-hero comic books. For instance, four months after *Marvels* wrapped up, the House of Ideas published a trio of painted prestige-format one-shots that paid tribute to series Marvel published in the 1960s: *Tales to Astonish* (written by Peter David, painted by John Estes and featuring the Hulk, the Wasp and Hank Pym), *Tales of Suspense* (written by James Robinson, painted by Colin MacNeil and starring Captain America and Iron Man) and *Strange Tales*

A 1994 Neil Gaiman/Michael Zulli comic complemented the latest Alice Cooper album. TM and © Nightmare, Inc.

(written by Kurt Busiek, painted by Richard Villamonte, and teaming up Doctor Strange, the Human Torch and the Thing). Marvel greenlit the three books before *Marvels* had been approved, but Ross produced his painted work much faster than any of the other artists, allowing *Marvels* to be published first.

A *Marvels* sequel was even planned, to be titled *Marvels II: Seduction of the Innocent*. The story would detail the encounters of two brothers—one a police officer and the other a petty criminal—with the darker heroes who emerged in Marvel Comics during the 1970s and 1980s. *Marvels II* would have begun with the first appearance of the Punisher, ended with the first appearance of the new Ghost Rider, and involved such characters as the Hulk, Wolverine, Dark Phoenix, Daredevil and Elektra, among other icons of the "Bronze Age" of comics. Ross had no fondness for any of those heroes, so replacing him on the project was Tristan Schane, who had delivered memorable painted work for Marvel's Clive Baker comics (Samsel 24). However, after the completion of half a script, most of the covers and several interior pages, Busiek backed out of the project because he didn't feel it was working. Years later, Busiek would vastly revise and repurpose *Marvels II*'s outline for a creator-owned project that once again involved Ross.

Neil Gaiman Rocks

Marvels provided a new look at traditional super-heroes. ***The Last Temptation*** was a decidedly different comic book project. It began when Epic Records executive Bob Pfeifer called **Neil Gaiman** to see if the writer was interested in creating the narrative for a concept album to be recorded by **Alice Cooper,** the rock star made famous for his edgy, often violent, songs and freak show-like performances. After meeting with Cooper to brainstorm ideas, Gaiman agreed to the assignment simply because he thought it would be fun. Gaiman's script, written with Cooper, casts the rock star as a Willy Wonka-style owner of a rundown old theatre staffed by dead people. "The Showman" (the name given to Cooper's character) tempts an impressionable homeless boy named Steven to join his freak show. Structurally similar to Charles Dickens' *A Christmas Carol*, *The Last Temptation* is a whimsical and demented story about faith and temptation (Campbell 174-177).

Cooper's album was released on July 12, 1994, but prior to that, a bidding war had ensued among three publishers to adapt Gaiman's plot into a comic book. Marvel won the rights because Cooper enjoyed his experience working on *Marvel Premiere* #50 (Oct. 1979), a one-issue adaptation of Cooper's 1978 concept album "From the Inside" about his stay at a New York sanitarium to treat his alcoholism. Michael Zulli, a frequent collaborator of Gaiman's and a big fan of Cooper, agreed to deliver the art for Marvel's three-issue mini-series, the first issue of which was included with the album (Grant 43).

The Last Temptation kicked off **Marvel Music**, an imprint edited by the former editor-in-chief of *Cracked* magazine and a man with an extensive background in both alternative comics and punk rock music, **Mort Todd**. Terry Stewart directed Todd to expand the scope of the imprint beyond "skinny white boys in black jeans" (Grossman). To that end, Marvel Music's offerings ran the gamut of music styles to include rap (*Break the Chain*, Kyle Baker's one-shot about the life of rapper KRS-One which came bagged with a free cassette tape), country (*Marty Stuart* and *Billy Ray Cyrus*, both of which were written by the prolific Paul S. Newman) and reggae (*Bob Marley: Tale of the Tuff Gong*). Marvel Music also released a collector's edition souvenir book for Woodstock '94 as well as Dave McKean's interpretation of the Rolling Stones' 1994 album, *Voodoo Lounge*.

Unfortunately, the Marvel Music imprint didn't last very long and for the simplest of reasons: it didn't sell very well. Todd believes Marvel had no one to blame but itself, "they just didn't have the marketing down. They didn't know how to sell anything that wasn't superheroes." Stewart, however, feels that the music artists themselves were at least partly responsible for Marvel Music not reaching its intended audience, "We tried getting artists to sell the books at shows, but that didn't work" (Grossman). Disgusted by the situation, Mort Todd didn't renew his contract, and by the end of 1995, Marvel Music was no more.

The Punisher Meets… Him? Really?!

Due to the success of Frank Miller and John Romita Jr.'s *Daredevil: The Man Without Fear*, Marvel put another origin story on its schedule, *Punisher: Year One* (first issue cover-dated Dec. 1994). Written by Dan Abnett and Andy Lanning, drawn by Dale Eaglesham and printed on glossy paper, the four-issue mini-series retells Frank Castle's transformation from Vietnam War veteran trying to raise a family to costumed vigilante waging a one-man war on crime.

Earlier in the year, **the Punisher** faced a "Suicide Run" in an eleven-issue story arc spanning all three of the character's on-going titles (*Punisher*, *Punisher War Journal* and *Punisher War Zone*). In the eventful tale, the Punisher's greatest surviving enemies come together to unleash a plan to crush the man they despise. The villains try to exploit Castle's greatest weaknesses: his hatred for criminals and his obsessive need to save innocents. In chapter one of the storyline, the Punisher is forced to bring a trigger that would explode a building resembling New York's World

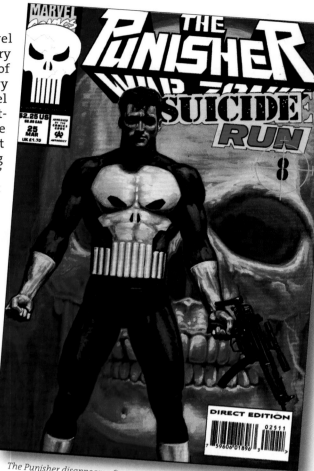

The Punisher disappears after an explosion in the World Trade Center in "Suicide Run." TM and © Marvel Characters, Inc.

Trade Center. After the bomb goes off but doesn't destroy the towers, the Punisher disappears. Several other people then throw on the skull emblazoned shirt to take their turn at being the Punisher. Among them are a mentally ill man, a Yuppie who wants to kill off his business rivals, a good cop gone bad, a British motorcyclist named "Outlaw," and a mob hitman. Eventually, Frank Castle becomes the Punisher again, but not before driving away all his erstwhile rivals and gaining his own revenge.

As momentous as "Suicide Run" was, nothing could top a different Punisher story from 1994, arguably the most bizarre intercompany crossover ever published in the history of comic books: *The Punisher Meets Archie*. Written by Batton Lash and drawn (in the Archie style) by Stan Goldberg and (in the Marvel style) by John Buscema, this oddball story begins with a notorious drug dealer on the run. That man's nickname is "Red," and he has some frightening problems: the mob is angry at him and the federal government is trying to arrest him.

In the most bizarre crossover in the history of comics, the Punisher travels to Riverdale to meet Archie.
The Punisher TM and © Marvel Characters, Inc. Archie and related characters TM and © Archie Comics Publications, Inc.

Worst of all for Red, the Punisher is hot on his heels, looking to turn him over to the FBI in exchange for a pardon. To escape the Punisher, Red flees to Riverdale, the wholesome town that is home to all-American teenager Archie Andrews. Unfortunately for Archie, he bears an uncanny resemblance to the red-headed fugitive criminal, so much so that the Punisher soon confuses the two, making Archie a target of Marvel's gun-toting vigilante.

The Punisher Meets Archie fits comfortably in both publishers' universes, with healthy doses of humor mixed with grim and gritty action. Perhaps as a concession to younger fans, though, there is less gunplay than was generally presented in Punisher stories. The concept for this wacky one-shot spawned from a dinner conversation between Tom DeFalco (then still Marvel's Editor-in-Chief) and Victor Gorelick (Archie Comics' Executive Editor) and several other longtime friends. Gorelick lamented to DeFalco that Archie didn't sell well in the Direct Market. As the discussion progressed, one of the men suggested a crossover with Marvel to help increase exposure. When someone proposed Archie meet the Punisher, the dinner table erupted in laughter. Several months later, while Lash and Gorelick were sharing a meal at a convention, Gorelick mentioned the Punisher/Archie idea. After considering the concept for a few days, Lash came up with an intriguing hook for a one-time meeting between the characters: "[The Punisher] goes to this town, which is a little more light-hearted than he's used to,

In a pair of one-shot crossovers, the Punisher met both the Bruce Wayne and Jean-Paul Valley version of the Batman. The Punisher TM and © Marvel Characters, Inc. Batman TM and © DC Comics.

and he enjoys it" (Johnson 47). Gorelick passed Lash's proposal on to Marvel whose executives approved the project. Marvel and Archie both released their own versions of the comic book on June 14, 1994. Marvel's had a cardboard diecut cover with the title *The Punisher Meets Archie* and cost $3.95. Archie's standard-format edition with the title *Archie Meets The Punisher* cost $2.95.

The Bat and the Bullets

The Punisher visited several surprising places in 1994. Along with Riverdale, Marvel's gun-toting vigilante also travelled to Gotham City where he teamed up with **Batman** in a pair of one-shot adventures proposed by someone who had extensive experience with both characters, **Chuck Dixon**. During the time he was writing several Batman and Punisher titles, Dixon approached his Marvel editor Don Daley and his **DC Comics** editor **Denny O'Neil** about an intercompany crossover involving both heroes. After conferring with their respective publishers, the two editors got the green light to produce the first DC/Marvel collaboration since 1982's *The Uncanny X-Men and the New Teen Titans*.

On the same day that *The Punisher Meets Archie* arrived in stores, DC released *Batman/Punisher: Lake of Fire*, written by O'Neil and illustrated by Barry Kitson and James Pascoe.

In the 48-page Prestige format comic the Punisher forms an uneasy alliance with the new Batman (a.k.a. Jean-Paul Valley) in order to stop the mobster Jigsaw from poisoning Gotham City's water supply. In the end, Jigsaw escapes imprisonment thanks to his new ally, the Joker, who wants Jigsaw to help him take control of the city's gangs. The story continues two months later in the Marvel-published *Punisher/Batman: Deadly Knights*, written by Chuck Dixon and drawn by John Romita Jr., and Klaus Janson, in which the Punisher returns to Gotham City to find Jigsaw. The Punisher finds himself at odds with Bruce Wayne, who unlike Valley, doesn't share his extreme crime-fighting methods.

Given how Frank Castle and Bruce Wayne both witnessed the deaths of their families, and how they both used their loss as their reason to combat crime, a Punisher/Batman team-up seemed not only natural but practically predestined. As O'Neil admitted at the time, "Punisher fits very, very comfortably into the Batman mythos" (Ringgenberg 75). Indeed, while most intercompany crossovers are considered inconsequential and having no bearing on the characters' personal histories (in other words, like exhibition baseball games, they don't really "count"), O'Neil actually incorporated *Lake of Fire* within Batman continuity, just in time for a crucial development in the Caped Crusader's life.

Bruce Wins Back the Bat Suit

Batman comics began 1994 with "Knightquest," an arc which split into two distinct storylines. "Knightquest: the Crusade" shows Jean-Paul Valley's increasingly violent approach in his war against crime. Driven by what he believes are commands from the ghosts of his ancestors, Valley massacres criminals with the nasty weapons in his armored uniform, including lasers, a flame-thrower and razor-sharp Batarangs. His cruelty causes deep friction between him and Batman's former allies. Longtime friends like Commissioner Gordon and Robin go so far as to shun Valley. The new Batman's actions come to a head when he encounters a serial killer named Abattoir who has imprisoned an innocent civilian in a secret torture chamber. After an intense battle, Valley allows Abattoir to die without determining the location of his hostage. Because of that decision, Abattoir's victim also dies. Knightquest's other storyline, "The Search", follows Bruce Wayne and Alfred through Europe as they try to find Tim Drake's father and Dr. Shondra Kinsolving. As the pair take part in thrilling adventures, Bruce's strength and confidence return. He is ready to go back to Gotham to reclaim his former title.

Upon the conclusion of "Knightquest," the ten-issue "KnightsEnd" immediately commences, involving nearly every Batman-affiliated title: *Batman*, *Detective Comics*, *Shadow of the Bat*, *Legends of the Dark Knight*, *Robin* and even *Catwoman*. In "KnightsEnd," Wayne comes home from Europe and confronts Valley, demanding he relinquish his role as Batman. Jean-Paul refuses, threatening to kill Wayne if he ever sets foot in the Batcave. Frustrated by his counterpart's hostility, Wayne makes a strategic retreat. To prepare himself for the coming war against his successor, Bruce seeks the mentorship of the assassin Lady Shiva, asking her to retrain him in the martial arts. After some rigorous training, the hero returns himself to fine physical form. This leads to the grand conclusion of years' worth of story arcs. In *Legends of the Dark Knight* #63 (Aug. 1994), Wayne and Valley confront each other in the caverns beneath the Batcave. Bruce, clad in the traditional Batman costume, challenges Jean-Paul, who wears his armored suit. Valley has cutting-edge weapons and a tenacious fighting spirit, but Wayne has experience and strategy on his side. Rather than battle his usurper in hand-to-hand combat, Bruce escapes into a cavern too small for his armored counterpart to climb into. When Valley takes off his armor to continue his pursuit, Bruce opens a hatch to the outside. Sunlight streams in, temporarily blinding his successor. In that instant,

The "KnightsEnd" story arc culminates Bruce Wayne resuming as role as Batman.
TM and © DC Comics.

Valley literally and symbolically sees the light, conceding, "You are Batman... and I am nothing." After a painful struggle that lasted nearly a year, Bruce Wayne is Batman once again.

Fan reaction at the time made it hard to tell if readers were more excited about Bruce Wayne's return or Jean-Paul Valley's defeat. As Chuck Dixon reported, "We wanted Jean-Paul to be despised, and I'm afraid we did our job all too well. The readers hate him, and we're not too fond of him either" (Shutt 75). Denny O'Neil, however, expressed sympathy for the character. Along with his *Lake of Fire* collaborator, Barry Kitson, O'Neil helmed an ongoing *Azrael* solo series (first issue cover-dated Feb. 1995) that sold moderately well. As far as the Batman titles went, sales drifted downward after Bruce reassumed his role as the Caped Crusader, a sure sign that readers were suffering from "event fatigue." Overall, though, the "Knightfall" saga sold better than issues that preceded Bane's breaking of Batman's back.

Though many fans were excited to see the return of the original Batman, an entirely different Batman comic won critical favor in 1994. *The Batman Adventures: Mad Love* by Paul Dini and artist Bruce Timm delivered a one-shot set in the world of *Batman: the Animated Series. Mad Love* told the origin of the Joker's companion and lover, **Harley Quinn**. As psychologist Harleen Quenzel treats the Joker at Arkham Asylum, she also falls in love with him – and then goes mad herself. Harleen dons a Harlequin's outfit and teams up with her lover to wreak havoc throughout Gotham City. The one-shot won an Eisner Award for "Best Single Issue."

Hal Jordan goes insane as a result of the events of "Emerald Twilight."
TM and © DC Comics.

The All-New Green Lantern

While Bruce Wayne had a challenging 1994, no DC character had a tougher year than Hal Jordan, a.k.a. **Green Lantern**. In fact, his problems started in 1993 at the end of the "Reign of the Supermen" saga. That tale of the return of Superman includes a decisive chapter in *Green Lantern* #46 (Oct. 1993) in which the powerful Mongul utterly devastates Hal's hometown of Coast City in order to turn it into an enormous engine that will transform Earth into a war world. Hal hurries to his city, only to find it completely annihilated and the voices of the dead crying out in his mind. Hal defeats Mongul in a titanic struggle, but the desolation of Coast City leads to the shattering **"Emerald Twilight"** story arc, beginning in *Green Lantern* #48 (Jan. 1994). A distraught Hal uses his ring to re-create Coast City and all the people he loves, restored from his memories. Seeking comfort, Hal visits with the hallucinations of an old girlfriend and his parents. The serenity lasts barely a moment before Hal is confronted by the image of one of his mentors, the Guardians of the Universe, who reprimands Hal for using his power ring for personal gain. The Guardian further orders Hal to surrender his ring. Hal is driven so mad by this command that he journeys to Oa, the Guardians' home planet, to murder them. Fellow Green Lanterns attempt to stop him, but when Hal defeats them, he steals their rings. Then in *Green Lantern* #50 (March 1994), written by **Ron Marz** and drawn by **Darryl Banks**, Hal has become so powerful he is able to destroy Oa's Central Power Battery, killing all the Guardians save one. Wearing a new costume, Hal streaks to the center of the galaxy, ready to wreak more destruction. Readers would have to wait a few months for the publication of DC's big 1994 event comic to learn of Hal's next move, but in the meantime, the sole surviving Guardian, Ganthet, visits Earth to find Hal Jordan's replacement. When he comes across a vain, young artist, he declares, "you shall have to do." He gives the young man a power ring and with that, **Kyle Rayner** becomes the new Green Lantern.

The decision to replace Hal Jordan came from editor **Kevin Dooley**. When monthly sales of *Green Lantern* dropped below 40,000 copies, Dooley concluded that comic book readers looked at Hal Jordan as a hero from a previous generation, seemingly out of step with the types of protagonists demanded by fans in the 1990s. Dooley and DC's editorial team then considered several options to reviving the series before ultimately deciding to follow a recent DC pattern. "The Death of Superman" and "Knightfall" had boosted the popularity of Superman and Batman comics by removing their title characters. A similarly radical change was needed to save *Green Lantern* from cancellation. To say the least, longtime Hal Jordan fans disapproved of the plot twist, but as Dooley put it, he had few alternatives in the matter, "Would [readers] rather have had it stay the same and have the book be cancelled, or try something different and keep the book and title with the essence of the character going?" (Darnall and Wenberg 73). Dooley recruited Ron Marz to script the adventures of the new Green Lantern, an apt choice considering the writer's three-year long tenure on Marvel's sci-fi super-hero series, *Silver Surfer*. Marz, however, had qualms about the assignment because it was a drastic departure from the status quo. After mulling over Dooley's offer, Marz decided the opportunity to create an entirely new Green Lantern was too good to pass up. As Marz explained to *American Comic Book Chronicles*, "the real trick, the real task, was creating a Green Lantern who could stand on his own and retain the audience in the wake of Hal giving up the mantle. That challenge was the attraction."

And without a doubt, Kyle Rayner was a completely different character from his gray-templed predecessor. Neither fearless nor completely honest, Rayner was a deeply flawed young man, forced to learn his skills on the job and mature into a true hero. Despite Darryl Banks providing Rayner with a flashy new costume that was more in line with the aesthetics of the times, fans were still slow to embrace the new Green Lantern in the aftermath of Hal Jordan's fall from grace. (Indeed, several fans upset with the course of events sent death threats to Marz on the mistaken belief that he pitched Hal Jordan's turn to evil rather than had it dictated to him by editorial fiat.) Acceptance of Rayner, though, grew gradually, evolving out of the new status quo. Kyle had no Green Lantern Corps to help him nor any experience in using his ring. In his early fights, Rayner often stumbled onto winning strategies. As Marz stated, "We wanted to get back down to one guy, one ring, and play this as something powerful and unique" (O'Neill 43).

Sales picked up with "Emerald Twilight," and for the remainder of the decade *Green Lantern* often sold in the

With Hal Jordan's fall from grace, Kyle Rayner becomes the new Green Lantern.
TM and © DC Comics.

month's top 50 comics. Though Rayner gained fans as he learned how to use his ring, the horrors in one issue angered many readers. In *Green Lantern* #54 (Aug. 1994), by Marz, Banks and Derec Aucoin, Rayner returns home after a battle to discover his girlfriend Alex murdered by a villain called Major Force. Making matters worse, Major Force had stuffed her body into a refrigerator. That cruel butchery became symbolic for a group of fans led by future comic writer **Gail Simone**. In 1999 Simone and her partners launched the website "Women in Refrigerators" in order to list the many ways women in adventure hero stories are killed, maimed or injured as springboards for a male hero's success. Simone's intention with "Women in Refrigerators" was to create a safe environment for women to read comics, and the site's commentary eventually provoked changes in the way the industry treated female characters.

After piranhas chew off his left hand, Aquaman puts on a hook, dons a new costume and develops a new attitude. TM and © DC Comics.

Green Lantern wasn't the only iconic DC hero to experience a dramatic transformation in 1994. Starting in *Aquaman* #1 (Aug. 1994), writer Peter David and artists Martin Egeland and Brad Vancata delivered a shocking new take on the King of the Seven Seas. Swimming out of the 1993 David-scripted *Aquaman: Time and Tide* mini-series, the first arc of the ongoing series concludes with a dreadful incident: piranhas chewing off Aquaman's left hand while he grapples with the evil Charybdis. The hero is furious at the vicious attack and at his betrayal by sea creatures. In a symbol of that anger, he replaces his hand with a harpoon. With unkempt long hair and a beard, Aquaman's very appearance demonstrates his fierce new approach to life. The previously moribund protagonist now embodied a defiant 1990s attitude. Nonetheless, David had to persuade his editors to agree to his ideas for the series: "We had to show that we really had creative concerns in mind and that we weren't desperate to do something to goose sales" (Shutt 60). The drastic change captured fans' attention. Aquaman was no longer a has-been super-hero. He was a formidable warrior who kicked as much butt as any other DC star.

The Clock Reaches Zero

Aquaman represented the latest DC super-hero to undergo a significant makeover. Unfortunately, by 1994, the disparate revamping of so many DC super-heroes caused the company's fictional continuity—which had been restarted barely nine years earlier with the publication of *Crisis on Infinite Earths*—to become overly convoluted and, in some cases, downright self-contradictory. No one seemed more frustrated by this fact than writer/artist **Dan Jurgens**. His annoyance dated back to a Superman story he created for *Action Comics* #650 (Feb. 1990), a celebratory issue which guest-starred many other DC super-heroes. In that story, Jurgens planned to reference a meeting that occurred between the Man of Steel and Hawkman in *Superman* #18 (June 1988). Jurgens was quickly informed, however, that Hawkman's personal history had been so completely overhauled by Tim Truman's 1989 *Hawkworld* mini-series that the 1988 meeting between the two characters was now out of continuity. In other words, by 1990, it was as if

Zero Hour reset the DC Universe for the 1990s and established Hal Jordan as the villain Parallax. TM and © DC Comics.

Superman and Hawkman had never met, despite evidence to the contrary. These kinds of problems only compounded with every passing year, and eventually, Jurgens couldn't make sense of DC's new continuity. And if Jurgens had a problem keeping everything straight, he knew the fans had to be even more confused: "I looked at the DC Universe as having a lot of problems with continuity. Even more important [was] the fan's ability to grasp and understand the characters. That was DC's biggest problem" (Fritz 44).

Jurgens felt something had to be done, so he voiced his concerns to DC's management, and after a series of conversations, he was tapped to write and pencil a five-issue, weekly mini-series that would clarify DC's past and present: *Zero Hour: Crisis in Time*. DC promoted the series as its most important event since *Crisis on Infinite Earths*. In fact, DC hoped *Zero Hour* would not only clean up some of the anomalies produced in recent years but also stimulate sales across the line.

Culminating a three chapter *Zero Hour* prelude, *Showcase '94* #9 presents Hank Hall, a.k.a. Monarch, the villain of 1991's *Armageddon 2001* event, stealing Waverider's temporal wristband to become a powerful entity called Extant. Two weeks later, *Zero Hour* officially launched with issue #4 (cover date Sept. 1994). (The five-issue series would "count down" to issue #0.) With his new powers, Extant goes to the end of time and begins to erase history. An alarmed Waverider travels through time to enlist allies who can help him combat the unprecedented threat. One of the most important heroes Waverider recruits is Wally West, the Flash. In a moment that echoes the death of his mentor Barry Allen in *Crisis on Infinite Earths*, Wally appears to perish in an attempt to stop Extant. Flash's apparent death pushes most of Earth's super-heroes to get involved, and the ensuing war between good and evil spans five increasingly desperate chapters before Hal Jordan, fully embracing his anger as the star-destroying Parallax,

Zero Hour presented a chance for DC to reform its tangled continuity around characters like Hawkman. TM and © DC Comics.

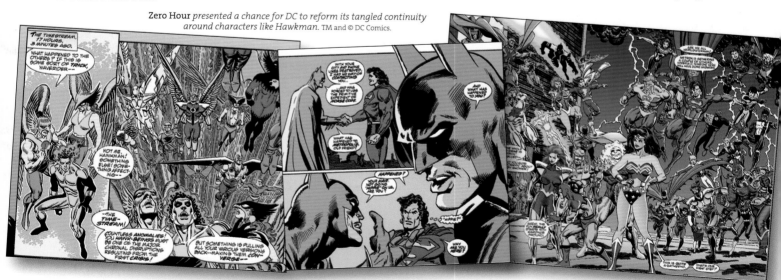

steals Extant's power so he can re-write the history of the universe as he sees fit. For a brief moment, it seems Parallax will succeed, but just as he declares himself ruler of the universe, Green Arrow shoots an arrow through Parallax's heart. Before dying from his wound, Hal Jordan repents of his evil by reversing all the devastation he caused and re-aligning history. Green Arrow has saved all of existence, but he has also killed his best friend. It was a bittersweet conclusion that resonated with many readers.

Though many debated whether *Zero Hour* ended up correcting or complicating DC's continuity, it sold extremely well. *Zero Hour* #4 was DC's best-selling comic book of 1994 according to Diamond Distributors. That achievement helped bring attention to some major changes to many of DC's titles. Wally West's apparent death launched the "Terminal Velocity" storyline in *Flash*, a six-issue arc that not only reveals that Wally didn't actually die but also spotlights the next generation of super-speedster, a hyperactive boy from the 30th century who happens to be Barry Allen's grandson, Bart Allen. With the codename **Impulse**, Bart becomes the Flash's sidekick (a partnership that Wally soon finds exasperating). Impulse would run into his own series in 1995. Elsewhere, the Team Titans are revealed to be Extant's brainwashed pawns. That group of super-heroes disappear from history only two years after their debut. Guy Gardner discovers his alien heritage and gains amazing new powers in the pages of *Guy Gardner, Warrior*. *Green Arrow* introduces Oliver Queen's son and eventual successor, Connor Hawke. As *Hawkman* resumed, the title character was meant to represent a consolidation of all earlier incarnations of the hero. No series was as profoundly affected as the Legion of Super-Heroes, whose old continuity was tied off during *Zero Hour* before a reconceived version of the team was unveiled in its eponymous book and its companion title, *Legionnaires*. Justice Society members Hourman, Atom and Doctor Fate met their demise while several of their teammates aged into senior citizens. Jurgens actually proposed the surviving JSA members receive their own alternate Earth to live on, but DC editorial ultimately rejected the idea (Cronin, #599).

The same month *Zero Hour* #0 arrived in stores (August 1994), DC delivered an unprecedented stunt. For all of its mainline super-hero titles, including 50-year-old series like *Action Comics* and *Detective Comics*, DC published a "zero issue" which re-told the origin of either the title's main character or a key villain.

Man of the Stars

DC launched six new series during "zero month." Five of the six didn't last long. *Fate* by John Francis Moore, Anthony Williams and Andy Lanning put the power of Doctor Fate in the hands of a cynical "procurer of rare artifacts," empowered to find a mystic balance in the DC Universe. *Manhunter* by Steven Grant and Vince Giarrano delivered a new take on the classic DC adventurer as a man possessed by a creature from British folklore. *Xenobrood* by Doug Moench, Tomm Coker and Keith Aiken centered on an archaeologist's discovery of four mystical characters. *Primal Force* by Steven T. Seagle, Ken Hooper and Barbara Kaalberg brought together a group of super-heroes who patrolled

the darker corners of the DC Universe. *R.E.B.E.L.S.* '94 by Tom Peyer, Arnie Jorgensen and James Pascoe set up the warriors from the earlier *L.E.G.I.O.N.* '94 series as fugitives from justice.

DC's sixth new book proved to be one of the most popular and acclaimed comics of the 1990s. It was the brainchild of writer **James Robinson**, who, after completing *The Golden Age* mini-series in 1993, wanted his next DC project to be something momentous, something that would appeal to a more mature reader and stand side-by-side with the most celebrated works from the previous decade like Alan Moore's *Swamp Thing* and Frank Miller's *Batman: Year One*, which Robinson considered "one of the greatest works of all time" (Curtin 36). After spending over a year brainstorming with editor Archie Goodwin, Robinson had formulated the groundwork for his magnum opus: **Starman**.

Intimately tied to DC's long history, *Starman* featured a legacy character while still maintaining a modern approach to heroism. Robinson wrote the series with passion and precise foreshadowing while **Tony Harris** supplied distinctive art deco-inspired visuals. As *Starman* #0 begins, David Knight, the son of the Golden Age

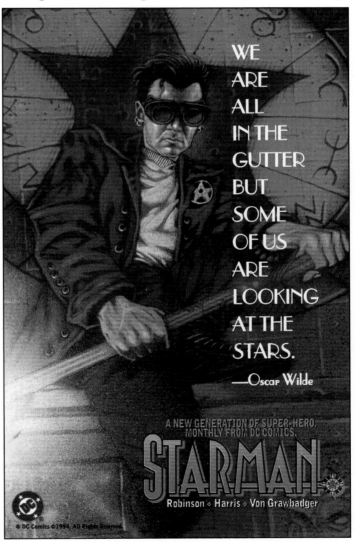

WE ARE ALL IN THE GUTTER BUT SOME OF US ARE LOOKING AT THE STARS.
—Oscar Wilde

A NEW GENERATION OF SUPER-HERO, MONTHLY FROM DC COMICS.

STARMAN

Robinson ◆ Harris ◆ Von Grawbadger

One of the key series spun out of Zero Hour *was* Starman *by James Robinson and Tony Harris.* TM and © DC Comics.

Starman Ted Knight, is ready to assume his valiant legacy. Proudly wearing his father's gaudy green and red costume, David prepares to patrol Opal City... but is suddenly shot down from the night skies by some petty criminals. When his body crashes to the streets below, David is dead. The Starman legacy thus falls to David's brother, but Jack Knight is poles apart from the rest of his family. He doesn't crave the super-heroic limelight. He just wants to run his antique shop, collect bakelite pottery, and live his own life. In the wake of his brother's murder, however, the reluctant twentysomething chooses to honor his family legacy, but on his own terms. Rather than wear a flashy lycra suit, Jack dons a t-shirt, a pair of jeans, a leather jacket and aviator goggles to fight his nemeses. Rather than use his father's old cosmic rod, he transforms the rod into an ornate staff. In fact, Jack really doesn't see himself as a hero at all. He never assumes the Starman moniker, and he is always a bit starstruck when around his fellow adventurers. Jack simply sees himself as an ordinary, flawed man doing his best to help improve the world. As such, he was the ideal protagonist for mature fans who appreciated tradition but who also delighted in doing things their own way. Like many men his age, the younger Knight loves his dad but remains frustrated by him. Jack craves Ted's love, though their approaches to the world are very different from each other. In one of the comic's most heartening series-long subplots, father and son ultimately bridge the emotional gap that separates them, each respecting the choices the other made with his life.

Starman was unlike any series produced by DC, or any other comic book publisher for that matter. Incidents were more unpredictable and presented in a more unconventional manner than in other comics. Romances took unexpected twists and turns, similar to experiences in real life. Jack's battles often lacked a clear hero or villain. Extended storylines frequently ambled into tangents before arriving at endings that often felt anticlimactic. Robinson would share Knight's thoughts in long, meandering monologues that provided ironic commentary on the issue's action. The series' expansive cast included David's ghost, who would pay Jack a visit once a year, and the two brothers would mainly talk for an entire issue. Periodically, Harris skipped a month on art chores while Robinson and a guest artist delivered a one-shot "Times Past" story that focused on some of the other characters who called themselves Starman throughout DC history. Most of all, Jack Knight matured over the course of the series' eighty-issue run, which set him apart from nearly all other super-heroes.

With One Magic Word!

The new Starman had deep roots in the past while looking towards the future. DC's 1994 reboot of **Captain Marvel** showed reverence for the past in a different way. Longtime DC creator **Jerry Ordway** wrote, drew and painted the 94-page deluxe graphic novel *The Power of Shazam*. In this origin story, a ghostly stranger entices young orphan Billy Batson into a mysterious Fawcett City subway tunnel. At the end of an abandoned section of track, the boy encounters a bizarre and seemingly ageless wizard named Shazam. Muttering the wizard's name, Billy transforms into a tall, muscled adult with a bright red costume and the powers of flight, super-strength and invulnerability. For an instant after he changes, Billy hesitates. He isn't ready to have these amazing abilities and doesn't want to be old, but when the wizard tells Billy his new persona will help him find his parents' murderer, Billy agrees to become a hero. He launches himself into a complex battle that includes his mighty nemesis Black Adam and Adam's billionaire ally, Dr. Sivana.

Ever since the publication of *Crisis on Infinite Earths*, various creators endeavored to make the former Fawcett Comics icon a major DC universe character. Most prominent among those creators was Roy Thomas, whose contract with DC granted him the right of first refusal to script a Captain Marvel comic book. In 1987, Thomas wrote a four-issue *Shazam!* mini-series that was intended as a springboard for an ongoing Captain Marvel title. Unfortunately, DC fumbled the launch of that comic, and Thomas's contractual exclusivity to the character expired (Sullivan 24). Up next was John Byrne who expressed his interest in rebooting the character, much like he did with Superman in 1986. But when Byrne faced resistance from DC's editors, he moved on to other projects (Smith). Ordway then stepped forward with his own plans. His take on the costumed character was originally planned for release in February 1992. However, the popular artist became sidetracked by the

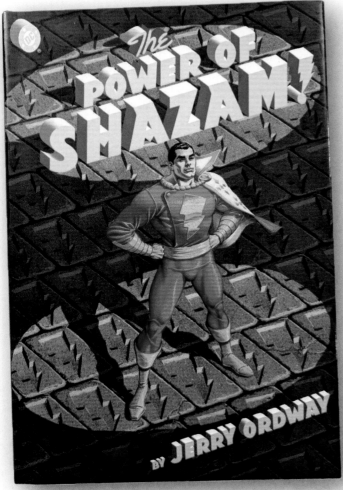

Jerry Ordway reformed Captain Marvel by embracing his 1940s roots in The Power of Shazam! *TM and © DC Comics.*

APRIL 1994

The much-anticipated rematch between Superman and Doomsday appeared in Superman/Doomsday: Hunter/Prey. TM and © DC Comics.

"Death of Superman" storyline and his creator-owned work for Image Comics, *Wildstar: Sky Zero*. Once those projects completed, Ordway devoted himself to *The Power of Shazam*. He wanted to incorporate retro-futuristic visuals as a way to contrast decades-old characters with modern day sensibilities. To that end, Ordway studied art deco designs, making them key visuals elements of his story.

The graphic novel Ordway ultimately produced presented an updated version of the legendary super-hero that still echoed his 1940s origins. A sales and critical success despite its $19.95 cover price, *The Power of Shazam* fulfilled its goal of generating significant reader interest in Captain Marvel. An ongoing *Power of Shazam* series, written by Ordway, launched with a March 1995 cover date. *Flash* artist Mike Wieringo was originally set to draw the title, but when he opted for an assignment on *Robin*, Peter Krause took his place and remained on the series for over three years (Smith).

Heavyweight Rematch

When Superman returned from the dead in 1993, readers naturally wondered when the monster responsible for his death, Doomsday, would also be resurrected for "round two" of his fight against the Man of Steel. The answer came

in 1994 with the three-part, squarebound mini-series ***Superman/Doomsday: Hunter/Prey***, courtesy of writer/artist Dan Jurgens. After he receives evidence that Doomsday is alive and on the distant planet of Apokolips, Superman vows to stop the mindless killing machine. With the aid of a Mother Box, Superman travels to Apokolips, only to find the planet—and its all-powerful ruler, Darkseid—devastated from Doomsday's attacks. As Superman prepares to confront the murderous juggernaut, the time-traveling Waverider informs him about Doomsday's origins, which had remained a mystery up until this point. Born on Krypton, hundreds of thousands of years before Superman's birth, Doomsday began his life as an evolutionary experiment, killed and cloned over and over again until he developed into an indestructible killing machine that hated all life. Because of his adaptive capabilities, Doomsday cannot be defeated the same way twice. This ominous revelation

forces Superman to figure out a different way to overcome the monster, all the while confronting his fears of dying again. Superman engages Doomsday, a losing struggle for the Man of Steel but just as all looks lost, Superman uses one of Waverider's temporal devices to transport Doomsday to the end of time where he is crushed by a force he can't adapt to: universal entropy. Relieved that he has ended the threat of Doomsday once and for all, Superman has also redeemed his own legacy.

Hunter/Prey was originally planned to launch in November 1993, one year after "The Death of Superman," but the busy creative team didn't have enough time to flesh out all the story details. DC finally released the three-parter

Overcoming his own insecurities and fears, Superman defeats Doomsday.
TM and © DC Comics.

beginning April 1994. Unusual for the time, the $4.95 cover-priced books contained no cover enhancements.

The Superman family of titles expanded in 1994 as three key supporting characters received their own titles. *Superboy*, an ongoing series by Karl Kesel and Tom Grummett, moved Superman's young clone to Hawaii where he fought super-villains in light-hearted adventures. The ongoing *Steel*, by Louise Simonson, Jon Bogdanove and Chris Batista, set the armored adventurer in Washington, D.C. while the four-issue *Supergirl* mini-series, written by Roger Stern and drawn by June Brigman, ended the Matrix Supergirl's romance with Lex Luthor when she discovered proof of his true villainy.

Another memorable DC event of 1994 was the **"Worlds Collide"** crossover, encompassing fourteen issues from eight different titles. The storyline brought the Superman family of heroes into contact with their counterparts from Milestone Media. The tale begins with Fred Bentson, a postal worker who has the power to traverse universes, traveling back and forth between Dakota, the home city of the Milestone heroes, and Metropolis, where Superman resides. One day an experiment causes him to lose control of his power, and the two universes merge, putting Dakota and Metropolis side-by-side each other. Inevitably, the Milestone and DC heroes meet, their contrasting personalities and approaches coming into conflict. Arrogant young Superboy and Static throw attitude at each other, Hardware and Steel argue about whether to execute a criminal, and the similarly-powered Icon and Superman come to realize how differently they operate. Eventually, the heroes put aside their differences in order to seal the rift that connects their worlds.

Louise Simonson and Milestone Publisher Dwayne McDuffie conceived the crossover one day when they agreed how fun it would be if the two characters they were handling, Steel and Hardware, met each other. After all, while both characters derived their power from armored suits, they had opposing personalities. That thought sparked further conversation as the possibility of more Milestone/DC team-ups stuck in everybody's heads. McDuffie and DC publisher Paul Levitz quickly approved the storyline, which appeared in issues of *Man of Steel*, *Superboy*, *Steel*, *Icon*, *Static*, *Hardware*, *Blood Syndicate* and a *Worlds Collide* one-shot. Milestone executives hoped the crossover would lead to increased sales for their line, which was greatly needed. As Creative Director Denys Cowan reflected at the time, "I have been completely surprised by the resistance our books have received from the direct market. I didn't expect the scale of resistance we've seen" (Shutt 81). Many believed the comics market just wasn't yet ready to embrace the multicultural approach Milestone took to its heroes. Unfortunate if true, since diversity was what made Milestone distinctive in the first place. Sales on the "Worlds Collide" issues were higher than expected, with many issues receiving second printings. Unfortunately, the bump proved short-lived as sales on Milestone series returned to their tepid levels once the event ended.

"Worlds Collide" crossed over the Milestone Comics heroes with the Superman line, in an attempt to spur sales on the flagging Milestone imprint.

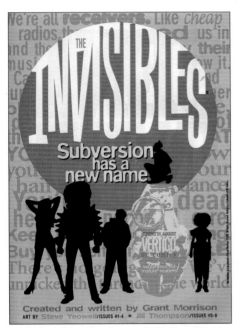

The Invisibles *offered a pure distillation of Grant Morrison's view of reality.* TM and © Grant Morrison.

A Comic Book Hand Grenade

Grant Morrison was one of the writers most responsible for the founding of DC's Vertigo line. He first gained attention for his bold, complex and often surreal writing on *Doom Patrol* and *Animal Man* from 1988 to 1992. That material presented state-of-the-art stories with postmodern approaches to character and plot. When DC announced a new Morrison Vertigo series, fans buzzed with excitement about his next innovations. Nobody was truly ready for the odd collection of ideas he delivered, though. In an era when many comics could be described in a mere handful of words, *The Invisibles* defied easy description. As one of the series' main characters, King Mob, describes the storyline: "it's a thriller, it's a romance, it's a tragedy, it's porno, it's neo-modernist kitchen sink science fiction that you *catch*, like a cold." Fittingly, the cover of the first issue (published with a cover date of September 1994) was a full-size illustration of a hand grenade because Morrison's opus resembled an explosion – or perhaps it reminded people of an idea delivered from outer space. That was appropriate, too, since Morrison claimed more than once that *The Invisibles* was a story told to him when space aliens kidnapped him in Katmandu.

On the surface, the bizarre series appeared to be a typical good versus evil adventure, presenting a war between The Secret College and the Invisible Kings of the World. The villains look like alien kings from another dimension who team with telepathic British aristocrats to hunt homeless people for sport. The heroes, on the other hand, are a trio that includes King Mob, a tough psychic superspy; Lord Fanny, a cross-dressing Brazilian Bruja; and Jack Frost, an anarchistic thug-slash-messiah from Liverpool. But there was much more going on in this series beneath the surface than some initially realized. As critic Douglas Wolk states, "It is, in a lot of ways, my favorite comic book ever, and I have never been able to recommend it to anyone else with a clear conscience, partly because it's such a ridiculous mess in so many ways" (Wolk 260). The reader's perception of heroes and villains, of truth and fiction, and even of the relationship between character and observer, shifts from issue to issue and sometimes from panel to panel. People who seem unimportant on a first read grow crucial on re-reading. Plot threads change significantly from page to page. All concepts of linearity shatter as the looping storylines deliver unique experiences. As such, *The Invisibles* is as much a meditation on the nature of reality and observation as it is a straightforward adventure tale. For this reason, many critics feel this series is the purest distillation of Grant Morrison's view of the world.

Perhaps not surprising given its unusual themes and unconventional narrative, *The Invisibles* suffered low sales at first. The deliberately oblique approach to plot alienated many casual consumers. In a wild idea to stimulate sales, Morrison suggested all *Invisibles* fans masturbate on the same day while meditating on the same magic thought to charge up sales. As ludicrous as Morrison's "wankathon" sounds, *The Invisibles* still lasted until its planned conclusion in 2000 and is a bestseller in trade paperback.

Men in Long Capes

Though Morrison gained the most attention for his work on *The Invisibles*, he also wrote other comics in 1994. Among them was a three-issue run on *Spawn*, with art by Greg Capullo. That trio of fill-in issues were necessary because **Todd McFarlane** was busy collaborating with writer **Frank Miller** on one of the best-selling books of the year. Ever since Spawn debuted in 1992, fans clamored for a team-up between that character and Batman. With a pair of one-shots cover-dated May 1994, that meeting transpired via two different creative teams. DC Comics published *Batman/Spawn: War Devil*, by Doug Moench, Chuck Dixon, Alan Grant and Klaus Janson while **Image Comics** published *Spawn/Batman*, by Miller and McFarlane.

Instead of meeting Valeria the She-Bat, Spawn met Batman in two major 1994 crossovers. Spawn TM and © Todd McFarlane Productions, Inc. Batman TM and © DC Comics.

War Devil brought Spawn to Gotham City, where the anti-hero searched for clues about his mysterious life before his resurrection. In the course of that search, Spawn encounters Batman, and the pair soon team up to combat a demonic force called the War Devil, the creature responsible for the disappearance of a legendary lost Gotham colony. *War Devil* reveals part of Spawn's origin as the two heroes battle zombies and other evil creatures – all the while loudly arguing with each other.

Different creative teams delivered each of the Batman/Spawn crossovers.
Spawn TM and © Todd McFarlane Productions, Inc. Batman TM and © DC Comics.

Spawn/Batman, Miller's first work on the Dark Knight since 1987's much-loved "Batman: Year One," presents an all-out action story as Batman and Spawn battle drifters and winos transformed into cyborg killing machines. Just as in the DC one-shot, the two iconic heroes hate each other. As McFarlane put it, the relationship was "like a buddy movie gone wrong" (Darnall 72). Miller described the team-up as "an action-packed, straight-ahead action story. There's not a lot of quiet scenes" (Cadenhead 35). As might be expected, fans had divergent opinions of each comic. For instance, *Sandman* and *A Distant Soil* artist Colleen Doran reviewed the two one-shots in *Hero Illustrated*. She called the DC team-up a "mega-yawner" while the Image one-shot was "fantastic entertainment" with "droll, black humor," a "quirky, energetic sense of design" and "clear, concise storytelling" (Doran 34).

Because of this major crossover, McFarlane cancelled a different team-up previously announced in magazines like *Comic Shop News*, *Hero Illustrated,* and *Wizard*. In fact, the event was even initially solicited through distributors. Spawn was slated to meet Continuity Comics' Valeria the She-Bat in a pair of special issues. McFarlane didn't just cancel the project because he wanted to concentrate on the much more lucrative Batman meeting; he also complained of Continuity Studios' chronic lateness. The canceled crossover hastened the demise of Continuity's line.

Besides Morrison and Capullo, McFarlane also hired several other creators to deliver work for him in 1994. One of them was **Alan Moore** who wrote a three-issue *Violator* mini-series, drawn by Bart Sears and Mark Pennington. Spawn and his nemesis Violator are forced to team up to fight a war against demons from Hell. Later in the year McFarlane gave **Neil Gaiman** the opportunity to return to Angela, the supporting character the writer created for *Spawn* in 1993, for a three-issue mini-series drawn by Greg Capullo. Gaiman enjoyed writing the straightforward adventure story that he

intended for his ten-year-old son, an avid fan of the *X-Men* animated cartoon (Campbell 147).

Angela, however, led to more problems than anyone could have expected. After the publication of the mini-series (and subsequent trade paperback collections), McFarlane refused to pay Gaiman any royalties from the project due to the absence of any written contract between the two men. (Evidently, McFarlane and Gaiman only had a verbal agreement.) What's more, McFarlane insisted that all the work Gaiman produced for *Spawn* was "work-for-hire," which meant Gaiman didn't own any rights to any of the characters he created for the series which includes not only Angela, but also Cogliostro and Medieval Spawn, all of whom continued to appear as major figures in future *Spawn* stories. McFarlane's toy company, Todd Toys, even manufactured action figures of all three characters. When pressed, McFarlane pointed to the legal notices that appeared in *Spawn* which indicated that all copyrights belonged solely to him. The irony of the situation seemed obvious to many observers: McFarlane formed Image Comics in part to protest how Marvel Comics treated its creators, and now McFarlane was treating Gaiman in the same manner. The legal battle over Angela, Cogliostro and Medieval Spawn extended well beyond the 1990s, complicated by McFarlane's quixotic attempts to buy the rights to Miracleman, a character which Gaiman partially owned.

The Thirteenth Generation

Jim Lee's Wildstorm Studios delivered Image Comics' biggest hit of the year: the five-issue *Gen¹³* by Lee, Brandon Choi and emerging superstar artist **J. Scott Campbell**. Described by Lee as "more offbeat" than most other superhero comics (Samsel 3), *Gen¹³* presents five super-powered teenagers, Eddie Chang, Caitlin Fairchild, Bobby Lane, Sarah Rainmaker and Roxy Spaulding, who escape a government prison for "gen-active teens." Rather than use their super-powers to fight evil, they mainly just want to hang out and party. Through their shared experiences, the teens develop close friendships and fall in and out of love with each other. Eventually, *Gen¹³* revealed its protagonists are the children of another Jim Lee group, Team 7, and the series shifted to the heroes learning about their heritages. These teens had complicated and ever-changing lives,

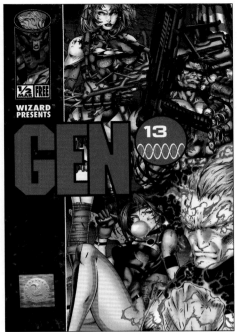

Gen¹³ was one of the hottest debut comics of 1994.
TM and © WildStorm Publications, an imprint of DC Comics.

displayed in an ongoing series that followed the miniseries. Within the first two years of their ongoing title, Fairchild and Spaulding learned they were half-sisters, while Rainmaker revealed she was bisexual.

Gen¹³ felt like a Marvel mutant title. Quite a few observers saw this new team as a version of the X-Men that fit Lee's approach to comics. Rainmaker had weather-controlling powers like Storm. Spaulding had a personality that resembled Jubilee's as well as an odd pet called Qeelocke which evoked Kitty Pryde's pet dragon Lockheed. Attentive readers noted other similarities, but *Gen¹³* was lighter-hearted than *X-Men* and its related titles. As Choi reflected, "[Lee] thought it would be interesting to take a different twist, more geared toward teenagers and the younger crowd, which wouldn't be so heavy into this grim storytelling" (Harris 69). Early ads promoted the series as

Generation X before Marvel announced its own new offering of the same name. Jim Lee and Brandon Choi cited other influences for their comic, such as Douglas Coupland's bestselling 1991 novel *Generation X* and DC's cheerful *Legionnaires* series. After the bestselling mini, Lee, Choi and Campbell quickly launched an ongoing. That first issue, *Gen¹³* #1 (March 1995), featured 13 variant covers which paid tribute not only to other famous comic book covers, like Todd McFarlane's *Spider-Man* #1, but also such pop culture items as a Janet Jackson album cover and the *Pulp Fiction* film poster, among others. Many of those variant covers appeared in a list of the most sought-after back issues throughout the remainder of the decade.

Though *Gen¹³* was a big hit for Image, the company faced plummeting sales across its line. In 1992 and 1993 many Image titles sold more than 500,000 copies per issue. By the middle of 1994, an Image comic that sold 250,000 copies was considered a bestseller. Besides their decaying sales, several Image founders also had to deal with struggles as they merchandised their characters. One of the most heated skirmishes occurred over animation produced for a proposed cartoon series featuring Rob Liefeld's *Youngblood*. At the beginning of the year, Liefeld's manager had preliminary commitments from both CBS-TV and a home video distributor to produce an animated version of his super-hero saga. Those deals fell through, and a lawsuit over the videos eventually resulted. Liefeld requested Roustabout, the studio that created the work, hand over 2,000 animation cells and master tapes. Roustabout refused, and the battle ended up in Los Angeles Superior Court, which ruled Liefeld had no rights to the work done on his creations due to the terms of their contract (Carlson 17).

Image released Gen¹³ #1 *with thirteen variant comics, including covers that paid homage to* Spider-Man *and* Pulp Fiction.
TM and © WildStorm Publications, an imprint of DC Comics.

In its third year of existence, Image Comics published work by some of the best-known creators in the industry. For instance, after ten years at Marvel, **Sergio Aragonés** moved his much-loved *Groo the Wanderer* to Image. After receiving offers from several publishers, Aragonés chose Image due to the freedom he would receive there. In his first issue at his new home, Groo remarks, "The *marvels* of the world are but *images* before me." *Groo* ran for twelve issues at Image before moving to Dark Horse.

Valiant Becomes Acclaimed

Comic heroes and video games had always been closely aligned with each other, so few observers were surprised when a video game company bought a comic book publisher in 1994. **Acclaim Entertainment** had an ad on the back cover of **Valiant Comics'** *Magnus, Robot Fighter* #1 (May 1991). Three years later, the company best known for such games as *Double Dragon*, *Mortal Kombat* and *NFL Quarterback Club*, purchased Voyager Communications, Valiant Comics' parent company, for $65 million in cash and stock. Consummated on April 7, 1994, after months of negotiations, the deal gave Acclaim control over a collection of properties that seemed well-primed to be translated into video games. In fact, one

of the reasons for the deal was that the game developer urgently needed to create new franchises. One week before acquiring Valiant, Acclaim failed to renew its licenses to produce new editions of their bestselling *Mortal Kombat* and *NBA Jam* games. *The New York Times* reported those two series of games represented as much as 75% of Acclaim's revenue. An analyst told the *Times* the Valiant acquisitions should help: "on the surface, the acquisition is positive because it addresses some of the revenue replacement relating to [the loss of the licenses]" ("Company News"). The deal was lucrative for Triumph Capital, the investors behind Valiant. Comic sales had been plummeting rapidly but Valiant still netted $30 million per year. Acclaim's offer presented the perfect opportunity for Triumph to exit the publishing business while Acclaim quickly went to work converting Valiant's heroes into video game stars. A 1996 game that teamed X-O Manowar with Iron Man was a steady seller. An even more popular 1997 game featured Turok, Dinosaur Hunter. Acclaim later produced games featuring Shadowman, among other characters.

Valiant's new owners retained the existing editorial staff, including Publisher/CEO Steven Massarsky, Senior Vice President Jon Hartz and Editor-in-Chief Bob Layton. All three had large equity stakes in Voyager, so each earned millions of dollars from the acquisition. Unfortunately for them, the money would be paid in one-fifth installments over a period of five years. That gave them "golden handcuffs" to remain at Valiant. As the sale closed, Valiant's sales were in deep decline from their 1993 levels. According to Capital City Distribution, *Magnus Robot Fighter* tumbled from a per issue average of nearly 200,000 copies sold in 1993 to 22,600 in April 1994. *X-O Manowar* dropped from a peak of 91,000 copies sold through Capital City in 1993 to 27,350 in April

The story of Defiant Comics was intimately tied to the life and career of publisher Jim Shooter. TM and © respective copyright owner.

1994. In a survey published in July 1994, eight of fourteen comic shop retailers reported sales slips for Valiant titles versus the year before ("Market Beat" 42-3). Hartz put a good face on the dip by bidding good riddance to the speculators who inflated revenues: "A year ago, we were selling approximately 300,000 to 400,000 copies per title, and that's too much. I know it's weird to hear a publisher say he would like to have fewer sales, but I know those sales weren't going into the hands of readers. They were going into the hands of speculators." Hartz also cited the fact Valiant's per-title average circulation was higher than either Marvel's or DC's (Grant 78). Sales, though, continued to decrease throughout the rest of the decade, aided by a bold experiment in 1995 that backfired on Valiant.

While Valiant Comics was in the process of being acquired, one of its founders, **Jim Shooter**, was valiantly trying to keep his newest venture afloat. Though his old company rode the industry's boom times, his new **Defiant Comics** debuted just in time for the industry bust. Throughout 1994, the company rolled out several

Acclaim/Valiant tried to boost sales with several 3D comics.
TM and © Valiant Entertainment LLC.

154

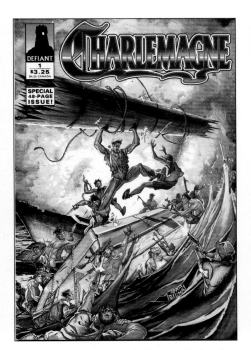
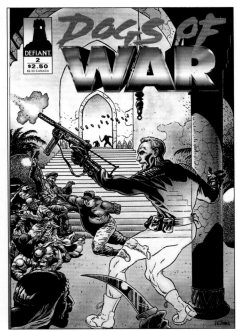

All the 1994 releases from Defiant Comics led up to the Schism crossover. However, the line ended before the crossover was published. TM and © respective copyright owner.

new Shooter-written titles, including *Charlemagne*, *Dogs of War* and *War Dancer* which was co-written by Alan Weiss. The only Defiant title not helmed by Shooter were Len Wein's *Dark Dominion* and Chris Claremont's *Prudence and Caution*.

All this output, though, didn't translate to any traction in the marketplace as retailers reported Defiant's titles didn't sell well in their shops. For instance, John Sedgwick of Norwich, Connecticut, claimed, "Our customers are defiant about buying Defiant Comics" (Sedgwick 54). Similarly, the owners of a shop in Champaign, Illinois, testified, "While *The Good Guys* is selling well for us, the rest of the Defiant line is sitting on our racks with no hope of moving any time soon" (Morris 60). Shooter had one last trick up his sleeve: an ambitious line-wide Defiant crossover called "Schism" that he hoped would, at least, echo the 1992 blockbuster success of Valiant's *Unity*. Unfortunately, *Schism* preorders were so poor that Shooter cancelled the event before any copies could reach stores. Only the first two parts of the grand event appeared, as the final issues of *Warriors of Plasm* and *Dogs of War*.

Rumors about Defiant's imminent demise abounded, becoming even more widespread when Shooter didn't attend the 1994 San Diego Comic Con in early August. Shooter skipped the

convention in order to meet with a film studio which he hoped would infuse his business with $3 million. The studio, however, stepped away from the transaction. Several potential partners considered investing but decided not to take a risk on the failing publisher. One of those companies was Broadway Video, which would make a separate deal with Shooter in 1995. On September 1, 1994, Defiant Comics closed its doors forever. Altogether, Defiant's investors lost $2 million (Grant 24).

Meanwhile, **Kitchen Sink Press** celebrated its 25th anniversary in 1994, a year in which publisher **Denis Kitchen** lost much of his autonomy when he took on a new partner. On May 24, 1994, Los Angeles-based investment banking company Ocean Capital Corporation announced its intent to acquire the publisher. Both Ocean and Kitchen described the transaction as a purchase of intellectual property made possible through the transfer of shares in a new version of Kitchen Sink. That infusion gave KSP a surplus of cash to help survive the contracting American comics market. Though sales were tough, Kitchen Sink received more Harvey Award nominations in 1994 than any

other publisher. With forty selections, Kitchen Sink received over a third of all possible nominations. Among those nominated were Jim Woodring for *Tantalizing Stories*, Simon Bisley for his work on *Melting Pot*, Shephard Hendrix for his inking on *Captain Sternn*, Eddie Campbell for *Graffiti Kitchen*, and Scott McCloud for *Understanding Comics*.

The Legend of Hellboy

Elsewhere, a different group of comic book artists—specifically Arthur Adams, John Byrne, Paul Chadwick, Geof Darrow, Dave Gibbons, Mike Mignola and Frank Miller—banded together to co-found **Legend**, a new **Dark Horse Comics** imprint. Legend grew from the idea of another partnership that was tentatively dubbed "Dinosaur," which would have presented a line-up of over a dozen fan-favorite pros. When the collected creators couldn't agree on their goals, Dinosaur split, with seven artists forming Legend while the others headed to Malibu to start Bravura. The Legend team nicknamed themselves "The Magnificent Seven," and as Miller explained at the time, they considered themselves an "alliance of artists": "It's not a publishing company and it's not a shared universe, but the seven of us feel that if you like one of our books, you will mostly enjoy the rest of them" (Cunningham 32).

Echoing the formation of Image Comics, every Legend title was creator-owned. The first two Dark Horse comics to carry the Legend logo were *John Byrne's Next Men* #19 (Oct. 1993) and the first issue of Frank Miller's second *Sin City* mini-series, *A Dame To Kill For* (Nov. 1993). Byrne and Miller produced the majority of Legend material in 1994, including Byrne's *Babe* and *Danger Unlimited* (a science fiction super-hero mini-series that evoked Byrne's *Fantastic Four* work) and Miller's third *Sin City* mini-series, *The Big Fat Kill*, and the sequel to *Give Me Liberty*, the five issue, Dave Gibbons-drawn *Martha Washington Goes to War*. Those works were joined by Paul Chadwick's latest *Concrete* mini-series, *Killer Smile*, and *Madman Comics* by Legend recruit, Mike Allred.

The other Legend offering of 1994 became one of its most successful. The fact that it was produced by **Mike Mignola**, arguably the least famous of all the Legend creators, made it all the more surprising. Mainly known for his cover art as well as his work

Mike Mignola's Hellboy made his debut in an issue of John Byrne's Next Men. Next Men TM and © John Byrne. Hellboy TM and © Mike Mignola.

on Marvel's *Hulk* and DC's *Cosmic Odyssey* mini-series, Mignola might have seemed like an odd choice to join Legend. That perception permanently changed with the creation of **Hellboy**, a red-skinned, cloven-hooved demon, pulled to Earth as a boy in 1944 by a group of Nazis. Liberated by the U.S. Army and placed in the care of the Bureau for Paranormal Research and Defense, Hellboy matures into one of the Bureau's most experienced occult investigators. Constantly reminded of his demonic heritage by the filed-down horns on his forehead and his gigantic stone right hand, Hellboy asserts his free will by denying his destiny as the destroyer of all mankind.

Mignola created Hellboy in 1991 as a throwaway sketch for a convention program book. At that point Mignola had no intention of doing anything with the giant, hideous demon, but the name "Hellboy," which he found humorous, stuck with him. A couple of years later, with the opportunity to produce his creator-owned comic book, Mignola opted for the genre that interested him the most: occult detective stories, with monsters thrown in for good measure. Mignola

Dark Horse Comics' Legend line included work by John Byrne and Frank Miller. TM and © John Byrne. TM and © Frank Miller, Inc.

realized that Hellboy fit perfectly into that book as he would be a monster fighting other monsters. As the artist explained years later, "I have a big collection of Victorian occult detective stories that are always just regular guys [with beards]. I knew that if I made my occult detective guy a regular guy, I'd be bored drawing him after 20 pages. It didn't matter how special a beard he had, I would just get bored drawing a regular guy. I made the main character a monster so that, even if he wasn't fighting a monster, I would be drawing a monster" (Irving 4-5).

As depicted by Mignola, the world of Hellboy was immersed in deep ominous shadows, emphasizing a dark Lovecraftian atmosphere. As far as writing went, Mignola lacked confidence in his own abilities, so he asked John Byrne to script Hellboy, first for a four-page story that appeared in *San Diego Comics* #2, a Dark Horse giveaway at the 1993 San Diego Comic Con, and then in the pages of *John Byrne's Next Men* #21 (Dec. 1993), which included ten pages of Mignola art featuring his fledgling character in a guest-starring role. Three months later, the first issue of *Hellboy: Seed of Destruction* appeared. After Byrne co-wrote that four-partner, he stepped away, leaving all writing chores to Mignola himself. Not that Mignola expected to have much to do since he figured *Seed of Destruction* would the first *and only* Hellboy mini-series (Irving 5). Much to his surprise, the character and his world immediately caught on with fans, so much so that the next Hellboy story, "The Wolves of St. August," ran as a four-part serial later in the year in *Dark Horse Presents* #88-91 (Aug. to Nov. 1994). Thanks to the inclusion of the Hellboy story, sales of *DHP* nearly doubled compared to previous issues (Bank 6). From there, Hellboy and his fellow members of the BPRD evolved into an ever-expanding supernatural epic. For his work on *Seed of Destruction*, Mignola won an Eisner Award for "Best Writer/Artist." (The collected edition of the mini-series won the "Best Graphic Album" category, while "The Wolves of St. August" was nominated for "Best Serialized Story.")

Dark Horse also offered a line of titles from African-American film director **Spike Lee**. Among the series published under the "Comics By Spike" imprint was *Colors in Black,* an anthology of short comic strips that focused on race and race relations. Lasting four issues, *Colors in Black* had genres that ran the gamut, from historical fact to science fiction, with work by such creators as Jason Lamb, Greg Simanson and Scott Tolson.

Dark Horse also celebrated a Hollywood breakthrough in 1994, as the movie adaptation of **The Mask** premiered in late July. *The Mask* boasted special effects by Industrial Light and Magic, but the real special effect was actor Jim Carrey's zany style and goofy facial gestures. *The Mask* finished as the ninth most popular movie of 1994 in ticket sales, earning almost $120 million. With an inevitable sequel in the planning stages and further Dark Horse mini-series in the works, there were dreams of making the Mask an iconic comic book character of the 1990s.

Bad Girls Mean Hit Comics

The **Topps Comics** revival of Zorro continued into 1994 with writer **Don McGregor** and artist **Mike Mayhew**. The two creators provided the roguish Old West adventurer with a new co-star, the tough, voluptuous, scantily-clad **Lady Rawhide**, who debuted in *Zorro* #3 (March 1994). Modeling the character after his daughter Lauren, who would go on to cosplay as Lady Rawhide at comic book conventions, McGregor went to great lengths to make the heroine an authentic part of Zorro's world: "I took a great deal of care with Lady Rawhide, to protect her identity, coming up with a way she could dye her hair, change her voice. I never could

understand how in costumed hero series, you put on a mask and even people who know you intimately haven't a clue who you are. And in Lady Rawhide's time, a male family member, even a brother, could have a woman confined to a Nunnery if they thought she was acting immorally" (Sacks). Though distinct in temperament and personality from many of the "Bad Girls" fashionable in 1994 (such as Harris Comics' Vampirella and Chaos! Comics' Lady Death), Lady Rawhide was like them in some ways. She wore a skimpy costume that emphasized her large breasts as she rode out to combat evil. She received her own strong-selling series in 1995.

The highest-profile Bad Girl of 1994 was DC Comics' **Catwoman**, who had an enduring love/hate relationship with Batman. Written by **Jo Duffy** and illustrated by **Jim**

Lady Death, Lady Rawhide and Catwoman were among the popular "bad girls" of 1994. Death TM and © Dynamite Characters, LLC. Catwoman TM and © DC Comics. Lady Rawhide TM and © Zorro Productions, Inc.

Balent, Catwoman dressed in a purple bodystocking that accentuated her bust. This anti-hero involved herself with petty grifts and crime-fighting exploits that always seemed to leave her as the winner of any battle.

A very different kind of Bad Girl came from newcomer comic book creator **Billy Tucci**. A graduate of Manhattan's Fashion Institute of Technology as well as a former U.S. Army paratrooper, Tucci's passion was to draw Marvel's *Daredevil*. An experience at the 1993 San Diego Comic Con changed his mind. Standing in line at a portfolio review, Tucci came to a realization: "everybody had the same stuff. The hell with that. I'm going to do my own thing. I decided to self-publish" (Golden 70). He went back home to his one-bedroom apartment in Queens, New York, and developed **Shi**, a.k.a. Ana Ishikawa, a martial artist trained by her grandfather after her father and brother are murdered by the Japanese mob. Seeking revenge, Shi (the Japanese word for "death") wields a traditional Japanese sword while wearing white kabuki face paint in order to resemble Tora No Shi, a legendary female warrior of medieval Japan.

After forming Crusade Entertainment Ltd., Tucci quickly learned the trials and tribulations of self-publishing a comic book. Not only did he have to spend day after day drawing page after page of his own work, he also had to take the time to arrange advertising, distribution and printing, and pay for it all out of his own pocket. Dead broke and six months late paying his rent, Tucci seemingly reached a breaking point when his car broke down during a blizzard as he tried to drive to a printer in New York City (Tucci). All of Tucci's hardships, though, eventually led to a big reward. While initial orders for *Shi: The Way of the Warrior* #1 totaled 37,000 copies, reorders surpassed 140,000. Evidently, Tucci's violent, emotionally conflicted heroine struck a chord with comic book fans, and *Shi* would defy the industry downturn with consistently high sales that often surpassed Batman and Superman titles. For the remainder of the decade, *Shi* #1 was a high-priced commodity in the back issue market, and the character starred in numerous intercompany crossovers, including a one-shot in 1997 in which Tucci finally fulfilled his dream of drawing his favorite Marvel Comics character: *Shi/Daredevil: Honor Thy Mother*.

Female comic creators had divergent opinions on the Bad Girls craze. For instance, Colleen Doran complained, "I think some of the characters are really great but some get up my nose. I think that some female readers find this stuff repulsive." Jo Duffy, on the other hand, stated, "I think it is so incredibly fantastic. I have always loved characters like Sue Storm, the Invisible Woman, who's such a good mommy, but I've always hated that *that's* all we really got" (Samsel & Kardon 44).

Even wholesome **Archie Comics** capitalized on the Bad Girl fad to an extent. In the four-part crossover "Love Showdown," the romantic triangle of Archie, Betty, and Veronica becomes disrupted when Archie receives a mysterious love letter in the mail. Each girl believes the other wrote it, which leads to an all-out war between the two. As the story wraps up in *Veronica* #39 (cover date Dec. 1994), writer Bill Golliher reveals that the person who wrote the letter was "bad girl" **Cheryl Blossom**, the curvaceous red-head who attends an elite private school and has been an Archie Comics supporting character since 1982. In a surprising twist, Archie chooses Cheryl over both Betty and Veronica.

The new romance received plenty of mainstream attention but ultimately was short-lived, ending in *Love Showdown Special* #1, published just two months after the end of the crossover. Archie Comics continued to get mileage out of the event, though. A trade paperback collection—almost unheard of at the publisher—was rushed into print by December and Cheryl received the first of several mini-series in 1995.

Shi is a martial arts master out for revenge in William Tucci's self-published comic. TM and © William Elliott Tucci.

Form and Void

After nearly 20 years of creating and publishing his own material, **Dave Sim** had achieved a reputation as the maverick lead of the self-publishing movement in North America. However, he lost much of his influence in the industry because of the contents of the controversial *Cerebus* #186 (Sept. 1994). The first five pages of that issue continued the epic "Mothers and Daughters" story arc, depicting Cerebus and his opponent Cirin slowly gliding to the moon. After that seemingly benign beginning, however, readers encountered something totally unexpected. In fifteen densely-written pages, Sim details his alter ego Viktor Davis's meditations on "the Female Void and the Male Light," in which he delineates men as logical creatures and women as emotional ones. Davis describes the struggle between the genders as a battle between thought and feeling with statements like, "The Male Light is jeopardized in all fronts, in my view. The Devouring Rapacious Female Void is not a thing to be taken lightly, to be explained away, to be rationalized into neutrality. I'm not here to make you feel good. I am here

to make you think. I have to make you see." By asserting that women are incapable of logical thought, seeking only to suck the creativity of men into their void, Victor Davis's beliefs are clearly misogynistic. In subsequent communications, Sim stated repeatedly that these observations were his own strongly held opinions. The reaction to *Cerebus* #186 was rapid and thunderous. Up to this point, Sim had been a well-respected leader of his industry, but now he faced near unanimous condemnation in the comics press. As a result, sales of his once-popular series cratered.

Ironically, strong female characters were the stars of the backup story in *Cerebus* #186: **Terry Moore's** *Strangers in Paradise*. First published in 1993 as a three-issue mini-series by Antarctic Press, and soon after through Moore's own Abstract Studios, *SiP* chronicles the lives of a pair of best friends – neurotic Francine and impulsive Katchoo – along with their complicated relationships and traumatic pasts. Their adventures, drawn by Moore with an obvious ardor, are clever, funny, and constantly surprising. As the story proceeds, the mysterious David joins the two women, forming a friendship triangle that provides a happy edge to the well-delivered stories. When asked to describe his unique series, Moore was a bit at a loss for words:

> Really and truly, if I have to describe it, it's the personal story of two young women, about their lives and their loves. But that's so lame. It's like saying *Batman* is about some vigilante who works at night. The appeal of a good story is not in sound bites, because that's a director's way of thinking. From the writer's standpoint, it's the subtleties. It's a book you have to read to appreciate. The charm is in the read and the emotional moments. (Allstetter 100)

Moore presented his characters as flawed people with complicated but compelling lives that make for

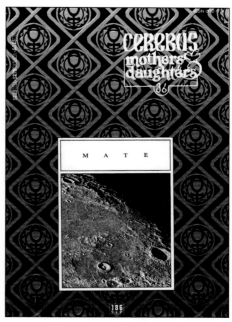

Dave Sim's controversial comments about women in *Cerebus* #186 caused sales on the title to plummet.
TM and © Dave Sim.

intriguing reading. With song lyrics mixed in with his clear black and white line art, *Strangers in Paradise* delivered an experience akin to watching a television show on the printed page, with light-hearted humor and a frantic but charming pace.

With creators such as Terry Moore leading the way, the self-publishing movement Dave Sim fostered continued unabated in 1994. Jeff Smith's *Bone* remained a bestseller, fueled in part by reprints in the popular *Disney Adventures Digest*, available at supermarket checkout stands nationwide. Popular mainstream artist **Bart Sears** started his own company in 1994. Despite copious advertising in industry magazines, Ominous Press only put out three issues of *Brute & Babe* before Sears folded the company after its October 1994 solicitations. Sears cited the difficult Direct Sales market as his reason for cancelling his book.

Due to fan-favorite work on *Batman: Sword of Azrael* and Valiant's *Ninjak*, among other series, artist **Joe Quesada** was a rising star. In 1994 he and **Jimmy Palmiotti** formed Event Comics in order to publish *Ash*, about a fireman turned super-hero. The first issue (cover-dated Nov. 1994) was the 54th bestselling comic book of the month. Event Comics lasted throughout the 1990s as a home mostly for Quesada and Palmiotti's creator-owned

Joe Quesada and Jimmy Palmiotti's **Ash** *starred a super-heroic fire fighter.*
TM and © Joe Quesada and Jimmy Palmiotti.

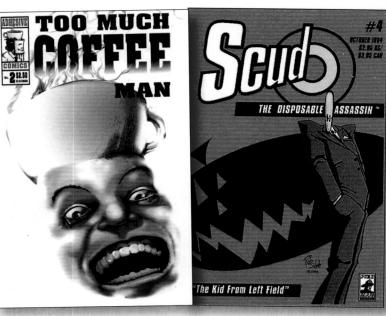

Among the most notable self-published comics of 1994 were Jar of Fools, Too Much Coffee Man *and* Scud. *Jar of Fools TM and © Jason Lutes. Too Much Coffee Man TM and © Shannon Wheeler. Scud, the Disposable Assassin TM and © Rob Schrab.*

properties, though they occasionally branched out with work by established professionals such as George Pérez's *Crimson Plague*. As time would tell, though, Quesada and Palmiotti were destined for bigger and better things.

Other writer/artists who self-published in 1994 included **Jason Lutes**, who received significant attention for his Xeric Award-winning *Jar of Fools*. First serialized in the Seattle weekly *The Stranger* and then released as a graphic novel through Lutes's own Penny Dreadful Press, *Jar of Fools* presents a depressingly beautiful meditation about

a magician down on his luck and the changes made in his life when he meets a stranger with whom he forms a close connection. Lutes's clean-line, European-influenced art style punctuated the melancholic mood of the book and earned him an Eisner Award nomination for "Best Writer/ Artist." At the same time, Shannon Wheeler produced *Too Much Coffee Man*; John Mitchell and Jana Christy collaborated on their Sinatra cool *Very Vicky*; and Donald Simpson released his silly *Bizarre Heroes*. Rob Schrab's *Scud the Disposable Assassin* was one of the small press' breakout hits of 1994. With a berserk sense of humor and a violent and irreverent flair in his work, *Scud* became a cult favorite and inspired a video game.

One attempt to offset the industry's downward trend was the "40 and 5" program. Proposed by Sim and Seattle retailer Preston Sweet, the program allowed retailers to purchase a minimum of five copies of an issue directly from a participating publisher and receive a 40% discount off cover price. The move was promoted by both publishers and retailers to help make sure stores could stock as many copies of a small-press book as they felt they could sell, while providing much-needed sales and attention for numerous publishers. Niche distributors, like the San Francisco-based Cold Cut Distribution, also cropped up to support indie comics and graphic novels.

No Heroes

Harvey Pekar was one of the most acclaimed and beloved of indie creators. By 1994, his *American Splendor* was a mainstay of autobiographical comics, especially after a series of popular appearances on *Late Night with David Letterman*. Pekar delivered stories that presented unflinching representations of his everyday life, with his flaws as much on display as his virtues. In his true-to-life tales, Pekar would be alternately kind and friendly, greedy and acerbic, angry and polite, just as most people are in real life. However, few of his fans were likely ready for the brutally honest *Our Cancer Year*. Pekar co-wrote this

Our Cancer Year *by Harvey Pekar, Joyce Brabner and Frank Stack chronicles Pekar's cancer and the toll it takes on his family's life.* TM and © Harvey Pekar Estate.

book with his wife Joyce Brabner and recruited classic underground cartoonist Frank Stack to illustrate it. As the graphic novel begins, Brabner and Pekar are looking to buy a house. To prep for their big move, Pekar goes to the doctor to have a lump in his groin checked to make sure it's not a hernia. While repairs on the new property ebb and flow and Brabner flies around the world to visit friends (becoming more and more worried about the upcoming Gulf War), Pekar's doctor delivers a devastating diagnosis: Harvey doesn't have a hernia. He has cancerous lymphoma. This harrowing book chronicles the emotional and physical stress the diagnosis has on Pekar and Brabner, chronicling the chemotherapy he receives, their deep stress about his condition, and the ravaging weaknesses Harvey experiences as part of his treatment. *Our Cancer Year* also unflinchingly details the effects that her husband's illness has on Brabner. She is forced to manage her despair over the changes Harvey's diagnosis causes in her life and in her social activism. This grim tome was critically acclaimed for its honesty and insight, though many found the painful details too tough to read. Ironically, considering the horrific incidents presented within, *Our Cancer Year* became the best-selling book of Pekar's career.

Other cartoonists found success with fictional stories about characters who had no super powers. **Daniel Clowes** wrapped up his dreamlike "Like a Velvet Glove Cast in Iron" story arc in 1993, then moved on to his next *Eightball* serial, "Ghost World," which told the nuanced story of two young women adrift in their lives. The serial was later collected into a well-reviewed graphic novel before being made into a successful independent film. **Chris Ware** released two issues of his *Acme Novelty Library* in 1994 through

Fantagraphics Books released two of the most critically acclaimed comics of 1994 with Daniel Clowes's Eightball *and Chris Ware's* Acme Novelty Library. *TM and © Daniel Clowes. TM and © Chris Ware.*

Fantagraphics. Each issue was produced in different sizes to fit the story being told, but all showcased Ware's trademark deadpan sense of humor and deep sadness. Fantagraphics also published three issues of *Pressed Tongue*, featuring Dave Cooper's surreal, sometimes disgusting, stories that bristled with energy and delight. After a six-month break, Peter Bagge continued his grungily satirical *Hate* with the addition of color.

A distinguished 1994 graphic novel emerged from the mind of one of America's most prominent literary authors with an adaptation of Paul Auster's acclaimed ***City of Glass***. Originally published in 1985, Auster's novel was a curious concoction: a 200-page meditation on identity and fiction in the guise of a literary-minded detective story. The novel tells the tale of Daniel Quinn, a crime writer haunted by the deaths of his wife and child. One day Quinn receives a phone call meant for a man named Paul Auster. Quinn ends up taking a job shadowing Auster, portrayed in *City of Glass* as a bookish lunatic. Readers watch Quinn disappear on the streets of New York before falling into madness. **Art Spiegelman**, best known for his Pulitzer Prize-winning *Maus* and a longstanding fighter for ambitious graphic material, approached Auster with the idea of adapting *City of Glass* into graphic story form to be published by Neon Lit, the graphic novel imprint of Avon

*Acme Novelty Library *used symbolism like animated characters to tell a multifaceted story. TM and © Chris Ware.*

David Mazzucchelli and Paul Karasik's adaptation of Paul Auster's **City of Glass** *took the avant-garde book to new levels of complexity.*
TM and © Bob Callahan Studios.

Books. Auster agreed to the adaptation but declined the offer to write new material for it, so Spiegelman tapped **David Mazzucchelli** to handle the project. A talented cartoonist who spent the early part of the 1990s working on his innovative *Rubber Blanket* comic, Mazzucchelli collaborated with fellow artist **Paul Karasik** to deliver a version of Auster's visionary fiction that maintained the spirit of the original book while functioning as a unique creation all its own. The *City of Glass* graphic novel is not a simple recitation of scenes in the prose book. The Mazzucchelli/Karasik adaptation is a visual tour de force, mingling maps and diagrams with symbolism and straightforward action sequences. *City of Glass* received a "Best Graphic Novel" Eisner Award nomination while Mazzucchelli and Spiegelman also earned nominations for their contributions (for "Best Penciller/Inker" and "Best Publication Design," respectively). More than that, the graphic novel also garnered widespread acclaim from mainstream critics, and in 1999 *The Comics Journal* included *City of Glass* in its list of "Top 100 Graphic Novels of the Century."

Neon Lit planned *City of Glass* to be the first in a series of graphic takes on classic modern literature. However, after Neon's second release, an adaptation of Barry Gifford's *Perdita Durango* that was scripted by Bob Callahan and illustrated by Scott Gillis, Avon quietly dropped the Neon Lit imprint. Editor Callahan had twenty more titles slated for the line, including *Nightmare Alley*, adapted from William L. Gresham's book by Tom DeHaven and Mark Zingarelli. In 1998 Fantagraphics published a version of *Nightmare Alley* with art by Spain Rodriguez.

DC courted mainstream audiences with its non-genre **Paradox Press** imprint. **Andy Helfer** helmed the line, which became well-known for its series of "Big Book" titles (like *The Big Book of Scandal*, *The Big Book of Hoaxes*, and *The Big Book of Conspiracies*, among many others). Each oversized black-and white book presented numerous stories that depicted events in contemporary or historical life, all drawn by a diverse team of artists. The series debuted with 1994's *The Big Book of Urban Legends*. Helfer conceived the series as a grownup version of a series of iconic children's books:

What I was thinking of was when I was a kid, we use to have these things called *The Big Book*s. *The Big Book of Dinosaurs*, *The Big Book of Insects*. Now that we've gotten older, what are the subjects that interest us? Subjects we're most interested in are urban legends, conspiracies, death, freaks, criminals, etc. So I combined that comprehensive compendium sensibility with these non-fiction subjects, and the *Big Book*s were born (Ray 80).

Paradox published other graphic novels intended for the bookstore market. *Brooklyn Dreams* by J. M. DeMatteis and Glenn Barr is a semi-autobiographical meditation on life. *La Pacifica* by Joel Rose, Amos Poe and Tayyar Ozkan depicts a cross-country odyssey of murder. In 1995, Paradox would release one of the finest original graphic novels of the decade.

The Information Superhighway Speeds Into the Future

One of the most important societal trends of 1994 had a lasting effect on comic books. For millions of Americans, the World Wide Web evolved from novelty to necessity. Usually accessed via dial-up modems that accessed America Online, CompuServe, Prodigy or another network, the "Information Superhighway" provided unprecedented opportunities for ordinary comic book fans to interact with their favorite pros, learn about plans for favorite characters, and engage each other in chat rooms and on message boards. Marvel, DC as well as smaller publishers hosted chat sessions with their writers and artists, but professionals also frequently visited the boards to make announcements about their work. For instance, in January 1994, subscribers to CompuServe's Comics Forum got a sneak preview of Marvel's *Ghost Rider 2099* #1. Though most comic books still included letters pages, editors began using email correspondence for letters of comment. Mitch Rubenstein, former head of the Sci-Fi Channel, went one step further. As he hyped, "Bell Atlantic has contracted Future Vision to develop software that will provide video and information on fiber optic cable. We are going to provide the network with the first ever electronic comic

The Tick, *based on Ben Edlund's comic book, was an oddball hit with kids and adults on FOX Kids.* TM and © Ben Edlund.

strip" (Fritz, "Big Plans" 47). Rubenstein would go on to co-found a Big new publisher.

Other publishers used computer technology in a different way. Voyager Company, a CD-ROM manufacturer unaffiliated with Valiant Comics, released three CD-ROMs of interest to fans of sequential art: Art Spiegelman's *Maus*, musicians The Residents' *Freak Show*, and the documentary film *Comic Book Confidential*. Malibu released CD-ROM versions of Ultraverse heroes such as Prime and Prototype.

Spooooon!

One of the most unexpected and best-loved shows of the 1994 fall TV season appeared on Saturday mornings with **Fox Kids'** *The Tick*. The animated series starred a buffoonish but lovable burly hero in a skin-tight blue suit with wiggling antennae on his head. Voiced by Townsend Coleman, the Tick teamed up with his sidekick, the bunny-suited Arthur (voiced by Rob Paulsen) to combat such absurd villains as The Breadmaster, Omnipotus (similar to Galactus), Professor Chromedome and the evil Chairface Chippendale, a villain with the head of a Chippendale chair who tries to carve his name onto the moon. A ridiculous and wacky alternative to some of the other super-hero cartoons on the airwaves, *The Tick* gained an immediate following among both kids and adults for its manic but benign humor. The series also showed the influence of super-heroes published by companies other than Marvel and DC as *The Tick* was based on the black-and-white series created by Ben Edlund and published by New England Comics (NEC). After meeting some Fox executives, Edlund jumped at the opportunity to put his series on the small screen, and he ended up writing or co-writing nearly all the scripts for the series, giving the show a consistently wacky tone which reflected the energy of his NEC comic.

The wacky *Tick* joined other comic book-oriented cartoons on Fox Kids Saturday mornings. The fledgling TV network continued to air *X-Men* and added *Spider-Man* to its 1994 lineup. Like *X-Men*, *Spider-Man* was true to its

title character's history, quickly attracting fan attention by featuring some of the web-slinger's most dastardly villains (such as the Lizard, the Scorpion, and the Kingpin) and his closest friends. Co-creator Stan Lee claimed he was hands-on with every aspect of the production's formulation, "In the beginning I checked every premise, every outline, every script, every model sheet, every storyboard, everything to do with putting the show together" (Lee 8).

The King is Dead

The turbulence of 1994 was presaged early in the year by a terrible event. On February 6, 1994, one of the greatest creators of all time passed away. **Jack Kirby**, the King of Comics, died of a heart attack at the age of 76. One of the undisputed titans of the industry, Kirby was beloved for his co-creation of the Marvel Universe and was a constant force for joy and happiness among fans. Many met Kirby during his annual pilgrimage to the San Diego Comic Con where they enjoyed Kirby's ebullient and generous personality. Though his health was failing for a long time, Kirby's passing hit the comics community hard. After his death, tributes came in torrents from thousands across the world, including people with no direct connection to comics.

Jack Kirby's death cast a sober shadow over an often challenging year. If 1994 was the year the comics industry counted down to zero, the "distributor wars" of 1995 would bring on an age of apocalypse. ◑

The death of Jack Kirby on February 6, 1994, was mourned by comic creators and fans worldwide.

1995

CHAPTER SIX

The Exclusivity Wars

As 1995 began, retailers could only reminisce about the comic book boom of a few years earlier. The downward sales slide that began in 1993 continued unabated two years later as consumers seemingly abandoned comic books for good in favor of other diversions, like video games or the ever-growing World Wide Web. In 1993, 9,400 comics specialty shops operated in the United States. By 1995, only 4,200 of them remained in business (Gray 26). If anything, comic sales were even worse than those grim numbers reflected. Series such as *WildC.A.T.s* and *Bloodshot*, which frequently sold close to 500,000 copies per issue when they premiered, struggled to sell a fraction of that number. Only the mighty X-Men and Spider-Man series maintained strong sales.

Many observers saw this prolonged drop in sales as a sign of the apocalypse for the entire industry. A common lament placed the blame for a "lost generation" of fans on the speculator boom of the early 1990s. As Capital City Distribution co-owner Milton Griepp testified,

> I've heard more than one retailer use the phrase "We've lost a generation" to describe what has happened. This lost generation seems to have come into specialty stores in huge numbers in '92 and '93, attracted by the publicity surrounding the death of Superman and the excitement around the new Image and Valiant lines. Unfortunately, much of their interest was related to the lottery ticket aspect of comic collecting – "How much will this be worth next month?" This interest dissipated as quickly as the presses could be cranked up to print more copies of the book with the "hot" designation. (Griepp 56)

A major paper shortage exacerbated the problem. Over the course of a few months, the cost of high-grade paper rose from under $400 to over $700 per metric ton. Several publishers passed that expense on to their consumers. DC raised its prices in April and May, with $1.50 series increasing to $1.75. (Superman and Batman titles were bumped up even higher, to $1.95.) Fantagraphics and Warp Graphics also raised their prices by a quarter per copy. The higher price points depressed sales even further because even the most devoted fans only had so much money in their wallets to spend on comic books, and as one Atlanta retailer explained, the mid-range selling titles were most severely hurt by the price increases: "Readers of those books seem to be subconsciously looking for a reason to drop the titles, and a price hike is a very good reason" (O'Neill 131).

Marvel, though, held the line. Many of its standard format series proudly boasted "Still $1.50" on their July through November cover-dated issues. But while Marvel's prices remained stable, the same couldn't be said for the rest of the company.

Marvel's New Heroes

Marvel Comics began the 1990s as the most popular comics publisher in America. In 1991, Marvel published 47.5% of all comics sold in America. By 1994, that number plunged to less than 32% (Howe 361). Marvel's executives blamed the drop on the inability of retailers to properly promote their series in a crowded marketplace. Furthermore, the executives believed retailers couldn't identify comics that held the potential to be hot sellers because they didn't receive the right level of support from their distributors. Marvel's sales managers approached distributors to request ideas on how to improve sales. According to Capital City Distribution co-owner John Davis, Marvel didn't like the answers that the distributors provided them: "We felt Marvel's core problems were too many titles, especially multiple titles overexposing the same character, like Ghost Rider and the Punisher. There was a perceived overall low quality, low value for the dollar spent on Marvels, both at the consumer and retailer level. Rightly or wrongly, that's how it was" (Reynolds 12). A retailer in Salt Lake City, Utah, concurred, "In our store, Marvel sales have dropped more than 25% in the last quarter, and the reason is not because we aren't paying attention to the Marvel line. It is because people just no longer care about Reed Richards and Tony Stark" (Gallacher 14).

Marvel management disagreed with those assessments. They believed the true problem was that distributors carried publications from all companies and therefore couldn't devote themselves full time to promoting Marvel Comics. Based on that line of thinking, Marvel executives concluded it was time to take matters into their own hands. In early 1994, they tried selling directly to consumers via the Marvel Mart mail order catalog. When that proved ill-fated, Marvel got more ambitious and acquired **Heroes World Distribution** in December 1994. The purchase set off all kind of alarms among retailers and

One way Marvel attempted to win back market share was by pricing a line of comics at 99¢. TM and © Marvel Characters Inc.

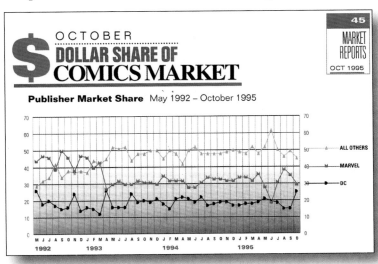

As this dollar share chart shows, between 1992 and 1995 Marvel struggled to maintain its market dominance.

distributors. Bill Leibowitz, head of retailer clearing house The Direct Line Group, summed up what their mood was like in January 1995: "the phones, faxes, e-mail [sic] and industry magazines and newspapers are burning up with speculation, prediction, and general paranoia. Some of the rumors and speculation say that Marvel is about to destroy the direct market, retailers will be hit with declining profit margins, increased cover prices, and erratic sources of supply" (Leibowitz 2). Many of the fears Leibowitz expressed turned out to be well founded. On March 3, Marvel publicly announced that effective July 1, 1995, Heroes World would become the exclusive distributor of Marvel Comics throughout the world. Essentially, Marvel became its own distributor, which meant that retailers who didn't have an account with Heroes World would no longer have access to new Marvel releases. Marvel executive Matt Ragone claimed the depressed comic book market made the change necessary: "The fact is that no segment in this industry is satisfied with 1994 performance, or early 1995 performance. Sales and profits are down at every level and retailers report that customer traffic is down" (Ragone 3). No one could deny that traffic and sales were down, but many believed Marvel's move to self-distribution would only make matters worse.

TIMELINE: 1995

A compilation of the year's notable comic book history events alongside some of the year's most significant popular culture and historical events. (On sale dates are approximations.)

January 16: The UPN television network launches with the pilot episode of *Star Trek: Voyager*, starring Kate Mulgrew as Kathryn Janeway, the captain of a Federation vessel lost in the Delta quadrant. Marvel Comics publishes a fifteen-issue "Paramount" series based on the show starting in 1996 as well as a four-issue mini-series in 1998 before Wildstorm acquires the license in 2000.

February 23: Don Heck—the comic book artist whose career spanned five decades and is best known for co-creating Marvel Comics' Iron Man and for a long run in the 1960s on *Avengers*—dies at the age of 66 of lung cancer.

March 1: Two Stanford University electrical engineering graduate students co-found Yahoo, soon to become the internet's most popular search engine.

March 3: Marvel Comics announces its products will be distributed exclusively by Heroes World, the company it purchased at the end of 1994.

March 9: Less than three years after acquiring Fleer, Marvel Comics buys Fleer's main competitor, trading card manufacturer Skybox International, for $150 million.

April 8: An adaptation of Sam Kieth's Image comic book *The Maxx* makes its debut as an animated cartoon as part of MTV's *Oddities* anthology series. Thirteen episodes of *The Maxx* air between April and June.

April 19: A truck bomb detonates outside a federal building in Oklahoma City, Oklahoma, killing 168 people, including 19 children. The main culprit, U.S. Army veteran Timothy McVeigh, seeks revenge against the government for its siege of the Branch Davidian compound, which occurred two years ago to the day. He is captured and eventually sentenced to death.

May 27: Actor Christopher Reeve, who portrayed Superman in four films from 1978 to 1987, is permanently paralyzed from the neck down after falling from his horse during a riding competition.

June 30: *Judge Dredd*—based on the character from Britain's *2000 AD* comic book and starring Sylvester Stallone as the titular law enforcement officer from the future dystopian city of Mega-City One—arrives in movie theaters. The film becomes a box office disappointment, grossing only $34 million domestically.

JANUARY	FEBRUARY	MARCH	APRIL	MAY	JUNE

February 14: Written by J.M. DeMatteis and drawn by Mark Bagley, Larry Mahlstedt and Randy Emberlin, the main story in *Amazing Spider-Man* #400 presents the death of Aunt May, just after she admits to Peter Parker that she's known for years that he is secretly Spider-Man.

February 28: The first issue of DC Comics' *Preacher*—written by Garth Ennis and drawn by Steve Dillon—arrives in comic book stores. The series stars Jesse Custer as a Texas minister who becomes possessed by an angel/demon half-breed. Endowed with "the Word of God," Custer goes on a road trip to find God who has abandoned his post in Heaven.

March 29: Comic book artist Mort Meskin dies at the age of 78. During a career that began in the late 1930s, Meskin worked for numerous publishers, including National (DC), MLJ/Archie and Marvel Comics, drawing such characters as Sheena, Queen of the Jungle, The Shield and Johnny Quick.

March 20: In Tokyo, Japan, members of a religious cult release poisonous sarin gas on five commuter trains, killing twelve passengers and injuring over 5,000 others.

April 26: Nearly two months after Marvel's Heroes World decision, DC Comics announces its products will be distributed exclusively by Diamond Comics Distribution, Inc.

June 16: *Batman Forever*—directed by Joel Schumacher and starring Jim Carrey as the Riddler, Tommy Lee Jones as Two-Face, Chris O'Donnell as Robin and Val Kilmer as the Caped Crusader—opens in movie theaters. It ultimately becomes the second highest grossing movie of the year, earning over $184 million domestically.

May 24: *Braveheart*—a historical drama directed by Mel Gibson who also stars as William Wallace, the legendary 13th century leader who helped free Scotland from English rule—opens in movie theaters. It will go on to win five Academy Awards, including Best Picture and Best Director.

Indeed, those predictions came true, in ways that most professionals could not have expected.

The radical move to an exclusive distribution model changed the way comics had been distributed in America for over two decades. From 1979 to 1995, retailers could buy a full line of publications from one distributor, who was often centered in the same region of the country as the comic shop. That model kept communications, reorders and bookkeeping simple for most stores. Retailers were eligible for discounts based on their total sales volume across all publishers. With the new system, however, all comic shops would have to use at least two distributors. They needed Heroes World to provide them with Marvel's books and another distributor to provide them with books from all the other publishers. As a result, most retailers could no longer take advantage of the highest possible discount threshold. Lower discounts meant lower profit margins. That vicious cycle in turn caused even more stores to close in 1995. As one observer stated, "good stores were also closing as well. The market has shrunk dramatically. People who used to be able to make a living can no longer sell enough comics to keep the doors open and the lights on" (Mariotte 93). In addition, the shift also required more complicated bookkeeping, reordering and communications systems. This was a problem that had no solution because no retailer could remain in business without selling Marvel Comics, even if doing so meant cutting profit

November 22: *Toy Story*—the Disney/Pixar animated film about children's toys that come to life—arrives in movie theaters. It will become the highest grossing movie of the year at the box office, earning over $191 million domestically.

July 20: One week after being fired from Penthouse Comix for suspicion of embezzlement, comic book writer/editor George Caragonne commits suicide by jumping from the 45th floor of a hotel in Times Square, New York City. He was thirty years old.

October 3: After a trial that lasted over eight months, a Los Angeles jury finds O.J. Simpson not guilty of the murder of his former wife Nicole Simpson and her friend Ronald Goldman. The verdict divides the nation along racial lines.

December 5: Comic book artist L.B. Cole dies at the age of 77. In a career that began in the early 1940s, Cole illustrated over 1500 covers on a variety of titles, including his own Star Publications.

July 24: Like DC Comics before them, Image Comics and Dark Horse Comics announce their products will be exclusively distributed by Diamond Comics Distribution, Inc.

November 4: At the conclusion of a rally in Tel Aviv, Israeli Prime Minister Yitzhak Rabin is assassinated by Yigal Amir, a 25-five-year-old Jewish fanatic who opposes peace efforts with the Palestinians.

December 30: Nestor Redondo—the Filipino comic book artist best known for his work on DC Comics' mystery titles during the 1970s—dies at the age of 67.

| JULY | AUGUST | SEPTEMBER | OCTOBER | NOVEMBER | DECEMBER |

August 10: Written by Kurt Busiek, drawn by Brent Anderson, with a cover by Alex Ross, the first issue of *Kurt Busiek's Astro City* arrives in stores. The Image Comics series will go on to win Eisner Awards for Best New Series and Best Single Issue.

November 17: *GoldenEye*—the first James Bond movie in six years and starring Pierce Brosnan as British secret agent 007—arrives in movie theaters. It will earn over $100 million domestically.

December 31: The final installment of Bill Watterson's *Calvin and Hobbes*, the popular daily comic strip about the friendship between a six-year-old boy and his stuffed tiger that began in 1985, appears in newspapers nationwide.

margin to the bone. "Marvel represents somewhere between the profit margin and the entire profit center for a great majority of comics stores," reported one magazine. "[The retailers] have to tighten their belts and try to make the new system work" (Spurgeon 2). One lifeline for many stores was a tremendously popular collectible card game called *Magic: The Gathering*. As retailer Michael Redman declared, "Our percentage of gross of *Magic* cards has almost equaled our percentage of gross from new comics" ("Retailer Conference Q & A" 44).

Adding insult to injury, the Northeast-based Heroes World had significant problems managing the large influx of new business from around the country. Its computer systems couldn't handle all the new retailers. Packages were slow to leave Heroes World warehouses, and retailers found it almost impossible to receive crucial reorders. Retailer Howard Beck described his problems after a year of using Heroes World:

In one year, my discount has dropped 10 percent (from 45% to 35%). I pay shipping for my books. Reorders stink. And Marvel has cancelled this year's retailer's meeting. Last August, they misplaced my order disk and while they had my hard copy, they did not think it necessary to contact me. That meant that I did not receive any new books that

month. When it was brought to their attention that this cost me almost $200 per week their response was, "These things happen." Soon after, I received my confirmation for September and discovered they had multiplied all my books by a factor of ten. (Beck 8)

Consensus grew in early 1995 that all publishers needed to counter Marvel's move by arranging their own exclusive relationship with a distributor lest they lose access to comic shops and become irrelevant. All eyes turned to DC Comics. As the country's second-largest comic book company, DC would pave the way for the remaining publishers. The industry's largest wholesaler, **Diamond Distribution**, quickly emerged as the leading contender for DC's business (Reynolds 11). On April 26, 1995, DC officially went exclusive with Diamond. DC Vice President and Publisher Paul Levitz declared in an internal memo, "We signed with Diamond yesterday. This deal has far-reaching benefits for DC, and although it was only possible in the wake of Marvel's acquisition of Heroes World, it leaves us in a far superior position to theirs." Though Capital City claimed the deal was "an inside joke in the industry," Levitz trumpeted the fact that "DC captures the benefits of exclusive distribution without either cost of acquisitions or cost of build up" in addition to the fact that "DC gets an immediate savings of $2 to $3 million annually on distribution fees" ("DC Leaves the Water Running" 5).

Diamond Distribution trumpeted its exclusivity with DC, Dark Horse, Acclaim and Image.

Besides receiving safe harbor at a friendly new home, DC also gained the opportunity to buy Diamond outright after ten years. Thus, Levitz and his team succeeded in signing a strategic partnership which would help provide long-term stability.

With Marvel and DC exclusive, most other publishers rapidly followed suit. Image (the third-largest publisher in America with a 12% market share) and Dark Horse (the fourth-largest with a 5% market share), each signed exclusive contracts with Diamond in July. Valiant, the fifth-largest publisher, with a 3% market share, joined them in August. When the dust finally settled, nearly every independent publisher went exclusive with Diamond. **Capital City**, the country's second-largest distributor, could only ink deals with Kitchen Sink Press, Viz Comics and a handful of others. The remaining publishers, including Warp Graphics and Fantagraphics Books, opted to ship with both Capital and Diamond, but the writing was on the wall: rebuffed by all the best-selling comic book publishers, Capital City's days were numbered, even after obtaining out-of-court breach-of-contract

settlements from Marvel and DC. All this change led to a mood of deep uncertainty among comics professionals. As one observer commented, "the computer bulletin-board systems are littered with apocalyptic predictions, as are the letters pages of every industry trade publication. Everyone is scared of the future, and nobody is devoid of an opinion of what that future will be" (Reynolds 1).

Marvel's decision made 1995 a very tough year for retailers and distributors alike. For completely different reasons, many of Marvel's employees had it just as bad.

Marvel Grows and Shrinks

Marvel's editorial team drove major changes in 1995. Starting with the February 1995 cover-dated issues, Bob Budiansky, Bobbie Chase, Mark Gruenwald, Bob Harras and Carl Potts began managing their own separate lines of comics inside Marvel. However, they each had a smaller team to help them with that work. After months of rumors about an impending downsizing, Marvel's leadership laid off nearly half the company's staff in early 1995. Editors Don Daly, Craig Anderson and Mike Rockwitz were among the professionals whose jobs were cut on management's justification that Marvel no longer needed as many internal team members as it had. By all accounts, staff morale before and after the axing was at an all-time low. Soon thereafter, executives also cancelled twenty-four of Marvel's lowest-selling series, including all the Punisher and Conan titles. Those cancellations were only the beginning. By December, Marvel's line had been trimmed nearly in half. Marvel released 170 new comics with a January 1995 cover date. Eleven months later, Marvel released 87 new comics with a December 1995 cover

date. The irony that didn't escape most observers was that the reason Marvel had dramatically increased its output of new series in the first place was to fortify itself against popular new upstart publishers (specifically Image and Valiant). Unfortunately, the maneuver backfired as Marvel mainly succeeded in damaging its own finances. Having learned a lesson about the extent of its readers' brand loyalty, Marvel separated its wheat from its chaff. Retailer Bill Christensen summed up the apathetic reaction to the cancellations: "Those titles have withered away and have lost almost all their readership. What's even more damning is that none of our customers have complained that a favorite book is being cancelled" (O'Neill, "Marvel Cancels Titles" 19).

Even as its comic book line was being reduced, Marvel completed its acquisition of trading card company SkyBox for $150 million, or $16 per share. An acknowledged leader in the card marketplace, SkyBox owned several lucrative licenses, including the NBA, Disney, Paramount (owners of *Star Trek*), and even DC Comics. Jill S. Krutick of Smith Barney Investments felt the acquisition "offers a strengthening of Marvel's position in the trading card business provided they are able to carry over key licenses they need, one of them being DC Comics" (O'Neill, "Marvel to Acquire Skybox" 23). Rumors also circulated that Marvel was considering buying nationwide toy store chain KayBee Toys, but that deal was never consummated.

Marvel Entertainment was spending millions of dollars to buy companies, but inside the offices of Marvel Comics, pennies were being pinched. Orders came down from management to avoid overnight shipping and to turn off lights to cut down on electricity usage. When staff was told to stop making expensive long-distance phone calls, communications between Marvel's editors and freelancers became very difficult because few creators used email. Some began to wonder how long Marvel could continue to operate in this manner.

Many observers thus found it ironic that Marvel's big 1995 crossover was called "The Age of Apocalypse."

Apocalypse Now

As 1995 dawned, the **X-Men** remained the most popular characters in comics. The vast line of series starring mutant heroes reflected that fact. For cover date January 1995, twenty-two Marvel releases featured mutant lead characters, representing 13% of Marvel's entire line. (Spider-Man starred in thirteen January-dated publications.) Mutants dominated the bestseller lists as retailers relied on the consistent sales the mutant titles enjoyed from weekly customers. Imagine retailers' panic then when rumors began to swirl in late 1994 that Marvel planned on cancelling its top-selling mutant series, including the newly-launched *Generation X*. In fact, the strange rumors proved true as Marvel *did* cancel all its mutant series... at least for the first few months of 1995 as Marvel's merry mutants shifted into a bizarre alternative universe called the "**Age of Apocalypse.**"

Editor **Bob Harras** conceived the initial idea for the epic crossover. He called **Scott Lobdell**, writer of *Uncanny X-Men* and *Generation X*, and asked, "What if Jubilee goes to the mansion and everyone she finds there are claiming to be X-Men, but they aren't really the X-Men?" Lodbell replied, "That would be cool! But what if they were right and she was wrong? What if something happened while she was out that all those people really were the X-Men!" (Siegel). In a series of conversations, the two men decided they wanted Professor X to die in the past, preferably at the hands of his own schizophrenic mutant son, Legion, which would radically alter who the X-Men were in the present day. When the duo couldn't figure out why Legion would kill his own father, **Fabian Nicieza**, writer of *X-Men*, suggested that the death could be the result of a terrible accident. That idea became the launching pad for "Age of Apocalypse."

The unparalleled four-month event began with "Legion Quest," which crossed over between *Uncanny X-Men* #320 and #321 and *X-Men* #40 and #41 (Jan. and Feb. 1995). In that grand adventure, Legion travels back in time to kill Magneto before the X-Men's arch-enemy could turn evil and commit any crimes against humanity. In the streets of 1970s Haifa, Israel, Legion confronts Magnus and rants, "My father spent so much time battling you — trying to stop your madness — that he couldn't help others — he couldn't help me! But I can change all that! If I kill you now, Magneto, things will have to get better in the future!" Legion then thrusts his psi-blade toward Magneto's head, but Charles Xavier won't allow the slaying of his best friend in cold blood. Xavier jumps in front of his son's attack and takes the full impact himself. Professor X dies, and with his

When Legion inadvertently kills Professor X in the past, he triggers the Age of Apocalypse. TM and © Marvel Characters, Inc.

death, the X-Men's timeline begins to unravel. Legion ceases to exist because his father dies before he is born. Xavier also never lived long enough to found his group of mutant heroes. Continuity as readers knew it was completely wiped clean. As "Legion Quest" concludes in a devastating wave of destruction, only the time-traveling mutant Bishop remembers the universe that existed before all reality shattered.

For the next four months, Marvel delivered an unprecedented stunt. At Harras's suggestion (which he couldn't believe Marvel's marketing department agreed to), nine X-Men related titles were put on pause. In their place was an interlocking collection of four-issue mini-series that showed the desolate world that resulted from Professor X's premature death. Put another way, all of Marvel's mainline mutant series were renamed to fit this new universe, their numbering restarted with issue #1, and their creative teams restocked with some of the rising stars in the industry. *Cable* was renamed *X-Man* (written by Jeph Loeb with art by Steve Skroce); *Excalibur* became *X-Calibre* (written by Warren Ellis with art by Ken Lashley); *Generation X* became *Generation Next* (written by Lobdell with art by Chris Bachalo); *Uncanny X-Men* was now *Astonishing X-Men* (written by

X-Men Alpha introduced readers to the dystopic Age of Apocalypse – and a rebranded set of X-Men titles (below and right).

from the strong. In fact, Apocalypse has destroyed much of the human race to create a refuge for mutants. Many of the surviving humans have been placed into breeding pens in New York that are patrolled by Beast and his Mutant Elite Force. A heroic Magneto and his ragtag team of X-Men resist Apocalypse's tyranny from their base at the former Xavier Institute. As the mutant series demonstrate, this dystopian world diverges from the Marvel Universe in other dramatically different ways. Cyclops is now Mr. Sinister's protégé and the rival to his brother Havok. Magneto and Rogue are married, which sets up an uneasy love triangle with Gambit. Weapon X, that universe's version of Wolverine, has lost a hand after battling Cyclops.

In a key moment in *X-Men Alpha*, Magneto has a fateful confrontation with a furious Bishop. Gazing into the time-lost mutant's mind, Eric sees the Apocalyptic world in which he lives is not the true reality. "The Age of Apocalypse" is fundamentally wrong. Magneto thus decides he must restore the timeline to its correct order. He starts a quest to find the materials needed to return everything back

Lobdell with art by Joe Madureira); *Wolverine* became *Weapon X* (written by Larry Hama with art by Adam Kubert); *X-Factor* turned into *Factor X* (written by John Francis Moore with art by Steve Epting); *X-Force* was transformed into *Gambit & the X-Ternals* (written by Nicieza with art by Tony Daniel); *X-Men* became *Amazing X-Men* (written by Nicieza with art by Andy Kubert). Finally, the double-sized anthology *X-Men Unlimited* was renamed *X-Men Chronicles*. The epic crossover was

bookended by two holofoil deluxe one-shots co-written by Lobdell and Mark Waid and drawn by Roger Cruz: *X-Men Alpha* (cover date Feb. 1995) served as part one of the tale while *X-Men Omega* (cover date June 1995) concluded the story.

As "Age of Apocalypse" unfolds within this sprawling array of publications, readers learn Apocalypse has conquered all of North America. The villain plans to execute his Darwinist goal of culling the weak

to the way it was supposed to be. As the war between Apocalypse and Magneto's grim team of concerned mutants proceeds, humans find themselves caught in the middle and flee North America as refugees. In Europe, the humans grow stronger and build Sentinels intended to protect them against a mutant attack. A war between humans and mutants seems inevitable, especially in *X-Men Omega* when Apocalypse captures Magneto and starts exercising his plans to conquer the remaining humans in Europe. However, the mutants play their ace in the hole. Nate Grey, a.k.a. X-Man, is that timeline's version of Cable. Grey attacks Apocalypse, which leads to a climactic battle in which Magneto uses his magnetic powers to literally tear Apocalypse apart. While the vicious fight rages, Illyana Rasputin opens a temporal portal that allows Bishop to go back in time and prevent Xavier's death. In a dramatic reversal of the scene that started "Age of Apocalypse," Bishop plunges Legion's psi-blade into his own body, engulfing Xavier's son in an energy force he cannot survive. Legion's final words sum up the terrors he unleashed: "In your mind... I saw... tomorrow. It was terrible... horrible... It was my fault. Just tried to... fix things. Give my father... his dream. Never meant to screw it up..." With those words of regret, the Age of Apocalypse begins to

reverse itself. In a final echo of the end of "Legion Quest," *X-Men Omega* finishes with a scene of Magneto, his wife Rogue and their son Charles speaking optimistically as their universe slowly fades away.

Though the reality was gone, "Age of Apocalypse" produced some lasting changes to the X-Men line. As they return to the main Marvel universe, Bishop and Nate Grey remember their tumultuous experiences in the alternate universe. Joining them is the evil version of the Beast, who infiltrates the X-Men and unleashes chaos. These changes added new spice to the

X-Men's universe, but all the mutant series essentially returned to their status quo. As Harras reported, "["Age of Apocalypse"] has definitely changed our perception of what we wanted to do with the X-Men. But I don't think it changed our basic foundation in any way" (Golden 60).

The massive crossover was a risky bet. Many Marvel executives fretted that fans would take the opportunity to drop the mutant titles. If they had done so, it would have been financially devastating. But "Age of Apocalypse" paid off on the sales charts. This alternate universe saga sold extraordinarily

X-Men Omega concluded the Age of Apocalypse in style, with a cataclysmic battle between Magneto and Apocalypse.

well, with a surge of interest in the mutant titles from many fans. For comics released in January 1995, AoA stories held nine of the top ten slots in the bestseller lists for both Capital City and Diamond Distribution (*Spawn* #28 occupied the ninth slot). For comics released April 1995, AoA titles held every one of the Top 10 slots. The momentum survived Marvel's shift to Heroes World, as 8 of the top 10 most popular comics listed in *Wizard* at the end of the year were mutant series.

Though many fans loved "Age of Apocalypse," a small but vocal minority of readers complained on the nascent internet message boards about the story. Labeling them "Internet psychotics," Fabian Nicieza dismissed them out of hand, "If we're going to worry about the people who are either A) not buying the books and complaining about them or B) stupid enough to keep buying the books even though they don't like them, then we're wasting our time" (Golden 102). On the other hand, *Gen13* co-creator J. Scott Campbell praised the crossover, saying, "I had a very negative slant going in, and they're pulling it off in a very cohesive and coherent way. I've been pretty impressed. Actually, I've been kind of almost jealous of how well they're doing it. More crossovers should be like this" ("Top 10 Comics" 139).

Receiving near universal praise was the artwork of **Joe Madureira**. A recent graduate of New York's High School of Art and Design, Madureira was only twenty years old when he pencilled *Astonishing X-Men* #1 (March 1995). Having already garnered significant attention by working on such assignments as *Deadpool* and *Uncanny X-Men*, Madureira became a superstar thanks to his fresh-feeling manga-inspired artwork on "Age of Apocalypse." As a result, "Joe Mad" (as he was nicknamed) arguably became Marvel's most popular artist since the Image Comics defectors. Scott Lobdell, among many other professionals, was a big fan: "He's incredibly talented and is changing and growing and pushing himself with every panel. Even his worst stuff is better than most" (Dillon 45).

While another mutant menace would provide the fuel for Marvel's major crossover in 1996, the Spider-Man titles stole some pages from the "Age of Apocalypse" playbook for their 1995 storylines.

Which Peter is Peter?

Peter Parker had an extremely tough 1994. Long-forgotten clone Ben Reilly reappeared, his Aunt May was hospitalized, and his parents appeared to have been raised from the dead before they were revealed as robots controlled by the villainous Chameleon. Little could **Spider-Man** (or his faithful readers) have predicted that both his and his clone's lives would get still more complicated as The Clone Saga ran through all of 1995 and took a dramatic twist as the year ended.

The year began with Spider-Man experiencing "Web of Death" in *Amazing Spider-Man* and *Spectacular Spider-Man* while Scarlet Spider worked though "Web of Life" in *Spider-Man* and *Web of Spider-Man*. Aptly named, "Web of Death" continued a key 1994 plotline in which Peter was poisoned by the Owl. Only one man seems to have an antidote to the poison, and he happens to be one of Peter's most hated enemies: Doctor Octopus. Ironically, Ock hates Spider-Man so much he refuses to let anyone other than himself kill his longtime nemesis. In an improbable turn of events, Doctor Octopus manages to save the man he hates only to be slain by the evil Kaine. Adding to the operatic feel of the story, Mary Jane Watson announces to Peter that she's pregnant, a situation that would add a level of power and responsibility to Spider-Man's life as the year goes on. Meanwhile, "Web of Life" depicts Ben settling into the role of hero, fighting the Grim Hunter and Kaine while gaining confidence in his abilities. In one crucial scene in both stories, both Ben and Peter have the same dream: of waking up in a strange lab, with glimpses of the Jackal and other clones. Attentive readers began to wonder which webhead was the true clone. The three-part "Smoke and Mirrors," which followed on the heels of the previous adventures, played further with that idea. In that crossover, the Jackal at first teased Ben and Peter that they both were clones

Aunt May dies in **Amazing Spider-Man** *#400. Marvel released an embossed tombstone cover to mark the event.* TM and © Marvel Characters, Inc.

and later that neither was a clone before revealing yet a third version of Peter was in a chamber inside a building. At the end of "Smoke and Mirrors" that building explodes, freeing that clone to wander New York, alone and confused.

As if all that craziness wasn't enough for the heroes, *Amazing Spider-Man* #400 (April 1995) saw them both lose the person they loved the most: Aunt May, who raised Peter from his childhood. As Peter's clone, Ben shared Peter's memories of the motherly way Aunt May raised him. In this fateful issue, May finally returns home from the hospital to recuperate and spend time celebrating Mary Jane's pregnancy. A week later, May persuades Peter to take her to the Empire State Building to help her get some fresh air and see the sights. As the sun sets behind them, May reveals the truth to Peter: she has known for years that her nephew was Spider-Man and has been very proud of his secret exploits. Writer J. M. DeMatteis was very pleased with Aunt May's dialogue: "It's one of those moments that come, not from the writer but from the character herself. I set the scene of Peter and May on top of the Empire State Building, then May started talking and there it was. I was surprised as anyone else. But it instantly felt right" (Johnson 19). As the words tumble out of her mouth, Aunt May collapses.

After they return home, Peter lays May in her sickbed. Murmuring "It's my time," Aunt May passes away. Peter, Mary Jane and Peter's Aunt Anna collapse in tears. Sitting on the roof of Parker's house, Ben feels crushed by the loss of the woman who was as much his surrogate mother as Peter's. Adding to Peter's pain, unexpected visitors come to the reception after May's funeral. They are two officers from the Salt Lake Police Department who arrest Peter for second degree murder. Hearing about Peter's arrest, Ben goes to his house and unmasks himself to the pregnant Mary Jane, offering to help track down the real killer.

A series of frantic crossover stories follows the shocking development, each one ratcheting up the tension. In "Aftershocks" and "The Mark of Kaine" Peter escapes from jail to save his wife from threats made to her by Kaine. Ben eventually takes Peter's place in jail because Peter believes Ben might be a murderer. Meanwhile, the third clone from "Smoke and Mirrors" re-emerges. As he puts on his own version of the spider-suit, he reveals himself to be nothing more than a genetically engineered killing machine yet swearing in his final dying breath that he was the real Peter Parker. The next tale, "The Trial of Peter Parker," has Peter proving Kaine framed Ben for murder, creating a par-

allel trial of Peter. While Ben is on trial in criminal court, a group of super-villains accuse Peter of being responsible for creating them. To no one's surprise, these super-villains find Peter guilty and sentence him to immediate death. Kaine, however, rescues Peter, and the hero flees from the prison. Peter then forces Kaine to come to Ben Reilly's trial. In a private room, Peter demands Kaine tell the truth about his identity. Removing his mask, Kaine claims he was Peter's first clone and has subsequently become the victim of clone degeneration. With that, Kaine is contrite. He enters court and admits the truth: he has framed Ben for murder, even going so far as to steal Ben's fingerprints. With Kaine's confession, Ben and Peter's names are both cleared, but "The Trial of Peter Parker" has one more twist as *Spectacular Spider-Man* #226 (July 1995) delivers one of the major climaxes to the clone saga. Ben and Peter undergo a series of tests to determine which one of them is the clone. Unexpectedly, the test results show that Peter Peter is a clone of Ben Reilly and not the other way around. Since 1975, then, fans had been following the exploits of an imposter.

Maximum Clonage *features hundreds of Spider-Man clones. The event ends with Peter Parker and Ben Reilly deciding which one of them should become the one, true Spider-Man.* TM and © Marvel Characters, Inc.

That revelation sets the stage for the **"Maximum Clonage"** storyline, which spanned all August 1995 cover-dated Spider-Man titles plus special *Alpha* and *Omega* one-shots. In this six part tale, the Jackal creates hundreds of Spider-Man clones who then attack our heroes. As Ben valiantly fights to defeat all the clones, Kaine is apparently killed by another evil clone named Spidercide. The story concludes with the Jackal plunging off a tall building. The arch-nemesis and clone creator is finally dead, and as *Maximum Clonage Omega* wraps up, Peter and Ben decide there must be a Spider-Man but they're not sure who should wear the mask. The next crossover, "Exiled," resolves the dilemma. Mary Jane declares she wants to stay in New York, so Ben jumps on his motorcycle to head out of town. Perhaps fighting a subconscious battle in his own head, Ben crashes the cycle and remains in New York. Using his time to resurrect some of his previous memories (and fight the Vulture), Ben also changes his mind and decides he wants to stay in New York to fight crime. *Spectacular*

Spider-Man #229 (Oct. 1995) resolves the question of who should wear the spider-suit once and for all. This double-sized issue, the concluding chapter of "The Greatest Responsibility" storyline, sets Peter and Ben against the new female Doctor Octopus, whose presence shakes Peter to his bones. He can't stop worrying about his life, or about leaving his unborn child an orphan. "Mary Jane... I've come to a decision!," he declares. "I have decided to quit being Spider-Man! I'm hanging up my webs forever." Handing the costume to his clone, Peter is finally ready to give up crime-fighting and become a fulltime dad. Peter and Mary Jane move to Portland, Oregon where the four-issue *Spider-Man: The Final Adventure* gives Peter one last escapade before his powers become inert in an accident and he is once again human. The course was clear for Ben Reilly to put on the blue and red costume and officially become Spider-Man. *The Final Adventure* was originally plotted to have Mary Jane

have a miscarriage in the final issue. However, editor Tom Brevoort refused to greenlight that story because he didn't want to be the person who killed Peter Parker's baby. Regardless, there would be much more conflict around Peter and Mary Jane's baby in Marvel's offices in 1996.

With Peter Parker 3000 miles away from New York, Ben Reilly was ready to become the official wall-crawler. Due to the massive success of "Age of Apocalypse," Marvel's marketing team mandated the November and December issues of the four main Spider-Man series be renamed to include "Scarlet Spider" in their title. Thus, readers could buy *Scarlet Spider, Web of Scarlet Spider, Spectacular Scarlet Spider* and *Amazing Scarlet Spider*. The initial four-parter presented "Virtual Morality," in which Ben battles cyber-criminals. The second tale, "Cyberwar," completes that adventure. The *Scarlet Spider* issues led to "Rebirth," released with January 1996 cover dates, with a new Spider-Man series and with Ben in a new version of the spider-suit. *Web of Scarlet Spider* continued for two additional issues before its brief run concluded.

By the end of 1995, many fans expressed their dissatisfaction with the seemingly never-ending clone saga. The revelation that Peter Parker was a clone, in particular, was not well received. In an interview for *Wizard* magazine at the time, Spider-Man group editor Bob Budiansky admitted, "We got a fair amount of negative reaction to the Clonage storyline. But the bottom line is Spider-Man is hot. Sales are way up and fan mail on the Spider-Man books is up ten-fold" (Griffen 132). Years later, former Marvel editor Glenn Greenwald similarly stated, "Despite popular belief, the clone saga significantly boosted sales on the Spider-Man books. At a time when the comics industry was starting to head downward, with sales dropping across the board on every title, the Spider-Man line was bucking the trend, with sales holding steady and even increasing each month" (Goletz).

Another Marvel hero saw a long storyline end and a new creative team take over in 1995.

Operation Rebirth

As 1994 ended, the very serum which gave **Captain America** his powers was now killing him. In *Captain America* #443 (Sept. 1995) writer **Mark Gruenwald** and artists Dave Hoover and Danny Bulandi chronicle the final day of Cap's life. Culminating Gruenwald's eleven-year-run on the title, the issue begins with the star-spangled Avenger lying in a grimy alley after being beaten by a mediocre villain named Nefarious. As Cap lies prone in his exoskeleton, weak and forlorn, mysterious hero Black Crow swoops down and declares, "24 hours from now, your super-soldier serum's deterioration will stop your heart... and you will die." Crow then flies away. Cap quickly decides to forego fighting Nefarious, allowing the Avengers to handle the villain. Instead Cap goes about putting his affairs in order. In a tearful visit, he says goodbye to his allies at his Brooklyn Heights staging area. Next, he has a final visit with his arch-enemy Crossbones in prison before looking in on his former girlfriend Bernie Rosenthal, his childhood friend Arnie Roth, and his longtime partner the Falcon. A tearful visit with his young friend and admirer Ram Riddley reminds Captain America that even a super-hero has his limits. That makes Cap choose to wander to Avengers Mansion to relax. While at the Mansion, the star-spangled Avenger has an unexpected encounter with

In 1995, Captain America received a new artist, Ron Garney.
TM and © Marvel Characters, Inc.

the rogue Batroc. Instead of fighting, the two men drink tea and have a long conversation about life philosophy before Cap decides to go to his room and lie down. As the issue concludes, the Avengers look in on their friend but discover the hero's body is gone with only his exoskeleton left behind. Readers could only wonder what happened to the hero, but many also admired the elegiac approach Gruenwald took to his final issue on the iconic character. In fact, Gruenwald's story can be read as a meditation on the difficulty of creating traditional comics storytelling in an increasingly hectic world.

With the following issue, *Captain America* #444, a decidedly different era premiered as scripter **Mark Waid** and artist **Ron Garney** assumed creative chores. The issue centers around a group of villains who take hostages at the Jefferson Memorial and demand Captain America be brought to them. But following on the events Gruenwald chronicled, Cap is missing and presumed dead. The Avengers must step in and solve the crisis without their ally. As the issue ends, readers discover Captain America's body has been encased in ice and held by a mysterious cabal. *Captain America* #445 begins with the hero's funeral, but the "Operation: Rebirth" story arc truly starts with the hero breaking out of his ice prison. Once awakened, he meets up with his old S.H.I.E.L.D. associate and lover Sharon Carter, miraculously revealed to be alive despite her supposed death in 1979. Cap and Carter join an unexpected ally, the Red Skull, on a mission to save all reality from the Cosmic Cube. In Waid and Garney's second arc, titled "Man Without a Country", Captain America is framed for murder and goes on the run to find Machinesmith, the evil cyborg who framed him. Cap and Sharon Carter must track down the cyborg in an action-adventure tale that evokes—and modernizes—classic Stan Lee storytelling. With its emphasis on slick, cinematic action, along with a modern new logo, Waid and Garney's run presented a patriotic hero that fit the zeitgeist of the mid-1990s.

Captain America was just one of several titles in which Marvel tried sweeping change to drive readership. In *Fantastic Four*, for instance, writer Tom DeFalco and artist Paul Ryan resurrected Doctor Doom and Reed Richards, which created some complicated team dynamics. Reed felt traumatized by his two-year imprisonment and became emotionally volatile. While Reed was gone, his wife Sue rekindled her relationship with the Sub-Mariner. New creative teams brought major changes to some of Marvel's other long-running series. Starting with issue #111 (Dec. 1995), *Silver Surfer* set the Fantastic Four's ally on his own unique path. Scripter George Pérez joined artists Tom Grindberg and Bill Anderson to reset the Surfer's status quo by moving him to a far-distant galaxy with a completely different group of supporting characters. The core concept of *Surfer*'s new direction was similar to that of *Star Trek: Voyager*, which premiered in January 1995 on the fledgling UPN television network. Elsewhere, *Daredevil* shifted from serious existential action-adventure under writer Dan Chichester to more standard action fare from J.M. DeMatteis. One of DeMatteis's first acts was to eliminate the hero's much hated "BMX racer" costume. Effective with *Daredevil* #344 (Sept. 1995, the premiere issue published under the "Marvel Edge" imprint), Matt Murdock returned to his customary red suit. DeMatteis also took over *Doctor Strange, Sorcerer Supreme* with issue #84 (Dec. 1995) after a short run by Warren Ellis. With artists Mark Buckingham and Kev Sutherland, DeMatteis focused Strange's attention on a novel concept: Catastrophe Magic based on the alignment of the planets.

Warren Ellis and Mike Deodato Jr. rebooted Thor's status quo after several years of traditional adventure. In "Worldengine," which ran from *Thor* #491 (Oct. 1995) to #494 (Jan. 1996), **Thor** is cast out from Asgard and made human by his father. Sick and dying, Thor gains redemption in the arms of the Enchantress while he saves Yggdrasil, the world-tree, from rot and destruction. Along the way, the hero gains a new costume and regains his lost powers. The rebooted *Thor* was a hit. One retailer in Chicago reported a major upsurge in sales for the series (Spurlock 123), and the title jumped into the top 100 list for the first time in many years.

Teen Tony Crosses Over

While Thor received a new costume and new creators in 1995, his longtime ally **Iron Man** had his world turned upside down. In "The Crossing," a 25-part crossover involving *Iron Man, Force Works, War Machine* and *Avengers*, readers discover revelations about Tony Stark they never could have imagined.

After two prequel issues, in which the Wasp loses her considerable fortune, the story begins in earnest in the deluxe, holofoil

In "The Crossing," Tony Stark kills the nanny to Crystal's daughter, among many others.
TM and © Marvel Characters, Inc.

The Avengers: The Crossing (Sept. 1995). Written by Bob Harras and Terry Kavanagh and drawn by Mike Deodato Jr., the issue briefly reintroduces Rita DeMara, the second Yellowjacket, who has returned from the future to Avengers Mansion. As she arrives, Yellowjacket sees visions of fugitive Avengers, of the team in different costumes and of the heroes battling to enter the mansion. Without warning, a mysterious stranger, shrouded in darkness, slays her. Soon after that murder, a battalion of strange beings attacks the Avengers. Disappearing before they can be defeated, the attackers leave behind a body. It is Gilgamesh, another former Avenger, now elderly and near death. As the vertiginous one-shot spins to its end, one more member of the Avengers family is killed. Marilla, nanny to Crystal's baby Luna, is slain by a man in the shadows. In the issue's shocking last page, that man reveals himself as Tony Stark.

Thor dons a new costume, courtesy of artist Mike Deodato, Jr.
TM and © Marvel Characters, Inc.

Over the next six months, "The Crossing" explores Tony's memory loss and his murderous, impulsive behavior. Besides being responsible for Wasp's bankruptcy, Tony also attempts to frame Hawkeye for the murder he doesn't even realize he has committed. As readers discover, the time-travelling villain Kang, allied with his wife and former Avenger Mantis, has been manipulating Stark for years to commit evil acts as a precursor for a time war he hopes to win. In *Avengers* #393 (Dec. 1995) the team confronts Stark in the halls of the Wasp's Southampton, New York home. A furious battle ensues between former friends, with Hercules beckoning, "It doesn't have to be like this. Just talk to us." Stark answers words with violence, but as he fires his repulsor beams at full blast at Hercules, the Wasp jumps in front of the rays. As her ex-husband Hank anxiously attempts to save her, the Wasp unexpectedly wraps herself into a cocoon, something she's never previously done. *Avengers* #394 reveals her body's immune system has turned her into a real human wasp, complete with majestic pink wings, antennae, an inhuman appearance and nasty stinger rays which can be shot from inside her body. As "The Crossing" moves into its grand denouement, the heroes seize upon a desperate plan to save lives. In the one-shot *Avengers Timeslide* (Jan. 1996), the team travels back in time and enlists a teenage version of Stark to help save the world. In the fateful *Iron Man* #325 (Feb. 1996), adult Tony faces his teen counterpart. Both men don advanced Iron Man armor for a vicious battle. Teen Tony fights as well as he can, but the clash concludes with the older Tony shattering the helmet of his young counterpart and then ripping out young Tony's heart. With that shocking development, the story shifts to *Avengers* #395 (Feb. 1996) as the heroes fight a final, frantic war against Kang, Mantis and their henchmen. The mature Tony repents of his evil ways just in time to bring an extradimensional version of the hero Swordsman to the fight. With Kang close to victory, Stark offers to sacrifice himself to help win the war. If the Avengers can charge up Stark's Iron Man suit, he can destroy Kang's weapons and win the day. In a final effort, the heroes push through and triumph over their nemesis. The defeated Kang flees, but Stark is near death. Before he dies, the adult Tony gives schematics for his chest plate to his allies. In the one-shot *Age of Innocence: The Rebirth of Iron Man* (Feb 1996), readers learn teen Tony's life was saved but the adult Tony Stark that fans knew for over thirty years has passed away. The younger version of Tony was now the new Iron Man. For any fans also reading the spider-clone saga, this turnabout came as no surprise. The super-heroic mantle was passed onto a new generation... at least until the lives of the Avengers and Iron Man faced an onslaught in 1996.

The action-oriented **Marvel Edge** imprint presented a story in 1995 that had a major impact on Marvel continuity. The crossover *Double Edge* has Nick Fury and S.H.I.E.L.D. arresting Frank Castle, a.k.a. The Punisher, in an attempt to rehabilitate him. Doc Samson tries using hypnosis to cure Castle's rage, but the treatment goes horribly wrong. In the middle of his treatment, the Punisher's therapy is stopped by an explosion. Instead of getting better, The Punisher becomes convinced Fury is responsible for the death of his family. The Punisher then embarks on a mission of revenge against Fury. He attacks S.H.I.E.L.D. headquarters, killing agents and Life Model Decoy robots until he confronts Fury himself. After a wild chase, Castle kills his enemy. Nick Fury is dead. The Punisher finds himself on his way to the electric chair for the murder, an incident that will kick off his new 1996 series.

And Under a Buck!

With all the changes to its main super-hero titles, it may have been a surprise that Marvel's most critically acclaimed comic of the year honored tradition. Beginning July 1995 (cover date September), Marvel premiered a set of comics with a 99¢ cover price that were each intended to promote a specific Marvel imprint. To that end, Marvel's Edge imprint produced *Over the Edge* (which carried the parenthetical subtitle "and under a buck!") featuring a rotating spotlight on Daredevil, Doctor Strange, Ghost Rider, the Hulk and the Punisher. The X-Men line, on the other hand, offered *Professor Xavier and the X-Men*, set in the 1960s as a continuity implant. The Avengers line provided *Avengers Unplugged*, and the Marvel Heroes line produced *Fantastic Four Unplugged*. Despite their affordable price tag, nearly every one of these series

As "The Crossing" reaches its climax, a teen version of Tony Stark comes forward to don the Iron Man armor.
TM and © Marvel Characters, Inc.

failed to catch on, mainly because fans recognized that most of the stories in these 99¢ books were essentially fill-ins or extraneous to the adventures going on in the main titles. As a result, the *Unplugged* series lasted only six issues each, while *Professor Xavier* and *Over the Edge* were both cancelled after ten issues.

One 99¢ release, though, broke free from the lackluster pack. Written with love and respect by Kurt Busiek and featuring art by Patrick Olliffe, ***Untold Tales of Spider-Man*** took place during carefully-considered gaps in the original Stan Lee-Steve Ditko run on *Amazing Spider-Man*. While the clone saga dominated most of the year's Spider-Man books, *Untold Tales* gave readers charming tales which reminded them why they loved the web-slinger in the first place. Busiek introduced new villains like the tragic Bluebird while emphasizing Peter's increasing maturity and his growing secret life as Spider-Man. The series was originally planned to cover Peter Parker's college years and play up the love triangle between Peter, Mary Jane Watson and Gwen Stacy. Busiek, however, submitted a six-issue outline that focused on Parker's high school years, allowing him to fill in continuity holes. For instance, Busiek had long wanted to tell a story that explained why Peter stopped wearing his glasses during the seminal original run of the title. Busiek, though, recognized that *Untold Tales* couldn't just pay homage to those 1960s comics that he and countless other Spider-Man fans loved. He had to tell stories that were entertaining in their own right, regardless of their reference to continuity. Nonetheless, Busiek was especially excited to "write Spidey back to when none of the power of the series had been diminished" (Mescallado 75). *Untold Tales* survived for 25 issues and two annuals.

Universes Collide

The Marvel and **DC Comics** universes crossed over again in 1995 with the squarebound $4.95 *Green Lantern/Silver Surfer: Unholy Alliances* by Ron Marz, Darryl Banks and Terry Austin. *Unholy Alliances* has its roots in DC's 1994 *Zero Hour* event. When Hal Jordan destroyed Oa, he created a breach in the fabric of reality that became a doorway into other universes. Thanos travels through that breach to the DC Universe. Once there, he tricks the gullible Kyle Rayner into recreating Oa as a precursor to Thanos accomplishing universal annihilation. Similarly, Hal Jordan, Parallax of the *Zero Hour* saga, travels to the Marvel Universe where he tricks the gullible Silver Surfer into relinquishing most of his cosmic power as a precursor to Hal recreating the universe in his image. Thanos dreams of death. Jordan dreams of life. Those attitudes place them in dramatic opposition. As Thanos and Jordan become more megalomaniacal, their strength grows exponentially. The godlings battle with their fists and their cosmic abilities through the recreated streets of Jordan's beloved Coast City. The only person who can initially save the two universes is Kyle,

Untold Tales of Spider-Man *presented a clone-free continuity implant.*
TM and © Marvel Characters, Inc.

who draws the villains' energy into his ring before he can transfer that energy back to the Silver Surfer. The crisis is averted when the Surfer closes the rift and everybody returns to their correct universe. Though the heroes were able to defeat the villains, the crossover set the stage for an even bigger meeting of Marvel and DC heroes in 1996.

In 1994 Superman flew into space for a rematch against Doomsday. In 1995 he flew into space to fight an equally terrifying creature when the Man of Steel went up against aliens from the famed Sigourney Weaver film franchise. Written and drawn by Dan Jurgens, inked by Kevin Nowlan and co-published by *Aliens* license-holder Dark Horse Comics, the three-issue, squarebound *Superman vs. Aliens* mini-series has the Man of Steel borrowing a spaceship to visit the lost Kryptonian city of Argo that has been invaded by the aliens only to discover that it is from a sister world called Odiline. Because Argo orbits a red sun, Superman loses all his super-powers when he lands there. In the city are a group of injured men and only one able-bodied survivor, named Kara. After he sends the wounded men back to Earth, Superman and Kara fight valiantly to destroy the aliens. Meanwhile, Lois Lane helps to care for the wounded men in a satellite orbiting the Earth before

Superman TM and © DC Comics. Aliens TM and © Twentieth Century Fox Film Corporation.

In a unique crossover, Superman squares off against the aliens from the famous film franchise.
Superman TM and © DC Comics. Aliens TM and © Twentieth Century Fox Film Corporation.

discovering they are all about to hatch newborn aliens. By the mini-series' conclusion Superman achieves victory, but it is an empty triumph as the aliens completely wipe out the Odiline refuge. Unknown to the hero, Kara rocketed to safety, setting the stage for a never-realized parallel to the 1959 origin of Supergirl.

While Superman was able to save himself from one dire fate, he wasn't able to do the same for Oliver Queen, a.k.a. the **Green Arrow**. Put more accurately, the Emerald Archer refused to let Superman save him. Written by Chuck Dixon with art by Rodolfo Damaggio, *Green Arrow* #101 (Oct. 1995) finds Queen on board a plane with his left hand attached to a bomb. If he removes his hand, the bomb will detonate and destroy Metropolis. Superman offers to resolve the situation by severing Green Arrow's arm, ensuring the survival of both hero and city (and echoing the archer's fate in 1986's *Batman: The Dark Knight* mini-series). Queen, however, can't stomach the thought of living the rest of his life as an amputee, unable to wield his bow and arrow. He instead detonates the bomb before the plane reaches Metropolis, sacrificing himself in the process. In contrast to the grand funeral provided for Superman, whose death shook the world, the lower-key Queen is remembered at a small wake at the back of Guy Gardner's bar. In the Batcave, Batman mourns his old friend, "He lived the way he wanted to. I can only hope he died the same way." With Oliver Queen's death, the legacy of the Green Arrow gets passed on to the next generation of archer: Queen's son, Connor Hawke.

Impulse Runs into his Own Series

Bart Allen, a.k.a. **Impulse**, represented the next generation of super-speedster, and in 1995, he was promoted from *Flash* supporting character to the lead in his own series. Written by Mark Waid and illustrated by Humberto Ramos, *Impulse* #1 (April 1995) describes the time-displaced Bart Allen as a "poster child for the judgment-impaired. Brought up in a world of virtual reality, Bart isn't good at distinguishing imaginary peril from genuine danger. He will learn the difference... just not today." That was all the information readers needed to understand that *Impulse*

went against the grain of dark, ultra-violent super-hero comic books that were trending at the time. As Waid explained in a 1995 interview, "People are less interested in seeing yet another superhero running around punching super-villains than they are seeing the real-life adventures of a 14-year-old dealing with the stuff a 14-year-old has to deal with, like family and friends" (Brady 86). To distinguish *Impulse* from every other DC title, Waid moved Bart far away from the hubbub of the DC Universe to the benign suburban neighborhood that Waid grew up in: Manchester, Alabama. Once there, Bart has to juggle fitting in with his high school classmates, concealing his super-heroic identity and absorbing the speed force lessons taught to him by his guardian and trainer, Max Mercury. Thanks principally to Bart's naïve recklessness, hijinks

Impulse, the next generation of Flash, ran into his own new series in 1995.
TM and © DC Comics.

ensue, all of them perfectly rendered by Ramos's cartoony art style. With its wacky, joke-a-minute approach—further emphasized by Bart's thought balloons which contained emoticons rather than words—*Impulse* garnered a devoted audience and became one of DC Comics' most beloved titles for the remainder of the decade.

Chris Claremont's New Royal Family

Since being unceremoniously removed from the X-Men books that had become synonymous with his name, **Chris Claremont** remained busy. He collaborated on a Star Trek graphic novel for DC Comics, guest wrote various Image Comics titles (after nearly becoming one of the company's founders), contributed to Jim Shooter's Defiant Comics and helmed a twelve-issue Aliens/Predator series for Dark Horse Comics, besides authoring several science fiction and fantasy novels. Claremont had even reached a deal with DC Comics to publish an adaptation of his acclaimed science fiction novel *First Flight* as a squarebound mini-series with art by Simone Bianchi. Unfortunately, the comic version of *First Flight* never took off.

In an unprecedented agreement with DC Comics, Chris Claremont owned all rights to his new super-team Sovereign Seven. TM and © Chris Claremont.

DC did, however, release Claremont's next big comic book, a groundbreaking project titled ***Sovereign Seven***. The unique deal Claremont negotiated with DC granted him full ownership of the characters he created for the series while at the same time allowed him to integrate these characters into the DC Universe. DC never permitted this kind of arrangement before, and Claremont saw the deal as a major step forward in creators' rights: "*Sovereign 7* [sic] establishes a fundamental benchmark, a precedent which says that for the right creator, the right project, the relationship between creator and publisher can be defined as a true partnership" ("The Sovereign Seven" 80).

As its title suggests, *Sovereign Seven* featured seven superheroes with royal blood: the super strong and super-fast Reflex; the occult, ninja-like assassin Finale; the high-flying psionic Rampart; the teleporter Cascade; the telepathic Network; the telekinetic warrior Cruiser; and finally Indigo, a master of disguise. Abducted from their dying worlds and brought to the DC Universe, these champions are naïve but powerful outsiders, forced to grow an awareness of their strange new world. The S7 take up residence in the town of Crossroads, Massachusetts, where they hang out at an inn that is the gateway to different dimensions. Paired with artist Dwayne Turner, Claremont's main focus was "the inherent mystery of the characters" rather than their integration into the DC Universe ("The Sovereign Seven" 78). Nonetheless, the Sovereigns met Darkseid in their first issue, and Power Girl joined the team in *S7* #25 (Aug. 1997), part of a string of issues that featured appearances by Superman, Hitman and Impulse. Claremont filled each issue with his trademark whimsy and angst, giving life and verve to his new creations. At times, he also indulged himself. The owners of the Crossroads bar were two singers from the folk duo Flash Girls, friends of the writer. The universe-spanning nature of the series allowed for cameos by a diverse collection of icons, including Pinky and the Brain, Neil Gaiman, reporters from National Public Radio, and even a pair of lightly disguised X-Men.

Sovereign Seven #1 (July 1995) was the eighth most popular comic of the month through Diamond Distribution. It was a short-lived ranking as by December, *S7* dropped to 43rd in the sales chart. A retailer from Virginia declared, "The big flop of the year has to go to *Sovereign Seven*, sorry DC" ("Market Beat"). A retailer in Newark, Delaware added, "Our customers simply couldn't follow where Claremont was going with it, and, eventually, everybody just gave up on it. We went from about 30 orders for the first issue down to zero by, I think, #6" (St. Lawrence 41). The series concluded with one of the oddest final issues ever published. After the team completes a victorious battle against its enemies, the last two pages of *Sovereign Seven* #36 (July 1998) reveal the Sovereigns were just fictional creations made up for tales told by two women to entertain their friends and family.

Claremont's former creative partner **John Byrne** also produced work for DC in 1995. Byrne assumed writer and artist responsibility on ***Wonder Woman*** with issue #101 (Sept. 1995) after a three-year run on the title by writer William Messner-Loebs. The Messner-Loebs issues placed WW and fellow Amazon Artemis at the heart of the bad girls movement, with the heroine briefly wearing a black

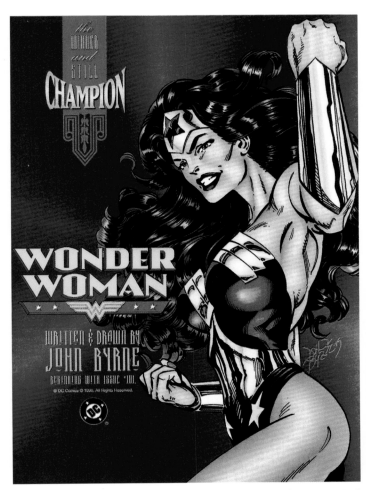
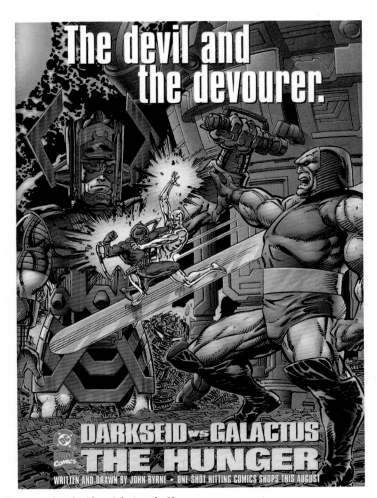

Two of John Byrne's 1995 releases were Wonder Woman *and* Darkseid vs. Galactus: the Hunger.
Wonder Woman, Darkseid and Orion TM and © DC Comics. Silver Surfer and Galactus TM and © Marvel Characters, Inc.

bustier, bicycle pants and punky boots as her costume. In one of his first moves, Byrne returned the heroine to her classic costume. He also made several other major changes during his time on the title, which lasted until *Wonder Woman* #136 (Aug. 1998). He moved Diana to a new city in which she created a new status quo. Byrne also introduced Cassie Sandsmark as the new Wonder Girl, and he established a connection between the New Gods and the Olympian Gods from which Wonder Woman descended. In a 1998 story, Byrne killed the title heroine and recast her mother Hippolyta in the role, retroactively revealing that she'd been the Golden Age Wonder Woman. Byrne saw his key task on *Wonder Woman* as making the character central to DC continuity. As he began his tenure on the title, he said, "I'm going to take [Wonder Woman] in I think a more traditional superhero direction than she's been [since] George [Pérez] relaunched her. I'm going to just be saying, 'Nah! She's number two to Superman.' She's gonna break some big stuff and fight some big villains. I have her up against Darkseid in the first issue" (Fielder, "Q&A John Byrne," 53).

Byrne also delivered a special one-shot in 1995. In *Darkseid vs. Galactus: The Hunger*, Galactus tries to consume Apokolips, a world central to the New Gods saga. That sets Galactus and Darkseid in conflict with each other and triggers a cataclysmic cosmic battle. Byrne was especially proud of the way the one-shot crossed over the two

powerful villains without involving the Fantastic Four or the New Gods. A fan gave Byrne the idea for the story, but the artist was unable to track the person down to give him credit for the suggestion. Byrne assumed the creative chores on a New Gods title in 1997.

DC's Deal with the Devil

While *Darkseid Vs. Galactus* crossed over two of Marvel and DC's greatest cosmic threats, a major 1995 crossover introduced a new supernatural threat to DC's fictional universe. Written by Mark Waid and pencilled by Howard Porter, the three-issue mini-series *Underworld Unleashed* (first issue cover-dated November 1995) begins with a massive escape of super-criminals from Belle Reve Prison. The jailbreak was engineered by a demonic trickster named **Neron** who brings the escaped villains to Hell to offer them a literal deal with the devil: they can all receive enhanced powers in exchange for their mortal souls. Not surprisingly, many villains accept Neron's terms, and with boosted powers (and confidence) they return to Earth to confront DC's super-heroes, with battles shown in a multitude of series. Among them, Major Disaster opposes the King of the Seven Seas in the pages of *Aquaman*; Dr. Phosphorous attacks Jack Knight in *Starman*; Satanus, Mr. Freeze and Blockbuster appear in *Primal Force, Green Lantern* and *Impulse* respectively. After dealing with the villains, Neron then turns to the heroes. He tempts the

When Absolute Evil Arises...

there'll be Hell to Pay!

UNDERWORLD UNLEASHED

a three-issue miniseries changing the face of villainy in the DC Universe forever!

Mark Waid · Howard Porter · Dan Green

BEGINNING IN September

In DC's Underworld Unleashed *crossover, many villains – and several heroes – have their powers enhanced by the demon Neron.* TM and © DC Comics.

Flash with the resurrection of Barry Allen and Batman with the resurrection of Jason Todd. He tempts Superboy with the chance to become Superman, and Green Lantern Kyle Rayner with the chance to bring his girlfriend Alex back to life. Most heroes resist Neron's temptation. The appropriately named Blue Devil isn't one of them. The longtime hero and Justice League member exchanges his soul for a chance to become the Hollywood movie star he has always dreamed of being. Because of his actions, though, Blue Devil's beloved friend Marla Bloom dies in a helicopter crash, devastating Blue Devil's life.

By *Underworld Unleashed* #3, the world has become enveloped in a war between Hell and Earth. Cities are under siege by demons. To battle the menace, the world's greatest heroes must enter Hell. Once there, they discover that only one who is pure of heart can defeat Neron. Thus, the innocent Captain Marvel offers the devil his soul, but his altruistic offering is a pure sacrifice which represents the opposite of Neron's evil. The goodness of the hero defeats the desolation of the villain and at long last, the world returns to its normal state. After three core issues and four dozen crossover issues, the horror has ended.

Though he enjoyed writing *Underworld Unleashed* at the time, Waid eventually realized that the story was wrong-headed in its attempt to modernize DC's established villains into something more formidable and sinister. As Waid explained in 1998:

> Knuckle-headed, well-intended creators ashamed of corny old characters have been, for most of a decade, dragging half-forgotten heroes and villains kicking and screaming into their own little hardware store of creativity. There, haunted by a guilty fear that these ancient superdoers aren't kewl enough for a generation of videogame-entranced readers, said knuckle-headed creators fool themselves into thinking they're doing them a good turn by bludgeoning all the innocent charm and colorful individuality out of them. I tried that once. Learned a lesson (Waid 202).

Batman Movie Recast

Veteran filmmaker **Joel Schumacher** could relate to Mark Waid's way of thinking. He was hired to replace Tim Burton as the director of the third Batman movie, *Batman Forever*. (Burton was relegated to producer after Warner Bros. executives found the box office returns from 1992's *Batman Returns* disappointing.) Differentiating himself from Burton, Schumacher sought to lighten up the film franchise as he explained in a 1995 interview for *Wizard* magazine: "I want Batman to be funnier and less dark. The TV series had a lot of humor in it that was missing from the first two films" (Pearlman 39). Aiding that approach was the casting of Jim Carrey—the most popular comedic actor of the decade—as the Riddler. Joining him were Academy Award winner Tommy Lee Jones as Two-Face, Nicole Kidman as criminal psychologist Chase Meridian and rising star Chris O'Donnell as Robin. However, Michael Keaton—the actor who wore Batman's cape and cowl in the first two films—no longer wanted any part of it. Reportedly concerned about Schumacher's approach for the film, Keaton bowed out and was replaced with Val Kilmer whose previous roles included singer Jim Morrison and Old West icon Doc Holliday (Gordiner).

In *Batman Forever* the Riddler invents a device that can drain information from a person's brain. Batman—now assisted by Robin, a newly orphaned circus acrobat—stops the Riddler and Two-Face from using this device on Gotham City. By movie's end, Two-Face has fallen to his death, and the Riddler has become so insane that he is convinced that *he* is Batman. Opening in cinemas nationwide on June 16, 1995, *Batman Forever* became the second most popular film of the year (trailing only the Pixar-animated *Toy Story*) and even performed better at the box office than *Batman Returns* did in 1992. The film, though, received mixed reviews from both movie critics and comics professionals. Kurt Busiek complained, "I kept checking my watch to see when it was going to end," and Peter David believed "there were some fundamental weaknesses in the script that the direction and acting couldn't surmount. But they produced exactly the movie they set out to produce." Dan Jurgens, on the other hand, felt "it was pretty enjoyable" while Alex Ross said, "I enjoyed the movie's look, it was very exciting and beautiful. But if I'd stopped to think about the plot, I'd have gone insane." Mark Waid was perhaps the most enthusiastic comics professional, gushing, "I loved it! I haven't enjoyed a comic movie so much since *Superman: The Movie*" (Shutt 21).

Texas-Flavored Vertigo

Despite all the attention paid to titles like *Sovereign Seven*, *Wonder Woman* and *Underworld Unleashed*, DC Comics remained a publisher devoted to releasing diverse material. For proof look no further than DC's line of **Star Trek** comics, edited by Margaret Clark. DC published eight Star Trek comic books with a December 1995 cover date. Four of those releases starred Captain Kirk's classic crew and four starred Captain Picard's *Next Generation* crew.

Meanwhile, the ethnically diverse **Milestone Comics** released a three-issue mini-series titled *Long, Hot Summer*, written by D.G. Chichester and illustrated by Denys Cowan. Like many of Milestone's story arcs, *Long, Hot Summer* could have emerged from a big city newspaper headline. A corporation seeks to build an amusement park on Paris Island, home to many of the Milestone heroes. The new construction forces families that live in the neighborhood to move, including *Icon* heroine Rocket and her family, prompting the Blood Syndicate to lead a revolt. *Long, Hot Summer* crossed over into all seven Milestone titles and included such developments as Hardware getting new armor and Static losing his virginity.

Over in the Karen Berger-helmed **Vertigo** line, writer Ed Brubaker and artist Eric Shanower combined for the 56-page one-shot *Vertigo Visions: Prez* (Sept. 1995). Subtitled "Smells Like Teen President," in an echo of the popular Nirvana song "Smells Like Teen Spirit," the story presents a group of slackers crossing the United States in search of the legendary first teen president. *Prez* captured Clinton-era ennui with a dramatic story of a slacker seeking his true father.

For all of Vertigo's relevance, variety and sophistication, the line's flagship title remained Neil Gaiman's *Sandman*, but that series was nearing the end of its distinguished run. In *Sandman*'s absence, another Vertigo title would have to step forward and carry the line, and the two creators responsible for that title were already within Vertigo's stable. Born and raised in Northern Ireland, writer **Garth Ennis** dropped out of a local university when he was nineteen in order to begin his comic book career. After writing several stories for U.K.'s Fleetway (most notably Judge Dredd serials for *2000 AD*), Ennis was hired to take over *Hellblazer* from the departing Jamie Delano, beginning with issue #41 (May 1991). It was on *Hellblazer* that Ennis first collaborated with British artist **Steve Dillon** (also a *2000 AD* veteran), and the two produced adventures of rogue John Constantine that combined empathy, horror, hatred and friendship in fascinating ways. While working on *Hellblazer*, Ennis was assigned to write the hysterically profane *Demon*, and his success on that title helped persuade Karen Berger to publish his—and Vertigo's—next great series.

Preacher (first issue cover-dated April 1995) stars Jesse Custer, a caustic small-town Texas minister who becomes possessed by the spirit of a half breed angel/demon named

Garth Ennis and Steve Dillon produced the next hit Vertigo comic book, **Preacher**. TM and © Garth Ennis and Steve Dillon.

Genesis that escaped from its prison in Heaven. Genesis endows Custer with "the Word of God," the ability to compel others to obey his verbal commands, but during Genesis's act of possession Custer's entire congregation is incinerated. Accompanied by his ex-girlfriend Tulip and an alcoholic Irish vampire named Cassidy, Jesse hits the road to find God (who has abandoned Heaven) to make him answer for his shortcomings as man's Creator. On the trail of Custer and his companions is an immortal gunslinger named the Saint of Killers who has been sent by God to retrieve Genesis by any means necessary.

Equal parts blasphemous and bloody, dark and disgusting, humorous and heady, *Preacher* embodied a variety of genres: American travelogue, supernatural horror and Western. As far as Ennis saw it, *Preacher* was about "the misuse of religion, and the misunderstandings that arise because of it, and God's responsibility to His creation. On the other hand, I see the book as being about loyalty and friendship, and standing by one's friends" (Samsel 100). Those themes in combination with a compelling cast of characters turned *Preacher* into a critical hit, earning five Eisner Award nominations for 1995: Best New Series, Best Continuing Series, Best Serialized Story, Best Writer and Best Penciller/Inker. Monthly sales on *Preacher* eventually settled in the high 40,000 copy range, only half the sales of the final issues of *Sandman*, but still enough to make it Vertigo's best-selling title, ensuring the viability of the line once *Sandman* ended. For Garth Ennis, *Preacher* marked the beginning of a very busy period in his career, as 1996 would show.

The Truth is Out There on the Comics Page

By 1995, **The X-Files** television show was a major cultural phenomenon, driving high ratings on the fledgling FOX network. The show enjoyed a rabid fan base anxious to learn as much as they could about FBI agents Mulder and Scully. Among those fans was **Stefan Petrucha**, then writing *Duckman* for **Topps Comics**. "I saw the first episode and fell in love with the series," Petrucha explained. "I decided to give [Topps editor] Jim Salicrup a call suggesting that it would make a great comic book and he should get the rights for Topps and that I would be the perfect writer for it" (Kurtz 83). Petrucha was a passionate follower of Forteana, the study of occult and bizarre happenings which provided much of the basis of show's mythology. With his interests, therefore, Petrucha could write his own Mulder and Scully stories while staying true to the conceptual framework of the TV program. In fact, he created a different conspiracy for the agents to pursue than the one Mulder and Scully investigated on TV. In the comic, the X-Files team deals with incidents such as the murders of UFO witnesses, the truth behind the 1908 Tunguska explosion, near-death experiences and vanishing Alaska cities, all under the guidance of the mysterious Project Aquarius. Salicrup paired Petrucha with artist Charles Adlard due to the latter's ability to draw believable human beings. Adlard started drawing *X-Files* even before the show began airing in his native England. Producers sent Adlard video cassettes so he could get a sense of the look and feel of the show.

X-Files sold well, with the first few printings selling out at the retail level. Sales were boosted by a special five-page story by the Topps team in the July 15, 1995 issue of *TV Guide*, America's best-selling magazine. Sales quickly

The X-Files, *an adaptation of the FOX TV series, was a hit for Topps Comics but suffered from interference by the show's production company.* TM and © Twentieth Century Fox Film Corporation.

dropped, though, because the comic was released on an irregular schedule. Those delays came because Topps editor Tony Isabella had major problems working with Ten Thirteen, the studio that produced the television show. Ten Thirteen took a painfully strict and slow approach to approving stories. As Isabella lamented, "I've worked on several licensed comics projects in my career; none were ever as – difficult – as *The X-Files*. Maybe it's because their people didn't know what they wanted from the comics, maybe it was because they didn't want the comics, period. But, if you ever asked why Topps was publishing *The X-Files* on such an erratic schedule, there's your answer" (Isabella 42).

From Out of the Shadows

By this time, the **Image Comics** creators already had a well-earned reputation for publishing their books on an erratic schedule, although **Jim Valentino** had been releasing his *Shadowhawk* series on a somewhat consistent bi-monthly basis. Initially, Valentino kept his hero hidden in the shadows, with his secret identity a mystery to everybody. Slowly, Valentino revealed the character's explosive backstory. Paul Johnstone was a troubled African-American growing up in Harlem. After some intervention, the boy turned his life around, growing up to become a lawyer and eventually a district attorney. In order to send Johnstone a message, mobsters hire a group of petty thugs to attack him, and during the ensuing fight, Johnstone is injected with HIV-infected blood. With the knowledge that the infection will eventually progress to full-blown AIDS, Johnstone vows to spend the rest of his life dispensing violent justice on criminals. To help him in this endeavor, one of Johnstone's friends provides him with an exoskeleton armor that he had been developing. With this armor, Johnstone becomes Shadowhawk, patrolling the city streets for felons and shattering their spines when he catches them in the act of committing crime. That level of savagery helped the anti-hero gain a reputation as an urban legend hunted by both law-enforcers and lawbreakers. Eventually, though, AIDS begins to ravage Johnstone's body. The six-part "The

Monster Within" chronicles his attempts to stop the disease. In *Shadowhawk* #12 (Aug. 1994) Johnstone meets up with fellow AIDS sufferer Chapel to see if they can work together to halt the disease. They cannot. Next the WildC.A.T.s put Johnson's brain into a robot body, but the body rejects the brain. A tragic trip to Alan Moore's "1963" universe unleashes the AIDS patient zero on that world. Meetings with Image heroes The Others, Supreme and Spawn also do nothing to stop the disease. Finally, *Shadowhawk* #18 (May 1995) presents Johnstone's demise. Rather than go out in a grand, super-heroic blaze of glory, Johnstone dies in a more conventional way: in a hospital bed.

While *Shadowhawk* focused on a terrible disease, another Image book took on an altogether different blight and garnered some odd publicity for its efforts. *Spawn* #30 (April 1995), written by Todd McFarlane and illustrated by Greg Capullo, depicts attempts by a group of KKK members to drive a black family off land they own, and of Spawn's attempts to stop the Klan. The violent story depicts cartoonish, almost maniacal KKK members at war with ordinary people. It was nearly impossible for any attentive reader to miss McFarlane's point about the evil of racism. That unsubtle subtext, however, was lost on at least one reader. When the seven-year-old son of Dr. Mary Williams Ahmed of Grand Forks, North Dakota, bought home his copy of *Spawn* #30, Ahmed was appalled by the story's violence. Ahmed wrote her state senator about the comic, wrote an article for her local newspaper, and even got the story featured on national TV. On the September 5, 1995 episode of the syndicated newsmagazine *A Current Affair*, reporter Mary Garofolo presented the comic in words that were intended to stir controversy, stating *Spawn* confronts "real-life horrors like homelessness, child abuse, and domestic violence. It's not your usual comic book fare and it's certainly not funny." Ahmed didn't believe comics were suitable for teaching children about life. "If this is the medium that we're going to be using in the future in terms of intervention and prevention measures in educating our children in relation to violence, crime, sexism, then this is a very sad day in America," she said (David). For his part, McFarlane defended his comic on *A Current Affair*, although he maintained that producers edited his comments so extensively that the show ultimately aired a one-sided version of the story.

Wicked Witchblade

The decision makers at **Marc Silvestri's Top Cow** studios were very impressed with the success Billy Tucci was

having with his creator-owned *Shi*. Besides collaborating with Tucci on an intercompany crossover (the two issue *Cyblade/Shi: The Battle for Independents*, published in August 1995), Top Cow also recognized that *Shi* represented something they needed to duplicate. As Silvestri explained, "We saw that [*Shi*] was popular and that there was a trend growing for strong female characters in comics" (Shapiro 6). With that in mind, writers David Wohl, Brian Haberlin and Christina Z. along with newcomer artist **Michael Turner** created one of the most popular comic book heroines of the 1990s. *Witchblade* #1 (Nov. 1995) introduces New York City police detective Sara "Pez" Pezzini. Tipped off to a secret meeting of crime bosses in an abandoned theatre, Sara investigates and finds the mysterious Ian Nottingham in possession of a strange, ornately-designed gauntlet called the Witchblade. When one of the mobsters tries to put on the mystically-powered glove, it destroys his whole hand. But when Sara is discovered and shot, she reaches for the Witchblade. The gauntlet bonds to her hand, and Sara becomes magically wrapped in armor. She declares, "I am the light. I am an angel of death. I am power. I am – insane!" Thus begins Witchblade's adventures, and while many observers could be excused for dismissing the protagonist as just another bombshell Bad Girl with skimpy clothing, what also lured in readers was Sara's down-to-earth, streetwise characterization. Christina Z. summed up her approach to the book: "We've all experienced weird and very real emotions and had experiences in our lives. For *Witchblade* to really work, Sara had to become an emotional confidante to readers in a very real way" (Shapiro 53). In fact, *Witchblade*'s earliest issues eschewed

Michael Turner art from Witchblade, *a major new release from Top Cow in 1995.* TM and © Top Cow Publications, Inc.

traditional super-heroics for a more mature look at police life. Silvestri compared the style of the comic book to top-rated TV show *NYPD Blue*. Fans also latched onto the series' premise—derived from Michael Moorcock's "Eternal Champion"—that only one woman per generation would be able to wear the enchanted gauntlet.

Witchblade established Michael Turner as a breakout star. A former karate professional and instructor as well as an avid diver and all-around athlete, Turner became an artist when his mother's friend dragged him to a comic convention. The con created a desire inside Turner to become involved in comics. He soon worked up some art samples and sent them to Top Cow editor David Wohl who rejected the initial submissions but encouraged Turner to develop greater skills by drawing as much as possible. Turner persisted and before long, Top Cow hired him to work on such titles as *Cyberforce* and *Ballistic* before giving him the opportunity to co-create *Witchblade*.

Summer Event Rising

Visionary artist **Sam Kieth** experienced multimedia success in 1995 when his strange ***The Maxx*** made its television debut as an ongoing cartoon segment in MTV's anthology series *Oddities*. Premiering Saturday, April 8, 1995, and often running multiple times per week, kids and comic fans alike praised "The Maxx" for its emotional honesty, its attractive animation and its dreamlike narrative. Abby Terkuhle, MTV's senior vice president for on-air creative and animation summed up the appeal of Kieth's work: "What I liked about *The Maxx* is that it was not your typical superhero story. It takes the conventions of a typical superhero comic and, as it unfolds, sort of turns them upside down" (Grant 45). *Oddities* faithfully adapted issues of Kieth's Image Comics series, providing the unique tale of a homeless man who is a super-hero in another dimension.

Maxx was still a comic star as well. He crossed over with popular Image/Wildstorm characters Gen13 in a December 1995 one-shot by William Messner-Loebs, Tomm Coker and Troy Hubbs. Despite events like this, however, the number of copies sold of Image Comics dropped dramatically from their high just three years earlier. Only *Spawn* was a constant presence in the *Wizard* Top 10 each month. Few Image titles even made their way into the Top 20. As a California shop owner reported, "The sales are quite decent on the average for this company, but way, way down from the glory days. For a hot year or so the Image mavericks could have sold even their used Kleenex, but not anymore. *Shadowhawk*, *Savage Dragon*, *Maxx* and almost all of Liefeld's books hardly sell at all" (Paterson 76).

The depressed sales only made Image rely even more on crossovers, and in 1995 both **Rob Liefeld's Extreme Studios** and **Jim Lee's Wildstorm** delivered separate events. *Wildstorm Rising* spanned two bookend issues, along with crossovers in all Wildstorm titles published in May and June 1995. Barry Windsor-Smith, James Robinson, Ron Marz, Kevin Maguire, Brett Booth, Terry Austin and Al Vey provided story and art. *Rising* first sets the WildC.A.Ts at odds with Stormwatch. Eventually the teams stop their fighting long enough to confront the villainy of Helspont and Defile who hope to collect the keys needed to unlock an alien Daemonite ship that could destroy Earth. Windsor-Smith hated his work on the bookend issues, stating a year later, "I should never have bloody done it, and I wish I hadn't. But I was talked into it, and kind of got caught up in it, and it had to do with – oh man, it's like a nightmare, only far remembered at this point – I was going through this hapless story where I couldn't understand what anybody's motives were" (Groth 73).

Liefeld's crossover, "Extreme Sacrifice," literally dragged readers to Hell and back. In *Extreme Sacrifice* #1 (Jan. 1995),

Prophet, Shaft, Deathstrike and Supreme starred in "Extreme Sacrifice," the crossover event from Rob Liefeld's Extreme Studios. TM and © Rob Liefeld Inc.

Rob Liefeld launched Battlestar Galactica, Glory *and* Avengelyne *through his new company, Maximum Press, which wasn't affiliated with Image Comics.*
TM and © Rob Liefeld Inc. TM and © Universal Studios.

gun-toting anti-hero Chapel dies and is sent to Hell — which he then takes over. Chapel unleashes a demonic villain who slaughters all the members of the long-running team Brigade, mostly off-panel. The story reaches its bizarre crescendo when Lucifer teams up with Superman-analog Supreme and a super-hero version of Jesus to battle Chapel for the control of Hell. Supreme is killed at the end of the fight. However, a quick resurrection in his solo comic showed that Supreme was as resilient as his DC Comics inspiration.

Liefeld looked to diversify his comic book enterprise beyond super-heroes, and in doing so, he stumbled upon a property that could be acquired for a very small royalty. **Battlestar Galactica** was a short-lived, fondly remembered science-fiction television show during the late 1970s. Rather than reboot the concept of a fleet of starships searching for Earth as they flee the robotic Cylons, Liefeld decided to continue the old TV show's timeline, with the comic taking place fifteen years after the TV show ended. Written by Liefeld and Robert Place Newton with art by Karl Altstaetter and Hector Gomez, the first *Battlestar Galactica* mini-series lasted four issues and has the humanoid fleet discovering an unpopulated Earth. Richard Hatch, the actor who played Apollo on the original program, then wrote a follow-up series, *Battlestar Galactica: Apollo's Journey*, in 1996. Liefeld's *Battlestar Galactica* also presented human-looking Cylons that infiltrated the human fleet — an idea that would later be at the center of a revival of the TV show in the 2000s.

Attentive readers noticed that *Battlestar Galactica* didn't carry the Image Comics logo. Instead, the series was part of Liefeld's new **Maximum Press**, created by Liefeld so he could have a comic book company unaffiliated with Image. With the aim of diversifying Liefeld's base of readers, Maximum released the "bad girl" series *Avengelyne* (based on former

Vampirella model Cathy Christian, then-fiancée to Image Publisher Tony Lobito), the science-fantasy *Warchild* and Dan Fraga's creator-owned science-fiction book *Black Flag*. All of these titles became victims of a terrible marketplace for new comics. While Maximum Press released fifteen issues of *Avengelyne*, *Black Flag* only lasted five issues, and *Warchild* even less than that at four issues. As far as sales went, *Avengelyne* fared the best — issue #3 (July 1995) finished in 45th place on Diamond distribution's sales chart. The highest *Galactica* placed on the sales chart was 78th but that was still better than Liefeld's other titles. Though Maximum Press got off to an inauspicious start, it would become an integral part of the biggest comics story of 1996, a story that would nearly overturn 1991's Image revolution.

Now Entering Astro City

Thanks to the smash success of 1994's *Marvels*, **Kurt Busiek** was one of the hottest writers in comics. He began contemplating a follow-up Marvel anthology series, one that would build on the core idea of *Marvels* by exploring different eras of Marvel history through the eyes of civilians. For example, Busiek considered presenting the stories of a nurse dealing with patients during a wild super-hero tussle, and of an Avengers battle seen through the eyes of one of the Wasp's society friends. The more Busiek considered the anthology, however, the more limiting the idea seemed to him. Such a book would require a daunting amount of research on a monthly basis. Furthermore, Busiek would not be fully free to explore the characters that intrigued him. The more he thought about it, the more Busiek realized that he should just create his own characters and embed them within a new fictional universe.

After inviting his former *Marvels* collaborator Alex Ross to commit to painting the covers for his new series, and choosing the name **Astro City** for its location, Busiek worked up a brief proposal. At first, Busiek wanted to have different artists illustrate each story arc, as Neil Gaiman did on *Sandman*. **Brent Anderson** committed to draw one storyline during a joint appearance at the World Science Fiction Convention in San Francisco. Other artists considered for *Astro City* included Steve Rude, Adam Hughes and Mike Wieringo. Dark Horse Comics felt Busiek's proposed series had potential, but one of its editors stipulated that Busiek create two books set in the same universe, with one of the books being an anthology. Busiek, though, demurred on that idea.

Shortly after dropping out of a Marvel Comics plan to produce a *Marvels* sequel, Busiek found himself on a shared plane flight with Dark Horse editor Bob Schreck. Taking advantage of the opportunity, Busiek suggested to Schreck that the story that would have been *Marvels II* might serve as a limited series with completely new characters. Schreck was enthusiastic about the proposal. Despite this, talks stalled between Busiek and Dark Horse, so the writer continued to shop his anthology around at conventions. When Image Comics expressed interest, Busiek went back to Anderson and asked the artist to draw the first five pages of a proposed first issue. Based on Anderson's art samples, Image agreed to publish the series.

In an interview with *American Comic Book Chronicles*, Busiek explained that someone at Image didn't like the title "Astro City." It was considered too "goofy." Busiek decided to add his name to the title (*Kurt Busiek's Astro City*) which would both undercut any perceived goofiness and remind readers that the series was being produced by the same person who wrote *Marvels*. Going with Image Comics, though, also meant the writer would have to pay for production of *Astro City* out of his own pocket. Thankfully for Busiek, he had received a large royalty check for his work on *Marvels*, which paid for Brent Anderson's art, Richard Starkings

Kurt Busiek's Astro City *featured some traditional super-hero action...*
TM and © Juke Box Productions.

and Comicraft's lettering and Steve Buccellato's colors for *Astro City*'s first six issues. It became money well spent with each contributor perfectly suited for the series. Regarding Anderson's work, Busiek said, "The anatomy of the characters is right, the faces are very detailed, but there's something that's just slightly larger than life about it" (Spaulding 68). Given this assessment, Busiek abandoned his initial plan to use a different artist for every *Astro City* story arc (which would have been a hassle to arrange anyway). Anderson could do everything Busiek needed, so he asked the artist to stay on *Astro City* beyond the first six issues.

In advance of publication, Busiek devoted an additional $35,000 of his own money toward promotion, and when *Astro City* #1 arrived in stores on August 10, 1995, the series became an immediate critical hit, receiving raves from fan magazines like *The Comics Buyer's Guide*, *Hero Illustrated* and even the notoriously picky *The Comics Journal*. *Overstreet's Fan* magazine called *Astro City* the best new series of 1995.

The ingenuity of *Astro City* was its casting of familiar super-heroic archetypes in an unfamiliar light. Busiek used these archetypes to both reveal and reconfigure the conventions of super-hero narratives. For instance, *Astro City* #1, titled "In Dreams,"

...but its main emphasis was on the humanity of its characters.
TM and © Juke Box Productions.

introduces the all-powerful Samaritan, who, like many other super-heroes, dedicates himself to safeguarding the citizens of Earth. But as the first issue reveals, Samaritan's dedication becomes a twenty-four hours a day/seven days a week responsibility as the hero races off to intervene in *every* crisis and threat. As a result, what little sleep Samaritan enjoys is dominated by dreams of flying, of a freedom from his never-ending super-heroics. Perhaps the most impressive story from *Astro City*'s first volume was issue #4 (Nov. 1995), which mixed immigration, history and the supernatural into a parable of the history of American comic books. That issue won the Eisner Award for Best Single Issue of the year, and *Astro City* also won the Best New Series award.

The first six issues of *Astro City* were published on a monthly basis, a schedule that Busiek and Anderson eventually couldn't maintain. To give themselves some time to catch up, Busiek scheduled *Astro City* #7 to be released a month late… but during that interim, the writer decided to put the series on hold as he began considering offers from publishers like Broadway Comics and DC Comics to move *Astro City* to their lines. Busiek ultimately decided to bring his comic to a brand new imprint in 1996.

The Lights Go On At Broadway

Broadway Comics happened to be **Jim Shooter**'s latest comic book venture. His previous enterprise, Defiant, folded in September 1994 when various suitors eventually declined to invest in the failing company. Those potential investors included New Line Entertainment, Savoy Pictures and Broadway Video Entertainment, a production company that delivered such popular TV series as *Saturday Night Live* and *Late Night with Conan O'Brien*. When Defiant went out of business, its publisher, Winston Fowlkes, made an arrangement with Broadway's president, Eric Ellenbogen, to hire members of Defiant's creative staff to develop a property based on Harley-Davidson motorcycles. Following the expiration of his contract with Defiant, Shooter received a call from Ellenbogen asking him to lead the development team. Before long, Ellenbogen offered to start a Broadway comics division, owned 50/50 by Broadway and Shooter, but with BVE's Lorne Michaels acting as the general partner.

Though comics industry sales continued to slump badly as 1995 dawned, Shooter hoped that Broadway's wealthy investors would enable the company to survive and thrive. "They had done a few licensing deals," reported Shooter, "one with Topps I think and one with Marvel. They liked the economics of the comic book business. They liked a lot of things about it" (Spaulding 16). With that backing, Shooter enlisted a group of friendly professionals and set about creating new intellectual properties. Echoing ideas he explored before, Broadway aimed to present the adventures of ordinary people who gain amazing powers in the "world outside your window."

Powers that Be #1 (Nov. 1995) was Broadway's first release. It featured two stories that spun off into their own series. One was "Star Seed," the story of the son of an amazing Earth woman and an alien father. The other story, "Fatale," was the Broadway character that attracted the most attention from industry observers. Fatale is gorgeous fashion model Desiree Hopewell, who has the power to leech memories and energy from people by kissing them. Chased by the evil organization The Brotherhood, Desiree fights to stay alive. Shooter relished working on *Fatale*, especially because it was a bit of a reply to a major industry trend: "*Fatale* was an experiment in many ways. *Fatale* was created to be Broadway Comics' answer to the 'Bad Girl' trend, popular in the 1990's. Being me, I wanted to do a Bad Girl who was every bit as extreme as those pneumatic vixens who led the charge but less puerile and more real" (Shooter). The Broadway creative team liked poking fun at

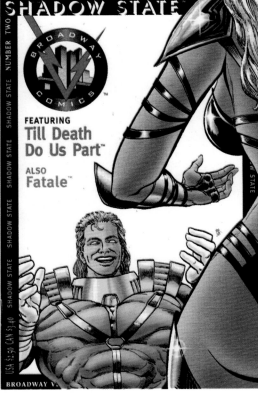

Jim Shooter's Broadway Comics launched with **Shadow State**, *an anthology series that introduced its ambitious line of titles.*
TM and © respective copyright owner.

Desiree's appearance. For several issues, the heroine had a bandaged, broken nose to show her vulnerability. Though many fans felt intrigued by the new heroine's irreverent attitude and personal growth, *Fatale* suffered from poor promotion. One observer noted *Fatale* was the focus of one of the biggest advertising missteps in recent memory: "An full-page ad [sic] appeared in Diamond's *Previews* distributor catalog. The picture: Fatale's bust. The caption: 'Shown actual size.' Smooth..." (Bickford 412).

At Broadway, all writing was done as a group. As Shooter recalls, "We wrote as a team. I thought, 'let's try this like TV writers.' We had four people writing, and every once in a while, we'd have a guest person that we called the fifth chair" (Sacks 224). That team was comprised of Shooter, Janet Jackson, Joseph A. James and Pauline Weiss. Broadway's artists included J.G. Jones, Geof Isherwood, Andrew Wendel, Art Nichols and Stefano Gaudiano. Everyone involved put in long hours to deliver a robust line. Despite all the hard work, Broadway would not survive beyond 1996.

Shooter's former company showed the comic industry's decline in stark terms in 1995. The newly rechristened "**Valiant Heroes from Acclaim Comics**" continued its steep sales drop, and in an attempt to reverse that course, publisher Steve Massarsky and editor-in-chief Bob Layton delivered "**Birthquake**," a line wide initiative that began after the cancellation of eight of Valiant's lowest-selling series: *Armorines*, *Geomancer*, *Harbinger*, *H.A.R.D. Corps*, *Psi-Lords*, *Rai and the Future Force*, *The Second Life of Doctor Mirage* and *Secret Weapons*. Then, starting with cover date July 1995, nine of Valiant's remaining series (*Bloodshot*, *Eternal Warrior*, *Magnus Robot Fighter*, *Ninjak*, *Solar*, *Timewalker*, *Turok*, *Visitor* and *X-O Manowar*) were promoted to a biweekly publishing schedule, to enable two-issue arcs by rotating creative teams. Valiant recruited some

of the industry's hottest creators to produce comics, several of whom had never worked for the publisher before: Dan Jurgens, Ron Marz, Bart Sears, Norm Breyfogle, Jackson Guice, Paul Gulacy, Keith Giffen, John Ostrander and Tom Grindberg, among others. Many of the new writers and artists took their assignments in new directions. For instance, on *Solar*, Dan Jurgens shook up the book's cast. Writer Ron Marz and artist Bart Sears gave *X-O Manowar* a new action-adventure spin which moved the comic away from its roots as a cross between Conan and Iron Man. The changes in story and talent, however, did nothing to improve sales. As a Chicago area retailer described, "The 'Birthquake' event was, naturally, a disaster. Perhaps it's not the best approach to go bi-weekly with titles that people aren't buying once a month" (Spurlock 248). Indeed, several months after the launch of "Birthquake" Acclaim represented only 3% of all comics sales through Capital City Distribution. That was a precipitous drop from two years earlier. One sign of Birthquake's failure was the layoff of half of Acclaim's staff in mid-September.

BIG Plans for Tekno

Broadway Entertainment wasn't the only Hollywood player to invest in the comic book medium in 1995. Sci-Fi Channel founders Mitchell Rubenstein and Laurie Silvers founded **Tekno Comix** under the corporate umbrella of BIG Entertainment. Comics, they reasoned, were an inexpensive way to explore new intellectual properties. Taking a cue from the world of conventional publishing, Tekno launched with a set of titles that all had initial inspiration from celebrity creators. *Isaac Asimov's I-Bots* was based on ideas Asimov had about super-powered robots trying to become human. *Gene Roddenberry's Lost Universe* dealt with a spaceship sent to a remote colony to preserve peace. *Neil Gaiman's Lady Justice* introduced a woman who was possessed by a revenge-seeking spirit. *John Jakes's Mullkon Empire* was a multigenerational science fiction saga while *Leonard Nimoy's Primortals* told a story of a first contact with aliens. Finally, *Mickey Spillane's Mike Danger* featured a hardboiled detective in a futuristic city. Connecting all the series in some way was *Neil Gaiman's Teknophage*, a series that starred a grungy lizard-like master manipulator who took a deep interest in various Tekno characters while he prepared to invade the Earth.

None of the celebrity creators actually wrote the comic books, and the extent of their involvement in each series varied widely. By 1995, Isaac Asimov was already dead, and according to Steven Grant, co-writer of *I-Bots* along with Howard Chaykin, Asimov, "didn't even come up with the name,

Acclaim Comics invested a lot of money and promotion in its "Birthquake" event, but sales remained anemic.
TM and © Valiant Entertainment LLC.

only the thinnest of concepts that, according to legend, was written on a cocktail napkin: robots as superheroes" (Steven Grant). Gaiman, on the other hand, sometimes called the writers assigned to his books. "I've let people run with [the books]", Gaiman stated in 1995, "I had a long chat with Jim Vance the other day, where I basically told him that I'm really enjoying what he's doing on *Mr. Hero*" (Stokes 76). Leonard Nimoy came up with the idea of *Primortals* while doing preparation work for *Star Trek IV*. That idea was planned as part of a short story anthology Nimoy was preparing with Isaac Asimov. Once Tekno launched, Nimoy didn't have any contact with his comic's writers or editors, but he claimed to speak daily to Laurie Silvers about story elements and approaches for his series.

BIG signed a deal with Warner Books to provide novelizations of the comic book concepts. Steve Perry (who also wrote prose versions of *Aliens*, *Conan* and *Star Wars*, among other film properties) adapted the worlds of *Primortals* and *I-Bots* to prose. Additional publications, such as a prose version of *Lost Universe*, were never released. BIG also opened futuristic-looking kiosks at the Mall of America in Minneapolis and at malls in Florida and Virginia that sold Tekno and other comics. Tekno even started a fan club before its line was even launched. For an annual fee of $15, subscribers received a button, a poster, a membership card and certificate, a newsletter, along with free giveaways at conventions. The first 1,000 members also received a free limited edition comic book.

Despite its hype, its strong financial backing and an unprecedented million-dollar marketing push, the new line had trouble attracting readers. Some early months saw a smattering of Tekno Comix break Diamond's Top 100 sales charts, but by 1996 sales were in freefall. Retailer Shaun Spurlock reported, "The original titles aren't selling well at all" (Spurlock 126). Other retailers said the line was nearly stillborn on arrival. Many readers who tried Tekno's books didn't enjoy them. *Gene Roddenbery's Lost Universe* "won" the dubious award for Most Incomprehensible Storyline for 1995 from *Overstreet's Fan* magazine. A rebranding of the line as BIG Comix in 1996 did little to improve matters, and the line died in 1997.

Spirits of Independence

In many ways, in 1995 it was better to be a small press publisher than a small comic book company. For one, iconic self-publisher **Dave Sim** led a "Spirits of Independence" tour with the purpose of spurring interest in small press books of all types. Joining Sim in such cities as Columbus, Kansas City, Chicago, Seattle and Austin were Stephen Bissette of *Tyrant*, Don Simpson of *Bizarre Heroes*, Steve Conley of *Avant Garde* and newcomer **Paul Pope** who had just begun publishing his opus, *THB*. The comic book stars HR Watson, a young girl on a bizarre version of Mars who is protected by her bodyguard, THB. Often surreal and emotionally moving in surprising ways, and animated by Pope's beguilingly intricate linework, *THB* was a star-making performance that earned an Eisner Award nomination for Best New Series.

Sim also spotlighted the work of many indie creators in a special "Cerebus Preview" section in the back of each issue of *Cerebus*. One of those works was *Hilly Rose's Space Adventures*, by B.C. Boyer, best known for *The Masked Man*, a series published by Eclipse in the mid-1980s. *Hilly Rose's Space Adventures* followed a spacefaring female reporter who becomes involved in a few scrapes and battles as part of her professional life. Boyer's series, which ran nine issues, contained classic E.C.-style science fiction art. Another small press standout that Sim promoted was Mark Oakley's energetic *Thieves & Kings*. M'Oak (as he called himself, partially in tribute to a much-loved *Cerebus* supporting character) delivered a sweet and complex fantasy with an eclectic mix of text and empathetic art. The approach gave Oakley's world a richly mythological feel.

Rick Veitch, former writer of *Swamp Thing*, launched an idiosyncratic self-published series in 1995. *Roarin' Rick's Rare Bit Fiends* was a dream diary, the chronicle of Veitch's subconscious mind channeled onto the comic book page. Through Veitch's kaleidoscopic eye, readers saw a multifaceted view of comics celebrities like Sim, Alan Moore, Steve Bissette and Neil Gaiman. They also received funhouse mirror views of Veitch's personal life.

Tom Hart published his Xeric Award winning *Hutch Owen's Working Hard*. Drawn in Hart's emotionally resonant childlike style, *Working Hard* tells the story of rapacious millionaire Dennis T. Worner and the eccentric Hutch Owen who stands in his way. A social satire and wistful daydream, *Working Hard* took the reader into unexpected

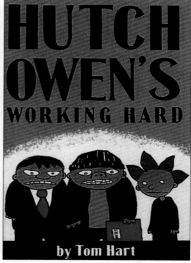

Paul Pope's THB *and Tom Hart's* Hutch Owen's Working Hard *captured the attention of indie comics fans.* TM and © Paul Pope. TM and © Tom Hart.

places and displayed Hart's potential. Another former Xeric Award winner received wider attention in 1995. **Adrian Tomine**, a 20-year-old student at the University of California at Berkeley, had his long-running slice of life comic *Optic Nerve* picked up by Drawn and Quarterly Press. The move to D&Q allowed Tomine time to focus on the production of his comic along with his studies. As time went on, the spectrum of Tomine's stories expanded and the title began to sell better due to its deadpan and thoughtful look at modern life. Under D&Q, *Optic Nerve* displayed stronger production values, tighter linework and more sophisticated storytelling.

And then there was **David Lapham** who previously worked alongside Jim Shooter on such series as Valiant's *Harbinger* and Defiant's *Warriors of Plasm*. Lapham learned the craft well with his work at those companies, but now he wanted to follow his own vision as he explained in 1995: "You break into the industry and you do everything you can get your hands on. Eventually I decided I wanted to do things for myself. The long-term plan was that I drew and liked comics and I wanted to be in comics. Once I started to grow, I discovered so many other possibilities" (Darnall 48). Lapham self-published a brutal, often hallucinatory crime drama called ***Stray Bullets***. Presented in stark, unembellished black and white with characters that had wildly dysfunctional lives, *Stray Bullets* became a surprise hit, earning three Eisner Award nominations (Best New Series, Best Continuing Series, Best Single Issue) while Lapham won the award for Best Writer/Artist.

Other self-publishers continued their runs in 1995. Among them were Don Simpson with his superhero parody *Bizarre Heroes*, Terry Moore with his slice-of-life *Strangers in Paradise*, Shannon Wheeler with his freewheeling *Too Much Coffee Man*, Teri Wood with her science fiction adventure *Wandering Star*, Batton Lash with his satirical *Wolff and Byrd, Counselors of the Bizarre*, James Owen with his fantasy *Starchild* and John Mitchell and Jana Christy with their unique *Very Vicky*. Virtually the only thing these publications had in common was the way they were funded and released. The range of material small press comics represented was vast, from Simpson's madcap super-hero silliness to Owen's delicate fantasy. Moore and Lash faithfully published their books every other month like clockwork. Wood, on the other hand, struggled to release two issues during the year.

Unsurprisingly in a down market, self-published titles typically had low sale numbers. For instance, B.C. Boyer's *Hilly Rose* #1 (May 1995) sold 7,500 copies while its second issue (July 1995) sold 4,500 copies. Those kind of figures meant slim profits, which, in turn, led to a disincentive

Former Valiant Comics artist David Lapham self-published his black-and-white crime drama Stray Bullets.
TM and © David Lapham.

for small press creators to continue their work. After all, if you could make more money working at McDonald's, why bother writing and drawing? At the same time, many creators expressed the optimism that the future was bright for small press comic books. A panel at the 1995 San Diego Comic Book Expo had Rick Veitch, Paul Pope, Maria Lapham, Don Simpson and Batton Lash extoling the virtues of self-publishing. Afterwards, Veitch pointed out, "We had over two hundred retailers show up while Marvel Comics were giving their panel right down the hall, and they only had seven retailers. They're finally ready to look at independent comics, because out of all the comics in America right now, the only growth is in independent and small press comics" (Braden 47). Teri Wood's *Wandering Star* demonstrated that upward trend. The series, which began with orders of 1,700 per issue, quickly climbed to 3,000 per issue and by early 1995 had sales that approached 5,000 per issue (Cook 14).

Deer Crossing the Road

Several creators, though, craved more security and support than what the world of self-publishing offered. One of those creators was **Jeff Smith**. His *Bone* debuted in July 1991 to universal critical acclaim and sales that were strong enough for Smith's wife Vijaya to quit her lucrative job in the technology industry so she could assist her husband in his endeavors. But even with Vijaya's help, the couple discovered they couldn't keep up with all the work involved in creating, publicizing, printing, soliciting and managing their burgeoning project. Jim Lee helped solve that problem. Smith and Lee reached an agreement for the latter to publish *Bone* under the Image banner. In return for a small payment to cover overhead, Lee's staffers handled most of the cumbersome solicitation and order management. That allowed the husband and wife team to focus on delivering their comic without having to be directly involved in the distributor wars. As Jeff Smith reflected, "Everybody's just like deer crossing the road at night, frozen in the headlights of a car. Cartoon Books is just not big enough to do much about this. I can't get the deer moving, know what I'm saying?" (Darnall 13). He added a warning for his peers in the self-publishing movement: "If somebody was looking for some meaning in my move, I would say that it means wake up! This is not the same world that existed when I started self-publishing *Bone*. It's an entirely different system, and you better really, really know what you're doing if you're going to self-publish" (Reynolds 21). The arrangement began with *Bone* #21 (Dec. 1995), and the move garnered Smith additional publicity and better distribution, which resulted in increased sales. *Bone* #21 finished in 87th place in Wizard's Top 100 chart for the month, the first issue of the series to appear on the list.

Elsewhere, **Charles Burns**, a veteran of the independent comics scene, had his dark horror stories frequently anthologized in magazines such as *RAW, Buzz, Death Rattle* and *Graphic Story Monthly*. In 1995 Burns began the comic serial which would define his career. **Black Hole**, which initially came out through Kitchen Sink Press, was a noir horror story that reminded many readers of the work of filmmaker David Lynch. *Black Hole* explores how the people in a small town react when a strange disease, dubbed the "Teen Plague," hits an affluent high school and turns students into freaks. Some have holes growing in different parts of their bodies, some teens grow reptilian tails, and others sprout large facial bumps. Drawn in Burns's characteristic deeply moody brush-driven style, *Black Hole* touches on themes more profound than those frequently found in horror comics. Burns explores body image, personal mutilation, the crushing effects of peer pressure and other problems that affect most teenagers. This ten-part comic, therefore, works as a metaphor for the angst people go through in their teen years. As Burns put it, "There's this whole idea that you're at a point in your life when you're a teenager, and you don't have a house to hang out in. You're in a kind of limbo, trying to come to terms with these horrific problems" (Kurtz 49).

Chris Ware's critically acclaimed **Acme Novelty Library** continued into 1995 with two issues, reformatted from their initial appearances in the Chicago *New City*. With his austere style and predilection for telling stories of "Jimmy Corrigan, Smartest Kid in the World" in a unique squarebound format, Ware presented stories less about living in the past as about living *with* the past. Ware's style has a hauntingly sad feel to it, with a metronomic rhythm that smartly depicts the sad world of Jimmy Corrigan. Ware saw his work as being a *tabula rasa* about which readers could make up their own minds: "If I could do a strip that... someone would think was funny and that someone else would think was really depressing, I would feel that's my true measure of success. If I make something that produces just a single emotional response, that's fine, but I like to provoke a variety of them" (Darnall 86). Another young creator began to gain his own unique voice as Caliber Comics released writer/artist **Brian Michael Bendis's** *A.K.A. Goldfish*. With dialogue influenced by playwright David Mamet and a complicated plot centered around a high-stakes card game, this comic earned comparisons to the work of noir crime novelist Jim Thompson. Newcomer Rich Tommaso also completed his first crime graphic novel with the street noir *Clover Honey*, published by Fantagraphics. Tommaso would go on to create several more crime graphic novels.

The Graphic Novel is a Serious Form

Tommaso admired the pioneering graphic novels of **Will Eisner**. In 1995 Kitchen Sink Press released the latest work by the 78-year-old cartoonist. In the 170-page softcover **Dropsie Avenue**, Eisner chronicled the human condition during several generations of settlement in New York. *Dropsie* spanned history from the original Dutch settlers to modern, multicultural city-dwellers. This epic tale told on a small scale present the men and women who shaped the existence of one city street over a period of decades. Eisner adroitly balances the story of New York's phenomenal growth and complex problems with a tight focus on the people living there. Reviewer Chris Ecker was effusive in his praise for Eisner's work, saying "This book should be required reading for humanities classes in high schools everywhere" (Ecker 40).

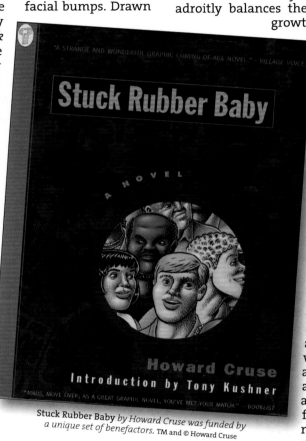

Stuck Rubber Baby *by Howard Cruse was funded by a unique set of benefactors.* TM and © Howard Cruse

Stuck Rubber Baby by **Howard Cruse** was also strongly influenced by Eisner's work. Released by DC imprint Paradox Press, this emotionally rich coming-of-age novel tells the story of Toland Polk, the young son of a carpenter reaching maturity in the 1960s in the fictional Southern city of Clayfield. Cruse juxtaposes Toland's emerging awareness of his homosexuality with the emerging civil rights struggle in the Deep South. Cruse's opus considers the effects of racism and class on Toland's experiences while showing the riots, explosions and daily struggles that happen all around him. Cruse's smartly semi-autobiographical style earned raves from critics. *Stuck Rubber Baby* made several "best of 1995" lists and garnered national attention from a wide range of publications. A *Village Voice* review was typical. The New York newspaper presented a four-page excerpt from the book, adding a comment that the book would end "once and for all" the question of whether "the graphic novel is a serious form, combining the complexities of narrative with the impact of cinema" ("Stuck Rubber Baby" 47). Cruse didn't serialize his 210 page story, even though that would have allowed him to earn money while he worked on it. To keep himself financially afloat, Cruse sought help from "sponsors" who subsidized production of the book by purchasing original art pages at high rates. Sponsors included playwright Tony Kushner, former Tundra Comics owner Kevin Eastman, and film and TV producer Martha Thomases. *The Comics Journal* rated *Stuck Rubber Baby* as the 86th greatest comic of the twentieth century.

Stuck Rubber Baby received extensive media coverage due to its mature approach to challenging subject matter. However, a great deal of the attention paid to comics in 1995 centered on the industry's financial problems. That attention would only increase in 1996, as Marvel made a leap into its past to in an attempt to boost sales.

1996

Crossing Over

In the months after Marvel Comics went exclusive with Heroes World Distribution, nearly every other publisher, including such major ones as DC Comics, Image and Dark Horse, opted to sell their products solely through **Diamond Comic Distributors**. That left **Capital City Distribution**, Diamond's sole remaining major competitor, handling only a handful of companies, most notably Kitchen Sink Press and game producer TSR. To remain in business, Capital needed to figure out a way to recover lost accounts, so in early 1996, Capital's owners boldly offered to take over distribution of Marvel Comics from beleaguered Heroes World. However, a deal never came to fruition, as Marvel signed with R.R. Donnelley, a company with no experience in comics, to help them get their books out (Stump, "Hello Again" 9). Capital's income continued to drop to the point where annual revenue was projected to be half the amount of the previous year. As Capital's president John Davis reported, "When we got our August numbers in this year, they were below our July orders, which were below our June orders. Since September is typically a down month, we thought we would be out of business within a month or two" (Stump 15-17). On July 26, 1996, after months of rumors about its impending demise, Capital City was purchased by Diamond. As part of the deal, Capital's owners sold Diamond their distribution centers and home office. In exchange, Diamond agreed to assume Capital's $7 million in debt and added key Capital staffers to its team in order to help provide continuity. After over fifteen years in the industry, Capital City Distribution was now relegated to the annals of comic book history.

By acquiring Capital's accounts, Diamond added much-wanted stability to the Direct Market as there were now only two distributors for retailers to deal with: Heroes World for Marvel Comics, and Diamond for everything else. The simpler cash flow and accounting brought about by Diamond's purchase of Capital City helped slow the weakening of store profitability, and within 18 months, Diamond retired all of Capital's old debt. On the other hand, with its purchase of Capital City, Diamond moved one step closer to becoming a de facto monopoly in the distribution of comic books. John Davis estimated more than half of the nation's 4500 comic shops dealt just with Diamond, a situation that made many shop owners uncomfortable. As retailer Bob Gray explained, "anti-trust laws were the first question that entered many thoughts about Diamond's market dominance. A comics distribution segment without competition is a frightening thought to many retailers and publishers" (Stump 9). That kind of dominance would eventually prompt an investigation by the United States Department of Justice's Anti-Trust Division in the summer of 1997.

The sale of Capital to Diamond had a major effect on all publishers and retailers, but it probably impacted struggling **Kitchen Sink Press** the most. Capital owed Kitchen Sink a significant amount of money at the time of Capital's dissolution, and though Diamond did eventually reimburse Kitchen Sink, the process took two years to play out. Kitchen also suffered due to disappointing sales from one of its key franchises. The company invested heavily in the film *The Crow: City of Angels*, expecting a windfall similar to the infusion of cash received in 1994 after the release of the original *Crow* film. But when *City of Angels* flopped, Kitchen Sink was left with thousands of dollars of unmarketable inventory. Unfortunately for Kitchen Sink, matters wouldn't improve any time soon.

Acclaim Comics, the parent company of Valiant, likewise suffered tough times. In 1993, at the peak of the comic book boom, Valiant enjoyed a market share of eight percent with some of its series selling a million copies an issue. Three years later, its market share had plummeted to 1.18%, and flagship titles like *X-O Manowar*, *Turok* and *Bloodshot* couldn't even muster 5000 copies an issue. Forays into crime comics and comic adaptations of the popular *Magic: the Gathering* game failed to generate much interest either. The decline on the comic side paralleled an even deeper plunge in Acclaim's video game division. Acclaim Games lost more than $140 million in the fourth quarter of the year alone. Summing up the year at Acclaim, *X-O Manowar* #68 (Sept. 1996) rather ironically displays the words "The End?" on its cover. In this climactic tale, writer Bob Layton (a Valiant founder) concludes the series with protagonist Aric feeling dislocated from reality as he suffers delusions while trapped in the spider alien ship from his origin story. The final issue ends with Aric breaking out of the ship and beginning his heroic cycle once again. It was an apt conclusion, one that both closed the original Valiant line and signaled

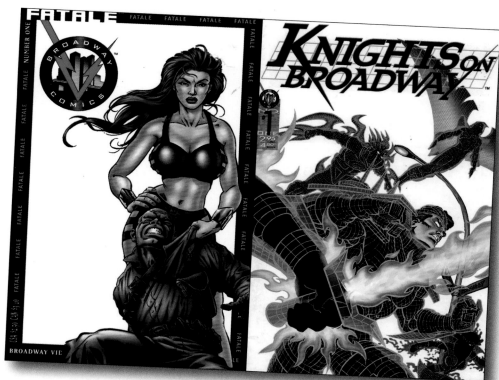

By November 1996, Jim Shooter's Broadway Comics had closed its doors with completed issues of Fatale and Knights on Broadway left unpublished. TM and © respective copyright owner.

that Acclaim wasn't completely out of the comics business. While readers wouldn't see "Conan in a can" again for several years, a different kind of X-O Manowar would be part of a Valiant Heroes rebirth, beginning in 1997.

Jim Shooter's Broadway Comics debuted in 1995 to much hype, but by November 1996, the company had closed its doors. Though its comics sold poorly, revenue was not the main cause of Broadway's demise. Instead, Broadway shut down due to the purchase of its parent corporation. On July 30, 1996, Golden Books Family Entertainment purchased Broadway Video Entertainment, a holding company that included Broadway Comics. Golden Books was interested in acquiring properties it could create books for and sell to young children. It had no interest in continuing Broadway's comics line and therefore cancelled all solicitations beyond October. Ironically, Golden Books owned the rights to Turok, Magnus and Solar, three properties Shooter licensed when he was in charge at Valiant Comics but could not publish at Broadway. Regardless, the decision to drop Broadway was likely easy for Golden Books executives since the comic line lost money. Monthly purchases of flagship book *Fatale* dropped from 21,800 on the first issue

to 14,000 soon after. Companion book *Shadow State* sold 18,200 copies of its first issue but 9,200 in August 1996. *Powers That Be* saw its preorders drop to 7,700 copies with issue #10, just a little more than a third of what the first issue sold. *Knights On Broadway* started at 15,000 copies before descending to 8,900 copies in December. Broadway needed to sell at least 25,000 copies of each issue to break even. Instead, the company failed to gain more than a 0.6% market share, despite its hype and high-powered staff. As influential retailer Rory Root reported, "Those projects never captured anyone's attention" (Stump and Spurgeon 32).

Broadway Comics only reached comic shops for seven months. Broadway's diligent creators completed several stories that now had to be abandoned, never to be published. Four future issues of *Knights on Broadway* were fully plotted when the book went under, with even more issues planned as a prelude for a universe-spanning crossover.

Chapter 11 of the Marvel Saga

It's one thing for independent publishers like Kitchen Sink and Acclaim to experience financial hardships. It's quite another for the market leader to be in the same kind of

TIMELINE: 1996

A compilation of the year's notable comic book history events alongside some of the year's most significant popular culture and historical events. (On sale dates are approximations.)

January 19: Bernard Baily, comic book artist who worked for several publishers including St. John and Atlas, but is perhaps best known for co-creating DC Comics' The Spectre and Hourman characters, dies at the age of 79.

January 28: Comic book writer and Superman co-creator Jerry Siegel dies at the age of 81.

February 28: Canadian alternative-rock singer Alanis Morisette wins four Grammy Awards, including Album of the Year. At the age of 21, she is the youngest performer to receive that award.

March 6: Prolific comic book inker Jack Abel, who contributed to such titles as DC's *Action Comics*, *Adventure Comics* and *Superman*, and Marvel's *Incredible Hulk* and *Iron Man*, dies as a result of a stroke he suffers while at his desk in Marvel's offices. He was 68 years old.

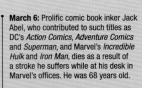

May 3: *Barb Wire*, adapted from the Dark Horse comic book and starring former Playboy Playmate Pamela Anderson, arrives in movie theaters. The film flops at the box office, earning less than $4 million domestically.

June 7: *The Phantom*, based on Lee Falk's classic comic strip character and starring Billy Zane as the crime-fighting "Ghost Who Walks," opens in movie theaters. The film is a box office flop, barely grossing $17 million domestically.

JANUARY	FEBRUARY	MARCH	APRIL	MAY	JUNE

January 28: Burne Hogarth, artist best known for his pioneering work on the *Tarzan* comic strip but also an influential educator who co-founded the institution that would eventually become the School of Visual Arts, dies at the age of 84 of heart failure.

April 3: At a cabin in rural Montana, the FBI arrests Ted Kaczynski, the suspected "Unabomber" responsible for killing three people and injuring twenty-three others in a series of mail bombings between 1978 and 1995 that were intended to protest the negative impact modern technology has had on human freedom.

June 19: Comic book artist Curt Swan, whose work on Superman comic books spanned six decades, from the late 1940s until the 1990s, dies at the age of 76. His final Superman contribution appears posthumously in 1996's *Superman: The Wedding Album*.

June 25: A bomb planted by Islamic terrorists explodes in an apartment complex in Khobar, Saudi Arabia, killing nineteen U.S. military servicemen.

trouble, but that's exactly how **Marvel Comics** started 1996: in a very bad state. Its experiment with exclusive distribution and five executive editors only exacerbated sales declines. Over the course of the previous twelve months, Marvel's market share fell to 34% while its stock price dropped by 66% (Leonhardt 44). Marvel only sold about five million comics to the Direct Market, its lowest sales since 1990. Facing strong headwinds, Marvel's executives laid off over 275 staffers in January, representing some 16% of the company's employees. Those dismissals simply represented the latest culling, following similar ones in 1994 and 1995. Though Marvel Entertainment reported losses of $48 million in 1995, the magnitude of these new staff cuts shocked many observers. Among those fired were members of the editorial, marketing and licensing departments. More significantly for comic fans, those layoffs also included long-time editors Bob Budiansky, Nel Yomtov, Joey Cavalieri and Carl Potts as well as Marvel archivist Peter Sanderson. Some former employees received severance packages but those under contract received the full amount of their contracts despite being fired (Ronan 11). The departures of so many editors ended Marvel's brief trial with five line-specific editors. The editor-in-chief role was once again the responsibility of one person, and the person assigned to that role was **Bob Harras**, the editor of the super-popular X-Men titles. What Harras oversaw, though, was a rapidly shrinking line of comics, as executives cancelled all unprofitable and marginally profitable series, which included the Malibu

July 2: Comic book artist Mike Parobeck, who received an Eisner Award nomination in 1995 for his work on *Batman Adventures*, dies at the age of 30 due to diabetes-related complications.

July 3: *Independence Day*—an alien invasion film directed by Roland Emmerich and starring Will Smith and Bill Pullman as the President of the United States—opens in movie theaters. It will become the highest grossing movie of the year at the box office.

July 5: An institute in Scotland unveils the first successfully cloned mammal, a sheep named Dolly.

July 19: The 26th Summer Olympics open in Atlanta, Georgia. Led by an injured Kerri Strug, the American women's gymnastics team (dubbed "The Magnificent Seven") wins its first gold medal, and American sprinter Michael Johnson wins gold medals in the 400 meter and 200 meter races, setting a new World Record in the latter event.

July 26: Diamond Comics Distributors purchases its sole remaining competitor, Capital City Distribution.

September 4: Rob Liefeld resigns his position at Image Comics just as Image's Board of Directors holds an emergency meeting to vote him out of the company. Liefeld subsequently sues Image for libel and defamation. Image countersues claiming Liefeld, among other transgressions, misappropriated funds for his own use. The two sides settle their differences out of court in February 1997.

September 6: *Superman: The Animated Series* debuts on the WB television network. Developed by the same team that produced *Batman: The Animated Series*, the show lasts three seasons, 54 episodes in total.

September 13: Influential rapper Tupac Shakur dies of internal bleeding resulting from gunshot wounds received six days earlier on the streets of Las Vegas. While no one is arrested for Shakur's murder, prime suspects include members of the Crips gang and rival rapper The Notorious B.I.G.

September 29: Nintendo releases the Nintendo 64 home video game console to the North American market with a suggested retail price of $199. Due to its fast graphics processing speed, *Time* magazine names the N64 1996's "Machine of the Year."

December 26: Six-year-old child beauty pageant contestant JonBenét Ramsey is found dead in the basement of her family's Boulder, Colorado home. The ensuing investigation becomes the fodder of massive nationwide media coverage as police suspect either JonBenét's mother or older brother strangled the child. The family asserts its innocence and is officially cleared several years later. No one is ever convicted of JonBenét's murder.

JULY	AUGUST	SEPTEMBER	OCTOBER	NOVEMBER	DECEMBER

August 12: Longtime Marvel Comics writer and editor Mark Gruenwald dies of a heart attack at the age of 43. As per his wishes, Gruenwald's ashes are mixed with the ink used to print the trade paperback version of *Squadron Supreme*, the twelve issue series he wrote in 1985.

August 30: *The Crow: City of Angels*, a sequel to 1994's *The Crow* and based on James O'Barr's graphic novel, arrives in movie theaters. The film only grosses $17 million domestically.

November 5: On Election Day, Democratic incumbent Bill Clinton remains President of the United States when he defeats Republican candidate Bob Dole. The Republican party retains control of both the Senate and the House of Representatives.

October 6: The third episode of the fourth season of ABC television's *Lois & Clark: The New Adventures of Superman* presents the long-anticipated wedding of Lois Lane to Clark Kent. Three days later, the couple tie the knot in the celebratory 96-page *Superman: The Wedding Album* with contributions from such creators as John Byrne, George Pérez, Al Plastino, Jim Mooney, Nick Cardy and Dan Jurgens, among many others.

July 27: During the Summer Olympics, a pipe bomb explodes at a park in downtown Atlanta, killing one person and injuring another 111. Nearly ten years later, an anti-abortion militant pleads guilty to the bombing and is sentenced to life in prison.

July 17: Twelve minutes after taking off from New York's JFK airport, the Paris-bound TWA Flight 800 explodes off the south shore of Long Island, killing all 230 passengers and crew on board. After a four year investigation, the National Transportation Safety Board rules the explosion likely resulted from a short circuit that ignited flammable vapors in the plane's fuel tank. Conspiracy theories persist, however, that the explosion was caused by a bomb or missile.

December 27: Marvel Comics' parent company, Marvel Entertainment Group, files for Chapter 11 bankruptcy. Several stockholders, most notably Carl Icahn, file lawsuits to block the move.

Comics titles acquired in 1995 as well as all licensed titles such as *Beavis and Butt-head* and *Barbie*. Furthermore, Harras led a deeply demoralized staff. By the middle of 1996, a skeleton crew was in place at the Marvel offices, simply doing what they could to get things done. Cost cutting was the rule of the day: travel was eliminated, and even photocopies were restricted to an as-necessary basis. Corporate revenues continued to drop steadily as the sports card market failed to bounce back from over-saturation and the 1994 baseball strike. Marvel's toy business slumped as Marvel characters failed to find their way to film and upstart companies like McFarlane Toys (owned by Image founder Todd McFarlane) upstaged Toy Biz in terms of quality. Flashy gimmicks and crossovers in the publishing division only cannibalized sales from lesser-selling titles. By October, company leadership cut yet another 110 staffers. Employees from all areas of the corporation, including Heroes World, continued to be fired in groups through March 1997, but even those cutbacks didn't make much difference as Marvel lost a staggering $400 million just in the fourth quarter of 1996. Total revenues at the corporation, including publishing, toys, cards, stickers and licensing, were down $100 million from 1995 to 1996, with the publishing division accounting for $7 million of that decline (Raviv 60). By the end of the year, Marvel stock had dropped an astonishing 90% from its high, forcing writer Mark Evanier to joke, "1996 was the year when you could buy a share of stock in Marvel for less than the price of a copy of *Iron Man*" (Evanier 22).

And then something happened that would have been considered unthinkable just a couple years earlier. On December 27, 1996 Marvel declared bankruptcy. Many readers and creators alike treated the news as if a bomb had been dropped on the entire industry, but others saw all the warning signs and recognized that bankruptcy was inevitable. In truth, though, the slump in Marvel's comic sales was only a small contributor to its bankruptcy. Marvel's most significant problems came from other sources, such as overpaying for its Fleer subsidiary during a deep slump in the collector's card market, ill-fated forays into theme restaurants and an emphasis on marketing over product. More than anything, though, the cause of Marvel's demise was its owner, **Ron Perelman**, a shark who cared little about the comics business and instead used his company as leverage for junk bonds and other shady financial products. In fact, in some ways Marvel's bankruptcy had nothing to do with its financial situation. Perelman and venture capitalist **Carl Icahn** were engaged in an intense behind-the-scenes battle for control over Marvel Enterprises. In November, Perelman unveiled a recapitalization plan that would infuse hundreds of millions of dollars into the company, but in doing so, company stock would be diluted by 80 percent (Howe 386). Icahn wasn't about to let that happen, so he and other bondholders filed lawsuits. By declaring bankruptcy, Perelman froze any large financial transactions involving Marvel, an effective counter-move against Icahn's attempts to oust him.

Onslaught Destroys the Marvel Universe

While Marvel may have officially filed for bankruptcy in 1996, many fans felt the "House of Ideas" became creatively broke a long time ago. From many readers' point of view, Marvel's characters no longer possessed the same attributes that made them so endearing in the first place. Fan Robert Moraes summed up his peers' frustration in a letter published in the in-house fanzine *Marvel Vision*: "Captain America's reputation has been destroyed, Iron Man betrayed the Avengers, Thor is no longer a god and the Fantastic Four are still trying to become a united team once more. Throw in the Spider-Clone nonsense and the death of Nick Fury and that about tops it" (Moraes 5). Virtually the only Marvel series fans embraced were the X-Men titles, still the best-selling line of comics after 1995's "Age of Apocalypse" epic. Thus, it was no surprise for the mutants to, once again, be the linchpin characters for Marvel's major annual crossover. What *was* surprising, however, was how **"Onslaught"** didn't just involve mutant characters. It involved—and affected—every major super-hero in the Marvel Universe.

Juggernaut informs the X-Men of the omnipotent new threat headed their way: Onslaught.
TM and © Marvel Characters, Inc.

"Onslaught" had its roots in 1993's "Fatal Attractions" mutant crossover. At the climax of that wild storyline, Magneto yanks Wolverine's adamantium skeleton out of his body — an incredible violation of one of the proudest X-Men. Professor Xavier can barely restrain his fury at the inhumane act so he lashes out and completely wipes Magneto's mind. Those actions devastate both Professor X and Magneto. Xavier remains wheelchair-bound, terrified by the power of his own anger. Magneto, on the other hand, manifests himself as the heroic and innocent Joseph. Though few knew it at the time, Xavier's anger would ultimately damage an entire universe. *Uncanny X-Men* #322 (July 1995) brought the first mention of Onslaught, when the Beast, Psylocke and Bishop discover the body of the invulnerable Juggernaut, seemingly thrown from a great height onto a New York City street. When Juggernaut wakes up, he rages in fear about a creature who hurled him across an entire country. The creature's name is Onslaught. If the unstoppable Juggernaut cannot defeat this mysterious menace, what hope do the X-Men have? Initially, even the most attentive readers had a challenging time making a connection between Xavier and the universe-shaking new villain Onslaught, but as 1995 gave way to 1996, the connection became all too evident.

When he is next mentioned, in *X-Men* #50 (March 1996), Onslaught seems just another incredibly powerful being. In that issue, Wolverine, Iceman, Cyclops and Storm struggle to defeat Onslaught's herald, Post. The heroes barely win in vicious combat, even though Post was the least of Onslaught's emissaries, and *X-Men* #50 ends with Post ranting, "The onslaught is coming. There is no power on this earth — or any other — capable of stopping it. No one... homo sapiens, homo superior, or otherwise, can turn back the onslaught." Three months later, in *X-Men* #53,

The war against Onslaught begins with a battle against one of his heralds in X-Men #50.
TM and © Marvel Characters, Inc.

Onslaught takes center stage in the Marvel Universe. He psychically abducts Jean Grey and shows her the hypocrisy and shortsightedness of Professor X. In doing so, Onslaught reveals details about the Professor nobody could possibly know, including romantic pangs for his young student when she joined his school. Jean is deeply hurt by the revelation but rejects Onslaught's request for her to become his consort. With a regal fury, Onslaught in turn rejects Jean, sending the heroine hurtling back to the physical plane with a warning tattooed on her forehead that Onslaught was coming. *X-Men* #54 (July 1996) then reveals Onslaught's shocking origin. Magneto's evil had been festering in Professor X's mind since he wiped Magneto's brain during "Fatal Attractions." That overwhelming malevolence, combined with the dark side of the Professor's personality, causes an entirely different creature to manifest: the horrific and invincible Onslaught. As Onslaught rants in the double-sized special *Onslaught: X-Men* #1 (Aug. 1996), "I was forged within the crucibles of his fear, his frustration, his rage at the injustices he saw perpetrated against his people! I was nurtured by his every darkest desire... for revenge... for control... for power – incubated in the suppression of those emotions." As that issue ends, it appears that little could prevent Onslaught from enslaving Earth and fulfilling Magneto's most evil desires.

As the story sprawls out into many of Marvel's August and September 1996 cover-dated titles, all of New York becomes prisoner to Onslaught's attacks. The all-powerful mutant destroys large sections of the city and sets his Sentinels to work patrolling for enemies. The Avengers, Fantastic Four, X-Men, Spider-Man and other heroes charge into action in a massive storyline that spans nearly all of Marvel's super-hero series. The heroes are able to defeat several of the Sentinels while in another corner of the battle, Captain America manipulates Post and another Onslaught lieutenant, Holocaust, into defeating each other. However, even as the heroes experience triumph in one battle, they begin to lose the larger war. Despite his losses, Onslaught becomes even stronger. He kidnaps young Franklin Richards (son of the Fantastic Four's Reed and Sue Richards) in order to use Franklin's reality-warping powers to reshape the Earth into a planet where evil mutants rule and the rest of the world is enslaved – a mirror image of 1995's Age of Apocalypse storyline. Marvel's heroes allied with villains like Doctor Doom as Earth's last line of defense, struggling as they seldom had before in order to defeat this evil, save the lives of everyone in New York and protect the planet from a horrific fate. As the conflict reaches its climax, the Hulk smashes open Onslaught's armor only to discover that the shattered armor does not bring the heroes closer to victory. Instead, readers learn that the villain no longer has a corporeal form. Onslaught has evolved into pure energy. The Fantastic Four, the Hulk, and most of the Avengers plunge into Onslaught's energy form in a final,

desperate attempt to salvage victory from the jaws of defeat. As those heroes rush into the abyss, Reed Richards orders the remaining heroes to attack Onslaught from the outside. The mightiest heroes of the Marvel Universe do not squander the opportunity. Under incredible pressure, Onslaught dissolves and disappears. The Sentinels are disabled, Franklin is rescued, and Manhattan begins to return to normal.

This was one of the greatest victories ever experienced in the Marvel Universe, but it came at a disastrous cost. Many of Earth's greatest heroes disappear as a result of the battle. To the surprise of nearly everyone, the Fantastic Four, Avengers and several other heroes don't return to New York after the dust of the battle begins to settle. In the wake of "Onslaught", Marvel cancelled such mainstay series as *Fantastic Four*, *Avengers*, *Iron Man*, *Thor* and *Captain America*. *The Incredible Hulk* was also slated for cancellation, but an outcry from fans and professionals saved that series (Brady 57). As far as readers—and residents of the Marvel Universe—knew at the time, the change could have lasted forever. The Marvel Universe became a "World Without Heroes," as the unofficial arc was nicknamed, and that fact added an element of despair and worry to Marvel's remaining ongoing series. Black Widow, former leader of the Avengers, feels a deep sense of survivor's guilt. Meanwhile, ordinary people need heroes more than ever, but they fear the ones who remain. The public scapegoats the Hulk and considers him the main suspect in the heroes' disappearance. Spider-Man is once again hated and feared by many New Yorkers. But more than anyone else, the X-Men bear the brunt of the anger. Because Onslaught emerged from the brain of Charles Xavier, ordinary people come to blame mutants for the disappearance of their greatest heroes. As 1996 moves into 1997, that hatred sets much of the status quo for the mutant books. In key storylines during that year, Bastion and his international team of mutant-hunters come after the X-Men in full force, while the presidential campaign of Graydon Creed leads to images of mutants rounded up in concentration camps. The impact of "Onslaught" was like an earthquake that sent shockwaves through the super-hero corner of the Marvel line for months to come.

Though the story was popular, lead X-Men writer **Scott Lobdell** found it a tough project: "'Onslaught' has been a difficult story for me to be involved in. Initially it was intended to be a story about a man [Professor X] who is trying real hard to do good. But what it's ultimately become is about an angry, frustrated person who is having to deal with rage and a damaged psyche. My own inclination is not to tell a story that's draped in this kind of cynicism." (Grant 64). Though Lobdell complained about the darkness of the adventure, "Onslaught" provided Marvel with a rare sales success amid a year of financial despair. One Virginia retailer reported "complete sell-outs on first-round 'Onslaught' issues." In fact, many retailers stated that Onslaught-related comics were positive surprises ("Market Beat: Comics" 24-27). Sales surged on the already successful X-Men line. *Uncanny X-Men*, for instance, had its average monthly sales of over 362,000 copies increased to over 455,000 by the end of 1996 (Stump, "Cutting Your Losses: Marvel's Sales Figures" 12).

Unfinished Business

As big as the "Onslaught" storyline was, it was mainly conceived as a setup for perhaps the biggest comic book event of 1996, an event as important for its creative staff as for the way Marvel managed its most iconic heroes.

It began in February 1995, when Marvel president Jerry Calabrese called Image Comics and requested a meeting with all its major creators. The Image founders complied, and in the subsequent session, Calabrese informed the former Marvel stars that he wanted to bury the hatchet between them by enticing the Image creators to work on some of Marvel's books. The Image stars doubted the sincerity of the offer, but Calabrese was serious. Facing decreasing revenues and a lack of attention for Marvel's largely moribund lineup, Calabrese saw the return of the Image creators as the kind of stunt that

As part of Marvel's "Heroes Reborn" event, Rob Liefeld's studio launched new volumes of Captain America *and* The Avengers...
TM and © Marvel Characters, Inc.

would bolster Marvel's finances. Perhaps unsurprisingly, most of the Image founders had no interest in a deal that would aid their former employer. Todd McFarlane, in particular, felt Calabrese's offer defied logic: "Why do you want to work for your competitor? I've got a toy company.... It would be like me making toys for Hasbro and Mattel.... I never understood it" (Khoury 83). Rob Liefeld and Jim Lee, however, proved more receptive than their comrades, so Calabrese and assistant Joe King courted them for over a year. At first the discussion between Calabrese, Liefeld and Lee involved the superstars doing some crossovers or even producing several comics as a co-venture (Fisher 29). From those conversations emerged the idea that Liefeld and Lee would license two Marvel books each to handle within their studios. Ultimately, the negotiations resulted in Lee and Liefeld signing personal services contracts for their studios to produce new versions of Fantastic Four, Captain America, the Avengers, Iron Man and other characters who would be unfettered by previous continuity thanks to the "Onslaught" storyline. In short, these longtime Marvel icons would be reborn for a new era: the Image era. The contracts, for twelve months each, gave each side the opportunity to opt out after six months. Marvel was obligated to pay an advance of $1 million to each creative team, plus 40% of the profit of the books, or an aggregate minimum of $2 million (Stump, "Liefeld vs. Marvel" 20). The contracts gave Marvel's editorial and management teams final veto power over storylines but otherwise allowed Liefeld and Lee full creative freedom. As Liefeld reflected, "It's a deal unlike any Marvel has ever cut. It's more than simply work-for-hire. There's a generous profit participation on these characters in all their different forms." From Marvel's viewpoint, the extra pay was just an incentive to deliver work that would strike a receptive chord with fans who had wandered from the industry. As Bob Harras reported, "We're hoping this deal with Rob and Jim gets people back to buying and enjoying comics, and that this will be the first step towards making comics a fun business again" (Shapiro 34-5). Liefeld and Lee both hoped to take Captain America, but Liefeld really wanted to draw that character's adventures. Giving way to his colleague, Lee chose to take the Fantastic Four instead (Shutt 66).

...while Jim Lee's studio launched new volumes of Fantastic Four *and* Iron Man.
TM and © Marvel Characters, Inc.

As "**Heroes Reborn**" begins, the world has been without super-heroes since Captain America disappeared decades before. But in *Captain America* #1 (Nov. 1996), by Rob Liefeld, Jeph Loeb and Jonathan Sibal, Pittsburgh steelworker Steve Rogers brings his dissolute past back in focus and remembers he is Captain America. In the opening arc of his new solo series, Cap and his friends stop a new American Civil War started by the Red Skull. Cap is literally reborn

Many fans despised Liefeld's redesign of Captain America's cowl.
TM and © Marvel Characters, Inc.

The Heroes Reborn version of Avengers *updated the team's origin with several new twists.*
TM and © Marvel Characters, Inc.

day Captain America is reborn, as four people sneak on board a rocket ship and launch into space, where they are irradiated with cosmic rays. Returning to Earth, the four figures discover they have their iconic powers, which leads to battles against the corrupt Storm Foundation and the anti-hero, Sub-Mariner.

From the start, the Heroes Reborn titles seemed smothered in controversy. Many fans despised the redesigns of characters, especially Liefeld's replacement of the iconic "A" from Captain America's cowl with a winged emblem. When asked about the alteration, Liefeld declared, "That 'A' on his forehead has bothered me since I was a kid. Superman's 'S' works, but Batman doesn't have a big 'B' on his chest. I tried leaving the forehead blank, but it doesn't look right" (Shutt 66). Fans also were livid that Mark Waid and Ron Garney had been removed from a fan-favorite *Captain America* run to allow Liefeld to take over, though they seemed less angry over the ends of comparatively humdrum runs on *Avengers, Iron Man* and *Fantastic Four*. In fact, Waid was first expected to stay on *Captain America* but turned down an offer to dialogue pages which were already drawn and plotted (Senreich, "Waid and Garney" 70). Waid and Garney weren't the only creators forced off Captain America. Steve Englehart had a squarebound Captain America mini-series cancelled, with the scripts for three issues written and art for six pages completed (Cook 61).

Professionals who worked on the Heroes Reborn titles were often as frustrated as the fans because of the haphazard way some stories were created. As Liefeld reported, "Chuck [Dixon] handed in the first pages and we were very disappointed with the direction that his script took. It was not in line with what we wanted and we just agreed to part ways" (O'Neill 17). Dixon countered that he plotted the first arc and turned the plot in to Liefeld, but when drawn, the comic had nothing to do with the plot as written. Dixon chose to leave the comic rather than submit to constant undercutting (Braden, "Untold Tales", 35). Valentino reported slowness in payment from Liefeld, and Liefeld's overall attitude towards his Image colleagues caused massive tension among the teams. In fact, Liefeld's behavior during "Heroes Reborn" would ultimately help contribute to a professional divorce from his Image colleagues.

Despite the frustration, the first issues of all four series reached the top of the sales charts due to the intense interest and hype around them. Indeed, sales on *Fantastic Four* nearly tripled their levels from before the reboot (Senreich, "Jim Lee" 68). On the other hand, like blockbuster movies with poor buzz, sales on *Avengers* and *Captain America* quickly plummeted as fan dissatisfaction increased. After some intense infighting, those plunging sales resulted in the termination of Rob Liefeld's contract after his team completed just six issues of their twelve-issue run. Overall, the whole experiment just felt strange. Perhaps the cleverest summation of "Heroes Reborn" came from a Connecticut comic shop owner, who said, "It's kind of like GM hiring Chrysler to design cars for them, because GM doesn't know how to make cars people want" (Cleary 208).

in his own series, as are many of the Avengers. *Avengers* #1 (Nov. 1996), by Liefeld, Jim Valentino, Chap Yaep, Jon Sibal and Marlo Alquiza, presents familiar but different versions of many of Earth's Mightiest Heroes, including the Vision, Hawkeye, the Scarlet Witch and Thor. In an echo of the original Avengers origin from 1963, Loki's evil machinations bring the team together. Iron Man joins the Avengers with issue #6, but a new take on the Armored Avenger premiered months earlier in *Iron Man* #1 by Jim Lee, Whilce Portacio, Scott Lobdell and Scott Williams. In that issue, an experimental gamma bomb explodes, turning Bruce Banner into the Hulk. In the subsequent fight, the Hulk fatally injures Stark. Only a suit of experimental armor can save him and give him the power to stop Banner's rampage. Lobdell was one of the few Marvel creators who worked on the "Heroes Reborn" titles. He agreed to write *Iron Man* after Alan Moore (who was nearing the end of his fourteen issue run on Jim Lee's *WildC.A.T.S.*) demurred. Lee's other series, *Fantastic Four*, co-written with Brandon Choi and co-illustrated by Scott Williams, begins the same

Marvel launched Starfleet Academy *after reacquiring the Star Trek license.*

Star Trek Treks to Marvel

In 1996 Liefeld and his studio actually also produced work for a different Marvel comic book. *Mission: Impossible* by Marv Wolfman, with art by Pino Rinaldi, Rod Whigham, Andrew Wildman, and Liefeld (who also drew the issue's cover), arrived in comic book stores two weeks before the film it was loosely based on premiered in movie theaters. However, it's not Liefeld's artwork or the relative rareness of this comic that makes it unique. Instead, Marvel recalled the first printing of this book because *Mission: Impossible* actor Tom Cruise complained his character Ethan Hunt looked too effeminate in several panels. Only a few copies survive of the first printing.

The *Mission: Impossible* comic was published due to a new deal Marvel reached with Paramount Studios, a deal which resulted in Marvel assuming publishing rights to several Paramount properties, including one whose comic book exploits had been published by DC since 1984: **Star Trek**. With series *Voyager* and *Deep Space Nine* going strong, and a series of *Next Generation* movies already begun, *Star Trek* seemed a logical license for Marvel to obtain. The new line of comic books debuted with *Star Trek: Voyager* #1 (Nov. 1996), arriving in stores the same day the television show's third season premiered. The following week, *Star Trek: Deep Space Nine* #1 was published shortly before the season five premiere of that series. *Star Trek Unlimited*, telling stories of the original and Next Generation crews, followed shortly thereafter, along with an adaptation of the film *Star Trek: First Contact*. The ongoing line wrapped with two more titles: *Starfleet Academy* (first issue cover-dated November 1996, based on a series of popular young adult novels) and *Enterprise: the Early Voyages* (first issue cover-dated February 1997, featuring adventures on the starship Enterprise before James T. Kirk became its captain). Many of the creators who worked on DC's *Star Trek* comics came over to Marvel to work on the new series. Several creators new to *Trek* joined that team as well. The line included one-shots like *Star Trek: Mirror Mirror*, a sequel to the acclaimed Original Series episode by Tom DeFalco, Mark Bagley and Larry Mahlstedt.

Perhaps inevitably, one of the first *Trek* comics to appear was the one-shot *Star Trek/X-Men*. That comic, written by Lobdell and illustrated by Marc Silvestri and a team of collaborators, transported Marvel's mutants to the future, where they teamed with the crew of the Enterprise to battle the cosmic villainy of X-Men villain Proteus and former Enterprise helmsman Gary Mitchell. That happens as Marvel's Shi'ar alien race get involved with *Star Trek*'s galactic Federation. The one-shot features such only-in-comics moments as the Imperial Guard hero Gladiator punching the hull of the Enterprise and Spock using his Vulcan nerve pinch to knock out Wolverine. While surprising to see Silvestri return to Marvel for the one-shot project, he did so for a simple reason: "It was something that appealed to me because I'm an old *Star Trek* fan and, obviously, I have an X-Men connection. Bob Harras approached me with the idea and I thought it was a good idea" (Shapiro 44).

In a special one-shot written by Scott Lodbell and drawn by Marc Silvestri, the X-Men meet the Star Trek crew. TM and © Marvel Characters, Inc. TM and © CBS Studios Inc

Broken Hearts

In the middle of a tough year at Marvel, the ultimate tragedy happened: longtime writer and editor **Mark Gruenwald** passed away on Monday, August 12, 1996 at his home in Pawling, New York, of a heart attack at the age of 43. Gruenwald became a Marvel mainstay after he joined the company in 1978 as an assistant editor and was well known as one of its continuity cops. He had a decade-long stint writing *Captain America*, as well as shorter runs on other titles like *Hawkeye*, *Thor* and the innovative *Squadron Supreme*. When Gruenwald walked out of his office on Friday, August 9, 1996, he brought with him a copy of Rob Liefeld's new *Captain America*. At 11:00 am on the following Monday, Vice President Terry Stewart announced via email that Gruenwald had passed away. The outpouring of grief and affection for Gruenwald was overwhelming. Stan Lee said Gruenwald had as key a place on the Marvel masthead as Lee himself.

It could escape few observers that Gruenwald passed away as his beloved Marvel went through some of the worst times in its history. A few wags went so far as to ruefully joke that Gruenwald died of a broken heart. According to people close to him, though, Gruenwald *was* devastated by the terrible turn of events at the company he loved so much. Many of his friends were unemployed, the comics market was contracting, and even his beloved *Captain America* was being vended out to a third party. As writer Mark Evanier remembered, "The last lunch we shared, he talked mainly of the upheavals and downsizing at Marvel: of what it meant to so many lives" (Evanier 15).

The comics veteran was remembered with a $10,000 donation in his name by the Comics Magazine Association of America (a confederation of comics-related companies that included Marvel, DC, Tekno Comix, Warner Publisher Services and Ronald's Printing) to the University of Wisconsin Oshkosh's Mark Gruenwald Scholarship Fund. His ashes were included in the ink for the 1998 trade paperback of his *Squadron Supreme* mini-series (Cronin). Gruenwald truly left all of himself in his comics.

The Battle You Always Wanted!

One of Gruenwald's final projects was one he would have relished as a fan. The four-part *DC Versus Marvel/Marvel Versus DC* depicted clashes that inspired many a childhood argument over the years. The ultimate crossover series featured combat between characters who were counterparts or contrasts to each

Longtime Marvel Comics editor Mark Gruenwald passed away August 12, 1996.

other. Writers Ron Marz and Peter David and artists Dan Jurgens and Claudio Castellini delivered fights between Elektra and Catwoman, Silver Surfer and Green Lantern, and Thor and Captain Marvel, among others. The comic's creators determined the victors of the fights in the first two issues of the series. What truly excited fans, however, was that they could determine the results of five other battles. Those contests included some of the most iconic characters from each company. Fans could decide who won in conflicts between Superman and the Hulk, Spider-Man and Superboy, Batman and Captain America, Wolverine and Lobo, and Storm and Wonder Woman. This was the first time fans had a say in a comics story since 1989, when calls to a custom phone number determined whether the Joker should kill Robin.

Marvel Versus DC begins with Ben Reilly swinging around New York City as Spider-Man. When a spark from a strange, glowing box hits him, Ben finds himself in a parallel universe where he confronts the Joker, who somehow seems to know him even though they never met. Next, the Juggernaut is suddenly transported from a battle against the X-Men to being punched by Superman. Those are the first of several events that tangle the Marvel and DC universes. As the story moves ahead, Bullseye clashes with Batman, J. Jonah Jameson takes control of the Daily Planet, and Captain America combats Bane. The climax of *Marvel Versus DC* #1 reveals the cause of the merger: two cosmic beings in opposition to each other. Rather than fight each other, the pair decide to fight by proxy. Their forces must battle to decide which universe to destroy. Thus, Captain America is forced to confront Batman as an adversary, Aquaman fights Sub-Mariner, Lobo and Wolverine have a brawl in a bar, and so on. Though the comics delivered the promised

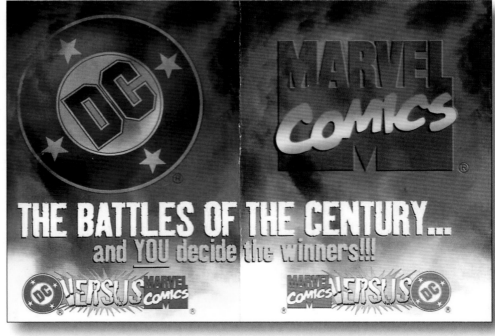

Fan voting determined who won some of the super-hero battles in the DC Versus Marvel *crossover.*

Along with fights between heroes, DC Versus Marvel *also presented such surprising events as a battle between Spider-Man and the Joker.*
TM and © Marvel Characters, Inc. TM and © DC Comics.

hype. Reader Jim Johnson's feelings typified fans' overall frustration: "While it was enjoyable, I think it's obvious that the entire thing had to be told too quickly and that the long-awaited battles of the century came across more as a series of 30-second TKOs" (Johnson 16). A writer to the letters page of *The Incredible Hulk* groused, "The whole crossover was a rip-off. The fights were short and cheap and letting the readers vote didn't prove anything. It actually turned everything into a giant popularity contest" (Shepherd 31). The comics sold well, though some fans resisted the $3.95 cover price. A retailer in Phoenix, AZ, reported they sold out of multiple reorders of issues #1 and #2, and his experience was common in shops around the country (Warren 101). That fulfilled the wish expressed by several professionals who saw *Marvel Versus DC* as a spark to drive traffic to comic shops. DC editor Mike Carlin reported, "We want to get some action going again and get some activity in comic shops. At the same time, it is a dream project" ("The Battle of the Century" 17). The two companies briefly contemplated trading characters between each other – Catwoman and Daredevil were on the trading block for a brief time – but the legal departments of each company nixed the idea. Logically enough, both SkyBox and Fleer released sets of trading cards for the series. Those cards featured additional battles not included in the comics, such as Doctor Doom vs. Cyborg, Killer Croc vs. the Abomination and Green Lantern vs. Green Goblin. Artists on the card set included John Byrne, Walter Simonson, Andy Kubert, Joe Quesada, Boris Vallejo and Stuart Immonen.

With the success of the first *Marvel vs. DC* crossover, both companies agreed to deliver a sequel. *DC Vs. Marvel: All Access* (first issue cover-dated December 1996) brought together even more battles than the first series. In each of the four issues, co-produced by Marvel and DC, written by Ron Marz and illustrated by Jackson Guice and Joe Rubinstein, a hero named Access struggles to separate the shared Marvel and DC Universes before their internal differences split all the cosmos apart. In the final issue, the Justice League and X-Men fight each other, then combine forces to destroy the common threat that could tear them apart. Though this crossover sold decently, *All Access* was nowhere near as popular as the original crossover mini-series.

bouts, many lasted just a page or two. Several of the combat scenes, such as the flirtatious fight between Jubilee and Robin, had sparks. Others, such as a struggle between Catwoman and Elektra, were less intriguing. In the end, of course, the heroes join together to combat the cosmic threat and are able to save both universes.

Expectations for the crossover were high, but many fans felt that *DC Versus Marvel* failed to live up the

An Amalgam of Heroes

Between issues #3 and #4 of *Marvel Versus DC*, an even more unprecedented event happened: the heroes of the two companies were combined into one universe under a shared imprint. **Amalgam Comics** combined various DC and Marvel characters into unique amalgamations. Altogether, twelve one-shots, all released on February 28, 1996, featured an array of intriguingly oddball super-heroes. Each publisher performed the editorial duties on six of the releases.

Super-Soldier by Mark Waid and Dave Gibbons combined Captain America and Superman. *Spider-Boy* by Karl Kesel and Mike Wieringo mashed up Spider-Man and Superboy. *Legend of the Dark Claw* by Larry Hama, Jim Balent and Ray McCarthy brought Wolverine and Batman together in a *Batman: the Animated Series* pastiche. *Bruce Wayne: Agent of S.H.I.E.L.D.* by Chuck Dixon and Cary Nord presented espionage adventures as

Batman's secret identity joined Marvel's famed spy agency. *Speed Demon* by Howard Mackie, James Felder, Salvador Larroca and Al Milgrom was a three-way merger of Ghost Rider, Flash and the Demon. *X-Patrol* by Karl and Barbara Kesel, Roger Cruz and Jon Holdredge combined Marvel's mutants with DC's "strangest heroes" in an oblique nod to the similarities between the original X-Men and Doom Patrol. *Amazon* by John Byrne and Terry Austin combined Wonder Woman with Storm. *Bullets and Bracelets* by John Ostrander, Gary Frank and Cam Smith paired Wonder Woman with the Punisher. *Magneto & the Magnetic Men* by Mark Waid, Gerard Jones, Jeff Matsuda and Art Thibert merged the Metal Men with Magneto's Brotherhood of Evil Mutants. *Assassins* by D.G. Chichester, Scott McDaniel and Derek Fisher brought together the overlapping pairs of Daredevil, Elektra, Catwoman and Deathstroke. *Dr. Strangefate* by Ron Marz, Jose Luis Garcia Lopez and Kevin Nowlan combined Dr. Strange and Dr. Fate. Finally, *JLX* by Waid, Jones, Howard Porter and John Dell blended the Justice League with the X-Men.

This oddball imprint proved popular with its creators. John Byrne, for instance, claimed, "People have asked me why I decided to do it, and I said, 'Well, I did it for the money,' but it turned out to be a lot of fun. I see this as being

The Amalgam line of comics merged Marvel and DC characters in a series of one-shots.
TM and © DC Comics. TM and © Marvel Characters Inc.

In Batman & Captain America, *John Byrne had the two heroes meet during World War II.* TM and © DC Comics. TM and © Marvel Characters, Inc.

The Legend Begins Anew!

By the end of 1996, the "old man **Spider-Man**" was back in his suit, though before he could wear that suit again, his story took some convoluted twists and turns.

The year began with just one man in the spider-suit. Ben Reilly was the one and only Spider-Man. Peter Parker and his pregnant wife Mary Jane moved to Portland, Oregon, to raise their baby in peace. To help celebrate the new status quo, a new Spider-Man title premiered with a superstar writer/artist newly recruited to Marvel Comics. *The Sensational Spider-Man* #0 (Jan. 1996) had **Dan Jurgens** as its writer and penciller, with inks handled by Klaus Janson. Jurgens was the key creator attached to some of the most popular DC events of the decade, including "The Death of Superman," *Zero Hour* and *Superman Vs. Aliens*, and Marvel hoped his contributions would add new life to the Spider titles. After encountering Mary Jane's Aunt Anna at Aunt May's gravesite, Ben realizes he must create a life separate from the one Peter Parker lived. Upon wandering into a local diner, the Daily Grind, Ben receives a job offer, and readers soon meet Ben's supporting cast, a completely new set of characters. Ben also dons a modernized costume, rejecting his previous hoodie suit that many fans despised. Designed by artist Mark Bagley, Ben's new costume was a modernized version of the classic Spider-Man suit, with the biggest change being a much larger spider emblem. The Scarlet Spider was no more. Now there was just one Spider-Man. To differentiate himself from Peter Parker even more, Ben dyes his hair blonde, an idea that originated with editor Bob Budiansky (Goletz, "Part 18"). Bagley was the artist for *Amazing Spider-Man* #407 the same month, which establishes that the Human Torch did not get along as well with the Ben Reilly Spider-Man as he did with the Peter Parker version. With that scene and many others, the creative

tremendously positive" (Ray 15). The line proved popular with fans, too. According to one trade magazine, if Amalgam had been an independent publisher, it would have enjoyed the second-largest price share of any publisher releasing comic books in February 1996. A second Amalgam run appeared in 1997.

Outside of the shared Amalgam universe, **John Byrne** also produced an iconic crossover with the December 1996 *Batman/Captain America*. Set during World War II, this Elseworlds adventure unite Cap and Batman as they try to stop the Red Skull and Joker from stealing the first atomic bomb. Byrne delivered "a story that [he'd] had in [his] head for about twenty years" – a rollicking, adventure-filled tale that brought light to both heroes (Braden 85).

As well as crossing over with DC characters, some of Marvel's greatest icons crossed over with Image Comics' heroes. Pastiche met original as Youngblood met X-Force with an August 1996 cover-dated crossover created by a team of Image creators including Eric Stephenson, Robert Napton, Stephen Platt, Dan Fraga, Richard Horie, Ching Lau, Michael Linchang, Mark Pajarillo, Andy Park, Marlo Alquiza, Eric Cannon, Robert Lacko, Sean Parsons, Norm Rapmund and Lary Stucker. Another crossover produced at Image paired Badrock and Wolverine by Jim Valentino and Chap Yaep. Peter David and Stuart Immonen delivered *Spider-Man/Gen13* with a November 1996 cover date. The 52-page, $4.95 squarebound comic has the evil Glider using Spider-Man to get at the Gen kids. The story stays light, with an emphasis on the division between "old man Spider-Man" and the spirited youngsters he meets.

staff made it clear Ben was a very different hero from the one most Spider-fans were used to.

For the first month, everything seemed to settle into place. The creative teams firmly established Ben as the new Spider-Man, and for a brief moment, fans had to be convinced the Spider-Man titles were finally going to move on from the turmoil involving Peter and Ben. Little did those fans know, behind the scenes, the Spider-Man editorial team was roiling with frustration about their choice to write Peter Parker out of the comics. The controversy came to a head after a meeting between Jurgens and Budiansky in which Jurgens strongly asserted that Parker must be the one and only Spider-Man. He believed the new lead character and his setting offended longtime fans. Simply put, Ben Reilly would never be fully accepted by fans as Spider-Man. Jurgens was persuasive, in large part because Budiansky had been wrestling with similar frustrations. Thus, as quickly as the status quo had settled into place to feature Ben as the sole Spider-Man, the editorial team reversed it. Peter would return to the spider suit and Ben would be gone forever. The only question was how to accomplish the change and how quickly the team could turn around the metaphorical ocean liner (Goletz, "Part 19").

The Spider-Man creators began their return to the classic status quo when Peter and Mary Jane show up at the Daily Bugle in *Amazing Spider-Man* #409 (March 1996). In that issue, J. Jonah Jameson requests them to return to New York to consider the enigma of a new skeleton found in the smokestack into which Spider-Man's clone body was sent. Ben and Peter reunite to try to solve the mystery together. A trip to Avengers Mansion in *Sensational Spider-Man* #3 (April 1996) for tests reveals the skeleton was in a smokestack for five years and was yet another clone of Spider-Man. If Ben is the original Spider-Man and the skeleton is the original clone, what does that make Peter? The next month Jameson announces he has hired a forensic

scientist to find the underlying cause of the mystery of the skeleton. The situation leads to an argument between Peter and Mary Jane about whether they should return to Portland. Peter wants answers, but Mary Jane yearns to return to their quiet, peaceful life. She wins the day, and the couple agree to return to Oregon. Just as they are preparing to leave, a mercenary squad called Cell-12 attacks Parker, intent on preventing him from investigating things he should not be looking into. At the same time, Ben returns to his apartment, which has been stripped bare. Rushing to the Daily Grind, Ben finds the cafe firebombed and burning to the ground. The drama gets heavier as Peter suffers a crisis of conscience about his heroism while Ben becomes blamed for the fire at his former employer. Several months later, Ben is acquitted of the accusation after Daily Bugle reporter Ben Urich records the Hobgoblin confessing to the fire. As Ben follows Peter's request and investigates the attack by Cell-12, he ends up fighting a cybernetically enhanced version of the Hobgoblin who reveals he has been orchestrating everything happening to Ben and Peter, at the instructions of his boss. When the battle ends, Ben and Peter get increasingly more desperate to discover the truth behind the mystery. No explanation for the skeleton was ever provided in the core Spider-Man comics.

After two years, the Spider-Man Clone Saga finally reached its resolution in 1996.
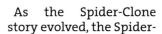
TM and © Marvel Characters, Inc.

As the Spider-Clone story evolved, the Spider-Man editorial team decided the master villain responsible for the events was going to be Harry Osborn, Parker's best friend and the former Green Goblin. However, that plan did not come to fruition. When Bob Harras was elevated to editor-in-chief at Marvel, he mandated a postponement of resolution of the Clone Saga until at least October 1996 in order to avoid competition with the "Onslaught" event. Harras also rejected the idea of Harry as the storyline's villain. Instead, Harras demanded *Norman* Osborn, the original Green Goblin, be the mastermind behind Peter's clone, an idea that the Spider-Man editors and creators opposed. Harras believed having Norman as the villain was the only logical resolution, despite the fact that the original Goblin died many years previously or the numerous plot holes the new revelation now exposed. Harras's edict caused the Spider-Man team to rework their stories and play a waiting game for an additional six months. That delay cost the project the stories and art of Dan Jurgens. The writer/artist already felt frustrated by having to create the adventures of Ben Reilly instead of Peter Parker. An additional six months' delay was the final straw for him. As he reflected, "I wanted to move to Peter Parker as the one, true Spider-Man as fast as possible. More than anything, I wanted to do stories that touched on classic Spider-Man themes. That was impossible under that time's editorial and character situation" (Goletz 25). Jurgens exited the project after producing *Sensational Spider-Man* #6 (July 1996).

After several months of feints, including a prolonged mysterious illness that caused Peter to lose his powers, the creative team finally resolved the long-running storyline. First, the team disposed of Mary Jane's pregnancy, as she is forced to take poison in *Sensational Spider-Man* #11 (Dec. 1996). Because of the poisoning, Mary Jane's baby is stillborn. It's a terrible tragedy, but those horrific events are just prologue to the grand conclusion. The endless epic ambled to its finale in a comic with a deliberately-worded new title. *Peter Parker, Spider-Man* #75 (Dec. 1996) was the new name for a comic which once was simply titled

Spider-Man. The title made a statement: with this issue, everything would return to normal at long last.

With writing by Howard Mackie (assisted by many editorial hands) and art by John Romita Jr., the final chapter of "Revelations" delivers a no-holds-barred battle that leaves no question about which man is the clone. Norman Osborn, the original Green Goblin, returns and reveals he had a hand in all problems of the previous two years, including the switched lab test results, the other clones who showed up, and even Peter and Mary Jane having a stillborn baby. Osborn says, "This thing here— this Ben Reilly. He is the clone, Peter. He always has been and a victory over him means nothing." Osborn also explains a never-before-mentioned healing factor allowed him to survive his impalement during the classic 1973 "Death of Gwen Stacy" storyline. In the end, the Goblin brings many of Spider-Man's friends and allies together at a Halloween party at the Daily Bugle offices, which he has wired with explosives. Reilly senses something is up, and heads to the Bugle to try to thwart the Goblin's plan. After a vicious struggle, though, Ben loses, impaled on the Goblin's glider as the Goblin himself once was. Ben suffers clone degeneration after his death, proving for the last time that he was the fake Spider-Man. Enraged by the death of a man he considered his brother, a furious Peter attacks the Goblin and the two enter a fiery confrontation. Parker throws the bag of bombs into the face of his enemy. "Goodbye, Green Goblin," he screams, but Osborn rants, "You think this ends it, Spider-Man? Not a chance! Never! Never! Never!" And with that, the villain vanishes. Peter limps away and gathers up Ben's body. As Ben falls into dust, Peter realizes, "This can't be happening. Osborn was telling the truth. You were the clone. I am the real Peter Parker. Rest easy... brother." The storyline wraps with a heartfelt scene between Peter and Mary Jane as Peter offers reassurances that give the haunting finale a bit of a happy ending: "We'll get through this. Through the tears. Through the pain. And

In Peter Parker, Spider-Man #75, Norman Osborn, the original Green Goblin, reveals he has been the villain responsible for all of Spider-Man's clone problems. TM and © Marvel Characters, Inc.

In an odd 1996 crossover, Howard the Duck appears in both Marvel Comics' Spider-Man Team-Up *and Image Comics'* Savage Dragon/Destroyer Duck. *TM and © Marvel Characters, Inc. Savage Dragon TM and © Erik Larsen. Destroyer Duck TM and © Steve Gerber.*

our love will be stronger. And we'll face all our tomorrows together. Husband and wife." With that, the Clone Saga finally comes to an end. Peter Parker was back in his spider suit, Ben Reilly was dead, and Norman Osborn was free to unleash his evil another day. The massive story was the longest Marvel had ever published. Altogether, the Spider-Clone story spanned 22 different story arcs and over 2300 comic pages in a period of two years.

Spider-Man line editor Ralph Macchio sounded contrite when discussing the ending of the Clone saga: "Readers who have left the books because of the clone material, we've heard you. We know where we went astray a little, and now we're coming back to making Spider-Man what he should be" (Brady 16). He also expressed remorse at killing Ben Reilly, whom a subset of fans mourned: "The main thing is that Ben developed a following, which I'm happy about. If you kill somebody and nobody cares or they want to see him dead, then you haven't really done anything interesting. But with Ben, when we decided early on that this was what we wanted to happen, I was determined that we were going to make him an interesting character" (Dillon 60). Writer Howard Mackie was defensive about the epic even two years later, stating, "I realize the 'Clone Saga' sucked. But it was a story. And a story that is now well over. Can't we move on?" (Senreich 49).

Marvel even attempted to exploit the fans' hatred of the interminable story arc, publishing *101 Ways to End the Clone Saga* in November 1996. This humorous 36-page one-shot shows the Spider-Man editors sitting around a table comparing ideas for ending their notorious mess, including having Peter use Doctor Doom's time machine to return

to the past, revealing all the characters are mere holograms, and simply having Ben Reilly melt as if he never should have existed (a resolution that many fans really wanted anyway).

Before the year ended, Ben did get to enjoy one last adventure, albeit a wacky one. At the behest of Bob Harras, the Scarlet Spider met none other than that irritable icon from the 1970s, Howard the Duck, in a tale published in *Spider-Man Team-Up* #5 (Dec. 1996). Initially, *Spider-Man Team-Up* editor Tom Brevoort had difficulty finding a writer for the assignment as everyone he contacted felt only the man who created Howard the Duck, **Steve Gerber**, should write the story. Brevoort took their advice and offered the assignment to Gerber, who, after mulling it over, told the editor he wanted to do an unofficial crossover with Howard appearing in *Spider-Man Team-Up* and Howard's doppelgänger, Destroyer Duck, appearing in Image Comics' *Savage Dragon/Destroyer Duck* one-shot. The two ducks wouldn't technically meet; they would just be simultaneously in the same place. Only readers who bought both issues would see the joke. That's at least how Gerber described the crossover to Brevoort. After receiving assurances from Gerber that nothing in the *Savage Dragon/Destroyer Duck* issue would get Brevoort in trouble with his superiors, the Marvel editor signed off on Gerber's idea. Gerber, however, had since learned that Marvel had planned on having Howard the Duck appear in other series, like *Generation X* and *Ghost Rider*, in issues that Gerber wouldn't be writing. Despite relinquishing ownership of Howard the Duck to Marvel during the mid-1980s, Gerber was still protective of his creation, and the notion that Marvel was now going to revive Howard the Duck without his involvement or approval didn't sit well with him. With this in mind, Gerber seized an opportunity to strike back. During a battle in *Spider-Man Team-Up* #5, Howard becomes surrounded by duck clones. When that same battle is presented one month later in the Image comic book, Destroyer Duck grabs Howard from the group of clones and removes him completely from the scene. Later in the *Savage Dragon* issue, Destroyer Duck puts Howard, among other Steve Gerber-created characters, in a witness protection program. The implication was that over in *Spider-Man Team-Up*, Howard had been replaced with an imposter. Gerber had essentially devised a way to remove Howard from Marvel Comics once and for all.

Upon learning what Gerber had done, Brevoort felt both betrayed and concerned that Marvel would fire him for allowing this to happen. When Brevoort confronted Gerber, the writer said the editor was just "in the way of the gunfire." Brevoort refused to work with Gerber ever again (Howe 382-4).

Dream's End, Dreaming's Beginning

Howard the Duck was one of the most critically acclaimed comics of the 1970s. Unquestionably, one of the most critically acclaimed comic books of the 1990s was **Neil Gaiman's** *Sandman*. It seemed appropriate, then, that *Sandman* #75 (March 1996) represented a landmark event in the history of the medium. For the first time ever, a long-running, popular series was cancelled not due to poor sales or because of company politics, but because the writer had finished his story.

Neil Gaiman had always imagined *Sandman* as a finite series, presenting a story that would eventually reach an appropriate conclusion. In fact, within the first two years of its run, Gaiman was pushing to end *Sandman* at a specific point: "I floated my little trial balloon along about issue twenty-two, twenty-three. We'd been doing this for a couple of years, and I remember saying to [editor] Karen [Berger] somewhere in there, 'I think I'm going to want *Sandman* to stop when I stop.' And she said, 'You know that will never happen'" (Campbell 120). After several years of repeating his wish, Gaiman finally persuaded Berger and her superiors to approve the plan. Unlike nearly every other comic released by DC or Marvel, *Sandman* ended on a definitive note. The elegiac double-sized issue "The Tempest" acted as a sequel of sorts to *Sandman*'s earlier Shakespeare-themed issues (#13, Feb. 1990 and #19, Sept. 1990), giving the series a feeling of closure. The issue alternates between Shakespeare's internal monologue and scenes from *The Tempest* itself.

Artist Charles Vess delivered penciled-and-inked pages for Shakespeare's thoughts and fully painted pages for the play's performance.

However, "The Tempest" was not the final *Sandman*-related comic Gaiman wrote during the '90s. A month after the final issue appeared, DC released the first issue of the three-part *Death: the Time of Your Life*. Written by Gaiman, with art by Chris Bachalo and Mark Buckingham, *Death* explores the relationship between popular *Sandman* supporting characters Foxglove and Hazel. Foxglove's music career is taking off while Hazel stays home with her young child. Gaiman depicts this dramatic split of life choices and relationships, as well as explores the music industry and humankind's relationship with death. Gaiman had planned to follow up *The Time of Your Life* with mini-series featuring two of Death's siblings, Delirium and Despair. Unfortunately, Gaiman's increasing popularity as a fantasy novelist caused him to move away from comics.

As Sandman *wound down, Neil Gaiman launched* Death: The Time of Your Life. TM and © DC Comics.

As readers soon learned, however, the world of *Sandman* didn't need Neil Gaiman to live on in other Vertigo series. For starters, DC's imprint continued publishing *Sandman Mystery Theatre*, which starred the Golden Age Sandman but was also tangentially related to Gaiman's series. Then there was *Essential Vertigo: The Sandman* (first issue cover-dated August 1996) which reprinted *Sandman* one issue at a time. Vertigo also launched a *Sandman*-themed anthology series; *The Dreaming* premiered with a June 1996 cover-dated issue and initially included arcs by rotating teams of writers and artists. Writer Terry LaBan and artist Peter Snejbjerg kicked off the series with

The acclaimed Sandman *saga concluded with issue #75, a Michael Zulli-illustrated issue that adapts Shakespeare's* The Tempest. TM and © DC Comics.

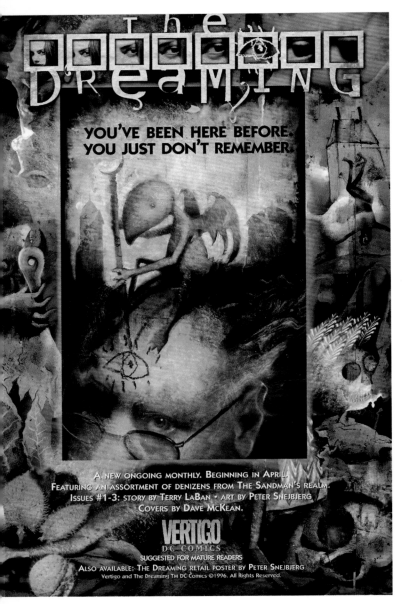

After Sandman *ended, DC launched* The Dreaming *to present more stories inside the Sandman universe.* TM and © DC Comics.

serial killer convention depicted in *A Doll's House*; Caitlin R. Kiernan's tale about Alvin-Wanda, the transsexual from *A Game of You*; George Alec Effinger's mash-up of the classic comic strip *Little Nemo in Slumberland* with *Sandman;* and a Gene Wolfe story showing a slightly skewed dreamlike perception of reality.

With the massive success of Vertigo Comics, DC editorial decided to start a similar science-fiction oriented imprint called **Helix**. Stuart Moore moved over from Vertigo to become chief editor for Helix's initial slate of titles. The imprint launched with three ongoing series. *Cyberella* by Howard Chaykin and Don Cameron tells the story of a twenty-year-old girl who becomes a virtual reality nightmare for the corporation that created her. *Gemini Blood* by Christopher Hinz and Tommy Lee Edwards presents the adventures of a combat squad trying to defeat genetically engineered assassins. *Vermillion* by Lucius Shepard and Al Davison features a man discovering the terrifying truth behind a form of interstellar travel that literally transforms its passengers. Reviewer Matt Bielby admired the first issue of *Gemini Blood*, praising its conceptual complexity and the pace in which it unfolded, "just like the best SF novels" (Bielby 94). Popular *Preacher* writer Garth Ennis brought Helix one of its pair of debut mini-series, *Bloody Mary* with art by longtime collaborator Carlos Ezquerra. While *Preacher* presented a gun-toting priest, this futuristic comic starred a gun-toting nun who seeks revenge for the death of her old commando team. The other debut mini, *The Black Lamb* by Tim Truman, stars a vampire who hunts the vampire hunters. Moore summed up his approach to the line: "When I started thinking about Helix, what I wanted were books with the same sort of seriousness and intellectual intent as the Vertigo titles, but with a little more color and futuristic detail" (Sodaro 110). Sadly for DC, science fiction comic books didn't sell very well, so the line died quickly... but not before launching a fan-favorite title in 1997.

A Preacher in the DC Universe

Thanks principally to his work on *Preacher*, **Garth Ennis** was a bona fide star in the comic book industry, but some readers may still have been surprised to learn that his next series wouldn't be part of Vertigo's adult-oriented line-up. Instead, **Hitman** was set squarely in DC's super-hero universe. The titular killer is Tommy Monaghan, first introduced in 1993 in the Ennis-scripted *Demon Annual* #2. As a result of that year's "Bloodlines" crossover, Monaghan became a "metahuman," gaining telepathic powers and X-Ray vision, which he puts to good use in his role as a contract assassin. With the launch of his own series (first issue cover-dated April 1996), Monaghan is hired to go to Arkham Asylum and kill the Joker. To be expected, the proposed hit puts Mongahan at odds with Batman. Accompanied by art by John McCrea, *Hitman* had a lot in common with the more serious *Preacher*: the new series was violent and

the four-issue "The Goldie Factor" in which the gargoyle Goldie runs away, only to be chased by the brothers Cain and Abel. The adventure grows larger after Goldie meets a character who turns out to be the snake from the Garden of Eden. Following LaBan and Snejbjerg's story were a four-issue arc by Steve Parkhouse and Peter Hogan and a three-parter by Dave Taylor and Bryan Talbot. Eventually a full-time creative team settled in on the series.

Warner Books even did its part with a *Sandman*-related prose book of its own. Edited by Gaiman and Ed Kramer, *Sandman: Book of Dreams* featured two dozen short stories set in the world of the Endless by prominent fantasy and science fiction authors. Contributions included John M. Ford's piece which adds context to Gaiman's very first *Sandman* issue; a story by Will Shetterly in which a splatter novelist attends the irreverent, filled with passionate character moments that stressed the importance of friendship. Some story arcs were grim and sobering, while others were silly or satirical, but through them all Monaghan—and Ennis—never lost their focus on the great friendships which grow out of a shared fellowship at a dive bar. Unlike Ennis's other series, *Hitman* featured appearances by such DC stalwarts as Green Lantern, Catwoman, Etrigan the Demon and, in an especially memorable 1998 issue, Superman.

Superman and Lois (Finally) Tie the Knot

One of the biggest events in the life of the Man of Steel finally occurred in 1996 on both television and in the pages of DC Comics. After nearly a full season of clones, feints and memory losses, "Swear to God, This Time We're Not Kidding" aired October 6, 1996 as the third episode of the fourth season of ABC TV's *Lois and Clark: the New Adventures of Superman*. Finally, viewers could enjoy the pleasure of a wedding that was a year overdue. Three days later, local comic book shop patrons could read an event nearly sixty years in the making when the comic book version of Superman put a wedding ring on Lois Lane's finger in *Superman: the Wedding Album*. The 96-page comic was produced by a who's who of Superman creators, including John Byrne, Jerry Ordway, George Pérez, Al Plastino, Jim Mooney, Nick Cardy, Roger Stern, Dan Jurgens, Louise Simonson, Karl Kesel, among others. Fans had been awaiting the wedding ever since 1990 when Lois first accepted Clark's marriage proposal. The couple were busy making plans for their nuptials, originally slated for November 1992, when Doomsday struck Metropolis and killed the Man of Steel in the epic "Death of Superman" storyline. After Superman's resurrection, DC editorial mandated any wedding in the comics happen simultaneously to the one on the *Lois and Clark* show. Considering how long it took the television show to wed

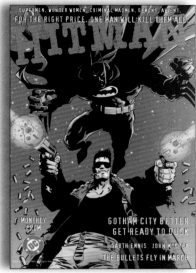

Hitman by Garth Ennis was often called "Preacher Lite." TM and © DC Comics.

its titular characters, several DC creators despaired of the event ever happening but when the big day finally came, they were thrilled they could be a part of it. As Kesel said, "It is kind of mind-boggling that 20 years from now, people will still look back at this wedding as a turning point that changed the status quo of Superman" (Brady, "Wedding of the Century" 42).

DC's editors made a strong effort to ensure many of Superman's most famous creators were included in *The Wedding Album*. Jurgens, who drew Superman's death, illustrated the wedding scenes. Longtime scripter Roger Stern wrote the story. *The Wedding Album* even included a never-before-published four-page tale by legendary Superman artist **Curt Swan**, who passed away just three months before the wedding was shown on television. One of the covers was monogrammed like a wedding invitation and all versions of the comic together sold about 350,000 copies through Diamond – the most copies of any Superman comic since he returned from the dead. The couple would remain married throughout the decade, but the change in the status quo didn't cause an uptick in interest in his series. The massive popularity of *The Wedding Album* was a momentary blip. Monthly sales on *Action Comics*, *Adventures of Superman*, *Superman* and *Superman: the Man of Steel* continued their steady drip of an average 20,000 copies per month through Diamond through 1996 (Beaty 18).

After a six-year engagement, during which the groom died and was resurrected, Clark Kent finally marries Lois Lane in Superman: the Wedding Album.
TM and © DC Comics.

As Superman was tying the knot, one member of his extended comics family returned to her own title, as *Supergirl* #1 (Sept. 1996) by Peter David, Gary Frank and Cam Smith arrived in comic shops. But as the first issue cover (featuring a close-up of a girl in a plaid button-down over a Superman T-shirt clutching a worn skateboard) announced, this was not the same old Supergirl. In this intriguing new series, the former blob of protoplasm known as Supergirl merges with a rebellious small-town girl named Linda Danvers. This new Supergirl has most of Superman's powers, but she is forced to fight a different mission: the small town of Leesburg sits on a ley-line for mystic energy in the world, and the combined new heroine is forced to battle that evil and keep her town safe. The series, which united David with one of his most beloved *Hulk* collaborators, was a solid hit for DC for many years, often animated by David's humorous dialogue. The debut issue ran through three printings.

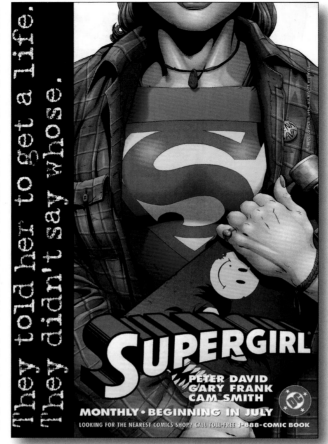

Peter David and Gary Frank's Supergirl *presented a decidedly different Girl of Steel.* TM and © DC Comics.

titles, including *Hitman*, *Supergirl*, *Sovereign Seven* and *Legion of Super-Heroes*, crossed over with *Final Night*, detailing the heroes' valiant efforts to save the world, but the dire situation becomes even worse with the realization that the energy-depleted sun will go nova. Lex Luthor, of all people, devises a plan to use small force field units to contain the sun's explosion. The only catch is that the person placing the units around sun will not survive the experience. A power-depleted Superman volunteers for the task, but Ferro Lad of the Legion of Super-Heroes decides that Superman is too important to be allowed to commit suicide. The young Legionnaire, therefore, takes matters into his own hands and races to the sun on his own. Before he can duplicate the heroic sacrifice that the original Ferro Lad made (in 1967's *Adventure Comics* #353), an unexpected savior arrives. Hal Jordan, formerly the evil Parallax, rescues Ferro Lad and then confronts the Sun-Eater on his own. As he defeats the strange creature, Hal's energy reignites the sun, causing his own apparent death. In doing so, Hal Jordan saves Earth, redeeming the crimes he has committed. With the conclusion in mind, few would be surprised the series was originally titled *Darkest Night*, after a line from Jordan's Green Lantern oath. The title was changed, though, to hide Hal's role as a major character.

As Supergirl was reborn for a new generation, the 1990s generation of *Justice League* titles died in 1996 to lay the ground for a dramatic reboot in 1997. Soon after *Extreme Justice* #18 (July 1996), *Justice League America* #113 and *Justice League Task Force* #37 (both Aug. 1996) wrapped up their respective series, DC launched a new mini-series, *Justice League: A Midsummer's Nightmare* (Sept. 1996). That three-issue series returned the headliners to DC's premier super-hero group after several years of absence. Written by the team of Mark Waid and Fabian Nicieza and drawn by Jeff Johnson, Darick Robertson, Jon Holdredge and Hannibal Rodriguez, *Nightmare* showed Superman, Batman, Green Lantern, the Flash, Wonder Woman, Aquaman and the Martian Manhunter struggling to regain the memories of their super-hero careers.

By the time *Midsummer's Nightmare* had concluded, DC had already begun its next intracompany crossover: *Final Night* (first issue cover-dated Nov. 1996). Written by Karl Kesel with art by Stuart Immonen, the four-issue weekly mini-series posed the threat of an extinguished sun on DC's super-hero universe. The story begins with an alien herald informing Earth of an approaching "Sun-Eater": "it will envelop your sun and steal its light and heat from you! Your crops will wither. Your waters will freeze. And that is only the beginning." The planet's greatest heroes gather to stop the Sun-Eater but their attempts are all in vain. Eternal nighttime grips the Earth as the lack of sunlight renders the whole planet frigidly cold. Twenty November-dated DC

Thy Kingdom Come

Four months before a near-Biblical catastrophe hit the Earth in *Final Night*, a near-Biblical catastrophe provided the impetus for a comic that caused one critic to declare, "this past summer, no other comic came even close to the amount of attention, praise, and controversy as *Kingdom Come*, the four-part DC mini-series by Alex Ross and Mark Waid" (Mescallado 109). As one of DC's Elseworld series, **Kingdom Come** drops readers into a near future in which a new generation of super-heroes are out of control, having pointless, flashy fights with each other while ignoring the destruction they cause to the lives of ordinary people. This depraved indifference to consequences reaches a devastating climax during yet another fight in Kansas when a hero named Magog rips Captain Atom's body wide open. The destruction of the cosmic-powered hero causes radiation to sweep over hundreds of kilometers in the Midwest, killing millions of people and rendering America's farm belt an irradiated wasteland. Superman leads many of his former Justice League compatriots out of retirement to combat the recklessness of the new generation of super-heroes. Pastor Norman McCay witnesses the events as the supernatural Spectre pushes him to pass judgment on the evil he sees. As Waid and Ross spin their tale of twisting alliances, massive super-hero battles and political intrigue, they explore the myth of the super-hero from multiple viewpoints. In the end, innocence, in the form of Captain Marvel, wins the day. All victories come with a price, though, and that price gives the book a resonating ending.

The response to *Kingdom Come*—both from fans and critics—was mostly positive. The series swept *Wizard*'s 1996 fan awards and won an Eisner Award in 1997 for Best Limited Series. (Ross also won Eisner awards for Best Painter and Best Cover Artist for his work on the series.) *Kingdom Come* also sold well despite its $4.95 price tag. Issue #4 finished a surprising third in a top 100 sales list dominated by lower-priced X-Men-related comics. Not everybody loved the series, however. One *Comics Journal* reviewer slammed *Kingdom Come* for its lack of originality: "The apocalyptic dread and cultural details of *Watchmen* meets the outsider narrator format of *Marvels* meets the fallen hero protagonists of *Dark Knight Returns* meets the basic plot structure and biblical shadings of Alan Moore's unused 'Twilight of the Super-heroes' proposal" (Spurgeon 37).

If *Kingdom Come* sounds like a commentary on the state of super-hero comic books during the 1990s, it is. As writer Waid reported, "Essentially it's the Image Universe taking over the DC Universe" (Russo 30). Waid saw *Kingdom Come* as a satire on the brutality of many of the decade's most popular super-heroes. As both a traditionalist and tremendous fan of Superman, Waid felt appalled by the kind of vicious heroism on display in many Image comic books, far removed from the ideals Waid believed in. The writer saw this project as an opportunity to comment on classic comic book history while also toppling icons in the same manner that Frank Miller did in *Batman: the Dark Knight Returns*. Collaborator Ross felt much the same. He relished his opportunity to explore the DC Universe from a different angle: "I wanted to pick up from what Alan [Moore] had done with *Watchmen* and Frank had done with *Dark Knight*, and show this wide-spanning kind of thing that had the entirety of the known fictional DC universe shown through this realistic, distorting mirror that's got everything just a little bit askew." Waid wedded his frustration with a story outline Ross had been working on since high school. DC editors connected the two creators and the comic resulted from the often stormy collaboration between them (Khoury).

Ross's moody and garish painted art in *Kingdom Come* is worlds away from the warm work he delivered in *Marvels*. He used darker colors, and he redesigned heroes with flasher and purportedly "edgier" costumes with increased grittiness. He showed the older heroes as being their actual age, with balding heads and expanding waistlines, and as such, their eventual triumph feels even more satisfying because of its improbability.

DC announced an ongoing *Kingdom Come* comic to launch in 1997 as a sequel to the blockbuster mini-series. Waid would have returned to write it, with art by Gene Ha and covers by Ross. Waid's intention was to help move the DC Universe of the current day towards the events shown in *Kingdom Come*, with Magog at the center of the storyline as the precipitator of the events to follow. The series never saw print, though DC did release a Waid-written sequel of sorts called *The Kingdom* in 1998. One *Kingdom Come*-related spinoff that *did* see print was a prose novelization of the graphic novel by longtime comic writer Elliot S. Maggin. The novelization shows a different approach to the story's events as Maggin lends depth and context that is only hinted at in the graphic novel via more extensive use of interior monologue and scene setting.

Batman Battles Ebola

In early 1996 **Batman** combatted a different enemy from the sort he usually brought to justice. In the 12-part "Contagion," Batman and his allies fight a deadly strain of Ebola called "The Clench," sent by Azrael's adversaries the Order of St. Dumas, which kills victims within twelve hours. In an increasingly stressful crossover that spans two months of Batman titles including *Detective Comics*, *Azrael*, *Catwoman* and *Robin*, Gotham's heroes must work together to prevent more infections and stop the Order.

Ever since 1993's momentous "Knightfall," the Batman line of comics had been involved in one crossover after another. By the time "Contagion" concluded, the Batman editorial team decided to put a stay on interconnected storylines in order to allow creators on books like *Shadow of the Bat* and *Catwoman* to follow their own direction. That stay, however, didn't impede the launch of a new Batman-related ongoing, perhaps the most requested new DC series in years. Following his successful 1995 mini-series, **Nightwing** received his own title, written by Chuck Dixon with art by Scott McDaniel and Karl Story. Dick Grayson, the former Robin, moves from Gotham to the port town of Blüdhaven, a city even more corrupt than his former hometown. Now all grown up and with a heroic style all his own, Nightwing starts to achieve his full potential as the main hero of the corrupt city. As writer Chuck Dixon stated, "He sees this town as rotten to the core, and has no one to

Collection of heroes from Mark Waid and Alex Ross's apocalyptic Kingdom Come.
TM and © DC Comics.

protect it. Everybody in Blüdhaven is a predator. There's no one there to protect the innocent. There's no Commissioner Gordon or Harvey Bullock or Huntress or Robin. He's alone, and if he leaves, he's left the town worse than when he arrived" (Brick 46). The series would prove to be extremely popular, and the version of Nightwing presented by Dixon and McDaniel became the definitive character take for many fans.

Meanwhile, one of Grayson's oldest allies, Oracle, appeared in *Black Canary/Oracle: Birds of Prey* #1 (Jan. 1996), a 54-page one-shot by Chuck Dixon, Gary Frank and John Dell. The issue has Oracle contacting Black Canary to ask for her help in taking down a group of eco-terrorists. Oracle provides the wisdom while Canary supplies the strength. Together, the pair form what soon will become an iconic partnership. As part of the event, Canary ditches her blonde wig and fishnets in favor of hair dye and a new costume designed by Oracle. It was understandable for a comic like *Birds of Prey*,

Birds of Prey brought together Black Canary and Oracle in a sell-out mini-series. TM and © DC Comics.

with two female leads, one in a wheelchair and neither of them a household name, to fly under the radar of many shop owners. For that reason, *Birds of Prey* received light orders. Regardless, the one-shot sold out in many shops and sold well enough overall to inspire a sequel four-issue mini-series just eight months later. *Birds of Prey: Manhunt*, also written by Dixon, with art by Matt Haley and Wade Von Grawbadger, added Huntress and Catwoman to the character mix. *Manhunt* also delivered solid sales results for DC, and after the mini-series wrapped, fans began clamoring for a *Birds of Prey* ongoing title. They got their wish by the end of the decade with a first issue cover-dated January 1999.

DC published two other notable Batman-related books in 1996. The first was conceived by longtime comic book colorist Mark Chiarello, who pitched a new Batman anthology printed in black-and-white with contributions from some of the industry's most talented creators. DC eventually accepted Chiarello's proposal, and **Batman: Black and White** became a four-issue mini-series that included short stories and pin-ups by such luminaries as Neal Adams, Mike Allred, Simon Bisley, Brian Bolland, Howard Chaykin, Richard Corben, Neil Gaiman, Klaus Janson, Mike Kaluta, Joe Kubert, Jim Lee, Frank Miller, Moebius, Kevin Nowlan, Denny O'Neil, Katsuhiro Otomo, Alex Ross, P. Craig Russell, Bill Sienkiewicz, Marc Silvestri, Walt Simonson, Alex Toth, Matt Wagner, Kent Williams, Barry Windsor-Smith and Jorge Zaffino, among many others. *Batman: Black and White* #1 (June 1996) offers both Bruce Timm's tale about Two-Face's failed rehabilitation and Ted McKeever's Eisner-

Award nominated story about Batman finding clues to a murder by doing an autopsy on a woman.

The other noteworthy Batman project of the year came courtesy of writer **Jeph Loeb** and artist **Tim Sale** who had been collaborating on annual *Batman: Legends of the Dark Knight* Halloween specials for the past three years. At first, Loeb did not plan to produce a Batman book for 1996. His position changed, however, when editor Archie Goodwin encouraged him to write a film noir gangster tale. As Sale and Loeb discussed the project, they came up with the idea of doing a Batman event that spanned a year's worth of holidays, starting and ending with Halloween. The thirteen issue **Batman: The Long Halloween** (first issue cover-dated Dec. 1996) takes place during the early years of the Dark Knight's career when he has to stop a serial killer who has earned the nickname of "Holiday" because of his penchant for murdering mobsters on the holiday of each month. Each chapter presents both a different holiday (i.e. Halloween, Thanksgiving, Christmas, Valentine's Day, etc.) and an often radically redesigned villain for Batman to fight (Catwoman, Solomon Grundy, the Joker, Poison Ivy, among others). By the end of the series, Holiday's true identity remains something of a mystery, with the prime suspects being the son of a Gotham City crime boss, District Attorney Harvey Dent, and Dent's wife Gilda. More thematic, however, is the series' depiction of the developing bond between Batman, Dent and Commissioner Gordon, a bond that is severed once Dent becomes Two-Face. Loeb's inspiration for exploring the dissolution of a group friendship came from a televised history of the Beatles and the famous break-up that music group had in 1970 (Senreich, "Jeph Loeb" 72).

Crossing Over to Film and TV

Comic book-related characters didn't make much headway in movies and TV in 1996. *Lois and Clark* foundered in the ratings after wedding its protagonists, and ABC cancelled the show at the end of the programming year. A pilot for the Marvel Comic *Generation X* aired on FOX in February during sweeps week but finished tied for 72nd out of 108 shows in the weekly ratings. Though the *GenX* pilot finished first in its time slot for males between 18 and 34, FOX didn't pick up the proposed series.

At least Marvel could boast that more people watched the *Generation X* pilot on TV than saw Dark Horse Comics' **Barb Wire** in theaters. Starring former Playboy Playmate and *Baywatch* star Pamela Anderson, the film has been described as a post-apocalyptic take on *Casablanca* set in a strip club. The film got green lit in 1994 when Dark Horse Publisher Mike Richardson, riding high on the success of the film adaptation of *The Mask*, met with Hollywood producer Brad Wyman to discuss possible new movies. When the idea of a film version of *Barb Wire* came up in their conversation, the producer showed Anderson's *Playboy* centerfold to Richardson and declared, "This is Barb Wire!" (Shapiro 32). Even though famous critic Roger Ebert gave *Barb Wire* a sympathetic review, stating "[it] has a high energy level, and a sense of deranged fun" (Ebert), the film ended up as one of the biggest financial flops in movie history, earning a paltry $3,794,000 in the United States. The movie was simultaneously nominated for an MTV Film Award (for a fight between Anderson and a villain) and for several Razzie Awards, including Worst Picture, Worst Screenplay and Worst New Star (which Anderson won).

Superman: the Animated Series was the most popular new comic-related media of the year. Produced by the same team that delivered the award-winning *Batman: the Animated Series*, the spinoff series maintained the same art deco look and loving reverence for the original characters demonstrated by *BTAS* while delivering a brighter color palette and more optimistic themes. Though the series was successful on weekday afternoons and became a staple of kids' programming for three seasons, its 90-minute premiere *Superman: the Last Son of Krypton* placed 100th out of 101 primetime shows for the week of September 2-8 (Alstetter 123). That pilot film presented Kal-El's rocket falling to Earth like fire from heaven.

An Homage to Independents

"Fire from Heaven" was the name of the major **Wildstorm/ Image** event of 1996, and it had long-lasting consequences for Jim Lee's Wildstorm Universe. "Fire from Heaven" brings the evil alien Damocles down to Earth, where he and a group of bounty hunters fight a furious battle with Wildstorm's greatest heroes. During the crossover, spanning all April and May cover-dated Wildstorm titles, Deathblow is killed, DV8 are sent on their first mission, and Stormwatch

Batman fights Catwoman in the pages of Jeph Loeb and Tim Sale's Batman: the Long Halloween. TM and © DC Comics.

discovers their member Flashpoint is a traitor. Coming out of the event, one of the most impactful changes to any series happened with *Stormwatch*. **Warren Ellis** assumed the series' writing chores starting with *Stormwatch #37* (July 1996). Beneath a cover homage to 1987's *Justice League #1*, Ellis delivers a new status quo for the team. He brings in new members Jenny Sparks, Rose Tattoo and Jack Hawksmoor and sets the new team against a serial killing, super-powered Nietzsche fan. Ellis grounded *Stormwatch* in the real world while providing its narrative with a gritty, cheeky tone. His style reflected a contemporary sensibility, with political commentary, sexually adventurous anti-heroes, and complex morality that brought in readers looking for more mature super-hero stories than they might find elsewhere. Heroes and villains died and stayed dead, political conspiracies ruled the world, and heroes had dark secrets slowly revealed over time. As *Stormwatch* artist Tom Raney reported, "[Ellis] turned in hugely imaginative scripts. A lot of fun to work with. A ton of work, tons, a lot of reference. It was always something different" (Hedges 135). Ellis's *Stormwatch* run climaxed in a cataclysmic 1998 crossover that led to a breakthrough 1999 series.

Besides working on *Fantastic Four*, *Iron Man*, and the "Fire from Heaven" crossover, **Jim Lee** premiered a new line of comics, dedicated to a select set of auteurs. **Homage Comics** became a home for creator-owned material as well as a safe haven from an increasingly challenging comic book market. **Kurt Busiek** was the first creator who signed on, agreeing to move his *Astro City* from Image Central to Homage. After negotiating with companies such as Milestone, Broadway and DC Comics, Busiek chose Homage because "[Jim Lee] pretty much gave us everything we wanted" (Hedges 120). *Kurt Busiek's Astro City* began its Homage run with a new first issue (cover date Sept. 1996).

Terry Moore followed in Busiek's footsteps, moving his self-published slice-of-life ***Strangers in Paradise*** to Lee's new imprint. Previously published in black and white, *Strangers in Paradise* could now be published in color, allowing Moore to expose his offbeat characters and story

Superman: the Animated Series was the most popular new comic-related media of the year. TM and © DC Comics.

to a new audience previously biased against black and white comics. Lee's hands-off editorial policy gave Moore the freedom to follow his own vision for his comic.

The final title in the initial Homage launch represented a genre popular in young adult fiction but rarely seen in comics. *Leave It to Chance* by James Robinson and Paul Smith featured teenager Chase Falconer and her pet dragon St. George in a world filled with monsters, ghouls and demons. Chance aspires to follow in her father's footsteps as a great paranormal adventurer, but her father opposes her ambitions because the very demons that made him successful also killed Chance's mother. Despite her dad's objections, Chance can't help herself: she engages in a series of delightful adventures that establish her as a force to be reckoned with. The series won both the Harvey and Eisner Awards for Best New Series for 1996.

Astro City *and* Strangers in Paradise *relocated to Jim Lee's Homage Comics, joined by the new* Leave It to Chance. *TM and © Juke Box Productions. TM and © Terry Moore.*

Roberts) and *Boondoggle* (by Steven Steglin). The move stimulated sales on all titles with Sirius publisher Robb Horan boasting "at worst, every book we've picked up has doubled its sales." Busiek could relate as sales of *Astro City* "shot up" once it became an Homage title (Shutt 121).

Of course, not all independent creators felt the need to abandon self-publishing in 1996. Many continued their ventures, including Dave Sim (whose *Cerebus* began the year with issue #202, just over two-thirds of the way to Sim's goal of three hundred issues), Rick Veitch (whose dream diary *Roarin' Rick's Rare Bit Fiends* was entering its third year of self-publishing existence), and David Lapham (who released four issues of his acclaimed *Stray Bullets* during the year). Writer James Hudnall took his *ESPers* series, formerly published by Eclipse and Epic Comics, to his own Halloween Comics. Linda Medley self-published her *Castle Waiting: the Curse of Brambly Hedge*, a 68-page traditional fantasy adventure with a witty, *Princess Bride* style while Carla Speed McNeil premiered her visionary science fiction comic *Finder*, the story of a depopulated world in which only a few people, named "Finders," traverse the landscape. McNeil constructed a complex and idiosyncratic world for *Finder*, making it a cult favorite series that lasted well beyond the 1990s.

Other prominent self-publishers also brought their comics to larger companies during 1996. **Colleen Doran** moved her *A Distant Soil* from her independent Aria Press to the safer confines of Erik Larsen's Highbrow Studios at Image Comics beginning with issue #15 (Aug. 1996). Doran explained the move as a pure financial necessity: "The printer depends on volume – that's the main reason I'm doing this" (Wilkofsky 22). In fact, self-publishing had left Doran deeply in debt, especially since some distributors constantly paid her late. Doran kept *A Distant Soil* at Image through 2006, with a final short sequence of issues in 2013. Fellow artist Teri Sue Wood also made a move in 1996 and summed up the self-publisher's dilemma thus: "Sales go down when you think they should be going up. Money goes tight so things come out late. [*Wandering Star*] #11 just barely came out. But the desperation and the determination just keeps you going. You go into self-publishing and small press wanting very much to tell your stories and, knowing all the while, that it's going to be hard to survive. But you keep at it because you want to do it so badly" (Shapiro 67). In 1996 Wood found her way to indie publisher Sirius which had added Drew Hayes's *Poison Elves* in 1995. Michigan's Caliber Comics picked up the formerly self-published *Dreamwalker* (by Jenni Gregory), *Adventure Strip Digest* (by Randy Reynaldo) and *Strange Attractors* (by Mark Sherman and Michael Cohen). Caliber also started an all-ages line, Tapestry Comics, in 1997, which took on additional refugees from self-publishing, including *Shades of Gray* (by Jimmy Gowned), *Patty Cake* (by Scott

a 68-page traditional fantasy adventure with a witty, *Princess Bride* style while Carla Speed McNeil premiered her visionary science fiction comic *Finder*, the story of a depopulated world in which only a few people, named "Finders," traverse the landscape. McNeil constructed a complex and idiosyncratic world for *Finder*, making it a cult favorite series that lasted well beyond the 1990s.

Light out of Darkness

Another major comic hit in 1996 came from **Marc Silvestri's Top Cow Productions**. Written by Garth Ennis and penciled by Silvestri, *The Darkness* (first issue cover-dated Dec. 1996) features a lonely hitman named Jackie Estacado who becomes the unwitting servant of "The Darkness." He gains the power to create anything, as long as he does so in darkness. This immortal hero is neither good nor evil, and as this character-based series progressed, it explored Jackie's complicated moral reactions to the changes in his life. *The Darkness* was long in gestation before finally reaching the printed page. Numerous writers, including Ann Nocenti, were attached to the project before the popular *Preacher* writer stepped up. Some of the company's representatives had some initial qualms about Ennis's work on the book. But as Top Cow's David Wohl explained, those qualms were quickly assuaged: "It was sort of shocking at first. Here's something you created, and then someone else comes in and puts their own, completely different spin on it, which in the end was probably the best thing that could've happened. You just learn to sit back and let others do their stuff" (Brady 39). Writers Christina Z and Wohl assumed writing chores with issue #7 and pulled the series in new directions that further developed the character. Sales started out strong and grew stronger in the first year, an unusual trend in the mid-1990s slumping comic book market.

Though Marc Silvestri helped found Image Comics and he formed Top Cow as an Image imprint, by the time *The Darkness* became a hit, Top Cow no longer had any connection to its former parent company. That's because Silvestri's comic line left Image in June, with a Top Cow spokesperson citing irreconcilable differences with fellow Image founder Rob Liefeld. Specifically, Silvestri accused Liefeld of attempting to poach Top Cow's star artist, Michael Turner, a clear violation of Image's internal rules. But to Silvestri, Liefeld's attempted poaching was just part of a protracted line of unacceptable behavior on Liefeld's part, and the other Image founders understood where Silvestri was coming from. Collectively and individually, they all had their reasons for being frustrated with Liefeld. For instance, as Image's Chief Financial Officer and Secretary, Liefeld was responsible for writing checks, a task that several of the Image founders felt he wasn't handling appropriately. As Image Executive Director Larry Marder reported, "[Liefeld] was making an increasing number of business decisions that were counterproductive to being a business partner. It was becoming ridiculous. He was a person it was impossible to deal with" (Dean 11). Fellow founder Jim Valentino complained Liefeld didn't pay him for writing done on the "Heroes Reborn" books. Adding insult to injury, Liefeld also angered his peers by spinning out his own Maximum Press imprint. The new line was like the comics he sold through Image but released without the Image "I" logo on the cover.

Facing mounting pressure from his peers, Liefeld resigned from Image with a letter to his fellow founders dated September 4, 1996. His resignation dodged an emergency vote by Image's Board of Directors, which planned to expel him from their ranks. Liefeld's letter was filled with bitter recrimination, stating in part, "it is your intent to not only drive me from the company I helped to found, but also to destroy my career in the process." The letter didn't win back any lost friendships. Todd McFarlane's reaction, in particular, was vicious: "I believe in life you reap what you sow. It's now harvest time for Rob." Valentino, on the other hand, said he was just sad about the turn of events: "It's been pretty difficult for me on a lot of levels personally because I feel very much like I've lost one of my dearest friends and that's really tough to take" (Senreich 24). Just as the dust was settling from Liefeld's resignation, he sued Image for $1 million for allegedly libelous and defamatory remarks about him, which he claimed cost him income. His former associates then responded with their own countersuits. The golden ideal of creative freedom that dawned in 1992 was beginning to turn into an attorney's paradise by 1996.

In their scathing legal response to Liefeld's accusations of libel and defamation, the Image team made several counter-accusations. First, they claimed Liefeld moved money from the company's central fund to Maximum Press. They also claimed he ordered Image employees to perform tasks for Maximum, including creating logos, designing posters, and reserving space at conventions. That would be illegal because the employees had with no formal connection to Maximum. They further claimed Liefeld designed Maximum to siphon money

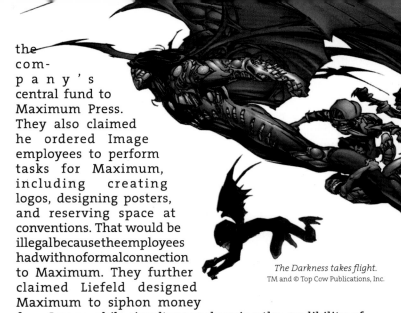

The Darkness takes flight.
TM and © Top Cow Publications, Inc.

from Image while simultaneously using the credibility of his Image connections to build up the independent imprint. Finally, they claimed Liefeld said he would prevent Image product from being sent to suppliers unless they extended the same credit to Maximum Press as they did to Image (Stump, "Now It Can Be Told" 16-17). The founders settled their suit out of court on February 19, 1997, with Image recovering all the money they claimed was due them (Stump, "Image, Liefeld Settle Lawsuit" 12). Liefeld, for his part, claimed to be innocent of the charges against him, saying he was, on some level, set up (Fisher 37).

The Supreme Alan Moore

Though he angered his business partners, Rob Liefeld at least kept one friend happy in 1996. That friend was **Alan Moore**, a man on a mission to change the tone and tenor of super-hero comic books. Nearly a decade after creating such epochal works as *Watchmen* and *V for Vendetta*, Moore was now feeling a fair amount of regret for ushering in an era of dark, cynical comic book stories. With Liefeld's assistance, Moore got to issue an apology of sorts. He took over the writing chores on *Supreme*, starting with issue #41 (Aug. 1996), and with Moore at the helm, *Supreme* became a love letter to 1960s-era DC Comics: "What I decided to do was recreate that sense of richness, something that has the same range and splendor as the original Superman mythos" (Rybandt 54). Little wonder then that the cover to *Supreme* #41 aped the cover to 1939's *Superman* #1 as the title experienced a true reboot. Moore discarded all the work delivered by previous creative teams on *Supreme*, so the previously psychopathic powerhouse suddenly became a paragon of positivity. Moore created a backstory for Supreme similar to Superman's, with love interest Judy Jordan standing in for Lois Lane and Darius Dax substituting for Lex Luthor. But this comic wasn't just an homage to the Superman comic books of yesteryear. Moore set Supreme's alter ego Ethan Crane as a cartoonist rather than a newspaper reporter. That twist allowed Moore to get meta with the character. In one tale, Crane must deal with a bearded British writer who wants to take a grim and gritty approach to his adventures – a clever satire on Moore himself. In other stories, Supreme sees a limbo in which castoff heroes are set aside. Moore won a "Best Writer" Eisner Award for his work on the series, and even though a devoted group of fans loved what Moore was doing with *Supreme*, Liefeld took a loss with each issue he published (Fisher 31). Nevertheless, Moore would continue to work with Liefeld for the next couple of years before launching his own line of super-hero comic books at the end of the decade.

Elsewhere at Image, *Gen13*, by Brandon Choi, J. Scott Campbell and Alex Garner, continued its popular run. In 1996, the heroes recovered from the trauma of the "Fire from Heaven" crossover, enrolled at the University of California at San Diego, and saw Grunge and Freefall fall deeper in love. The series spawned one of the most oddball gimmicks of 1996: for issue #13 (Aug. 1996), the Gen13 team released three completely distinct comics. Issues #13A, 13B and 13C cost $1.30 each, and the story in each issue contained 13 guest stars from indie comics, including Hellboy, Foney Bone from *Bone*, Spawn, the Teenage Mutant Ninja Turtles, Francine and Katchoo from *Strangers in Paradise*, and even Jughead from Archie Comics. In an even more oddball twist, motivational speaker Tony Robbins helps hero Grunge win the day – a clear sign of why fans loved the random wackiness and character-centered action of this unique series. In fact, *Gen13* was popular enough to inspire an anthology spinoff. In the spirit of DC Comics' *Batman: Legends of the Dark Knight* and *The Dreaming*, *Gen13 Bootleg* presented stories by creators who had never worked on Image's teenage heroes before. The series debuted with a two-parter by Mark Farmer and Alan Davis. Subsequent issues contained tales by Dan Norton, Louise and Walter Simonson, Terry Moore and Tomm Coker, among others. The Teenage Mutant Ninja Turtles also returned to comics under Erik Larsen's Highbrow Studios with a new first issue cover-dated June 1996.

Archie Comics, which stopped publishing Ninja Turtles comics in 1995, delivered a shocking development in *Betty* #43 (Nov. 1996). Written by C.J. Anderson and Bob Bolling, drawn by Doug Crane, Mike Esposito and Bob Smith, and with a cover that announces the issue contains a story "you'll never forget," "For One Brief Moment" shows kind and sweet Betty Cooper falling in love with Riverdale's bad boy, Reggie Mantle. After Reggie saves Betty's life, the two end up dating every weekend. This new romance would seem to open the door for Veronica and Archie to be together at last, but instead they both become jealous of the pairing.

Kubert's Fax from Sarajevo

One of the most devastating world events of the 1990s was the war in the European country of Bosnia. Set loose from the former Yugoslavia after the collapse of Communism in Europe, a horrific conflict erupted between different ethnic groups living in that once-peaceful land, resulting in the deaths of over 100,000 soldiers and civilians. One of the people most changed by the war was **Ervin Rustemagic**,

The cover to Supreme #41 *deliberately evokes 1939's* Superman #1. *TM and © Rob Liefeld Inc.*

who operated his Strip Art Features artist representation agency out of Sarajevo when the war erupted. He and his family quickly moved to America; however, homesick and convinced the war was close to an end, Rustemagic, his wife and their two children soon returned to their native country. Two days after they returned, authorities closed off the Bosnian border. Rustemagic and family thus found themselves trapped as the conditions in Sarajevo grew more hellish. For the next two years, the family was stuck in the country as bullets whizzed around their heads and survival became treacherous. Their only dependable means of communication with the outside world was via faxes Rustemagic sent to friends in France, the Netherlands and the United States. One of those friends was legendary comic book creator **Joe Kubert** who reported he "must have thousands of faxes giving me a detailed story of their entire time under siege" (Shutt 58). Rustemagic's terrifying experiences compelled Kubert to write and illustrate a 144-page color graphic novel about them. Published by Dark Horse Comics, **Fax from Sarajevo** became widely acclaimed as an unflinching portrayal of the desolation of war, and is a landmark in Kubert's celebrated career. *Fax* earned both the Harvey and Eisner Awards for Best Graphic Novel of 1996, but seldom has a creator wished for acclaim less than Kubert did for chronicling the suffering of his friend.

No More Love (and Rockets)

Gilbert, Jaime and Mario Hernandez completed their fourteen-year run of **Love and Rockets** with issue #50 (May 1996). The magazine-sized comic was deeply influential to a whole generation of comic artists who embraced the complex worlds and interesting characters presented by "Los Bros." In the final issue Gilbert, who frequently presented stories of the fictional Central American town of Palomar, illustrated the effects of an earthquake on the town. Jaime provided a temporary wrap up for the story of his main characters Maggie and Hopey. Meanwhile, Mario, who last contributed to *L&R* in issue #40 (Jan. 1993), included a political thriller titled "Love and Rockets... When the Muse is Not Amused." Though both Gilbert and Jaime would return to their characters and settings repeatedly, the end of the first volume of *Love and Rockets* represented a major landmark in indie comics. It also helped free the brothers to do work away from their main characters. Jaime created a mini-series for Fantagraphics centered on wrestling titled *Whoa Nellie!* (July to Sept. 1996) while Gilbert created the light adventure *Girl Crazy* (May to July 1996) for Dark Horse Comics as well as the often surreal six-issue *New Love* (Aug. 1996 to Dec. 1997) for Fantagraphics.

Bill Willingham began a fantasy series for Fantagraphics titled *Coventry* (first issue cover-dated November 1996) which presented an America where magic and sorcery never went away and where mythic heroes, licensed by the government and assigned to keep peace, are treated like celebrities. The series introduced Claudia Nevermore and her partner "Max" Maxwell as they solve cases that included a plague of frogs triggered by a great god and an angel who commits random violence like killing twenty men named Bob in one day. Though much loved by those who read the series, *Coventry* did not sell enough copies for Willingham to continue past issue #3.

In 1996, Fantagraphics published one issue of **Daniel Clowes's** critically acclaimed *Eightball*: #17 (Aug. 1996) which included one of Clowes's most revered stories: "Gynecology." This challenging 22-page tale explores the nature of reality and identity through its main character Epps, a man with an affectation for items from the past and for his own eccentricity. As usual, Clowes's characters resonate and stick in the mind, and Clowes's preciseness of image and word shows the power of creators taking their time with their comic art. Fantagraphics also published the very different but equally devastating *Daddy's Girl* by Debbie Drechsler. The emotionally honest graphic novel with clear line work is a semi-autobiographical story of a pre-teen girl's abuse at the hands of her father.

Xeric Award-winner **James Sturm** delivered his first substantial work in 1996 with the self-published *The Revival*. The 24-page black-and-white tale focuses on a 19th century couple, in despair after the death of a child, attending a religious revival meeting. Sturm's art is earthy and precise while his story sketches a work deeply respectful of his characters' experiences. Artist/writer Jeff Nicholson provided some profoundly disturbing comics with his one-shot graphic novel *Through the Habitrails*. First serialized in the pages of *Taboo*, Nicholson imagines a group of workers for The Corporation, rendered faceless by their work and forced to wander rodent-like habitrails to do their job. The despairing story delivers a strong satirical punch for anyone who has had to work a job they hate.

Meanwhile, packager and entrepreneur **Byron Preiss** launched two lines of comics which embraced several technologies that were relatively new in 1996. Preiss's CD-ROM comics included *Will Eisner's The Spirit* and *The R. Crumb Screensaver and Companion*. Preiss's Virtual Comics provided some of the first webcomics, comics presented first on the internet, with *They Call Me...the Skul* by Danny Fingeroth, Ron Lim and Jimmy Palmiotti and *The Suit* by Dan Chichester, Greg Wright, Shawn McManus and Dan Pension. Both series premiered March 18, 1996. The online

comics offered features readers couldn't find in print comics, including context-sensitive menus, a navigable 3-D space and the ability to quickly scroll through the stories. Virtual Comics later collected these online stories into print comics – minus, of course, the multimedia components. Virtual also sold CD-ROMs of the comics and included video games on the disks. Other publishers sold CD-ROMs of comics, including Kitchen Sink's *The Crow: The Complete Interactive Collection*, which offered a virtual sketchbook, interviews, production designs and internet access software.

Master Storyteller

Barry Windsor-Smith, one of the main forces behind the original Valiant titles, began a unique solo series through Dark Horse Comics. *Barry Windsor-Smith: Storyteller* was a 40-page, large format (9x12) omnibus featuring three ongoing tales: "The Freebooters", a Conan-style saga of a quest to find the warrior who would destroy the world; "Young Gods", the tale of a war between two groups of gods; and "The Paradoxman", about a time traveler in search of his lost love. Providing lavishly detailed artwork, Windsor-Smith saw the series as a kind of culmination of his career: "*Storyteller* is the main event of my career. I've been doing this stuff for a quarter century; I've always wanted to just tell it the way I wanted to tell it, without intervention. It's the first time in my career that I'm doing something that I don't have to apologize for. If the script is crud, then it's my fault. If something else doesn't work out, then blame me" (Blumberg 68). The project was a long time in forming. Smith had actually penciled the opening two-page spread for "The Freebooters" in 1980, sixteen years before the project premiered. Though the comic received fan and press acclaim, the enormous size made *Storyteller* awkward for

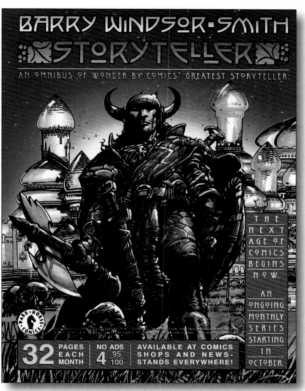

Barry Windsor-Smith delivered the oversized Barry Windsor-Smith: Storyteller *for Dark Horse Comics.*
TM and © Barry Windsor-Smith.

many dealers to carry. Some complained they did not have an appropriate space to display the book. Many readers also felt they couldn't find good-fitting bags and boards for the comics. All those frustrations depressed sales. Though the notoriously slow Windsor-Smith was able to release nine issues in the space of ten months between October 1996 and July 1997, *Storyteller* could not continue.

That cancellation was just another experiment that didn't work out in 1996. Just as a phoenix must turn to ash before it is reborn, so too did the American comics industry have to begin to hit bottom before showing signs of bouncing back. 1997 would begin to show the potential for comics' eventual future.

1997

Change or Die

In the waning years of the twentieth century, the American comic book industry felt like it was well on its way toward extinction. The already-plummeting industry-wide sales decreased by an additional 25% between 1996 and 1997 with some of the most popular titles now selling only a fraction of what they had earlier in the decade. In June 1997, for instance, only twenty-five titles sold over 70,000 copies and only five of them sold over 120,000. As recently as September 1993, a comic book that sold 120,000 copies would have barely earned a spot on a list of the top one hundred best-selling titles. At DC, many ongoing series (including such iconic titles as *Wonder Woman*, *Azrael* and *Teen Titans*) hovered around 40,000 copies sold per month. Some long-running Vertigo titles, like *Hellblazer*, *House of Secrets* and *Sandman Mystery Theatre*, lingered even lower, around the 20,000 copy mark. At Image, the once-hot *Gen13* saw its sales drop precipitously, decreasing by 50,000 copies within a year. Still, *Gen13* was one of only five Image titles (along with *Spawn*, the *Spawn* spin-off *Medieval Spawn*, *Darkness* and *Witchblade*) that consistently sold over 70,000 copies per issue. Monthly sales for *Amazing Spider-Man* were half of what they were in 1992, and aside from X-Men related comics and "Heroes Reborn," most of Marvel's titles suffered anemic sales. For small press publishers, things were even worse. Sales of perennial bestseller *Bone* dropped around 40%. In fact, only thirty comics released by a publisher other than Marvel, DC, Image, Acclaim and Dark Horse sold more than 9,000 copies per issue. As one analyst put it, "It is possible that things have never been this bad in the American comics market, and it is not yet possible to say that the worst is over" (Beaty 17-19). As a result of the cratering sales, several prominent publishers retrenched or closed completely in 1997.

In the midst of this deep decline, DC Comics earned a pyrrhic victory. For the first time in the history of the Direct Market, DC topped Marvel in terms of overall market share for an entire year. DC finished 1997 with a 21.58% share of all products shipped to comics and specialty stores while Marvel finished over two points lower, with a 19.38% share. Image finished in third with a 12.1% share followed by Dark Horse at 5.4%. In a telling sign of how comic shops stayed in business during this turbulent year, Wizards of the Coast, manufacturer of collectible card games like *Magic: the Gathering*, held a 2.52% share and toy manufacturer Kenner/Hasbro earned a 1.29% share ("Diamond reports DC" 6).

CHAPTER EIGHT

For the first time in recent memory, DC also released more total comics than any other company. DC published 956 individual issues, over a third of all comics released during the year. Marvel published 591, Image 430, Dark Horse 275 and Acclaim 213. Archie Comics was the only other company to release over 200 comics in 1997, with 203 issues bearing the Archie logo.

Unfortunately, DC didn't have much reason to celebrate its resurgence because the harsh reality was that the comics industry had to change or it was going to die. Many believed growth would develop from increased diversity in the comics medium. As Dark Horse Comics Publisher Mike Richardson stated, "All of that euphoria of the late 1980s has been washed away... The industry is right where it was 15 years ago, despite some of the outstanding books that are out there... For our market to survive, we need to look to expand the market, and it cannot be done with superheroes. It cannot be done" (O'Neill 32). While many comic book retailers, creators and executives shared Richardson's conviction, the irony was that innovative super-heroes would, in fact, propel comics out of their deep financial depression. Leading the way was the revival of a recently declining DC title now guided by a rock star writer.

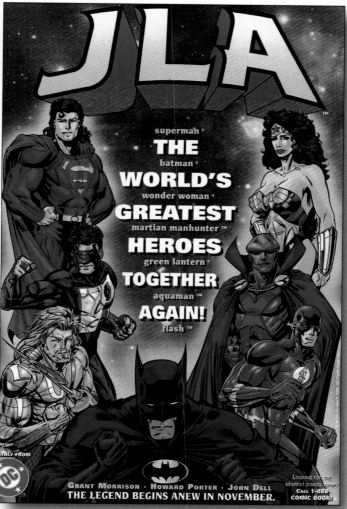

DC Comics house ad for Grant Morrison and Howard Porter's *Justice League* relaunch, *JLA*. TM and © DC Comics.

Three Letters Say It All

The biggest hit of the year restored **DC Comics'** most iconic super-heroes to their most legendary series. *JLA* #1 (Jan. 1997) by **Grant Morrison**, **Howard Porter** and John Dell begins with a flying saucer above the White House. Inside that ship are a group of apparent world-savers called the Hyperclan, who promise to make a utopia of Earth by creating an Eden in the Sahara Desert and executing unrepentant super-criminals. As these alleged saviors transform the planet, some of Earth's bravest defenders voice their concerns. Superman speaks out against the Hyperclan on the network news but finds the tide of public sentiment against him. As opinion shifts, the Hyperclan reveal their true intentions: a group of Hyperclan fighters attack the Justice League satellite, where former Justice League members such as Metamorpho, Nuklon, Ice and Obsidian are residing. The attack destroys the satellite and those Justice League members plummet to Earth, resulting in their near death. At the same time, a band of Earth's

frontline crimefighters, including Superman, Batman, Wonder Woman, Aquaman, the Flash, Green Lantern and Martian Manhunter, discover the truth behind the Hyperclan. Far from being avatars of justice, the extraterrestrial visitors are survivors of the Martian Manhunter's race who intend to lead an all-out Martian invasion of Earth. The new roster of Justice Leaguers come together to defeat the Hyperclan, and in the final pages of *JLA* #4 (April 1997), they build a Watchtower on the moon to replace the old JLA satellite. The subtext is clear: the former Justice League, populated by second-rate super-heroes, crashed to Earth, and now DC's most iconic characters would reclaim their rightful place. With a roster of superstars, the new JLA had adventures that showed deference to the past with a kinetic energy that befit the upcoming millennium. In subsequent storylines, delivered at breakneck speed, the team undertakes a membership drive, gets in the middle of a battle between Heaven and Hell, and becomes involved in an Elseworlds-inspired adventure. Morrison and Porter's widescreen approach emphasized world-spanning—or even universe-spanning—conflicts that fit the importance of the heroes and resulted in smartly-created science fiction stories. In addition, Morrison often took existing second-rate villains (like the Key and the Lord of Time) and transformed them into real threats through a deeper consideration of their powers and abilities. Before *JLA* premiered, Morrison expressed deep confidence in his ideas: "I know that you can't go wrong with it because we're dealing with the major superhero icons of the last 50 years" (Beatty 14). From its launch, *JLA* topped the sales charts, selling over 200,000 copies per issue – ten times what its predecessor, *Justice League America*, sold in 1996.

Morrison's classic approach represented a departure from his previous work like *The Invisibles* and *Doom Patrol*. "There would be no obtrusive postmodern meta-tricks in *JLA*," he reflected, "just unadulterated, gee-whiz, unadorned sci-fi myths in comic form, giving back to the super-heroes respect and dignity a decade of 'realism' and harsh critique had stripped away" (Morrison 292). More than one reader remarked that the new Justice League evoked a mythical, almost Biblical, vibe. That idea pleased Morrison, who

TIMELINE: 1997

A compilation of the year's notable comic book history events alongside some of the year's most significant popular culture and historical events. (On sale dates are approximations.)

January 25: Dan Barry, comic book artist whose career spanned six decades and included work on such titles as *Action Comics*, *Air Fighter Comics* and even Dark Horse's *Predator* and *Indiana Jones* series, dies at the age of 73.

February 5: A civil jury in Santa Monica, California finds O.J. Simpson liable for the wrongful death of Ron Goldman and Simpson's ex-wife, Nicole Brown. Simpson is ordered to pay over $33 million in damages.

February 7: Marvel Comics shuts down Heroes World Distribution. Like every other American comic book publisher, Marvel will now be exclusively distributed by Diamond Comics Distributors.

March 10: *Buffy the Vampire Slayer*—a supernatural drama created by Joss Whedon and starring Sarah Michelle Geller as the titular heroine—premieres on the WB network. The show will become one of the most acclaimed television shows of the decade, lasting seven seasons and spawning several spin-off series.

March 12: In *Superman* #123—written by Dan Jurgens and drawn by Ron Frenz and Josef Rubinstein—the Man of Steel dons a blue-and-white costume that harnesses his new energy-based powers.

April 15: Major League Baseball honors the late Jackie Robinson, the first African-American professional baseball player, by requiring all of its teams to retire his uniform number (#42).

June 26: Bloomsbury publishes *Harry Potter and the Philosopher's Stone*, the first of many novels written by British author J.K. Rowling about a boy who studies at the Hogwarts School of Witchcraft and Wizardry. Released a year later in the United States, the book will reach the top of the *New York Times* bestseller list and eventually spawn a film franchise.

June 20: *Batman & Robin*—directed by Joel Schumacher and starring Arnold Schwarzenegger as Mr. Freeze, Uma Thurman as Poison Ivy, Alicia Silverstone as Batgirl, Chris O'Donnell as Robin and George Clooney as the Caped Crusader—opens in movie theaters. The film is both critically panned and a box office disappointment, earning only $107 million domestically. As a result, the next Batman film won't be released until 2005, by a completely different creative team.

JANUARY	FEBRUARY	MARCH	APRIL	MAY	JUNE

January 31: Nearly twenty years after its original release, *Star Wars* returns to theaters with added scenes and updated special effects. It grosses an additional $138 million at the box office, making it the eighth highest-grossing movie of the year. Special Editions of the other two Star Wars films, *Empire Strikes Back* and *The Return of the Jedi*, are released later in the year.

March 26: In a mansion outside San Diego, California, police discover the bodies of thirty-nine members of the Heaven's Gate cult, the victims of a mass suicide. The deceased killed themselves in the belief that their souls would be transported to a spacecraft that was trailing the Hale-Bopp comet which was passing through the solar system.

March 3: Marvel removes Rob Liefeld's Extreme Studios from *Avengers* and *Captain America*, effective with the seventh issue of each series. Jim Lee's Wildstorm Studios, already producing *Fantastic Four* and *Iron Man*, assumes the reins on all four Heroes Reborn titles.

May 16: *Todd McFarlane's Spawn*—an animated series based on Todd McFarlane's comic book—premieres on HBO. The show will last three seasons, totaling eighteen episodes.

---

conceived the lineup as hewing close to the Greek gods. Superman served as the counterpart of Zeus, Wonder Woman was Hera, Aquaman was Poseidon, and Green Lantern paralleled Apollo, and so on. Thus, the JLA was set up as virtual gods in their own Olympus, gazing down on the Earth. (While the JLA was "above" humanity, they didn't consider themselves "better" than humanity as one of *JLA*'s subtexts was the idea that super-heroes reflect the best in all of us, that anyone could take off his shirt to reveal a Superman "S" beneath.)

Befitting the blockbuster popularity of the new series, DC quickly added JLA-themed one-shots and specials. In July 1997 alone, DC published *JLA Gallery*, *JLA Secret Files and Origins* and the Morrison-scripted crossover *JLA/WildC.A.T.s*. With art by Val Semeiks and Kevin Conrad, the 68-page comic explored a topic typical for *JLA*: "time bifurcation," i.e. the idea that a cosmic event may trigger a split in time. The bifurcation allows the two super-hero teams to meet across different universes. Besides giving Morrison the chance to have the Justice League fight dinosaurs at the dawn of time, this one-shot changed the WildC.A.T.s heroes as they began to more fully understand the concept of true heroism.

Also during the year, Morrison joined with his protégé **Mark Millar** to write a comic intimately related to *JLA*. The two assumed co-writing duties on **The Flash**, starting with issue #130 (Oct. 1997) while the series' regular writer, **Mark Waid**, took a one-year sabbatical from the title. In Morrison and Millar's debut storyline, a new villain called The Suit breaks Wally West's legs and forces him into a wheelchair. Now crippled, Wally must use all his skills as the Flash to save his friends and city from destruction. Readers could easily imagine the story idea being published in the 1960s, but Morrison and Millar delivered a set of twists that felt simultaneously classic and modern. Other Morrison and Millar stories featured the Golden Age Flash (in a story in which he fills in for Wally), the Mirror Master, and a foot race across the cosmos.

Even though Waid took a break from the main *Flash* monthly, he still spearheaded one of the most notable Flash comics of the year, *The Life Story of the Flash*. Written by Waid and Brian Augustyn, with art by Gil Kane, Joe Staton and Tom Palmer, this 96-page standalone graphic novel recounts the life of the Silver Age Flash, Barry Allen, as a tell-all biography narrated by his wife, Iris. The hardcover describes Barry's entire career: from his childhood to the day he gained his super-powers to his death in *Crisis on Infinite Earths* to the legacy that succeeded him. *Life Story* was a loving tribute highlighted by Waid's obvious affection for the characters and Kane's Silver Age style art.

July 2: *Men In Black*—directed by Barry Sonnenfeld, and starring Tommy Lee Jones and Will Smith as secret government agents who protect Earth from extraterrestrial threats—opens in movie theaters. Loosely based on the 1990 comic book of the same name, *Men In Black* will become the second highest-grossing film of the year, earning over $250 million domestically.

August 15: *Steel*—based on the DC Comics character and starring basketball player Shaquille O'Neal as the titular character—opens in movie theaters. A complete flop, the critically panned film earns only $1.7 million domestically.

August 31: Diana, the internationally beloved Princess of Wales who championed dozens of charities, dies at the age of 36 of a car crash in Paris, France. For several months afterwards, the entire world mourns her loss.

November 1: *Titanic*—directed by James Cameron and starring Leonardo DiCaprio and Kate Winslet as star-crossed lovers on board the infamous passenger liner when it sank in 1912—opens in movie theaters. Besides winning eleven Academy Awards (including Best Picture and Best Director), the film will also earn over $600 million domestically, both records at the time.

JULY	AUGUST	SEPTEMBER	OCTOBER	NOVEMBER	DECEMBER

July 9: The first issue of DC Comics' *Transmetropolitan*—written by Warren Ellis and drawn by Darick Robertson—arrives in stores. The dystopian series stars Spider Jerusalem, a foul-mouthed, drug-addicted, anti-authoritarian journalist determined to bring "The Truth" to his readers.

August 1: *Spawn*—based on Todd McFarlane's best-selling Image comic book and starring Michael Jai White as the titular character and John Leguizamo as the Violater—opens in movie theaters. Distributed by New Line Cinema, the movie will gross over $54 million domestically.

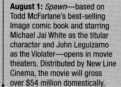

September 16: Marvel reaches a tentative agreement with its lenders to settle its debt. As part of the deal, Marvel agrees to sell its sticker subsidiary Panini and pay its creditors $385 million in cash.

November 13: Samm Schwartz, comic book artist best known for his work on Archie's Jughead stories, dies as the age of 77.

Change or Die

While Morrison and Porter's *JLA* proved the continued appeal of super-heroes, **Warren Ellis and Tom Raney's** *Stormwatch* showcased a different approach to the genre. The first phase of Ellis's run climaxed with a three-part storyline whose title seemed to sum up the stakes of the entire comic book industry: "Change or Die." Running in *Stormwatch* #48-50 (May-July 1997), the arc focuses on a group of powerful beings called The Changers, led by a super-hero from the 1940s named The High, who seek to save the world from itself. Ellis cast the conflict in a morally ambiguous light. On one hand, The High and his team are transforming Earth into a utopia. On the other hand, their actions stifle democracy and free will.

Without question, *Stormwatch* was one of the most ambitious titles published by **Image Comics**, a company that now had **Marc Silvestri** back in its fold in the wake of Rob Liefeld's departure. That was good news for Image as Silvestri's Top Cow line delivered the most popular comic of the calendar year. *Darkness* #11 (cover-dated January 1998), with eleven different variant covers, sold more copies than any other book released in 1997.

Surprisingly, the latest series by Silvestri's fellow Image superstar, **Jim Lee**, didn't make the comics bestseller list. *Divine Right: the Adventures of Max Faraday*, released through Lee's Wildstorm imprint, starred an unassuming young adult who downloads the Creation Equation, a binary number string that dates back millions of years and spans the societal relationship between religion and science. The Creation Equation imbues Faraday with the mystical power of "Divine Right," transforming him from a normal Internet-obsessed college student who delivers pizza to make a buck to a god-like being who becomes the target of different groups trying to take the Equation away from him. Despite a compelling story that juxtaposes a cosmic battle with the quotidian life of an ordinary college kid, *Divine Right* under-performed. Its first issue (Sept. 1997) only ranked nineteenth on the monthly retail chart, and sales didn't significantly increase from there. One of the long-term problems with the series was Lee's chronic tardiness. Only seven issues were released in fifteen months, and as time went on, Lee even fell further behind schedule. A series that was planned to last twenty to twenty-five issues was finished after twelve, with the final two issues (cover-dated November 1999 and February 2000) acting as a crossover event for the Wildstorm Universe. Lee was sanguine about the shift: "I thought the story would hold itself for up to 25 issues, but I found the pacing was losing people's interest. I figured out a way to resolve it in 12 issues, which makes for a more compact story. A two-hour movie versus a four-hour movie" (Brick 7).

Valiant Efforts at Revival

By all appearances, as 1997 began, **Acclaim** had a thriving video game division. Indeed, its *Turok: Dinosaur Hunter*, the first-person shooter game released in January 1997 for the nascent Nintendo 64 console, garnered rave reviews from video game magazines and sold an impressive 1.5 million copies. As Acclaim editor Jeff Gomez reported, "The game's first day gross sales in dollars exceeded most blockbuster movies! It was huge!" (McLelland). Despite this success, Acclaim's games division was hemorrhaging money, mainly due to mismanagement and the high cost of video game production. Acclaim's comics line wasn't faring well either. Although the Marvel Comics/Acclaim crossover, *Iron Man/X-O Manowar: Heavy Metal*, was a solid 1996 comics hit that coincided with the video game release of the same name, sales of just about every other Acclaim comic book were, at best, lackluster. The terrible performance of Acclaim's crime books, *Magic: the Gathering* adaptations and *Baywatch* photo novels showed deep weakness in the Direct Sales market. In fact, sales were so bad the company even closed down its core super-hero line with the September 1996 cover-dated issue of *X-O Manowar*, and only released three crime comics per month over the subsequent three months.

One of the ways Acclaim hoped to breathe new life into the company was through rebooting its comics line. This makeover would allow them to get out from under expensive contracts signed during the ill-fated "Birthquake" event and provide new storylines for future video games. Acclaim's working theory was that fans had grown bored with its older style Valiant heroes and would be attracted to new talent on familiar-sounding titles. To pursue that goal, popular writer **Fabian Nicieza**, who often appeared in the *Wizard* Top Ten Writers list, was brought on board to help brainstorm new ideas. Nicieza spearheaded the launch of a new set of Valiant Heroes for the late '90s. "The decisions on how to approach the titles were pretty open. It wasn't an autocratic decision-making system. I presented my thoughts on relaunching the 'new universe' for a variety of reasons. For every argument I had in favor of doing that, of course there were equally valid arguments against. It wasn't an ego-thing, it was a business decision. How can we make the most noise? How can we get fresh creative voices on our books? How can we best reposition our properties for the marketplace and for the needs of our parent company?" (McLelland). Premiering with February 1997 cover-dated issues, the new **"Valiant Heroes"** spanned ten ongoing monthlies and two quarterlies, none of which referenced the original series. The new *X-O Manowar*, conceived and written by Mark Waid and Brian Augustyn and illustrated by Sean Chen and Tom Ryder, was more a cross between Captain America and Iron Man rather than Conan and Iron Man. *Ninjak* by Kurt Busiek, Neil Vokes and Michael Avon Oeming mashed-up video games and ninjas rather than James Bond and ninjas. *Bloodshot* by Len Kaminski, Sal Velluto and Jeff Albrecht brought conspiracy theories into the story of an avenging, gun-wielding hero. *Magnus* by Tom Peyer, Mike McKone and Mike McKenna didn't star a robot fighter in the 50th century but a man who travels back in time to save our world. Nicieza and collaborators also produced new versions of *Shadowman*, *Solar Man of the Atom*, *Turok* and *Eternal Warriors*. Along with the rebooted Valiant heroes, Nicieza and team launched three new series. *Troublemakers*, by Nicieza, Kenny Martinez and Anibal Rodriguez, sets teenagers as adventurers looking to save the world. Kevin Maguire's *Trinity Angels* delivered his customary mix of deadpan humor and wacky charm to the story of three heroic but bickering sisters. The breakout hit of the relaunch was the madcap *Quantum & Woody* by Christopher Priest and Mark Bright, billed as "the worst superhero team of all time." The series combined deadpan blackout humor, heartfelt friendship, and an intriguing look at race relations in a postmodern take on the hero genre.

In 1997, Acclaim Comics reinvented X-O Manowar as part of its "VH2" reboot. TM and © Valiant Entertainment LLC.

For a fleeting moment, the relaunch caught readers' attention. Most of the "VH2" titles (given that nickname to differentiate them from the original "Valiant Heroes", or "VH1" series) were successful with their first issues, achieving sales of around 30,000 copies per issue.

BIG Becomes Little

By 1997, **BIG Entertainment** (previously known as Tekno Comics) couldn't live up to its name. Most BIG titles could barely muster sales of 5,500 copies an issue, and its bestselling title, *Mike Danger*, only sold 8,600 copies in December 1996 (Beaty 19). After two years and massive hype, BIG closed down with its February 1997 cover-dated releases. Though the company announced comics emerging from the imaginations of such best-selling authors as Arthur C. Clarke, Tom Clancy (with *Net Force*) and Margaret Weis (tentatively titled *Wyrm*), none of those series ever made it to America's comic book shops. However, BIG/Tekno *did* follow through on its pledge to diversify its offerings beyond just comics. In 1996, it released an interactive CD-ROM of *Primortals* which could be played on PCs and Macs. The company also packaged several prose novels based on BIG characters, including *Primortals* and *I-Bots*, both written by former comic book writer Steve Perry.

Slumping sales likewise doomed **Milestone Comics**. Despite a unique distribution deal that placed Milestone series alongside DC Comics on newsstands and comic shops, all of Milestone's series had plummeted towards the bottom of the sales charts. For instance, while *Hardware* #1 sold 225,000 copies in early 1993, four years later *Hardware* #47 (Dec. 1996) only sold 4,500 copies, an astonishing 98% decline. More recently, sales of Milestone's bestselling series, *Static*, plunged from 11,000 per issue to 6,500 within one year. In January 1996, *Xombi* #20 was the lowest-selling DC release through Diamond, finishing below a Looney Tunes comic. While some retailers blamed Milestone's demise on bad DC marketing, others blamed competing premiere dates. One thing the majority of comic shop owners could agree on was that perception was partly at fault since Milestone was primarily aimed at minority readers. As one retailer put it, "there are some people who won't go to those books because they feel closed off from them." (Stump, "Milestone Comics" 18). Publication of Milestone Comics ended after *Hardware* #50 (April 1997).

One of the decade's most dramatic falls was that of **Kitchen Sink Press** (KSP), which had never recovered from what KSP employee Robert Boyd called, "some bad luck and some disastrous management level decisions" (Stump, "Kitchen Sink" 7-8). With terrible cash flow and very little money in the bank, KSP management laid off Boyd and nearly all his fellow employees during the summer of 1997. By the beginning of September, however, Kitchen Sink had secured new ownership. The company was able to rehire some of its previous employees and that team delivered an aggressive publishing schedule in 1998. Unfortunately, it wouldn't be enough and 1998 would prove to be Kitchen Sink's last hurrah.

Even the publishers who survived the year did so with major decreases in their line. **Warp Graphics**, for instance, published seven *Elfquest*-related comics with cover dates

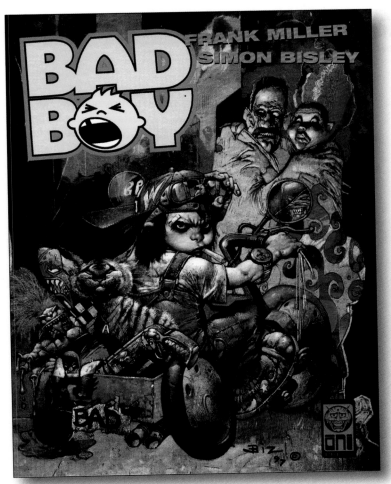

Frank Miller and Simon Bisley delivered the outrageous Bad Boy *for new publisher Oni Press.* TM and © Frank Miller Inc. and Simon Bisley.

of February 1996. By early 1997, however, publishers Wendy and Richard Pini were down to two comics per month. The Pinis kept their line alive through smart worldwide marketing. German comics publisher Carlson commissioned new Elfquest stories which were published in Europe before appearing in the United States. This was enough to keep Pini's creative juices flowing during a time of overwhelming bad news in the comics industry.

During this prolonged slump, at least one new publisher proved comics were still a viable business endeavor. Longtime Dark Horse Comics editor **Bob Schreck** paired Portland, Oregon-based **Oni Press** with partner Joe Nozemack. Oni, named for the Japanese word for demon, debuted in 1997 with a radically different set of titles. One of the first was the outrageous *Bad Boy* (December 1997) by Frank Miller and Simon Bisley. Reprinted from the pages of the British *GQ* magazine, *Bad Boy* portrays a ten-year-old boy who tries to escape an enclosed community that promises to keep its citizens safe but restricts their freedom. The next year, Oni published bestselling crime writer Greg Rucka's *Whiteout* and gained a license to adapt characters from Kevin Smith's *Clerks*. In 1998, Oni's miniseries *Jay and Silent Bob* #1 (July 1998) sold 40,000 copies, making *Jay* the 50th bestselling comic of the month. Smith loved the comic stating, "The characters and situations transfer easily from the movies to comics, and comics are a big enough medium to hold everything. In a world where *Hate* can exist, so can *Clerks*" (Anderson 25).

The debut of Oni Press brought a sliver of good news to the comics industry but a major move by Marvel would instill some long-needed peace and stability.

Marvel Returns

On February 7, 1997, **Marvel Comics** announced a change that most industry experts felt was inevitable: the company closed down Heroes World Distribution and joined every other American comic book publisher by shipping exclusively through Diamond Comics Distributors. This move provided a lifeline to many of the nation's comic shops, who had a seemingly endless set of problems working with Heroes World. During its first several months as the exclusive distributor of Marvel Comics, Heroes World struggled in managing its sales, delivery and customer support operations. In fact, Heroes World's problems strongly factored in the closing of hundreds of comic shops. Though Heroes World had begun to improve its performance and processes substantially by mid-1996, many retailers still expressed frustration with the service and the distribution system became more and more of an albatross for a company struggling to stay solvent. Marvel's late 1996 bankruptcy allowed the company to liquidate Heroes World, but in the days after the news broke, response from the comics industry was sobering. Retailer Brian Hibbs summed up the feelings of many insiders by saying, "Marvel Comics owes the direct market an apology for what they did. They destroyed an entire business" (Stump, "Hello Again" 10). Diamond President Steve Geppi concurred, "In 1993, when Diamond was 45% of the business, the entire business was $500 million at wholesale. After Marvel came back and we were just about the whole world, we were only $186 million at wholesale. The industry capsized in the middle" (McLauchlin, "A Wedding"). At least one Marvel executive admitted the Heroes World endeavor was ill-conceived: "Our theory was that we could do a better job publicizing and displaying our books. That theory was totally wrong.

Heroes World just gave people one more reason to hate Marvel" (Raviv 68).

On the bankruptcy front, Marvel and its lenders reached a tentative agreement on September 16, 1997 to settle Marvel's debts. As part of the deal, Marvel management agreed to sell its sticker subsidiary Panini and pay its creditors $385 million in cash. Despite Marvel's financial turmoil, the worst fears of its fans didn't come to pass; Marvel would not go out of business. Indeed, even while under bankruptcy protection, the company continued to publish several dozen comics per month and pay high rates to its key writers and artists. Though Marvel slipped behind DC in market share during 1997, the company's major event of the year helped it gain the momentum it would need to seize 1998.

Fighting Words

After their smash debut in late 1996, sales on the "**Heroes Reborn**" comics, produced by Image Comics' Jim Lee and **Rob Liefeld**, quickly plummeted. Despite the fact each of the four titles sold better than they did before the reboot, Marvel's executives were disappointed with the sales numbers. The critically acclaimed Mark Waid/Ron Garney run on *Captain America* that was cancelled for Heroes Reborn sold about 40,000 copies per issue. Liefeld far exceeded that number but sales still weren't high enough to justify the expensive contract (Fisher 29). As a result, Marvel attempted to renegotiate its agreement with Liefeld... to no avail. Under the terms of the contract, Marvel could fire Liefeld—and/or Jim Lee—if their books underperformed saleswise. Therefore, on March 3, 1997, Marvel removed Liefeld from *Avengers* and *Captain America*, effective with issue #8 of the former and issue #7 of the latter. Jim Lee's Wildstorm Studios, already producing *Fantastic Four* and *Iron Man*, assumed the reins on all four Heroes Reborn titles.

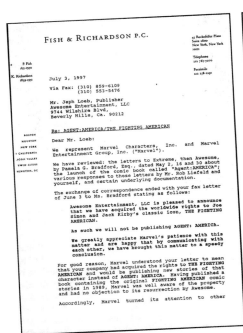

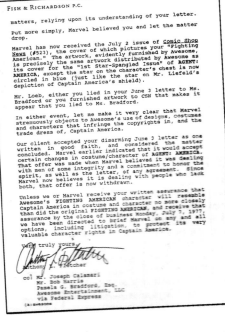

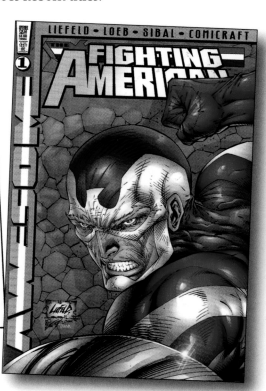

In 1997, Marvel's lawyers threatened to use Rob Liefeld on the basis that his proposed Agent: America *series was too similar to Captain America. Liefeld's licensing of Joe Simon and Jack Kirby's* Fighting American *didn't appease them. TM and © Joseph H. Simon and the Estate of Jack Kirby.*

Liefeld didn't handle his dismissal from Heroes Reborn gracefully and quickly began planning an unauthorized continuation of his *Captain America* run. After work on *Cap* wrapped up, Liefeld's Extreme Studios crew began drawing a character that looked remarkably similar to Marvel's star-spangled Avenger. He was called "Agent: America" and his exploits would be published through Liefeld's Awesome Comics line. Once Marvel got wind of Liefeld's plans, however, one of its attorneys, Pamela Bradford, sent Awesome a letter that claimed the Agent: America samples that Liefeld shared at the 1997 WonderCon "lent credence to rumors we had been hearing that *Agent: America* was simply a reworking of what Liefeld had planned [...] for *Captain America*." Though the artist believed Marvel's claims had no basis in fact, he took a bold counter-step. In June, Awesome Comics licensed a different star-spangled super-hero that Joe Simon and Jack Kirby had created, **The Fighting American**, and quickly announced plans to produce a comic starring the patriotic character. That move didn't mollify Marvel, and after more legal back-and-forth, a federal judge determined on August 21 that if Liefeld made some minor changes to Fighting American, he could go ahead and publish his comic. The judge's position was reinforced by Marvel's lack of objection when DC Comics published its own licensed version of Fighting American in 1994 (Stump, "Liefeld vs. Marvel", 17-20). Awesome Studios subsequently proceeded with its plans, and *Fighting American* #1 was published soon thereafter. Written by Liefeld and Jeph Loeb, with art by Liefeld and Awesome stalwart Stephen Platt, the first issue revives the classic hero as he joins forces with an android named Spice (the spitting image of the young female Bucky from the Heroes Reborn *Captain America*) in order to battle a Russian super-villain. In an essay included in the back of the first issue, Liefeld proclaims himself furious at Marvel and looking for revenge, "If you only knew the lengths to which Marvel has gone to make sure this book would not make it into your hands. Lawyers. Lawsuits. Harassment. More anger. More fuel. Keep it up, Marvel; at this rate, I'll be ready to take a nuclear warhead." Awesome published two issues of *Fighting American* in 1997, followed by two sequel mini-series over the next two years.

As Liefeld battled Marvel, Jim Lee's Wildstorm Studios brought stability to *Avengers* and *Captain America*. Lee installed Walt Simonson and Michael Ryan on *Avengers* and writer James Robinson on *Captain America* who "came up with a nice little six-part *Captain America* story that, with the exception of the female Bucky, could've just as easily happened in the Marvel Universe" (Hedges 117). Sales rebounded as older fans began returning to the series, and Marvel's executives took notice. Lee and his team had their runs on the Heroes Reborn titles extended from twelve to thirteen issues, and Marvel also considered having Lee spearhead a revival of *Defenders*, *Dr. Strange*, *Punisher* and *Nick Fury* as a kind of "executive producer." The idea was that the comics would take place in the real Marvel Universe – no pocket universe as with the "Heroes Reborn" titles – and Lee would only serve as a consultant rather than as a creator (McLauchlin, "Lee Extends" 18).

Ultimately, though, that didn't come to pass as Marvel, instead, stuck to its own script: from the moment the Heroes

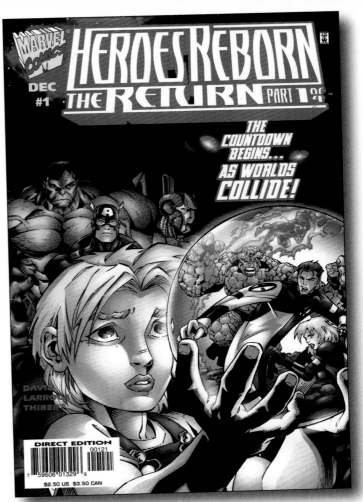

Franklin Richards returned Marvel's most iconic heroes to the Marvel universe in Heroes Reborn: the Return. TM and © Marvel Characters, Inc.

Reborn titles were first announced, Marvel emphasized that its contracts with Lee and Liefeld would only last one year, after which the Heroes Reborn characters would return to the Marvel Universe. As early as three months into Lee and Liefeld's projects, rumors circulated that popular writers like Mark Waid and Kurt Busiek would be taking over the Heroes Reborn titles once its temporarily displaced heroes returned to the core Marvel Universe. (Waid kept himself busy at Marvel by writing a new *Ka-Zar* series with artist Andy Kubert. This new series had the barbarian warrior of the Savage Land squaring off against Thanos in an extended storyline titled "Urban Jungle.")

As his tenure on the Heroes Reborn titles came to an end, Lee expressed his frustration that his and Liefeld's work wasn't duly appreciated by Marvel management: "If anyone goes out there and takes groups of books that no one seems to care about, triples sales and gets the readers excited by it, everyone will be slapping him on the back and saying great job. That wasn't there for us. I am looking forward to seeing what Marvel does with the characters after they get them back, because they have all these great ideas that may never have happened unless 'Heroes Reborn' happened" (Senreich 68).

All four Heroes Reborn titles ended in September 1997 (cover-dated November), but before *Avengers*, *Captain America*, *Fantastic Four* and *Iron Man* could be re-launched, **Peter David** was tasked with bringing their heroes back

The revelation at the end of Thunderbolts #1 *shocked many readers.*
TM and © Marvel Characters, Inc.

to the proper Marvel Universe in a weekly four-issue mini-series titled **Heroes Reborn: the Return.** Published in October 1997, *Return* reveals that Franklin Richards, son of the Fantastic Four's Mr. Fantastic and the Invisible Woman, was responsible for creating the pocket dimension in which the Heroes Reborn characters reside. When the almighty Celestials come to Earth and discover Franklin has near godlike powers, they threaten to destroy the planet and send an emissary to bring young Franklin into space with them. Ultimately, Franklin returns the parallel universe heroes back to his Earth and saves the main Marvel Universe. With Marvel's January 1998 cover-dated issues, the former exiles have been re-inserted into the core Marvel Universe. David saw the mini-series as an opportunity to explore the psychology and philosophy of power: "*Heroes Reborn* is an exploration of learning how to deal with power and the responsibility that power brings. And what better way to bring the heroes back into the Marvel firmament than with a story that explores one of the simplest, most elegant philosophies to come out of Marvel Comics — 'With great power comes great responsibility'" (Cunningham 8).

Justice, Like Lightning...

As Heroes Reborn played out over the course of a year, the New York City of the Marvel Universe found itself bereft of many of its most iconic champions. The void was filled by a new team called the **Thunderbolts.** Led by the chivalrous, sword-wielding Citizen V, the team included: Meteorite, who can channel extraterrestrial energy to fly and shoot energy blasts; Songbird, who can harden sound waves into shapes; Atlas, a giant muscleman; Techno, a mechanical genius who can cybernetically control a set of weapons; and MACH 1, who wears a skintight fighter jet suit. Unfortunately for New York's citizens, these new super-heroes weren't quite what they seemed.

First appearing in *Incredible Hulk* #449 (Jan. 1997) by Peter David and Mike Deodato, the Thunderbolts appeared to be the new forces of justice for a deeply fractured world. In that issue, the six-member group attempts to stop the Hulk during an angry rampage through the American Southwestern desert. They put forth a solid effort against the green goliath, but are forced to break off their attack when the Hulk smashes a major dam. While the new heroes act quickly to save lives downriver, the Hulk escapes.

Three months later, the Thunderbolts spun out into their own title, written by **Kurt Busiek** and drawn by **Mark Bagley.** The double-sized first issue begins with a TV news reporter lamenting the lack of heroes for the world's seemingly insurmountable threats. She sums up her concerns with a simple question: "who's going to save us now?" The answer, the issue seems to suggest, is the Thunderbolts, who draw enthusiastic cheers from New York City's residents after they successfully prevent the Wrecking Crew from destroying the Statue of Liberty. Soon Manhattan street vendors are selling Thunderbolts T-shirts and caps, and other Marvel super-groups like the New Warriors are praising their fellow adventurers. But as the issue ends—with a scene that *Wizard* magazine called "The Best Comics Moment of 1997"—Citizen V pulls off his mask to reveal he is actually long-time Captain America villain, Baron Zemo. He's not the only Thunderbolt masquerading as a hero. In fact, every single one of them is actually a disguised member of the Masters of Evil. Songbird is Screaming Mimi, Meteorite is Moonstone, Atlas is the evil Goliath, Techno is really the Fixer, and MACH 1 is the Beetle. As the series continues, the T-Bolts find their motives alternating between good and evil. They waver in their commitment to take over the world, finding valor to be a powerful intoxicant.

Everyone involved in the comic was extremely careful to keep the first issue's shocking revelation under wraps. As Busiek explained, "We fought like hell to keep the ending of *Thunderbolts* #1 a secret. We yanked copy from solicitations and promotional write-ups. We played interviews as if the team was what it appeared to be. It was a delicious feeling to know that we had an actual, honest-to-God surprise coming. I couldn't wait for the book to come out and see if it worked" ("Thunderbolts Revealed!" 106).

Initially, Busiek had no intention of helming a new comic book project since he already had his creator-owned *Astro City*, Marvel's *Untold Tales of Spider-Man* and Acclaim's *Ninjak* on his schedule and wanted to give those series his full attention. However, when Marvel invited him to a creators' conference to chart the post-Onslaught Marvel Universe, Busiek figured there was no harm in taking part in the discussions. First, though, he dusted off his original concept for the Thunderbolts. As originally conceived, a group of villains disguise themselves as heroes in order to become Avengers. They reveal themselves as infiltrators only after they gain full membership. The idea sounded even more intriguing in a post-Onslaught Marvel Universe: "What if a new team of heroes emerged from the rubble – a bold, splashy, noble-seeming team – but they were all frauds, and were actually scamming the public in order to get access to whatever it is they needed to take over the world?" Before the conference even began, Busiek pitched the idea to editor Tom Brevoort. The two of them then approached editor-in-chief Bob Harras at the retreat's bar after the first day's events where Harras immediately gave *Thunderbolts* the green light (Mescallado 85-6). Busiek describes it as the fastest sale of his career (Greenberg 24). With its jaw-dropping premise, the new series became a big hit for Marvel.

Meanwhile, Professor Xavier, whose psychic temper tantrum created Onslaught, had new problems to deal with. In *Onslaught Epilogue* (Feb. 1997), Professor X has been stripped of his psychic powers and imprisoned by Bastion, the leader of Operation Zero Tolerance, an organization devoted to exterminating all mutants worldwide. Bastion has two goals in mind: first, he wants to see if the Professor has any vestige of his original powers, and second, if he does, Bastion wants to return Onslaught to destroy all the mutants in the world. Bastion's plans ultimately lead to Marvel's major mutant crossover of 1997.

Who Killed Grayson Creed?

In the wake of "Onslaught", Marvel's mutants found themselves more despised and hated than ever before. This anger came to a head in *X-Factor* #130 (Jan. 1997), when popular Presidential candidate Grayson Creed is assassinated, literally disintegrated by a plasma burst. A mystery ensues: who killed Creed or is he possibly faking his own death to stir up anti-mutant hysteria? As 1997's mutant titles roll along, Creed becomes a martyr for the cause of discrimination, inspiring the international organization Operation Zero Tolerance to track down and exterminate all mutants. The story starts with great intensity as Jubilee is tortured and mentally abused, Cyclops has a bomb

After two popular mini-series, Deadpool finally received his own ongoing series.
TM and © Marvel Characters, Inc.

implanted in his chest, and Operation Zero Tolerance takes control of the X-Men's mansion. In the end, though, the X-Men, led by Iceman, completely discredit Operation Zero Tolerance, Bastion is arrested, and the agency is forbidden to operate on American soil. Many fans disliked the ending, slamming it as anticlimactic. As one reviewer put it, "It all feels rather shallow and generic and unambitious. It's excessive and bombastic, but it also feels strangely empty" (Mooney). The end of the storyline also coincided with the end of Scott Lobdell's tenure on Marvel's X-Men books. After chronicling the mutants' adventures for six years, Lobdell decided it was time to move on to other projects. His respective replacements on *X-Men*, *Uncanny X-Men* and *Generation X* were Joe Kelly, Steven Seagle and Larry Hama.

While the X-Men titles focused on the hysteria around Creed's assassination, another mutant series delivered a different kind of madness. After two limited series, **Deadpool** finally received his own ongoing title beginning with the January 1997 cover-dated issue #1. With writing by Joe Kelly and art by Ed McGuiness and Nathan Massengill, the Merc With a Mouth finds himself in Antarctica fighting Sabretooth in a tale teeming with wild action and ridiculous one-liners. Meanwhile, over in *Cable*, **Jose Ladrönn** assumed the art chores for the time-lost character beginning with issue #48 (Nov. 1997). Ladrönn was a natural fit for the series with a style that channeled the work of Jack Kirby. Soon joined on the series by writer **Joe Casey**, Ladrönn's art became influenced by the French artist Moebius. With that creative team in place, Cable's adventures felt both strongly grounded in the real world and full of time-spanning Kirbyesque adventure. Casey and Ladrönn remained on the comic until 1999. Along the way, they redesigned Cable's costume, provided him with a love interest, and involved him in massive, earth-shattering battles which allowed Ladrönn to display his obsessive love for detail.

With the seemingly interminable Clone Saga finally over, the **Spider-Man** comics tried to establish a new status quo with Peter as a professor at Empire State University and Mary Jane also enrolled there as a student. In addition, Spider-Man's adventures no longer crossed over between his various titles. Even the original Doctor Octopus (believed dead during the Clone Saga and replaced by a younger and more vicious counterpart) returned in 1997. Unfortunately for Marvel, none of this helped turn around the declining sales. Some fans were frustrated with the revival of Norman Osborn as the Green Goblin, a character that had been dead for decades. Others decried the series' lack of humor or even the fact that Peter no longer worked at the *Daily Bugle*. To overturn this, Marvel would take radical steps to shake up Spider-Man's world in 1998.

Back to the Future

One of the more prevalent gimmicks of the 1990s was the "zero issue," a comic that often served as a prelude for an ongoing series. Publishers such as Image embraced the idea, and DC included "Zero Month" as part of its *Zero Hour* event in 1994. Marvel's "Flashback Month," cover-dated July 1997, took the "zero issue" concept one step further, delivering "-1" editions for nearly every Marvel super-hero title: twenty-six of the forty-four Marvel comics released that month. Each of the stories, hosted by a wacky, cartoony version of Stan Lee, provides origins or never-before-revealed information about various characters. For instance, *Uncanny X-Men* #-1 reveals the origin of current X-villain Bastion while *Sensational Spider-Man* #-1 recounts the story of Peter Parker and his Uncle Ben battling classic Marvel monsters. *Daredevil* #-1 describes Matt Murdock's first day at college where he meets Elektra, while *Elektra* #-1 shows the title character meeting her mentor, Stick. Peter David used *Incredible Hulk* #-1 to explore the link between Bruce Banner's split personality problems and his incredibly abusive father. In maybe the most popular of all the flashback issues, *Untold Tales of Spider-Man* #-1, written by Roger Stern with art by classic Spider-Man artist John Romita Sr., provides the full

Marvel's Flashback issues presented previously untold tales of the Marvel Universe.
TM and © Marvel Characters, Inc.

backstory of Peter Parker's parents as agents of S.H.I.E.L.D., establishing the fact that Peter follows a heroic tradition.

Adding to the feeling of nostalgia, all the flashback comics featured old-fashioned cover designs, with classic logos and Comic Code seals. For newer titles, Marvel's staff created new logos in a 1960s style pastiche. The "-1" idea originated with Scott Lobdell who proposed it as an X-Men crossover, but when editor-in-chief Bob Harras brought the idea to an editorial meeting, all the Marvel editors wanted to take part as a way of providing a light-hearted kickoff to summer. The oddly numbered flashback issues, though, proved too easy for fans to skip, and although Marvel's creators were excited about the ideas they presented, sales were disappointing. A retailer in Maryland stated, "This Flashback thing is without a doubt the least popular and worst selling series of comics from a major publisher that I have seen in my 15 years in this business" (Beckner 14). Likewise, *Comics Retailer* magazine reported, "The failure of Marvel's 'Flashback Month' in many responding retailers' stores contributed to the worst unit-sales month for retailers' Top 25 titles since we've been keeping records" ("Negative Impact" 23).

Later in the year, Marvel launched a different set of titles with its "Strange Tales" horror sub-line. It began in October with J.M. DeMatteis and Liam Sharp's *Man-Thing*, which cast the title character as the protector of the Nexus of All Realities. *Werewolf by Night*, by Paul Jenkins and Paul Lee, then debuted in December. Finally, Don McGregor and Brian Hagan's *Blade* premiered in 1998. A fourth Strange Tales title, *Satana*, by Warren Ellis and Ariel Olivetti, was cancelled before it was published. Ellis later reused his unpublished script for a 1999 Avatar Press comic (Cronin). With sales hovering around 20,000 copies, *Man-Thing* was cancelled after eight issues. *Werewolf* and *Man-Thing* were then combined into a single *Strange Tales* comic which too was cancelled before its storylines wrapped up. Marvel also hyped two other series, *Orleans* and *Endtime*, as part of the Strange Tales line, but they never saw print.

Devil's Reign

The crossover mania of 1996 continued unabated into 1997 with Marvel participating in six of them just in the month of January. As Wildstorm Studios' Jim Lee put it, "I think there is a real need to create excitement in the industry for such events that are a big deal," adding, "There's definitely overkill right now, but I still don't think that invalidates a story or project that's well done. I think there'll always be crossovers. Just not as many as there are now. Maybe we'll be a little more discriminating about them than we are now" (Sodaro 51-2).

Some of the Wildstorm team-ups made major differences in their universes, such as the aforementioned *JLA/WildC.A.T.s*. Likewise, in the eight-part "Devil's Reign," Marvel villain Mephisto attacks heroes of Marc Silvestri's Top Cow universe to gather their souls and build strength to take over the Marvel Universe. In part one, *Weapon Zero/Silver Surfer* by Walter Simonson, Marc Silvestri, Billy Tan and Kirk Van Wormer, Mephisto tricks the Silver Surfer into opening a gateway into the Top Cow universe where he encounters the team Weapon Zero. In chapter two, *Cyblade/Ghost Rider* by Ivan Velez Jr., Anthony Chun and David Finch, Eternity sends the Ghost Rider to the Top Cow Universe to battle Mephisto and team up with the heroic Cyblade. As the crossover unfolded, the heroes alternated issues. *Ghost Rider/Ballistic* led to *Ballistic/Wolverine*, which then led to *Wolverine/Witchblade*, *Witchblade/Elektra*, *Elektra/Cyblade*, and then back to *Silver Surfer/Weapon Zero*. In the crossover's finale, the Top Cow heroes and Silver Surfer unite to defeat Mephisto and Top Cow hero Heatwave sacrifices himself to rid the world of the Marvel Universe's devil.

The two-part *Daredevil/Shi* and *Shi/Daredevil* united Marvel's blind crimefighter with William Tucci's Japanese warrior for an adventure in which Daredevil's ninja enemies The Hand try to recruit Shi to join their cult. Tucci, who created and self-published *Shi* through his Crusade Comics imprint, was thrilled to get the opportunity to create and write the meeting of the two heroes, declaring, "when I first tried to break into comics, all of my submissions were about Daredevil. This crossover is a dream come true" (Blumberg, "Shi, DD" 89).

Dan Chichester, Scott McDaniel and Derek Fisher collaborated on a January one-shot in which Daredevil and Batman joined forces to battle the united villainy of Two-Face and Mr. Hyde. When Frank Miller, who was initially contacted to work on the comic, declined due to his obligations on his own *Sin City*, editor Ralph Macchio got Chichester and Lee Weeks to sign on. The pair then had to wait a year for Marvel to finalize their contracts, a delay which pushed artist Lee Weeks away from the project (Mithra). One clever angle Chichester added to the special was the notion that Daredevil and Two-Face knew each other before they adopted their alternative identities since Matt Murdock and Harvey Dent were both lawyers.

The *X-Men/WildC.A.T.s* crossover spanned four bookshelf-format comics. The first chapter, "The Golden Age" by Scott Lobdell and Travis Charest, was released in February and has Wolverine meeting the WildC.A.T.s' Zealot. The

"Devil's Reign" teamed up the heroes of the Top Cow and Marvel Universes.
TM and © Marvel Characters, Inc. TM and © Top Cow Publications, Inc.

second issue, "The Silver Age" by Lobdell and Jim Lee, was published in June. It unites the original X-Men with some of the longer-lasting members of Lee's team to fight an alien invasion. In August, James Robinson, Adam Hughes and Mark Farmer delivered "The Modern Age" in which the early 1980s version of the X-Men joins forces with the WildC.A.T.s, despite the tension produced by the WildC.A.T.s' violent ways and the X-Men's more traditionally heroic approach. The saga wrapped up in May 1998 with "The Dark Age" by Warren Ellis and Mat Broome. This finale presents a dystopian future in which the evil Daemonites have taken over the Earth and killed many of the super-heroes. Jim Lee planned all the details of the series, designing it to show how the teams progressed in different directions: "I wanted to show the growth of the two teams in a realistic way. The story makes it clear the X-Men and the WildC.A.Ts exist on the same Earth, so naturally, they would've run into each other before. We wanted to intertwine the histories of the two teams a little" (Brady 16).

The former *Hulk* team of Peter David and Dale Keown reunited for a 52-page squarebound crossover in which Marvel's green goliath battled the Pitt. The book begins as Timmy lands in an orphanage with no knowledge of where he's from. The only clue to his past is his repeated comment that a large "hulking" creature follows him. Timmy is clearly connected to the Pitt, but when Rick Jones visits Timmy, the Hulk shows up as well. From there the two giant characters trade punches before teaming up to help their friends. Writer David had a fun time with both the plot and the differences between the two characters: "We're dealing with characters who are polar opposites. You have Pitt, who is an alien character moving towards humanity, and you have Hulk who is a human character moving away from humanity – they actually see that in each other and don't like it" (Senreich 17).

Spider-Man and Batman teamed up in August in a one-shot by J.M. DeMatteis and Graham Nolan. The two flagship characters match up against the combined menaces of Ra's al Ghul and the Kingpin, in a story which journeys back and forth between New York and Gotham City. The contrasts between the grim Batman and the whimsical Spider-Man made for an intriguing tension and delivered a crossover that fans enjoyed.

At least the ones who bought it did. The fact of the matter was that many comic book readers found themselves overwhelmed by the number of intercompany crossovers and began tuning them out. After twenty-six appeared in 1996 and an additional sixteen followed in 1997, the whole idea seemed overdone. That sentiment didn't bode well for **Amalgam**, the line of comics which mashed up Marvel and DC characters in a series of one-offs. Amalgam was a major hit in 1996, so the two companies decided to produce a second set of crossovers, all of them released on April 2, 1997. The dozen new stories had some overlap with the 1996 characters, with Dark Claw, Spider-Boy, JLX and Magneto and the Magnetic Men returning for a second round.

The Amalgam comics of 1997 included: *Dark Claw Adventures*, merging Batman and Wolverine in an animated-style story by Ty Templeton and Rick Burchett; *Challengers of the Fantastic*, combining the Challengers of the Unknown with the team they influenced, the Fantastic Four, written by Karl Kesel and illustrated by Tom Grummett; *Super Soldier, Man of War*, a fusion of Superman and Captain America by Mark Waid and Dave Gibbons; *Generation X*, a Jonah Hex/Generation X mashup by Peter Milligan and Adam Pollina; *Lobo the Duck*, featuring the improbable pairing of Howard the

A new set of Amalgam Comics was published in 1997.
TM and © DC Comics. TM and © Marvel Characters, Inc.

Duck and Lobo by Alan Grant and Val Semekis; *Iron Lantern*, a merger of Iron Man and Green Lantern by Kurt Busiek, Paul Smith and Al Williamson; *Bat-Thing*, a combination of Man-Thing and Batman by Larry Hama, Rodolfo Damaggio and Bill Sienkiewicz; *Magnetic Men Featuring Magneto* by Tom Peyer, Barry Kitson and Dan Panosian; *Spider-Boy Team-Up*, starring 1996's Spider-Man/Superboy combination alongside a pastiche of the Legion of Super-Heroes, by Karl Kesel, Roger Stern and Jose Ladrönn; *Thorion of the New Asgods*, a fusion of Thor and the New Gods' Orion by Keith Giffen and John Romita, Jr.; *The Uncanny X-Patrol*, a merger of the Doom Patrol and the X-Men by Barbara Kesel and Bryan Hitch; and *JLX Unleashed* by Christopher Priest, Oscar Jimenez and Hannibal Rodriguez.

During the summer, *Comics Retailer* magazine reported, "Amalgam II titles sold well in some stores, poorly in others – but nothing like 1996. This year's top Amalgam, *Iron Lantern*, sold fewer copies per store than last year's worst-selling Amalgam, *Speed Demon*" ("Market Beat" 33). As a result, Marvel and DC put their shared universe on hiatus.

Faerie Dust

By 1997, **Neil Gaiman** and **Charles Vess** had collaborated several times, most notably on *Sandman* #19 (Sept. 1990), which had won a World

Neil Gaiman and Charles Vess delivered the four-issue fantasy Stardust.
TM and © Neil Gaiman and Charles Vess.

Fantasy award for its adaptation of William Shakespeare's *A Midsummer Night's Dream*, and on *Sandman*'s final issue (#75, March 1996) which adapted Shakespeare's *The Tempest*. Vess next wanted to work with Gaiman on an illustrated novel rather than a comic book, and the writer provided him with *Stardust*, a four issue adult fairy tale that DC began publishing in October via its **Vertigo Comics** imprint. Starring a young protagonist who promises to retrieve a falling star for his lover by journeying into a magical realm, *Stardust* features 175 Vess illustrations alongside Gaiman's exquisite prose.

While *Stardust* may have seemed typical for DC's Vertigo line, the two-issue **Uncle Sam** was very different. For one thing, the book featured art by **Alex Ross**, best known for his spectacular depictions of super-heroes in *Marvels* and *Kingdom Come*. For another, the comic was an explicitly polemical bit of liberal agitprop from writer **Steve Darnall**. The first issue opens with a derelict version of Uncle Sam—the iconic image of America from James Montgomery Flagg's famous "I Want You" poster—reaching to the reader for help. As it progresses, the story migrates through a dreamlike landscape composed of scenes from American history, from a Southern lynching, to the Kennedy Assassination, onto the Revolutionary War, and then finally back to the present day. The unusual series came, in part, from Ross's ambition to produce something both truly unique and radically different from anything he had worked on before. The politically charged series sold about 70,000 copies per issue—decent numbers for a non-super-hero comic book but still only a third of what *Kingdom Come* sold in 1996.

Spider Jerusalem Delivers the News

Besides publishing new Vertigo series, DC also expanded its science fiction **Helix Comics** line with several new titles. Garth Ennis and Carlos Ezquerra's *Bloody Mary* returned for a sequel mini-series with Mary battling a madman who wants to kill children in order to send them to Heaven. Dave Gibbon's one-shot, *The Dome: Ground Zero*, has completely computer-generated artwork by Angus McKie, the first such comic from DC in several years. Another new Helix release featured the work of acclaimed veteran fantasy and science fiction writer **Michael Moorcock**. With art by Walt Simonson, John Ridgway and Mark Reeve, *Michael Moorcock's Multiverse* unifies the author's Eternal Champion characters Elric, Moonbeams and Roses, and The Metatemporal Detective. The twelve-issue run won critical raves but because of poor sales, no sequel was commissioned.

The biggest hit from DC's Helix line involved a very different hero from Moorcock's Eternal Champion. **Transmetropolitan by Warren Ellis and Darick Robertson** portrays Spider Jerusalem as a journalist who fled the dystopian, urban grime for a hermit-like existence in the mountains. When Jerusalem is forced to return to the city to fulfill a book contract, he quickly finds himself an agent of change in the dysfunctional society. Ellis's scripts delivered delirious satire on everything from religion to consumer culture with bizarre sci-fi concepts mixed in (such as the ability to get an alien "race change"). Ellis saw Jerusalem as an important

In Warren Ellis and Darick Robertson's Transmetropolitan *journalist Spider Jerusalem is an agent of change in a broken society.* TM and © Warren Ellis and Darrick Robertson.

hero: "There are moments of pure, heart stopping beauty in the most tragic and broken environments. And the loveliest community on earth will not be able to eliminate the dog turd. I have attempted to reflect this in *Transmet*: the understanding that the world can be neither perfect nor doomed. But that it can be better. And the people who get to decide if it's going to be better or not are the people who show up and raise their voices" (McBride). Robertson's detailed depictions of urban misery gave the series a grungy, urgent feel. *Transmet* moved over to the Vertigo line after issue #12 and became one of its most iconic series.

DC's **Paradox Press** also continued to publish adult graphic novels, including *100% True*, *The Big Book of Losers* and *The Big Book of the Unexplained*. One of Paradox's standout books of the year was **A History of Violence**, a gritty, violent crime story written by John Wagner and illustrated by Vince Locke that recounts the life of Tom McKenna, owner of a small-town diner stalked by Brooklyn gangsters. When the turbulent truth beneath McKenna's seemingly placid life gets revealed, he is forced to confront his violent past. The book was adapted into a feature film in 2005.

The Genesis of the DC Universe

DC's big crossover event of the year was **Genesis**. Illustrated by Ron Wagner and written by John Byrne as a tie-in to his *Jack Kirby's Fourth World* title, the four-issue weekly mini-series (published in August) begins as the heroes of the DC Universe experience the diminishment of their powers. Green Lantern's ring malfunctions. Captain Marvel loses his connection to magic, and the Flash runs at a much slower pace. In the face of this confusion, only the New Gods have an idea of what is happening. As aliens amass to attack an Earth weakened by its nearly powerless champions, New God leader Highfather gathers Earth's heroes and explains that the problem stems from a godlike force called the Godwave that has twice passed across the universe. The first time the Godwave passed, gods and planets were created in its wake. The second time it passed, it bounced off the edge of the universe and created super-humans. Now on its third pass, the Godwave is beginning to contract. At a certain point this contraction will cause the Godwave to explode outward and destroy all life in the universe. A group of heroes, led by New God Takion, fly inside The Source, the genesis of all power on Earth, to stop the explosion. In the end, the group wins its incredible cosmic battle but not without experiencing some frustrating losses. Some two dozen DC titles crossed over with *Genesis*, but the event was generally criticized for being poorly coordinated. Tie-in issues frequently conflicted with each other or even with the overall main storyline. *Genesis* was also panned for the way Byrne unified all the DC heroes' origins under the same aegis, for its unwanted retroactive changes to continuity, and for altering the abilities of several super-heroes. *Genesis* received the second-highest orders for any DC comic the month of its release (*JLA* was first) but the event was quickly forgotten in DC continuity.

Electric Blue Superman

Arguably, the 1990s was **Superman**'s most eventful decade. First, he died, then he got married, and then in 1997 he received a completely new set of powers. The controversial storyline began in the aftermath of 1996's *Final Night* crossover as the Man of Steel struggled to regain his lost powers. In an act of desperation, Superman agrees to submit himself to a lab experiment that will charge him with new radiation. Unexpectedly, he is transformed into a being of pure energy, losing his super-hearing and x-ray vision but gaining the ability to harness light and heat. In order to contain his new energy-based powers, Superman ditches his traditional red and blue costume and replaces it with a blue and white suit built by S.T.A.R. Labs scientists. In a story written by Dan Jurgens and drawn by Ron Frenz and Joe Rubinstein, "Superman Blue" made his debut in *Superman* #123 (May 1997) with two covers, one for newsstand release and the other for the Direct Market. The costume change was a radical move for one of comics' most

iconic characters, perhaps even more radical than his death. Superman line editor Joey Cavalieri explained the reason for the change: "We thought it was time to make things a little tougher for Superman. And since we've already killed him, it seemed the way to do it was to get him powers he was unfamiliar with and have him learn to walk again" (Senreich 26). "Superman Blue" was covered by such mass media outlets as CNN and *Entertainment Tonight* which temporarily increased newsstand sales. Comic shop sales, on the other hand, slumped as many fans frowned upon the change, derisively referring to it as "Electric Blue Superman." Undaunted, the Superman creative team would take the costume change one step further in 1998.

While Superman journeyed into a new status quo, readers were also able to discover the history of his adoptive family. Written by John Ostrander and illustrated by Tom Mandrake, the twelve-part *The Kents* told a dramatic story rich in American history. Presented as letters from Jonathan Kent to his son Clark, the series includes such figures as Jesse James, Wild Bill Hickok and Sojourner Truth as they battled for truth, justice and the American way long before Kal-El was rocketed to Earth. The message of the series was clear: Clark Kent followed in a long family tradition of heroism.

Going on a Tangent

One of the more unusual ideas to emerge from DC in 1997 was the **Tangent** line of comic books. In the Tangent universe, new super-heroes have familiar names but the events that involve them unfolded differently from what happened in either the real world or the DC Universe. For instance, in the Tangent universe, the 1962 Cuban Missile Crisis led to a nuclear exchange between the United States and the Soviet Union. The creator responsible for the Tangent line was Dan Jurgens who conceived it as a way of resurrecting the spirit of the past and applying those ideas to the present: "What we're trying to do here is what Julie Schwartz got to do as a DC editor in the '50s when he restarted characters like the Flash in *Showcase* #4. Back then, creators had to take the names of super-heroes — sometimes classics or even sometimes forgotten — that existed before and use them to rebuild, entirely from scratch, the kind of book they wanted. That's what we're doing now" (Senreich 14). For his Tangent collaborators, Jurgens composed a thirty-page bible, detailing his complex and interlocking universe.

TM and © DC Comics.

Tangent Comics launched different versions of familiar DC titles.
TM and © DC Comics.

DC released all nine Tangent comics on October 1st. *The Atom*, written and drawn by Jurgens, tells the story of the world's nuclear apocalypse while focusing on the third-generation Atom. The other Tangent titles included: *Doom Patrol*, written by Jurgens with art by Sean Chen and Kevin Conrad, features a group of heroes who return from the future to warn people about the end of the world; *The Flash*, written by Todd Dezago with art by Gary Frank and Cam Smith, introduces a woman composed of living, sentient light; *Green Lantern*, by James Robinson with art by J.H. Williams and Mick Gray, stars a mysterious woman who can raise the dead to seek revenge; *The Joker*, written by Karl Kesel with art by Matt Haley and Tom Simmons, presents a female counterculture leader in post-nuclear Atlanta; *Metal Men*, written by Ron Marz with art by Mike McKone and Mark McKenna, tells the story of the 1969 ground war between the U.S. and U.S.S.R. and how that war affected its veterans nearly twenty years later; *Nightwing*, written by John Ostrander with art by Jan Duursema, unveils a clandestine organization and its plans for changing the world; *Sea Devils*, written by Kurt Busiek with art by Vince Giaranno and Tom Palmer, features sea creatures made intelligent and powerful by nuclear radiation. Finally, *Secret Six*, the super-team book of the line written by Chuck Dixon with art by Tom Grummett, unites the Atom, the Flash, the Joker and three other members.

Sales on the Tangent titles were middling, with no single title breaking the top 60 on the sales charts, but the Tangent Universe would return in 1998.

Before then, DC published a different group of thematically-linked one-shots. Released on the last day of 1997, each **"New Year's Evil"** special starred a key DC villain, many of them already familiar to devoted DC fans, like Darkseid, Mr. Mxyzptlk, Scarecrow and the Flash's Rogues Gallery. Other one-shots, like *Body Doubles* and *Dark Nemesis*, presented villains only recently introduced in the DC universe. Two "New Year's Evil" specials, however, had a more ambitious purpose. *Gog*, written by Mark Waid with art by Jerry Ordway and Dennis Janke, was designed as a prelude to

a *Kingdom Come* sequel series that had been in the works for several years. *Prometheus*, written by Grant Morrison with art by Arnie Jorgenson, debuted a villain Morrison called "the Batman of evil," a super genius who can mimic the moves of any master fighter thanks to a computer that is wired directly into his brain (Aubrey 23). One month after his introduction in "New Year's Evil," Prometheus appeared in *JLA #16* to become a major thorn in the side of the Justice League.

Bone Leaves Image

After making a big splash by joining Image Comics in 1995, **Jeff Smith** chose to return to self-publishing beginning with *Bone* #28 (Aug. 1997). Though his time at Image was short, Smith didn't leave due to any problem he had with the publisher. Instead, with the comic book industry now being serviced by only one distributor, Smith realized he could release his work without needing Image's help: "We went to Image in the Spring of '95 during the distributor wars and the wars between exclusives. It's now at a point where it's reached a pinnacle. Certainly the distributors can only consolidate so much. It can't get any narrower" (Woodward 18). Before Smith joined Image, *Bone* was selling just over 50,000 copies per issue. By the time he went solo again, his sales had dropped to 35,000 copies per issue, a decent showing which Smith was able to supplement with merchandise and trade paperback sales.

Fellow Homage team member **Terry Moore** also took his *Strangers in Paradise* back to a self-publishing status. Moore did so after discovering his move to Image didn't significantly improve his income. After Moore signed with Image, *Strangers in Paradise* was made available in 4,000 stores, double its previous exposure. Sales, though, only increased by 7,000 copies from their original level of 20,000 per issue. Since Moore had higher expenses by publishing through Image, these costs ate into his profit from the title, and his net income stayed the same at Image as it had through Moore's own Abstract Studio. Regardless of sales, Moore continued self-publishing *Strangers in Paradise* for the remainder of the decade.

Once Smith and Moore left Image, **Jim Valentino** expanded the company's commitment to the kinds of independent and idiosyncratic comics exemplified by *Bone* and *Strangers in Paradise*. He added over a dozen black-and-white series to the company's roster. While some of those additions were formerly self-published, others were released by small publishers like Caliber Press. All the creators shared a common goal, though: to see increased sales and distribution by being included in the Image section of the Diamond *Previews* catalog. In order to participate in the "non-line," as Valentino called it, each creator was required to pay $2,500 per book, of which $2,000 was paid to Image and $500 to Valentino's Shadowline imprint to cover overhead costs. Other than the $2,500 fee, the creators owned all rights to their intellectual properties and received revenues from the sales their series generated.

Valentino keynoted the collection of titles in his autobiographical memoir *A Touch of Silver*. Other members of the "non-line" included James Hudnall's *ESPers* and *Age of Heroes*, Aaron Warren's *The Adventures of Aaron*, C.S. Morse's *Soulwind*, James A. Owen's *Starchild*, Zander Cannon's *Replacement God*, James Pruett and Andrew Robinson's *Dusty Star*, Jimmie Robinson's *Amanda & Gunn*, Mike Baron and Michael Avon Oeming's *The Badger*, Joe Pruett and Phil Hester's *The Nameless*, Bryan J.L. Glass and Michael Avon Oeming's *Ship of Fools* and Rob Walton's *Ragmop*. At first, sales of many of these series jumped substantially under the arrangement. For example, Hudnall cited increases from 2,000 copies per issue to 17,000 copies of his *ESPers* before sales declined again. Zander Cannon received sales of 10,000 on the first Image issue of *Replacement God* but they dropped to 3,700 copies by issue #5 in March 1998. The industry's weak market conditions rapidly proved too much for Valentino's pet project as he reported, "After a year of attrition and living off of my own savings trying to give this the best shot I could, it is time for me to cut my considerable losses" (Spurgeon 7).

Brian Michael Bendis also moved from Caliber to Image but not to be part of Valentino's "non-line." Instead, Bendis continued writing and illustrating *Jinx*, a series about a bounty hunter who falls in love with a crook and the complications which emerge from that relationship. Through textured, snappy dialogue, *Jinx* presents conversations that are sometimes elliptical, sometimes

Former Batman Azrael met Joe Quesada's Ash in a 1997 one-shot.
TM and © DC Comics. TM and © Joe Quesada and Jimmy Palmiotti.

straightforward and sometimes deceptive, giving the story an intriguing complexity. Bendis's art emphasizes the noir darkness of the story, and *Jinx* became a gateway for Bendis to move to other, more high-profile projects. For instance, in 1999, he helmed a *Spawn* spin-off title before launching one of Marvel's biggest successes in 2000.

Other individualistic creators struck their own ground. Small San Antonio, Texas-based Antarctic Press published Alex Robinson's quirky *Box Office Poison*, a comic book that simultaneously presented a multifaceted romance between a cartoonist and his girlfriend and satirized the comics industry through the cartoonist's curmudgeonly boss. *Box Office Poison* won raves for Robinson's naturalistic storytelling and emphasis on characters and their everyday struggles. Another unique artist, **Frank Cho**, created *Liberty Meadows* which hit newspapers in 1997 and soon found its way into comic shops via the Baltimore small press publisher, Insight Studios. Cho's whimsical story takes place in a nature reserve, where beautiful Brandy is in charge of keeping the anthropomorphic animals happy. Mark Crilley's *Akiko*, published through Sirius Entertainment, was another prominent small press title of 1997. The science fiction adventure places a fourth-grade girl on the wondrous planet Smoo where she encounters strange creatures while searching for a kidnapped prince. Akiko was an indomitable heroine who resonated with young girls and Crilley eventually expanded her adventures into a series of popular young adult novels.

Meanwhile, **Joe Quesada and Jimmy Palmiotti** had successfully evolved their slick **Event Comics** into a notable independent publisher. In doing so, Event became more consistent with its shipping schedules and attracted big-name talent to its roster. This year also marked the launch of one of Event's most popular series, **Painkiller Jane**. Written by Mark Waid and Brian Augustyn with art by Rick Leonardi and Jimmy Palmiotti, *Jane* stars an ex-New York City police officer who emerges from a coma with her life completely changed: she's lost her family, her fiancée and her career but she's become virtually indestructible. As bullets fly through her body, she undertakes a film noir type struggle to regain her previous life. Quesada and Palmiotti also announced plans to publish *The Hour of Reckoning* by Tony Harris, *Thrax* by Dave Ross and *Crimson Plague* by George Pérez. While Harris's work never appeared, Event released single issues of Ross's and Pérez's series, at which point Quesada and Palmiotti put Event on hold late in the year. Rumors spread that the pair were on the verge of a lucrative deal with Marvel similar to the contract Rob Liefeld and Jim Lee signed with Marvel two years earlier. The truth wouldn't be revealed until 1998.

The Hero Defined

Another creator who followed his own artistic vision became a bestseller at Image. After over a decade of buildup, **Matt Wagner** delivered *Mage II: the Hero Defined*. A sequel to his beloved 1980s series, *The Hero Discovered*, Wagner's new story reunited Kevin Matchstick, the reincarnation of King Arthur, with some super-powered friends for an action/adventure story that resonated with real-world charm and quirkiness. In *The Hero Defined*, Kevin Matchstick must face the demons freed by the destruction caused at the end of the first *Mage* saga. Thankfully, Kevin has a team of allies to help him. His sidekicks, all men in t-shirts, were modeled after comic book creators, all of whom believe they are the re-embodiment of different historical legends. As with the first series, the sequel was based deeply on Wagner's life: "You go through various stages in your life that are generally familiar, but also new if you look in the right manner" (Rybandt 52). Although many fans loved the series, *Comics Journal* reviewer Gil Roth dubbed the team-up elements "Justice League of Mage," complaining about what he saw as Wagner's lack of direction (Roth 38).

Over at **Dark Horse Comics, Michael Allred** produced his own wacky seven-part book, *Red Rocket 7*, about an alien from another planet named Red Rocket who sends six clone sentinels to Earth. While all the clones have extraordinary skills – one is an award-winning author, another has brilliant math skills, another great athletic prowess – Red Rocket 7 has tremendous music talents. As the science fiction adventure unfolds, Rocket infiltrates the music industry and tracks the history of rock and roll, Forrest Gump style. This unique mini-series was printed in an unusual size (12"x12"), meant to emulate record albums. A musician as well as an artist, Allred also released a companion CD.

Before being removed from *Avengers* and *Captain America*, Rob Liefeld co-published two Marvel Comics crossovers with his **Awesome Comics** characters: *Prophet/Cable* (written and drawn by Liefeld with help from Robert Place Napton and Mark Pajarillo) and *Spider-Man/Badrock* (written by Dan Jurgens with art by Liefeld, Marat Mychaels and Dan Fraga). Once divorced from Marvel, however, Liefeld approached **Alan Moore** to write a three-issue limited series that would allow Moore to reset the entire Awesome Comics universe, just as he did for *Supreme* the previous year. Moore seized the opportunity: "It struck me that I could come up with something that was interesting and dynamic and also allowed for a greater range of sensibilities to grow out of it" (Rybandt 16). *Judgment*

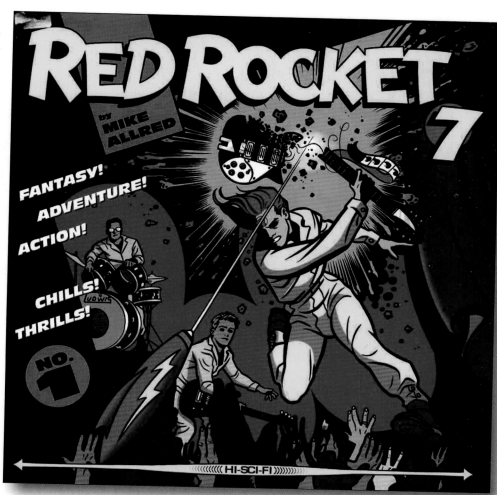

Mike Allred's Red Rocket 7 *plants an alien as a Forrest Gump-style viewer of the history of rock and roll. TM and © Michael Allred.*

Day centers on a trial in which a member of Youngblood is accused of murdering one of his teammates. As various super-heroes testify, flashback sequences realign Awesome's continuity. In some ways, *Judgment Day* acted as a counterpoint to Liefeld's work on *Captain America* and *Avengers*; it added a sense of history and tradition to new characters rather than stripped history away from existing characters. Drawing the flashbacks was an all-star lineup of new and veteran artists, including Terry Dodson, Keith Giffen, Dan Jurgens, Stephen Platt, Chris Sprouse, Jim Starlin, Rick Veitch and even the legendary Gil Kane. Liefeld drew each issue's main sequence, and it was work that Moore found wanting: "There were some great artists working on [*Judgment Day*], but I don't really think that Rob Liefeld was one of them.... Liefeld never seemed to put an enthusiasm into any of these drawings; he wouldn't put enough backgrounds or anything like that. It was pointless writing scripts for him because he'd just ignore most of them because he wanted to do the easiest, simplest thing" (Khoury 172-173).

Once *Judgment Day* concluded in October, Moore and artists Steve Skroce and Lary Stucker introduced their new Youngblood team in December's *Awesome Holiday Special*. Moore's Youngblood then returned for an abortive two-issue 1998 run intended to be the foundation for a new line of comics. However, financial struggles at Awesome led Moore to seek a new home for his ideas.

Bill Black's Femforce *is one of the longest running independent comic books, having been published since 1985.* TM and © AC Comics.

Star Wars Stays Put

Soon after acquiring the rights to the moribund *Star Wars* comic book license in 1991, Dark Horse Comics turned it into one of its biggest moneymakers. Dark Horse steadily expanded its line of *Star Wars* books all the way until 1997 when the license came up for renewal. By this time, several other comic book companies, most notably DC and Marvel, wanted to throw their hat into the ring. Wildstorm even proposed a six-year publishing plan which would include work by Jim Lee, J. Scott Campbell, Peter David, James Robinson, among many other prominent creators. Ultimately though, the rights to the franchise remained with Dark Horse and *Star Wars* comic book sales surged as "Special Edition" versions of the original trilogy hit theatres between January and March.

Ditko at Fantagraphics

While Dark Horse held on to a legendary property, **Fantagraphics Books** published work by one of comics' most legendary creators. With a bold cover that conjured memories of his classic work on *Doctor Strange*, **Steve Ditko's Strange Avenging Tales** delivered a mix of heroic adventure stories and politically-oriented tales. Though there were hopes *Strange Avenging Tales* would become an ongoing series, Ditko's uncompromising approach to his material limited Fantagraphics' endeavor to a one-shot

presentation. Afterward, Ditko moved into small press publishing, in which he was able to deliver his political and social views uncensored.

Another major Fantagraphics publication delivered work by a cartoonist who had achieved the mastery of his form. *Ghost World* **by Daniel Clowes** depicts two smart and funny teenage girls, Enid and Rebecca, on the edge of adulthood and struggling to understand the purpose of life. Clowes flawlessly explores the sense of loss that pervasively hangs on the girls, ghosts of a brief moment of time as they transition from youthful freedom into the ambiguity of adulthood. Drawn in an empathetic, post-ironic style that emphasizes character, Clowes's graphic novel resonated with many readers. *Ghost World* would be adapted into a film in 2001.

A longstanding comic book series hit its 100th issue in 1997, but few readers likely noticed. *Femforce*, published by Florida-based AC Comics since 1985, accomplished this milestone in February 1997. In the landmark issue, writer Bill Black and artist Brad Gorby presented the resolution of a tragic love story that had been running for over 60 issues. The black-and-white series, starring an all-female cast, had a small but devoted following. As Black stated at the time, "We are appealing to a lot of female readers and think we have good role models for women. Our women are not victims or counterparts of male heroes who take to the forefront. They are beautiful, buxom, yet intelligent, take-charge type of women" (Senreich 23).

Another Florida-based company, Alternative Press, published *Detour*, **Ed Brubaker**'s story of a strange and lonely man living in a world that seemed to have experienced an environmental catastrophe. The claustrophobic black-and-white tale was projected to be a three-part story but only the first issue was published. Nonetheless, *Detour* was nominated for a Harvey Award for "Best New Series."

The Web Expands Its Tendrils

By 1997, nearly all comic book publishers had one thing in common: a presence on the ever-expanding internet. BIG Entertainment, for one, had forums and interactive content on the Prodigy and America Online services. Marvel's internet involvement was one of the most prominent, earning America Online's Member's Choice Award, which combined data on return visits and "stickiness" (how long a user stays on a page). Placing in the top 50 of all sites worldwide for every category, Marvel Online offered such features as "CyberComics," which combined traditional comics with animation so Web surfers could watch Spider-Man spin a web or Wolverine pop out his claws as they read a heroic adventure. Marvel also offered trivia rooms, a news page (called "The Daily Bugle"), an online store, and the chance to interact with professionals and fellow fans in chats and message boards which helped foster a strong sense of community. For the most part, DC's site included many of the same features as Marvel's. Other comics professionals, including Peter David, Steve Gerber and Mark Evanier, maintained strong web presences, posting and commenting in online forums. Even *Wizard* had its own online forums. The magazine also included AOL disks with several of its 1996 and 1997 issues.

Holy Bat-Nipples

Overall, it was not a good year for super-hero movies. The fourth Batman film, **Batman and Robin**, arrived in theaters on June 20 and pitted Batman (now played by George Clooney), Robin (Chris O'Donnell) and Batgirl (Alicia Silverstone) against Mr. Freeze (Arnold Schwarzenegger) and Poison Ivy (Uma Thurman). Due to its campy tenor, cringe-worthy dialogue, and overcrowded cast, the movie was panned by film critics and comic book fans alike. (One need not look further than the nipples on the Dark Knight's costume to gauge the film's quality.) Even though it basically broke even on its massive $125 million budget, *Batman and Robin* was a box office disappointment, especially when compared to the previous three installments which grossed considerably more money. Prior to *Batman and Robin*'s release, rumors circulated that Warner Bros had greenlit a fifth Batman movie. *Batman Triumphant* would have once again featured Clooney and O'Donnell as the Dynamic Duo, facing off against Harley Quinn (rumored to be played by pop singer Madonna) and the Scarecrow (rumored to be played by radio shock jock Howard Stern). Unfortunately (or perhaps fortunately), *Batman Triumphant* was never produced as Warner Bros. put the franchise on hold after the lackluster performance of *Batman and Robin*. The Caped Crusader wouldn't return to cinemas until 2005.

Less than two weeks after *Batman and Robin* premiered, another comic book-inspired movie arrived in theaters. Based on the 1990 Malibu comic book by Lowell Cunningham and Sandy Carruthers, **Men in Black** starred Will Smith and Tommy Lee Jones as two secret government agents who track down aliens on Earth. Considering that the sci-fi/action comedy had endured years of Hollywood "development hell," and that it was based on a work that even devoted comic book fans weren't familiar with, no one could have predicted that *Men in Black* would more than double the domestic box office gross of *Batman and Robin*. Even more impressive, the only other 1997 movie to earn more money in America than *Men in Black* was James Cameron's blockbuster *Titanic*. Indeed, *Men in Black* became a cultural phenomenon, not only spawning several movie sequels and an animated television show, but various merchandise as well.

While many of his Image counterparts developed their comic books into kids' cartoon shows, **Todd McFarlane** pursued a different path. The animated *Todd McFarlane's Spawn* didn't appear on Saturday mornings but rather on prime time HBO, where it didn't have to adhere to network standards. Premiering on May 16, 1997, the series hewed close to the dark, violent themes of the source comic book, complete with mature language. In the opening story arc, Spawn battles child killer Billy Kincaid with the evil Clown lurking in the background. The series was acclaimed by fans and critics

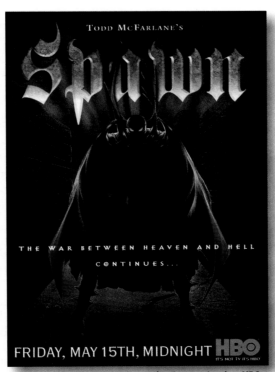

Todd McFarlane's Spawn *animated series premiered on HBO May 16, 1997.* TM and © Todd McFarlane Productions, Inc.

as breaking new ground in animation, but McFarlane just wanted to scare people: "In the best-case scenario, I hope it's so dark that people will have to watch it with the lights off" (Beatty 38). Keith David, the voice of Al Simmons, a.k.a. Spawn, provided a deep, emotional tone that emphasized the show's dark sense of horror. Eric Radomski, who directed the award-winning "Robin's Reckoning" for *Batman: the Animated Series*, worked with McFarlane to deliver a storyline that remained true to the spirit of the comic book but also took a different approach. That approach emphasized horror but also highlighted Al Simmons's introspection and complex inner life. As Radmonski reported, "We're taking you inside Spawn's head. You'll see what's going on around him, but you'll also feel what he's thinking and feeling. I'm a big fan of Scorcese, Coppola and Oliver Stone, and I used their films for inspiration more than comics" (Fritz 43). HBO aired three seasons of *Todd McFarlane's Spawn* for a total of eighteen episodes.

Three months after the animated series premiered, the **Spawn** live action movie arrived in theatres. Starring Michael Jai White as Al Simmons/Spawn, with John Leguizamo as the Clown and Martin Sheen as Jason Wynn, this adaptation was more linear and, perhaps surprisingly, less mature than the animated series. Al Simmons, an operative of a secret government agency, finds himself betrayed and then killed by his boss. He returns to life five years later to find his wife remarried and his world turned upside down. As Spawn struggles with whether or not to accept a deal with the Devil, his former boss and the evil Clown conspire to ravage the planet with a terrible virus. Spawn must stop the villains, which leads to a hellish battle with the Violator. Filmed for $40 million, *Spawn* grossed nearly $55 million—a modest hit, but not enough to inspire sequels.

One of the most bizarre super-hero flicks of all time premiered in theatres two weeks after *Spawn*. **Steel** starred basketball player (and rapper) Shaquille O'Neal as John Henry Irons, an inventor who learns the hi-tech weaponry he designed for the U.S. military has wound up in the hands of street gang members. With the help of his uncle (played by Richard Roundtree), Irons builds and dons a powerful suit of armor to become the super-hero Steel and confront the gangs. Eventually, Steel learns a disgraced soldier has been auctioning his weapons to criminal organizations.

Although based on a DC Comics character, the film treats Steel as if he is the only super-hero in the world. His connections to Superman are nowhere to be found, which ultimately discouraged comic book fans from seeing the movie. That perhaps played a factor in *Steel*'s abysmal performance at the box office, grossing a mere $1.7 million on a budget of $16 million.

In a way, though, *Steel* served as a perfect metaphor for the comics industry during 1997: the attempts being made to lure readers back to comic books fell way short.

CHAPTER NINE

The Heroes Return

In some ways, the American comic book industry returned to stability in 1998. Marvel emerged from bankruptcy, DC continued its steady production, and even the crossover craze of 1996 and 1997 subsided as fewer inter-company events saw print in 1998. Perhaps the most promising news came from the *Comics Buyer's Guide* which reported, "we have more publishers in the field than ever before" (Thompson 4). Unfortunately, an abundance of publishers didn't equate to a prosperity in the market. Comic book sales continued their dramatic decline with the top 300 comics selling a cumulative 84.45 million copies in 1998, a drop of 16% from the previous year, and they retailed for a total of $210 million dollars, a drop of 14%. Former distributor Frank Mangiaracina put these numbers in perspective: "Measured in dollars, the comics market is about the size it was in 1983, measured in units it is about one-fifth as large" (Mangiaracina 1).

For many, running a comic shop barely paid their expenses. In response to a summer 1998 survey, 76% of store owners stated they earned $22,300 in annual take-home pay. That was over 25% less than the national average salary of $30,500. Tellingly, no respondent reported they were very satisfied with their compensation ("Viewpoint Report" 22). It's no surprise then that 9% of Diamond accounts stopped working with the distributor in 1998, an indication that they went out of business. That left approximately 3,600 active comic shops in America by the end of 1998 (Field 30).

Not every retailer seemed to be suffering, however. Indeed, some stores claimed to be flourishing. One Denver retailer reported sales in 1998 were "better than the last three years" (Bennett 58). Similarly, Boston store owner Tom Devlin boasted, "[we] made more money [in 1998] than [we] ever had before. Talking to other stores that stock a lot of alternative comics [...] everybody seems to be doing better than they ever have" (Groth 10). The question that needed to be asked was if these thriving stores were merely anomalies or harbingers of more prosperous times.

Toy Biz buys Marvel

When **Marvel Comics** filed for bankruptcy in December 1996, months of rancorous legal wrangling ensued with intensified acrimony amongst shareholders Carl Icahn and Ron Perelman and Toy Biz executives Avi Arad, Ike Perlmutter and Joe Ahearn. For a brief period interested parties had the chance to acquire Marvel, its intellectual properties, SkyBox Cards and Panini Stickers. Companies such as MGM, Sony and Time Warner (owner of DC Comics) reviewed Marvel's financial paperwork as did a team of investors led by former Marvel editor-in-chief Jim Shooter and retailer Chuck Rozanski. They all came to the same grim conclusions: the comic book market was shrinking, Marvel had an insurmountable amount of debt, and its bankruptcy slowed the marketing of its heroes while its SkyBox and Panini subsidiaries experienced massive losses. In the face of those realities, each potential bidder decided Marvel was a poor investment. As Rozanski related, "What an exercise in futility. The lawyers involved love it, but the rest of us are just so burned out" (Raviv 238).

The matter began to get resolved only when Toy Biz first won the right to take over Marvel's management, effective October 1, 1997. Then, in June 1998, Toy Biz merged with Marvel to bring the publisher out of bankruptcy once and for all. They formed **Marvel Enterprises** and quickly relisted its stock on the New York Stock Exchange using the symbol MVL. The protracted legal battles had taken its toll, however; MVL opened at a mere $7 per share, down from the $17 price it sold at before the bankruptcy.

Peace in the boardroom didn't ease the stress inside Marvel's editorial offices. The new management team, led by tight-fisted Toy Biz executives, quickly set to work cutting Marvel's staff, including employees from marketing, front office and the field representative team. Among those fired were Executive Vice President of Publishing Shirrel Rhoades, Vice President of Editorial Planning Jim "Ski" Sokolowski, Editorial Director Jackie Carter and editors Kelly Corvese, Glenn Greenwald, Jim Kreuger and Tim Tuohy. Many of those who remained likely wished they were let go too, especially since the new executives implemented rules that were seen as arbitrary, extreme, and aimed at cutting costs without consideration of editorial quality. They required employees to punch time clocks, removed free coffee and bottled water from the offices and mandated the offices' electricity be turned off at 5PM. As with previous management, Marvel's new executives forbade unnecessary long-distance calls and even forced employees to reuse paper clips. Mandatory drug testing was even considered. Office tensions were so high that one senior employee remarked, "it was like being in a war zone" (Howe 399).

The Return of the Good Guys

Despite the poor office morale, Marvel launched two major 1998 initiatives that laid the roots for long-term success. "Heroes Return" and "Marvel Knights" added much-needed luster to several of Marvel's most iconic heroes and reasserted the power of Marvel's intellectual properties. Though 1997's Heroes Reborn returned *Avengers, Iron Man, Captain America* and *Fantastic Four* to the top of the sales charts, many fans felt the kind of style the Image creators used was inappropriate for the classic heroes. Therefore, 1998's **"Heroes Return"** brought fan-favorite creators back to those titles. These writers and artists used more traditional storytelling approaches which simultaneously embraced modern styles and respected tradition. *Fantastic Four* #1 and *Captain America* #1 were cover-dated January 1998. *Avengers* #1 and *Iron Man* #1 followed one month later with *Thor* debuting with a July cover-dated issue.

Scott Lobdell took on the task of writing **Fantastic Four** with Alan Davis handing art. The creative pair delivered a slick first issue that paid tribute to 1961's original *Fantastic*

Captain America returned to the main Marvel Universe in 1998 with his former creative team of Mark Waid and Ron Garney. TM and © Marvel Characters, Inc.

Four #1 by casting Mole Man as its feature villain. Lobdell and Davis also added healthy dollops of contemporary humor and family antics, but the creative team only lasted three issues. Starting with *FF* #4 (April 1998), Chris Claremont scripted Lodbell's plots before taking over full writing duties with *FF* #6. This was an ironic inversion of what happened in 1992 when Lobdell replaced Chris Claremont on *X-Men*. At the same time Davis handed over art responsibilities to Salvador Larroca after *FF* #3, and under Claremont and Larroca, *Fantastic Four* became a consistent Top 15 seller. Fans enjoyed both the familiar FF family interaction and the clever ways Claremont played with the heroes' powers. For instance, the Invisible Woman, besides training with martial arts master Iron Fist, began using her force field powers for new purposes like creating weapons or forming invisible sliders. Claremont was also inclined to separate the team from each other during their cosmic adventures, reuniting them for grand finales.

For **Captain America**, Marvel turned to a creative team that had already made a significant mark on the character: writer Mark Waid and artist Ron Garney. As Waid said, "I actually got the impression from Marvel that things never [were supposed] to go any other way [once Heroes Reborn ended]. It was also nice to have people excited about the prospect of us coming back even after a year of not being on the title" (Senreich 70). Unfortunately, readers who were expecting the kind of extended run that the creative pair

TIMELINE: 1998

A compilation of the year's notable comic book history events alongside some of the year's most significant popular culture and historical events. (On sale dates are approximations.)

January 1: As of this date, smoking is prohibited in all bars and restaurants in the state of California.

January 11: Win Mortimer, comic artist whose career spanned five decades including work on the *Superman* newspaper strip as well as such titles as *Action Comics*, *Adventure Comics* and *Spidey Super Stories*, dies at the age of 78.

March 1: Archie Goodwin, arguably the most respected comic book writer and editor of his time, dies of cancer at the age of 60. Over the span of thirty years, Goodwin made his mark on dozens of titles for DC, Marvel and Warren Publishing. He served as Marvel's editor-in-chief in the mid-1970s, after which he wrote the *Star Wars* comic strip as well as shepherded Marvel's Epic Comics line.

April 7: Alex Schomburg, comic book artist who produced some of the Golden Age's most vivid covers, particularly on titles featuring Captain America, Human Torch and the Sub-Mariner, dies at the age of 92.

April 8: Lee Elias, comic book artist whose career spanned five decades including work for DC, Marvel, Harvey and Warren Publishing, dies at the age of 77.

May 26: David Hasselhoff is *Nick Fury: Agent of S.H.I.E.L.D.* in a two-hour made-for-television special that airs on the FOX network.

May 27: Written and drawn by Frank Miller, the first issue of *300* arrives in stores. Published by Dark Horse Comics, the five-issue mini-series tells the story of three hundred Spartan soldiers defending ancient Greece from Persian invaders.

June: Toy Biz merges with Marvel Entertainment Group to bring the latter out of bankruptcy. They form Marvel Enterprises, and the New York Stock Exchange relists its stock with the symbol MVL.

JANUARY	FEBRUARY	MARCH	APRIL	MAY	JUNE

January 26: During a televised press conference, President Clinton reacts to publicized rumors that he had an affair with a White House intern by defiantly declaring, "I did not have sexual relations with that woman, Miss Lewinsky."

March 18: Jim Lee's "Cliffhanger" imprint debuts with the release of J. Scott Campbell's *Danger Girl* #1. Joe Madureira's *Battle Chasers* and Humberto Ramos's *Crimson* follow in April and May respectively.

May 20: A remake of *Godzilla*—directed by Roland Emmerich and starring Matthew Broderick and Jean Reno—opens in movie theaters. Despite significant promotion and moviegoer anticipation, the film disappoints at the box office, only grossing $136 million domestically.

Sub-Mariner TM and © Marvel Characters, Inc. Superman TM and © DC Comics.

provided in 1995 and 1996 were in for a disappointment as Garney only drew the first five issues of the new *Captain America* volume. In that time, however, he depicted one of the most significant calamities in the Star-Spangled Avenger's storied career: the loss of his iconic shield, which sinks to the bottom of the Atlantic ocean during a battle against Hydra. At first, Cap uses a replica of his original triangular shield, but once Andy Kubert became the series' new artist, Cap acquires a shield composed of photonic energy. Waid made the "gut-wrenching" decision to have Cap lose his shield because he wanted to shake up the comic's status quo as part of the reboot (Troglen 61). As the months wore on, though, Waid grew more and more frustrated with what he saw as editorial meddling in his work. According to Waid, *Captain America* #14 (Feb. 1999) was extensively rewritten by editor Ralph Macchio at the request of editor-in-chief Bob Harras. Waid wanted his writer credit removed from that issue, but his request came too late as the book had already been sent to the printer. Scarred a bit by the experience, Waid left *Captain America* by the end of 1999, remarking "we had a few nice moments in year two, but I'm tempted to say I should have never returned to *Cap* for a second go-around" (McLaughlin 22).

Several years after pitching to take over *Iron Man*, **Kurt Busiek** finally got his chance to write the title. Together with artist Sean Chen, Busiek turned the Golden Avenger's new volume into a globetrotting series that was one part super-hero adventure and one part James Bond espionage thriller. "I think *Iron Man* should be a book about suspense and intrigue," Busiek stated at the time. "I think there should be enemies all around, whether it's corporate enemies or villains like the Mandarin. I think there should be a healthy dose of shadows, intrigue and paranoia in the book" (Kardon 53). With a new suit of armor designed by Chen, Alex Ross and Allen Bujak, Tony Stark became the leader of Stark Solutions, a global nonprofit, which provided the hero with a pretext for traveling around the world and, coincidentally, uncovering super-villains' plots. Early chapters found Stark in Switzerland, the Caribbean, Russia and Paris, where he fought updated versions of classic villains like Firebrand and Whiplash while dealing with treacherous lovers, erupting volcanos and complex political intrigue. All these battles led to a decisive clash with a redesigned version of the Mandarin. Busiek played up the danger of being Iron Man. In one memorable issue, Tony Stark is beaten to within an inch of his life by a gang of thugs and by the end of the new volume's first year, Stark discovers he is being killed by toxins released in his own armor.

Busiek applied much of the same "back to the future" approach from *Iron Man* to his collaboration with **George Pérez** on another iconic title: *Avengers*. The team's new

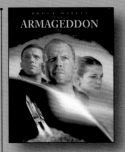

July 1: *Armageddon*—directed by Michael Bay and starring Bruce Willis and Ben Affleck as members of an oil drilling team that is recruited to destroy an asteroid before it impacts the Earth—opens in movie theaters.

August 7: Trucks laden with explosives are detonated almost simultaneously outside two U.S. embassies in east Africa, one in Tanzania and the other in Kenya. Over 200 people die in the attacks which are linked to Osama bin Laden's terrorist organization, Al-Qaeda.

August 21: *Blade*—starring Wesley Snipes as Marvel Comics' vampire hunter—opens in movie theaters. The film will gross over $70 million at the box office and spawn two sequels.

September 2: Written by Grant Morrison and drawn by Val Semeiks and Prentis Rollins, the first issue of *DC One Million* arrives in stores. The four-issue weekly mini-series features the Justice League of the 853rd century. Throughout September nearly three dozen DC Comics titles have their regular numbering interrupted in order to present a special #1,000,000 issue.

October 6: Outside Laramie, Wyoming two men rob and then torture Matthew Shepard, a 21 year old homosexual who dies of his injuries six days later. The murder draws national media coverage and inspires federal legislation that classifies offenses committed on the basis of a victim's sexual orientation as prosecutable hate crimes.

October 16: Bob Rozakis steps down as the manager of DC Comics' production department, a position he's had since 1981.

November 3: Bob Kane, comic book writer and artist who co-created Batman and guided his adventures until the mid-1960s, dies at the age of 83. Besides being honored by DC Comics as one of its most important creators, Kane also served as a consultant on the four Batman films that were released between 1989 and 1997.

| JULY | AUGUST | SEPTEMBER | OCTOBER | NOVEMBER | DECEMBER |

July 24: *Saving Private Ryan*—directed by Steven Spielberg and starring Tom Hanks as the captain of a U.S. Army squad during World War II—opens in movie theaters. The film will become the highest grossing movie of the year at the box office and earn eleven Academy Award nominations, winning the Best Director, Best Cinematography, Best Sound Mixing, Best Film Editing and Best Sound Effects categories.

September 9: Marvel Comics' "Marvel Knights" imprint debuts with the first issue of *Daredevil*—drawn by Joe Quesada and Jimmy Palmiotti and written by independent filmmaker Kevin Smith. The first issue of MK's three other inaugural series—*Black Panther*, *Inhumans* and *Punisher*—arrive in stores later the same month.

September 7: Two Stanford University Ph.D. students found Google, soon to become a leading provider of internet-related services and products.

August 20: In retaliation for the attacks on two U.S. embassies in east Africa, President Clinton authorizes cruise missile strikes against suspected al-Qaeda camps in Afghanistan and a chemical plant in Sudan.

August 17: After making a statement on tape for a grand jury, President Clinton admits to the American public that he had an extramarital affair with former White House intern, Monica Lewinsky.

December 17: The United States and Great Britain begin four days of limited air strikes against Iraq for its continued obstruction of United Nations weapon inspections.

December 19: The Republican controlled House of Representatives impeaches President Clinton for lying under oath to a federal grand jury and obstructing justice. The case moves to a trial in the U.S. Senate.

December 23: Joe Orlando, comic book writer, artist, editor and executive whose career spanned six decades, dies at the age of 71. Besides contributing to dozens of EC, Marvel and Warren Publishing titles, Orlando served as DC Comics' Vice President and near the end of his life became *MAD* magazine's Associate Publisher.

---

roster included founding members Captain America, Iron Man and Thor, along with such Avengers mainstays as Hawkeye, Vision, the Scarlet Witch and Warbird (the super-heroine formerly known as Ms. Marvel). Rounding out the lineup were two former members of the New Warriors: Justice and Firestar. While Busiek and Pérez provided the obligatory colossal clashes that one would expect from an *Avengers* series (i.e. an opening story arc which has sorceress Morgan LeFay transporting over three dozen super-heroes to a medieval village in an alternative universe), Busiek asserted that the new volume was more about the protagonists' human emotions than their super-human conflicts: "*The Avengers* is not a book about the big cosmic battle; it's a book that uses the big cosmic battle as the crucible in which the character drama happens. The character interaction and the drama of the team is at least as important as the adventures they get into" (Sanderson 9). In the title's

first year, not only did the Avengers confront such opponents as the Squadron Supreme and a group of dead Avengers who had been revived by the Grim Reaper, but they also had to deal with such personal matters as Warbird's alcoholism and a new hero named Triathlon who believes his faith in a Church of Scientology-like cult has unlocked his superhuman potential. What received the most fan attention, however, was the resurrection of Wonder Man, the former Avenger who died in *Force Works* #1 (July 1994). He is brought back to life through the power of Scarlet Witch's magic and Wonder Man's love for her. Wonder Man's return only further distances the Scarlet Witch from her ex-husband, Vision. Busiek and Pérez's collaboration on *Avengers* was immediately popular. In fact, *Avengers* consistently placed within the top ten bestselling titles of the month. In addition, Busiek and Pérez won the *Comics Buyer's Guide* fan awards for favorite writer and artist for 1998.

After almost eighteen months without his own title, **Thor** returned with a Heroes Reborn banner on the cover of the first issue of his new series. Assigned to the relaunch were writer Dan Jurgens (beating out such distinguished contemporaries as Peter David, David Quinn and Roger Stern) and artist John Romita Jr. who passed on the opportunity to return to *Iron Man* in order to draw the kind of titanic, unearthly battles that *Thor* would feature (McLaughlin 20). Jurgens envisioned a new status quo for Marvel's God of Thunder, something more down-to-earth that will help connect readers to the otherworldly protagonist: "We need to add a sense of personal loss. That's what's made so many classic characters like Spider-Man popular. We can identify with them. There's a personal connection. Our job is tough. We have to make people care for a god" (McLaughlin 51). To that end, the giant-sized *Thor* #1 features a destructive clash between Thor and the enormous

George Pérez delivered amazingly detailed art for the Heroes Return version of The Avengers.
TM and © Marvel Characters, Inc.

armored Destroyer in New York City. As paramedic Jake Olson responds to the scene of the fight in order to evacuate a wounded civilian, he is struck and killed by flying debris. Because Thor pays no mind to Olson's demise, a mysterious mystical entity called Marnot teaches the God of Thunder a lesson in humility. He forces Thor to live a mortal life in Jake Olson's body while having none of Olson's memories. As a result, Thor has a fiancée he doesn't know, a job which requires skills he doesn't have, and coworkers he's unfamiliar with. In a throwback to his days as Donald Blake, Thor must once again deal with all the entanglements of everyday life.

Sales on all five "Heroes Return" titles exceeded expectations. Four months in, a shop owner from Bloomington, Indiana applauded Marvel's efforts: "The relaunch of *Avengers*, *Cap*, *FF* and *Iron Man* have been successful for us... These new books have readers excited about what's going to happen next. I hope [Marvel realizes] quality writers and artists will *earn* solid sales. *Please* don't screw this up" (Edwards 30).

Meanwhile, Marvel's breakout series from 1997, *Thunderbolts*, began 1998 with the team's secret revealed to the public. In *Thunderbolts* #10 (Jan. 1998), a battalion of armed S.H.I.E.L.D. agents interrupts a press conference intended to reward the Thunderbolts with high-level

security clearance. When the agents announce that the supposed heroes are really the Masters of Evil, the Thunderbolts flee the scene. In a dramatic "parting gift for the good people and heroes of New York City," Baron Zemo blows up their former home at Four Freedoms Plaza. After issue #11 reveals Zemo's desire to achieve Hitler's dream of ruling the entire world, the double-sized *Thunderbolts* #12 brings the series' first year to an appropriate conclusion. Guest-starring the Avengers and Fantastic Four, "Endgame" features a massive battle aboard a cramped satellite. As the combat ends, the heroes, along with several rebellious Thunderbolts, triumph. A furious Meteorite takes her anger out on Zemo, destroying his hand, smashing his ribs and leaving his face a bloody pulp. Zemo, however, would not submit to defeat. He manages to engineer his own escape before he can be sent to jail. The rest of the team are unexpectedly transported to a different dimension, where a strange adventure leads them to another major twist in 1999.

At this time, no other comic book writer matched Kurt Busiek's production. Besides being attached to three Marvel series (*Avengers*, *Iron Man* and *Thunderbolts*), he continued writing his own *Astro City*. And then artist Carlos Pacheco asked Busiek to collaborate with him on yet another Marvel project. Tired of drawing *X-Men*, Pacheco wanted instead to work on an Avengers project. He and Busiek eventually developed a pitch which featured the time-travelling antagonist, Kang the Conqueror. Mark Waid suggested that the Avengers team that opposed Kang's schemes could be composed of members from different time periods. **Avengers Forever** then became a twelve-issue adventure, co-plotted by Roger Stern, which thrust seven Avengers from different eras (Captain America, Wasp, Giant-Man, Hawkeye, Songbird, Yellowjacket and Captain Marvel) into a strange war that involves longtime Marvel sidekick, Rick Jones. Over the course of the series, this oddball Avengers team participates in the metamorphosis of Kang into Immortus, opposes a quixotic attempt by Immortus to prevent humans from journeying

Thunderbolts #12 brings the series' initial storyline to its conclusion. TM and © Marvel Characters, Inc.

to the stars, and takes part in a dimension-spanning battle where they must fight against their alternative future selves. Eventually, the motley team triumphs over travails deeply embedded in Avengers history, and Busiek seemed to relish the opportunity to clean up inconsistencies in Marvel lore. Among them was the chance to decontextualize the much-despised "Tony Stark, Murderer" tales from 1995's *The Crossing*.

Knights Take the Devil

Even though Jim Lee and Rob Liefeld's work on 1997's Heroes Reborn was a mixed bag, Marvel management continued searching for independent creators who could be contracted to take over some of its titles on an interim basis. To aid that endeavor, Marvel president Joe Calamari asked *Wizard* magazine publisher Gareb Shamus to recommend some up-and-coming talent. Shamus had two people in mind: **Joe Quesada** and **Jimmy Palmiotti**. The Brooklyn-based creators were Valiant Comics veterans who left the freelance life to form their own company, Event Comics. Over the previous four years, Event released such notable books as Quesada's *Ash*, Fabian Nicieza's *22 Brides*, and Mark Waid and Brian Augustyn's *Painkiller Jane*. Unquestionably, Quesada and Palmiotti were experienced at producing high-quality comic books on tight budgets, but they also had strong relationships with movie producers and directors, the kind of high-profile Hollywood talent that Marvel wanted to attach to their properties. As a result, Calamari signed Palmiotti and Quesada to one-year contracts. While they wouldn't be earning as much money as Lee and Liefeld had during Heroes Reborn, Palmiotti and Quesada did receive an attractive perk: penthouse offices several floors above the editorial teams that were delivering Marvel's other series. Though some staffers resented Quesada and Palmiotti's executive roles, feeling the pair hadn't earned their positions, the new editors paid immediate dividends.

Quesada and Palmiotti were handed the reins to four titles – *Black Panther*, *Daredevil*, *Inhumans* and *Punisher* – which became branded under a new imprint called **Marvel Knights**. Compared to many of Marvel's other titles, Marvel Knights provided a more mature and cinematic approach. Movie director **Kevin Smith** (of *Clerks* and *Chasing Amy* fame) wrote the initial story arc in *Daredevil*, with art by Quesada and Palmiotti. *Quantum and Woody* writer Christopher Priest wrote *Black Panther*, with art by Mark Texeira. Paul Jenkins and Jae Lee presented a 12-chapter *Inhumans* series while writers Christopher Golden and Tom Sniegoski and artists Bernie Wrightson and Palmiotti collaborated on a four-part *Punisher* tale. While there was general interest in each of the four titles, everyone saw *Daredevil* as the one most likely to expand readership. As

Film director Kevin Smith revived Daredevil *for the new Marvel Knights imprint. Issue #2 variant cover by J. Scott Campbell.* TM and © Marvel Characters, Inc.

Quesada reported, "Comics do nothing but preach to the converted. That's why it's really important to bring Smith in, and why his movies are so important to the comic industry." Kevin Smith wasn't the only movie industry veteran that Quesada and Palmiotti reached out to. Directors Richard Rodriguez, John Singleton and Quentin Tarantino all expressed interest in writing for Marvel Knights but only Smith made it past the talking stage. Quesada and Palmiotti used their deep experience in advertising to launch a strong push for Smith's *Daredevil* outside the comics press. The editors hyped the book at music festivals, appeared on MTV and even included their faces in advertising as a way of attracting new readers. The publicity effort paid off (Brady 41).

Smith had never written comics before, but he delivered a script with a tantalizing hook: what if Daredevil was asked to protect a seemingly innocent baby from evil, but the baby itself might be evil? Smith incorporated guest appearances by Doctor Strange, the Black Widow and Spider-Man as Daredevil attempted to understand the truth about the infant. The struggle had lasting consequences as his longtime girlfriend Karen Page is killed by Bullseye with Daredevil's own billy club. The secret mastermind of the story turns out to be longtime Spider-Man nemesis Mysterio who is fighting off the end stages of cancer and wants to bring down one of New York's greatest heroes with him. The story reads like a print version of a big-budget action movie. Frequent and casual readers alike were intrigued by both the mystery Smith created and his unique take on iconic characters. Though Smith felt "comics are the hardest thing I've ever written," his *Daredevil* was well received (St. Lawrence 32). In fact, it was a bestseller, selling out on its first day of release despite an extra 10,000 copies sent to shops. A 1999 trade paperback collection of Smith's run sold good numbers as well. In 1998, Smith also scripted the adventures of his cult favorite *Jay and Silent Bob* in a four-part mini-series published by Oni Press. The black-and-white series sold decently but nowhere near the heights of *Daredevil*.

The other three Marvel Knights titles also took unique approaches to their material. *Inhumans* explored the question of how to exist in a Utopian society that could be doomed by its own flaws. Many reviewers admired Jenkins's deft characterization and relentless plot while Jae Lee received praise for his precise and angular artwork that had a photo-realistic feel. *Black Panther* set the African Avenger in Brooklyn as a millionaire hero with a pair of fierce female warrior aides (the Dora Milaje), dragged into a complicated plot which begins with Mephisto, a rebellion in Wakanda and a comical U.S. State Department liaison named Everett K. Ross. Priest and his artists present a dizzying and intriguing epic that eventually opens up to an outright war between Wakanda and the U.S. Though *Panther* didn't attract the same hype as *Daredevil* when first published, at least one reviewer called Priest's *Black Panther* run "one of the great comic-book writing stretches" (Riesman). The final Marvel Knights title, *Punisher*, sets Frank Castle as an avenging angel battling demons who want to destroy innocent lives. Reaction to this series was mixed with many fans objecting to the grafting of supernatural elements onto Marvel's most famous vigilante protagonist.

Sales on the Marvel Knights titles were solid, an impressive achievement considering they starred second-string super-heroes. *Daredevil* was a top 20 hit under Kevin Smith, while *Inhumans* landed between 30th and 40th place each month. *Black Panther* averaged around 40th place, and *Punisher* placed 50th in the charts. As Quesada said, "We knew we had flash. But it's been a surprise beyond expectations" (McLaughlin, "Boogie Knights" 24). While Smith's presence helped the line get attention outside the standard comic-reading audience, readers stayed for the unique stories with the flashy artwork. Quesada thus had good reason to stand by his loud boast that "We wanted to show Marvel that we could do their characters better. It's an arrogant thing, but it was our goal, to do the best we can and show them how it could be done" (Howe 393).

A different Marvel outreach resulted in a separate set of outside creators producing a unique four-issue weekly mini-series. Chaos! Comics president Brian Pulido and

his stable of creators, including writer Marc Andreyko and artist Ivan Reis, created *The Supernaturals*. The series imagines a world where all the super-heroes disappeared thirteen years earlier. Now, around Halloween, the same incidents that resulted in the murders of Marvel's icons are happening again, and only the team of supernatural heroes that includes Ghost Rider, Brother Voodoo, Black Cat, Satana and Gargoyle are able to stop them. Pulido and his team delivered modern redesigns for many of the supernatural heroes, and each issue included a free cardboard mask, appropriate for a series released around Halloween. The series finished with sales of around 28,000 copies per issue and marked the only book Pulido packaged for Marvel.

Traditional Heroes in Traditional Styles

While Marvel Knights debuted with a style that appealed to older readers, a proposed **Marvel Kids** imprint never came to fruition. Helmed by longtime publishing industry veteran Jackie Carter, the "Interactive Adventure Series for Beginning Readers" would have consisted of 32-page saddle-stitched comic formatted stories with a retail price of $3.49 each, all mainly sold through traditional book stores. Before taking on the Interactive Adventure Series, Carter worked as an editor at Scholastic Books, where she specialized in books for young readers. As she said, "One of the goals of the [Marvel Kids] program is to put books in a comics format back in the hands of kids 5 to 8. Comics are still out there, but young people are unable to read them. These books are written for beginning readers" (Thompson 42). Titles would

Marvel house ad for Spider-Girl *and* J2, *two key titles in the MC2 line.*
TM and © Marvel Characters, Inc.

248

have included *Fantastic Four Franklin's Adventures*, *X-Men Mutant Search R.U. 1*, *Hulk Project H.I.D.E.* and *Spider-Man Mysteries*. The only aspect of this line to see print was an August 1998 Happy Meal promotion at McDonald's. Marvel Kids never appeared because Carter was laid off when Toy Biz management took over.

Marvel also planned a small set of science-fiction-focused comics but only one ever saw print. Writers Dan Abnett and Ian Edginton and artist Andrew Currie delivered the four-issue *Seeker 3000* which revived the one-shot concept from *Marvel Premiere* #41 (April 1978). Revivals of the Guardians of the Galaxy, Killraven, and Micronauts were also announced and promoted but never reached shops. The new *Micronauts* was to be written by Shon C. Bury and illustrated by Cary Nord. As Bury describes, *Micronauts* would have depicted universe-shaking events: "There is a big war going on, the fate of the Microverse hangs in the balance and Homeworld is under attack. Baron Karza will also be back. Basically, what's going on is that there's a threat so ominous that the threat of Karza pales in comparison" (Cairns 10). Bury and Nord completed three never-published issues. Furthermore, the Micronauts were scheduled to star in a cartoon on Sci-Fi Network, but rights concerns on the toy-based heroes prevented any plans from moving ahead.

Although Marvel ultimately abandoned those two projects, a completely different imprint got launched nearly by happenstance. It began in *What If?* #105 (Feb. 1998) with the introduction of **Spider-Girl**. Written by Tom DeFalco with art by Ron Frenz and Bill Sienkiewicz, the issue starred May "Mayday" Parker, daughter of Peter Parker and Mary Jane Watson. Mayday is not only the star of her high school basketball team but extremely smart as well. One day, Mayday discovers she's inherited her father's powers and when Normie Osborn, grandson of the first Norman Osborn, attacks Peter Parker, Mayday dons a costume similar to her dad's and saves his life.

The *What If* tale was intended to be a clever one-shot. Unexpectedly, the issue sold out its 29,000-copy run on the day of its release. The next time DeFalco met with his editor, they agreed an ongoing *Spider-Girl* title needed to be put on Marvel's schedule, but that idea soon mushroomed into a set of unified series that all took place in the near future

Gifted with psychic claws, Wild Thing was the daughter of Wolverine and Elektra. TM and © Marvel Characters, Inc.

of an alternative version of the Marvel Universe. Thus was born "Marvel Comics 2," better known by its abbreviation of "**MC2**."

Debuting in August (cover date October 1998), MC2 had three inaugural titles, each of them written by DeFalco. Joining *Spider-Girl* (now drawn by Patrick Olliffe) were *A-Next* (drawn by Frenz) and *J2* (drawn by Ron Lim). As DeFalco said of the imprint, "I'd love to say there's a master plan here, but there's not. We've got heroes' kids, villains' kids... we're just here to have a good time" (Brick 75). To that end, *J2* delivers a slapstick tale about a hero determined to restore his father's reputation. Wimpy Zane Yama, the son of X-Men nemesis Juggernaut, discovers he can transform into a super-strong fighter for short periods of time. *A-Next*, on the other hand, presents the next generation of Avengers, which includes not only J2 but also new versions of familiar heroes like Speedball, Jubilee and Thunderstrike. The team is led by Mainframe, an armored powerhouse who keeps secret the fact that he is actually an android created by Tony Stark.

DeFalco originally planned each series to conclude with its twelfth issue. In early 1999, Marvel gave fans the opportunity to determine which books would become the next wave of MC2 titles. Ballots appeared not only in print (in the seventh issue of *A-Next*, *J2* and *Spider-Girl*) but also online at the rec.arts.comics.marvel. universe Usenet discussion group. As a result of the fan vote, the first issues of *Wild Thing* (written by Larry Hama, drawn by Ron Lim and starring the daughter of Wolverine and Elektra) and *Fantastic Five* (written by Tom DeFalco and drawn by Paul Ryan) arrived in stores in August 1999, one month after the release of the final issues of *A-Next* and *J2*.

Spider-Girl was also slated to end after its twelfth issue but the fan devotion to the title kept *Spider-Girl* in Marvel's lineup for over a decade.

Spider-Man's New Chapter

After the Clone Saga finally wrapped up in 1996, **Spider-Man**'s adventures seemed a bit adrift. Peter and Mary Jane attended Empire State University and Norman Osborn returned from the dead with little logical explanation. The sense of disconnection reached its apex with 1998's "Identity Crisis" crossover. When Norman Osborn frames Spider-Man for murder and puts a million-dollar bounty for his apprehension, Peter Parker finds himself besieged by bounty hunters willing to do anything they can to earn the money. Fearing he's endangering the people he's trying to save, Peter concludes his best solution is to assume four new super-heroic identities. In the May cover-dated issues of *Amazing Spider-Man*, *Sensational Spider-Man*, *Spectacular Spider-Man* and *Spider-Man*, Peter respectively appears as the disc-throwing Ricochet, the high-flying armored Hornet, the super-strong Prodigy and the ninja-like Dusk. Peter believes that with these identities, he can infiltrate the criminal underworld. In the end, he triumphs and has the bounty removed from his head. "Identity Crisis" led to a temporary ten percent sales boost in the participating titles as curious readers checked out the latest changes to the Spider-Man's status quo.

(Right) Original art to John Byrne's cover for the first issue of Spider-Man: Chapter One. TM and © Marvel Characters, Inc.

However, that bump in interest didn't last long and sales declined once again. Spider-Man line editor Ralph Macchio decided to return the hero to the ideas that made the web-slinger popular in the first place. He turned to someone who had already distinguished himself for rebooting super-heroes: writer/artist **John Byrne**. In the thirteen-part **Spider-Man: Chapter One** Byrne set about retelling classic Stan Lee/Steve Ditko stories. As Byrne elaborated, "*Chapter One* conceived as a kind of 'What If?' project -- what if Stan and Steve, like so many more recent writers, had planned out the first year of *Amazing Spider-Man* in detail, instead of making up each story pretty much on the fly? One of the first things I thought would reflect this would be to combine elements where possible. The Chameleon working for Doctor Doom, for instance. Or Spider-Man and Doctor Octopus being 'born' in the same accident" (Byrne). In the course of the series, the appearances and origins of many of Spider-Man's most iconic villains got revised. For instance, Doctor Octopus acquired cybernetic legs. Byrne also made the controversial decision to insert modern references into stories first published in the 1960s. In one issue, Peter receives an Apple Macintosh as a birthday gift from Aunt May and Uncle Ben, and another issue mentions 1990s icons Stephen Hawking and Bill Gates. Byrne claimed sales on *Chapter One* warranted a *Chapter Two*, but he didn't want to risk acquiring a reputation as "a transcriber for Stan Lee."

Elsewhere, after a twelve-year run writing *The Incredible Hulk*, **Peter David** left the title with issue #467 (Aug. 1998). Citing irreconcilable differences with his editors, David chose to leave the series synonymous with his name: "I was told that I'd be required to come up with Hulk-centric plots that would have ramifications throughout the Marvel Universe. I don't like originating those. I feel guilty if I screw with other writers' plans for their own titles" (McLaughlin 26). David later clarified that he was pushed off the series because his editors wanted higher sales: "The powers that be, bottom line, weren't satisfied with the sales on the title. They felt it should be pulling the same numbers as *Avengers*, *Iron Man*, et al: titles that had been relaunched with new creative teams and much hoopla" (David 62). In fact, *Incredible Hulk* frequently finished among the top twenty-five bestselling comic books with average monthly sales of around 65,000 copies. David left his signature title with a final tale that allowed him a graceful goodbye. Ten years in the future, a Hulk-like character speaks with a writer (shown in the shadows) about events in the past that represent storylines David planned for future issues. Joe Casey assumed writing chores on the title but for a short-lived run. Seven issues after David's departure, *The Incredible Hulk* was discontinued with issue #474 (March 1999) to make way for a notable relaunch.

The what known as Sabretooth?!

In one of the odder events of 1998 an issue of *Wolverine* inadvertently contained an anti-Semitic slur. It happened when editor Mark Powers was searching for a new writer to take over the title. As a stopgap, Todd DeZago was assigned to write some fill-in issues, starting with *Wolverine* #129 (Oct. 1998). DeZago plotted three issues and scripted two of them, but once he saw all the changes Powers made to *Wolverine* #130, he refused to script the final issue he had plotted. Consequently, Powers had to find someone else to finish *Wolverine* #131 and fast because the issue was already running behind schedule. Enter **Brian K. Vaughan**, a 22-year-old college student who distinguished himself in New York University's "Stan-hattan Project," a class sponsored by Marvel Comics for fledgling comic book writers. Once Vaughan finished the script, Powers revised some of his dialogue, including a line that read "the assassin known as Sabretooth." Powers crossed out "assassin" and wrote "killer" and then faxed the edited script pages to Richard Starkings' Comicraft lettering studio. Evidently, the fax transmission garbled Powers's handwritten marks because after lettering, the dialogue now read, "the *kike* known as Sabretooth." Since the issue was so late, Powers didn't have the time to proofread Comicraft's work, so the anti-Semitic remark ended up getting printed. Once the issue arrived in stores, Marvel learned what happened and recalled all copies in order to replace them with corrected ones some weeks later. (Ironically, *Wolverine* #131 was scheduled to be released on the Jewish holy day of Yom Kippur.) Of course, some retailers kept the "racial slur misprint" as a unique rarity, but DeZago regrets the event for a different reason: "The saddest part of this whole incident is that many people told me that they didn't even know what the word meant—we may have inadvertently re-introduced a hateful word back into a culture that had forgotten it." (Cronin)

Another "Stan-hattan Project" participant, **Ben Raab**, wrote the three-issue mini-series *Union Jack* (first issue cover-dated Dec. 1998) where the eponymous hero battles vampires in England. The real star of the series, though, may have been artist **John Cassaday** whose work was beginning to attract significant attention. As one *Union Jack* review stated, "All praise is due to John Cassaday, whose art is simply superb" (Nelson 64). Cassaday would become attached to one of the most important new series of 1999.

Sunfire & Big Hero 6 *hovered under the radar of many Marvel fans.*
TM and © Marvel Characters, Inc.

The three-issue *Sunfire & Big Hero 6* by Scott Lobdell, Gus Vasquez and Bud LaRosa introduced readers to Japan's very own super-group, **Big Hero Six**. Led by genius teen inventor Hiro Takachiho, the team includes his robotic bodyguard Baymax, a cancer-ravaged Sunfire, the Silver Samurai, GoGo Tomago (whose rage creates fire) and Honey Lemon (whose purse allows her to retrieve objects from another dimension). Together, they must save Tokyo against the threats of the villainous Everwraith. This slapstick team was originally intended to be foils for Alpha Flight, but scheduling snafus abandoned that plan. A significantly altered version of the concept became a Disney animated motion picture that arrived in movie theaters in 2014.

Marvel followed up its 1996 *Star Trek/X-Men* crossover with an appropriate sequel: *Star Trek: The Next Generation/X-Men: Second Contact*. Written by Dan Abnett and Ian Edginton and drawn by Cary Nord and Scott Koblish, the sixty-four page graphic novel has Captain Picard and his crew teaming up with Marvel's mutants to battle the Borg. Oddly, the comic book only told the first half of the entire story. The second half was presented in the prose novel *Planet X* by Michael Jan Friedman. *Second Contact* was one of the final *Star Trek* comics produced by Marvel. Effective with the July 1998 cover-dated issues, the starship Enterprise was grounded.

The First Mighty Marvel Movie

For years, Marvel seemed cursed in its inability to sell its properties to Hollywood film studios. Even when success looked imminent, a monkey wrench always got thrown into the works. For proof, look no further than filmmaker James Cameron. The director/producer of the record breaking *Titanic* had a contract to bring Spider-Man to the big screen, but on December 17, 1997, Cameron appeared on Howard Stern's radio show to explain that while he had both completed a script and spoken to rising star Leonardo DiCaprio to play the iconic web-slinger, production couldn't move forward due to legal issues that arose from the bankruptcies of several film studios. MGM, Viacom Pictures, Sony Pictures and Twentieth Century Fox all claimed they owned the exclusive rights to distribute a Spider-Man movie. It would take a few years before this matter untangled itself and by that point, a different director would be attached to the project.

Marvel's own bankruptcies woes contributed to the cancellation of a Captain America cartoon that would have aired on FOX Kids. As written by Steve Englehart, the series would have been set during World War II, but FOX's

Standards and Practices department stipulated that Cap couldn't kill anyone. That might have made sense for a show targeting children. More head-scratching, however, was FOX's decision to forbid the display of swastikas on Nazi uniforms. Regardless, producer Will Meuginot claimed the creators "decided we would approach [the cartoon] more like it was 'Indiana Jones,' a period adventure, big stakes, one man against the world" (Allstetter 8). Ultimately, production of the series was halted due to Marvel's Chapter 11 status, which also caused the cancellation of a second season of FOX Kids' *Silver Surfer* cartoon.

As far as Hollywood success was concerned, Marvel couldn't win for losing. The best that seemingly could be done was *Nick Fury: Agent of S.H.I.E.L.D.*, a schlocky made-for-television special that aired on FOX on May 26, 1998. As portrayed by *Baywatch* hunk David Hasselhoff, Nick Fury comes out of retirement to stop the terrorist organization Hydra from releasing a deadly virus into Manhattan. At the end of the special, former Hydra leader Baron Von Strucker is brought back to life, but if any viewers were intrigued about the evil machinations he had in store for

the world, they were left wanting as no sequel was ever made.

Just as Marvel's Hollywood futility seemed to have no end in sight, the unexpected happened. At the very end of an extraordinarily busy summer movie season a film was released to theaters featuring a minor Marvel Comics character: *Blade*. Action movie veteran Wesley Snipes stars as the African-American vampire who faces off against the evil Deacon Frost, played by Stephen Dorff, in an attempt to prevent Frost and the Assembly of Vampire Lords from invoking a sinister vampire god. As Snipes described his character, "Blade's a bad guy who's a good guy who's a bad guy who's kind of sort of a good guy... who's really just misunderstood" (Allstetter 122). Snipes—who initially wanted to star in a movie featuring the Black Panther—also was one of the film's producers. Thanks to its choreographed, blood-soaked fight scenes and gun play, *Blade* grossed over $70 million at the box office, an impressive showing considering it was competing against such blockbusters as *Saving Private Ryan*, *Armageddon* and *There's Something About Mary*.

First appearing as Dracula's adversary in *Tomb of Dracula* #10 (July 1973), Blade's relative obscurity as a comic book character perhaps helped during a time when super-hero movies had lost their luster among film audiences. Indeed, even the name "Marvel Comics" was absent from much of *Blade*'s promotional advertising and only received a small mention in the screen credits. The exclusion irked executive producer Avi Arad who complained, "It was an idiotic move – and you can put that in bold letters – not to put the Marvel name on *Blade*. I have a feeling that

someone at Marvel asked that the credit not be put on, and I think that was insane. You know, sometimes you have a hit, sometimes you have a miss, but the fact is, it's still a Marvel property, and we should be proud of it" (Russo 56). The lack of prominent credit didn't stop Hollywood from recognizing the viability of Marvel's properties, and a plethora of Marvel movies was about to receive the coveted Hollywood green light.

As *Blade* was released to theaters, comic book writer **Marv Wolfman** filed suit against Marvel and production house New Line Cinema. Wolfman believed he and artist Gene Colan deserved creators' credit and royalty for Blade and his supporting cast. While nobody denied that Wolfman and Colan co-created Blade, whether or not they could claim ownership was a thorny legal debate. In an intriguing parallel to Steve Gerber's 1979 suit for ownership of Howard the Duck, Marvel claimed it owned full rights to the characters under the work-for-hire agreement in place when Blade was created. However, Wolfman believed he had ownership because he didn't sign an agreement at the time and over the years, he had challenged Marvel's assertion of ownership whenever the vampire hunter appeared. Ultimately, after a jury trial which frayed emotions and friendships, Wolfman lost his suit.

Hanging from a Cliff

As the year began, **Homage Studios** was thriving, publishing critically acclaimed material, like *Kurt Busiek's Astro City* and *Leave It to Chance*, but **Jim Lee** wanted to expand his roster of titles to include the work of a trio of ultra-popular artists: *Gen13*'s J. Scott Campbell, *Uncanny X-Men*'s Joe Madureira and *Impulse*'s Humberto Ramos. The only question was where to place their creator-owned series. They wouldn't fit within the Wildstorm Universe (i.e. *Stormwatch* and *WildC.A.T.S.*), and as Lee saw it, Homage Studios was "more retro in feel" (Senreich 26). Lee's solution was to create a new Image Comics imprint.

He called it **Cliffhanger**, and **Joe Madureira** didn't need much convincing to jump on board. After drawing *Uncanny X-Men* for the

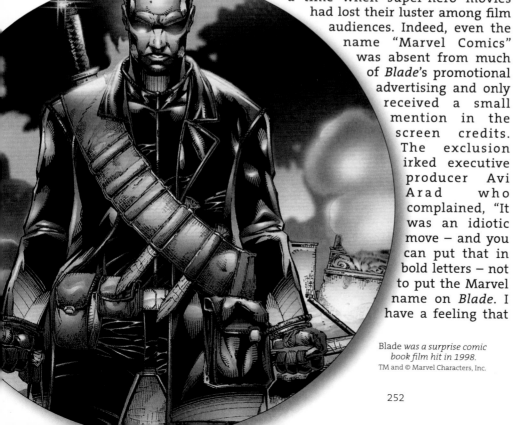

Blade was a surprise comic book film hit in 1998.
TM and © Marvel Characters, Inc.

previous two years, Madureira was anxious for a change, especially since the X-Men series had gotten too dark for him. Madureira quit *Uncanny X-Men* with issue #350 (Dec. 1997) in order to create **Battle Chasers**, a fantasy adventure involving five characters: the warrior woman Red Monika, the swordsman Garrison, the wizard Knolan, the war golem Calibretto and ten-year-old Gully, who inherits magical gloves from her mysteriously missing father. Together, the team has Dungeons & Dragons-style adventures in a strange new world.

J. Scott Campbell stopped working on *Gen13* in order to deliver **Danger Girl**, a non-stop action thriller with shallow but delightful plots. Campbell himself described it as "an amalgam of James Bond, Indiana Jones, but primarily G.I Joe" (Hedges 122). The comic features a trio of spies – Abby Chase, Sydney Savage and Natalia Kassle – who are aided in their missions by a computer whiz named Silicon Valerie. By the second issue, they join forces with charismatic C.I.A. agent Johnny Barracuda to retrieve a powerful mystical artifact that seems destined to be used for world domination.

Humberto Ramos provided **Crimson**, which put a modern spin on vampires by presenting them as pawns in an eons-long war between Lilith, who sides with the devil, and Ekimus, who has the ability to see the future. Ekimus recruits a human named Alex Elder who has the power to defeat Lilith by becoming a vampire himself. Alex attempts to handle his transformation as his girlfriend is murdered and Lilith's followers stalk him. *Crimson* stood out from most vampire comics due to its hip late '90s feel that was accentuated by Ramos's light, manga-flavored art.

All three Cliffhanger titles became immediate smash hits in the Direct Market. Shops ordered 109,000 copies of *Danger Girl* #1, making it the fifth best-selling release of the month. *Battle Chasers* #1 completely sold out its 76,000 copy print run. Sales on the second issue dropped to 64,000 then immediately bounced back up as the series became a hot commodity in the back issue market. Some issues sold for double the cover price within days of their release (Pearson 128).

The only problem with the Cliffhanger titles was that Campbell and Madureira, like some of their Image Comics mentors, couldn't release their work on a regular schedule. A ten-month period yielded only four issues of *Danger Girl*, and while the first three issues of *Battle Chasers* were published on a monthly basis, readers had to wait four months for issue #4 and then five months for issue #5.

Joe Madureira's Battle Chasers *was set in an arcane punk world and had vivid and exciting characters.* TM and © Joe Madureira.

J. Scott Campbell's Danger Girl *was an amalgam of James Bond, Indiana Jones and G.I. Joe.* TM and © J. Scott Campbell Ltd.

One other popular artist almost joined Cliffhanger, *Witchblade*'s **Michael Turner**, who created a concept that would become the most iconic work of his career: *Fathom*. It starred a young girl named Aspen Matthews who was found washed up on a beach as a child with no memory of her past. She grows up to become a marine biologist for Deep Marine Discovery, researching a mysterious underwater race. As she soon discovers, Aspen is actually a member of that race, with the ability to mold shapes and create objects out of water. *Fathom*'s aquatic premise was no accident. Turner had a deep love for the ocean. He was an avid scuba diver, water skier and boater who was frequently happier on the waves than on dry land. He brought his love for the waters to his illustrations.

Rather than take *Fathom* to Jim Lee's Cliffhanger imprint, Turner instead decided to remain with the Image founder who helped him break into the comic book industry, Marc Silvestri. As a Top Cow Production release, *Fathom* #1 (Aug. 1998) sold an astonishing 257,000 copies, boosted by three different versions of the comic with alternate interiors. Those versions made *Fathom* #1 the bestselling release of the year. However, many readers were frustrated they had to buy multiple copies to read the whole story. As a store in Edmonds, WA, reported, "I'm getting major feedback from

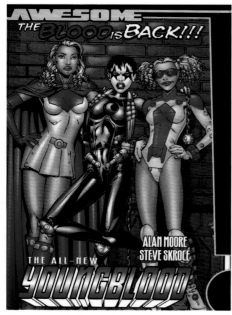

customers on the *Fathom* #1 variants. Nobody is pleased that they feel they have to buy three issues of #1 to read the whole thing. At least with the regular variants, you can choose which cover you want, but this is going too far" (Meredith 42). Nonetheless, successive issues of Turner's aquatic adventure consistently placed among the top fifteen bestselling comic books for the months they were released for the remainder of the decade ("The Buzz Bin" 26).

Over in the Wildstorm Universe, editor Scott Dunbier conceived a unique Image Comics/Dark Horse Comics crossover that would have lasting repercussions. Written by Warren Ellis and drawn by Chris Sprouse and Kevin Nowlan, *WildC.A.T.S/ Aliens* #1 (Aug. 1998) sets up a bloody confrontation between Jim Lee's cast of super-heroes and the deadly creatures from the Sigourney Weaver films. During the course of their battle on Stormwatch's orbiting satellite, the WildC.A.T.S. discover that the aliens have slain most of the Stormwatch team, including members Fahrenheit, Fuji and Hellstrike. As Dunbier explained, he wanted to use the crossover to kill off the remaining Stormwatch characters that wouldn't be used for a new Wildstorm comic book that would debut in 1999 (Dunbier). Though *WildC.A.T.S/Aliens* was planned to be the first of several crossovers between Wildstorm and Dark Horse, this was the only one that appeared.

With Cliffhanger, Homage and Wildstorm, Jim Lee had a very successful year, and as 1999 would prove, the best was yet to come. The same couldn't be said for **Rob Liefeld**. Early in the year, Liefeld's **Awesome Comics** seemed to be gaining momentum after 1997's *Judgment Day* event. Alan Moore was happily writing *Youngblood* and *Supreme*, with art by Steve Skroce and Rick Veitch, among others, and other series, like Jeph Loeb and Jeff Matsuda's *Kaboom*, a new *Fighting American*

Fans dove deep with their love for Michael Turner's Fathom. TM and © Aspen MLT, Inc.

mini, and Moore's new take on *Glory*, were being prepared for 1998 debuts. Liefeld gained a reputation for paying some of the best rates in the industry, but his gains proved to be short-lived. Awesome's expansion was fueled by an investment from Crossroads Communications, a venture capital entertainment financing firm, and in 1998, Crossroads decided to pull all its financing from Liefeld's unprofitable titles. That meant that creators like Moore, Skroce, Matsuda, Alex Ross, Jim Starlin and Brandon Peterson had their series cancelled. Skroce's comments summed up many creators' opinions of the situation: "I worked with Alan Moore for two issues and it was terrific. I never felt so fulfilled as an artist. But I'm not independently wealthy. I've got to move on" (McLaughlin, "Awesome" 24). Only three titles remained, all of which were cancelled before the end of the year. Hollywood actress Jada Pinkett Smith wrote *Menace*, with art by Dan Fraga, about a woman caught up in a world of drugs and violence who becomes transformed into a mighty warrior in a battle between Heaven and Hell. Only one issue of *Menace* appeared, which was used to shop the idea around to movie studios.

Moore's ideas for *Supreme*, *Youngblood*, *Glory* and other characters became the inspirations and lynchpins for a new line of comics that would debut in 1999. Those new heroes would both embrace the past and show a clear vision of the future.

Superman Red and Blue Reunite

It was a weird year for **Superman**. It began with pre-production well underway on a new Superman feature film with *Batman* director Tim Burton at the helm and Nicolas Cage set to star as the Man of Steel. With a screenplay written by Kevin Smith, **Superman Lives** would have greatly evoked the "Death of Superman" comic book arc from 1992. The movie opens with Superman being killed by Doomsday only to be later resurrected to defeat the villainous team of Brainiac and Lex Luthor. But in April 1998, just as filming was set to begin in Pittsburgh, Warner Bros. executives grew so concerned about the movie's astronomical budget (projected to be in excess of $190 million), they put production on hold. As a result, Burton opted to direct a different film (*Sleepy Hollow*). Months passed by, and while various proposals to reduce the cost of the movie were presented to Warner executives, none of them gained traction. Eventually, even Cage abandoned the project, and the whole process had to be started over.

Back at **DC Comics**, the Superman creative team doubled down on their controversial decision to turn DC's flagship character into "Superman Blue," a hero composed of pure energy. In 1998, he also became "Superman Red." It happened in the 64-page one-shot ***Superman Red/Superman Blue*** (Feb. 1998), courtesy of writers Dan Jurgens, Stuart Immonen, Karl Kesel and Louise Simonson and artists Jon Bogdanove, Ron Frenz, Tom Grummett and Paul Ryan. In the story the Cyborg Superman and Toyman capture Superman Blue and disperse his energy across the cosmos. To pull his consciousness back together, Superman splits himself into two separate beings: one blue and one red. Technically, the concept was not new. *Superman* #162 (July 1963) presents an "imaginary story" in which Superman has split himself to be the protector of two worlds: Superman Blue for Earth and Superman Red for Krypton. For four months in 1998, however, Superman Blue and Red despise each other because each believes he is the one, true Superman. Their attitudes correspond to their colors: Superman Red is prone to bursts of anger while Blue is more placid. The so-called "Electric Blue Superman" saga finally concluded in the deluxe 84-page, $5.95 one-shot *Superman Forever* (June 1998), released for the 60th anniversary of Superman's first appearance. As the story begins, Superman crashes onto the Kent family farm after purging himself of his energy powers in order to stop the destruction of Earth. Back in the flesh, naked and renewed, Clark once again dons his iconic costume and, with the help of Supergirl, Superboy and Steel, stops a crashing airplane using his traditional powers. Though Superman was back in his old costume, many readers voiced their displeasure with the Superman Blue story arc. Editor Mike Carlin felt annoyed by that anger: "Why so many people were mad about this costume change I'll never know. One — we've done worse things to Superman; two — it was fairly obvious where we were going with it" (O'Neill 31). Alex Ross painted the *Superman Forever*'s lenticular cover which showed an animation of Clark Kent changing into Superman and then flying away. The special concluded with a teaser about a new story that celebrated the long history of the Man of Steel, a decisive nod to disgruntled fans who wanted a return to the status quo.

The history of Superman was also a key aspect of a much-loved 1998 four-issue prestige format series. After achieving massive sales and fan acclaim for their work with Batman, Jeph Loeb and Tim Sale turned their attention to the Man of Steel. *Superman: For All Seasons* explored Clark Kent's small-town roots with each issue set in a different season of the year. Appropriately, Loeb and Sale used the Kent family farm and his all-American hometown of Smallville, Kansas, as the foundation for Superman's personality and attitude to the world. When "country mouse" Kent moves to big city Metropolis, he gains new experiences, but at heart, he is a small-town boy. After the intricately-plotted *Batman: The Long Halloween*, the mythical-feeling *For All Seasons* intrigued fans for its unique approach, especially those who missed the traditional Superman costume. A panel of four *Comics Buyer's Guide* reviewers gave the first issue an A+, praising the book for its intriguing characterization and lovely painted art.

Alex Ross was at the top of the comics industry in 1998. After the accolades he received for *Marvels* and *Kingdom Come*, he could work on any project he wanted. In November, Ross released his latest opus, this time a collaboration with Paul

The tension was electric between Superman Blue and Superman Red.
TM and © DC Comics.

Dini.

Superman: Peace on Earth was an oversized, 64-page tabloid in which Superman fights the most evil menace imaginable. The villain wasn't Brainiac or Lex Luthor but the worldwide plight of human hunger. Inspired by lessons from his father and a compulsion to make a difference, the Man of Steel decides he should lead an effort to donate America's tons of surplus grain to impoverished countries around the world. Many nations willingly accept the gift. Others refuse it. One despot uses hunger to oppress his people. In other countries, the people are too scared to take the gift. In the end, Superman is chastened, reminded that even a man of his nearly boundless powers has his limits. He learns mankind must learn to be generous with each other to truly solve the problem of world hunger. The oversized $9.95 special sold a surprising 80,000 copies. A companion volume starring Batman arrived in stores in 1999.

While Superman tried tackling the world's problems, a tragedy brought many difficulties to **Batman**. In *Shadow of the Bat* #73 (April 1998), an earthquake measuring 7.6 on the Richter scale centers on Wayne Manor, destroying both it and the Batcave. Batman must swim blindly through an underground river to escape his family home, and when he finally emerges in Gotham Harbor, he discovers the unimaginable: the earthquake has completely levelled Gotham City. Thus begins the 16-part **"Cataclysm"** crossover, and as the saga unfolds, the writers and artists of *Batman, Shadow of the Bat, Detective Comics, Catwoman, Robin, Azrael, Nightwing* and three one-shot specials show how the Batman family of heroes ally themselves with first

responders to deal with the crisis and save ordinary people from the terrible calamity. But even with Oracle at the center of the crisis management team, many of the heroes' efforts are in vain. As "Cataclysm" moves into its sequel crossover "Aftershocks," the heroes learn to deal with their failures and the fact that no super-villain is responsible for the catastrophe (despite a blackmail threat by The Ventriloquist, who tries to extort $100 million from Gotham by masquerading as The Quakemaster). Appearances by Poison Ivy, Killer Croc and the Joker are mere sideshows for the deep despair that hits Gotham in the wake of the disaster. With the city dealing with the daunting complexity of recovery, citizens find themselves facing trials few humans can long endure. Gotham has no electricity or fresh water. All businesses and schools are closed. Rats and wild dogs overrun the city while violence soars. No surprise, then, that millions of Gothamites choose to flee their homes and become refugees. However, even their simple decision to abandon their shattered city has tragic consequences, as massive amounts of foot traffic causes one of Gotham's bridges to collapse in *Batman* #559 (Oct. 1998), appropriately titled "Dead City." Gotham City quickly becomes

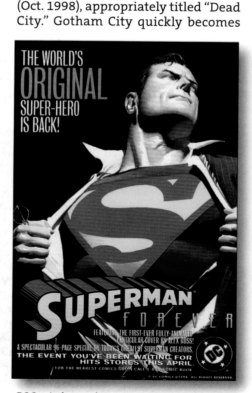

DC Comics house ad promoting the return of the Man of Steel to his traditional red and blue tights in Superman Forever. TM and © DC Comics.

a no man's land. As Bruce Wayne goes to Washington at the end of the year to seek money from Congress to rebuild the city, he faces bipartisan opposition with polls showing that 82% of Americans don't want to spend the trillion dollars necessary to rebuild Gotham (70% even favor another earthquake). Decisions made at the end of Wayne's Washington trip would set up a memorable Batman crossover in 1999.

The idea for "Cataclysm" came from freelance writer/artist Chris Reynaud who read an article in *New York* Magazine which described the unbelievable devastation an earthquake would bring to New York: "It was a very frightening article. They made a lot of references to Kyoto, Japan, and the devastating effects the quake had on the city. New York had, in a lot of ways, been built on the premise that there won't ever be an earthquake here."

With every month the changes to Gotham seemed more and more permanent. As Associate Editor Darren Vincenzo declared, "With 'Cataclysm', we *can't* return to the status quo. A story like this will have repercussions for months and years to come" (Lang 32). *Shadow of the Bat* writer Alan Grant felt he was delivering a major change: "It was a bit of a shock, the Batcave being established for such a long time, to make it come crashing down. I believe the other writers felt the same way I did — that we were smashing an icon" (Lang 30-1). Sales were excellent for the crossover with one retailer in Milford, Connecticut reporting, "Cataclysm doubled sales on Bat-books" (Toth 32).

Justice League Expansion

DC's most popular ongoing series of 1998 continued to be **Grant Morrison**'s hyperkinetic *JLA*. Morrison upped the ante with the time-spanning "Rock of Ages" story arc which enlisted several new super-heroes, such as Steel, Oracle, Huntress and New Gods Orion and Big Barda, to the Justice League while exploring fascinating and unique corners of the DC Universe. When fans clamored for more Justice League action, DC released several spin-off series. The twelve-part *JLA: Year One* was the first to appear. Writers Mark Waid and Brian Augustyn and artist Barry Kitson recounted how the original members of the Justice League joined together for the first time. Uniting the post-*Crisis* version of the Justice League, including Martian Manhunter, The Flash, Green Lantern, Aquaman and Black Canary, *Year One* filled in a crucial hole in DC continuity while also remaining faithful to the Justice League's 1960s roots. Set ten years prior to the events of *JLA* #1, the creators included emblematic details which got to the heart of the characters. For instance, they showed Aquaman having trouble adjusting to living on dry land, the Flash in a leadership role, and a villain who was a smart fit for traditional JLA mythos. In addition, *Year One* was significant for the fact that Superman, Batman and Wonder Woman don't join the team even while other 1960s-era DC notables like the Blackhawks, the Challengers of the Unknown and Green Arrow make guest-star appearances. Kitson's expressive artwork added an essential sense of whimsy.

The other Justice League spinoff DC launched was Alan Davis's *JLA: The Nail*, an Elseworlds tale that postulates the consequence to the DC Universe if Jonathan and Martha Kent never found the baby Kal-El as a result of a nail causing the Kent's truck tire to go flat. Many of DC's heroes still exist, but the absence of Superman causes them to be just slightly different from the heroes DC readers are familiar with. These heroes are more feared than loved, and a bald madman named Lex Luthor serves as mayor of Metropolis. First proposed by Davis in 1993 as a one-shot, the story wasn't picked up by DC at the time because the Justice League wasn't popular. With the success of Grant Morrison's *JLA*, however, Davis's pet project was given the green light. Davis proposed *The Nail* as a 64-page one-shot but editor KC Carlson wanted a 12-issue story. The two sides compromised. In the end *The Nail* was told in three 48-page chapters, which Davis enjoyed filling with ideas which fulfilled his goals "to tell a simple, accessible story where you don't have to be a rocket scientist or DC historian to understand what's happening" (Shutt 46).

Other JLA-related comic books released in 1998 included *JLA Secret Files* and *JLA 80 Page Giant*, which told backstories of some of the JLA heroes; *JLA: Paradise Lost* by Morrison protégé Mark Millar and artist Ariel Olivetti, which starred new JLA member Zauriel; *JLA: World Without Grown-ups* by Todd Dezago and Humberto Ramos, a slapstick two-parter that set Impulse, Robin and Superboy as the only heroes on a planet from which all adults have been sent to a parallel universe; and *JLA/Titans* by Devin Grayson and Phil Jimenez, which reunited the two super groups.

DC Comics house ad promoting the next Batman crossover event, "Cataclysm." TM and © DC Comics.

One of the Justice League's oldest and most enigmatic heroes received his own title in 1998. Writer John Ostrander and artist Tom Mandrake, the team behind the supernatural *Spectre*, delivered *Martian Manhunter* (first issue cover-dated Oct. 1998), which gave readers a chance to understand who the Manhunter really is, including the reason he's considered a great hero in Australia and why he acts as a liaison for aliens migrating to Earth. As such, Martian Manhunter works as one of Earth's first lines of defense against alien invasion. The series played up Manhunter's shape-shifting abilities, placing him in the body of a Denver detective, a Japanese salaryman and a super-villain (and that's only in the first three issues). Ostrander and Mandrake brought a dark and mysterious approach to the Manhunter's adventures, presenting a brooding hero who saves the Earth without most humans having an idea he even exists.

One Million Months in the Future

Grant Morrison was responsible for DC's biggest event of the year, the four-issue weekly mini-series that crossed over into every DC Universe title: **DC One Million**. Drawn by Val Semeiks and Prentis Rollins, the first, double-sized issue (cover date November 1998) shows the modern day Justice League being visited by Justice Legion A, their doppelgängers from the 853rd century (i.e. one million months in the future). The future JLA's membership includes a strange new incarnation of Hourman, an android who carries the DNA of Rex Tyler, the Golden Age Hourman. The modern day Justice League are invited to travel to the future to celebrate the return of "The Prime Superman" who has spent the last one hundred centuries in the core of the sun. Justice Legion A vows to safeguard the 20th century during the JLA's absence. Immediately after the modern heroes have been spirited away, however, Hourman unwittingly unleashes a techno-virus that could infect everyone on Earth. Meanwhile, in the future a malevolent artificial sun named Solaris threatens to end the "Superman dynasty forever." As the end of the first issue reveals, the villain operating in both time periods is the immortal tyrant Vandal Savage. After two long and furious battles, both bands of heroes defeat their adversaries, and the futuristic ceremony proceeds as planned. In a moving ending, Superman (turned gold by the sun) is reunited with Lois Lane (turned silver) along with doppelgängers of Jor-El and Lara.

The same month that the *DC One Million* mini-series was released, nearly three dozen DC comics flashed forward to the 853rd century and celebrated their millionth issues. Some, like *Martian Manhunter*, *Starman* and *JLA*, continued their stories directly from the events of *DC One Million*. Others, such as *Young Heroes in Love* and *Robin*, told side-tales. *Hitman* even satirized the event (as one would expect from a series written by Garth Ennis). *DC One Million* also spun out a 1999 series starring Hourman, written by Tom Peyer and drawn by Rags Morales. After the events of the time-spanning adventure, the android settles in the 20th century where he fights Amazo, meets the original Hourman and joins the JSA.

With the runaway success of *JLA*, DC's younger heroes decided to band together as their own super-team with **Young Justice**. Written by Peter David, with art by Todd Nauck and Lary Stucker, this wildly silly comic presents the adventures of six teenage heroes – Robin, Superboy, Impulse, Wonder Girl, Secret and Arrowette – who join forces to be something like a junior Justice League. Working out of the old Justice League headquarters, with former Justice Leaguer Red Tornado as their mentor, Young Justice fight evil everywhere they find it. David deliberately kept the series light-hearted and full of jokes, befitting a comic starring a group of carefree teens. Far from the angst-filled world of the X-Men and their allies, *Young Justice* encounters villains like the Mighty Endowed, who can't stand up because her breasts are too large, the government agents Fite 'n' Maad, a young Mr. Mxyzptlk and the sword-wielding Harm (Motto: "Stay out of Harm's way"). David and Nauck's whimsical approach resonated with many readers as *Young Justice* finished towards the middle of the monthly Top 100 list.

Peter David, by the way, stopped his fan favorite run on *Aquaman* around the same time that he stopped working on *Incredible Hulk* and for really the same reasons: creative differences with his editors. After four fill-in issues by writers Dan Abnett and Andy Lanning, *Aquaman*

THE REVELATION OF A UTOPIAN FUTURE.
a PROMISE OF HEROISM UNTAINTED BY TIME.
a DARK ALLIANCE DETERMINED TO LAY WASTE TO IT ALL.

COMICS YOU NEVER THOUGHT YOU'D LIVE TO SEE!

a MONTH LONG event FEATURING a FOUR-ISSUE MINISERIES BY GRANT MORRISON, VAL SEMEIKS, and PRENTIS ROLLINS.

ON SALE IN SEPTEMBER

DC ONE MILLION

Grant Morrison spearheaded DC One Million, *an event that leaped one million months into the future.* TM and © DC Comics.

received a new ongoing creative team, one that raised the eyebrows of many fans. The person taking over the title was one of Peter David's most vocal critics: *Savage Dragon* creator **Erik Larsen**. Aided by artists Eric Battle and Norm Rapmund, Larsen's *Aquaman* run started with the double-sized issue #50 (Dec. 1998), and it didn't take long for the title's new writer to dismantle Peter David's legacy. For starters, by the issue #51 Aquaman's distinctive harpoon hand became replaced with a golden prosthetic. The series also acquired an overall "campy" tone, which irritated many fans. Larsen later claimed that DC's editors directed him to make *Aquaman* less serious. If the assumption was that a drastic change in tone would result in a boost in sales, the plan backfired. Sales actually plummeted, and Larsen's run on *Aquaman* ended after issue #62 (Dec. 1999).

Wally West Gets Married

After her introduction in *Flash* #28 (July 1989), the romantic relationship between Wally West and Linda Park developed for the better part of a decade. First, the pair became friends while investigating a scam together. By the time Wally freed Linda from her possession by an 800-year-old Irish spirit, the couple were passionately in love. During much of 1997 and 1998, Wally had considered proposing to Linda and finally did so at the end of the "Human Race" story arc, in *Flash* #138. The couple quickly moved on to their wedding, and in *Flash* #142 (Oct. 1998), Wally West and Linda Park finally married. The event was peaceful and happy, with the only real drama coming from Wally's bickering divorced parents. Some of Wally's best friends from the Justice League and Teen Titans attended, and the event was all smiles... until the very end of the issue. In a terrifying dénouement that led to an extended storyline, Wally forgets who Linda is. The villainous Abra Kadabra kidnaps Linda and erases her from history. After a long and terrifying struggle, the couple are reunited in 2000 with their memories intact.

DC's April 1998 skip week event was called "Girlfrenzy!" Each of the seven releases starred a different female lead in a solo story which included a distinctive color design. For *Batgirl*, writer Kelley Puckett and artists Jim Balent and Rick Burchett collaborated on a flashback featuring Barbara Gordon in her pre-Oracle persona. *Birds of Prey: Ravens* by Chuck Dixon, Nelson DeCastro and Drew Geraci saw the allies of the Birds of Prey fight a terrorist. In *Tomorrow Woman*, by Tom Peyer, Yanick Paquette and Mark Lipka, the JLA's robot female member from *JLA* #5 finds her humanity. *The Mist* spun off from *Starman*, with scripting by regular series writer James Robinson and art by John Lucas and Richard Case. *Lois Lane* by Barbara Kesel, Amanda Conner and Jimmy Palmiotti showed the intrepid reporter uncovering a mystery. *Donna Troy* recounted how Wonder Woman's former Wonder Girl found peace within herself in a story written and drawn by Phil Jimenez and inked by John Stokes. *Young Justice: The Secret* by Todd Dezago, Todd Nauck and Lary Stucker had Young Justice members Robin, Superboy and Impulse investigate the evacuation of a small town in upstate New York where they find a young female "secret." Though some of these specials garnered positive reviews, only Birds of Prey eventually received its own ongoing series.

In 1998, DC's Paradox imprint published its most acclaimed graphic novel, **Road to Perdition**. Written by Max Allan Collins and illustrated by John Piers Rayner, *Road to Perdition* takes place in Depression-era America as Michael O'Sullivan, a ruthless but honorable assassin, is betrayed by his employers and forced to flee with his son on a quest for revenge. Collins included echoes of the classic Japanese comic and movie series *Lone Wolf and Cub*. Two sequels were published including the same cast of characters, *On the Road to Perdition* and *Return to Perdition*. The story was adapted for a well-reviewed 2002 film starring Tom Hanks, Paul Newman and Daniel Craig, a project that inspired two further prose novels by Collins: *Road to Purgatory* and *Road to Paradise*.

DC's Vertigo and Paradox imprints continued to survive in a tough market, but the plug was pulled on science-fiction oriented **Helix Press**, which suffered from low sales because of a sense that Helix books were too intellectual for the average comic reader. By the end of the year, only one Helix comic survived the cut: *Transmetropolitan* which steadily increased its readership. *Transmetropolitan* #13 (Sept. 1998) begins the "Year Two" story, which moved the title to DC's Vertigo line. There, along with fellow Vertigo mainstay *Preacher*, Warren Ellis and Darick Robertson's epic of a dystopian future came to symbolize a cheeky sort of subversive approach to character and story fans associated with Vertigo.

Sex Doesn't Sell

Fantagraphics Books, publisher of some of the most prominent art comics of the 1990s, also suffered the impact of decreasing sales, but in its case, the decline had little to do with intellectualism. On May 21, 1998, the Seattle-based publisher announced cutbacks of its own. Five employees were laid off and eight low-selling comics were cancelled, including *Meat Cake*, *Poot* and *Zippy Quarterly*. None of the series sold over 2,000 copies per issue and at least one only sold 1,000 copies, not nearly enough to break even. However, the deeper reason for Fantagraphics' cutback was its declining Eros Comix imprint. That line of pornographic comics, which debuted in 1991, had boosted Fantagraphics' revenues to such a degree that it helped keep the company out of bankruptcy during low financial ebbs. By 1998, the adult material was no longer profitable. Popular pornographic Japanese comics had prohibitively high built-in costs, and publications like *God of Sex* and *New Bondage Fairies* no longer drove sales like they used to because more and more consumers were using the Internet to access porn (Spurgeon 8-9).

Fantagraphics wasn't the only publisher of sexually explicit comics to experience financial troubles. In June, the editorial board at Penthouse magazine decided to cancel *Penthouse Comix* after four years. The anthology, which had included work by such prominent talents as Adam Hughes, Kevin Maguire and Keith Giffen, had begun to see sales pick up but high production values meant the magazine wasn't earning

"Girlfrenzy" presented a series of one-shots starring some of DC's most intriguing female characters.
TM and © DC Comics.

adequate profits at 50,000 copies sold per issue. *Hustler Comix*, which presented highly graphic stories by creators such as Jim Sherman, Gray Morrow and Tom Sutton, among others, also ended in 1998. *Hustler* even crossed over with the adult film industry without much of a rise in sales as the premiere issue featured a comic adventure starring porn star Kristi Myst.

Publishers of other adult comics fared slightly better. London Night, Verotik and new publisher Avatar experienced decent sales with comics that included explicit nudity as well as explicit violence. The November 1998 cover-dated Avatar release *Dreamwalker* #0 was relatively innocuous and featured a notable debut in a four-page backup: Eric Powell's **The Goon**. Powell would spin his anti-hero into his own solo comic in 1999, and the character became much-loved in the 2000s. Boneyard Press, which earlier in the decade released gothic horror comics like *Jeffrey Dahmer vs. Jesus Christ* and *Kill Image*, was another publisher that walked the tightrope between good girl art and horror, teasing readers with comics like *Dead Grrl* ("The Ultimate Party Vampire!!!"). Revisionary Press found success selling series such as *True Stories of Adult Film Stars* at adult bookstores. Small publisher Cabbage Comics attempted to exploit this market in a different way with its *Halle the Hooters Girl*. Seven thousand copies of *Halle* reached comic shops and other outlets before the Hooters restaurant sued the publisher.

The Spirit of Comics Anew

The most star-studded comic of 1998 featured a hero created fifty years earlier. The anthology series **The Spirit: The New Adventures** included work by a roster of the finest creative teams of the 1990s. Among those contributing were Paul Chadwick, John Ostrander and Tom Mandrake, Neil Gaiman and Eddie Campbell, *Watchmen* creators Alan Moore and Dave Gibbons, the classic Judge Dredd team of John Wagner and Carlos Ezquerra and the *Astro City* pairing of Kurt Busiek and Brent Anderson. They all paid tribute to one of the greatest comic book heroes of all time, in stories that reflected the oftentimes experimental nature

ALAN MOORE AND DAVE GIBBONS

WILL EISNER'S
THE SPIRIT
THE NEW ADVENTURES

$3.50
$4.90 CAN

SMASHING 1ST ISSUE!

MOORE AND GIBBONS REUNITE!
•
ALL NEW COLOR SERIES!
•
THREE THRILLING TALES OF THE SPIRIT'S ORIGIN!

The Spirit: The New Adventures had a variety of writers and artists presenting their take on Will Eisner's classic character.
TM and © Will Eisner Studios Inc.

of Will Eisner's work. The eighty-one-year-old legend gave creators a completely clean slate to produce their stories, and many of them rose to the occasion, delivering some of the finest work of their careers. (Alan Moore's contribution to the anthology would inspire a new character who would first appear in 1999.) Readers responded with interest; the first issue finished in 36th place in the sales charts for the month, the most popular release from **Kitchen Sink Press** in quite some time. *The Spirit: The New Adventures* ultimately ran eight issues, though two further issues were solicited through Diamond but never published. Besides *New Adventures*, Kitchen published a handful of other comics during the year but sales on those releases were dire. The anthology *Mona* sold a mere 3,181 copies to comic shops. Sales of the autobiographical *Skin Eater Comics* were even more meager at 1,086 copies. In fact, the failure of Kitchen Sink's comics line was just one of the many problems the publisher faced in 1998. After years of bouncing between different ownership groups, Denis Kitchen held only a small percentage of the company he founded thirty

years previously. When Jim Lee passed on an opportunity to buy Kitchen Sink due to problems with Kitchen's brother James, Kitchen allied himself with Fred Seibert, former President at Hanna-Barbera Animation. Seibert negotiated with Kitchen's former partner, Ocean Capital, but the resulting company foundered on disagreements about Kitchen Sink's future. Seibert wanted to concentrate on the company's lucrative candy business while Denis Kitchen wanted to focus on comics. By December 1998, the argument reached a head. Kitchen was fired from the company he had created and kept alive for decades. Renaming itself True Confections and devoting itself to the candy business, the former Kitchen Sink Press closed before the end of the decade (Cooke 97-99).

As 1997 ended, the reboot of Valiant heroes at **Acclaim** was faring decently. However, by March 1998, *Quantum & Woody*, their most popular title, sold only 11,500 copies per issue, and four of Acclaim's ten releases that month sold under 7,000 copies. That was an unsustainable level and each issue incurred a loss. Even *Turok*, which sold millions of video games, sold only 10,000 copies after debuting at 23,000 (Stump 23). The problem was that the new versions of the Valiant heroes were hitting a bad chord with many consumers. For instance, Kurt Busiek described the fan reaction to his *Ninjak*: "Readers who liked it, liked it a lot – but old Ninjak fans hated us for not doing something like the Bondian *Ninjak* vol. 1, lots of fans ignored the line completely, and there was a hefty number of people who refused to even look at Ninjak" (Mescallado 86). Though *Comics Buyer's Guide* listed Acclaim as the fifth-largest American publisher in 1997, the VH2 heroes saw their final releases in October 1998. Some Acclaim comics were cancelled after they were solicited and had work completed and paid for. *Concrete Jungle: The Legend of the Black Lion* was solicited as a six-chapter mini-series by Christopher Priest and James Fry, but only the first issue of this urban noir tale saw print after advance orders for issue #3 dropped under 5,000 copies. A

final valiant effort would be made to resurrect the Acclaim heroes in 1999.

While Kitchen Sink closed down and Acclaim cancelled nearly all of its series, a different publisher never even saw print. In August 1998, **Jim Shooter** announced the formation of Daring Comics. Created in alliance with comic shop owner Chuck Rozanski, Shooter announced two launch titles, both of which would be limited to print runs of 5,500 copies. Of that, 5,000 copies would retail for $2.95 and the remaining 500 copies would be autographed and retail for $14.95. Daring's first intended release was the Joe James-illustrated *Anomalies*, a "hard science"-based adventure starring teen super-heroes. The second scheduled title was *Rathh of God*, starring an executioner during a time when life was held as sacred. Shooter expressed optimism about Daring, saying "I see the comics world poised for a turnaround, and I want to make that bright future come to pass" (Doran 6). Again, neither series saw print.

Trojans and Spartans

Frank Miller took a break from his ever-popular crime noir *Sin City* to deliver a five issue mini-series that was set in a completely different time-frame: ancient Greece. Dark Horse Comics' *300* (first issue cover-dated May 1998) told the story of Spartan soldiers defending Greece against a Persian invasion force. Three hundred men heroically fought a force over ten times their size in the narrow mountain pass of Thermopylae. Drawn in a style similar to his work on *Sin City*, this time colored by Lynn Varley, Miller's stark and striking vision mostly received critical raves. Some reviewers, however, criticized, what they saw as, Miller's hyperbolic storytelling. Miller responded to those criticisms by claiming, "My intent was misunderstood because in many ways *300* was a deliberate propaganda piece. When I work on a story I choose a point of view. For this story, the approach was to tell this story the way the Spartans told it around the campfire. That's the reason they were fighting against 80-foot elephants and that's why Xerxes was portrayed as much larger-than-life figure and given these traits

Frank Miller's *300* chronicled a titanic and heroic defense in Ancient Greece. TM and © Frank Miller Inc.

that the Spartans would [project on to] their enemies" (Boucher).

Where Miller's work was steeped in hyperbole, another comic took a different approach to presenting ancient Greek society. *Age of Bronze*, published by Image and written and drawn by **Eric Shanower**, aimed to tell the story of the Trojan War based on archaeological research along with insights into the era and characters. As Shanower declared, "*Age of Bronze* is different than past retellings of the Trojan War. My goal is to present a complete version of the story, synthesized from the many versions of the legend, while making it as consistent as possible with the archaeological record" (Shanower 22). Indeed, in his first issue, Shanower thanks several professors and researchers for their help in making the work as true as possible. Thus, *Bronze* was applauded by both comics critics and experts in classical history.

Cartoonist **Daniel Clowes** released one of his most sure-handed graphic novels with the hard cover *Caricature*. Published by Fantagraphics, this collection of nine short stories offers a multi-tiered exploration of perception and truth with a title story that presents the interior monologue of Mal Rosen, a caricaturist who has a complicated encounter with a woman at an arts festival.

Following his earlier *Palestine*, **Joe Sacco** produced another well-reviewed graphic novel. Drawn & Quarterly's *Tales from Bosnia: Soba* describes the atrocities and devastation during the war in the former Yugoslavia. Presented as a profile of a young Bosnian man, the story depicts Soba's terror under an exploding sky and as he defuses landmines. Sacco's work also shows Soba's reactions after the cease-fire as he finds peace in his art, dancing and womanizing. In his portrayal of a complex man, Sacco finds a larger truth while delivering indelible and powerful images.

Though he finished his long-running *Hate* earlier in the year with issue #30 (May 1998), **Peter Bagge** continued telling his characters' stories with annual one-shots. October 1998's *Hate Jamboree* was a 64-page, $3.95 collection of short comic stories, photos, illustrations and ephemera along with a

Bagge bibliography. He would continue to release *Hate* Annuals each year.

Many creators took their own paths to indie prominence. Among them were Jill Thompson, whose *Scary Godmother* was published by Sirius Entertainment, and Linda Medley, whose fantasy comic *Castle Waiting* was published by Fantagraphics. Self-published works included Xeric Award-winning writer Anton Jew's *Saturday Nite*, John Gallagher's *Buzzboy* (an indie take on super-heroes) and Xeric winner Garrett Hinds's *Bearskin*, an adaptation of an obscure Grimm's fairy tale.

As the Internet became more of a force by the turn of the century, websites such as pets.com began attracting enormous investments. The dot-com boom also hit comics, as Diamond Distribution owner Steve Geppi invested in an online comic shop, AnotherUniverse.com, to prevent its folding. The successor to popular mail-order retailer American Entertainment, the website aimed to be a top retail specialty outlet for comics and collectibles. It also was Diamond's biggest account when Geppi bought an interest in it. AnotherUniverse and competitor NextPlanetOver would experience financial troubles along with many other dot-com stocks in 1999 and 2000. In August 1998, Rick Veitch and Steve Conley launched Comicon.com as a virtual comic book convention, with an artist's alley, hangouts and panel rooms. The site attracted dozens of creators who set up virtual tables as a way of meeting their fans, selling wares, and sharing industry news and legends. It grew in popularity and was an industry staple through the early 2000s.

Rediscovering an Alter Ego

Fan interest was cultivated in a different way in 1998 with the revival of Roy Thomas's longtime fanzine **Alter Ego**, in the pages of the TwoMorrows nostalgia fanzine *Comic Book Artist*. Edited by Jon B. Cooke, *CBA* explored the history of American comics. The first issue, for instance, included an exhaustive roster of interviews devoted to the history of DC Comics circa 1967-1974. Thomas became involved in the project when he saw an ad flyer for the 1970s Marvel Comics-themed *CBA* #2 which noted the magazine would cover the careers of "forgotten" creators like himself and Gil Kane. Thomas wrote Cooke requesting his own space in the magazine; Cooke replied with the offer of an ongoing 14-page "flip magazine" with its own cover. After a few successful releases, publisher John Morrow requested that Thomas move his section into its own ongoing magazine. The new volume of *Alter Ego* launched in the summer of 1999 and went on to become one of the most important magazines covering the history of the comic book medium. Editor Thomas and his staff presented interviews and articles that chronicled the twists and turns of the industry over the decades.

Though the late 1990s were a tough era for comic book publishers, they were terrific for those interested in nostalgia. A new line of comics debuting in 1999 would explore nostalgia with a decidedly postmodern perspective. ◐

1999

CHAPTER TEN

No Man's Land

If the story of the comics industry in the late 1990s was low sales, then 1999 represents the nadir of that tale. The grim truth was that monthly comics sales in America were at their lowest levels in decades. As one anonymous publisher reported at the beginning of the year, "My 1999 publishing plans are literally on hold at the moment while I try to digest the disintegration of the comic market week by week. I am leaning more and more towards halting comic book publication altogether" ("A bleak forecast" 8). Only a handful of comics, including *Uncanny X-Men*, *X-Men*, *Danger Girl*, *Tomb Raider* and *Battle Chasers*, sold over 100,000 copies per month. Worse, sales on the next tier of titles were way down as well. By December 1999, only twenty-five ongoing comics sold over 50,000 copies per issue. Overall for the year, sales for the top 300 comics were down 8% compared with the already anemic 1998, and industry-wide retail levels were a third of what they were five years earlier. While sales of trade paperbacks went up by 9%, they only represented $17 million of the $270 million comic book industry. In a sign of the times, Marvel released fewer comics in 1999 than any other year since 1984. In one striking month Marvel released only thirty-six comics. The same month DC put out ninety-six comics. Marvel had emerged from bankruptcy, but as far as everyone could tell, its future was still uncertain.

However, the American comics industry wasn't all grimness and depression. A new generation of comic series seemed to present an alluring vision for the next millennium. Comics like *Transmetropolitan*, *Astro City*, *Black Panther*, *Inhumans* and *Preacher* shined a promising light, with modern storytelling that struck a chord in receptive readers. One of comic book's most iconic characters even proved that all wasn't hopeless, that fortunes could be turned around with the right creative decisions. Or put another way by **DC Comics** editor Jordan Gorfinkel, "If any one character can lift this industry out of its doldrums, it's Batman" (Morrisard 43).

Batman: No Man's Land

Gotham City had suffered cataclysms in its long history, but nothing prepared the citizens of Batman's home town for the earthquake that struck in 1998. Even worse was the quake's aftermath. As described in the *No Man's Land* one-shot (March 1999), by writer Bob Gale and artist Alex Maleev, the formerly civilized city gave way to anarchy. Prior to this storyline, Bruce Wayne failed to persuade the U.S. Congress to fund the restoration of his beloved city. Instead, the federal government chose to cordon off Gotham, forbidding anybody from entering or leaving it. To do so, the government blew up all the bridges and tunnels into the city and made Gotham a true "No Man's Land." As the epic storyline kicks off, the military has surrounded Gotham's perimeter. The city has no fresh food, no clean water supply and no working police department, other than a rogue team of police officers. Gotham's only inhabitants are the poor, those who were too stubborn to abandon their homes, and the criminals. Batman has been missing for 93 days as whole sections of Gotham are now controlled by some of his most vicious enemies, such as the Penguin, Two-Face and Poison Ivy. Territories have been marked with spray paint, but as the issue ends, a caped figure spray-paints the bat symbol on walls across the city. *No Man's Land* continued into several overlapping storylines that encompassed *Batman*, *Detective Comics*, *Legends of the Dark Knight* and *Shadow of the Bat*.

As "No Man's Land" proceeds, Batman returns to his home town, but his beloved Gotham is different from anything he had ever expected to encounter. Wayne Mansion was destroyed in the earthquake, along with the Batcave. Though Batman has allies – including an important new one – the scope of the destruction and gang violence puts the Caped Crusader in a completely new situation, where the conflicts he faces are more confusing, ambiguous and bizarre than he had ever faced before.

Batman's new status quo came about in part because the character's editors simply felt bored. After all the turmoil of "Knightfall," "Knightquest" and "Knightsend" in 1993 and 1994, the Batman comics had settled into a predictable groove, but by 1998 the editors' concern was that their own boredom would spill over to their readers. Facing that ennui, editor Jordan Gorfinkel walked into Batman group editor Denny O'Neil's office one Monday morning with a 12-page proposal that detailed how "Cataclysm" could lead into the "No Man's Land" event. Gorfinkel expected O'Neil to hate the idea, but the veteran editor actually embraced the gamble: "it seemed like a dangerous story to try. It's a story that has never been told, as far as I know, certainly not in comics. That's always a reason to do something" (Morrisard 43-9). One of the reasons why the changes seemed new to Batman was because of the new writers and artists who had never written Batman comics before. Besides the aforementioned Bob Gale, the screenwriter for *Back to the Future*, crime novelist Greg Rucka was brought on to write "No Man's Land"'s third story arc. He would become a mainstay of the Batman books into the new millennium. Other writers new to the Batman line included Devin Grayson, Kelley Puckett, Larry Hama and Bronwyn Carlton. Longtime Batman writer Doug Moench was one of the few who opted out of the storyline, complaining "I didn't think it was a good story and didn't want to write it. I thought it was absurd that the U.S. government would deliberately cut Gotham off from the rest of the country."

Sales for the storyline were extremely strong. A retailer from Seattle reported, "Sales on the 'No Man's Land' storyline continue to amaze us. We increase our orders, place reorders, and still can't fill customer demand on these titles" (Halstead 22).

"No Man's Land" is also significant for introducing a new version of a familiar hero. As the story arc begins, Helena Bertinelli abandons her Huntress identity to assume Barbara Gordon's former alter ego of **Batgirl**. The change was short-lived, however, as in *Legends of the Dark Knight* #120 (Aug. 1999), an argument between Bertinelli and Batman leads to someone else donning the Batgirl costume. Her name is Cassandra Cain. Unable to read, talk or write, because of her assassin father's uncaring approach to her, this silent Batgirl can only communicate through body language. With Barbara Gordon's blessing, the new Batgirl

After 1998's "Cataclysm," Batman faced a "No Man's Land" in 1999.
Batman TM and © DC Comics.

helps Batman in the "No Man's Land" fray. Afterwards, DC provided her with her own ongoing title in 2000.

For many fans, even more exciting than a new Batgirl was the insertion of a popular *Batman: The Animated Series* character into the DC comic universe. **Harley Quinn** first appeared in a 48-page one-shot written by *B:TAS* co-creator **Paul Dini** and drawn by Yvel Guichet and Aaron Sowd. In *Batman: Harley Quinn* (Oct. 1999) psychologist Harleen Quinzel falls in love with the Joker while caring for him at Arkham Asylum. After being committed to the asylum herself, Quinn walks out when the earthquake hits Gotham. She then seeks out the Joker and happily teams up with him as he tries to carve out his own section of Gotham during "No Man's Land." *Batman: Harley Quinn* sold a solid 55,000 copies through Diamond.

With Alex Ross, Paul Dini also delivered a new tabloid one-shot, reminiscent of their 1998 *Superman: Peace on Earth*. But where *Peace on Earth* pontificates on Superman's sense of idealism, **Batman: War on Crime** expresses the Caped Crusader's sense of dread. *War on Crime* tells a story of loss and retribution on a much more intimate level than Dini and Ross's previous comic. In it, Batman witnesses the aftermath of a murder in which a young man is orphaned in the same way that young Bruce Wayne was many years previously. However, the boy is poor and lacks the ability to escape the urban hell that continually drags him into dangerous situations. The dramatic contrast between the

TIMELINE: 1999

A compilation of the year's notable comic book history events alongside some of the year's most significant popular culture and historical events. (On sale dates are approximations.)

January 1: The euro, the official currency of the European Union, is established.

January 10: The premiere episode of *Batman Beyond* airs on Kids WB. Developed by *Batman: The Animated Series* creators Alan Burnett, Paul Dini and Bruce Timm, the cartoon takes place fifty years in the future where Bruce Wayne mentors the next generation's Caped Crusader, a teenager named Terry McGinnis. The show will run for three seasons for a total of 52 episodes.

February 3: Vin Sullivan—Golden Age-era comic book artist, editor and publisher, best known for drawing the cover to *Detective Comics* #1 as well as being Superman's first editor—dies at the age of 87.

February 12: The Monica Lewinsky scandal concludes with the U.S. Senate acquitting President Bill Clinton of perjury and obstruction of justice charges.

February 26: MLJ/Archie Comics co-founder John L. Goldwater dies at the age of 83. Goldwater also served as the president of the Comics Magazine Association, which oversees the Comics Code Authority, for 25 years.

March 12: Lee Falk—cartoonist most famous for creating *The Phantom* and *Mandrake the Magician* comic strips—dies at the age of 87.

March 14: Comic book writer John Broome—best known for his DC Comics work during the 1950s and 1960s including co-creating the Hal Jordan version of the Green Lantern and a signature run on *The Flash*—dies at the age of 85.

May 3: A series of tornadoes strikes Oklahoma, killing over 50 people and causing over $1.4 billion in property damage. The tornado outbreak produces the highest wind speeds ever recorded on Earth: over 301 mph.

May 19: The first new *Star Wars* film in sixteen years, *The Phantom Menace*, arrives in theaters. Starring Natalie Portman as Queen Amidala, Ewan McGregor as Obi-Wan Kenobi, and Liam Neeson as Jedi Knight Qui-Gon Jinn, *Star Wars: Episode I* earns over $431 million at the box office, far and away the highest grossing movie of the year.

June 1: Napster, an online digital audio file sharing service, debuts. At the peak of its popularity, 80 million people use Napster to download music.

June 2: *Batman: Legends of the Dark Knight* #120, written by Greg Rucka and drawn by Mike Deodato, Jr. and Sean Parsons, introduces the new Batgirl, Cassandra Cain.

JANUARY	FEBRUARY	MARCH	APRIL	MAY	JUNE

February 3: Written by Warren Ellis and drawn by John Cassaday, the first issue of Wildstorm Comics' *Planetary*—about a group of adventurers on a mission to discover the Earth's secret history—arrives in stores.

January 27: Alan Moore's America's Best Comics—an imprint of Jim Lee's Wildstorm—debuts with the publication of *League of Extraordinary Gentlemen*. Other ABC titles released this year are *Tom Strong*, *Promethea*, *Top 10*, and the *Tomorrow Stories* anthology.

January 10: The premiere episode of *The Sopranos*—starring James Gandolfini as a New Jersey-based mobster who is trying to balance his family life with his criminal activities—airs on HBO. The show will run for six seasons, winning numerous awards along the way, including an Emmy for "Outstanding Drama Series," the first cable series to do so.

April 20: In one of the worst school shootings in American history, Eric Harris and Dylan Klebold murder twelve of their fellow students and one teacher in Columbine High School, outside Denver, Colorado. Twenty-four other students suffer gunshot wounds and injuries before the two shooters commit suicide. The incident sparks national debate on gun control, high school bullying, goth culture and violence in video games.

March 31: Directed by the Wachowski brothers, *The Matrix*—starring Keanu Reeves as Neo, a computer hacker who learns that reality is a mirage generated by sentient machines that have enslaved humanity—arrives in movie theaters. Comic book writer Grant Morrison accuses the filmmakers of copying his Vertigo series *The Invisibles*.

May 30: Paul S. Newman, prolific comic book writer whose career spanned six decades, dies at the age of 75. While having worked for several publishers, Newman is best known for co-creating Western Publishing's Doctor Solar and for scripting *Turok* for 26 years.

lives of Wayne and the boy makes Batman wonder what he would have done if he didn't have all the money that his parents bequeathed to him after their passing. Delivered as an extended interior monologue, *War on Crime* distills the essence of Batman in a long meditative piece. Ross and Dini portrayed a Batman that, as Ross described him, is "a regular man who swore an oath to fight crime" (Brick 28). The $9.95 softcover sold nearly 50,000 copies through Diamond upon its release.

After their one-shot and mini-series sold extremely well in 1996, the **Birds of Prey** finally got their own ongoing series in 1999. Written by Chuck Dixon with art by Greg Land, *Birds of Prey #1* (Jan. 1999) has Oracle sending Black Canary to the remote island country of Rheelasia to battle the evil plans of Hellhound and his fellow oppressors. The strong warrior Canary provides an intriguing contrast to the wheelchair-bound Oracle. As the series evolved in

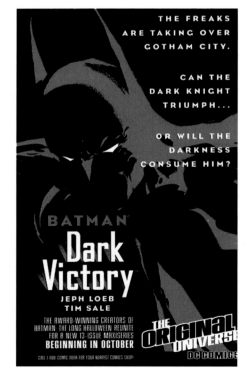

Batman: Dark Victory *was Jeph Loeb and Tim Sale's latest thirteen-part murder mystery.*
TM and © DC Comics.

its first year, so too did the friendship between the two heroines as they learned more about each other during Canary's globe-spanning adventures. Editor Jordan Gorfinkel was the main force behind bringing the comic to the stands. As Dixon recalls, "The book was really his brainchild. Oracle was a popular character but was a hard sell for a solo title. Canary's own monthly had just failed but she remained beloved with readers. Teaming them was an elegant solution for the team's creation" (Mullins). Dixon and Land played up the heroines' connections with the DC universe. Tim Drake (Robin) was a frequent presence, Oracle had an online friendship with Blue Beetle, and villains R'as al Ghul and the Joker showed up in the title as well.

In 1999, Jeph Loeb and Tim Sale delivered a new Batman mini-series. *Batman: Dark Victory* was a thirteen-part murder mystery that echoed their well-received *Batman: the Long*

July 16: John F. Kennedy Jr., the son of President Kennedy, dies along with his wife Carolyn Bessette-Kennedy and her sister Lauren Bessette when a plane he is piloting crashes off the coast of Martha's Vineyard, Massachusetts.

August 6: Haley Joel Osment is a boy who sees dead people in M. Night Shyamalan's *The Sixth Sense.* Co-starring Bruce Willis as a child psychologist, the movie becomes the surprise hit of the summer, earning over $293 million at the box office.

November 25: Fishermen off the coast of Fort Lauderdale, Florida rescue Elián Gonzalez, a five-year-old boy who is clinging to an inner-tube. His mother, along with eleven others, drowned while fleeing Cuba. A contentious international custody battle ensues as several of Gonzalez's relatives want him to stay in America as a political refugee, but eventually the boy is returned to Cuba to be reunited with his father.

JULY	AUGUST	SEPTEMBER	OCTOBER	NOVEMBER	DECEMBER

August 6: Loosely based on Bob Burden's *Flaming Carrot Comics, Mystery Men*—an action comedy about a group of bumbling super-heroes trying to stop a super-villain from destroying their city—arrives in movie theaters. The film earns less than $30 million at the box office.

October 10: The premiere episode of *Spider-Man Unlimited*—which has the webslinger traveling in space to a planet called Counter-Earth—airs on Fox Kids. The animated series only lasts thirteen episodes.

October 31: EgyptAir Flight 990, en route from Los Angeles to Cairo, Egypt, crashes in the Atlantic Ocean south of Nantucket Island, Massachusetts, killing all 217 people on board. The cause of the catastrophe comes in dispute as an American investigation team determines that the flight's relief pilot deliberately crashed the plane while an Egyptian investigation team blames it on mechanical failure.

Halloween of 1996 and '97. Like *Long Halloween*, *Dark Victory* centers around a serial killer who strikes on holidays throughout the year. However, this killer's modus operandi is different from his predecessor: he kills police officers by hanging them, attaching a partially completed hangman game as a sadistic clue to the crime. Along the way villains like the Joker, Mr. Freeze and Poison Ivy are enmeshed in the criminal plot while Selina Kyle (a.k.a. the Catwoman) begins a complicated affair with Bruce Wayne. The series works as much as a psychological portrait of Commissioner Gordon and Batman as it does a murder mystery. Bruce Wayne struggles to come to terms with the descent of his friend Harvey Dent into the sadistic killer Two-Face just as Gordon struggles to come to terms with his wife leaving him with their son. Another key hero joins the cast halfway through the year-long crossover. At first, Robin also struggles to cope with the murder of his parents

but eventually comes to peace with their deaths and helps provide some closure for Batman as well. As writer Loeb described *Dark Victory*, "At the end of *The Long Halloween*, Batman is left empty; Gordon has lost his best friend; and Harvey Dent has lost everything he once held dear. With *Dark Victory*, there is the chance to tell the other half of the tale... to begin with futility and end with hope and possibilities once more" (Cohen 15).

One out-of-continuity Batman story that received a lot of attention was the 48 page one-shot *Darkness/ Batman* (Aug. 1999) which teamed the Dark Knight Detective with a man who literally *is* the darkness. Written by Scott Lobdell and Jeph Loeb, with art by Marc Silvestri and David Finch, the special issue begins as Jackie Estacado, who carries the Darkness, moves with his mob boss uncle Don Franchetti to Gotham City to gain some of Gotham's underground business. At the same time, Batman

investigates a series of murders that have a supernatural element to them – an element that leads him back to the Darkness. The creative team spun iconic Batman villains like the Joker and Two-Face into a story that crosses over two of the darkest characters in comics.

The Batman of Beyond

Paul Dini and Alan Burnett brought Batman back to television screens, but their latest cartoon was much different from their retro-feeling *Batman: the Animated Series*. **Batman Beyond** features a brand-new Batman named Terry McGinnis who fights his own set of criminals fifty years in the future. In this world, an 80-year-old Bruce Wayne has retired after a heart attack and is living alone in his mansion. Bruce has been abandoned by all his former companions. The only one left to comfort him is his dog, Ace. One day, though, a teenage boy named Terry comes to Bruce's doors, pleading

265

for help. Bruce sends the boy away, but not until after Terry steals an experimental bat-suit. When Terry returns, he tells Bruce about his father's murder. Feeling empathetic, Bruce agrees to mentor Terry as the Batman of a new generation. *Batman Beyond* was truly a unique take on the Caped Crusader. Terry was Bruce's opposite in many ways. He was less brooding and more fun-loving though also serious when situations demanded. His futuristic world uses new technology and new approaches to crime fighting, and the bat-suit he wears is streamlined with a full-face mask and dark red glider wings. Barbara Gordon, the former Batgirl, has been installed as police commissioner of a Gotham City which is no longer terrorized by the Joker but by a violent street gang that calls itself the "Jokerz." The series launched January 10, 1999, on Kids WB with a premiere episode that earned the highest rating of any WB show in the Sunday night timeslot. The cartoon became such a smash hit that it earned an unusual 25-episode renewal after its initial 13-episode first season. Ultimately, *Batman Beyond* enjoyed a three-year run.

Later in the year, Fox Kids premiered **Spider-Man Unlimited**, a cartoon in which Spider-Man stows away on a flight to "Counter-Earth," a parallel Earth located on the far side of the sun. Though *Unlimited* earned decent ratings, Fox Kids cancelled it after three October 1999 episodes, then revived the series in December 2000. Fox Kids also aired another comics adaptation in the form of Frank Miller and Geof Darrow's *Big Guy and Rusty the Boy Robot*. Unlike the comic, which offered a surface exploration of the characters and their world, the 26-episode animated series delved deep into their backstory and added depth to the characters' universe.

A comic book that explored alternative versions of iconic DC characters was John Byrne's **Superman & Batman: Generations**. Cover billed as "an imaginary tale" (along with the "Elseworlds" label that DC used for its alternative universe comics), the four-issue mini-series presents Batman and Superman as if their careers truly began in the late 1930s and they've been aging ever since. As such, each square-bound issue features not only DC's most famous characters but their descendants as well. In chapter one, taking place in 1939, the two heroes meet at the Metropolis World's Fair and defeat the Ultra-Humanite. In 1949 Lex Luthor and the Joker kidnap the pregnant Lois Lane. The heroes defeat the villains, but in the process Lois and Clark's unborn son is exposed to gold kryptonite and loses his powers forever. In 1959 Batman contemplates retirement and passing the cape and cowl on to Dick Grayson. In 1969 Bruce Wayne Jr. dons the bat-suit while Superman's daughter Kara Kent helps him in his adventures. By 1999 the Batman suit is worn by a third-generation crimefighter while Superman leaves Earth in the hands of his grandson, Clark. The final chapter takes place in 2919, where an amazingly long-lived Superman and Batman have turned the galaxy into a paradise under their protection and care, a fitting ending for the world's greatest protectors. *Generations* was popular enough that DC published two sequels: *Generations II* in 2001 and *Generations III* in 2003.

The man from Krypton had a busy year making new friends and allies. The 64-page *Superman/Fantastic Four* (March 1999) by Dan Jurgens and Art Thibert has Superman traveling to the Marvel Universe when he discovers a clue that Galactus may be responsible for the destruction of Krypton. The Cyborg Superman follows as Superman teams with the FF to investigate. It turns out that Galactus didn't devour Krypton, and the Man of Steel briefly serves as the world eater's herald. Another crossover, the July cover-dated *Incredible Hulk vs. Superman*, by Roger Stern, Steve Rude and Al Milgrom, sets Superman against the Green Goliath during the early days of each of their careers. One reviewer said of the comic, "This is the best, most faithfully written, carefully crafted intercompany crossover yet" (Keeney 24). Superman also met Savage Dragon in a madcap one-shot later in the year that had the two heroes battle an insurrection on Apokolips. Writer Karl Kesel and artist Jon Bogdanove clearly relished the chance to deliver a wacky team-up that breezed through its 48 pages.

The Original Super-Team Returns — for a New Millennium

With the massive success of *JLA*, DC decided to add an ongoing partner title that starred the original super-hero team: the **Justice Society of America**. To promote a new JSA monthly, DC released a multi-comic event in March. "The Justice Society Returns" took place during World War II with the JSA battling the seven minions of the evil Stalker in the backdrop of such real world events as the Yalta Conference and the Manhattan Project. Following the classic Golden Age trope of splitting up the team in order to deal with a crisis, "The Justice Society Returns" unfolded throughout seven one-shots and two bookended issues of *All Star Comics*. All released on March 24, 1999, each one-shot paid homage to the titles of yesteryear: *Adventure Comics* (starring the Golden Age Starman and the Golden Age Atom and written by James Robinson and David Goyer with art by Peter Snejbjerg and Keith Champagne), *All-American Comics* (starring the Golden Age Green Lantern and Johnny Thunder by Ron Marz and Eduardo Barreto), *National Comics* (starring the Golden Age Flash and Mr. Terrific by Mark Waid and Aaron Lopresti), *Smash Comics* (starring Doctor Mid-Nite and Hourman by Tom Peyer, Steve Sadowski and Michael Bair), *Sensation Comics* (starring the Golden Age Wonder Woman and Hawkgirl by Robinson and Goyer with artist Scott Benefiel), *Star Spangled Comics* (starring the Golden Age Sandman and the Star-Spangled Kid by Geoff Johns and Chris Weston), and *Thrilling Comics* (starring the Golden Age Hawkman and Wildcat by Chuck Dixon and Russ Heath). "The Justice Society Returns" performed well on the stands, with all issues landing in the top fifty best-selling comics for the month.

Three months after the event, the Justice Society re-formed in the modern day in *JSA* #1. The debut issue became DC's second best-selling comic for June, and ranked 13th among all new releases for that month. The new Justice Society was a mix of old and new heroes, including Golden Age standbys like the original Green Lantern (now known as Sentinel), the Flash and Wildcat, and new characters based on classic JSA members, like Starman, Hourman and Atom Smasher. The initial storyline begins when a villain tries to steal Dr. Fate's power, which triggers a new team to jump into action. Robinson and Goyer collaborated on scripts for the early issues with Stephen Sadowski and Michael Bair delivering the art. By issue #6, however, Robinson departed, and Goyer's new writing partner was someone who would quickly become one of DC Comics' most popular creators, **Geoff Johns**. A lifelong comic book fan, Johns graduated from Michigan State University in 1995 and then moved to Los Angeles where he became an assistant to film director Richard Donner (the man who brought Superman to the big screen in 1978). While in New York for the production of Donner's 1997 film *Conspiracy Theory*, Johns invited some DC editors to the set. Once there, the editors asked Johns to pitch them some story ideas. The end result was a new on-going series titled *Stars and S.T.R.I.P.E.* (first issue cover-dated July 1999), a light-hearted series drawn by Lee Moder about a teenage girl named Courtney Whitmore who finds the Star-Spangled Kid's cosmic belt and uses it to become a costumed crime-fighter. Based on Johns's sister Courtney, who died when TWA Flight 800 crashed in 1996, this new Star-Spangled Kid is joined by her stepfather, the original Stripesy, who dons a suit of armor and renames himself S.T.R.I.P.E.

Unfortunately, *Stars and S.T.R.I.P.E.* didn't become a bestseller and was cancelled after fourteen issues. From such humble beginnings, however, blossomed one of the most important careers in DC Comics history. As Johns recalled, "[writing comic books] was supposed to be just a side thing, but I had a great time doing it, and when other opportunities came up, like *JSA* [...] and everything else, I really just ran with it" (McCaw).

The Long Redemption of Hal Jordan

One of the opportunities that Johns ran with was DC's major crossover event for 1999: the five-issue mini-series *Day of Judgment*. Written by Johns, drawn by Matt Smith in an art style that evoked the work of *Hellboy* creator Mike Mignola, and released weekly throughout the month of September, *Day of Judgment* followed up on the events of DC's 1995 crossover *Underworld Unleashed*. As the story begins, the human host of the Spectre, Jim Corrigan, has died. Seizing

James Robinson co-wrote the early issues of JSA but was soon replaced by Geoff Johns. Justice Society and related characters TM and © DC Comics.

Hal Jordan finally achieves redemption in Day of Judgment. TM and © DC Comics.

the chance to sow some chaos, Etrigan the Demon arranges for the fallen angel Asmodel to bond with the Spectre. When that happens, Asmodel uses the Spectre's power to freeze Hell and unleash demons onto Earth. The planet's super-powered guardians are quickly overcome, so a team of magic-based heroes, including the Phantom Stranger, Deadman, Raven, Sentinel and Zatanna, band together to save the Earth. At first, they go to Heaven to convince Corrigan to reunite with the Spectre. When Corrigan refuses, the angel Michael directs the team to Purgatory where they can find a lost soul who regrets the choices he made in his life: Hal Jordan, the former Green Lantern who became the villainous Parallax. Returning to Earth, Spectre accepts Jordan as his host under the logic that it would be a fitting punishment for the crimes Jordan committed as Parallax. With a costume that is an amalgam of both the Spectre and Green Lantern, DC's new Spirit of Vengeance resolves the conflict. The story ends with Hal Jordan vowing to use the Spectre's power to become the "Spirit of Redemption." With that, the former Green Lantern's life has come full circle in the course of a decade. He began the 1990s with one of DC's lowest-selling super-hero titles. By mid-decade, he became a mass murderer and was stripped of his power ring. Now at the dawn of a new millennium, Hal Jordan has been restored as a hero again.

Day of Judgment crossed over into thirteen ongoing DC titles, including *JLA*, *Supergirl* and *Young Justice*, but the mini-series itself only averaged sales of around 55,000 copies per issue. Based those disappointing numbers, DC produced no crossover event in 2000—the first time in several years that happened.

DC's decision was probably made easier by the lackluster performance of an earlier event. After the massive success of *Kingdom Come* in 1996, a sequel was planned as a monthly ongoing series starting in 1997. Unfortunately, writer **Mark Waid** and artist **Alex Ross** argued over creative direction until finally Ross threw in the towel and moved on to other projects. As Ross put it, "I felt that as the original creator – by that I mean I was the first guy to put anything down on paper – my ideas were being met with little or no respect" (McLaughlin 28). Waid was now free to do as he wished with the concept, and thanks to a retailer's suggestion, he produced *The Kingdom* as a month-long event (cover date February 1999). Continuing from the events of *Kingdom Come*, *The Kingdom* #1 (drawn by Ariel Olivetti) begins with a super-powered madman from the future named Gog who hates Superman with such intensity that he travels back in time, one day at a time, just to kill Superman over and over again. The resulting havoc these murders have on the space-time continuum draws the attention of those who watch over it, particularly Rip Hunter. He convinces the Batman, Superman and Wonder Woman from the *Kingdom Come* future to travel to 1998 and confront Gog. From there, the story continues in five one-shots, all written by Waid and all released on the same day: *The Kingdom: Kid Flash* (with art by Mark Pajarillo and Waldon Wong), *The Kingdom: Nightstar* (with art by Matt Haley and Tom Simmons), *The Kingdom: Offspring* (drawn by Frank Quitely), *The Kingdom: Planet Krypton* (drawn by Barry Kitson) and *The Kingdom: Son of the Bat* (with art by Brian Apthorp and Mark Farmer). The following week, DC published *The Kingdom* #2 (with art by Mike Zeck and John Beatty) where the various heroes of the one-shots not only aid the Batmen, Supermen and Wonder Women from two time periods in defeating Gog but also discover the existence of "Hypertime," which Rip Hunter describes as "the vast interconnected web of parallel time-lines which comprise all reality." In other words, while the DC Universe no longer had "alternate Earths" (thanks to 1985's *Crisis on Infinite Earths*), it did have "alternate timelines" where anything that *can* happen *has* happened. Through Hypertime, Waid sought to resolve the contradictions in DC's continuity once and for all. Indeed, Hypertime allows for contradictions because anything that didn't make sense can be attributed to overlapping timelines. Fan reaction to the concept was mixed: some welcomed it while others saw it as an excuse for writers to create even more contradictions. Waid joked that fandom had two minds on the idea – one half sent him death threats while the other half wanted to build a statue of him (Frankenhoff 40).

Regardless of how Hypertime was appreciated, the overall *Kingdom* event was poorly received. As one analyst reported: "Almost everyone expressed disappointment with this sequel. Its structure of bookended one-shots lacked the grandeur and narrative unity of *Kingdom Come*, and its stories seemed far sillier and far less consequential. *The Kingdom* also lacked *Kingdom Come*'s real star, Alex Ross's painted art" (Darius 18).

100 Bullets and No Prosecution

With *Preacher* and *Invisibles* continuing their monthly marches towards their final issues in 2000, writer **Brian Azzarello** and artist **Eduardo Risso** launched the next iconic **Vertigo** series in 1999 with *100 Bullets* (first issue cover-dated Aug. 1999). The series had a seemingly simple premise: What if someone gave you a gun, 100 bullets and the freedom to kill anyone you wanted without getting arrested? Each chapter in this highly acclaimed series presented that scenario while building up a more complex storyline. As the series proceeded, Azzarello and Risso's grungy world evolved into two tracks: one explored the fascinating revenge story of each arc's lead character while the other slowly parceled out details behind the mysterious agency that provided the gun and bullets. Azzarello's stories seemed crossed between daily news headlines and classic crime novels, and Risso's gritty art added to the intensity of the stories Azzarello created.

Several other Vertigo releases received critical acclaim. Indie comics darling **Ed Brubaker** joined with artist Michael Lark to deliver *Scene of the Crime*. The four-issue crime noir tale focuses on Jack Herriman, a former police officer turned private eye who investigates the disappearance of a young woman who was involved in a New Age cult in her childhood. In doing so, Herriman uncovers some shocking secrets and comes to peace with his own complicated past actions. Though *Scene of the Crime* didn't sell well, the comic received a grade of "A" from a panel of *Comics Buyer's Guide* critics. Other major Vertigo releases included the mystical *Books of Magic*, the popular *Sandman* spinoff, *The Dreaming*, and the quixotic *Happydale: Devils in the Desert* by writer Andrew Dabb with blissfully busy art by Seth Fisher. The most successful Vertigo title of the year, however, starred its most iconic lead character. *The Sandman: The Dream Hunters* (cover date Oct. 1999) returned **Neil Gaiman** to the series he launched a decade ago. Joined for the deluxe $29.95 hardcover by artist Yoshitaka Amano (designer of the *Final Fantasy* game series), Gaiman morphs the classic Japanese tale of "The Fox, the Monk and the Mikado" into the Sandman universe. Reviewers raved about Amano's lush artwork as well as Gaiman's mythic tone. The graphic novel won the 1999 Bram Stoker Award for Best Comic Book or Graphic Novel and the 2000 Eisner Award for Best Comics-Related Work.

Offspring was one of several one-shots tied to Mark Waid's The Kingdom *event. TM and © DC Comics.*

As 1999 proved, DC was simultaneously proud and wary of its provocative comics. In one incident, DC management banned Glenn Fabry's drily humorous cover planned for *Preacher* #52 (Aug. 1999) which showed Tulip's father giving her a machine gun for a Christmas gift. DC editorial considered the image too distasteful in the wake of the Columbine school massacre. The replacement cover, also painted by Fabry, had a design similar to that used for *Preacher* #50 and was similar in style to a set of covers Fabry would produce for the final few issues of the series. A comparable fate hit a story planned for *Hellblazer* #141 (Oct. 1999). Written by Warren Ellis, with art by Phil Jimenez, "Shoot" follows a researcher who searches for the causes of school shootings. John Constantine provides her with an inflammatory explanation: America's youth have become apathetic to own lives because their parents, their government and their culture have failed them. School shootings are just the expression of youthful nihilism. After the issue had been completely scripted, drawn, lettered and colored, Vertigo's editors prepared photocopies to send out to media outlets. But then DC publisher Paul Levitz got wind of the story, and after he perused the contents, he refused to let the issue be released. Vertigo head Karen Berger wanted the story to be published but understood that Levitz had final say in the matter. Ultimately, the issue was pulled – though copies of it quickly appeared on the Internet. Because of Levitz's edict, Ellis lost his interest in writing *Hellblazer* and consequently quit the assignment (Riseman).

A much sillier story triggered DC to recall thousands of copies of the one-shot *Elseworlds 80-Page Giant*. In this case the cause was concerns about the story "Letitia Lerner, Superman's Babysitter" by Kyle Baker and Elizabeth Glass. In that madcap tale, baby Superman gets electrocuted, falls off a roof, falls asleep on a busy highway, and gets put in a microwave, among other events. Fearing backlash and charges of cruelty to children, all 26,000 copies of the *Elseworlds Giant* were ordered shredded. However, somewhere between 300 and 2000 copies avoided destruction when Diamond shipped copies to England. Prices for this $4.95 cover-price comic quickly ballooned to $45 on the back issue market.

The notoriety of "Letitia Lerner" helped it win an Eisner Award for Best Short Story in 2000 and the tale was subsequently published officially by DC as part of the edgier *Bizarro Comics* hardcover anthology (2001). The contents of *Elseworlds 80 Page Giant* were ultimately released in full in a 2012 one-shot. Two years prior to that, Ellis and Jimenez's "Shoot" was finally released by DC as well, appearing in *Vertigo Resurrected* #1 (2010).

Archaeologists of the Impossible

Despite his angry departure from *Hellblazer*, **Warren Ellis** remained one of the most respected writers in the industry, thanks to his work on such series as *Stormwatch* and *Transmetropolitan*. His new 1999 series, though, put Ellis in a class all by himself. At first glance, both **The Authority** and **Planetary** seemed typical offerings from Jim Lee's Wildstorm universe, with morally complex heroes fighting bizarre and often incomprehensible menaces while cracking

House ad promoting Vertigo's latest blockbuster series: Brian Azzarello and Eduardo Risso's 100 Bullets. TM and © Brian Azzarello, Eduardo Risso and DC Comics.

wise and displaying outlandish superpowers. A closer look revealed that Ellis's new comics presented a new approach to storytelling for a new millennium. *The Authority* and *Planetary* were different in style from any other comic book at the time. In contrast to the classic Marvel Comics action found in *Avengers* or the hyperkinetic thrill ride of *JLA*, Ellis's *The Authority* and *Planetary* combined widescreen adventure with decompressed storytelling. Ellis and his artists took their time telling stories, with lingering scene-setting shots interspersed with intensely dynamic bursts of action. Both series demanded attention to background information in order to understand the story's subtext. In that way, Ellis transformed eager fans into knowing cognoscenti who were partners in the storytelling approach.

The Authority, illustrated by Bryan Hitch and Paul Neary, was the more traditional super-hero series. Spinning out of 1998's *WildC.A.T.s/Aliens* one-shot that cleared the deck for a new super-team, *The Authority* #1 (May 1999) begins with a scene of loss, as the leaders of the decimated Stormwatch contemplate their uselessness in the face of a vicious superhuman attack on Moscow. As those bureaucrats mournfully mumble on with each other, a woman steps through an extraspatial gate to speak to them. She is Jenny Sparks, dressed all in white and wearing a Union Jack t-shirt. Jenny tells the bureaucrats that the attackers will answer to an authority higher than mere government. Returning to the other side of that gate and on board an astonishing ship called the Carrier, Sparks speaks to the team that represents that new authority, one that consists of former WildC.A.T.s members and altogether new characters. The team's members are Jack Hawksmoor, the spirit of the cities; Swift, a woman who turns into a fearsome bird; the Engineer, a woman with astonishing mechanical powers; the Doctor, the psychedelic spirit of the Earth; and Apollo and Midnighter, analogues of Superman and Batman (and, incidentally, a gay couple). The new team quickly goes to work to defeat the cloned attackers sent by the evil Kaizen Gamorra, but just as important as the Authority's victory is the fun they have during the fight, accented by Ellis's cheeky writing. In fact, *The Authority* was full of both joys and clever ideas. Some of Ellis's concepts were complex (the Carrier is a massive living creature stranded in Earth orbit as it waits for its family to find it). Others were satirical and absurd (Kaizen is a scenery-chewing satire of "yellow menace" villains from Golden Age comics and adventure fiction).

Warren Ellis's work on Stormwatch *continued into* The Authority.
TM and © WildStorm Publications, an imprint of DC Comics.

More than anything, *The Authority* was a high-concept idea machine. In the second four-issue arc, the team fights off an invasion from another dimension in which England and Italy are the only remaining countries on Earth. In the third arc, the team defeats an invasion of Earth by going inside the bloodstream of a Godlike creature larger than the moon and destroying its brain. As fellow writer Grant Morrison explained the series:

> ...the members of the Authority were comfortable with their powers, using them to sensibly fight "bastards" and improve the lot of everyone on planet Earth. It was the utopian vision of Siegel and Shuster strained through British cynicism and delivered on the end of a spiked leather glove. It took the accusations of fascism that had haunted Superman and suggested a new kind of superfascist, one that was on our side (Morrison 311).

The other debut Ellis series of 1999, *Planetary*, was even more ambitious than *The Authority*. Illustrated by **John Cassaday** in the series that made him a star, *Planetary* #1 (April 1999) introduces readers to the "Archaeologists of the Impossible," as the first issue cover blurb declares. Jakita Wagner visits a strange man named Elijah Snow in a freezing cold diner in the middle of a desolate desert. She entices Snow to join her with the offer of a paid salary, anonymity and something far more intriguing: "You have an idea of what's really been going on this century. The secret history. Help us uncover the rest." Snow meets another teammate, the Drummer, and hears talk of the mysterious "Fourth Man" who funds the team before Snow embarks on his first mission. The team flies to the Adirondack mountains where they rescue a man born January 1, 1900, a spirit of the century. He is a desiccated resemblance of the classic pulp hero Doc Savage and as he relates his life story – his own take on the secret history

Before DC Comics bought Jim Lee's Wildstorm,
Planetary *was promoted as an Image comic book.*
TM and © WildStorm Publications, an imprint of DC Comics

of the twentieth century – he introduces some key story themes such as the complexity of the multiverse. In *Planetary* #2, the team journeys to a graveyard for old Japanese monsters. Issue #3 resembles a Hong Kong crime film. Issue #4 has the team encounter a living sentient spaceship that can sail "The Bleed" like the ship from *The Authority*. Casual readers enjoyed the sideways references to pop culture icons like the Fantastic Four, Vertigo comics heroes and James Bond. More committed readers loved the concepts Ellis and Cassaday presented about the nature of reality and the mysteries of the Fourth Man. As Alan Moore declared about the book, "It is at once concerned with everything that comics were and everything comics could be, all condensed into a perfect jeweled and fractal snowflake" (Moore 5). Both *Planetary* and *The Authority* could be seen as comics that fulfilled the promise of Ellis's earlier work: they respected tradition yet demonstrated the potential of an exciting new generation of comics.

Alan Moore is America's Best

Despite being labeled Wildstorm titles, neither *The Authority* nor *Planetary* was published by Image Comics. That's because as of October 5, 1998, Wildstorm was no longer part of Image. On that day, Wildstorm, along with its Cliffhanger and Homage imprints, were purchased by DC Comics.

DC had been looking to add another comics line to its portfolio for at least the past few years. In 1996, DC executives initiated talks with both **Jim Lee** and Rob Liefeld about the acquisition of their respective companies. Once DC reviewed Awesome Comics' financial accounting, though, negotiations with Liefeld broke off. DC then focused all of its attention on Lee and Wildstorm, and eventually a deal was consummated. The benefits of the transaction to both publishers were clear. With DC as its parent company, Wildstorm received safe harbor from slumping industry sales, but it also essentially remained an autonomous publisher. Wildstorm's base of operations stayed in La Jolla, California, and now it could enjoy DC's marketing muscle, gaining featured space in Diamond Distributing's monthly catalog. For its part, DC Comics improved itself in several ways with the purchase. First and foremost, with Wildstorm now in its stable DC increased its market share. Secondly, DC added a line of comics that readers considered to be more cutting-edge than most DC titles. Thirdly, DC now had access to Wildstorm's coloring department, generally considered the best in the business.

DC had one other incentive to purchase Wildstorm: a series of titles being produced by one of the most innovative and popular writers in the history of the comics medium, **Alan Moore**. As 1998 began, Moore was delivering a new universe to Awesome Comics, including such titles as *Supreme, Judgment Day* and

Youngblood. However, by mid-year, when rumors abounded about the financial collapse of Liefeld's company, Moore found himself inundated by calls from companies looking for him to write for them. As Moore recalled, "the best offer seemed to come from Jim Lee. And Jim was someone I'd enjoy working with and whom I'd always found very gentlemanly" (Millidge 210). Entering a handshake agreement with Lee, Moore set out to create a new set of characters for Wildstorm. As he began planning, Moore found an old note with a list of character names he'd considered for future series: Tom Strong, Promethea, Greyshirt, Cobweb, Jack B. Quick, among others. Over the course of one weekend, Moore conceptualized those names into a set of different series that would be published under a new Wildstorm imprint called "**America's Best Comics.**" Moore chose that deliberately corny name as a reaction to the changes he helped bring to comics in the 1980s: "I wanted something that sounded like it had been around since the '40s" (Edwards 84). Each new series riffed on classic character concepts. *Tom Strong* was an homage to Doc Savage with art by former *Supreme* collaborator Chris Sprouse. Cop drama *Top 10* was originally planned for Steve Skroce to draw, but when Skroce declined the opportunity, Moore connected with artist Gene Ha. For *Promethea*, which at first was similar to *Wonder Woman*, Alex Ross recommended J.H. Williams III, late of DC's *Chase*. The fecund Moore furthermore created

the anthology series *Tomorrow Stories*, which included Greyshirt (his and Rick Veitch's take on Will Eisner's The Spirit) as well as the sexy Cobweb with wife Melinda Gebbie and the kid genius Jack B. Quick with Kevin Nowlan. Many of these characters were similar to the Awesome creations Moore worked on. For instance, the mystical *Promethea* shared concepts Moore had in mind for his updated version of Awesome's *Glory. Tom Strong* had elements in common with Moore's proposed new take on *Prophet*.

Moore imagined ABC as a unique sort of "alternative future" for the comics industry. He conceived the titles as representing a type of heroism that would have emerged if the super-hero hadn't taken precedence:

You have to trace comics' roots back to the point of which the modern super-hero was born: Superman. If you go back to the stage right before that, you'll find pulp magazines and newspaper comic strips. The 19th century fantasy novel. Mythology. Early science fiction. These were the things the comic grew out of. I've tried to return that to a pre-Superman territory and extrapolate a different future from there. They're the parallel world comic books, if you like. (Hutchins 42).

There was just one problem with the deal between Moore and Lee. Moore vowed in 1987 to never again work for DC Comics due to his objections to a proposed content rating system. Moore believed a rating system was one step away from censorship and thus was anathema to him. And now DC owned the company that Moore was producing comics for. To assuage Moore's concerns, Lee and another Wildstorm representative flew to the writer's home in Northampton, England. While there, they negotiated a plan to institute a "firewall" between Moore's "America's Best Comics" and the rest of the Wildstorm line. Under that arrangement, all editorial work on Moore's imprint would be performed out of Wildstorm's La Jolla office. DC's New York office was forbidden from overriding that work. As Moore said, "As long as I could be kept as far away from DC as possible, then I can live with that and honor my commitment" (Spurgeon 14). Thus, Moore's America's Best Comics premiered in late January 1999 as a

Alan Moore and Kevin O'Neill used classic characters from Victorian-era literature for The League of Extraordinary Gentlemen.
TM and © Alan Moore and Kevin O'Neill.

self-governing imprint, proudly displaying the distinctive ABC logo and an indicia that mentions neither DC nor Wildstorm.

Intriguingly, Moore did not own the full intellectual property rights to any of the aforementioned four series. Instead, Moore delivered *Promethea*, *Tom Strong*, *Top 10* and *Tomorrow Stories* to Wildstorm under work-for-hire contracts. That meant Wildstorm owned the copyrights on the characters, but that Moore and his artists would receive a contractually-mandated page rate. Moore felt responsible for ensuring his artists were well-paid and did not want them waiting for royalties. At the same time, Moore and collaborator Kevin O'Neill *did* retain copyright on the fifth series Moore created for Wildstorm: **League of Extraordinary Gentlemen**. This was somewhat ironic since the Victorian-age characters in that series—including the Invisible Man, Alan Quatermain, Captain Nemo and Mina Harker—all came from the public domain.

Some of Moore's unpublished work for Awesome continued to trickle out in 1999. *Awesome Adventures* #1 (Aug. 1999) features a Moore-written Youngblood tale which was originally slated for *Youngblood* #3. Alex Ross painted that issue's cover, with Steve Skroce and Lary Stucker delivering the art. Moore also wrote *Glory* #0 (March 1999), with art by Brandon Peterson, and since Moore was well ahead on his work on *Supreme,* that allowed for the six-issue *Supreme: The Return* (which ran from May 1999 to June 2000), featuring art by Chris Sprouse, Jim Starlin, Rick Veitch and others. The final issue was a special treat for comics fans as it shows Supreme in the Himalayas meeting doppelgangers of Jack Kirby characters – and Kirby himself as a godlike figure hovering above the mountains. No better way to end a nostalgia-oriented comic than to have the ultimate nostalgia story.

While America's Best Comics was debuting a set of series which emphasized traditional American heroes, Jim Lee's Homage Comics debuted a miniseries that read like a sitcom. *Ball and Chain* by Scott Lobdell and Ale Garza, stars a couple who call their relation-

ship quits... just as they are nearly hit by a meteor. Now endowed with superpowers, the angry couple quickly don costumes and call themselves Chain Lightning and Thunderball. Lobdell and Garza show the couple's humorous travails as they try to simultaneously stop a terrible threat and keep their marriage from completely sliding off the rails.

Image Comics After the Storm

Though the loss of Wildstorm took its toll on **Image Comics'** market share, the company still published around thirty comics each month throughout the year. Co-founder Todd McFarlane continued to plot each issue of *Spawn* (with writing by Brian Holguin and art by Greg Capullo and Danny Miki) even while expanding his line of action figures and collecting expensive sports memorabilia. (In January 1999 McFarlane spent $3 million to win an auction for the baseball that Mark McGwire hit for his 70th home run in 1998.) Co-founder Erik Larsen delivered *Savage Dragon* month after month despite his commitments to DC's *Aquaman* and Marvel's *Wolverine* and *Nova.* Co-founder Marc Silvestri's Top Cow also thrived, with *Darkness*, *Witchblade* and *Fathom* selling well, even if Silvestri rarely drew comics anymore. Co-founder Jim Valentino assumed Image's publisher role in 1999, and he brought on more creator-owned series. One of them was *Tellos* by writer Todd Dezago and artist Mike Wieringo, an adventure/fantasy tale about a planet called Tellos that becomes threatened by a darkness that spreads across its continents. Only three mismatched heroes, named Jack, Serra and Koj, seem able to stop the darkness and they embark on a quest to end it. Another new Image title was *Chassis* by Joshua Dysart, William O'Neill and Larry Welch. This retro-future adventure about a race car driver helped launch Dysart's career in comics. Image also released Jimmie Robinson's charming all-ages super-hero story *The Adventures of Evil and Malice* as well as Larry Young and Matt Smith's *Astronauts in Trouble* (originally published as as a five-issue mini-series through small press Gun Dog Comics). With creators such as Tony Daniel, Brian Michael Bendis, Judd Winnick, Matt Wagner, Matt Hawkins and Don McGregor

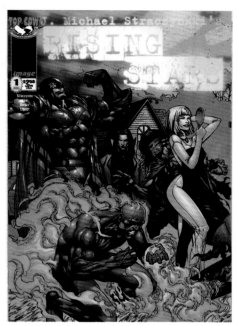

J. Michael Straczynski's Rising Stars *was a decidedly different – and darker – look at super-heroes.*
TM and © J. Michael Straczynski and Top Cow Productions. Inc.

within its stable, Image bolstered its reputation in 1999 as the place to find the highest quality creator-owned material.

Image was such an enticing publisher, in fact, that Top Cow landed one of the hottest writers in television science fiction for one of its new series. **J. Michael Straczynski** (or "JMS," as he was nicknamed) was best known for his work writing almost every episode of the hit syndicated science fiction series *Babylon 5*. For his Top Cow comic, JMS delivered a decidedly different look at super-heroes with **Rising Stars**. In the 1960s, an extraterrestrial energy source hits the small town of Pederson, Illinois. Soon thereafter, 113 children there are born with super-powers. *Rising Stars* tells the story of the lives of those 113 children. Some use their powers for good, some don't have their lives changed at all, and some even become megalomaniacal menaces. The small-town setting was important for Straczynski because it added an uncommon element to the adventure: "The setting is essential because I want to explore what happens when the good guys and bad guys all know each other. They grew up together. There are no secret identities in the classical style" (Castro 26). When one of the weaker kids is murdered, a mystery begins. The long tendrils that led to that murder eventually

threaten the existence of the entire world. Straczynski had been a comic book fan since childhood. He chose Top Cow because Silvestri's company maintained strong relationships with Hollywood and offered the chance to get *Rising Stars* in front of movie and TV producers (Goldman 45-8). Keu Cha illustrated the first two issues of the series, which was projected as a 24-issue complete novel. It premiered in third place in the sales charts upon its August 1999 debut.

Even more popular than *Rising Stars* was Top Cow's new **Tomb Raider** comic. Based on the smash hit video game franchise, Top Cow released *Tomb Raider* #1 right at the end of the year, selling an amazing 194,000 copies. Thanks in part to its nine variant covers, the issue became the best-selling comic of the year. Dan Jurgens, Andy Park and Jonathan Sibal sent Lara Croft on a mission to find the Medusa Mask. *Tomb Raider* fit well alongside such other female-centered Top Cow comics as *Witchblade* and *Fathom*.

Other creators had happy homes elsewhere. Over at **Dark Horse Comics**, Mike Mignola wrote and illustrated the next *Hellboy* installment – the two-part *Box Full of Evil* – and then collaborated with Bill Wray, Dave Cooper and Pat McEown on the decidedly different *Hellboy, Jr.*. Stan Sakai continued delivering striking tales of his rabbit ronin in *Usagi Yojimbo* while Paul Chadwick produced a new fantasy adventure, *The World Below*. Frank Miller's next *Sin City* story was the nine-issue *Hell and Back*. Mike Allred returned to *Madman Comics* after a two-year hiatus, but he also teamed up with writer Shane Hawks on a nightmarish one-shot titled *Feeders*. These were all fine pieces of comic art, but Dark Horse's many adaptations helped keep the company paying its bills. Its *Buffy the Vampire Slayer* comics, based on the popular TV series, continued strong with the addition of a new *Angel* series (following a successful mini-series) as well as a three-issue mini-series starring supporting characters Spike and Dru. As popular as those series were, Dark Horse's most important releases in 1999 were

its diverse *Star Wars* comics. When prequel *The Phantom Menace* was released to theatres in May, Dark Horse was ready with a slew of related books, including movie adaptations, manga versions of *Star Wars*, spotlights on heroes and villains, and graphic novel collections of previous *Star Wars* comics. The momentum of fan enthusiasm for *Star Wars* in May propelled Dark Horse above Image in sales at levels half of Marvel's numbers. That month produced the company's largest market share in its twelve-year history.

Other American comics publishers also snapped up work from some of the most innovative cartoonists in the industry. New publisher Top Shelf published a set of up-and-coming cartoonist Dean Haspiel's punk-styled Billy Dogma stories under the title *Daydream Lullabies*. Antarctic Press released both Richard Moore's fantasy adventure *Far West* and Alex Robinson's soap operatic *Box Office Poison*. Scott Morse brought his crime drama *Volcanic Revolver* to Oni Press. A surprising new creator for the small

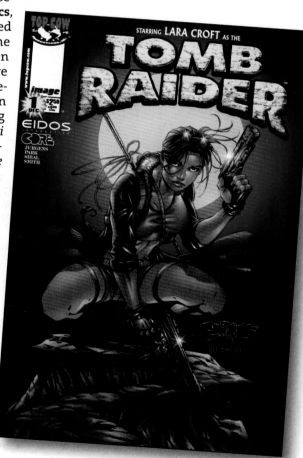

Video game heroine Lara Croft, Tomb Raider, was a 1999 bestseller for Top Cow.
TM and © Square Enix.

press was Jim Starlin. Famed for iconic work on *The Infinity Gauntlet* and *Warlock*, Starlin produced the six-issue *Wyrd, the Reluctant Warrior* for tiny Slave Labor Graphics. *Wyrd* tells the story of an ordinary man chosen to be this reality's champion. Upon leaning magic, he becomes the mystic warrior Wyrd who confronts the evil Nexus Combine, a corporation that engulfs whole worlds to improve its profit margins. "The series is a satirical look at big business and how corporations influence our lives," explained Starlin. "This is stuff that would be too risky for a lot of publishers, but Slave Labor isn't afraid to take chances on this type of material" ("Starlin's Wyrd").

Craig Thompson debuted his first full-length graphic novel through Top Shelf with *Goodbye, Chunky Rice*. Thompson's languid opus is a sweet and poetic meditation on friendship and was named one of the Books of the Year by *The Comics Journal*. Among the other American comics appearing on *TCJ*'s list was *Cave-In* by Brian Ralph. Published by Fantagraphics Books, the wordless graphic novel depicts a nameless caveman who continuously discovers new civilizations as he wanders deeper below the Earth.

Rob Liefeld returned to Cable *in 1999, but his tenure was extremely short.*
TM and © Marvel Characters, Inc.

One of the most important stories of the comics industry in the 1990s was the rise of the self-publishers. Creators such as Jeff Smith, Terry Moore, Carla Speed McNeil and Dave Sim worked without a financial safety net, and dozens more creators tried their hands managing all aspects of their own comics business. The small press also continued to be a means for publishing projects that followed creators' dreams. As Sim, Moore, McNeil and Smith continued their series, Jim Ottaviani assembled a well-intentioned graphic novel anthology that explored the history of women in scientific fields. Drawn by prominent creators like McNeil, Lea Hernandez, Marie Severin, Ramona Fradon and Linda Medley, *Dignifying Science* presented short biographies of women such as Marie Curie, Rosiland Franklin, Britte Galdikas and Hedy Lamarr. Ottaviani was no stranger to these sorts of projects, having previously delivered the similar *Two-Fisted Science*.

Marvel in Recovery

After several challenging years of corporate turmoil, **Marvel Comics** was on the slow road to recovery. The year began with Marvel divesting itself of some of the deadwood acquired earlier in the decade. In February, Marvel sold trading card manufacturer Fleer/Skybox to a privately held company led by the former CEO of Rite Aid Pharmacies for $26 million. The sale represented a huge loss for Marvel who bought Fleer in 1992 for $265 million and Skybox in 1995 for an additional $150 million, but at least Marvel got rid of a company which seemed near death, and the losses Marvel took from the sale could be written off tax wise. In September, Marvel signed a new card and sticker contract with Topps and then one month later divorced itself from Panini (the Italian sticker maker that Marvel couldn't find a buyer for) for what the two companies called "a nominal fee" as well as an $11.2 million payment from Marvel to erase a $27 million debt guarantee.

Significantly, Marvel finally stopped distributing comics to newsstands in 1999, since outlets other than comic shops and bookstores represented only 14% of monthly revenues. Net sales from publishing and licensing weren't considerably affected. Indeed, Marvel's sales increased from $65 million in the third quarter of 1998 to $89.9 million in the third quarter of 1999, an upswing that continued through the end of the year.

Marvel's offices remained chaotic, however. As one freelancer reported, "The offices are virtually deserted. Even senior editorial are rushing around doing intern jobs" ("Movers and Shakers"). Many of Marvel's new titles often felt like tired rehashes of older series, but none of them lasted long anyway. *New Warriors* by Jay Faerber, Steve Scott and Walden Wong restored the teen super-hero team but only ran ten issues. Similarly, Erik Larsen revived his childhood favorite *Nova*, but the title was cancelled after seven issues. That's one more issue than the new volume of *Blade* got. After Wizard provided a twenty-page preview of the new series written and drawn by Bart Sears, *Blade: Vampire Hunter* was cancelled after six issues. New volumes of *Squadron Supreme, Champions, She-Hulk, Ghost Rider* and *Defenders* (that would have featured the original team of the Hulk, Doctor Strange, the Silver Surfer, Namor and a female fifth member) were all considered, but none of them ever went into production. Instead, Marvel retrenched by focusing on well-known characters and creators.

Rob Liefeld returned to Marvel for a character he co-created, **Cable**. Issue #71 (Sept. 1999) featured Liefeld's first work on the mutant from the future since he left *X-Force* seven years earlier. When Liefeld was contacted by editor Mark Powers to become the artist on *Cable*, he at first thought he was being pranked. He soon learned the offer was sincere: "Any book other than *Cable* and I wouldn't have considered it. But he's like my first-born son" (McLaughlin 21). Liefeld assumed the art reins from an artist whose style and approach was his opposite. Jose Ladrönn had been illustrating *Cable* since 1997, gaining acclaim for a style which seemed to combine Jack Kirby and Moebius.

WOLVERINE/PUNISHER: REVELATION #1 (of 4)
Christopher Golden, Tom Sniegoski, Pat Lee & Alvin Lee

BLACK WIDOW #1 (of 3)
Devin Grayson & J.G. Jones

MARVEL KNIGHTS WAVE II HITS IN APRIL
From The Creators of DAREDEVIL, BLACK PANTHER & INHUMANS

The Black Widow, Wolverine and the Punisher were included in the second wave of Marvel Knights releases. TM and © Marvel Characters, Inc.

Once Powers removed Ladrönn in favor of Liefeld, writer Joe Casey left *Cable* as well. "Jose and I had a nice run," Casey explained at the time. "On a different book, I would have gladly worked with Rob. But Jose and I had a 50/50 partnership" (McLaughlin 21). With Casey gone, Liefeld teamed with writer Joe Pruett to bring the "Prophecy of the Twelve" storyline to an end before setting up Cable's next confrontation with the villain Apocalypse. To no one's surprise, though, Liefeld immediately began missing deadlines. He drew *Cable* #71, then writer Shon Bury and former Liefeld studio-mate Chap Yaep provided a filler story for issue #72. Pruett and Liefeld returned for issue #73 but Bernard Chang had to fill in for Liefeld for issue #74. *Cable* #75 (Jan. 2000) proved to be Liefeld's swansong on the title as Michael Ryan became the title's regular artist, starting with issue #78.

Longtime Marvel writer **Fabian Nicieza** returned to Marvel in 1999 with *Gambit* #1 (Feb. 1999). It was familiar territory for Nicieza who wrote several X-Men titles earlier in the decade. With art by fellow former X-Men creator Steve Skroce, Nicieza had Remy LeBeau running missions for the mysterious New Son, who turns out to be an alternate universe version of Gambit. Though all involved knew the comic would sell well, Marvel hedged its bets by releasing five different variant covers for the premiere issue. Nicieza had two years' worth of stories planned as he joined the title and concluded his run with an apocalyptic tale which shed light on the character's previous mini-series.

Uncanny X-Men was the bestselling comic in 1999 just as it was in 1990. In fact, from issues #366 to #375 (Jan. 1999

– Oct. 1999), *Uncanny X-Men* was Diamond Distributing's best-selling comic book for ten consecutive months, an unprecedented achievement. Writer Alan Davis finally resolved the long-lingering mystery over Magneto look-alike Joseph in 1999, as Joseph was revealed to be merely a clone of the long-time nemesis before he died in the "Magneto War" crossover. After four years, fans finally had answers about one of the X-Men family's most mysterious characters.

In other Marvel mutant news, *Wolverine* #145 (Dec. 1999) celebrated the 25th anniversary of the title character's first appearance in *Incredible Hulk*. The issue, by Erik Larsen and Leinil Francis Yu, has Apocalypse forcing Wolverine to fight Sabretooth. As Wolverine's reward for winning the battle, Apocalypse transfers Sabretooth's adamantium skeleton to Logan, restoring what Magneto had pulled out of the feral mutant's body in *X-Men* #25 (Oct. 1993). Still under Apocalypse's control, Wolverine becomes one of the Four Horsemen and then battles the Hulk before casting off the control and trying to stop Apocalypse on his own.

Though the mutant line sold well in 1999, Marvel's M-Tech imprint was less successful. Spinning out of a 1999 X-Men storyline and created as a home for hard science fiction comics, the imprint included three titles. *Deathlok* by Joe Casey and Leo Manco reinvented Marvel's cyborg hero as a S.H.I.E.L.D. agent with identity problems. *Warlock* by Louise Simonson and Pascual Ferry starred the former New Mutant "Douglock" in his own solo series and had no relation to the similarly-named Adam Warlock. *X-51* by Michael Higgins, Karl Bollers, Pascual Ferry and Andrew Pepoy revived Machine Man in a redesigned costume as one of the most powerful cybernetic constructs on the planet. None of the series lasted longer than twelve issues and all sold towards the bottom of the Marvel sales chart.

The nascent Marvel Knights line continued to expand in 1999. Writer Devin Grayson and artist J.G. Jones delivered a three-part mini-series featuring a new Black Widow who dons the black leather jumpsuit and takes on a mission to track down the previous Black Widow. *Black Widow* #1 (June 1999) sold 90,000 copies. Marvel Knights took its first step into the world of Marvel mutants with *Wolverine/ Punisher: Revelation* by Christopher Golden, Tom Snegozi, Pat Lee and Alvin Lee. Pat Lee's manga-influenced art gave the two protagonists a unique look, and the three-issue mini-series acted as a bit of a sequel to Marvel Knight's

1998 *Punisher* mini-series, as it presented a mystically-powered Punisher.

Meanwhile, in the perennial top-five selling *Avengers*, writer Kurt Busiek and artist George Pérez delivered an epic storyline quickly acclaimed as an Avengers classic. The saga debuted with an intense cover on *Avengers* #19 (Aug. 1999), with its menacing outline of Ultron's face, eyes and mouth glowing red against a stark black background. That issue presented the first part of "Ultron Unlimited," a nail-biting tale in which the evil robot exterminates every single living thing in the small Baltic country of Slorenia as a first step to destroying all life on Earth. Only the Avengers stand in Ultron's way. Their cause grows ever more desperate as Ultron discovers he can clone his adamantium body and send an almost unlimited army after Earth's Mightiest Heroes. As the tale reaches its climax, Ultron's inventor Henry Pym feels tortured by all the souls killed by his robot creation. Pym's pain, fear and frustration nearly lead him to a nervous breakdown, but as an exhausted and valiant team of Thor and several of his fellow Avengers launch a frontal assault against Ultron in *Avengers* #23 (Nov. 1999), Pym finds reserves of courage inside himself. The weakest man becomes the strongest hero as he comes up with a plan to defeat his murderous creation. Fitting Busiek's plan of juxtaposing action with characterization, "Ultron Unlimited"

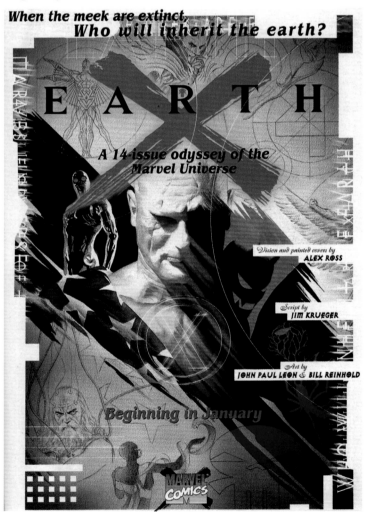

Earth X *imagines a world in which a plague transforms every person into a super-hero.*
TM and © Marvel Characters, Inc.

combined a furious battle, some deliriously detailed art by Pérez and Al Vey, and deep emotional turmoil to produce a stirring and memorable conclusion. The story was immediately praised by critics and fans alike and frequently makes the lists of greatest Avengers stories.

Kingdom Come creator Alex Ross, along with writer Jim Krueger and artists John Paul Leon and Bill Reinhold, spearheaded a new series that explored a possible future for the Marvel Universe and formed a theoretical basis for its foundations. Set twenty years in the future, the 14-part *Earth X* imagines a world in which a plague transforms every man, woman and child on Earth into a superhuman. Because of that, some older heroes are lost and don't know what to do because they have nobody to protect. The proliferation of superpowers both impacts societal order and challenges traditional notions of heroism. As he did in *Kingdom Come*, Ross imagined different futures for the heroes: Spider-Man has retired; Captain America becomes a demoralized shell of his former self; Reed Richards blames himself for the mutation of mankind. The comic was acclaimed for the way it created a comprehensive and well-thought-out foundation for the Marvel heroes based around Jack Kirby creations the Celestials and their eternal battles with the Deviants. The new series debuted in fifth place in the sales charts, no doubt boosted by Ross's presence on the book, and stayed in the top ten throughout its fourteen-issue run. Marvel commissioned a sequel mini-series titled *Universe X*, which debuted in July 2000.

Byrning Up the Comic Shops

One creator who maintained a steady presence on comic shop shelves throughout the 1990s was **John Byrne**. He started the decade helming *Iron Man* and *Namor*. He ended it by being involved in several new Marvel series.

As part of editor Ralph Macchio's effort to get Spider-Man back to basics, Marvel consolidated the number titles that starred the friendly neighborhood wall-crawler. As of cover date January 1999, Spider-Man only had two regular series—in the form of relaunched volumes of *Amazing Spider-Man* and *Peter Parker*—and an anthology series titled *Webspinners*. Joined by writer Howard Mackie, Byrne drew *Amazing Spider-Man*, in which Peter, Mary Jane and a resurrected Aunt May reside in a beautiful penthouse funded by MJ's earnings as a globetrotting supermodel. Peter gets a job at a lab while maintaining his work as a photographer, and a lot of the new series' tension came from a promise Peter makes to Mary Jane to give up the super-hero life so he can concentrate on his family instead.

Spinning (literally) out of the new Spider-Man volumes was a new Spider-Woman whose alter ego, Mattie Franklin, gains spider-like powers during a bizarre ceremony that involved Norman Osborn. Byrne wrote her new series (first issue cover-dated July 1999) with Bart Sears on pencil duties. Byrne also wrote the relaunch of *Hulk* (first issue cover-dated April 1999). With art by Rob Garney and Dan Green, the new Hulk series was like a rougher version of the 1970s *Incredible Hulk* television show, as Bruce Banner's attempt to find peace and happiness in a small farm community are ruined by the widespread destruction cause by his bestial alter ego. Though the book sold well, at around 50,000 copies per issue, Byrne was removed after issue #7 due to an editorial change. By the end of 1999, the series was retitled *Incredible Hulk* and its new writer, Paul Jenkins, abandoned Byrne's TV-inspired vision.

At least Byrne now had the time to create, write and draw *X-Men: the Hidden Years*. Premiering with a December 1999 cover-dated issue, the new series featured the original X-Men and began filling the five-year gap between that team's last appearance in *X-Men* #66 (March 1970) and the new X-Men's introduction in *Giant Size X-Men* #1 (July 1975). *Hidden Years*—which Byrne said "has been on [his] wish list for 30 years" (Frankenhoff 37)—gave him a playground in which he could fill in holes in Marvel continuity. With guest appearances by Ka-Zar and the Fantastic Four, among others, the series sold around 50,000 copies per issue.

Stan Lee Doesn't Present

For over six decades, the name "**Stan Lee**" was synonymous with Marvel Comics, even earning him a place in most issues' masthead with the declaration "Stan Lee Presents." But the dotcom boom of the late 1990s, which made ordinary people millionaires virtually overnight, swept Lee up as well. Before starting his own dotcom, Lee needed to update his Marvel contract. In 1999 that process concluded. In exchange for agreeing not to contest the ownership of Marvel's iconic characters, Lee was granted a non-exclusive contract, a generous salary for himself and his wife and a percentage of profits on Marvel movies. Lee remained on the company Board of Directors and retained his "Chairman Emeritus" title. With controversial co-founder Peter Paul at his side, Lee then launched Stan Lee Media, envisioned as an online portal to create intellectual properties that could be converted to film, television and, of course, comics. Lee's first work for Stan Lee Media was a massive multimedia project called *The 7th Portal*, which presented a comic book story with animation, narration and music. *The 7th Portal* features a group of seven heroes from different corners of the Earth who get superpowers from the Internet itself. They battle a team of seven villains from another world,

with the fate of Earth at stake. Duncan Rouleau provided the art for the project, with Paul Mounts doing colors and Shawn McManus the art direction. As a public company, Stan Lee Media was sold on the NASDAQ stock exchange. The stock opened at $7.25 a share but went up to $9 per share by the end of the first trading day. By February 2000 the company had 165 employees and a market capitalization of over $370 million before the entire project ended up in bankruptcy and acrimony.

The dotcom boom involved comics in a different way in 1999, as two graduates of the Wharton School of Business opened NextPlanetOver, an ecommerce site aimed at comic collectors. NextPlanetOver offered comic news, forums and previews as well a storefront from which readers could buy comics at a discount. Diamond announced that it would work as a fulfillment agent for the company, but like many startups of the era, NextPlanetOver folded by spring 2001. Before it went under, many retailers worried out loud that the upstart site would cause the end of comic shops in America. NextPlanetOver wasn't the only online comic shop to open during the dotcom boom. Fandom Shop and TheComicStore.com also launched during that era but neither stayed in business for very long. Denver-based retailer Chuck Rozanski's Mile High Comics started a relationship with Amazon.com, selling comics via Amazon's zShops small business engine, which even gave fans a chance to start their own online comic shops for the cost of $9.99 per month. The Internet ended up saving Rozanski's business. Facing deep declines in his retail sales due to the industry downturn, Rozanski doubled down and created one of the largest online retail sites for comic books in the world.

In another sign of progress in the comics industry, attendance at the annual San Diego Comic Con continued to grow. In 1990, the convention had over 13,000 attendees. By 1999, that number more than tripled to over 45,000 attendees. Especially pop-

Stan Lee became part of the late 1990s dotcom boom with The 7th Portal. *TM and © respective copyright holder.*

ular during 1999's SDCC were panels tied to Hollywood, including ones on "How to Break into Hollywood" and "Fundamentals of Acting for Television." Studios such as Warner Brothers Animation, Troma Entertainment and Miramax Films had booths at the con. It was even reported that actor Leonardo DiCaprio (whose father was a cartoonist) attended the show incognito.

One company that would soon be exhibiting at San Diego Comic Con was founded in 1999. For as long as they have been around, comic collectors have been debating the "true" condition of the books they own. Various price guides included detailed evaluation scales, but there was no professional service to provide an objective consideration of a comic's condition. That changed in 1999 as New Jersey-based Numismatic Guaranty Corporation founded the **Comics Guaranty Corporation** (CGC). As it did with coins and trading cards, CGC aimed to remove the ambiguity about a comic book's condition by offering to determine it based on a specific set of criteria. For a fee, CGC would grade a comic book and then encase it in a hard plastic shell so that the book's condition couldn't be altered. The CGC's rating was prominently displayed on a label at the top of the case. Comic book collectors soon began referring to this service as "slabbing." CGC also kept a registry of all comics that came through its system, so a census of the number of comics in certain grades was maintained. This became especially important for comics from the pre-World War II era that were extremely scarce.

Not Feeling Particularly Optimistic

As people prepared for the new millennium, the widespread fear was that a "Y2K bug" was going to wipe out computers across the world. The comic book industry didn't have to wait until January 1, 2000, to see what damage was done. It already felt pretty much wiped out. In fact, in terms of comic book publishers going out of business, 1999 was one of the worst years ever. Sales had dropped to their lowest ebb of the decade and all publishers suffered financial concerns. While it wasn't immune from those concerns, longtime Disney comics publisher **Gladstone Comics** released its final comics with *Walt Disney's Comics and Stories* #633 and *Uncle Scrooge* #318 (both Feb. 1999). Though the company was earning reasonable profits, owner Bruce Hamilton revealed, "The simple truth is that we have found it no longer tolerable to deal with the Walt Disney Company any more than is absolutely necessary. When we first made contact with Disney almost 20 years ago, we found the company to be honorable. The biggest areas of concern that I have about dealing with them and about their future mostly concerns middle management and their legal department" (Thompson 6). Hamilton cited the fact that a simple contract renewal turned into a six-month ordeal that included a clause that would allow Disney to search Gladstone's office any time it liked.

As regrettable as Gladstone's situation was, it paled in comparison to what was happening at **Acclaim**. After the "VH2" line flamed out in 1998, editor James Perham attempted to revive the Valiant Comics heroes the following year, delivering a trio of series with familiar titles. Perhaps the most anxiously awaited one was *Quantum and Woody*, still written by Christopher Priest and drawn by Mark Bright. Rather than resume the series' numbering where it left off in 1998, with issue #18, the next issue of *Quantum and Woody* that got published was #32 (Sept. 1999). The series had jumped ahead fourteen issues,

as if it had never stopped being published in the intervening months. The following month, Acclaim published *Quantum and Woody* #18. Priest's intention going forward was to fill the gap so readers could see how the series progressed to what they read in issue #32. Unfortunately, only three more issues were published before the series was cancelled for good after issue #21 (Feb. 2000).

The second Valiant series that was renewed was *Shadowman*, now written by Dan Abnett and Andy Lanning with art by Mat Broome and Ryan Benjamin. This dark tale of crime and vengeance was greenlighted due to Acclaim's plans for a corresponding video game. *Shadowman* lasted six issues, the final one containing a December 1999 cover-date. The final Valiant series to get relaunched was *Armorines* by Omar Banmally, Michael Marts, Jim Calafiore and Peter Palmiotti. It proved to be a massive flop. *Armorines* #4, the new volume's final issue, sold only 2500 copies (McLelland).

All remaining hopes for an Acclaim/Valiant Comics renaissance were pinned on a mini-series titled **Unity 2000**, a deliberate allusion to 1992's *Unity*, the crossover that triggered Valiant's massive popularity in the first place. Fittingly, the person tapped to write *Unity 2000* was former Valiant co-founder and editor-in-chief **Jim Shooter**. He was teamed up with artists Jim Starlin and Josef Rubinstein. As described by editor Michael Marts, the mini-series was intended to "bring into conflict the characters of the more recent Acclaim Universe and the original Valiant Universe, while simultaneously generating new ideas and characters that will carry Acclaim Comics into the future" (McNeeley 27). Bringing in themes from the very first Valiant stories, Shooter sets Doctor Solar in a vicious battle with Master Darque and Morningstar to prevent the entire multiverse from collapsing. In the end, Solar succeeds, but many alternative universes are devastated. As a result, all the disparate versions of the Valiant heroes that have been introduced throughout the 1990s become unified. In other words, all the variations of Solar, X-O Manowar, Ninjak, etc., get reduced to one definitive version. A new Valiant universe is established, effectively wiping out the continuity of the entire decade. Shooter seemed to relish the opportunity to obliterate everything that was established after he left Valiant, with characters casually dismissing the changes that happened over the past several years. Not everyone shared Shooter's enjoyment.

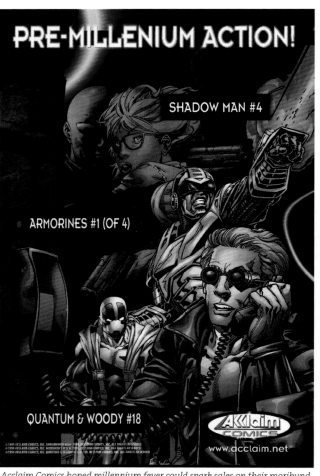

Acclaim Comics hoped millennium fever could spark sales on their moribund comics line. TM and © Valiant Entertainment LLC.

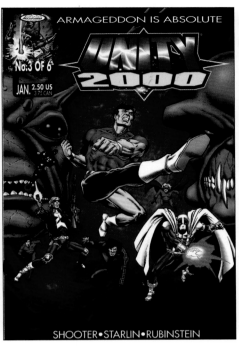

Jim Shooter returned to the Valiant Comics line with Unity 2000, *a failed attempt to duplicate Valiant's success during the early 1990s.*
TM and © Valiant Entertainment LLC.

Indeed, former Acclaim editor Jeff Gomez was horrified at what Shooter was doing:

> I read Shooter's content before it was published, and I called Acclaim, and I said: 'please don't do this. You are destroying your intellectual property... this is vindictiveness, and this is a person who is acting out of anger toward the past.' With his treatment of the VH2 Master Darque and Sandria Darque, Jim was undoing everything that Fabian and I had been trying to do to bring things back around. The universe was becoming a farce, unrecognizable." (D'Orazio).

Even though all six issues of *Unity 2000* were solicited in Diamond Distribution's *Previews* catalog, Acclaim only published three of them due to extremely poor orders. (Fragments of the final three issues eventually surfaced on the Internet.) Also solicited in 1999 and 2000 but never published were one-shots starring Valiant mainstays Harbinger, Bloodshot, Magnus and Doctor Mirage as well as an *Acclaim Comics Web Anthology*, presenting the Valiant heroes in a web comic format. Ultimately, fan apathy doomed the revival of the Valiant heroes, and the line went down for the third and final time.

Comics at the end of the 1990s

Acclaim's mistake was hoping that a comic book event that succeeded in 1992 would do so again in 1999. The comic book market had changed dramatically, and one need only look at the sales data to see how much it had worsened over the course of the decade. In January 1990, retailers ordered 10.6 million comics through over a dozen distributors. By the end of 1999, sales were barely half that, a mere 5.58 million units, all ordered through Diamond Distributors. Put even more bleakly, industrywide sales by the end of 1999 were a mere 11% of what they were at the indus-

try's April 1993 peak of 48.2 million copies. Comics and creators that once were the most popular in the early 1990s cooled off as the decade went on. When the Image rebels walked out of Terry Stewart's office in December 1991, only the most starry-eyed optimists could have predicted their early massive success. Between 1992 and 1994, their best-selling titles made the Image founders—and many of their staffers—millionaires virtually overnight. But the popularity of comics in the early 1990s also earned huge amounts of money for creators like John Romita Jr., Scott Lobdell, Louise Simonson, Denny O'Neil, Alex Ross and a slew of others who were both known and unknown as the decade began. For a brief time, comics were hip treasures fated to pay for college educations. That fad died as suddenly as it was born. By the end of the 1990s, Beanie Babies were the valuable collectible that everybody craved. Million-copy selling comics like *X-Men* #1, *Spawn* #1 and *Superman* #75 gathered dust in attics and storage lockers waiting for the elusive day they would be worth more than their cover price—let alone provide a return on investment.

The silver lining to the comic industry's dark cloud is that the new millennium began with creators at the forefront. Publishers were no longer preoccupied with gimmicks like holographic or die-cut covers. There seemed to be a greater emphasis on quality story-telling rather than dazzling artwork. Writers like Garth Ennis, Grant Morrison, Brian K. Vaughan, Warren Ellis, Ed Brubaker and Greg Rucka stepped to the forefront and broke the conventions of the comic book format in sophisticated and innovative ways, and a new X-Men movie was about to legitimize superheroes in the public's eyes.

While very few comic book creators, retailers or fans in 1999 could foresee this, a phoenix was poised to rise from the ashes of a seemingly dead industry.

Chapter 1: 1990: Swing Time

Barnum, Gary. "Foolkiller." *Marvel Age* (No. 90). July 1990: 14.

"The Beginning of the Valiant Era." *Wizard: the Guide to Comics Special Edition: The Beginning of the Valiant Era*, 1994: 6-14.

Byrne, John. "Questions About Aborted Storylines." *Byrne Robotics*. 6 Feb. 2105. <http://www.byrnerobotics.com/FAQ/listing.asp?ID=3&T1=Questions+about+Aborted+Storylines#59>.

Cronin, Brian. *Comic Book Legends Revealed* (#201). 2 April 2009. <http://goodcomics.comicbookresources.com/2009/04/02/comic-book-legends-revealed-201/>.

---. *Comic Book Legends Revealed* (#271). 29 July 2010. <http://goodcomics.comicbookresources.com/2010/07/29/comic-book-legends-revealed-271/>.

"DC in the 90's." *Beyond Zero Hour: A Comprehensive Look at DC Comics*. Wizard Press, 1994: 38-41.

Dean, Michael. "The Image Story, Part One: Forming an Image." *The Comics Journal* (No. 222). April 2000: 11-15.

DeFalco, Tom and Tom Brevoort, Matthew K. Manning, Peter Sanderson. *Marvel Chronicle: A Year by Year History*. New York: DK Publishing, 2008.

Duncan, Andrew. "Chris Oliveros." Indiebound.org. 2003. <http://www.indiebound.org/author-interviews/oliveroschris>.

"From Hither and Yon..." *The Comics Journal* (No. 143). July 1991: 23.

Groth, Gary. "Kevin Eastman." *The Comics Journal* (No. 202). March 1998: 38-99.

---. "So Far, So Bad: The Schlockification of the Comics Market." *The Comics Journal* (No. 140). Feb. 1991: 5-10.

Hall, Kevin W. "Slutburger Stories #1." *Amazing Heroes* (No. 185). Nov. 1990: 79.

Harrington, Tom and Sheldon Wiebe. "Tempus Fugitive." *Amazing Heroes Preview Special* (No. 10). Feb. 1990: 119.

Henkel, Franz. "Illustrated Spirits." *Comics Scene* (No. 15). Oct. 1990: 9-12.

Howe, Sean. *Marvel Comics: The Untold Story*. New York: HarperCollins, 2012.

Humphrey, M. Clark. "Comic Business Faces Uncertain Future." *The Comics Journal* (No. 140). Feb. 1991: 15-17.

---. "It's So Long for NOW." *The Comics Journal* (No. 140). Feb. 1991: 11-12.

---. "Records for Marvel and Dark Horse." *The Comics Journal* (No. 137). Sept. 1990: 20.

King, Susan. "'Flash' Suits Up for a Sizzling TV Ratings Race." *The Los Angeles Times*. 19 Sept. 1990. <http://articles.latimes.com/1990-09-19/entertainment/ca-726_1_tv-ratings>.

Kreiner, Rich. "Strip Mining the Alternatives." *The Comics Journal* (No. 137). Sept. 1990: 3-5.

McElhatton, Greg. "The Busiest Man in Comics." *Wizard: the Guide to Comics* (No. 17). Jan. 1993: 42-5.

Millidge, Gary Spencer. *Alan Moore: Storyteller*. New York, NY: Universe, 2011.

Nolen-Weathington, Eric and Roger Ash. *Modern Masters Volume Eight: Walter Simonson*. Raleigh, North Carolina: TwoMorrows Publishing, 2006.

Nutman, Philip. "Storytelling Days." *Comics Scene* (No. 15). Oct. 1990: 14-18.

Offenberger, Rik. "Comic Book Biography: Keith Giffen." Newsarama. 23 Feb. 2015. <http://web.archive.org/web/20060525000607/http://www.newsarama.com/images/interviews/2006/giffen/GiffenBio.htm>.

Powers, Thom. "Shooter Launches New Company." *The Comics Journal* (No. 135). April 1990: 13-14.

Raviv, Dan. *Comic Wars: Marvel's Battle for Survival*. New York: Broadway Books, 2002.

Sacks, Jason. "Guardians of the Galaxy." *Amazing Heroes Preview Special* (No. 10). Feb. 1990: 57.

Sally, Zak. "'Your Theory Is More Than a Theory': Zak Sally's Interview with Peter Bagge (Part One)." TCJ.com. 10 June 2013. <http://www.tcj.com/your-theory-is-more-than-a-theory-a-peter-bagge-interview/>.

Sanderson, Peter. "The Non-Mutant Report: Spider-Man." *Marvel Age* (No. 90). July 1990: 18-19.

Sellers, Dennis. "Whither Thou Ghost." *Amazing Heroes* (No. 195). Oct. 1991: 26-33.

Shooter, Jim. "Ditko at Valiant and Defiant—Part 1." JimShooter.com. 7 Nov. 2011. <http://www.jimshooter.com/2011/11/ditko-at-valiant-and-defiant-part-1.html>.

---. "The Web of the Snyder—Part 1." JimShooter.com. 11 Jan. 2012. <http://www.jimshooter.com/2012/01/web-of-snyder-part-1.html>.

Thompson, Kim. "Bissette: Back to the Drawing Board." *The Comics Journal* (No. 185). March 1995: 42-99.

Wheeler, Andrew. "Fabian Nicieza: Working for the Man." PopImage. 10 Feb. 2015. <http://www.popimage.com/industrial/062000nicezaint.html>.

Wong, Len. "Spider-Man Artist: Todd McFarlane." *Amazing Heroes* (No. 179). May 1990: 24-40.

Chapter Two: 1991: X-Year

Best, Daniel. "Interview with Jim Starlin." *Adelaide Comics and Books*. 2003. <http://www.adelaidecomicsandbooks.com/starlin.html>.

Bishop, David and Karl Stock. *Thrill Power Overload: 2000 AD – the First Forty Years*. London, UK: 2017.

Brayshaw, Christopher. "Frank Miller." *The Comics Journal* (No. 209). Dec. 1998: 44-71.

Bruck, Dylan. "The Great Cover-Up." *Wizard: the Guide to Comics* (No. 179). July 2006: 49

Byrne, John. "JBF Reading Club: OMAC #1." Byrne Robotics. 16 Nov. 2007. <http://www.byrnerobotics.com/forum/forum_posts.asp?TID=22003>.

---. "Questions About Aborted Storylines." *Byrne Robotics*. 6 Feb. 2105. <http://www.byrnerobotics.com/FAQ/listing.asp?ID=3&T1=Questions+about+Storylines#59>.

Chun, Alex. "Marvel: The Marvel Age of Fanzines." *Amazing Heroes* (No. 195). Oct. 1991: 74-75.

"From Hither and Yon..." *The Comics Journal* (No. 145). Oct. 1991: 29.

Groth, Gary. "Kevin Eastman." *The Comics Journal* (No. 152). Aug. 1992: 36.

---. "Comics: the New Culture of Illiteracy." *The Comics Journal* (No. 202). March 1998: 38-99.

Gustines, George Gene. "Where Superheroes Go For Industry News." *New York Times*. 2 Aug. 2005. <http://www.nytimes.com/2005/08/02/books/where-superheroes-go-for-industry-news.html?_r=0>.

Howe, Sean. *Marvel Comics: The Untold Story*. New York: HarperCollins, 2012.

Humphrey, M. Clark. "Marvel 1991: The Biggest Gets Bigger." *The Comics Journal* (No.147). Dec. 1991: 13-15.

---. "The State of the Comics Industry 1992." *The Comics Journal* (No.149). March 1992: 11-13.

Johnson, Kim Howard. "Inside Cages." *Comics Scene* (No. 19). June 1991: 25-28.

McCallum, Pat. "Comics's New Image." *Wizard: the Guide to Comics* (No. 14). Oct. 1992: 54-57.

---. "Wizard Exposed." *Wizard: the Guide to Comics* (No. 50). Oct. 1995: 74-80.

McLelland, Ryan. "Valiant Days, Valiant Nights: A Look Back on the Rise and Fall of Valiant." *Sequart.Org*. 15 Feb. 2006. <http://sequart.org/magazine/28120/valiant-days-valiant-nights-a-look-back-on-the-rise-and-fall-of-valiant/>.

Miller, John Jackson. "The Print Age of Wizard Ends." *ComiChron.com*. 24 Jan. 2011. <http://blog.comichron.com/2011/01/print-age-of-wizard-ends.html>.

Nicholls, Stan. "Conversations in Judgment." *Comics Scene Yearbook* (No. 1). 1992: 75-59.

Nolen-Weathington, Eric. *Modern Masters Volume Two: George Pérez*. Raleigh, North Carolina: TwoMorrows Publishing, 2007.

O'Neill, Patrick Daniel. "Mutants Aren't Everything." *Wizard: The Guide to Comics* (No. 4). Dec. 1991: 4.

---. "War of the Gods." *Comics Interview* (No. 104): Winter 1991: 4-13.

Roth, Gil. "David Mazzucchelli's Short Stories in Rubber Blanket." *The Comics Journal* (No. 210). Feb. 1999: 50.

Sacks, Jason. "Fanzines: *Wizard*: Pay No Attention to the Fan Behind the Curtain." *Amazing Heroes* (No. 202/203). July 1992: 62-3.

Salerno, Tom. "Jim Starlin Now Claims: 'Robin's Death Was Planned.'" *Comics Buyer's Guide* (No. 805). April 21, 1989: 1, 3.

Sellers, Dennis. "V is for Valiant." *Amazing Heroes* (No. 199). Feb. 1992: 28-38.

Shooter, Jim. "Traci Adell, the WWF, Fatale on TV, and the Web of the Snyder – Part 1." JimShooter.com. 3 Jan. 2012. <http://www.jimshooter.com/2012/01/traci-adelle-wwf-fatale-on-tv-and-web.html>.

Chapter Three: 1992: Nirvana

Bartilucci, Vinnie. "Rage, Rage Against the Dying of the Light." *Wizard: the Guide to Comics* (No. 14). Oct. 1992: 32-4.

Braden, Scott. "Untold Tales: the Marvel World of Tomorrow." *Overstreet's Fan* (No. 23). May 1997: 34-5.

Byrne, John. "What's the connection between Marvel 2099 and John Byrne's 2112?" *Byrne Robotics*. 3 Nov. 2105. <http://www.byrnerobotics.com/FAQ/listing.asp?ID=15&T1=John+Byrne%27s+Next+Men#234>.

Cadigan, Glen. *The Titans Companion*. Raleigh, North Carolina: TwoMorrows Publishing, 2005.

Chrissinger, Craig W. "Secrets of Shadowhawk." *Comics Scene* (No. 29). Oct. 1992: 43-46.

Christensen, William A., and Mark Seifert. "Doomsayer." *Wizard: the Guide to Comics* (No. 27). Nov. 1993: 84-87.

"The Comics Break New Ground." *The New York Times*. 24 January 1992. <http://www.nytimes.com/1992/01/24/opinion/the-comics-break-new-ground-again.html>.

Cooke, Jon and Eric Nolen-Weathington. *Modern Masters Volume Seven: John Byrne*. Raleigh, North Carolina: TwoMorrows Publishing, 2006.

Cronin, Brian. *Comic Book Legends Revealed* (#96). 29 March 2007. ‹http://goodcomics.comicbookresources.com/2007/03/29/comic-book-urban-legends-revealed-96/›.

David, Peter. "But I Digress....." *Comics Buyer's Guide*. 14 Feb. 1992: 99-100.

"DC in the 90's." *Beyond Zero Hour: A Comprehensive Look at DC Comics*. Wizard Press, 1994: 38-41.

Duin, Steve and Mike Richardson. *Comics Between the Panels*. Portland, OR: Dark Horse Books, 1998.

Fiore, R. "Funnybook Roulette." *The Comics Journal* (No 152). Aug. 1992: 19-22.

Fisher, Hart. "Well, I Feel Like I've Had a Fun Ride." *The Comics Journal* (No. 195). April 1997: 27-41.

Furey, Emmett. "Homosexuality In Comics - Part II." *ComicBookResources.com*. 17 July 2007. ‹http://www.comicbookresources.com/?page=article&id=10809›.

Gerosa, Melina. "Odd Woman Out." *Entertainment Weekly*. 30 Jan. 2007. ‹http://www.ew.com/article/2007/01/30/agony-and-ecstasy-sean-young›.

Groth, Gary. "Kevin Eastman." *The Comics Journal* (No. 202). March 1998: 38-99.

—. "The Two Daves." *The Comics Journal* (No. 155). Jan. 1993: 3-8.

Hansen, Neil A. "Phantasm of the Knight: An Interview with Paul Dini." *Comic Values Monthly* (No. 89). Jan. 1994: 10-16.

Harvey, R.C. "Round and Round with Scott McCloud." *The Comics Journal* (No. 179). Aug. 1995: 53-81.

Howe, Sean. *Marvel Comics: The Untold Story*. New York: HarperCollins, 2012.

Irving, Christopher. "It's All Gold: Jim Shooter's Return to Gold Key." *NYCGraphic.com*. 26 April 2010. ‹http://www.nycgraphicnovelists.com/2010/04/its-all-gold-jim-shooters-return-to.html›.

Jankiewicz, Pat. "Animated Knights." *Comics Scene* (No. 29). Oct 1992: 33-40.

Johnson, Dan. "Remembering the Super-Hero Comic About Nothing: Giffen and DeMatteis Talk Justice League." *Back Issue* (No. 3). April 2004: 3-23.

Kanalz, Hank. "Wetworks." *The Malibu Sun* (No. 18). Oct. 1992: 4-10.

Kass, Douglas. "Pow! Smash! Ker-plash! High-Flying Marvel Comics May Be Heading for a Fall." *Barron's*. 17 February 1992: 64.

Khoury, George. *Image Comics: the Road to Independence*. Raleigh, North Carolina: TwoMorrows Publishing, 2007.

Lesly, Elizabeth. "A Burst Bubble at Topps." *Businessweek*. 22 Aug. 1993: 24.

Liefeld, Rob. "Image Comics & the Death of Superman." *Robservations*. 22 Oct 2020.

Lissau, Russell. "Image Booster." *Wizard: the Guide to Comics* (No. 93). May 1999: 184.

Mangels, Andy. "Hollywood Heroes." *Wizard: the Guide to Comics* (No. 18). Feb. 1993: 34-41.

Mason, Tom. "Image Comics." *The Malibu Sun* (No. 14). June 1992: 1.

—. "Interview with Erik Larsen." *The Malibu Sun* (No. 14). June 1992: 18-22.

—. "The First Image Press Conference." *The Malibu Sun* (No. 14). June 1992: 14-15.

McCallum, Pat. "WildC.A.T.S. Covert Action Teams." *Wizard: the Guide to Comics* (No. 12). Aug. 1992: 29.

McLelland, Ryan. "Valiant Days, Valiant Nights: A Look Back on the Rise and Fall of Valiant." *Sequart.Org*. 15 Feb. 2006. ‹http://sequart.org/magazine/28120/valiant-days-valiant-nights-a-look-back-on-the-rise-and-fall-of-valiant/›.

McTigue, Maureen. "Buying, Selling & the American Way." *Comics Scene Yearbook* (No. 2). 1993: 5-8.

Meredith, Randy. "Anatomy of a Crossover: The Making of 'Operation: Galactic Storm.'" *Avengers Anniversary Magazine* (No. 1). Nov. 1993: 24-25.

Miller, John Jackson. "Nov. 17, 1992: A $30 Million Day — And The Days After." CBGXtra.com. 12 Dec. 2005. ‹http://www.cbgxtra.com/knowledge-base/for-your-reference/the-1900s-the-century-in-comics›.

O'Neill, Patrick Daniel. "Claremont Returns with the Write Stuff." *Wizard: the Guide to Comics* (No. 22). June 1993: 28-35.

Pedeto, Joseph. "On the Scene at the Sotheby's Auction." *The Comics Journal* (No. 148). Feb. 1992: 20-21.

Powers, Thom and Gary Groth. "Revolutionary in Financial Disarray." *The Comics Journal* (No. 164). Dec. 1993: 11-17.

Sacks, Jason. "Image Comics 20th Anniversary Panel: Plain, Stupid, Insanity." *ComicsBulletin.com*. 23 April 2012. ‹http://comicsbulletin.com/image-comics-20th-anniversary-panel-plain-stupid-insanity/›.

---. "Jim Valentino: Broadening the Base and Raising the Bar." ComicsBulletin.com. 17 April 2012. ‹http://comicsbulletin.com/jim-valentino-broadening-base-and-raising-bar/›.

Shooter, Jim. "Traci Adell, the WWF, Fatale on TV, and the Web of the Snyder – Part 1." JimShooter.com. 3 Jan. 2012. ‹http://www.jimshooter.com/2012/01/traci-adelle-wwf-fatale-on-tv-and-web.html›.

Sodaro, Robert. "Foiled Again." *Wizard: the Guide to Comics* (No. 20). Apr. 1993: 70-72.

Stephenson, Eric. "Under the Shadow of the Hawk." *Wizard: the Guide to Comics* (No. 12). Aug. 1992: 22-26.

Swan, Curt. "My Life with Superman." *Wizard: the Guide to Comics: Superman Tribute Edition*. 1993: 8-9.

Todorovich, Lisa. "A Comic Event At The Ramada O`hare." *The Chicago Times*. 3 July 1992.

Voger, Mark. *The Dark Age: Grim, Great & Gimmicky Post-Modern Comics*. Raleigh, North Carolina: TwoMorrows Publishing, 2006.

Walko, Bill. "Rob Liefeld's Titans Series." *TitansTower.com*. 14 Dec. 2011. ‹http://www.titanstower.com/rob-liefelds-titans-series/›.

Chapter Four: 1993: Feeling Vertigo

Amash, Jim. "Conan, Cthulhu, Cross Plains, Kryptonians, & Cadillacs (Or, 'You've Got To Play All The Cards You're Dealt!'): Roy Thomas on Freelancing in the 1990s—Part 2." *Alter Ego* (No. 139). May 2016: 4-74.

Barlow, Stephanie. "Close-ups." *Orange Coast*. June 1993: 34.

Bell, Blake. "Terry & Annie Reissues: An Interview with Dean Mullaney (P1)." 28 March 2007. *Internet Archive Wayback Machine*. ‹https://web.archive.org/web/20071012001015/http://www.bestofmostof.com/07mar/index070328.htm›.

Berry, Michael. "Birth of a Barkerverse." *Wizard: the Guide to Comics* (No. 25). Sept. 1996: 80-83.

Braden, Scott. "Scott Braden's Untold Tales: David Quinn's Doctor Strange." *Overstreet's Fan* (No. 24). June 1997: 30-1.

Brown, Jeffrey A. *Black Superheroes, Milestone Comics, and Their Fans*. Jackson, MS: University Press of Mississippi: 2001.

Butler, Don. "Todd McFarlane: Late comics, firings, bootlegs, pogs, and the Image implosion." *Comics Buyer's Guide* (No. 1037). 1 Oct. 1993: 28, 34, 38.

Cronin, Brian. *Comic Book Urban Legends Revealed* (#122). 27 Sept. 2007. ‹http://goodcomics.comicbookresources.com/2007/09/27/comic-book-urban-legends-revealed-122/›.

Curtin, Jack. "The Spin on Vertigo." *Wizard: the Guide to Comics* (No. 23). July 1993: 44-49.

David, Peter. "After the Great Debate." *PeterDavid.net*. 2 Sept. 2010. ‹http://www.peterdavid.net/2010/09/02/after-the-great-debate/›.

Dean, Michael, "The Image Story Part Three: What Went Wrong." *The Comics Journal* (No. 225). July 2000: 7-11.

DeMatteis, J.M. "Darkness, Light... And Free Food." *Spider-Man: Maximum Carnage*. New York: Marvel Comics, 1994.

Deppey, Dirk. "A Comics Journal History of the Direct Market, Part Three." *TheComicsJournal.com*. 17 Feb. 2010. ‹http://classic.tcj.com/history/a-comics-journal-history-of-the-direct-market-part-three/2/›.

Dixon, Chuck. "Ben Bennett Interview." Facebook. 22 Nov 2015. ‹https://www.facebook.com/chuck.dixon.779/posts/10207890096147720?pnref=story›.

Grant, Paul J. "Final Fate of the FF?" *Wizard: the Guide to Comics* (No. 27). Nov 1993: 21.

---. "Germinal Velocity." *Hero Illustrated* (No. 18). Dec. 1994: 78-81.

---. "Looking for Another Big Bang." *Wizard: the Guide to Comics* (No. 24). Aug 1993: 83-86.

Groth, Gary. "Kevin Eastman." *The Comics Journal* (No. 202). Mar. 1998: 38-99.

---. "The Room's Spinning: Vertigo Roundtable." *The Comics Journal* (No. 163). Nov. 1993: 46-58.

Herman, Ben. "David Quinn's Doctor Strange, Part Three." *BenjaminHerman.wordpress.com*. 14 Aug. 2013. ‹https://benjaminherman.wordpress.com/2013/08/14/david-quinns-doctor-strange-part-three/›.

Howe, Sean. *Marvel Comics: The Untold Story*. New York: HarperCollins, 2012.

Johnston, Rich. "Fanboy Rampage: Rob Liefeld Vs Stephen Platt." *BleedingCool.com*. 20 Jan. 2014. ‹http://www.bleedingcool.com/2014/01/fanboy-rampage-rob-liefeld-vs-stephen-platt/›.

Khoury, George. *Image Comics: the Road to Independence*. Raleigh, North Carolina: TwoMorrows Publishing, 2007.

Martin, Anya. "The Making of the Avengers/X-Men Crossover." *Avengers Anniversary Magazine* (No. 1). Nov. 1993: 8-13.

Markley, Wayne. "Where's My Book Year End Wrapup." *Internal Correspondence* (Volume XIV No. III). March 1994: 16.

McDevitt, Todd. "What's Hot and What's Not." *Overstreet's Comic Book Monthly* (No. 3). July 1993: 36, 38.

McElhatton, Greg. "The Busiest Man in Comics." *Wizard: the Guide to Comics* (No. 17). Jan. 1993: 42-45.

McLelland, Ryan. "Valiant Days, Valiant Nights: A Look Back on the Rise and Fall of Valiant." *Sequart.Org*. 15 Feb. 2006. ‹http://sequart.org/magazine/28120/valiant-days-valiant-nights-a-look-back-on-the-rise-and-fall-of-valiant/›.

Meth, Clifford. "Azrael As It Gets." *Wizard: the Guide to Comics* (No. 24). Aug. 1993: 28-35.

Millidge, Gary Spencer. *Alan Moore: Storyteller*. New York, NY: Universe, 2011.

Nazzaro, Joe. "Welcome to Dakota: Milestone Unwraps a New Universe of Urban Realities." *Comics Scene* (No. 36). Aug. 1993: 46-51, 64.

Ogg, Doug. "Some Milestone Comics Drop Comics Code." *The Comics Journal* (No. 160). July 1993: 12.

O'Neill, Patrick Daniel. "Deathmate Comes Alive." *Wizard: the Guide to Comics* (No. 23). July 1993: 28-35.

Pinkham, Jeremy. "Image Cuts Back." *The Comics Journal* (No. 161). Aug. 1993: 27.

Powers, Thom. "Comic Book Packagers Seek Money from Eclipse; Lawsuit Filed." *The Comics Journal* (No. 166). Feb. 1994: 38-9.

---. "Eclipse Copes with Divorce and Back Debt." *The Comics Journal* (No. 165). Jan. 1994: 12.

---. "Innovation Goes Under Leaving Substantial Debt to Creators, Printers, and Investors." *The Comics Journal* (No. 163). Feb. 1994: 34-37.

Powers, Thom and Gary Groth. "Three Comic Store Chains on the Horizon." *The Comics Journal* (No. 163). Nov. 1993: 9-11.

Reynolds, Eric. "Comics Publishers Suffer Tough Summer." *The Comics Journal* (No. 172). Nov. 1994: 13-18.

---. "Industry Sales Records in 1993 Shadowed by Collapse of Speculator Boom." *The Comics Journal* (No. 166). Feb. 1994: 27-33.

Robson, Eddie and Sean Phillips. *The Art of Sean Phillips*. Mt. Laurel, NJ: Dynamite Entertainment.

Rosenberg, Howard. "TV Reviews: 'Lois & Clark' Soars, and So Does Townsend." *Los Angeles Times*: 11 September 1993.

Samsel, Rob. "Continuity Comics... Poised to Continue!" *Wizard: the Guide to Comics* (No. 18). Feb. 1993: 56-57.

Sims, Chris. "Comics FutureStars: The High School Yearbook of the Comics Industry." *Comics Alliance*. 1 Sept. 2010. <http://comicsalliance.com/comics-futurestars-the-high-school-yearbook-of-the-comics-indus/?trackback=tsmclip>.

Sodaro, Robert. "Bucking the Superhero Odds." *Wizard: the Guide to Comics* (No. 23). July 1993: 36-43.

---. "Spotlight On: Jim Shooter." *Hero Illustrated* (No. 2). Aug. 1993: 74-76.

Spurgeon, Tom. "James Robinson: Rising Star." *The Comics Journal* (No. 199). Oct. 1997: 58-90.

Tucker, Ken. "Lois & Clark: The New Adventures of Superman." *Entertainment Weekly*: 8 Dec. 1995.

Wells, John. "Mark Waid: Igniting the Speed Force." *The Flash Companion*. Raleigh, North Carolina: TwoMorrows Publishing, 2008: 154-166.

Zuranski, Ralph. "Real-Life Good Guy Inspiration." *Wizard: the Guide to Comics* (No. 31). March 1994: 20.

Chapter Five: 1994: Counting Down to Zero

Allstetter, Rob. "Katchoo and Francine Get Dressed Up." *Combo* (No. 20). Sept. 1996: 98-100.

Amash, Jim. "Conan, Cthulhu, Cross Plains, Kryptonians and Cadillacs." *Alter Ego* (No. 139). May 2016: 4-74.

"An Interview with Valiant's Steve Massarsky." *Internal Correspondence*. (Vol. 14 No. 8). Aug. 1994: 7-9.

Bank, Lou. "Thanks, Lou." *The Comics Journal* (No. 192). Dec. 1996: 6.

Cadenhead, Rogers. "Send in the Clones." *Wizard: the Guide to Comics* (No. 36). Aug. 1994: 30-34.

---. "The Dark Knights." *Wizard: the Guide to Comics* (No. 32). April 1994: 30-36.

Campbell, Hayley. *The Art of Neil Gaiman*. New York, NY: Harper Design, 2014.

Carlson, Eric. "Extreme Versus Roustabout." *Hero Illustrated* (No. 15). Sept. 1994: 17.

"COMPANY NEWS; Acclaim Entertainment Deal For Comics Publisher Near." *The New York Times*. 8 April 1994.

Cronin, Brian. *Comic Book Legends Revealed* (#578). 3 June 2016. <http://goodcomics.comicbookresources.com/2016/06/03/comic-book-legends-revealed-578/2/>.

---. *Comic Book Legends Revealed* (#599). 28 Oct 2016. <http://www.cbr.com/comic-book-legends-did-kurt-vonnegut-almost-write-silver-surfer/>.

Cunningham, Brian. "The Magnificent Seven." *Wizard: the Guide to Comics* (No. 31). March 1994: 32-38.

Curtin, Jack. "Reaching for the Stars." *Wizard: the Guide to Comics* (No. 43). May 1995: 31-38.

Darnall, Steve. "The Devil Went Down to Gotham." *Hero Illustrated* (No. 10). April 1994: 70-73.

Darnall, Steve and Brian Wenberg. "Life Springs Ever Green." *Hero Illustrated* (No. 9). March 1994: 72-73.

David, Peter. "But I Digress..." *Comics Buyer's Guide* (No. 1321). 12 March 1999: 56-8.

Davis, John. "Market Reports: Monthly Market Wrap." *Internal Correspondence* (Vol. 14, No. 8). Aug. 1995: 55.

Doran, Colleen. "Guest Review: Spawn/Batman." *Hero Illustrated* (No. 12). June 1994: 34.

Fritz, Steve. "Countdown... Zero Hour for the DC Universe." *Hero Illustrated* (No. 14). Aug. 1994: 42-49.

---. "Big Plans for Information Superhighways." *Hero Illustrated* (No. 13). July 1994: 47.

Funk, Joe. "Comic Sales Sluggish This Fall." *Hero Illustrated* (No. 8). Feb.1994: 22-4.

Golden, Chris. "Something in the Way Shi Moves." *Hero Illustrated* (No. 25): July 1995: 70-72.

Goletz, Andrew. "Part 24." The Life of Reilly. 5 March 2008. <http://lifeofreillyarchives.blogspot.com/2008/03/part-24.html>.

Grant, Paul J. "Defiant Halts Operations." *Wizard: the Guide to Comics* (No. 40). Dec. 1994: 24.

---. "Fables & Reflections." *Wizard: the Guide to Comics* (No. 40). Dec. 1994: 38-45.

---. "Valiant After Shooter: Twelve Tough Questions." *Hero Illustrated* (No. 9). March 1994: 76-81.

Groth, Gary. "Marder for the Cause." *The Comics Journal* (No. 170). Aug. 1994: 11-16.

Grossman, David. "Marvel Music's Strange, Brief, and Totally Doomed Rock-Comics Revolution." *Spin.com*. 12 March 2014. <http://www.spin.com/2014/03/marvel-music-rock-comics-revolution-1994-billy-ray-cyrus-onyx/>.

Harris, Andrew Steven. "Gen-erating Excitement." *Wizard: the Guide to Comics* (No. 38). Oct. 1994: 68-72.

Howe, Sean. *Marvel Comics: The Untold Story*. New York: HarperCollins, 2012.

Irving, Christopher. "The Genesis of Hellboy." *Back Issue* (No. 21). April 2007: 3-5.

Johnson, Kim Howard. "Blood and Choklit." *Comics Scene Yearbook* (No. 3). 1994: 45-47.

Lee, Andrew Thomas. "The Spider & the Fox." *Overstreet's Comic Book Monthly* (No. 20). Dec. 1994: 8-11.

"Market Beat." *Comics Retailer* (No. 28). July 1994: 42-3.

McLaughlin, Shaun, "'Breed: A Walk on the Dark Side." *Malibu Sun* (No. 33). Jan. 1994:4-8.

Morris, Brian and Carol Morris. "What's Hot and What's Not." *Overstreet's Comic Book Monthly* (No. 10). Feb. 1994: 58-60.

Neal, Jim. "Harvey 4th Quarter Loss Blamed On Film Revenue Drop." *The Comics Buyer's Guide* (No. 1064). April 8, 1994: 6.

O'Connor, Paul. "Twenty Years Ago Today: Marvel Buys Malibu Comics." *Longbox Graveyard*. 3 Nov. 2014. <https://longboxgraveyard.com/2014/11/03/twenty-years-ago-today-marvel-buys-malibu-comics/>.

O'Neill, Patrick Daniel. "In Darkest Night..." *Wizard: the Guide to Comics* (No. 34). June 1994: 42-47.

Raab, Benjamin. "Mermaids, Monsters & Magic Carpets: Disney's Cartoon Comics." *Marvel Age* (No. 137). June 1994: 10-11.

Ray, Benn. "Big Books Are Big." *Overstreet's Fan* (No. 20). Feb. 1997: 80-2.

Ringgenberg, Steve. "Batman Punisher." *Hero Illustrated* (No. 14). Aug. 1994: 74-7.

Sacks, Jason. "The Woman with a Whip: Why Lady Rawhide Matters." *Comicsbulletin.com*. 6 June 2013. <http://comicsbulletin.com/woman-whip-why-lady-rawhide-matters/>.

Samsel, Rob. "Genetics." *Wizard Presents: Gen13 ½*. March 1994: 3- 6.

---. "Marvel's Marvels." *Wizard: the Guide to Comics* (No. 28). Dec. 1993: 24.

Samsel, Rob and Andrew Kardon. "Bad fad?" *Wizard: the Guide to Comics* (No. 38). Oct. 1994: 44.

Sedgwick, John. "What's Hot and What's Not." *Overstreet's Comic Book Monthly* (No. 10). Feb. 1994: 52-54.

Shutt, Craig. "Dark Knights." *Wizard: the Guide to Comics* (No. 35). July 1994: 74-81.

---. "If It Ain't Broke... Fix It!" *Wizard: the Guide to Comics* (No. 38). Oct. 1994: 80-86.

---. "Making Change." *Wizard: the Guide to Comics* (No. 68). April 1997: 56-62.

Smith, Zack. "An Oral History of Captain Marvel: Secret Shazam." *Newsarama*. 25 Feb. 2011. <http://www.newsarama.com/7118-an-oral-history-of-captain-marvel-secret-shazam.html>.

Sodaro, Robert J. "I Was a Teenage Mutant!" *Wizard: the Guide to Comics* (No. 34). June 1994: 30-36.

Straub, L.D. "Company Town: Comic Book Giant Marvel Buys Upstart Rival Malibu." *The Los Angeles Times*. 04 November 1994.

Sullivan, Darcy. "The Power of Shazam." *Comics Scene* (No. 40). Feb. 1994: 21-25.

Tucci, William. "Crusade: The Impossible Dream." *CrusadeFineArts.com*. <http://www.crusadefinearts.com/aboutus/yearzero.php>.

"Wizard Market Watch." *Wizard: the Guide to Comics* (No. 36). Aug. 1994: 141.

Wolk, Douglas. *Reading Comics*. New York, NY: Da Capo Press, 1997.

"You Say You Want a Marvelution..." *Hero 1994 Special* (Vol. 8 No. 1). 1995: 13-17.

Chapter Six: 1995: The Exclusivity Wars

Beck, Howard. "We Told You There'd Be Days Like This." *The Comics Journal* (No. 186). April 1996: 8-9.

Bickford, Peter. "Fatale." *The Standard Catalog of Comic Books*. Iola, WI: Krause Publications, 2002: 412.

Braden, Scott. "Neil Gaiman's Tekno Titles." *Overstreet's Fan* (No. 4). Sept. 1995: 46-50.

Brady, Matthew. "America, Good Guys, & A Couple of Flashes in the Pan!" *Overstreet's Fan* (No. 4). Sept. 1995: 84-87.

Cook, Brad. "A Talk with Teri S. Wood." *indy* (No. 11). Jan. 1995: 14-5.

Darnall, Steve. "David Lapham: #1 with a Bullet." *Hero Illustrated* (No. 22). April 1995: 48.

---. "For Bone, Image is Everything." *Hero Illustrated* (No. 25). July 1995: 13.

---. "Is Chris Ware a Hopeless Romantic" *Hero Illustrated* (No.24). June 1995: 84-86.

David, Peter. "Drawing the Line." *Comic Buyer's Guide* (No. 1142). 6 Oct. 1995. <http://www.peterdavid.net/2011/08/08/drawing-the-line/>.

"DC Leaves the Water Running." *Internal Correspondence* (Vol. XV, No. VII). July 1995: 5-6.

Dillon, Jeff. "Secret X." *Overstreet's Fan* (No. 17). Nov. 1996: 42-4.

Ecker, Chris "Dropsie Avenue." *Hero Illustrated* (No. 26). Aug. 1995: 40.

Fielder, Joe. "Q&A John Byrne." *Hero Illustrated* (No. 24). June. 1995: 53.

Gallacher, David. "Dialog." *Comics Retailer* (No. 41). Aug. 1995: 10-14.

Goletz, Andrew and Glen Greenwald. "Part 7." *Ben Reilly Tribute*. 17 May 2017. <http://www.benreillytribute.x10host.com/LifeofReilly7.html>.

Golden, Chris. "Shattered Mirror: the Alter X Universe." *Hero Illustrated* (No. 19). Jan. 1995: 98-102.

---. "X-Men: A Post-Apocalyptic Future." *Hero Illustrated* (No. 25). July 1995: 52-60.

Gordiner, Jeff. "Val Kilmer Takes Over 'Batman Forever.'" *Entertainment Weekly*. 15 July 1994. <http://ew.com/article/1994/07/15/val-kilmer-takes-over-batman-forever/>.

Grant, Paul. "MTV to the Maxx." *Wizard: the Guide to Comics* (No. 45). May 1995: 44-5.

Grant, Steven. "Permanent Damage." ComicBookResources.com. 4 Nov. 2009. <http://www.comicbookresources.com/?page=article&id=23589>.

Gray, Bob. "Distribution fallout." *Comics Buyer's Guide* (No. 1188). 23 Aug. 1996: 22-32.

Griepp, Milton. "The World According to Griepp: Cool Wind." *Internal Correspondence* (Vol. XV No. X). Oct. 1995: 56.

Griffen, Christopher. "Send in the Clones." *Wizard: the Guide to Comics* (No. 53). Jan. 1996: 132.

Groth, Gary. "The Barry Windsor-Smith Interview." *The Comics Journal* (No. 190). Sept. 1996: 59-99.

Howe, Sean. *Marvel Comics: The Untold Story*. New York: HarperCollins, 2012.

Isabella, Tony. "Tony's Tips!" *Comics Buyer's Guide* (No. 1353). 22 Oct. 1999: 42.

Johnson, Dan. "The Many Deaths (and Returns) of Aunt May." *Back Issue* (No. 48). May 2011: 16-20.

Kurtz, Frank. "Q&A Charles Burns." *Hero Illustrated* (No. 22). April 1995: 49.

---. "The X Files." *Hero Illustrated* (No. 20). Feb. 1995: 82-83.

Leibowitz, Bill. "Direct to the Masses." *The Comic Journal* (No.174). Feb. 1995: 2-3.

Mariotte, Jeff. "The Year in Review Sort of." *Overstreet's Fan* (No. 8). Jan. 1996: 93.

"Market Beat." *Comics Retailer* (No. 46). Jan. 1996: 22-26.

Mescallado, Ray. "Kurt Busiek." *The Comics Journal* (No. 216). Oct. 1999: 50-98.

O'Neill, Patrick Daniel. "Marvel Cancels Titles." *Wizard: the Guide to Comics* (No. 45). May 1995: 19.

---. "Marvel to Acquire Skybox." *Wizard: the Guide to Comics* (No. 46). June 1995: 23.

---. "The Price Crunch: Paper Pushes Cover Prices Up." *Wizard: the Guide to Comics* (No. 53). Jan. 1996: 131.

Paterson, Geoffrey. "What's Hot and What's Not." *Overstreet's Comic Book Monthly* (No. 21). Jan. 1995: 74-76.

Pearlman, Cindy. "Inside Batman Forever." *Wizard: the Guide to Comics* (No. 46). June 1995: 38-39.

Ragone, Matt. "June 95." *Mega Marvel The Marvel Comics June 1995 Catalog*: 3.

"Retailer Conference Q & A." *Internal Correspondence* (Vol. XV, No. VII). July 1995: 44-47.

Reynolds, Eric. "Bone Joins Image Comics." *The Comics Journal* (No. 177). May 1995: 21.

---. "Marvelution: The Art of the Deal." *The Comics Journal* (No. 176). April 1995: 11-15.

---. "Pro/Con Politics." *The Comics Journal* (No. 178). July 1995: 1-2.

Sacks, Jason, Dominick Grace and Eric Hoffman. *Jim Shooter: Conversations*. Jackson, MS: University Press of Mississippi, 2017.

Samsel, Rob. "Comfortable with Controversy." *Combo* (No. 20). Sept. 1996: 98-100.

Shapiro, Marc. "Top Dog." *Wizard's Top Cow Special*. 1997: 4-9.

---. "Witchful Thinking." *Wizard: the Guide to Comics* (No. 63). Nov. 1996: 52-54.

Shooter, Jim. "More About Broadway and Fatale." JimShooter.com. 2 Jan. 2012. <http://jimshooter.com/2012/01/more-about-broadway-and-fatale.html/>.

Shutt, Craig. "Pros React to Batman Forever." *Wizard: the Guide to Comics* (No. 49). Sept. 1995: 21.

Siegel, Lucas. "AGE OF APOCALYPSE: The Secret Origins of a One-of-a-Kind Event with Scott Lobdell." *Newsarama*. 31 Oct. 2014. <http://www.newsarama.com/22592-age-of-apocalypse-the-secret-origins-of-a-one-of-a-kind-event-with-scott-lobdell.html>.

"The Sovereign Seven." *Hero Illustrated* (No. 24). June 1995: 78-81.

Spaulding, Steve. "Genre Blender." *Hero Illustrated* (No. 25). July 1995: 66-69.

---. "He's Baaaack..." *Hero Illustrated* (No. 20). Feb. 1995: 16.

Spurgeon, Tom. "Witness at the Marvelution." *The Comics Journal* (No. 177). May 1995: 1-2.

Spurlock, Shawn. "What's What." *Overstreet's Fan* (No. 4). Sept. 1995: 126.

---. "What's What." *Overstreet's Fan* (No. 5). Oct. 1995: 123-4.

---. "What's What." *Overstreet's Fan* (No. 8). Jan. 1996: 247-8.

St. Lawrence, Gary. "Ever Feel Like a Market Beat Misfit?" *Comics Retailer* (No. 64). July 1997: 40-42.

Stokes, Mike. "Wheel of Worlds." *Hero Illustrated* (No. 22). April 1995: 76-79.

"Stuck Rubber Baby Excitement Builds." *Dialogue*. Sept. 1995: 47.

"Top 10 Comics." *Wizard: the Guide to Comics* (No. 44). April 1995: 138-9.

Waid, Mark. "Afterword." *Underworld Unleashed*. New York, NY: DC Comics, 1998.

Chapter Seven: 1996: Crossing Over

Alstetter, Rob. "Trailer Park." *Wizard: the Guide to Comics* (No. 64). Dec. 1996: 122-5.

---. "The Battle of the Century." *Wizard: the Guide to Comics* (No. 52). Dec. 1995: 16-17.

Beaty, Bart. "Don't Ask, Don't Sell." *The Comics Journal* (No 197). July 1997: 17-19.

Bielby, Matt. "Gemini Blood." *SFX* (No. 17). Oct. 1996: 94.

Blumberg, Arnold T. "Curtain Rising: Setting the Stage for Barry Windsor-Smith Storyteller." *Overstreet's FAN* (No. 17). Nov. 1996: 68-9.

Braden, Scott. "War Story." *Overstreet's Fan* (No. 20): Feb. 1997: 84-6.

---. "Untold Tales: Chuck Dixon's Captain America." *Overstreet's Fan* (No. 22). April 1997: 34-35.

Brady, Matt. "Magic Act." *Wizard: the Guide to Comics* (No. 76). Dec. 1997: 36-40.

---. "Send Out the Clone." *Wizard: the Guide to Comics* (No. 59). July 1996: 16.

---. "The Wizard Q&A: Peter David." *Wizard: the Guide to Comics* (No. 66). Feb. 1997: 54-8.

---. "Wedding of the Century." *Wizard: the Guide to Comics* (No. 63). Nov. 1996: 40-45.

Brick, Scott. "Freebird." *Wizard: the Guide to Comics* (No. 74). Oct. 1997: 42-46.

Campbell, Hayley. *The Art of Neil Gaiman*. New York: Harper Design: 2014.

Cleary, Kevin. "What's What." *Overstreet's Fan* (No. 20). Feb. 1997: 208-9.

Cook, Brad. "Steve Englehart talks about Marvel, Malibu, and the future of comics." *Comics Buyer's Guide* (No. 1210). 24 Jan. 1997: 61.

Cronin, Brian. *Comic Book Legends Revealed* (#425). 28 June 2013. <http://www.cbr.com/comic-book-legends-revealed-425/>.

Dean, Michael, "The Image Story Part Three: What Went Wrong." *The Comics Journal* (No. 225). July 2000: 7-11.

Dillon, Jeff. "Web Slinging." *Hero Illustrated* (No. 22). April 1997: 60-63.

Ebert, Roger. "Barb Wire." *RogerEbert.com*. 3 May 1996. <http://www.rogerebert.com/reviews/barb-wire-1996>.

Evanier, Mark. "Oh, So?" *Comic Buyer's Guide* (No. 1190). 6 Sept. 1996: 15.

---. "POV." *Comic Buyer's Guide* (No. 1212). 7 Feb. 1997: 22.

Fisher, Hart. "Well, I Feel Like I've Had a Fun Ride." *The Comics Journal* (No. 195). April 1997: 27-41.

Goletz, Andrew. "Part 18." The Life of Reilly. 5 March 2008. <http://www.benreillytribute.x10host.com/LifeofReilly18.html>.

---. "Part 19." The Life of Reilly. 5 March 2008. <http://www.benreillytribute.x10host.com/LifeofReilly19.html>.

---. "Part 25." The Life of Reilly. 5 March 2008. <http://www.benreillytribute.x10host.com/LifeofReilly25.html>.

Grant, Paul. "The Wizard Q&A: Scott Lobdell." *Wizard: the Guide to Comics* (No. 65). Jan. 1997: 62-67.

Hedges, Joseph. *Wild Times: An Oral History of Wildstorm Studios*. Esposito & Hedges, LLC: 2017.

Howe, Sean. *Marvel Comics: The Untold Story*. New York: HarperCollins, 2012.

Johnson, Jim. "Oh, So?" *Comics Buyer's Guide* (No. 1170). 19 Apr. 1996: 16.

Khoury, George. "A Look at 'Kingdom Come.'" *ComicBookResources.com*. 24 Sept. 2010. <http://www.cbr.com/a-look-at-kingdom-come/>.

---. *Image Comics: the Road to Independence*. Raleigh, North Carolina: TwoMorrows Publishing, 2007.

"Market Beat: Comics." *Comics Retailer* (No. 54). Sept. 1996: 24-27.

Leonhardt, David. "What Evil Lurks in the Heart of Ron?" *Business Week*. 22 January 1996: 44.

Moraes, Robert. "Insights." *Marvel Vision* (No. 6). June 1996: 5.

Mescallado, Ray. "Everything Old is New Again." *The Comics Journal* (No. 190). Sept. 1992: 109-112.

O'Neill, Patrick Daniel and Matthew Senreich. "Loeb Replaces Dixon on Captain America." *Wizard: the Guide to Comics* (No. 61). Sept. 1996: 17.

Raviv, Dan. *Comic Wars: Marvel's Battle for Survival*. New York: Broadway Books, 2002.

Ray, Benn. "A Sneak Peek at the Amalgam Universe. *Overstreet's FAN* (No. 9). Feb. 1996:15.

Ronan, John. "Marvel Axes Editorial Department, Slashes Titles." *The Comics Journal* (No. 183). Jan. 1986: 9-11.

Russo, Tom. "First Look *Kingdom Come*." *Wizard: the Guide to Comics* (No. 52). Dec. 1995: 30.

Rybandt, Joseph. "Moore Is Always Better." *Overstreet's Fan* (No. 16). Oct. 1996: 54-5.

Senreich, Matthew. "Image Conscious." *Wizard: the Guide to Comics* (No. 63): Nov. 1996: 24.

---. "Jim Lee the Wizard Q&A." *Wizard: the Guide to Comics* (No. 75). Nov. 1997: 66-72.

---. "The Wizard Q&A Howard Mackie." *Wizard: the Comics Magazine* (No. 84). Aug. 1998: 48-54.

---. "Wizard Q&A Jeph Loeb." *Wizard: the Guide to Comics* (No. 70). June 1997: 68-73.

---. "Wizard Q&A: Mark Waid & Ron Garney." *Wizard: the Guide to Comics* (No. 72). Aug. 1997: 68-72.

Shutt, Craig. "The Big 10." *Wizard: the Guide to Comics* (No. 65). Jan. 1997: 116-125.

---. "Business Plan." *Wizard: the Guide to Comics* (No. 60). Aug. 1996: 66-70.

---. "Fax of Life and Death." *Wizard: the Guide to Comics* (No. 56): Apr. 1996: 58.

Shapiro, Mark. "The Art of the Deal." *Wizard: the Guide to Comics* (No. 55). March 1996: 34-7.

---. "High Wire." *Wizard: the Guide to Comics* (No. 58). June 1996: 30-32.

---. "Small Wonders." *Wizard: the Guide to Comics* (No. 58). June 1996: 65-68.

---. "'Star Trek' Meets the X-Men." *Wizard: the Guide to Comics* (No. 61). Sept. 1996: 44.

Shepherd, Matt. "Green Mail." *The Incredible Hulk* (No. 444). Aug. 1996: 31.

Sodaro, Robert. "Enter DC's New Science-Fiction Helix." *Combo* (No. 20). Sept. 1996: 108-110.

Spurgeon, Tom. "Firing Line: *Kingdom Come* #1." *The Comics Journal* (No. 187). May 1996: 37.

Stump, Greg. "Cutting Your Losses: Marvel's Sales Figures." *The Comics Journal* (No. 193). Feb. 1997: 12.

---. "Diamond Buys Capital." *The Comics Journal* (No. 189). Aug. 1996: 15-20.

---. "Department of Justice Investigates Comics Distribution Industry." *The Comics Journal* (No. 199). Oct. 1997: 9-12.

---. "Hello Again: Marvel Goes with Diamond." *The Comics Journal* (No. 193). Feb. 1997: 9-10.

---. "Image, Liefeld Settle Lawsuit, If Not Their Differences." *The Comics Journal* (No. 195): Apr. 1997: 12.

---. "Liefeld Vs. Marvel." *The Comics Journal* (No. 199). Oct. 1997: 17-20.

---. "Now It Can Be Told: Image Lashes Back." *The Comics Journal* (No. 194). March 1997: 16-17.

Stump, Greg and Tom Spurgeon. "Shooter, Fowlkes Finishing Run Off Broadway as Golden Books Cancels Comics Line." *The Comics Journal* (No. 192). Dec. 1996: 31-2.

Warren, Jon. "What's Up?" *Wizard: the Guide to Comics* (No. 56). April 1996: 101.

Wilkofsky, Marc. "Doran Plants Soil at Image." *Wizard: the Guide to Comics* (No. 58). June 1996: 22.

Chapter 8: 1997: Change or Die

Anderson, Paul M. "Rare Miller/Bisley Comic Hits America." *Wizard: the Comics Magazine* (No. 75). Nov. 1997: 25.

Aubrey, Scott A. "DC Wraps Up 1997 with 'New Year's Evil.'" *Wizard: the Comics Magazine* (No. 76). Dec 1997: 23.

Beaty, Bart. "Don't Ask, Don't Sell." *The Comics Journal* (No 197). July 1997: 17-19.

Beatty, Scott. "Batman and Superman Headline Justice League Revamp." *Wizard: the Guide to Comics* (No. 57). May 1996: 14.

---. "First Look: Spawn." *Wizard: the Guide to Comics* (No. 60). Aug. 1996: 38.

Beckner, E. "Dialog." *Comics Retailer* (No. 65). Aug. 1997: 14, 16.

"Best Moment Thunderbolts Revealed." *Wizard: the Comics Magazine* (No. 77). Jan 1998: 106.

Blumberg, Arnold T. "Shi, DD; DD, Shi: Crusading Marvels Meet." *Overstreet's Fan* (No. 20). Feb. 1997: 88-91.

Brady, Matthew. "X-Men/WildC.A.T.s Crossover to Have WWII Flavor." *Wizard: the Guide to Comics* (No. 66). Feb. 1997: 16.

Brick, Scott. "On the Ball." *Wizard's Wildstorm Special*. 1999: 4-9.

Cronin, Brian. *Comic Book Legends Revealed* (#376). 20 July 2012. <https://www.cbr.com/comic-book-legends-revealed-376/>.

Cunningham, Brian. "The Second Coming." *Wizard's Heroes Return Special*. 1997: 8-12.

"Diamond reports DC as top dollar earner in direct market." *Comics Buyer's Guide* (No. 1265). 13 Feb. 1998: 6.

Fisher, Hart. "Well, I Feel Like I've Had a Fun Ride." *The Comics Journal* (No. 195). April 1997: 27-41.

Fritz, Steve. "Spawn of the Media." *Overstreet's Fan* (No. 24). June 1997: 42-3.

Greenberg, Glenn. "Justice, Like Lightning... Thunderbolts Strike!" *Marvel Vision* (No. 14). Feb. 1997: 22-5.

Hedges, Joseph. *Wild Times: An Oral History of Wildstorm Studios*. Esposito & Hedges, LLC: 2017.

Khoury, George. *Image Comics: the Road to Independence*. Raleigh, North Carolina: TwoMorrows Publishing, 2007.

"Market Beat Comics Report April 1997." *Comics Retailer* (No. 64). July 1997: 33.

McBride, Melanie. "The Transmetropolitan Condition: An Interview with Warren Ellis." Mindjack.com. 28 Oct. 2002. <http://www.mindjack.com/interviews/ellis.html>.

McLauchlin, Jim. "A Wedding, Bankruptcy & KINGDOM COME - More From The Crazy Year of 1996." Newsarama. 5 Dec. 2016. <https://www.newsarama.com/32216-a-super-wedding-big-two-bankruptcy-kingdom-come-more-from-the-crazy-year-of-1996-in-review.html>.

---. "Lee Extends 'Reborn Run.'" *Wizard: the Guide to Comics* (No. 72). July 1997: 18-9.

McLelland, Ryan. "Valiant Days, Valiant Nights: A Look Back on the Rise and Fall of Valiant." *Sequart.Org*. 15 Feb. 2006. <http://sequart.org/magazine/28120/valiant-days-valiant-nights-a-look-back-on-the-rise-and-fall-of-valiant/>.

Mescallado, Ray. "Kurt Busiek." *The Comics Journal* (No. 216). Oct. 1999: 50-98.

Mithra, Kuljit. "Interview with D.G. Chichester." ManWithoutFear.com. 1998. <http://www.manwithoutfear.com/daredevil-interviews/Chichester>.

Mooney, Darren. "X-Men: Operation Zero Tolerance (Review/Retrospective)." The M0vie Blog. 29 July 2013. <https://them0vieblog.com/2013/07/29/x-men-operation-zero-tolerance-reviewretrospective/>.

Morrison, Grant. *Supergods*. New York, NY: Spiegel & Grau, 2011.

"Negative Impact." *Comics Retailer* (No. 65). Aug. 1997: 23.

O'Neill, Patrick Daniel. "Publishers 50: Dark Horse Comics." *Comics Buyer's Guide* (No. 1265): 13 Feb. 1998: 32.

Raviv, Dan. *Comic Wars: Marvel's Battle for Survival*. New York: Broadway Books, 2002.

Roth, Gil. "Mage #6." *The Comics Journal* (No. 203). April 1998: 38.

Rybandt, J. Patrick. "Judgment is at Hand." *Overstreet's Fan* (No. 23). May 1997:16.

---. "What Color is Magic... This Time?" *Overstreet's Fan* (No. 23). May 1997: 50-3.

Senreich, Matthew. "DC to Introduce 'Tangent Universe.'" *Wizard: the Guide to Comics* (No. 71). July 1997: 14-5.

---. "'Femforce' Hits 100 Issues." *Wizard: the Guide to Comics* (No. 64). Dec. 1996: 23.

---. "Hulk and Pitt Get Ready to Rumble." *Wizard: the Guide to Comics* (No. 66). Feb. 1997: 17.

---. "Jim Lee the Wizard Q&A." *Wizard: the Comics Magazine* (No. 75): Nov. 1997: 66-72.

---. "A New Look Up in the Sky." *Wizard: the Guide to Comics* (No. 66). Feb. 1997: 26-7.

Sodaro, Robert. "Together Again, for the First Time." *Marvel Vision* (No. 13). Jan. 1997: 50-2.

Spurgeon, Tom. "Publishers in Flux." *The Comics Journal* (No. 205). June 1998: 7-10.

Stump, Greg. "The End of the Road for Milestone Comics." *The Comics Journal* (No. 193). Feb. 1997: 18-21.

---. "Hello Again: Marvel Goes with Diamond." *The Comics Journal* (No. 193). Feb. 1997: 9-10.

---. "Liefeld Vs. Marvel." *The Comics Journal* (No. 199). Oct. 1997: 17-20.

---. "Teetering Towards a Shutdown, Kitchen Sink Searches for a Savior." *The Comics Journal* (No. 196). June 1997: 7-14.

Woodward, Christopher. "Jeff Smith & Bone Depart from Image." *Overstreet's Fan* (No. 20). Feb. 1997: 18.

Chapter 9: 1998: The Heroes Return

Allstetter, Rob. "Captain America Defeated." *Toons: the Animation Magazine*. Fall 1998 Special: 8.

---. "Special Report: Blood on the Big Screen." *Wizard: the Guide to Comics* (No. 72). Aug. 1997: 122-3.

Bennett, Reece. "Market Beat Comics Report August 1998." *Comics Retailer* (No. 80). Nov. 1998: 58.

Boucher, Geoff. "Frank Miller returns to the '300' battlefield with 'Xerxes': 'I make no apologies whatsoever.'" *Hero Complex*. 1 June 2010. <http://herocomplex.latimes.com/movies/xerxes-300-frank-miller-300-zack-snyder-300/>.

Brady, Matthew. "Beginning again: Why restart?" *Comics Buyer's Guide* (No. 1355). 5 Nov. 1999: 40-2.

Brick, Scott. "Separate Assemblies." *Wizard Avengers Special.* 1999: 75-9.

"The Buzz Bin." *Wizard: the Comics Magazine* (No. 85). Sept. 1998: 26.

Byrne, John. "Spider-Man: Chapter One." *ByrneRobotics. com.* 7 May 2013. <http://www.byrnerobotics.com/forum/forum_posts.asp?TID=44465&PN=0&TPN=1>.

Cairns, Bryan. "To the Microverse and Beyond." *Marvel Vision* (No. 30). June 1998: 10-12.

Cooke, Jon B. *Everything Including the Kitchen Sink.* Raleigh. NC: TwoMorrows Publishing, 2016.

Cronin, Brian. "An Issue of Wolverine Was Once Recalled Over an Ethnic Slur." *ComicBookResources.com.* 25 Oct. 2016. <https://www.cbr.com/when-an-issue-of-wolverine-was-recalled-over-an-ethnic-slur/>.

David, Peter. "But I Digress..." *Comics Buyer's Guide* (No. 1355). 5 Nov. 1999: 62.

Doran, Michael. "Jim Shooter gets Daring." *Comic's Buyer's Guide* (No. 1291). 14 Aug. 1998: 6.

Dunbier, Scott. "The Only Real Drawback." ScottDunbier Blog. 16 Oct. 2007. <http://scottdunbier.blogspot.com/2007/10/only-real-drawback.html>.

Edwards, Brandon. "Market Beat Comics Report." *Comics Retailer* (No. 74). May 1998: 30.

Field, Joe. "The Big Picture: The numbers game." *Comics Retailer* (No. 87). June 1999: 30-1.

Groth, Gary. "Dialog." *Comics Retailer* (No. 87). June 1999: 8, 10, 12.

Hedges, Joseph. *Wild Times: An Oral History of Wildstorm Studios.* Esposito & Hedges, LLC: 2017.

Howe, Sean. *Marvel Comics: The Untold Story.* New York: HarperCollins, 2012.

Kardon, Andrew. "The Wizard Q&A: Kurt Busiek." *Wizard: the Guide to Comics* (No. 71). July 1997: 50-4.

Lang, Jeff. "Batman and Gotham City Shake Rattle & Roll." *Comics Buyer's Guide* (No. 1263). 30 Jan. 1998: 30-2.

Mangiaracina, Frank. "How a 25-Year-Old Deal is Killing the Comics Industry." *The Comics Journal* (No. 204). May 1998: 1-2.

McLaughlin, Jim. "Awesome Suspends Titles." *Wizard: the Comics Magazine* (No. 82). June 1998: 24.

---. "Boogie Knights." *Wizard: the Comics Magazine* (No. 89). Jan. 1999: 24-5.

---. "Hulk's World Smashed." *Wizard: the Comics Magazine* (No. 82). June 1998: 26.

---. "Rolling Thunder." *Wizard: the Comics Magazine* (No. 80). April 1998: 50-4.

---. "Romita Jr. Hammers for 'Thor'." *Wizard: the Comics Magazine* (No. 74). Oct. 1997: 20.

---. "Waid Out, Jurgens In On 'Cap.'" *Wizard: the Comics Magazine* (No. 96). Aug. 1999: 22.

Meredith, Brian. "Market Beat Comics Report April 1998." *Comics Retailer* (No. 76). July 1998: 42.

Mescallado, Ray. "Kurt Busiek." *The Comics Journal* (No. 216). Oct. 1999: 50-98.

Nelson, Lee. "Union Jack 1." *Comics International* (No. 102). Christmas 1998: 64.

O'Neill, Patrick Daniel. "DC Comics." *Comics Buyer's Guide* (No. 1265). 13 Feb. 1998: 31.

Pearson, Lars. "Market Watch." *Wizard: the Comics Magazine* (No. 84). Aug. 1998: 128-130.

Raviv, Dan. *Comic Wars: Marvel's Battle for Survival.* New York: Broadway Books, 2002.

Riesman, Abraham. "The Man Who Made Black Panther Cool." *Vulture.com.* 22 Jan. 2018. <http://www.vulture.com/2018/01/christopher-priest-made-black-panther-cool-then-disappeared.html>.

Russo, Tom. "The Wizard Q&A Avi Arad." *Wizard: the Comics Magazine* (No. 89). Jan. 1999: 50-6.

Sanderson, Peter. "When the Heroes Return Part Two." *Marvel Vision* (No. 23). Nov. 1997: 8-11.

Senreich, Matthew. "The Next 'Image'?" *Wizard: the Comics Magazine* (No. 77). Jan. 1998: 26-7.

---. "Wizard Q&A: Mark Waid & Ron Garney." *Wizard: the Comics Magazine* (No. 72). Aug. 1997: 68-72.

Shanower, Eric. "Linear B." *Age of Bronze* (No. 1). Nov. 1998: 22-24.

Shutt, Craig. "On the Brink." *Wizard: the Comics Magazine* (No. 81). May 1998: 42-6.

Spurgeon, Tom. "Publishers in Flux." The Comics Journal (No. 205). June 1998: 7-10.

Stump, Greg. "Acclaim Downsizes." *The Comics Journal* (No. 203). April 1998: 23.

Thompson, Maggie. "50 comics companies? What about the other 450?" *Comics Buyer's Guide* (No. 1265). 13 Feb. 1998: 4.

—-. "Marvel's 'Kids' Line Aims at Youngest Readers." *Comics Buyer's Guide* (No. 1302). 30 Oct 1998: 42.

St. Lawrence, Gary. "Keep Things Anything But Quiet." *Comics Buyer's Guide* (No. 1287). 17 July 1998: 32-4.

Toth, Brandon Vangor. "Market Beat Comics Report." *Comics Retailer* (No. 74). May 1998: 32.

Troglen, Dugan. "Putting Cap's Can-Do Spirit to the Test!" *Captain America 75th Anniversary Magazine* (No. 1). 2016: 61-66.

"Viewpoint Report: Retailer Quality of Life Results: 'So, Are You Happy?'" *Comics Retailer* (No. 80). Nov. 1998: 22.

Chapter 10: 1999: No Man's Land

"A bleak forecast." Comics International (No. 102): Christmas 1998: 80.

Brick, Scott. "First Look Batman: War on Crime." *Wizard: the Comics Magazine* (No. 95). July 1999: 28.

Castro, Nachie. "Straczynski to Write Series for Top Cow." *Wizard: the Comics Magazine* (No. 90). Feb. 1990: 26.

Cohen, Ivan. "Sketchbook and Interview with *Batman: Dark Victory's* Jeph Loeb and Tim Sale." *Wizard Presents Batman: Dark Victory* (No. 0). 13-18.

Darius, Julian. *Classics on Infinite Earths: the Justice League and DC Crossover Canon.* Edwardsville, IL: Sequart Organization, 2015.

D'Orazio, Valerie. "The Second Life of Valiant Comics? (Part One)." *Valiantfans.com.* 11 Aug. 2006. <http://valiantfans.com/forum/viewtopic.php?t=11551>.

Edwards, Gavin. "The Lost Alan Moore Interview." *Full Bleed* (No. 1). Spring 2018: 76-89.

Frankenhoff, Brent. "No Longer 'Incredible'?" *Comics Buyer's Guide* (No. 1321). 12 Mar. 1999: 36-7.

---. "The Write Stuff: From fan to fan-favorite: Mark Waid." *Comics Buyer's Guide* (No. 1351). 8 Oct. 1999: 40-1.

Goldman, Michael. "The Wizard Q&A J. Michael Straczynski." *Wizard: the Comics Magazine* (No. 96). Aug. 1999: 44-50.

Halstead, Kevin. "Market Beat Comics Report July 1999." *Comics Retailer* (No. 91). Oct. 1999: 22.

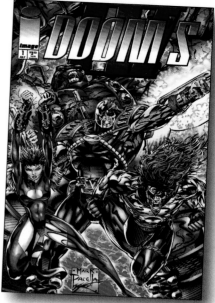

Doom's IV TM and © Rob Liefeld, Inc.

Hutchins, Chris. "The Wizard Q&A Alan Moore." *Wizard: the Comics Magazine* (No. 95). July 1999: 40-4.

Keeney, Mike. "Comics in Your Future." *Comics Buyer's Guide* (No. 1325). 9 Apr. 1999: 22, 24.

McCaw, Derek. "An Interview with Geoff Johns." *FanboyPlanet.com.* 17 Aug. 2001. <http://fanboyplanet.com/an-interview-with-geoff-johns/>.

McLaughlin, Jim. "Liefeld Hooks Up with 'Cable.'" *Wizard: the Comics Magazine* (No. 93). May 1999: 21.

---. "The 'Kingdom' that Didn't Come." *Wizard: the Comics Magazine* (No. 90). Feb. 1999: 28-29.

McLelland, Ryan. "Valiant Days, Valiant Nights: A Look Back on the Rise and Fall of Valiant." *Sequart.Org.* 15 Feb. 2006. <http://sequart.org/magazine/28120/valiant-days-valiant-nights-a-look-back-on-the-rise-and-fall-of-valiant/>.

McNeeley, Trent. "Acclaim Seeks Unity with Shooter." *Wizard: the Comics Magazine* (No. 98). Oct. 1999: 27.

Millidge, Gary Spencer. *Alan Moore: Storyteller.* New York, NY: Universe, 2011.

Moore, Alan. "Planetary Consciousness." *Planetary: All Over the World and Other Stories.* New York, NY: DC Comics Inc., 2000.

Morrisard, James A. "Risky Business." *Wizard: the Comics Magazine* (No. 89). Jan. 1999: 42-9.

Morrison, Grant. *Supergods.* New York, NY: Spiegel & Grau, 2011.

"Movers and Shakers." *Comics International* (No. 104). Feb. 1999: 69-70.

Mullins, Mike. "Looking Back with the Birds: A Birds of Prey Retrospective." Newsarama.com. 27 April 2009. <https://www.newsarama.com/2755-looking-back-with-the-birds-a-birds-of-prey-retrospective.html>.

Riseman, Abraham. "The Secret History and Uncertain Future of Comics Character John Constantine." *Vulture.com.* 23 Oct. 2014. <http://www.vulture.com/2014/10/secret-history-of-john-constantine.html>.

Spurgeon, Tom. "DC/Wildstorm." *The Comics Journal* (No. 207). Sept. 1998: 13-14.

"Starlin's Wyrd for Slave Labor." Comics International (No. 106). April 1999: 15.

Thompson, Maggie. "Gladstone runs out of luck." *Comics Buyer's Guide* (No. 1313). 15 Jan. 1999: 6-8.

American Comic Book Chronicles The 1990s
Index

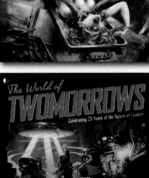

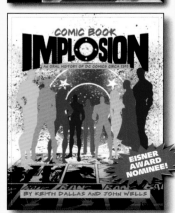